D1071874

MASS VIOLENCE IN AMERICA

Advisory editors:

ROBERT M. FOGELSON   RICHARD E. RUBENSTEIN

MASS VIOLENCE IN AMERICA

THE CRIPPLE CREEK STRIKE

A HISTORY OF

INDUSTRIAL WARS IN COLORADO

Emma F. Langdon

ARNO PRESS & THE NEW YORK TIMES

New York · 1969

Editorial Note

Nations, like men, are sometimes interested in burying the past.

In early 1968, after more than five years marked by political assassinations, racial uprisings, campus disorders, mass demonstrations and the violent suppression of protest, *The New York Times Magazine* asked a group of distinguished scholars to reply to the question, "Is America by nature a violent society?" In answer, University of Chicago anthropologist Clifford Geertz wrote:

> "We do not know very well what kind of society we live in, what kind of history we have had, what kind of people we are. We are just now beginning to find out, the hard way . . ."

The proposition was astonishing but correct: what was least understood about domestic political violence was its role in American history. It was common knowledge that the United States had had a Revolution, a Civil War, some trouble with the Indians and a period of labor-management conflict. But one could search the shelves of the nation's great libraries without discovering more than a handful of works on the subject of violence in American history, and these hopelessly out of date.

Historians had generally ignored or soft-pedaled the history of farmer uprisings, native vigilantism, labor-management struggles, ethnic conflicts and race riots; comparative work in the history of social conflict was particularly weak. Sociologists and political scientists in the grip of "consensus" theory tended to treat episodes of mass violence in America as insignificant or aberrational—temporary exceptions to the norm of peaceful progress. Psychologists and behavioral scientists discussed "mob violence" in terms which suggested that riots, revolts, insurrections and official violence were the products of individual or group pathology. All such interpretations had the effect not only of minimizing group violence in America, but of depriving it of political content—hence, of relevance to the present.

As a result, as late as 1968, the rich, multifarious and often terrifying history of domestic political violence was still largely *terra incognita*. So long as most Americans wished to keep certain skeletons locked away in their closets, few scholars would attempt to open doors. Conversely, once the American people, frightened yet emboldened by the sudden reappearance of intense social conflict, began to ask new questions about the past, so did the scholars.

Our purpose in helping Arno Press and *The New York Times* select and publish significant documents in the history of political violence has not been to compound past errors by overemphasizing the role of conflict in American history. On the contrary, our aim has been to provide materials which will aid in the search for an accurate perspective on the present. MASS VIOLENCE IN AMERICA includes eyewitness reports, government documents and other descriptive and analytic material relating to mass political violence in the United States. These documents not only provide information—they give the "feel" or "flavor" of past eras of civil disorder by evoking the emotional and political context in which revolts took place. Most of them have long been out of print and are obtainable, if at all, only in the nation's largest libraries.

The scope of this series is wide, ranging from accounts of Indian warfare to descriptions of labor-management violence, from narratives of colonial insurrections to reports on modern racial uprisings. It is not, however, limitless, nor were the constituent volumes carelessly selected. The principle of coherence which guided the selections is implicit in the phrase "mass political violence." "Mass" denotes activity engaged in by large groups rather than individuals acting alone; "political" suggests a relationship between such activity and competition among domestic groups for power, property and prestige; and "violence" is narrowly construed as resulting in physical damage to persons or property. In short, the materials reproduced herein are intended to illuminate the resort to violence by American groups seeking to change or to preserve the status quo. Although historical, they are of interest to any who wishes to understand the causes, nature and direction of domestic political violence, whether they be social scientists, historians or just interested Americans.

Of course, we are particularly hopeful that these volumes will prove useful to those now engaged in curriculum-revision and the teaching of high school and college courses in the area of American studies. What Christopher Jencks and David Reisman term "the Academic Revolution" has made difficult demands on all educators, not the least of which is the demand for courses which are both relevant to the condition of modern America and of the highest academic quality. These volumes are meant to provide raw material for such courses— primary source matter which will help both instructors and students to deepen and enrich their views of the American experience.

Most important, the editors and publisher recognize that these volumes appear during a national crisis which is also a crisis of the spirit, a time in which the public response to various manifestations of civil disorder is increasingly governed by anger, fear and hysteria. In such an atmosphere it is important to recognize that one is not alone in time—that such events have taken place before in America and, unless fundamental changes in our social and political life take place, will probably recur in the future. Our fondest hope is that this work, and others like it, will help to keep alive, in a time of growing unreason, the spirit of reasoned inquiry.

RICHARD E. RUBENSTEIN
The Adlai Stevenson Institute
Chicago, Illinois

ROBERT M. FOGELSON
Harvard-MIT Joint Center
for Urban Studies
Cambridge, Massachusetts

THE CRIPPLE CREEK STRIKE

A HISTORY OF

INDUSTRIAL WARS IN COLORADO

Yours in Unionism,

Emma F. Langdon

THE
CRIPPLE CREEK STRIKE

BY EMMA F. LANGDON

A HISTORY OF

INDUSTRIAL WARS IN
COLORADO

1903-4-5

*Being a Complete and Concise History of the Efforts of
Organized Capital to Crush Unionism*

THE GREAT WESTERN PUBLISHING CO.
DENVER, COLORADO

DEDICATION

In view of the fact that the Western Federation of Miners has
made a law-abiding and manly fight against the lawless,
corrupt and un-American methods of those against
whom they have a grievance, to the Western
Federation of Miners and loyal labor
organizations of the state of
Colorado, I respectfully
dedicate this work.

INTRODUCTION

TO PART ONE

THE state of Colorado ceased under the administration of
James H. Peabody, to be republican in its form of government, and became a military oligarchy. The expressed
will of the people was ignored by their chosen representatives;
thus bringing upon the state a series of calamities, the magnitude of which may now readily be seen.

It is deplorable that the state, at that time, was dominated
by public officials who conceived that they were the masters and
not the servants of the people; of a coterie of men who cast law,
decency and that innate fairness which distinguishes the statesman of capacity from the truckling politician, to one side, and
dropping to the level of a Machiavelli, pursued those policies which
obtain for success, regardless of the principles upon which the
American Republic is founded—in short, that "the end justifies
the means."

Again, the instrumentalities employed in that crisis in this
state were not such as would be employed by a statesman, and
were such as would rather be used by one whose hands are stained
with questionable commerce. The writer used to think it singular
that the merchant prince, A. T. Stewart, was denied a position in
Grant's cabinet, because, as was asserted at the time, his hands
were stained with commerce, but the brilliant galaxy of statesmen in control of the government knew well their business; knew
that statesmen are not made of the calibre of men who are accustomed to hiding the world from their vision with that small
coin, the nickle.

The commonwealth of Colorado experimented with such an
one. The experiment was costly. The people of the state elevated
to the highest position within their gift one who dared not deny
that he was a Shylock, a money monger, such an one as Jesus
Christ scourged from the temple with thongs—James H. Peabody
—cheap (except when spending public funds on eastern junketing

trips), and, as Macauley said of a certain potentate, "little in war, little in government, little in everything but the art of simulating sturdiness of purpose." Such is Peabody. All that is lacking to make him as contemptible as James II or Charles I is a Judge Jeffries or Judge Impeys.

This man was the mere puppet, the chiefest instrumentality, of that coterie of men who, while they shouted law and order, throttled liberty and subverted courts of justice. His proclamation, like those bulls launched against distant empires by the mediaeval church of Rome startled the country and brought discredit on the state; but those who live amidst the scenes of his anathemas; to those who were on the ground and are familiar with the mechanism that moved the puppets of his wretched devices; to all such his fearful maledictions were a source of amusement and contempt.

General John C. Chase was, for a time, a very potent and "fierce" factor in what the governor ascribes as that "rebellious territory of Teller county;" but the fierce extractor of old ladies' teeth was too strenuous even for his Excellency and Bell, and, consequently, the doughty general was disgraced and retired to the sanctity of his dental parlors in the capitol, where he might practice without let or hindrance the "fierce" art of wrestling with decayed teeth.

John C. Chase, in some mysterious manner, had the title of soldier thrust upon him; but there is much diversity of opinion as to the justness of the thrust. If, with a couple of hundred rookies, to chase ladies and gentlemen up and down the street who are out for a Sunday afternoon's stroll, is a characteristic of a soldier, then he is worthy of the title; if to place sharp-shooters on the roofs of buildings, command the approaches to the district court of Teller county with Gatling guns, invade the aforesaid court with an armed force in order that he might have the courage to defy its decrees; if, from any possible viewpoint, these acts can be construed into those qualities which go to make up the soldier, then must the writer admit that Chase is a soldier; if with a troop of cavalry and a company of infantry, to invade a printing office, seize its inmates at a late hour of night (one would suppose that only thieves and burglars choose midnight hour for acts of outrage), and thrust them into a foul tent out of which to make room a number of drunken members of the guard had been removed; and it must be remembered that these men were not even provided with blankets. If to these acts can be ascribed the character of a man of honor, the just citizen, the humane general, then, indeed, is John C. Chase a soldier.

John C. Chase (the writer will not call him general, for, having resided for many years at one of the greatest military posts in the United States, and having been partially educated at aforesaid fort, she knows those qualities which constitute, first, the gentlemanly officer; second, the man who is always a gentleman; third, the soldier; fourth, those fine qualities which distinguish an officer of the United States Army from one whose military career has been confined within the limits of a mere tin soldier on state occasions), will not deny that he headed the aforesaid predatory expeditions.

Another "soldier" who was conspicuous in the "proscribed area" is Adjutant General Bell, brigadier general, adjutant general, state of Colorado—"It" of the iron jaw, and let it not be forgotten that it takes a heavy head to support an iron jaw. Bell rose to fame from the humble position of a deputy United States marshal—professional thief taker and adept in the art of unraveling and creating dark and bloody plots. Too valuable was he to remain in the field, and after the shelving of the warrior Chase, he was returned to the capitol, for, be it remembered, squawking geese saved the capitol of Rome, and might not Bell be used in a like manner to save Peabody and the credit of his administration. At any rate shortly after his return to the capitol, according to the public press, numberless mines in the district were to be dynamited, miners were in danger of being lynched and men fell over themselves in their efforts to make confessions of grave crimes. That was a stroke of policy worthy of a Richelieu. As a matter of fact, the original policy of intimidation and violence outlined by the cabal had utterly failed. The press and public sentiment throughout the state, it was seen, was decidedly against the policy of ruffianism instituted. Hence, Bell's recall to the capitol, where his peerless art as a fictionist—his superior abilities as a manufacturer of mountains out of mole hills—was given free rein. Then were mines to be dynamited; then were men to be lynched; then had men made fearful confessions—all phantoms of Bell's imagination.

These fictions were given wide publicity for the purpose of preparing the public mind for a new policy, about to be introduced—that of martial law.

Thomas McClelland, major, was another "aggressive" factor of the war of extermination. The position assigned McClelland seems to have been the real "dirty work," such as breaking into halls and printing offices and seizing the inmates thereof; thrusting civil officers out of hallways in their efforts to serve papers upon officials—in short to perform all those menial offices which an officer of the regular army would spurn with contempt.

But the meanest, lowest, most vile of the instrumentalities employed by this honorable cabal in the accomplishment of its purposes was one Frank Vannick, ex-convict, No.——; a man of whom it is said, that to shield himself from prison walls, turned states' evidence and sent his own brother to the institution which he thereby avoided for a tiime only. Peabody, the chiefest; Vannick the least; both of Canon City, Colo., one, a banker, a resident of the town, the other, an inmate of a prison. Fit instrumentalities to subvert courts, suppress free speech, censor the press, thrust citizens into bull pens without warrant of law, invade public halls, break into dwellings and rifling them of their contents during the absence of the owners thereof.

Such are the atrocities that the people of this district have suffered, and yet maintained a calm dignity that gives the living lie to Peabody, Bell and the Mine Owners' Association.

So far as the writer has been able to observe, organized labor of the Cripple Creek district sought to maintain law. Organized labor sought to enforce the laws against gambling, and when convictions were secured James H. Peabody, governor of Colorado, intervened with executive pardon—probably on the principle that gambling and Shylocking are not widely different occupations. Organized labor has sought to close those scourges of civilization —the dance halls—wherein more disorder and brawls originate than in any other institution in the mining camp. It was not observed that James H. Peabody or the military closed them. Presumably this commerce in woman's virtue did not appeal strongly to the governor's fine sense as an evil that should be suppressed, for, according to Judge Owers, one may rise from the position of a dance hall proprietor to be even a banker; yea, even as James H. Peabody.

THE CONTENTS

PART ONE

PART TWO

THE ILLUSTRATIONS

"This work received the unanimous endorsement of the Colorado State Federation of Labor by 350 delegates representing 50,000 union men and women of the state of Colorado, in convention assembled at Denver, Colo., January 11 to 14, 1904.

J. C. SULLIVAN, President.

"H. B. WATERS, Secretary."

The Cripple Creek District

N speeding toward the west, after many days of the same monotonous view of rolling prairie, stretching onward, ever onward, bounded only by the distant blue of the horizon, the weary traveler is startled by what at first appears to be an enormous white and blue cloud. The sight holds one spell bound with awe and admiration and it is many minutes before one can realize that the mighty mass looming up apparently from the prairie and piercing the sky is the first glimpse of that Titan sentinel among Titans, Pike's Peak, over seventy-five miles still to the westward.

The name is reminiscent of another time, and as the tourist of today is whirled across the continent, enjoying all the comforts of his home, he can hardly appreciate the hardships, the privations of those early Argonauts, whose slogan was "Pike's Peak or Bust" in the days of 1859. Words cannot adequately portray the vicissitudes and dangers of the time. The journey was made in what was commonly termed a prairie schooner. The dangers of such a trip were manifold, but the greatest source of anxiety arose from the hostile tribes of Indians. Along the line of the great transcontinental railroads, the bones of thousands lie bleaching, countless graves dot the prairie, graves of men and women who left their Eastern homes, who turned their backs on all they held dear in life and braved the terrors of an unknown country for gold.

Twenty years later, in 1879, the Mt. Pisgah excitement swept over the West, and a rush was made for the new Eldorado. This was an illusion, pure and simple, and the authors narrowly escaped well-deserved lynching. But the bitterness and irony of fate is evinced in both of these rushes. Almost in the shadow of Pike's Peak, the riches of Golconda awaited the prospector's pick;; while the fortune hunters who rushed to Mt. Pisgah walked over the Gold Coin, Portland, Independence, Vindicator, El Paso, Ajax, Last Dollar, Isabella and hundreds of other rich mineral deposits. The Cripple Creek district, contributing as it does, the vast sum of $24,000,000 in gold annually to the world's wealth, has been for the last few years an object of great interest to the entire commercial world. The richness and magnitude of the treasure so cunningly hidden by the hand of nature in this store-house, has attracted the attention of both foreign and American capital, and the tourists who visit this wonderful gold camp are amazed at the extent of the great enterprises that he sees developing before . him. Many discoveries have been made in the past ten years, of which I will speak very shortly, but first a word about the early prospectors. Mountains in the immediate vicinity of the mining belt were dotted, a few years ago, with little homes made preparatory for the wives and children who had been left behind and were coming to make their homes in the new camp. The number of these huts and cabins grew so rapidly that it soon became necessary to incorporate them into towns.

The prospector, with his old-fashioned windlass, slow method and hand drills, was rapidly displaced by the capitalist, monster steam and electrical appliances, steam hoist and steam drill. Railroad companies vied with each other in the display of wonderful and heretofore unheard of engineering feats in competition for the enormous receipts for ore transportation. The mines were surrounded with a net-work of steel rails, thrown over the mountain tops, and connecting the great gold producers with the smelters and mills in the valley below. The speculator and capitalist came to get that which the prospector had found, and from then until now every inch of valuable ground, staked as a claim by the miner, has in some manner found its way into the hands of corporation capital.

As has been shown in the foregoing, Cripple Creek and Victor owe their present prosperous lives to the indomitable will and perseverence of a few early prospectors, who, notwithstanding the adverse opinions of experts, stuck doggedly to their claims. Gold was first discovered in 1889, but it was not until 1890-91 that its true worth was appreciated. The camp owes its prosperity to the financial panic of 1893, which brought thousands of unemployed to the district, owing to the fall in silver. About this time the fame of the district began to attract the attention of the experts, who, after thorough and exhaustive examinations, were almost a unit in their disapproval of it. Gold could not occur in this formation, they argued;pockets might be opened up, but as for continuous ore bodies, it was ridiculous. Never in the history of mining was the truth of the old axiom more sharply verified: "Gold is where you find it."

From an unknown, obscure and doubtful mining camp—from a ranch where cattle browsed quietly day by day, where the cow-

VICTOR AVENUE, Victor, Colorado.

boys lived and dreamed of fortunes to come, all unconscious of the millions beneath their feet, there has sprung, as if in a night, a mining district whose richness and extent has astonished the world. From a few huts and cabins have sprung cities—Victor and Cripple Creek—that compare favorably with any in the world for population. They are beautiful little cities of brick and stone buildings, fine homes, modern schools, morning and evening daily papers, churches of all denominations and hotels with all modern accommodations.

It is a common mistake made by people who have never lived in a mining town, to associate the name "mining camp" with a mushroom town, rough, rowdy men, who prefer outlawry to a good square meal. Imagine their surprise, when they visit the camp, to find instead,· a beautiful city, with quiet, respectable and law-abiding citizens.

Cripple Creek is the county seat of Teller county, and ranks first in size of the ten incorporated towns of the district, having a population of from 12,000 to 15,000.

Victor is located in the extreme southern limit of the district, ranking next to Cripple Creek in size with a population of about 7,000. Goldfield, also has the honor of being a city of the second

ALTMAN, Highest City in the World, on Bull Hill.

class in the district of ten incorporated towns. Goldfield has a population of nearly 2,000 and is only a nice walk from Victor.

Altman, upon the very crest of Bull Hill, enjoys the distinction of being the highest incorporated town in America, if not in the world. It is strictly a mining town and affords homes for the miners of that famous hill, who had rather live the year round at an altitude of nearly 11,000 feet above sea level than to be compelled to travel far from their place of employment. All of the other incorporated towns in the district are of more or less interest, but for lack of space I will pass them by.

At 1 o'clock a. m. of April 25, 1896, a woman of Cripple Creek, in a quarrel, overturned a gasoline stove and in that way started a conflagration which almost completely destroyed that city during its greatest boom. But soon the enterprising citizens of the flourishing little city were busy rebuilding.

Victor also had a fire which came near banishing it from the face of the earth, August 21, 1899. The fire will always be remembered and talked of by those who happened to be in the district at that time. The great Victor fire destroyed property to the value of a million dollars and rendered 3,000 people homeless at that time. The fire spread through the frame, pioneer build-

BENNETT AVENUE, City of Cripple Creek.

ings of the city as if it had been a heap of kindling wood. But there is no pluck like the pluck of the man who has upreared the cities and towns of the West. Calamity can not discourage him, for, checked in one direction, he will expend his energies in another. Victor was then, as now, the city of the mines, and as such she had reason for living. Her citizens brushed the smoke from their eyes, shoveled away the embers from their lots, and proceeded to build a bigger and more substantial city, the frame buildings which had been destroyed being replaced by stone and brick structures.

Victor became incorporated in 1894, and in 1898 was elevated to the dignity of a city of the second class.

The two cities, Victor and Cripple Creek, are entirely surrounded by mountains of more or less note, with Pike's Peak in plain view twelve miles away. The cities just named are connected by two electric and three steam lines, one of the steam lines being a narrow gauge. The suburban train service is perfect, and as you ride between the two little cities, you will find along the lines smaller towns nearly every mile.

During normal conditions, there is, counting all trains, a service of 222 separate and distinct trains running into Cripple Creek and Victor every twenty-four hours. It seems marvelous but it is nevertheless true.

The scenery viewed from any of the local points of interest is grand and surpasses description. The cars round the spur of a mountain, now through a gorge, now over high trestles, now through tunnels and then hundreds of feet up the mountainside, and ever rising higher and higher, the snow-covered mountains, dotted with working mines and abandoned prospect holes. While away to the south and west, some sixty miles, stands the pure, white, eternally snow-capped Sangre de Christo range, sharp and clear against the blue azure of the sky, a glorious monument to the vast and mighty beauty of the handiwork of God.

The ore producing area of the district embraces approximately thirty square miles, with a population of 50,000 people.

Following is a brief summary of the largest producers in the district located in Victor:

The famous Gold Coin mine was discovered while excavating a foundation for a hotel. A description of the Gold Coin will apply to other mines of the district, therefore a few words in reference to this great mine might prove of interest. In '95, the Woods Bros. secured a bond and lease on a portion of the Gold Coin claim for the sum of $50,000. They offered the stock to the public at five cents per share and found few takers. At an early stage in the development of the property, rich ore was found and the Gold Coin started on an upward career, which did not terminate until the price reached the sum of $6.50 per share. The mine is a steady dividend-payer. The character of the Coin ore is a granite quartz, between granite walls. The mine has attained a depth of over one thousand feet, and the average value of the ore has increased. The Gold Coin has produced a total of $6,-000,000 in about eight years, and in addition to paying for the most expensive development and equipment, which includes a very large chlorination plant, has distributed $1,500,000 in dividends to its stockholders. The Gold Coin is located right in the heart of Victor.

The Ajax Gold Mining Company, E. A. Colburn president and general manager, which bounds Victor partly on the north, is worthy of mention. This mine has a modern and up-to-date assay and chemical laboratory where all the mine assaying and chemical work has been performed for the past year, proving to be more satisfactory than having the work done elsewhere. This company has a machine shop of which it is very proud. Everything except casting can be done there, which does away with the inconvenience of sending out of the district when any special article is needed.

The equipment of the Ajax company is of the best and there are few mines in the district better fixed for hoisting and compressor facilities.

Last Dollar mine, located on Bull Hill, is a very rich mine and the company owns a total of eighteen acres territory. This mine is said to contain the richest ore at the greatest depth of any mine in the district.

The Wild Horse is also located on Bull Hill, near Altman, the highest incorporated town in the United States. This mine is one of about twenty-five controlled by the Woods' Investment Co., owners of the Gold Coin.

About three years ago, the Woods company merged a number of the mines promoted by them into a great consolidation, with a capitalization of $5,000,000.00, divided into 5,000,000 shares of $1.00 each. The consolidation formed greatly reduced the expense of handling them and the stockholders were thereby benefited.

Upon the slopes of Bull Hill, the activity upon the Hull City placer caused a town to spring up, which received the name of Independence. As time elapsed the town grew in the direction of Goldfield, until it was thought best to consolidate the two, but the two towns still retain their own names even if the distance is short between the two. At Independence the Vindicator mine will be found, right in the heart of unionism. There is no section in the district more loyal to the unions than the set of men on and around Bull Hill.

The Vindicator is one of the many large mines of the district. The development for the last three years has been of the most satisfactory character and the future outlook is all that could be asked by the most sanguine.

The estate of the company comprises about twenty-eight acres of territory, and that great ore-bearing veins and dykes cross it from all directions, which yield considerable ore, is best evidenced by the dividends that are sent quarterly to the various stockholders.

The Strong mine is located just on the northeast boundary of Victor. It is one of the most remarkable mines in the district, and mainly for the fact that its enormous production has been mined from one vein; it being the only property known to have but one producing vein.

The Strong mine is situated in the granite, a portion of the country that the experts said in the early days, would not yield pay ore.

The Strong is a close corporation, owned by four people— William Lennox, E. W. Gidding, E. A. Colburn and Senator N. B. Scott, of West Virginia. The company was organized in 1892.

This mine has produced a fortune for its owners and is an example of what can be found in the granite and the owners, in not heeding the advice of would-be friends, benefited the camp, and proved that experts, who were so ready to condemn the granite, can see no farther into the ground than the ordinary man.

The Elkton Consolidated Mining and Milling Company is located about midway between Cripple Creek and Victor. on the

Low Line electric. Around the mine has sprung the little town of Elkton. But the village has no municipal organization, its population being made up principally of miners employed at the big Elkton mine.

This company has many good lessees operating on various parts of the big estate, and the royalties received from their ore sales each month averages about $3,000.00.

The Elkton company is managed by an executive board, each member of which is a very large stockholder in the company. The following gentlemen compose the management: E. M. De la Vergne, Sherwood Aldrich, Dr. J. W. Graham and George Bernard.

The record made by the El Paso Consolidated Gold Mining Company has been a remarkable one, and well may the officers be proud of their achievement, from a financial point of view, while the stockholders are certainly to be congratulated for the showing their officers have made. During the past two years a vast amount of money has been expended in improvements on this mine. In 1902 the new equipment installed on the property alone cost $104,000. And 1903 was a banner year in the history of improvements for this mine. Not one penny has been drawn from the treasury to pay for the equipment, and besides buying other property and paying all operating expenses, it has all been paid from ore taken from the ground of the company.

The El Paso Consolidated Company is capitalized for $2,500,-000, divided into 2,500,000 shares, each having a par value of $1.

The El Paso Consolidated Company owns close to seven acres of territory and already there has been proven and determined eight veins, five of which contain ore yielding splendid values.

The company's estate is located on Beacon hill and the ore bodies revealed as depth is gained are remarkable. The officers of this company are: S. S. Bernard, president; H. H. Barbee, vice-president and J. M. Jordan, secretary-treasurer; William M. Bainbridge is superintendent and has charge of the actual development of the mine.

In speaking of mines famous for the amount of ore produced, we must not forget to mention the famous Coates prospect hole

known as the St. Patrick—famous because of the fact that there
has been nearly a million dollars expended in prospecting in this
mine and not one ounce of ore as yet received in return. The St.
Patrick was started about April, 1899. It is owned at present by
the St. Patrick Gold Mining Syndicate, of Scotland. The shaft
is 700 feet deep, with 3,500 feet of lateral work. This property
has been almost totally destroyed by fire three times, but would
at once repair all damage or rebuild shaft house and soon be at
work again If perseverance will make a success of an undertaking this mine will yet strike it rich. The St. Patrick is located
in the southwestern part of Victor, four blocks from the post-
office.

STRATTON'S INDEPENDENCE.

Just a word about the discoverer of the great Independence
mine and then I will tell you something of the mine itself.

The late W. S. Stratton, who passed away in 1902, came to
Colorado in the summer of 1872, and was considered a poor man.
He was possessed of an ambition to become a lawyer, and this one
thing more than any other induced him to come to Colorado,
where he hoped to make quickly enough money at mining to study
law. His father could not afford to give him a college education,
but when the youth decided to start out to seek his fortune his
father gave him $500. Young Stratton had been apprenticed to
a carpenter and was well equipped for making his way with the
capital he possessed. He came to Colorado Springs in 1872 and
soon after his arrival he went out and dug in the hills, not far
from the city.

Thus he early began the years of prospecting and study of
the formations of the rocks which finally resulted, in 1891, at
Victor, Cripple Creek district, so successfully. He spent the days
working at his trade and at night studied the intricacies of mining. He devoted nineteen years to the toil of prospecting in the
hills from one range to another, persevering with almost super-
human endurance. On July 4, 1891, Mr. Stratton located two
mining claims, and in honor of the day he named one the Independence and the other Washington.

W. S. STRATTON.

The late Winfeld Scott Stratton was a quiet, taciturn, self-contained man of the simplest manners. He vied with Diogenes in the ability to reduce his wants as the occasion of health and fortune required. His manner was plain, straightforward and unaffected. He was a man whom success and riches did not alter, either in modes of life or disposition. In his days of prosperity he never forgot any of his friends of his toiling, suffering days, and remembered them substantially. It was truly said of him that he was absolutely void of vanity, perhaps the rarest trait known to human kind.

Mr. Stratton came to Colorado in 1872 a poor youth with $500 and a prospector's pick and passed away in 1902 a multi-millionaire.

Stratton's Independence is known everywhere. It has proved to be a phenomenal mine in a phenomenal camp. Some time ago it was generally reported as played out. The real fact of the situation was that the mine was "gouged" in order to pay enormous monthly dividends, without a proportionate amount of development work. Recent developments are gratifying to a high degree.

Stratton, early in the camp's history, made the assertion that any patented claim within the mineral belt was worth $25,000. He backed that statement by purchasing over $4,000,000 worth of unproducing inside territory at an average value of over $40,-000 per claim. . With development, it appears as if a mine can be opened up anywhere.

The daily output of the mine under normal conditions is 260 tons of ore.

This property was purchased by the Venture Corporation and Stratton's Limited of London for the enormous sum of $10,000,-000 and because of its failure to produce that amount to date it has been involved in numerous litigations and controversies.

The old bonanza has had a stormy career since it passed into English ownership. It has been made the subject of stock manipulation on a scale which has seriously hurt the industry of Colorado's foremost camp; it has been experted and denounced frequently, in a manner which appeared ridiculous to onlookers and despite the frequent assertions that it had "played out," the old mine is still doing business and is a good producer.

THE PORTLAND.

In January, 1892, the first stake was set, claiming the Portland claim. The locator had no idea then that the day would soon come when all the surrounding property would be owned, and the claim would be a part of the most gigantic mining corporation in the state of Colorado, if not in the United States.

The original location of the Portland company, which was the Portland claim, consisted of one-tenth of an acre and the Bobtail No. 2, the total of the two being less than three acres of ground.

After the location of the property, James F. Burns, John Harnan and James Doyle commenced operations on it, and in January of 1893, they made their first shipment of ore, which consisted of thirty-two sacks, to Pueblo. For this ore they received $640.00 a ton in gold. The first ore was obtained while sinking the shaft from the surface to the depth of thirty-five feet.

Just a year after the first shipment was made, the owners gave an option on the property to T. J. Condon and Walter F. Crosby, who, a month later, in February, 1894, organized the Portland company. It was capitalized for $3,000,000 divided into 3,000,000 shares of a par value of $1.00 each. The purchase price of the property was $250,000.00. The sum of $15,000.00 was made as the first payment, which meant $5,000.00 to each of the owners. They failed to meet the second payment when it became due, however, and then Messrs. Burns, Harnan and Doyle took charge of the company. A special meeting was called, at which the resignations of the old officers and board of directors were accepted and new officers elected, James F. Burns being elected president and treasurer; the late W. S. Stratton, vice-president and F. J. Peck secretary.

The Portland has had litigation after litigation to contend with. But in a very short time after the company was organized, they paid out, besides the amount expended in litigation, acquir-

THE GREAT PORTLAND MINE.

ing more property, the sum of $2,000,000. All of which they took from the ground during the course of development.

The Portland, as time went on, bought property after property and at the end of five years from the time the first stake of the original claim of less than three acres was staked as the Portland, the company owned close to two hundred acres of rich territory. Every penny paid for the additional property being realized from the sale of ore taken out of the ground; not to mention the fortunes that had to be spent during the first five years in litigation.

The Portland company has the distinction of never having sold one share of treasury stock for the purpose of acquiring money for development. From the first time that ore was encountered they commenced to mine, and as development proceeded, more ore was opened, and the prospects of the mine looked better every day.

The Portland of today stands the best developed mine in the state. Above the 1,100-foot level there are twenty-five miles of workings, which have exposed fifty ore-bearing veins.

This company has the finest equipment in the state. Three shafts furnish the exit for the great tonnage of ore. The Portland up to Jan. 1, 1903, had paid the enormous sum of $4,297,-080.00 in dividends to the stockholders, and the Mining Reporter of Oct. 15, 1903, reported a three cent dividend, making a total of $4,500,000 that has been declared by the company within ten years on a capitalization of $3,000,000.

At the beginning of this year, 1903, the Portland company had hoisted 400,000 tons of ore, that had yielded in gold the sum of $17,000,000.00. In ten years there has been produced $17,000,-000.00 worth of gold-bearing ore.

The mill owned by the Portland, located at Colorado City, Colo., for the treatment of the company's ore, is one of the finest, best appointed and most scientifically constructed chlorination plants in the world. The cost of this institution, which is the consummation of technical skill and energy, was much more than $500,000.

The actual management and development of the great bonanza has always been in the charge of James F. Burns.

Among the distinguished traits of Mr. Burns' character, not the least predominant and praiseworthy, is his philanthropy.

Not of the sentimental sort is the liberality of the great mine owner. Not an instant will he tolerate imposition. He demands of his employes both skillful and conscientious work, and rewards that work in the measure of its merit. Opportunity is the tool of genius and the career of James F. Burns has been its demonstration. Many, perhaps, feel that, had the opportunity been presented to them, they too could have improved it to as good advantage as Mr. Burns. Possibly they could, had they his genius; but their number is not many.

Mr. James F. Burns is looked upon as a hero in the Cripple Creek district, especially by the unions, on account of the stand taken by him in all labor troubles that have as yet confronted the miners of the district. Of his attitude toward organized labor, I will deal more fully in the "strike of 1903."

The Cripple Creek district is dotted everywere with other mines of more or less note, but I cannot undertake the task of describing all the mines in the district. My book's mission is to relate the labor troubles of the camp, and the mines given in detail, were only intended to give the outside public some idea of one of the **greatest gold camps in the world—the Cripple Creek district, Teller county, Colorado.**

Following are a few of the richest mines that have not been mentioned, located in the district: Gold Sovereign, Modoc, Isabella, Independence T. & M. Co., Golden Cycle, Gold King, Mary McKinney, Finley, Theresa, Anaconda, Mary Cashen and many others.

The Cripple Creek district is a $3.00-a-day camp. That is, no one receives less than $3.00 a day for eight hours work. Many receive more, making the average wage per day paid for labor amount to $3.44.

The pay roll for the entire district each month, under normal conditions, amounts to $652,189.41. This does not include the salaries of the managers and superintendents, their salaries amounting to many thousand dollars each month. The total number of men employed in mines in the district January 1, 1903, was about 6,270. This number included coal haulers, ore haulers, power plants, mills, sampling works, timber haulers, assayers and helpers, mining supply men, lumber supply men, etc.

The employes of the camp believe in patronizing home industry, and for that reason very little of the $652,189.41 paid each month to them goes beyond the limits of the district. With such conditions existing, it is readily seen that the merchants enjoy a good trade.

In the latest mining report of the United States the Cripple Creek district takes the lead of any camp in the United States.

VICTOR, THE CITY OF MINES.

(The following applies to the entire district as well as Victor.)

Where the massive granite boulders rear their heads to sun-kissed
    heights.
Where the eager mountain tourists view nature's grandest sights,
Where the summer's sun and winter's snow mingle the whole
    year round,
Where the gold in nature's treasure vaults, by the delving miners
    found,
There is the city of Victor, the city of the mines.

Where progress is our motto and prosperity our lot,
Where our spirits never daunted are, and failure we know not,
Where the people of all nations are as one in enterprise,
Where as evidence of industry, lowering smokestacks pierce the
    skies,
There is the city of Victor, the city of the mines.

Where a host of sturdy miners wrench the gold from nature's
    grasp,
Where the hand of any stranger always meets with friendly clasp,
Where the people work together, all as one in firm accord,
Where the laborer for his labor gets his full and just reward,
There is the city of Victor, the city of the mines.

Where the bells of Sabbath morning call the faithful to the fold,
Where the charity of the people shield the helpless from the cold,
Where the young and old together, the Almighty's praises sing,

Where with song and music always, mountain crags and canons
    ring,
There is the city of Victor, the city of the mines.

Where we do not curse the country every time a thing goes wrong,
Where we do not get discouraged, to that class we don't belong.
Where in future we will prosper as we've prospered in the past,
Where a strike our heads don't worry, for it will not always last,
There is the city of Victor, the city of the mines.

CITY OF VICTOR.—The Smokestack in the center shows location of the famous Gold Coin mine.

The Strike of 1894

It is little less than a dozen years since the deceased multi-millionaire, W. S. Stratton, was tramping the desolate, barren hills of the Cripple Creek district, in search of gold which resulted in his discovering the great Independence mine, which formed the nucleus of a great mining camp. And yet within this short space of time, so stirring have been the scenes enacted within the borders of this district and so determined and constant the struggle for the equalization of power between capital and labor, that twice the military forces of the state of Colorado have invaded the district. They were ordered out in 1894 by Governor Waite to prevent an armed conflict between union miners and mine owners' deputies; and again ordered out in 1903 by Governor Peabody to disrupt the union. I want to give the 1894 strike a few pages, in order to compare the action taken in the two controversies by the chief executives of the state of Colorado.

In the very infancy of the camp, the mine owner capitalists attempted to overthrow the established wage for the miner of $3.00 for an eight-hour day; but they reckoned without their host.

The metalliferous miner of the West is a very different man from the Italian and Hungarian that used to be employed in the eastern coal mines. The most of them are American born. Those who have emigrated came from Germany, Sweden and Ireland. Many had been among those sturdy pioneers, who blazed away and made it possible to speak to the wilderness beyond the Rocky mountains as "The Great West." Such men are not easily subdued.

Although a large per cent of the men were union miners, no particularly active work had been done at this time, 1894, in the way of organizing by the Western Federation of Miners. But, when a common danger threatened alike the union and non-union miner, the membership of the Federation grew by leaps

and bounds. A most determined stand was taken which culminated in the strike of 1894.

A threat was made by the mine owners to import cheap labor
to take the places of the striking miners and the threat backed
up by sending into the district 1,200 deputy sheriffs from the
county seat, then Colorado Springs.

A fort was established on Bull Hill, a well nigh impregnable
point, in the very center of the mining camp. The striking
miners, who, by some mysterious process were well armed, entrenched themselves within the fort. Then followed a series
of the most startling and dramatic events ever known in the history of labor and capitalistic controversies. Riot reigned
supreme.

The 1,200 deputies, who were sent into the district at that
time to enforce the will of the mine owners, made themselves
so intolerable to the citizens generally, by methods pursued by
them in trying to suppress the Western Federation of Miners,
that Governor Waite was petitioned to intercede.

He did so at once; walking from the terminus of the D. & R.
G. railroad, which at that time was being constructed but did not
reach the city of Victor by several miles, through a deep snow, in
the night to interview, personally, the strikers barricaded in the
fort on the crest of Bull Hill.

Take note of the fact that he did not send a ''commission to
investigate,'' but came himself, and walked a long distance in the
snow. He, too, arrived at night but did not leave before day, but
consulted both sides to the controversy. This is well to remember.

Governor Waite was received with the greatest enthusiasm.
He addressed the assembled miners in no uncertain terms. He
exacted a personal promise, which was given willingly and fulfilled faithfully, that the law should be respected. ''And I,'' said
he, ''will see that your rights are respected also, if it takes every
soldier in the state of Colorado to do it.'' His address to the
miners on that memorable occasion is treasured in the heart of
every Cripple Creek miner today for its justice and sound advice,
though it bristled at times with stern reprooff and the assurance of

speedy punishment for every lawless act, regardless of the provocation.

On the governor's return to Denver, troops were sent into the district, not to assist the deputies in their acts of oppression, but to restore law and order. This was promptly accomplished. In a very short time the militia had restored order and ended in a satisfactory manner the strike of '94. Governor Waite occupies the unique position in history of being the only governor in the United States who ever ordered out state troops to protect the rights of the working man against his oppressor.

Though the mine owners resisted at that time with unlimited vigor, and upon the governor's head visited bitter maledictions, Governor Waite's power of penetration and the wisdom of his act has been proven in the fact that for nine, long, prosperous years the Cripple Creek district has been a $3.00, eight-hour camp. The mine owner has enjoyed every luxury. The miner, who risks his life in the bowels of the earth for the precious metal, that procures these luxuries, has enjoyed a comfortable and happy home for himself and family.

Meanwhile the Western Federation of Miners grew in members and power and at the time of this writing, 1903, the organization embraces between 150,000 to 200,000 with a substantial treasury. It has spread its organizations over the states and territories of Utah, California, Nevada, Idaho, Colorado, Arizona, New Mexico and British Columbia.

Not only has the Western Federation's strength grown in its own ranks, but it has fostered, encouraged and assisted, as an elder brother, all other trades and laborers to organize, till there is scarcely a craft in the district that has not its flourishing union.

The local branches of the Western Federation of Miners are located in different towns of the district, each owning its own hall. The two largest unions, located at Cripple Creek and Victor, have established public libraries and reading rooms to which the public, as well as their members are welcome. Each union has a sick benefit fund and buries its deceased members.

Not only have the miners representatives in their own national federation, but in the District Trades and Labor Assembly. This local, central body, composed of delegates from every union in the district, meets once a week, arbitrating, adjusting and deciding all questions pertaining to the general welfare of all. Thus they are practically affiliated with all other unions. The Trades Assembly is a power, may well be added.

Naturally, the corporations have viewed with considerable alarm the growing intelligence and executive ability displayed by the workmen in their employ, and they began some time ago to quietly make plans for combatting that which might eventually be inimical to their interests.

Since the strike of '94, some two or three years ago, there was formed by the mine owners a trust, which included every big producer in the district, with the great Portland as a notable exception. This trust became known as the Mine Owners' Association. It was the supposition that the purpose of the Mine Owners' Association was the subjugation of the Mill and Smeltermen's trusts, which, it was claimed, were most unfair and exorbitant in their prices for the treatment of ore. But they have shown that they organized for other purposes than was at first thought. I will deal more fully with the Mine Owners' Association in the strike of 1903.

The following contribution on conditions of labor in the Cripple Creek district from its inception until up to and after the strike of 1894, explains the situation at that time more fully than I have been able to do:

"By request of the author to contribute something of my experience during the labor troubles of 1894, I submit the following article:

"During the early period of labor in the Cripple Creek district no attention was given to the number of hours employers of labor demanded their men should work; or, in fact, the amount of wages paid the men. Although, with few exceptions, the miners were paid at the rate of $3.00 per day. Outside men received $2.50, $2.75 and $3.00 per day, according to the character of labor performed and the hours they were required to work. In the fall of 1893 a communication was received by Alexander McIntosh, of Aspen, who was at that time duly elected organizer of the Western Federation of Miners for the state of Colorado, to institute a union in Altman, that being the strongest point in the district.

"Mr. McIntosh immediately began corresponding with the men at Altman who were taking the lead in forming a union with the result that a

union comprising about three hundred miners was instituted in the fall of
1893. Mr. McIntosh returning to Aspen shortly afterward, appointed myself his deputy with instructions to organize the remainder of the district.
I at once threw my whole force and energy into the work of thoroughly
organizing the miners of the district, with the result that in less than sixty
days I had instituted unions in Cripple Creek, Anaconda and Victor. This
achievement, in so thoroughly unionizing the district, was rewarded
by a request for me to become president of Altman Miners Union No. 19.
I did so. Although four unions had been organized in the district,
only one charter had as yet been granted by the Western Federation, that
to Altman No. 19. Each of the other unions elected a full set of officers
with the exception of president, working under the Altman charter; the
president of that union presiding over the remaining unions in the district.
The conditions which had allowed men to make their own agreement with
the employers as to hours and wages, soon began to make itself felt. The
owners of the mines which were working eight hours a day claimed their
money was as good as that of the other mine owners, and that unless the
men compelled the other employers to work their men only eight hours
they would likewise demand ten hours from their men.

"This argument was reasonable on the part of the mine owners who
were receiving only eight hours from the employes while others were
receiving ten hours for the same wages. The men at the head of the
unions were quick to comprehend that such conditions could not stand
without a struggle for only a short time. Committees were appointed to
wait on the owners and managers of mines working their men nine and
ten hours a day to induce them to adopt an eight-hour day; but these
committees in each instance met with a refusal to comply with the proposition, in effect, or received an evasive answer that they would present the
proposition to the directors of their companies.

"The strained relations existing between the mine owners and miners
employed on mines working eight hours soon came to a crisis, for on
January 17, 1894, the owners of the mines working their men only eight
hours per day posted a notice in effect that all men who desired to work
for that company on and after February 1, 1894, would be required to work
ten hours for $3.00; or, if the men preferred, $2.50 would be paid for eight
hours work. A similar notice was posted a few days later on the Zenobia
and Buena Vista mines, owned principally by J. J. Haggerman, and both
working eight hours for a shift, the men receiving $3.00 per day. Thus the
clouds were fast darkening the horizon of the industrial world for the
miners of the district. A battle was imminent. The unions had but recently been organized and were still in their infancy, with no money in
their treasuries. Several attempts were made by the unions, with the aid
of the business men, to bring about a conference between the mine owners
and the unions, but without success.

"Finally, on February 1, 1894, a general strike was declared, and, with the exception of the Victor mines, the men responded to the call to a man. The men working on the Victor mines, however, fell in line with their brothers three days later. The number of miners working in the entire district, when the strike was ordered, would not exceed twelve to thirteen hundred. About eight hundred were members of the different unions and about one-half of all the men employed were, up to February 1, working eight hours and receiving $3.00 per day; the other half working nine and ten hours and receiving $3.00 for the same. In thus outlining the early conditions with which the miners had to contend in this district, the writer desires to be fair and treat both sides with impartiality.

"The strike continued from February 1, 1894, until June 10, 1894, a period of five months and ten days, and went down into history as the most bitterly contested strike in this country. But, in order that the reader may more fully understand the true state of affairs as it then existed in the district, it will be necessary to give some idea as to what the miners had to contend with at that time regarding the cost of living. A two-room house, built of rough boards and paper cost $15.00 per month; wood, which was the only fuel to be had, was $4.50 per cord; water, 40 cents per barrel. Provisions had to be hauled by wagons from Canon City or the Divide. Therefore, the cost was nearly one-half more than the present prevailing prices. Clothing was at least 25 per cent higher than at present. Taking into consideration all of the above facts, a man with a family to support was indeed fortunate who could make ends meet. The men, knowing this to be true, banded themselves together as one man and determined to fight for what they considered a right to earn sufficient compensation to properly care for those dependent upon them, and the 'laborer was worthy of his hire.' How nobly they maintained their position is a matter of history. The mine owners, such men as J. J. Haggerman, D. H. Moffatt, Irving Howbert and others, were rated as millionaires, with unlimited money at their command. The county commissioners of El Paso county, this district being in that county, were very active in showing their interest in behalf of the mine owners; also, the sheriff of the county. Feeling ran high, and for a time it looked as though blood would be shed in abundance; but, luckily for all concerned, there were enough cool, conservative men to hold down the hot heads on both sides to the controversy. Some of the business men in Cripple Creek, petitioned the governor for the militia to be sent at once to the district. Accordingly, Governor Waite ordered out the militia and they arrived on the morning of March 7 in Cripple Creek. The miners, in company with business men, considered there was no need for the state guards and that it was only increasing an unnecessary expense that would fall upon the tax payers of the state, petitioned the governor to withdraw troops from the district. The governor then ordered a committee to investigate the situation of affairs and report its findings, which it did. After the committee reported, Governor Waite ordered the troops home. No serious trouble had been committed by either side.

"Immediately upon the troops being withdrawn, the sheriff began deputizing men to fight the miners, and he gathered the scum from nearly all the cities in Colorado. He numbered as his deputies nearly thirteen hundred men. These he placed in the field to intimidate the miners, using nearly three hundred as cavalry under the command of General Adams. The remainder as foot soldiery, equipped with the finest, improved fire-arms, two field pieces and two Gatling guns. All of this war display only tended to cement the union miners more closely together, they determined to meet force with force, if necessary, and prepared to that end. In the meantime a number of the smaller mines had conceded the demands of the unions for eight hours and $3.00 per day. The owners of the Portland mine, having leased and bonded several mines, paid the union scale of wages and acquiesced in the demand for eight hours, and kept their mines at work. A number of leasers also commenced operating in favor of the unions. The total number of men working at this time now numbered three hundred. These men were assessed $10.00 per month, this being the only money the striking men had with which to support themselves and families. One of the most remarkable things was that during all the time this strike was in progress not to exceed ten men left the district. I urged at every opportunity the necessity of every man remaining in the district until a final settlement could be made and peace restored. Many conferences were held between the mine owners and the unions, but no settlement could be arrived at, the mine owners giving their ultimatum at one of these consultations that they were willing to pay $3.00 for nine hours work, or $2.75 for eight hours. When the committee made its report to the unions of the proposition of the mine owners they voted unanimously to turn it down. About May 20, while the miners were attending the funeral of a deceased member, a man by the name of Rabideau who had made himself particularly obnoxious to the miners, and one Ferguson, undertook to call a meeting at Anaconda with a view to getting a number of the deputies there to pass a resolution and have it published in the press of the state, to the effect that a majority of the men were in favor of accepting the proposition of the mine owners and returning to work but were prevented from so doing by intimidation from the union men. But the members of the union were alert and assembled in large numbers to watch the proceedings. When Rabideau addressed the meeting he was asked the object of calling the same, and, upon stating the purpose, he was handled roughly. Both Ferguson and he were taken to Bull Hill, and upon their promising to leave the district for all time, they were released.

"On May 24, the deputy sheriffs were taken via Florence, over the

Florence & Cripple Creek railroad to Wilbur, the road being completed to that point. The miners were early apprised of this move on the part of the deputies, and were assembled by the blowing of whistles, this being a signal arranged to assemble the union men in case of danger. A bitter feeling existed at this time between the miners and the deputies, and they were anxious to give them a chance to fight. About one hundred miners ordered the railroad to get an engine and cars and take them to Wilbur, where the deputies were located for the night, which the railroad men did. The deputies, upon learning of the action of the miners, commenced moving down toward Florence. However, the miners overtook part of the deputies and a running fight took place with the result next morning that the body of the man Rabideau, who had agreed to leave the district two weeks before, was found with a bullet in his heart; also, one of the Herman Crowley miners was killed. This encounter is known as the 'Battle of Wilbur.'

"The following morning a number of men quietly entered the building of the Strong mine and ordered Sam McDonald, Charles Robinson and Jack Vaughn to come out. They declined to do so and retreated down the shaft. Dynamite was then deliberately placed in the boiler inside the shaft house, and with an electric battery, the same was exploded, demolishing the building together with its valuable machinery. Great interest in the fate of Sam McDonald and the two men with him in the shaft of the destroyed Strong mine was felt, but twenty-six hours after the calamity, voices were heard in an old shaft connected with the main shaft of the mine by a drift, and the imprisoned miners were taken out. After getting washed and something to eat, they were taken to what was known as 'Bull Hill stronghold.' Charles Robinson suffered considerably as a result of his terrible experience, but none of the others suffered to any extent. Who was responsible for the destruction of the Strong mine is still a mystery. R. J. Lyons and Nichols Tully were both arrested and convicted for the crime, but the general belief among the people was that some one had to pay the penalty, and on account of the feeling against them they were railroaded to the penitentiary. None of them, however, served out their terms. The owners of the mine afterward brought suit against Sam Strong for being the instigator of destroying the property himself.

"The war spirit had been aroused, but still there were some left who believed and hoped that a meeting could be arranged and moral suasion prevail for peace. The district had taken on the aspect of a military camp. It was impossible to reach the miners' headquarters without proper credentials. May 21, a committee from Colorado Springs, composed of President Slocum, Rev. Evans Carrington, who was a strong sympathizer with the labor movement, and Charles Collais, president of the Trades Assembly, of Colorado Springs, came to Cripple Creek, and called up the officers of the union at Altman by telephone, stating they wished to visit Bull Hill

in hopes of arranging for an arbitration committee. Men were selected to
go to Cripple Creek and escort the distinguished guests to Altman. They
made a hurried trip up the hill and were respectfully received. Professor
Slocum made an extended address. Rev. Carrington and President Collias
also made short speeches which were well received by the men. The
following day a mass meeting of miners was called and I informed the
men of the request of the mine owners for an arbitration committee. The
miners, believing in the justness of their cause, had at all times been
ready to submit their cause to a fair and reasonable committee, so they
readily consented.

"On the following day Governor Waite left the capitol and came to
Altman to make a personal investigation of the situation for himself. This
was a most unusual undertaking, but Governor Waite was an exceptional
governor, entirely fearless in the performance of what he believed to be his
duty—not to one class of citizens in the state, but to all, whether rich or
poor, alike. A meeting was arranged for him to take place in the school
house at Altman, the door being thrown open so all could listen to his remarks. At the conclusion of his speech a committee on arbitration was
appointed , consisting of Governor Waite and myself, this showing the men
had full confidence in the governor. Early the following morning the committee started for Colorado Springs, but failed to reach Adilade, finding
the heavy rains had washed out the roadbed. The party remained in the
car through the day and night, then walked the following day to Florence
through rain and water. Think of the hardships encountered on this trip
in behalf of humanity by the governor of the state, who was then over
seventy years of age.

"Arriving at Florence we were informed that the railroad was washed
out between Florence and Peublo, but through the kindness of Mr. Johnson, of the Florence & Cripple Creek, and Mr. Slack, of the Denver & Rio
Grande, a special train was secured to carry us by way of La Junta to
Colorado Springs.

"The party went to Colorado college and met r resident Slocum, who
notified the mine owners of their presence in the city. Arrangements were
made for a meeting the same afternoon. An agreement was made between
the mine owners on the one side, and Governor Waite and myself on the
other, that J. J. Haggerman be selected to represent the mine owners' side
of the question, and Governor Waite the miners' side, under conditions
that I should remain in the adjoining room and advise the governor upon
all points under discussion with which the governor was not familiar.
After a session of four hours an agreement was reached, Mr. Haggerman,
however, refused to sign until after lunching. During the interval, a
number of mine owners and politicians requested Mr. Haggerman not to
sign the agreement, stating he had given up everything the miners had
contended for. Mr. Haggerman then refused to put his signature to the

document. However, June 5, Mr. J. J. Haggerman, D. H. Moffat and the governor got together and signed the same agreement that was made in Colorado Springs three days before, to the effect that the miners receive $3.00 for eight hours work, and no discrimination be made between union and non-union men, provided the latter were paid the scale of wages. The trouble was not ended, however.

"The county officials were foaming with rage by reason of their utter defeat to intimidate the miners with their twelve hundred deputies, their cannon and Gatling guns. Bob Mullen, who was the real commander at the deputy camp, ordered his men to march on Bull Hill and storm the miners' stronghold. The latter learning of the intention of Mullen, prepared to defend their houses and families to the last. It looked as if the long delayed clash between the miners and deputies was at hand, and hundreds of lives were to be sacrificed. In the meantime, the governor, hearing of the serious condition of affairs, ordered the state militia to assemble at once and proceed to Altman with orders to take a position between the miners and deputies and fire upon the party who persisted in firing a gun. The Leadville company signalized itself by capturing a Midland train in its haste to arrive on time; but the deputies made no determined effort to take Bull Hill until after they saw the state militia assembled between them and the miners.

"General Brooks notified Mullen if he attempted to go on the hill he would fire upon his men. Mullen and Commissioner Boynton, who was really the acting sheriff as well as commissioner, marched the deputies through Cripple Creek and over to Victor, where they camped for the night, near the Independence mine, returning to Colorado Springs the following day. The militia remained in the district about five days. A grand jury was summoned and brought in about forty indictments. Trials dragged along for two years; but, with the exception of Lyons and Tully, no convictions were had. Thus ended one of the most bitterly contested struggles ever fought between capital and labor. The commissioners had used the county's cash with a lavish hand until its treasury had been depleted. A new court house, which the county was about to build, had to go by default; but a lesson had been given both sides to the dispute, and a better feeling soon sprang up between both sides to the dispute, and a better feeling soon sprang up between employers and employes, the same having remained untarnished up to the commencement of the present strike.

"The mysterious man of the 'Bull Hill War,' was General Johnson, who was a West Point graduate—quite an unassuming man, but every inch a soldier, as his record in the Spanish-American war proves. He was commissioned an officer by the governor of Arkansas, and died about three years ago. A number of accidents occurred to the deputies by the accidental discharging of their weapons, Charles Steele, who was manager for W. S. Stratton, lost his life in this manner, as did Columbus Wright. The tarring and feathering of General Tarsney was a disgrace to the state, and showed the class of men the sheriff had enlisted as deputies. A great many of them have since served time in the state penitentiary for offences committed by them.

"When we view the action of Governor Waite, during the strike of 1894 in the district, and compare it with the position taken by Governor Peabody in the present strike, we can not help but say, what fools the toilers are! Governor Waite believed the National guards of the state were to protect life and property, but not for the purpose of farming it out to any man or any class of men. Governor Peabody's actions indicate that he believes the ₁.ational guard is created for the purpose of being farmed out to men possessing wealth, and to oppress the laboring man in the former's interest. The workingmen and their families have the power to select whom they please as governor, and unless they use that prerogative they must suffer. The toilers should raise a monument over the last resting place of all that remains of the best and noblest friend they ever had as governor of the state of Colorado—*Davis H. Waite.*

"JOHN CALDERWOOD, President of No. 19, in 1894.   Dec. 8, 1903.
"Victor, Colorado."

The Strike of 1903

Regarding the strike in the Cripple Creek district, it is necessary to go back nearly a year that we may understand the actual conditions and causes leading up to the main strike.

In the fall of 1902, shortly after the mill workers of Colorado City had been organized by a representative of the Western Federation of Miners, C. M. MacNeil, vice-president and general manager of the United States Reduction and Refining Company, which was operating the Standard mill at Colorado City, started the same tactics that had been used previously in breaking up a union of mill workers of Colorado City—that of discharging the union men as fast as his paid spotters reported their names. This policy on the part of Mr. MacNeil was pursued from about the middle of August, 1902, when the union was formed, until the 14th of February, 1903, when it was found that about forty-two of the most effective members had been discharged for no apparent reason other than being members of organized labor. If this policy was to be pursued by MacNeil, the union would soon be dissolved. The situation in Colorado City is fully described under the caption: "The Strike in Colorado City" which appeared in the April (1903) number of the Miners' Magazine as follows:

"THE STRIKE IN COLORADO CITY."

"On February 14, 1903, the Mill and Smeltermen's Union No. 125, of the Western Federation of Miners, was forced to strike a blow on the industrial field against the arrogance of the mill trust, whose employes were denied the right to organize for self-protection under the penalty of a forfeiture of employment. Previous to the Western Federation of Miners sending an organizer to Colorado City to establish a local of the W. F. M., the employes of the mills had maintained a local union which was disrupted and shattered through the employment of Pinkertons by the corporations. * * *

"When the Western Federation of Miners invaded the domain that was considered sacred to MacNeil, Fullerton and Peck, and organized the Mill and Smeltermen's Union, corporation coin secured the services of a Benedict Arnold in the union by the name of A. K. Crane, who, for Judas money, prostituted his manhood and betrayed his fellowmen by furnishing tne corporations the names of every man who sought shelter in the membership of the Western Federation of Miners. As rapidly as the names of members of the union were furnished by the traitor to Manager MacNeil of the mill trust, they were discharged without ceremony. The union at Colorado City bore with patience this discrimination until patience became so abused 'that it ceased to be a virtue.' The representatives of the Western Federation of Miners called upon the management of the mills, protesting against discrimination, but all efforts to bridge the gulf that lay between the union and the mill owners were fruitless, and the strike was declared on February 14, against the United States Reduction and Refining Company. It was but a short time when the Telluride mill owners joined hands with MacNeil and entered into a compact that was backed and supported by the Mine Owners' Association of Colorado, to fight to a finish any and all efforts of the Western Federation of Miners to establish the right of the mill men to organize for their mutual welfare and collective prosperity. * * *

"Secret meetings of the mill owners and representatives of the Mine Owners' Association were held, and a plot was ..atched that would bring the state militia to the scene of action to assist the corporations in their infamous assault upon the right of labor to organize. The governor of the state became a willing tool to serve the interests of the corporate masters, who, in all probability, a few months before furnished the 'sinews of war' to aid him in reaching the goal of his political ambition. The reason and the cause which led to the strike can be conveyed to the readers in no more abbreviated manner than to quote the language of Secretary-Treasurer Haywood to a reporter of the Denver Post of March 4:

" 'The occasion for the strike was the absolute refusal of the mill managers at Colorado City to treat with or recognize the union. Our men were discharged because they belonged to the union; they were so informed by the managers. We then asked the operators to reinscate these men and consider a wage scale. They would do neither.

" 'We object to compulsory insurance, and claim the constitutional right to organize as do the operators, and want wages that will enable our men to move into houses and not rear their families in tents. The scale asked is lower than in any milling or mining camp in Colorado.

" 'During the bitter cold weather the wives and children of many of the men were huddled togethher in tents because the wages paid would not suffice to pay house rent and provide other necessities.

" 'The minimum scale paid is $1.80 per day, from which is deducted 5 cents for compulsory insurance and one per cent discount. Checks are drawn in favor of merchants with whom the men trade.'

"When the mill owners and the representatives of the Mine Owners' Association realized that the strikers were masters of the situation and their places, a picture was drawn by the corporations to present to the governor that would justify the legality of the state militia being used to break the strike. The governor, in his message to the legislature after having taken the oath of office, was emphatic in his assurance that he would uphold 'law and order.' Such words coming from the chief executive of the state were wisely interpreted by the capitalistic anarchists, who knew that the governor would never call out the state militia to prevent the employer from starving his serfs. On the third of March, at the hour of noon, the governor, who but a few months before was living on usury in the convict city of the state, issued an order that swelled the plutocratic heart with gratitude and joy.

THE GOVERNOR'S ORDER.

" 'Denver, Colorado, March 3, 1903.

" 'Executive Order.

" 'Ordered—It being made to appear to me by the sheriff of El Paso county and other good and reputable citizens of the town of Colorado City and of that vicinity in said county, that there is a tumult threatened, and that a body of men acting together by force with attempt to commit felonies and to offer violence to persons and property in the said town of Colorado City and vicinity, and by force and violence to break and resist the laws of the state, and that the sheriff of El Paso county is unable to preserve and maintain order and secure obedience to the laws and protect life and property and to secure the citizens of the state in their rights, privileges and safety under the constitution and laws of this state, in such cases made and provided.

" 'I therefore direct you, in pursuance of the power and authority vested in me by the constitution and laws of the state, to direct the brigadier general commanding the National guard of the state of Colorado to forthwith order out such troops to immediately report to the sheriff of El Paso county, as in the judgment of the brigadier general may be necessary to properly assist the sheriff of that county in the enforcement of the laws and constitution of this state and in maintaining peace and order.

" 'Given under my hand and the executive seal this third day of March, A. D. 1903.

JAMES H. PEABODY, Governor.

To the Adjutant General, State of Colorado.'

"The order of the governor calling out the state militia to proceed to Colorado City came upon the people of the state of Colorado 'like a peal of thunder from a cloudless sky.' Many doubted the story that was flashed from one to another, but as soon as President Moyer and Secretary-Treasurer Haywood ascertained the truth of the report, the following address and appeal was drafted and furnished to the Denver Post and Rocky Mountain News for publication:

" 'The chief executive of the state of Colorado has ordered the militia to Colorado City. The governor of this great commonwealth, after giving audience for several hours to Manager MacNeil and the representatives of the Mine Owners' Association, men who are pecuniarily interested in the degradation and subjugation of labor, send the armed power of the state to aid the merciless corporations in demanding their 'pound of flesh' from the bone and muscle of men who have borne the tyranny of greed until 'patience has ceased to be a virtue.'

" 'Manager MacNeil acted as a deputy of the sheriff, and handed to the governor the following letter:

" 'I hand you herewith a communication from the Portland Gold Mining Company, operating a reduction plant in Colorado City, and from the United States Reduction and Refining Company, from which I have received requests for protection. I have received like requests from the Telluride Reduction Company. It has been brought to my attention that men have been severely beaten, and there is grave danger of destruction of property. I accordingly notify you of the existence of a mob and armed bodies of men patrolling this territory, from whom there is danger of commission of felony.'

"It does not appear from the letter of the sheriff that he made a personal investigation of the conditions existing at Colorado City. The communications from the corporations to the sheriff of El Paso county actuated the sheriff in placing in the hands of Manager MacNeil, a member of the corporations, an order to Governor Peabody, and upon the strength of this letter, the armed force of the state is to be placed at the disposal of the corporations, to be used in intimidating labor to fall upon its knees in mute submission to the will of oppressors. No word came from the citizens of Colorado City to the governor, stating that there was a mob or insurrection. Depending absolutely upon the unsupported representations of the corporations and a letter from the sheriff, an official, who, from his letter, had failed to make a personal investigation, the governor of this great state has become a willing tool in the hands of corporate masters to place the armed machinery of Colorado in the hands of corporations.

"The governor listened attentively to the gory story of MacNeil, the representative of the corporations. Why did he not summon the representatives of labor, and hear their evidence, as to the conditions at Colorado City? Is there only one side to a story when the interests of corporations are to be subserved and labor humiliated?

"The Western Federation of Miners, through its executive officers, appeal to the laboring hosts of Colorado, to denounce this unpardonable infamy of the governor by pouring into the present legislature an avalanche of protests. The hour for action on the part of labor is at hand, and the voice of the producing class must be heard in thunder tones in the legislative chambers of the state, branding this shameless abuse of gubernatorial power, with the malediction of their resentment.

"CHARLES MOYER, President W. F. M.

"WM. D. HAYWOOD, Secretary-Treasurer.

"As soon as it was learned by the citizens of Colorado City that the state militia had been called out by the governor, and ordered to Colorado City, the mayor and members of the city council held a meeting and the following protest was telegraphed to the governor:

" 'Governor Peaoody—It is understood that the militia has been ordered to our town. For what purpose we do not know, as there is no disturbance here of any kind. There has been no disturbance more than a few occasional brawls since the strike began, and we respectfully protest against an army being placed in our midst. A delegation of business men will call upon you tomorrow with a formal protest of the citizens of the city. (Signed) J. F. FAULKNER, Mayor; GEORGE G. BIRDSALL, Chief of Police; JOHN M'COACH, City Attorney.'

"J. F. Faulkner, the mayor of Colorado City, made the following personal statement to a representative of the Rocky Mountain News:

" 'The only trouble we have had since the strike began was yesterday afternoon, when there were a few street fights. These disturbances were quickly quelled and the offenders were arrested. There were no gun plays. The men simply fought with their fists and probably the employes of the mills who came down town were given the worst of it.' * * * *

"Chief of Police George G. Birdsall, of Colorado City, was interviewed by a reporter of the Rocky Mountain News and spoke as follows:

" 'I have talked with a number of people during the afternoon and they are all exceedingly indignant at the thought of having the militia come among us. If some trouble had arisen which we experienced difficulty in handling, then there might have been some excuse for sending soldiers over here, but nothing of the kind has taken place. I am sure the strikers do not care to employ force to win their victory.'

"In the face of the protests that came from the mayor, chief of police, city attorney and the citizens of Colorado City, the governor attempted to defend his position and his action in the following words:

" 'If I had not considered that the situation warranted the order I would not have issued it. The sheriff is an officer of the court and does not have to make an affidavit. He asked for immediate help and he got it. Those people must learn that they have got to be law-abiding citizens, the same as you and I.

" 'I will protect the property and lives of the people of this state if I have to call out every able-bodied man in the state.'

"This statement of the governor demonstrates that he placed more reliance on the mere assertion of the sheriff than the protests of the mayor, the city council, chief of police and city attorney, whose interests are identified with the city, in which the sheriff assumed without evidence, the threatened destruction of life and property. * * *

"The citizens of Colorado City, to the number of more than 600, signed a petition which was presented to the governor, requesting that the militia be recalled, but the governor remained as adamant to the written appeal of that citizenship. * * *

"The governor is quoted by the Rocky Mountain News in its issue of March 5 as giving expression to the following:

" 'I will not withdraw the troops until the trouble is settled. They are at Colorado City to protect the rights of the miners as well as of the smeltermen. There are no agitators running this administration. This administration is to be run for the benefit of the people. If a man wants to work he has a perfect right to do so and the troops are there to see that everybody's rights are protected.'

"The above proves beyond the question of a doubt the antipathy of the executive of the state against organized labor. 'Agitators' are particularly objects of his vindictiveness. He seems to forget that the 'agitator' in every age of our civilization has been the advance guard in the conflict that humanity has waged against injustice. Philips, Garrison and John Brown were the advance agents of the rebellion, whose 'agitation against chattel slavery lifted the 'lamp of hope' to the trembling black man and made an Abraham Lincoln grasp the pen with the hand of a hero to liberate from slave pen and master's lash 4,000,000 serfs that were bound to the bench of unpaid toil.

"*Christ was an 'agitator,' and we regret to say that it was the Peabodys of his day and age that put upon his brow the crown of thorns, nailed him upon a cross, plunged the spear into his side and mocked him in the agony of death.* * * *

"Previous to the strike being declared, the following letter was presented to the mill managers by the Mill and Smeltermen's union of Colorado City:

" 'We respectfully present for your consideration a schedule relating to employment and wages in and about the mills. This schedule has been carefully considered by members of the Colorado City Mill and Smeltermen's union No. 125, W. F. M., and they deem it a fair and reasonable minimum scale for the services in the various lines of work, and inasmuch as throughout the immediate surrounding places a like or higher scale is in effect, it is evident that both the employer and the employes regard a scale not lower than the one presented as just and equitable. Should there be any part of the schedule, however, which appears to you as not being fair and just, we will be glad to take the matter up with you, and assure you of our willingness to look at things from the company's standpoint as well as our own, and do that which will promote harmony and justice.

" 'We are greatly aggrieved over the discharge of individuals who have been, so far as we are informed, faithful employes of the company, and the only reason for their dismissal being the fact of their membership in this union.

" 'We do not object to the company discharging men whose services as workmen are unsatisfactory. We are not now, nor do we intend to uphold incompetent men nor insist that they be either employed or retained in the employment of the company, but we must protect the men in their rights to belong to the union, even to the extent of discontinuing to work for any company which so discriminates against them.

" 'Realizing that you will require some time to consider the accompanying scale, the committee will call upon you on the 25th inst. and expect a definite answer.'

"This letter was signed by the official committee of the union, but the letter received but little courteous consideration from the managers. When all overtures of the union failed to bring about an amicable adjustment of differences, the strike was declared as a last resort for justice. The mill managers exhausted every resource to fill the places of the strikers, but their efforts were unavailing. The governor then came to the rescue by recognizing the order of the sheriff, who wears the collar of the corporations. The Denver Post contained the following in its issue of March 6:

" 'This is the telegram sent to the Colorado City mill managers by the Denver Post:

" 'Are you willing to submit to arbitration the trouble between your company and the mill workers employed by you, the arbitration board to be appointed by joint arrangement of parties involved? Please answer at our expense.   THE DENVER POST.'

" 'This is the reply:

" 'There is no trouble between our company and mill workers employed by us. Our employes are now and have been perfectly satisfied with wages and treatment. Wages paid by us more and hours of labor less than ore reducing plants with whom we compete. Our employes don't ask to arbitrate. Our plants are full-handed and all our employes and plants require is protection from the violence of outsiders not employed by us. We would be pleased to have your representative visit our plants and fully investigate.   C. A. MACNEIL.

" 'Vice President and General Manager United States Reduction and Refining Company.'

"In the same issue of The Post the following editorial appeared:

" 'C. M. MacNeil, stand up!

" 'Was not this telegram of yours indorsed by the other mine managers?

" 'Is it not true that it is a subterfuge?

" 'Is it not a brazen falsehood from beginning to end?

" 'Is it not a carefully worded telegram, prepared to hoodwink the people of Colorado?

" 'Is it not intended to make the people believe the mill managers are more sinned against than sinning?

" 'Are you not laughing at your own cunning and flattering yourself that you have made a master stroke and have fooled the people?

" 'Your answer to each of these questions, if you are truthful, must be:

" 'Yes.'

" 'Read your own telegram, Mr. MacNeil.

" 'There is no trouble between our company and mill workers employed by us.'

" 'Is it not a fact that your employes are on a strike?

" 'You must answer 'Yes.'

" 'Our employes are now and have been perfectly satisfied with their wages and treatment.'

" 'Is it not a fact that your wages were so low that the men were hungry more than half of the time?

" 'Is it not true that your employes were forced to pay insurance and medical assessments and trade in your stores?

" 'Is it not true that many employes were forced to live in tents because you would not pay them enough to pay for a house?

" 'To each of these questions you must answer 'Yes.'

" 'You say 'wages paid by us are more and hours of labor less than ore reducing plants with whom we compete.'

" 'You know that is a barefaced lie, don't you?

" 'Is it not a fact that the Woods Investment Company pays higher wages for less hours of work than do you?

" 'Answer 'Yes.'

" 'You say, 'our employes don't ask us to arbitrate.'

" 'Is it not a fact that they have offered to arbitrate and you refused?

" 'Is it not a fact that you say, 'there is nothing to arbitrate' to these men?

" 'Is it not a fact that you are trying to break up the union?

" 'Is it not a fact that you have refused and do refuse to recognize the rights of men to organize?

" 'Do you not know this right is guaranteed by the Constitution of the United States that gives to every man the right of liberty and pursuit of happiness?

" 'Do you know that you are seeking to deprive these men of their liberty and deprive them of their happiness by grinding them down to the level of serfs?

" 'You must answer 'Yes' to these questions or tell a deliberate lie.

" 'You say, 'our plants are full-handed and all our employes and plants require is protection from the violence of outsiders not employed by us.'

" 'Do you know that lies teem in every word of that sentence?

" 'Craftily as you have couched that sentence, do you not know that it will not fool the people of Colorado?

" 'Is it not a fact that your plants are not full-handed?

" 'Is it not a fact that there has been no violence?

" 'Is it not a fact that you had the troops called out to awe men who were asking only that you pay them money enough for their labor to allow them to live decently?

" 'Is it not a fact that citizens of Colorado Springs and Colorado City to the number of hundreds have signed petitions to Governor Peabody declaring that there was no violence?

" 'Do you know that these troops are costing the state of Colorado $2,000 a day and that there is absolutely no use for them in Colorado City?

" 'Is it not a fact that you have those troops there just to excite violence?

" 'You must answer 'Yes.'

" 'Is it not true that your company has $12,000,000 of watered stock and pays dividends on starvation wages?

" 'Answer 'Yes'.

" 'Don't you know that you must answer 'Yes' to these questions?

" 'This is what the Western Federation of Miners stands for:

" 'To secure compensatioin fully commensurate with the dangers of our employment and the right to use our earnings free from the dictation of any person whomsoever.'

" 'Do you indorse that for yourself, personally?

" 'Answer 'Yes.'

" 'Is there any reason why every man should not indorse that?

" 'You must answer 'No.'

" 'Here is another point the miners stand for:

" 'To establish as speedily as possible and so that it may be enduring, our right to receive pay for labor performed, in lawful money and to rid ourselves of the iniquitous and unfair system of spending our earnings where and how our employers or their agents or officers may designate.'

" 'Is that not right?

" 'Will you consent to anybody dictating to you how or where you will spend your salary?

"Here is another point the miners stand for:

" 'To use all honorable means to maintain and promote friendly relations between ourselves and our employers, and endeavor by arbitration and conciliation or other pacific means to settle any difficulties which may arise between us, and thus strive to make contention and strikes unnecessary.'

" 'Does this not show that our employes are ready to arbitrate?

" 'Is that not an honorable and fair stand for a man or men to take?

" 'You must answer 'Yes.'

" 'Mr. MacNeil, stand up.

" 'You are the Baer of Colorado.' * * *

"Secretary-Treasurer William D. Haywood, on March 10, expressed himself as follows:

" 'The rights of personal freedom and the liberty of speech are being violated. The strikers' pickets are being arrested on the public domain, when not attempting to encroach on the company's property. They are not permitted to speak to the men who work in the mills, although their purpose is the peaceable one of persuading the men to quit work. So many of the non-union men have left the mills that the company is getting desperate.

" 'Now, the situation is this: The miners of this state do not propose to submit to such oppression. They are advocates of law and order, and they will not long permit it to be violated even by the state's chief executive. There is grave danger in pushing oppression too far, and it is certain that the miners are now in a mood to strike back. They will preserve their liberties and retain their rights if it is necessary to pass through the red sea of revolution in order to do so. Colonists had less occasion to rebel against the authority of King George than have the miners of Colorado to resist the oppression of Governor Peabody.' * * *

"As soon as it became known throughout the state that the militia had been ordered to Colorado City, organized labor in every hamlet, village and city of the state, acted as a unit, in carrying out the instructions that were conveyed in the address that was issued by President Moyer and Secretary-Treasurer Haywood. The first petition that was presented to the legislature in condemnation of the governor, was laid upon the table by a vote of twenty-nine to nineteen. The members of the legislature did not seem to realize that organized labor throughout the state was thoroughly aroused, and when petition after petition came into the chambers of the law-makers, the corporation-owned lackeys of the Peabody administration felt 'a change of heart.'

"The governor for a few days played the role of the parrot to Manager MacNeil, and echoed the slogan of the corporations: 'There is nothing to arbitrate.' 'Nothing to arbitrate,' exclaimed the governor, when the state militia, at an expense of $1,500 per day are located at Colorado City to give assistance to the mill trust in binding the shackles of a more galling bondage on the limbs of the serfs, who rebelled against czarism in

Colorado. Nothing to arbitrate, wnen mill managers ride in $14,000 auto-mobiles, and their employes live in hovels, surrounded by squalor of the most abject poverty? Nothing to arbitrate while misery is the legacy of the mill workers, and fabulous dividends, for the trust? Governor, in the language of the street, 'you are a corker.' The sentiment of the people of Colorado was expressed in the numerous petitions that poured into the state capitol, and the governor showed symptoms of receding from his former position. * * *

"Sherman Bell, the adjutant general, who was recently appointed by the governor, at the urgent request of the Mine Owners' Assoc.ation, and whose salary in the capacity of adjutant general is $1,800 per year, plus $3,200, which is to be appropriated by the Mine Owners' Association, has assumed the attitude of a military autocrat. This imperial bum hero, who won a questionable reputation in the Spanish-American war, by crawling behind the breastworks of black men, who stormed San Juan hill, vomited the burning lava of his pent-up indignation in the following words to a correspondent of the Denver Post:

" 'You may say for me, in the most emphatic and unqualified terms, that while President Moyer, of the Western Federation of Miners, is in Denver carrying a white flag of truce and asking for the good offices of Governor Peabody to relieve him and his factional Coeur d'Alene followers from their present embarrassing predicament, he is acting with a double purpose here by waving a red flag under a black flag and at the same time is endeavoring to be relieved of any and all responsibility for the firing at our sentries by Moyer's assassins and forcing his ideas of arbitration. There is nothing to arbitrate with us on this matter, and everybody concerned might just as well understand it. That is all there is to that.'

"Sherman Bell is not supposed to assume the duties of adjutant general until Gardner of 'Wrath of God' and 'Snowslide Fame,' steps down and out at the expiration of his term in the month of April. But Bell is anxious to impress the mine owners with the fact ι.αt their princely donation of $3,200 per annum in conjunction with the regular salary is duly appreciated, and that no effort will be spared on his part to fully meet their expectaιions in serving the interests of the corporations.

"President Moyer, in the same issue of the Denver Post, which quoted the belligerent verbosity of Bell, had the following to say to a Post correspondent:

" 'The Mill and Smeltermen's union agreed to submit their differences to a board of arbitration, and were willing to abide by the decision of such a board. The terms submitted for arbitration by the Federation are as follows:

" 'First—That eight hours shall constitute a day's work in and around the mills.

" 'Second—That all men now on strike or who shall have been

discharged by the different milling companies for no reason other than that they were members of Colorado City Mill and Smeltermen's union, be reinstated.

" 'Third—That members of organized labor be not discriminated against, but be privileged to affiliate with a labor organization, and that they be not discharged for said affiliation.

" 'Fourth—That the scale of wages as set forth in the demands of the Mill and Smeltermen's union be paid.

" 'Fifth—The Colorado City Mill and Smeltermen's union is willing to submit the above demands to a board of arbitration, selected as follows: The first member of the board to be selected by the governor or the mill managers; the second member to be selected by the Western Federation of Miners, and the third to be selected by the two; and the Colorado City Mill and Smeltermen's Union No. 125, agrees to abide by the decision of the said board, providing that pending their deliberations, the state militia, armed guards, strike breakers and all pickets be withdrawn from in and around the above mentioned mills.

" 'CHARLES MOYER,
" 'Representing Mill and Smeltermen's Union No. 125.'

"The Post in its issue of March 13, said editorially:

" 'WHAT WOULD YOU DO, GOVERNOR, WERE YOU A MILL HAND?

" 'GovernorPeabody, do you wish to learn the difference between the men working in the strikers' places at Colorado City and the strikers? You did not see the strikers when you visited the military camp there. You talked with the men at work in the mills.

" 'Governor, there is a profound difference between those—and that difference represents the truth. * * *

" 'You talked with the men at work in the guarded mill, governor, and they told you that they had no complaints to make.

" 'At that moment a woman, sent by The Post, was doing a natural and practical thing. She was at the homes of the strikers talking with their wives.

" 'They were very poor, governor, so poor that the check you pay in a fashionable cafe for one meal would mean the very affluence of food for a striker's family for one week.

" 'And yet the men had worked very, very hard, governor. They had given every muscle and all the endurance they possessed to the mill— every bit of it—and yet their children would have shouted for joy and their wives wept over the sum of a restaurant check carried by a bowing waiter to the proud cashier of a fashionable cafe. * * *

" 'And then this woman, who writes for The Post, went to the homes of the 'scabs' and saw their wives and children and the men when they returned gloomily home—the men who told you, governor, that they had no complaints to make. * * *

" 'Theirs are the homes, governor, where, after the credit at the store is cut off in the middle of the month, the women live on crusts of bread so that the men may have an egg or a bit of meat to keep up their strength to work for the mill until next pay day, when credit is restored and they can have enough to eat for another half month.

" 'But the men are working—they have no complaint to make.

" 'Governor Peabody, imagine that you were shorn of your power, your fortune, your home—imagine that you had nothing wherewith to support your family, save a chance to earn enough to keep them half alive.

" 'And suppose, governor, that you might lose that chance by a complaint. What would you do? Possibly you would cling to it; possibly you would try to smile through the cold sweat in your face and say:

" 'I have no complaint to make. Let me alone!' * * *

" 'Or perhaps, Governor Peabody, if you found that there were beside you good and true comrades, brave men, who would stand by you, you might throw down your tools and say to your employers:

" 'You must pay us living wages—By God, you must!' * * *

" 'That is the difference, governor, between the men who are striking and those who have no complaint.

" 'Read Dora Desmond's story in The Post today, the story written in the laborers' poor homes, written in the pure light of the sacrifice of their wives, written on the very heart of unrequited toil.

" 'Nothing to arbitrate!'

" 'Why, Governor Peabody, don't you know that if you and the rest of the men who sit in their artistic homes with one hand fondly caressing sweet, sunny-haired children and the other holding up the newspaper wherein they read the news of the strike, don't you know what you and they would do were the conditions reversed?

" 'What would the so-called 'ruling classes' do if they found themselves giving their lives for one-half of a right to live? * * *

" 'How long would 'the great conservative, intelligent citizenship' stand it? How long would the mill owners toil in weary silence? How long would you endure slavery?

" 'Did it ever occur to you what the men would do who demand that union labor shall be crushed were they the toilers?

" 'Did it ever occur to you, governor that they might say:

" 'We can't arbitrate poverty and suffering.'

" 'But union labor offers to arbitrate, governor.'

"The Rocky Mountain News had the following editorial in its issue of March 14, 1903:

" 'SOME ADVICE BY REQUEST.'

" 'Governor Peabody said yesterday that the News had been criticising him so freely that he would like that paper to tell him what it thought he should do to bring about arbitration of the Colorado City strike.

" 'Whether the governor's expressed wish was an outburst of petulance or was caused by a real desire to receive a suggestion, the News does not know, but it will try to give the best advice it can.

" 'The first thing the governor should do to bring about arbitration is to believe that there ought to be arbitration, and then to act as if he believed it. So far as the press and public have been able to discover from the governor's words and actions, he has never given any intimation to the mill owners that he thought they should recognize the union and arbitrate tne differences. Never has he made any declaration to the public that he thinks there should be arbitration.

" 'As a first step toward facilitating arbitration, let him make the public statement that he thinks the mill owners should accept the proposal of the Western Federation of Miners and that they will deserve to be condemned if they fail to accept it.

" 'The governor should understand that the people of this state, almost without exception, look on him as a partisan of the mill owners and think that the mill owners would have agreed to arbitration long ago were it not that they expect to have his full support whether they be right or wrong. This belief in the minds of the people may do the governor an injustice, but if it does he is responsible for it, and he only can remove it.

" 'The conviction that the governor stands with the mill owners took deep root when he called out the National guard and rushed it to Colorado Springs. Manager MacNeil of the mill trust came to Denver, carrying in his pocket the request of Sheriff Gilbert for troops. Nobody had any idea that troops were to be asked for. There had been no disorder to warrant their entry on the scene. The sheriff of El Paso county had made no effort to employ the peace force of the county. The municipal authorities of Colorado City were prepared, alone, to keep order.

" 'But the governor and Manager MacNeil went into private con- ference and when they came out the order to the troops came with them. The governor did not go to Colorado City himself, he did not send anybody to investigate, he took the ex parte statements of the manager of the mill trust and the request of an incompetent sheriff as his warrant for sending a small army to Colorado City at an expense of over $1,500 a day to the state.

" 'Then the governor pushed aside the recognized officers of the National guard and gave some kind of a personal commission to Sherman Bell and James H. Brown, both of whom have conducted themselves in exactly the right way to provoke trouble. The appointment of Sherman Bell to be adjutant general of the state troops, beginning in April, is in itself an indication of the most extraordinary ignorance or recklessness on the part of the governor. A hair-brained adventurer like Bell is about the last man in the state who should be placed in a position so responsible as that of adjutant general.

" 'The public conviction as to the governor's mental attitude was fixed by his recent trip to the scene of the strike. He talked with the men working in the mills, but refused to go to a meeting of the strikers to which he was invited. Instead of spending the evening talking with the strikers and learning their opinions he chose to hold a social function in the Antlers hotel. At another time a public reception in the Antlers would have been in good taste. Under the circumstances which took the governor to Colorado Springs it was in the worst possible taste, and no man with an ounce of good judgment in public affairs ever could have been led into such an indiscretion.

" 'If the governor has any wish to invite public confidence in himself and his administration, he will recall Bell and Brown from Colorado City, revoke Bell's appointment as adjutant general and require Brown to confine himself strictly to the duties of his proper rank in the guard.

" 'The proposition of the union is that the mill owners shall select one arbitrator, the Western Federation of Miners the second and those two the third, the finding of the board to be binding on both sides.

" 'If the governor believes that proposition to be fair, let him say so.

" 'Then let the governor notify the mill owners that if they will not accept that proposition at the meeting this afternoon he will withdraw the National guard from Colorado City and will issue a statement to the public saying that the mill owners are not disposed to be fair.

" 'If the governor will take that attitude an agreement to arbitrate will be reached before today's sun goes down. If he says there must be arbitration there will be arbitration.'

"The governor could no longer maintain his position that 'there was nothing to arbitrate.' Public sentiment became so strong that he was forced to use his office in bringing together both parties to the controversy. The governor requested the mill managers and the representatives of the Federation to meet at his office on the afternoon of March 14, for the purpose of obtaining further personal information. The Federation was represented by President Moyer and Secretary-Treasurer Haywood, who secured the temporary services of an attorney. The mill owners were represented by their managers and attorneys. The conference lasted from 2 o'clock Saturday afternoon until 3 o'clock Sunday morning, with the following result:

"Terms of the Portland mill:

"First—that eight hours shall constitute a day's work, in and around the mills, with the exception of the sampling department, which may extend to ten hours per day.

"Second—That in the employment of men by this company there shall be no discrimination between union and non-union labor, and that no person shall be discharged for reason of membership in any labor organization.

"Third—That all men now on strike shall be reinstated within twenty days from Monday, the 16th day of March, A. D. 1903, who shall have made application for work within five days from said date.

"Fourth—That the management of the Portland Gold Mining Company will receive and confer with any committee of the Colorado City Mill and Smeltermen's Union No. 125 at any time within said twenty days upon the subject of a scale of wages.

"Dated at Denver, Colorado, this 14th day of March, A. D. 1903.

"FRANK C. PECK,

"For the Portland Gold Mining Company.

"CHARLES MOYER,

"For Mill and Smeltermen's Union.

"Terms of the Telluride mill:

"First—That eight hours a day shall constitute a day's work in and around the mills, with the exception of the sampling department, which may be extended to ten hours per day.

"Second—That in the employment of men by this company there shall be no discrimination between union and non-union labor, and that no person shall be discharged for reason of membership in any labor organization.

"Third—That all men formerly employed by the Telluride Reduction Company shall be reinstated in the same positions which they occupied in the mill at the time it closed down, it being understood that in the new mill now under constructionn by the Telluride Company that there will be certain positions in the new mill which did not exist in the mill as formerly operated, and that the agreement of the Telluride Company to the reinstatement of men shall apply to the positions in the new mill which were in existence in the old mill.

"Fourth—That the management of the Telluride Reduction Company will receive and confer with any committee of the Colorado City Mill and Smeltermen's Union No. 125, within any time after thirty days from the date upon which the mill is placed in operation to consider a wage scale.

"Fifth—The Telluride Reduction Company further agrees that during the period of construction of this mill that it will employ as many of its old employes as it finds practicable so to do.

"Manager MacNeil, of the Standard mill, who has at all times maintained a stubborn attitude, practically forced himself out of the conference with the Portland and Telluride mill managers. President Moyer and Secretary-Treasurer Haywood, at the request of the governor, accepted an invitation to meet the manager of the Standard mill on Sunday, March 15, at 11 o'clock. The meeting took place at the governor's office, but all efforts on the part of the Federation representatives to bridge the gulf were unavailing. Manager MacNeil refused to reinstate the strikers, made no mention of the wages he would concede to his employes, nor would he consent to a recognition of the union.

"The governor agreed that he would withdraw the state militia, providing the Western Federation of Miners would withdraw the suits that were entered against officers of the Colorado National Guard. If the representatives of the Federation had refused to accede to the demands made by the governor, the people of Colorado would have the inestimable privilege of continuing to donate $1,500 per day as an expense account for soldiers on dress parade. The people of the state have sized up the present executive, and have concluded that he is smaller mentally than he is physically. In the words of a prominent mining man, 'He is a Reuben from the country who shies at an electric light.' He has lived so long in the rural districts of Colorado that bunches of alfalfa have grown on the gray matter in his think dome, and the war horses of the G. O. P. are endeavoring to disclaim responsibility for the political accident that nominated and elected the present apology as governor of the state.

"After it became known that the Telluride and Portland mill managers and the representatives of the Federation had arrived at a satisfactory settlement, there was a general rejoicing, but amidst the jubilation there could be heard strong words of condemnation for Manager MacNeil of the Standard, who repudiated with haughty arrogance the reasonable demands of the Federation representatives.

"The Cripple Creek Press, the official organ of organized labor of the Cripple Creek district, (since suspended) had the following to say in its editorial columns of March 15: (1903.)

" 'The announcement of a settlement of the differences between the Mill and Smeltermen's Union No. 125, of Colorado City, and the managers of the Portland and Telluride mills is pleasing to the people of this district, but the failure of the United States Reduction and Refining Company to enter into the agreement made by the other mills means something which is not pleasing. It means that unless the mines shipping to the Standard mill accede to the demands made upon them by the executive board of the Western Federation of Miners, that they quit shipping their ores to the said United States Reduction and Refining Company on Monday, that the miners employed by them will be called out by the Federation. It means that when these men are called out in support of their brothers on strike against the Standard mill, they will go out and tie up those mines so tight that Manager MacNeil will have a difficult time in getting material to keep his pet scabs at Colorado City employed. The Western Federation has done everything in its power to bring about an amicable settlement, and when Manager MacNiel refuses to accept the terms made by the managers of the other mills he places himself behind the pale of public consideration and the only thing now left for the mine managers who are shipping to his mill will be to whip him into line or submit to a strike of miners employed by them. There is no middle ground with the miners on this question. They will be compelled to insist upon the demands made by them being complied with or walk out.'

"The governor failed to keep his proimse that he would immediately withdraw the troops, and the delay of the governor in issuing his order recalling the state militia caused the following to be issued from the headquarters of the Western Federation of Miners ōn March 17:

" 'The representatives of the Western Federation of Miners, since the strike was declared at Colorado City, have at all times held themselves in readiness to confer with the mill managers for the purpose of bringing about an amicable adjustment of differences. ʀʼor months previous to the strike, the officers of the Federation labored early and late to bring about an honorable settlement, which would . prevent any open rupture between the mill managers and their employes. The officers of the Federation have given a respectful hearing to representatives in all departments of business, and at all times have shown a disposition to submit their grievances to a board of arbitration. Had the mill managers manifested as earnest a desire to pour oil upon the troubled waters as the Western Federation of Miners, the people of the state oî Colorado would never have been compelled to forward protests against the executive of the state for his loyalty to corporate interests.

" 'Had the mill managers exhibited even tne slightest disposition to act in a spirit of justice to their employes the strike would have been averted and the treasury of the state would not have become a graft for military officials who are 'bug house' when clothed with the uniform of blue. The militia of the state has been used for the purpose of inciting riot, but with all the infamous schemes concocted by Bell and Brown, the strikers have remained unruffled, and have shown to the people of Colorado that they are law-abiding, and that even uniformed ruffians could not goad them to acts of violence. The sheriff of El Paso county has demonstrated that he has been a willing auxiliary in the hands of the mill managers to exaggerate the conditions of the situation at Colorado City so that corporations which refuse to arbitrate could secure the militia to perform picket duty at the expense of the state.   *   *   *

" 'The governor, toward the close of the interview ꝃunday morning, admitted without any solicitation, that the representatives of the Western Federation of Miners had gone more than three-fourths of the way and had been more than fair in bringing about a settlement and that he would at once issue an order to withdraw the troops. The governor admitted, after his personal investigation of affairs at Colorado City, that he was unable to connect the strikers with any violation of the law. In the interview that was held Sunday at the governor's office to arbitrate with Manager MacNeil, the governor receded from his former agreement to withdraw the troops. He asked the representatives of the Western ꝛ·ederation of Miners for a further concession, namely, that he would immediately withdraw the troops providing that the Federation would withdraw all suits against the officers of the state militia. The representatives of the Federation were again maganimous and accepted the proposition of the governor.

" 'The governor and attorney general asked that these suits be withdrawn as a personal request, owing to the fact that tne office of the attorney general was crowded with business and that no funds were available for engaging special attorneys to defend the military officials. The governor and the attorney general remembered the opinion that was rendered by Rogers, Riddle and Helm during the ౼eadville strike of 1896, and knew that the legal opinion rendered by tnis trio of constitutional lawyers would have far-reaching effect on some of the brainless nonenities that are now connected with Colorado's National guard. The governor has violated every syllable and letter of his agreement by sending his private secretary to Colorado City to make a personal investigation and report. The private secretary to the governor, when reaching Colorado Springs, placed himself under the supervision of Bell and Brown, so that his report to the governor would be of such a character as would enable militia grafters to live a little longer on 'easy street' at the expense of the state.

" 'The action of the governor has shown him to be weak and vacillating, and that he is a man who has no conception of the dignity of his office. The Western Federation of Miners, through its representatives, have used every honorable effort to bridge every chasm, notwithstanding the fact that the Mine Owners' Association, the mill managers, the state militia and even the governor himself have been arrayed against them.

" 'The governor is now intimating that we promised there would be no strike in the Cripple Creek district. We never made any such promise. It would have been an impossibility for us to make a promise of that character while MacNeil, the 'Baer of Colorado,' refused to recognize the Western Federation of Miners. We gave the governor to understand that we would fight ౼acNeil to a finish, and under no circumstances could he construe our meaning that a strike would not be declared upon the mines that would ship ore to unfair mills. We have been willing and are now willing to arbitrate with Manager MacNeil. He has refused to arbitrate with us as an organization, and he alone is responsible for the situation that confronts the people of the Cripple Creek district. We have been more than fair, and have gone three-fourths of the way, according to the governor, and we are now willing to place the justice of our cause in the hands of the whole people of the state, and let ౼em be the jury to bring in the verdict.

(Signed) " 'CHARLES MOYER, President W. F. M.
" 'WILLIAM D. HAYWOOD, Sec-Treas. W. F. M.'

"Charles Moyer took his departure for the Cripple Creek district on the afternoon of March 16, to hold a conference with the members of

District Union No. 1, as to future action in reference to .he Standard mill, whose manager absolutely refused to recognize the Western Federation of Miners or their representatives in the settlement of the strike.

"President Moyer, after arriving in the Cripple Creek district, immediately went into conference with the district members, and it was agreed at said conference that the mines that were shipping ore to unfair mills should be requested to refrain from so doing, or that the men on such mines would be called out. The conclusion arrived at by the meeting was not put into execution until 4 o'clock in the afternoon of March 17, at the request of a committee of business men who labored with MacNeil for a settlement of the strike. The committee of business men failed to induce MacNeil to accept the terms proposed by the representatives of the Federation, and the ultimatum of District Union No. 1 went into effect. * * *

"The governor, after receiving telephone communication from his private secretary, whom he had dispatched to Colorado City to report on the situation, issued the following order at 7 p. m. March 17:

" 'Denver, March 17, 1903

" 'Colorado City, Colo.,

" 'Sir—You will immediately recall the troops under your command, now at Colorado City, to their company stations, together with all quartermaster, ordnance and commissary stores, the property of this state, and report to the adjutant general.   JAMES H. PEABODY.

" 'Governor and Commander-in-Chief.'

"Sherman Bell, the adjutant general-elect, whom Governor Peabody has slated, has been unanimously condemned, not only by members of organized labor, but men in every department of business have covered the hair-brained, strutting, burlesque on a soldier with the odium of their contempt. The delegates in the Republican convention that was held recently in Cripple Creek denounced the utterances of Sherman Bell as 'idiotic, revolutionary and un-Republican.' Resolutions have been passed and forwarded to the state senate demanding that his appointment shall not be confirmed by that body. Blow-hard Bell is a Republican and a resident of the Cripple Creek district and this repudiation by men who know him best should cause the governor to hesitate in placing the state militia in the hands of a man who has proved himself an irresponsible wind bag with nothing to him but 'hot air' and feathers.

"During the strike at Colorado City, while the commanding officers of the state militia were ignoring the rights and liberties of citizenship, Judge F. W. Owers threw a bomb in the shape of a judicial opinion, that caused the state administration to clip the wings of the verdant captains and colonels whose heads were expanded through self-importance. The legal opinion that was written by Judge Owers and published in the Denver papers, defining military and civil authority, was unanswerable, and the minions who craved to serve their masters were put up against a stone wall. F. W. Owers commands the respect of every laboring man in the state, who recognizes in him one of the highest types of that incorruptible manhood whose unswerving loyalty to justice gives dignity and honor to the judiciary.

"March 1, at 9 o'clock in the morning, Camp Peabody passed into history, and the 'boys in blue' returned to their homes to discard the uniform and become peaceable and law-abiding citizens"—Miners Magazine, April, 1903.

On March 31, in order that Manager MacNeil might be placed on trial before the people of the state to see if he would keep his word to the governor's commission, President Charles Moyer, of the Western Federation of Miners, acting for the union declared an armistice until May 18. The news of this armistice was received in the Cripple Creek district with unalloyed enthusiasm by the entire population. Bells were rung, mine whistles were blown, bands of music paraded the streets to the accompaniment of plenty of red fire and fire crackers. The terms of agreement, as stated in the public press, were that the union should be recognized and those who had been discharged reinstated by May 18, an eight-hour clause was also added, but we are all familiar with the terms on which MacNeil agreed to settle at that time.

But as soon as the strike was declared off and the miners of the Cripple Creek district began breaking ore to supply the plants of the United States Reduction and Refining Company, Mr. Mac-Neil apparently forgot he ever made any promises to the governor's commission, for he failed to keep the promises he made on March 30, when the armistice was declared and the strike raised. The minimum wage of $2 for outside and $2.65 for inside work had been established in the Portland and Telluride mills, but at the Standard mill the wages were only $1.75 per day. Early in August, District Union No. 1, again took up the case with the United States Reduction and Refining Company, and endeavored to adjust the differences. They sent a committee to Colorado City and held a conference with Mr. MacNeil, and tried to induce him to pay the same wages as prevailed at the Portland and Telluride mills, and to stop discrimination against members of the union. While Mr. MacNeil received the committee and freely discussed conditions, and even admitted that $1.75 a day was not enough for any man to raise a family on, he positively refused to grant the request of District Union No. 1. After MacNeil's answer was received it was decided to call a strike on all mines in the Cripple Creek district that were shipping ore either direct or indirect to any of the plants of the United States Reduction and Refining Company.

THE STRIKE.

The Western Federation of Miners started its fight on these lines August 8, while the men were not officially called out so early the work was going on. President Moyer, of the Western Federation came to the district and held a conference with the district committee of miners. The matter was discussed at length, and the decision reached was to call out all the miners of the Cripple Creek district Monday forenoon of Aug. 10. This was found necessary in order to bring the mills at Colorado City in line on the question of hours and wages in the Standard Reduction company mills. This came as a great disappointment to the business men of the district who had hoped and about concluded that there would be no strike in the mines of the district, but the Federation felt that it needed the assistance of the miners of the district to win the fight and called upon them to take an active part. It was understood that there was no grievance in this district and that the miners here were quite satisfied with conditions but they were obliged, as members of the Western Federation of Miners, to act on the matter.

There were many also who were glad to see the matter come to a square issue, as it had been "hanging fire" for some time, and both the business men and the miners were uneasy as to the continuation of the uncertainties that existed for some time. They felt that even the worst was better than the continued suspense. They also felt that it would soon be settled permanently and that the miners would not go to work again until it was settled satisfactorily to all. The Western Federation of Miners was well prepared for the fight and had little difficulty in raising the amount of money needed to make the strong fight they have made.

THE CALL.

"All members of the Western Federation of Miners and all employes in and about the mines of the Cripple Creek district are hereby requested **not to report for work Monday morning, August 10, 1903, except on properties shipping ore to the Economic mill, the Dorcas mill at Florence and the Cyanide mills of the district. BY ORDER DISTRICT UNION NO. 1.**"

The foregoing notice expresses concisely the action taken on the night of Aug. 8, by District Union No. 1, of the Western Federation of Miners, upon the return to the district of the committee which attempted to secure from MacNeil the promise that the Standard mill men should be paid the union scale of wages. During the stay of the committee Mr. MacNeil absolutely ignored all requests of its members, leaving the declaration of a strike at the mines their only alternative. The order embraced all miners in the district except those shipping to the Dorcas and Economic mills or to the cyanide mills situated within the district, and called out fully nine-tenths of the miners employed.

Before the order was issued, when it was known what Manager MacNeil's attitude would be, the committee discussed the matter in all its phases with President Moyer and members of the executive committee, and the order was the result of the discussion. Its sweeping character and its workings were thoroughly canvassed and it was regarded by all as being the only means to attain the end. The committee on being asked why they had taken the foregoing action said:

"Manager MacNeil's refusal to treat with us left us nothing to do but to order a strike and in so doing we adopted the only plan which promised certain success. In our proposals to him no mention was made of his failure to re-employ men who went out in the former strike, as he had agreed. We confined ourselves strictly to the question as to whether he was willing to pay the union wages demanded by his striking employes, and when he absolutely refused to do so or to recognize us in any way, our mission was ended."

It was confidently believed and predicted at that date by

labor leaders, and hoped by all, that the strike would be of very short duration, though the Federation even at that time stated that they were in every way prepared for a long hard fight if necessary. They considered the question thoroughly before they took the action, and would not have ordered the strike had they not been fully prepared. A prominent official said on being interviewed shortly after the order was issued:

"While the strike just ordered is directed primarily at the unfair Standard mill, it may be regarded as but the precursor of a fight all along the line for an eight-hour day. For months the Federation has been gathering funds from its members and from the friends of unionism all over the globe for such a fight, and it is now determined that the eight-hour day shall prevail throughout its jurisdiction. Should the fight be now precipitated and should extreme measures be necessary, it would not surprise me to see the miners throughout the entire state called out. Such a course would tie up every thing in the state, but it would soon bring the enemies of labor to their senses."

In Victor when it was known positively that the long talked of strike was at our door at last, it was the one topic of conversation. Little crowds gathered here and there and everywhere and discussed the situation. While the necessity for a strike was generally regretted, sentiment, too, was almost unanimously with the miners in their fight for living wages for their fellowmen.

August 11, found the strike in full swing, men at Independence, Ajax, Findley, Vindicator and a score of others had responded to the call and quit work. The Portland at this time was still working, pending a conference to be held the following morning. President Burns was in the district and felt confident that the Portland would not be put under the ban. The committee in charge of the strike held a conference with Mr. Burns August 10, and while no decisive action was taken, it was agreed that the men should continue work at the mine until another meeting should be held August 11, and some course of action decided upon.

President Moyer was in the district giving the strike his personal attention, and on being questioned on the subject said:

"There seems to be no reason for a prolonged struggle, as

the Standard mill matter is a small one which should be easily adjusted. It was simply a demand of the union men of this district that their brethren of Colorado City should be paid fair and living wages."

The Woods properties which ship to the Economic mills were not affected by the strike order, and were working as usual. The Deadwood, employing a small force of men, was closed down Aug. 10, but from reasons entirely foreign from the strike. The Gold Coin and the other properties maintained the force employed.

All day August 10 and 11 and until late at night the strike was the sole topic of conversation on the streets. The general view seemed to be a hopeful one—a view which was encouraged by the reports from the railroads that no unusual number of tickets to outside points were being sold. A special effort was made by union officials and union men to avoid friction or trouble of any kind, and the first day of the strike passed quietly without a disturbance. Sheriff Robertson was in Victor on the above date and said: "Aside from the unusual number of men on the streets he encountered nothing in his rounds in the district which would excite even the slighest apprehension."

Manager Cornish, of the Independence, that was shut down August 10, by reason of the strike, said:

"He did not know what his company would do should the strike continue longer than a few days. That the mine had been employing about 500 men and should he receive orders to resume work with a strike on, he could hardly hope to resume with anything like that number. It would be less expensive to remain closed down than to resume with a fraction of the regular force. For that reason I do not expect an order to resume."

After the men employed on the drainage tunnel were called out, Superintendent Bainbridge, of the El Paso, announced to newspaper men that the tunnel would be pushed to completion, even if he and other officers of the company were obliged to don overalls and run the machines themselves.

Governor Peabody, even so early in the strike as August 11, said: "If an emergency arises I shall be prompt to order out the troops in the Cripple Creek district.'' He said, however, that he did not apprehend trouble from the striking miners.

It was said at that time that the governor had determined not to move hastily this time, as in the case of the Colorado City strike, and that he would not send troops into the Cripple Creek district until there was a general demand for them.

Manager MacNeil was in the district on August 11, viewing his work. He, however, declined to be interviewed, and refused to answer any and all questions as to the object of his visit.

August 12 found the tie up in the Cripple Creek district complete. The committee was able by that time to reach the mines that they had not been able to reach before. The reader will at once understand that it would be utterly impossible to visit every mine in the district in less than forty-eight hours, but as fast as it could be attended to the men were called out, with the result that on Aug. 12 the El Paso, Golden Cycle, Last Dollar, Modoc, and all that had not been visited at that date walked out. There was hardly a break in the ranks of the Western Federation of Miners to obey the call. The committee and Mr. Burns, president of the Portland, through a false report that had been circulated, failed to come to satisfactory terms to both sides and the 550 men on the Portland were also called out. Mr. Burns addressed the men, reciting his long friendship for them and for organized labor. The men listened respectfully and attentively. But as the committee and Mr. Burns had failed to agree at that time, they went out as ordered to a man. Thus it will be seen that the great industry of the district at the above date was practically at a standstill with the exception of the Woods properties, which at that time were considered fair. By evening of Aug. 12 there were at least 3,000 men out. C. G. Kennison, president of Miners' Union No. 40, of Cripple Creek, said on the night of Aug. 12, that things were progressing nicely and satisfactory to the W. F. M. He and other local officers were busy all day handling the details of the strike. Mr. Kennison stated on that date that ever since the first declaration of the strike the secretaries of the different unions of the district had been kept busy writing receipts for union dues. The announcement of trouble was a forcible reminder to the men that they should see to it that they were in good standing with their unions, and at no time in the history of the district had the payments been so prompt and so large.

Along about August 12 or 13 a meeting of the mine owners and mill managers was held in Victor and was attended by representatives of nearly every property in the district. The existing conditions were discussed at length, but no announcement was made at that date of any decisive action having been taken. A committee was appointed to act for the mine owners in all matters pertaining to the strike

August 14, 1903, the following article or statement was published by the Mine Owners' Association:

"A general strike has been called on the mines of the Cripple Creek district by the executive heads of the Western Federation of Miners. At the time this strike was called, and, in fact, ever since the settlement of the labor difficulties of 1894, the most entire harmony and good will has prevailed between the employers and the employed in this district. Wages and hours of labor have been satisfactory and according to union standards, and general labor conditions have been all that could be wished.

"Notwithstanding all this, the heads of the Western Federation have seen fit to compel the cessation of all labor in the district, not because of any grievance of their own against the Cripple Creek operators, but for reasons entirely beyond our control. A no more arbitrary and unjustifiable action mars the annals of organized labor, and we denounce it as an outrage against both the employers and the employed.

"The fact that there are no grievances to adjust and no unsatisfactory conditions to remedy, leave the mine operators but one alternative, and that alternative they propose to adopt fearlessly. As fast as men can be secured, our mining operations will be resumed, under former conditions, preference being given to former employes, and all men applying for work will be protected to the last degree.

"In this effort to restore the happy conditions which have existed so long, we ask and confidently count on the co-operation and support of all our former employes, who do not approve the methods adopted, as well as of the business men of the district who are equal sufferers with us.

"In the resumption of operation, preference will be given to former employes, as before stated, and those desiring to resume their old positions are requested to furnish their names to their respective mines at an early date."

The foregoing was signed by about thirty properties.

The mine owners' statement was issued after a conference of

the committee appointed at the meeting of the day before and occasioned much comment. The committee was composed of William Bainbridge, of the El Paso, chairman; Samuel Bernard, of the Elkton; J. S. Murphy, of the Findley; Charles Aldron, of the Last Dollar; Thomas Cornish, of the Independence; C. C. Hamlin and A. E. Carlton.

Just what the mine owners expected to gain by the foregoing statement is hard to understand.

Their statement would indicate that the Federation was composed only of the miners in this district; that it began and ended here. They forgot during the time of writing their statement that the Western Federation of Miners has hundreds of members outside of the state of Colorado as well as in it. There would be just as much folly in the miners of this district going alone as it would for the mine owners of one of these hills, exclusive of a united organization, such as they have here now, making their fight alone. The Western Federation of Miners extends beyond this district and when its members need help at Colorado City, or any where else, it is the duty of the members here to go to the assistance, and the mine owners know that as well as they know that there is an organization. The members of the Federation at Colorado City were entitled to just as much protection there as they are here or elsewhere and there was, therefore, no mystery about the strike that needed any explanation to the people of the Cripple Creek district, although an effort was made by outside newspapers to create that impression. Up to August 15, the Mine Owners' Association had held two meetings in Victor, at least, they held one and their committee another. Does any one propose to claim that if they had devoted the same length of time with Charles MacNeil that they would not have succeeded in causing him to meet the wages of his competitors at Colorado City? What was the difference between the fight that began in August and the one that was made last spring? It was the same identical fight with the exception that we had the failure of Mr. MacNeil to keep his former promise with the Federation in reinstating men and paying wages.

The mine owners' statement is the usual corporate appeal to union strikers, when making a stand for justice, or fair conditions, to renounce their union, (the only protection that the wage earner has under the present system of corporate rule), and return to work under armed protection of the professional deputy thugs and corporation vassals. It is needless to say that the union man stood firm and true to his obligation and hurled back in the face of the would-be bribers, the offer to sell his manhood for corporation gold. The position taken by the Mine Owners' Association, that the strike was a sympathetic one, is known to all, whether members of the Federation or not, to be untrue and only those who had given little or no thought to the subject would give publication over their signature to such shallow argument. There was no disposition on the part of the membership of the Western Federation of Miners to depreciate the spirit of fairness shown by some of the mine operators of the district in the past, and they held only the kindest regard for them. But the Mine Owners' Association in their statement would have the members of organized labor, as well as the public, believe that they, the miners, were being coerced by their officers to take part in an unjust and unreasonable strike. This, however, was too flimsy to be taken seriously by any members of the W. F. M.

August 14, the Victor Daily Record became the official organ of the local unions of the Western Federation of Miners. From that date it contained several columns of information concerning conditions of the strike over the signature of the executive committee of District Union No. 1. In this manner, there was given out daily all official news in the district concerning all matters pertaining to the strike.

If the reader will go back a few years, or to 1898, we will find the legislature elected in '98 which convened early in '99 passed an eight hour law. It will be remembered that Thomas was the governor at that time (Democrat) and Cary, lieutenant governor. There was a strong labor constituency in the legislature of 1899. As will also be remembered, the supreme court later declared the law unconstitutional. But the laboring people did not give up the matter of making an eight-hour law at this, but at once put a move on foot to send legislators to the legislature to frame an amendment to the constitution, thereby making possible the creation of an eight-hour law. This was accomplished. In 1900 the amendment was framed, which was one of six others. Orman was at that time governor and D. C. Coates lieutenant governor. The amendment was put before the people and although a Republican ticket was elected, the people of the state declared themselves in favor of the eight-hour law by the astonishing majority of over 46,000.

All residents in this state know the history of the attempt to pass such a law in the Fourteenth General Assembly and they realize that there is no hope for such a measure, at least, until another legislature is elected and possibly then the law passed would be tied up in the courts for an indefinite length of time. There is, therefore, no opportunity for an eight-hour day except through the force of organization.

About August 13, the rumor to the effect that the merchants of the district were going on a strictly cash basis was confirmed by the majority of the grocers refusing to supply their regular customers as usual. This came as an unexpected blow to the miners, as pay day was but two or three days past and many had turned over to the business men the greater part, if not all, of their cash, with the expectation and in many cases the promise of being carried on another month as usual. There were some exceptions but they were very few.

The miners met this announcement by at once starting a move to organize co-operative stores. The movement was carried out in a few weeks by the Western Federation of Miners in the establishment of union stores in Cripple Creek, Anaconda, Victor and Goldfield. From the day they opened the trade was more than could be conveniently handled. In brief, the union stores have been more than a success, and have proven a great competition for the grocers that refused to carry the families that had paid them almost a fortune in the past for groceries and other household supplies. The ease with which all arrangements were made to start and maintain these stores and the great saving that has and will accrue therefrom, leads union men to think that the action of the business men, in cutting off the credit to their customers, was a blessing in disguise, and they owe the business men a vote of thanks for teaching them this lesson of self-reliance in time of trouble.

August 15, the miners' unions gave a big picnic at Pinnacle park which was attended by a multitude. Regardless of the fact that thousands were out of employment at the time, everybody seemed to thoroughly enjoy the day. President Moyer, of the Western Federation of Miners, John C. Sullivan, president of the Colorado State Federation of Labor, William D. Haywood, secretary-treasurer of the Western Federation of Miners, and D. C. Copley, member of the executive board of the Western Federation of Miners and other prominent labor leaders attended the picnic and made addresses.

Mr. J. C. Sullivan was first introduced to the audience and said in part, after excoriating the business men for their action in declaring no more credit would be given their customers so soon after the strike was called:

"The business man is prosperous with the money he puts in his till received from the miner, but immediately upon the first cloud of trouble showing on the horizon, he cuts the miners off without notice, at the behests of mine managers. Are they worthy of any consideration at the hands of the miner? Would it not have been better if the business men had said to the men who had traded with them and paid their bills for years to have said to their customers: 'Our finances will not permit us to carry you, but we will sell goods at cost price for cash.'"

After paying his respects to the Citizens' Alliance and Pinkerton thugs, he closed with the remarks:

"It is time the laboring men thought about more than wages and hours."

President Moyer was the next speaker. He was greeted with prolonged applause. He said in part:

"The responsibility for the present conditions has been laid by most of the newspapers at my door. I wish to say that I am ready at this time to assume any responsibility in a fight for humanity and living conditions for the miners of the Cripple Creek district. All I ask is that the other people in the state, who are responsible for the present conditions in this district, shall be saddled with like responsibility. The facts are that the legislature of 1899 passed an eight-hour bill, the supreme court declared it class legislation and unconstitutional. Notwithstanding this, the representatives of organized labor went before the men who were working twelve hours in the smelters and urged them to wait, and a future legislature would do something for them. The eight-hour constitutional amendment was carried by 40,000 majority, 70,000 votes being cast for the amendment. The Fourteenth Colorado legislature went into session pledged to the enactment of an eight-hour day. The representatives of the mill and smelter trusts went into session with them. The result was no law was passed. Upon this legislature I place the responsibility for the present trouble. Had this legislature performed its duty there would now be no strike in the Cripple Creek district. * * *

"A small per cent of the press has been clamoring that this is a sympathetic strike. This I most emphatically deny. It is a strike of the Western Federation of Miners. The mill men are a part of the Federation, and to deny them support at this time is the same as denying one of the unions here support should it be attacked by a corporation. The men have pledged themselves to support their brothers of the Federation and they will do it." * * *

The next speaker introduced was William D. Haywood, who addressed the audience in part as follows:

"Ladies and Gentlemen, Brothers of the Western Federation of Miners, Members of the Citizen's Alliance, Members of the Mine Owners' Association and Pinkerton Detectives:"

(He said he desired to include all, as he knew all were in the audience and he mentioned the latter as he held them responsible for the strike.)

"The Federation was born by oppression of the mine owners, which had sometimes been worse than the Spanish Inquisition. The Federation has now more thousands of members than it had hundreds in 1893, having at this time 207 affiliated unions.

"The laws of Colorado are good enough for a union man but they are not good enough for the corporations, else they would not spend a fortune to corrupt every legislature that is elected. * * *

Mr. Haywood ridiculed the statement of the mine owners to the effect that they would start the mines if they had to work themselves. He said the miners would give them their cast-off overalls to work in. The statement of the mine owners, that affairs in this district had been all that was asked for since 1894, Mr. Haywood denied. He said discrimination had been practiced against the union miners on the Strong, Ajax, El Paso, Gold King and other mines, that the owners had never lived up to their agreement made at that time. He cited the union conditions that existed in some union camps where all union men are employed. "Why," he asked, "can not the same conditions prevail here?" He illustrated his remarks with several humorous stories that fit the cases and concluded with an earnest appeal to the miners to be loyal to the organization, "**which is the only friend you have against corporate oppression.**"

W. F. Davis, president of Free Coinage Miners' Union No. 19, and a member of the committee of District Union No. 1, was next introduced. Mr. Davis was one of the committee who waited upon Mr. MacNeil at Colorado Springs before the strike was called. He said Mr. MacNeil had stated that he (MacNeil) thought eight hours was long enough for any man to work in a mill or smelter and that $1.80 was not enough for a single man to live on, saying nothing of married men. MacNeil said, however, that he could do nothing for the committee, as his company would not permit it.

Mr. D. C. Copley was the last speaker. He said in part:

"I have been a resident of this district for the past eight years and can, therefore, sympathize with the men in this strike. The strike is being managed by the men whom the miners have elected for that purpose. * * * I am confident that the men I have known for the past eight years will not go back on the Federation and all that is necessary to be done is for the men to stand shoulder to shoulder and we will win the victory." * * *

I would be glad to give each address verbatim, but space will not permit. The talks by all were good and to the point.

August 17, the beginning of the second week of the strike opened very quietly. It had been rumored that a number of mines intended starting up on Monday of the second week. However, no men attempted to go to work on any of the mines where the men had been called off or at the El Paso drainage tunnel, that was nearly completed at that time. It was understood that several tools of the corporations, at that time had been endeavoring to hire men to "scab" on the properties, but the parties were carefully watched, and their efforts were in vain. There was no trouble of any kind, everything around the mines being quiet.

The city of Victor was never known to be so quiet, as it was during the first three weeks of the strike. There was absolutely "nothing doing." Groups of union miners stood about on the corners in the sunshine, laughing, talking, joking each other good naturedly, telling experiences of past strikes and troubles. As far as business was concerned, the last of August found business practically at a standstill.

The El Paso mine management, being the most aggressive in the fight against organized labor, by indefatigable efforts secured enough men, composed of a few deserters from the union ranks, inexperienced men, men unfamiliar with the strike situation, and men gathered from the too large ranks of hangers-on of various resorts, whose debt to humanity and the welfare of a community consists of the vapid and rancorous plea, "the world owes me a living" without hard work, inclusive of a few reform school graduates, by August 20, announced they would commence work.

Among the distinguished members that were employed on the El Paso, were to be found such celebrities in the criminal history of the state as the Gibson brothers, who had just returned from a sojourn in the state's institution at Canon City, for wholesale robbery and holdups. They had been residents of Canon City (against their will) for five years and returned on parole to help break the strike. Another gentleman (?) with a criminal record that was of invaluable service to the association was Frank Vannick, who had also served the state with distinguished dishonor to himself at Canon City, and was also at large on parole. (The reader will learn more of Vannick before my story ends.) Dumps Benton, Esq., the man who killed George Potts, is still another in the galaxy of notables that was engaged to guard the slopes of Beacon hill against a mythical foe that existed only in the putrid imagination of a few prejudiced and misguided men.

The El Paso fiasco was the first blot upon the history of the strike.

The first work of the men I have mentioned as employed on the El Paso was to build a fence around the property. It was said the men were formerly employed on the Gold King mine. It was also said, by people in a position to know, that in order to get even that class of men to work, the El Paso company paid them at the rate of $1.00 an hour. The first twelve non-union men were guarded by seventeen imported men, worse, if possible, than the ones employed to build the fence. The guards carried rifles and upon inquiry at the sheriff's office, it was found that none of the men had been deputized to carry arms, and were doing so and holding up people whose business caused them to pass by the mine, in open violation of the law.

It is a sad commentary on human nature, that there are always some parodies for men who are ready and willing to sell themselves for gold.

From the date given, when the first non-union men began the work of building a fence at the El Paso, until the completion of the El Paso tunnel, Sept. 2, 1903, there were enacted at the mine many disgraceful scenes of lawlessness. Guards at the mine had fights among themselves; insulted passers-by; stopped respectable people that had business to pass that way, at the point of rifles. They were, it was said, caught stealing. They made indecent exposures before innocent children; for which some of the men employed were arrested. The home of Mr. Dennison, a union miner, was destroyed by incendiaries on the night of Sept. 2, and while it was not proved positively, that it was the work of the El Paso crew, the evidence was strong against them. If they did not actually light the fire that destroyed the property, they, at least, made plain the fact that they were glad to see Mr. Dennison and family made homeless. While the house was in flames and the work of saving some of the household goods was in progress, the guards stood by and laughed and jeered. They did not offer to assist the unfortunate people. For that reason, I say if they were not instrumental in the burning of the building, at any rate, they made no secret of their joy at the sight of Dennison's home being in flames.

It was good union men who had made it possible for these men to enjoy the benefits of union hours and wages without contributing to bring them about. The English language does not contain expletives sufficiently strong to express the contempt felt by all true men and women for such persons. The history of the world proves that all momentous occasions has produced their heroes and traitors.   The American revolution gave us a Washington and a Benedict Arnold.   The Benedict Arnolds had appeared so early in the fight, and as the fight went on there were others appeared on the field of battle.

Along about August 21, there was brought to light a dastardly plot to blow up the El Paso.   Fortunately it was reported to the executive committee of District Union No. 1 in ample time who, upon investigation, found that no guards had been posted at shaft house No. 2, and this, coupled with other suspicious circumstances, caused them to promptly notify Sheriff Robertson of the facts in the case, and the necessary measures were taken by him to stop the commission of the dastardly outrage.

Constant vigilance was displayed by the executive committee of District Union No. 1 to see that no overt act of any kind should be committed by the strikers, that no chance should be given the mine owners for a pretext for a call for the troops from **a too willing tool they had in the present governor of the state.**

On the evening of August 19, the executive committee received information of a ''job'' put up by the Mine Owners' Association to destroy some of their own property and thus have the needed excuse for a call for troops. The diabolical crime proposed, as reported to District Union No. 1, was for the shaft house No. 2, of the El Paso to be blown up by some of the leading members of the association, and, of course, the union men were to be charged with the crime.

The foregoing rumor and a few similar reports were the only incidents of interest at that date.   There were many rumors of all kinds of mines that were to start up and of men working here or there, but when investigated it was found there were no mines ready to resume.   With the exception of the men on the El Paso, there were no mines that the strike affected working at that time.

The city council met on the night of August 20 and dispensed with one of the city's regular policemen.   As I have just stated, the next thing of any interest to the reader that occurred was on August 22, when there was a settlement brought about between the executive committee and the Portland management.

PORTLAND SETTLEMENT.

There was a meeting arranged between Mr. Burns and John Harper and Dan Griffis, of Miners' Union No. 32. These gentlemen met Mr. Burns at the Portland by appointment August 21 and discussed differences. Before they left Mr. Burns invited President Charles Moyer, of the Western Federation, Sherman Parker, Dan Griffis and John Harper to dine with him at the mine the following day. President Moyer and Mr. Parker did so. Before the dinner was over, an agreement was entered into by which the great Portland was declared fair. Mr. Burns was willing to ask the men to join the union and willing that the secretary of the union go on the property at any time. There was practically no contention between Mr. Burns and the committee, they simply came to an understanding.

The whole city went into a state of jubilee. Extra editions of daily papers were gotten out and the glad tidings spread quickly over the district. Everybody rejoiced. Mr. Moyer stated, on being interviewed, that he thought the settlement of the Portland difficulty was a great step toward a final settlement by the mines of the entire district.

Had a vote been taken at that date upon whom was the most popular man in the Cripple Creek district, James F. Burns, of the Portland company, would easily have been the winner. His broad and liberal policy has endeared him not only to the miners, but to all the residents of this community. What a contrast between this man and the average member of the inner circle of the Mine Owners' Association.

The following poem was written by Mr. William McCormick upon the announcement of the stand taken by Mr. Burns toward organized labor in the strike of 1903:

HERE'S TO YOU, JIM.

Here's to you, Jim, you've proved a friend,
    Our grateful thanks we owe you.
We're pleased to see this trouble end,
    And better now we know you.
A gentleman—you've met us fair,

In friendly consultation;
Who merits and receives our share
Of warmest approbation.

Here's to you, Jim, if in the past
　　There's been misunderstanding;
The stormiest voyage ends at last
　　With greater joy on landing.
When murky clouds obscure the sky
　　The lightning flash can clear it;
When to the rocks the ship is nigh,
　　Some skillful hand must steer it.

Here's to you, Jim, you did not need
　　The aid of thugs with rifles,
Though well you know we never heed
　　Such unimportant trifles.
But you're the "hero of the hour,"
　　(I read that in the papers)
Oh, if you had the governor's power,
　　You would soon stop these capers.

Here's to you, Jim, in sparkling wine,
　　Or if you wish it—water,
A humble, homely muse is mine,
　　That never aims to flatter;
But still we wish some we could name
　　From you would take a lesson,
The "Overall Brigade" looks tame,
　　With aye a Sunday dress on.

Here's to you, Jim, the best of luck
　　We hope will still attend you,
Be sure we will not see you stuck
　　For aught we can befriend you.
You've stood by us, we'll stand by you,
　　No more a fence divides us,
So here's to Burns, mine, mill and crew
　　Until the green sod hides us.

The United States Reduction and Refining Company are well
able to pay the same scale of wages as is paid by Mr . Burns at the
Portland mill and if the Mine Owners' Association had told them
so in unmistakable language and informed this mill that it would

receive no more ore from their mines until the union wage scale was paid, the whole trouble and strike would have been settled at the very beginning of the strife.

Everybody expressed themselves as greatly pleased at the starting up of the Portland. Mr. Burns met with an ovation everywhere. He left on the Short Line late in the afternoon after the settlement and there was a crowd of 500 union miners at the depot to see him off. The miners cheered him heartily as the train pulled out. He tipped his hat and smiled in reply.

On the night of August 26, the first shift of two hundred and twenty-five men were put on. There was a little difficulty over a record the men were asked to sign, but the strike committee met Mr. Burns and the matter was soon adjusted. Mr. Burns changed the record to be signed to suit the committee, and in every case more than complied with the wishes of the Western Federation.

At the mine that evening, when the men reported for work, Mr. Burns addressed them, stating that it was "very evident that they were good union men or they would not have gone down the hill when they were called out. And hoped that they would pay up their dues and continue loyal to the union." He spoke of the pleasant relations between the management and the men and hoped that they would continue so. At the conclusion of his remarks he was heartily cheered.

Sherman Parker, representing the Western Federation of Miners, responded to Mr. Burns. He stated that he wanted to express the thanks of the men to Mr. Burns for his courteous and reasonable treatment of them.

The men took their stations and the biggest gold mine in the Cripple Creek district was soon running full blast and as a union mine.

The Portland in a few days had all its old men back, consisting of 575 of the best miners in the Cripple Creek district. The writer is willing to confess to a feeling of partiality for the Portland.

The general public experienced a belief that the starting of the Portland with all union men would have a great influence on the mine owners. It was expected at that time that the other mines would soon fall in line and at once settle all differences existing. But the strikers soon found to the contrary. Mr. Burns was so kind as to write the following statement upon request. He plainly defines his feeling toward organized labor over his own signature.

JAMES F. BURNS.

Colorado Springs, Colo., November 14, 1903.
Mrs. Emma F. Langdon, Victor, Colorado.
    Dear Madam: Agreeable to your request that I furnish a statement of the position of the management of the Portland mine during the labor troubles of '94 as well as during those of the present year, for your "History of the Cripple Creek District," I take pleasure in submitting briefly as follows:
    During the time of what was known as the "Bull Hill War," or more correctly speaking, the labor troubles of 1894, the Portland was working

about 125 men, while the principal officers and stockholders—including myself—lived at the mine and were in the closest possible touch with all employes, knowing each other personally. During the time that trouble existed elsewhere in tne district, everything went smoothly at the Portland. We had been paying $3.25 per shift of nine hours, which permitted the working of only two shifts. We promptly made a new scale of $3.00 for eight hours, which was accepted by the union and three instead of two shifts were put to work. Our mine was the only one of any consequence to operate continuously during this strike and the scale then adopted has governed ever since.

The strike of the present year was called in support of the mill strike then on in Colorado City, and through a wrong impression on the part of the unions that the Portland was shipping to an "unfair" mill, the men were called out on our property as well as the others. But upon learning their mistake, the matter was soon adjusted, putting more than 500 men back to work.

Aside from a kindly feeling that every humane employer must naturally have for his employes, we have always looked upon these matters as a strictly business proposition.

The employe goes into the labor market to sell his labor, and as employers desiring to purchase this labor, we have always been willing to treat with him individually or with any person or concern he may appoint as his agent, whether it be union or otherwise. Always recognizing that labor has an equal right with capital to organize or combine; we feel that we have no more right to dictate whether or not our employes ong to a union than we have to dictate whether or not they belong to some church. What we desire is efficiency in the labor we employ and we know we have it to a higher degree in the present union force than could be obtained from any new set of men until after they had been schooled for a long time in our employ. Therefore we are content, and believe we have at the mine and mill about 700 of the best men in the Rocky mountains. I remain,

Yours very truly,

JAMES F. BURNS,

President of the Portland Gold Mining Company.

I will ask the reader to go with me for a short time and we will leave the Cripple Creek district for a few moments and make a trip to Idaho Springs. It may seem just a little foreign at first to the reader, but I think there are several points pertaining to law and lawlessness in that case too good to omit from my little history of labor troubles. The destruction of the Sun 'and Moon property and the action of the sheriff of Clear Creek county, the "Citizens' Protective league," and the part Judge Owers played in the game attracted widespread attention. I am sure there was not one loyal union man in the state that did not deplore the de-struction of the Sun and Moon property at Idaho Springs, and would like to see the person or persons who perpetrated so dastardly a crime punished to the fullest extent of the law. And yet the W. F. M. was condemned at once for this crime and their officers and members at once dragged from their homes and families.

It will be remembered that in the latter part of July, 1903, after the destruction of the Sun and Moon property by unknown persons, the sheriff of Clear Creek county, biased in his judgment by his prejudice against labor unions, showed by his action in ar-resting innocent men, peaceable and law-abiding citizens of Idaho Springs, dragging them from their beds at night and next day turning them over to a band of capitalistic anarchists, known as "Citizens' Protective League," that his only reason for such arrest was that they were members of the W. F. M. If, even supposing they were guilty of the crime, why did he not hold them in jail until they were tried by the proper court as provided by the laws of the state of Colorado, and let the law take the proper course? The sheriff's action at that time was denounced everywhere. There were few unions that failed to have printed resolutions con-demning the outrageous action of the sheriff in turning over to the "Citizens' Protective League" these men, who were "innocent" at least, "until proven guilty."

It will also be remembered that the action of the so-called "Citizen's Protective League" was roundly scored for usurping the functions of the properly constituted authorities of the county of Clear Creek, and becoming a law unto themselves, without even the formality of a trial; have exiled, a la Czar of Russia, several of the old-time residents of that city; men of family and property holders, who had always merited and had the respect and con-fidence of their fellow citizens in that community.

Judge Owers, as soon as he could do so, issued an injunction against every member of the "Citizens' Protective League, re-straining them from in any way interfering with the eighteen members of the Idaho Springs Miners' union, who were driven out of town just after the blowing up of the compressor of the Sun and Moon mine.

Immediately after the issuance of the restraining order the attorney representing the eighteen miners and the Western Federation of Miners offered criminal complaints against the members of the "Citizens' Protective League," of Idaho Springs. Warrants against each of them were issued and the sheriff was instructed to arrest all of them and instruct each one to appear before District Judge Frank Owers, at Georgetown. In issuing the order Judge Owers said, August 10:

"This complaint states nothing but that which is a right of every citizen of the land, the right to attend to his business and stay at home if he desires. The restraining order must be granted."

In brief, I will state, it is said that before the night of August 11 there were forty-two citizens prisoners, all arrested under warrants issued by Judge Owers. It was said that among the number arrested were some of the most wealthy and prominent citizens of Idaho Springs, the president of the First National bank, cashiers of banks and other prominent business men; in fact, the judge in issuing the warrants was no respector of the positions the men held. Every man suspected of being implicated in the disgraceful affair was placed under arrest.

Judge Owers claims that for officers of the law ever to be overpowered by a mob is a shame to any community that claims to be civilized. Judge Owers said the action of the Idaho Springs mob—he took pains to use the accurate term—in running out of town with threats of violence, the officials of the miners' union was "sheer anarchy, an outrageous violation of rights guaranteed by the Constitution to the humblest person."

The stand taken by Judge Owers created a great sensation. Much was said and written on both sides of the question. Sermons were preached in Denver and other cities, upholding the action of the judge. The minister of Bethany Baptist church (Denver), Rev. Henry W. Pinkham, preached on the subject and ended his sermon in the following words:

"**The remarks of Judge Owers on the situation and principles** involved have been most refreshing. There is no need to add to them, but it is fitting to say, thank God for such a man on the bench at such a time.''

OWERS' REPLY TO GOVERNOR PEABODY.

Replying to a published interview with Governor Peabody on the Cripple Creek strike, Judge Owers at once answered as follows:

"To His Excellency, Hon. James H. Peabody, Governor of Colorado:

"Dear Sir:—In the News of Saturday, Aug. 15, 1903, you are reported as having in an interview of the labor troubles at Cripple Creek, spoken as follows:

" 'I anticipate no trouble, however, either here or at Cripple Creek. The miners are beginning to understand that they cannot violate the law. They cannot assassinate men, neither can they destroy property. Not even if they do have the protection of District Judge Owers. For that reason I do not think we will have to order the militia out any place. But they must all understand that order must be preserved if they do not want the state to take a hand.'

"When I casually read the interview, I dismissed it from my mind as an error, on the theory that no man occupying the position of governor of this state, could be so lacking in all sense of decency and justice as to make such a statement about a member of the judiciary. It occurred to me, that you, as a gentleman, would naturally seize the first opportunity to correct the error in the evening papers, and thus attempt to acquire some portion of the public esteem.

"This you have not done, and I now realize that you are not entitled to the benefit of the doubt, and that even had you done so, your effort would have been futile, as the matter would have then resolved itself into a question of veracity between yourself and the reporter. In your interview you give the miners credit for 'beginning to understand that they cannot violate the law.' Do you fix the intelligence of the Idaho Springs rioters at so low a standard that you were unable to state that they, too, 'are beginning to understand' and, if so, when will you inform them in the words used to the miners that they, also, must understand that order must be preserved, if they do not want 'the state to take a hand?'

"In the interview you directly charge the miners of the state as a body, with violation of the law, assassination and destruction of property, and me, as a district judge, with protecting them in the commission of each and all of these crimes.

"The law presumes all innocent until proven guilty. I am not aware and have not heard that any miner has as yet been tried, let alone convicted, of any crime connected with recent labor troubles in this state. I have not heard that any miners, either as individuals or as a union or otherwise, have openly boasted of the commission of any crime or misdemeanor, or openly avowed responsibility for, or approval of the same in any manner, let alone by adopting and publishing resolutions approving thereof, and offering to aid and abet the same. On the other hand it is a matter of common knowledge that in Denver, Idaho Springs and elsewhere throughout the state, an organization has openly assumed the responsibility, and boasted of its pride in the recent mob violence and outrage at Idaho Springs, and concerning which you have not so far raised your voice in condemnation or protest.

"I regret, that lacking the advantages of blood, breeding and education which are yours to an eminent degree, I am not gifted with that delicate sense of discrimination which enables you to distinguish so nicely between a mob led by a banker and a dance hall proprietor, and one led by a miner, and which makes it possible for you to regard an actual trespass upon human right with equanimity, while you look upon every threatened invasion of property rights as by comparison an unpardonable sin.

"When the expelled men from Idaho Springs appealed to you to be restored to their homes, you were prompt with a denial of help, based upon technical interpretation of your duty. You advised them with many platitudes, to appeal to the courts for redress. They asked for bread and you gave them a stone, yet they followed your advice and when the court appealed to restored them to their families, doing in two days what you dared not attempt in two weeks, you hasten with characteristic vacillation to serve your masters by expressing your chagrin and disapproval of the action of the court by publicly insulting the judge who presided, and who had the courage to perform the duty you recognized, but shirked.

IF I WERE GOVERNOR.

"I fear had fate been so kind to Colorado as to have made me governor, I should be brutal enough to disregard the frantic appeals of hysterical sheriffs for militia, whenever the destruction of a chicken house should be threatened, and I might even insist that the powers of a county should be used, before disgracing the state by ordering militia at an enormous expense to climb a hill and then climb down again. I might even, through lack of moral sense, were I governor, if appealed .o by men claiming to have been expelled from their homes by a mob, feel it my duty, in defiance of precedent, use the militia to restore them to their wives and children, and enforce the rights guaranteed my fellow beings by the constitution and the law. I might even, in such event, be impolitic enough to disregard the fact that the expelling mob was composed of 'our best and most prominent citizens.'

"Not having passed my life in the arduous toil of calculating interest at 2 per cent per month, I naturally have not that fellow feeling which, judging from your conduct, exists among bankers as a class, and I might, thereiore, if I were governor, do as I am doing, enforce ᴜᴊe law without fear or favor, treat a riot as a riot, call a mob a mob, whether led by a banker or a pauper, order the militia to restore men to their homes and instead of writing platitudes and insulting the courts and judges, I should endeavor to prove that through the courts sure and swift punishment will be visited upon offenders, of both low and high degree, and thus in the only way possible, as I believe, stop mob violence and the appeal to that 'higher law,' which is but another name for anarchy. Permit me to thank you for the compliment you pay me, by your disapproval of my attempt to enforce the law.

"In conclusion, may I venture to hope for a reply to ᴜᴊis letter through the press as soon as you can get some one to write an answer for you, and will you kindly particularize your grounds of complaint against me?

"Respectfully,

"FRANK W. OWERS."

The writer watched the public press for the answer to this interesting article, but if the governor ever answered the writer failed in some manner to see it. In fact, like the mere puppet of a cabal the distinguished governor gulped down the accusation of Owers' and like a "yellow boy" said: 'I have nothing to say.''

About September 1 there were many rumors of an alliance being formed in Victor. Upon investigation it was found there was an organization known as the "Citizens' Alliance" in Cripple Creek. If there was at the above date, such an organization in Victor, there could not be one member located. Just what this organization hoped to accomplish in the Cripple Creek district was hard to understand, but it was not hard to understand from whence the spirit of the movement came. It required but little investigation into the membership to convince one that it was inspired by the mine owners; at least, the most prominent members are their lieutenants in the district. These men, it appears, first interviewed Victor merchants but received a decided "turn-down," for which all friends of organized labor were grateful. The situation is different here from what it is in Denver. The great mass of people here are union people and just how a "Citizens' Alliance" could hope to accomplish any good for itself or anybody else is hard to understand. Just think of it; the idea of the business men, or any one else of this district, organizing to fight organized labor. What has made the Cripple Creek district from a business standpoint? Has it been the generosity of the mine owners, or the work of organized labor in establishing a wage-scale here that would put enough money in circulation to make business here in place of going elsewhere.

In the city of Victor the news of the organization caused much amusement at that time, be it said to the credit of Victor's business men.

On the night of September 1, T. M. Stewart was taken from his home and beaten and shot by a party of five unknown men. His condition at first seemed very serious, but did not prove fatal. This lawless act was greatly deplored by every one, especially union miners, as they knew a few prejudiced people would at once lay the crime at the door of the men on strike. It was afterward said that the outrage was perpetrated by men that had held a personal animosity against Mr. Stewart for several years past. There were other reports to the effect that he came to grief in a manner that had occurred at other times before the strike was called. A strong effort was made by the officers of the entire district to apprehend the persons guilty of the assault. The officers made several arrests of suspects, but there was no evidence sufficient at this writing to convict any one. Mr. Stewart soon recovered from his injuries and was out in a short time.

Mr. Hawkins was also rather roughly handled about the same time by unknown persons. Large rewards were offered by the county officials and citizens for evidence leading to the arrest of the guilty ones. Here the writer will state that there was no reward offered for the villains that burned the home of Mr. Dennison, a union miner, and there was very little said of the matter by the enemies of organized labor.

The executive committee of the District Union, in their official statement about September 2, said that they deplored the outrage perpetrated upon Mr. Stewart and Mr. Hawkins on Sept. 1; also that they realized that outrages of this character would be charged to the unions, no matter if perpetrated by outside, irresponsible parties, etc.

September 3 found the strike situation looking quite serious. There seemed to be a strong likelihood of state troops being ordered to the district. It was understood that the Mine Owners' Association had asked for the state militia. It was also understood that some of the militia officers were very anxious to receive a call to the Cripple Creek district. It was said that Sherman Bell was so desirous to get into the district with his militia that he sat up nights courting the telephone in a night robe. It was feared by his friends that if he did get a call that he would embarrass them by not taking time to dress.

Victor on Sept. 3 was the quietest city in the state of Colorado. Just what the militia would or could do if they should be sent was a mystery to everyone that was disposed to express an honest opinion. There was no lawlessness in the district and the tax payers expressed indignation at the mere suggestion of state troops being sent to the quiet little law-abiding cities of Cripple Creek and Victor. It was known that strong pressure was being brought to bear on the governor by the mine owners, to send troops. There was a strong feeling that the governor would be conservative and be very careful after the mistake made in the spring, in sending troops to Colorado City. When it was announced that an investigating committee was to visit the district, a general expression of satisfaction was heard on every side. But, alas, that investigating committee—what a farce.

The members of the committee arrived over the Short Line Sept. 3, at 9:30 p. m. They were hastened through an alley by F. M. Reardon to a rear entrance into the Bank of Victor, where they were met by Mayor French and a few other prominent citizens and held a short consultation, when they left for the residence of Nelson Franklin. The committee remained at the residence of Nelson Franklin about a half hour and then took the Low Line electric car for Cripple Creek, where they went into session and held a long interview with Sheriff Robertson. They refused to talk for publication. After the meeting with the mine owners they returned to Victor on a special car.

A telegram received at the Victor Daily Record office from Denver, shortly after midnight, said that the commission was in session at the National hotel in Cripple Creek and would not be ready with the recommendation for several hours. The commission consisted of Attorney General N. C. Miller, Brigadier General John C. Chase, of the National guard and Lieutenant T. E. McClelland, an obscure lawyer of Denver. No intimation was given out as to the possible conclusions.

The commission returned to Denver early the following morning, being in the district less than eight hours and only interviewing one side of the question.

September 4, about noon, the news reached the district that troops had been ordered to the gold camp and would arrive that night. The people were seized with consternation at this news. A wail of indignation went up from at least two-thirds of the entire population. The people at once understood the mission of the "investigating committee" and why they did not consult all parties concerned. The first of the state troops arrived in the district Sept. 4, before midnight, and from then on, for twenty-four hours, they came until there was located, in one of the quietest, most conservative, law-abiding districts in the world, over 1,000 men with munitions of war sufficient to fight a small nation.

The all absorbing subject on the streets of Victor and in the entire district was the arrival of the troops. The farce committee sent by Governor Peabody to secure an excuse to bring the troops, returned to Denver Sept. 4, early in the morning, and immediately advised the governor to send the troops. Adjutant General Bell had his men in readiness. In fact, they were wearing their uniforms around Denver early in the morning and were simply waiting for the farce committee to report what had been agreed upon the day before.

Indignation in the district ran high at the presence of troops. There was scarcely a man who could be found that approved of their presence. They were unwelcome guests in the district and the men who were eager to secure their presence realized that more than others. Mr. P. J. Lynch, chairman of the board of county commissioners, made the following statement in the Victor Daily Record on the morning of Sept. 5:

"I am a resident of Victor, and expected that I would be invited to at tend the meeting which was held in the Bank of Victor, but evidently they thought that the men who are constantly advising with the sheriff in the matter of preserving the peace during the strike, could throw no light on the subject and that they could get better information elsewhere. I do not know what opinion these persons have formed from the interviews which they have had during the night, as do a number of our most conservative citizens, and it would be a shame to have the troops called in here when there is no need of their help. I was glad to learn of the remark which was made by former Mayor Franklin, when the commission asked him to make a statement to them. He informed them that the sheriff was the peace officer of the county and that he could give them all the necessary information they would require."

Governor Peabody's order calling out the troops read as follows:

EXECUTIVE ORDER.

"Ordered:—It having been made to appear to me by reputable citizens of the county, by the constituted civil officers and by the honorable commission appointed by me to investigate the matter, that an insurrection is threatened in the county of Teller, in the state of Colorado, and that there is a tumult threatened and imminent, and that a body of men are acting together, by force, with attempt to commit felonies, and to offer violence to break and resist the laws of this state, and that a number of persons are in open and active opposition to the execution of the laws of this state in said county, and that the civil authorities are wholly unable to cope with the situation.

"I therefore direct you, in pursuance of the power and authority vested in me by the constitution and laws of the state of Colorado, to direct the brigadier general commanding the National guard of the state of Colorado, to forthwith order out the First regiment of infantry, together with company H of the Second infantry, Colonel Verdeckberg, commanding, together with the First squadron of cavalry, consisting of troops B, D and C, also battery A, and the signal corps and the medical corps of the state, and to prevent said threatened insurrection; and he will protect all persons and property in said county of Teller, from unlawful interference, and will see that threats, assaults and all sorts of violence cease at once, and that public peace and good order be preserved upon all occasions, to the end that the authority and dignity of this state be maintained and her power to suppress lawlessness within her borders be asserted.

"Witness my hand and the executive seal, at Denver, this 4th day of September, A. D. 1903.   JAMES H. PEABODY,

"To Sherman M. Bell, Adjutant General of the State of Colorado."

PEABODY'S STATEMENT.

"I have sent the guard to the Cripple Creek district because I saw no way in which it could be averted. I opposed it all I could, but the situation is such that I did not think it policy to delay any longer. My special committee sent me very alarming telegrams, but I did not act until the men came and made a verbal report. Their report was even more alarming than the telegrams that they had sent.

"The order was issued on the representation of the business men of the district, the mine owners and the mayor of Victor. At no time did Sheriff Henry Robertson ask for the guard. I have heard he maintained they are not needed. He also refused to join in the request. From the present outlook the men will stay there indefinitely. Of course, we cannot know when matters may quiet down. I did not act rashly in the matter. I did everything to avert sending the troops, but I have been forced from the circumstances of the case to do so."

COMMISSION'S REPORT.

"Santa Fe Depot, Colorado Springs, Colo., Sept. 4, 1903.
"Governor James H. Peabody, State Capitol, Denver, Colo.:

"Have visited Cripple Creek and Victor, and after careful inquiry among representative citizens and property owners, including mayors of Cripple Creek and Victor, we are of the opinion that the lives of the citizens of the district are in imminent danger and property and personal rights are in jeopardy. Prompt action is imperatively demanded by the above people to protect the lives and property of the citizens. We find that a reign of terror exists in the district. We do not believe that the civil authorities are able to cope with the situation.

"JOHN CHASE,
"N. C. MILLER,
"TOM E. M'CLELLAND."

The sheriff of Teller county published the following plain statement Sept. 5:

SHERIFF ROBERTSON'S PLAIN STATEMENT.

"TO THE PUBLIC—The commission sent by the governor of the state of Colorado to investigate the strike situation in Teller county, called me at midnight Thursday, the 3rd inst. I went to the National hotel at Cripple Creek, and reached there about 12:30 a. m. Friday morning Sept. 4. I was with the commission about two hours and fully explained the situation. I stated to the commission I had authority to employ all the deputies I needed; that I had the situation in hand; that I had made arrests and was going to make more; that there was no trouble. Within three hours after I left the commission, the members thereof departed for Denver. There is no occasion for the militia here. I can handle the situation. There is no trouble in the district, and has been none. No unusual assembly of men. Saloons closed at midnight. The sending of

H. M. Robertson, Sheriff of Teller County.

troops here is a usurpation of authority on the part of the governor. I believe the action of the governor will have much to do toward injuring the district to such an extent that it will be a long time before a recovery will be had.

"As sheriff of Teller county, I do solemnly protest against the militia being sent here at this time.   H. M. ROBERTSON."

District Union No. 1, W. F. of M., published the following statement in its official organ September 5, which speaks for itself:

"The executive committee wishes to state that they were not invited to appear before the 'special committee,' or 'commission,' appointed by Governor Peabody, neither were they in any manner consulted. So far as learned, the committee arrived in the district over the Short Line a few minutes after 9 o'clock, on last Thursday evening, Sept. 3, and after meeting certain persons in Victor, went to Cripple Creek where they were accompanied by bankers and sampling works men. At Cripple Creek they talked only with the sheriff of Teller county, but did not meet any of the representatives of the Western Federation of Miners, neither did they intimate any desire to hear the Federation side of the difficulty, but departed for Colorado Springs at 4:30 Friday morning, Sept. 4.

"DISTRICT UNION NO. 1, EXECUTIVE COMMITTEE."

MAYOR FRENCH ASKS FOR TROOPS.

Everybody was surprised at the action of Mayor French in the matter and it was believed that if he wanted to do anything like that he should have conferred with the council. It was generally believed that he was forced to it; that influences that stood over him in a business way, allowed him no alternative but to ask for the militia, as he had always held the respect of the public generally up to this time. A resolution was prepared to be introduced into the council Sept 4, demanding an explanation and condemning his actions. There was some question in the minds of Mayor French's friends as to the report that he had wired for the troops, but the following settled that question:

Victor, Colo., Sept. 3, 1903.

"His Excellency, Jas. H. Peabody, Governor of Colorado, Denver.

"There is in and near the city of Victor, Teller county, Colorado, a body of men acting by force and violence to resist and break the laws of the state, and that a riot and violence and bloodshed and destruction of property are seriously threatened and are imminent. The sheriff and other peace officers are utterly unable to preserve order and protect lives and property. I therefore request and demand that you send the National guard of Colorado to this city and community immediately, for the purpose of protecting the lives and property of the citizens of this community. F. D. FRENCH,

"Mayor City of Victor, Teller County, Colorado."

Mayor French sent another dispatch with much the same wording from Cripple Creek, urging the governor to give assistance at once.

There was sent out in the district a few circulars, anouncing a meeting on the corner of Fourth and Victor avenue, Sept. 5, at 4 o'clock for the purpose of making a formal protest against the outrageous proceedings and declaring against the threatened establishment of martial law, and for the purpose of placing the community in the proper light before the world. The meeting was called for the purpose of passing a resolution that would express the sentiment of the people of the district. In answer to the few circulars sent out, hundreds of representative citizens gathered and held a rousing enthusiastic meeting.

J. E. Ferguson, of Victor, was elected chairman of the meeting and delivered the following address:

"It is a very extraordinary occurrence which has, on such short notice, called out this vast assemblage of law-abiding citizens. We are today confronted with a condition which calls forth from the breast of every peace loving, law-abiding citizen expression of condemnation such as he has never before felt.

"Without any provocation whatever, we have in our midst an army of soldiers but for what purpose has not yet been declared. Last night while the community was asleep, this body of armed men were unloaded in our midst. Up to this hour, I am informed, they have not officially made known to the sheriff or any other peace officer that they are here. Why are we thus afflicted? Why this array of soldiery and munitions of war? It is said that the governor of this state sent them here and that he has been notified of the existence of that necessity. What peace officer has called for the aid of the state militia? I hear the name of Mayor French mentioned. Whether he is guilty or not I am not prepared to say, but if he is, his actions do not show that he acted in good faith. Mayor French is the mayor of this city. His authority as an executive officer extends only to the limits of his municipality. If there existed in his jurisdiction a necessity for troops, why has he not had them sent to Victor? Not a single soldier is stationed within the city limits or so far as I am informed, in any other city of the county. Your sheriff has called for no militia. He has need of none. The constitution of the state of Colorado gives power to the governor to call out the militia to execute the laws, suppress insurrection or repel invasion. Can it be said that any oi these constitutional conditions existed as a basis for his recent action? Under the laws of the state which follow this constitutional authority, he has the power to 'call out the militia when there exists in any town, city, or county any tumult, riot, mob, or body of men acting together by force with attempt to commit felony, or to offer violence to persons or property, or by force or violence to break or resist the laws of the state, or when such tumult, riot or mob is threatened and the fact is made known to the governor.;' and when the militia is so called it is to aid the civil authorities to suppress such violence and support the law. Did this condition exist in our midst? There was not a community in the entire county where such conditions existed. It is now over three weeks since the present strike was declared and such a condition has not at no time existed. I want to say to you as a citizen of your city, and as an officer of the law, for I am an officer of the court, that in over four years that I have resided in Teller county, I have not seen three consecutive weeks that were fraught with as little violence, as little disturbance, as little breaking of the law as the past three weeks have been. It has been charged that the mayor has been guilty of assisting in perpetrating this wrong upon this city and county.

Frank P. Mannix, County Clerk.

If the necessity existed, when did he wake up to his duty? Mr. French was mayor of the city last April, and at that time there was not a property holder or renter of property who was not nightly and daily in fear of incendiary fire. House after house was fired all over the city, many of which were burned to the ground. Murder was committed by the setting of the fire. Yet this law-abiding mayor did not think of calling in the militia.

"The purpose of this meeting, ladies and gentlemen, is to adopt a set of appropriate resolutions, which I am informed has been prepared. It is proper that you should do so. Some action should be taken at once to show the powers that reign over us that we have been misrepresented. That we have no need of martial law, and I hope that proper resolutions will be adopted."

Frank P. Mannix was then introduced and went over the situation with a few appropriate remarks. Among other things he stated that he was responsible for the nomination of F. D. French, whom he condemned for what he, as mayor, had done. He said that French had to do it and that he did it against his will. Mr. Mannix said: "Frank, since you have done it, you ought to have the honor to resign."

The remark was heartily cheered. Mr. Mannix scored the parties that had the troops brought here in strong terms and received hearty applause at the conclusion of each sentence. At the conclusion of the meeting it was announced that the petition or resolution would be left at the Record office and at Judge Kavanaugh's store where people flocked by the hundreds to sign the petition. By 7 o'clock that evening at least 1,000 people had signed the petitions in Victor and others were being circulated over the district. When the resolution was finally sent to the governor it had the signatures of at least 5,000 of the representative citizens of the district attached. The governor utterly ignored the appeal.

Following is the resolution drafted, which expressed fully the public sentiment in the entire district:

RESOLUTION.

Whereas, a certain detachment of the Colorado State militia have already been landed in the Cripple Creek district with others to follow, and,

"Whereas, according to published statements of Adjutant General

Bell, printed this morning, martial law is threatened in every incorporated or unincorporated town in the Cripple Creek district; and,

"Whereas, the vilest sort of misrepresentation has been employed in the effort to have the same camp invaded by soldiery, now therefore, be it

"Resolved by the people of Victor and the entire Cripple Creek district, in mass assemblage in Victor, this 5th day of September, A. D., 1903, that we deplore the action taken by Governor Peabody in sending troops into Teller county, and condemn the same as unwarranted by the facts and as anarchistic in its conception, spirit and consequence.

"We do hereby most emphatically protest against the threatened declaration of martial law in the communities of the Cripple Creek district, as a further invasion of our rights and liberties as American citizens.

"We protest that Mayor French, Postmaster Reardon and Banker Rollestone, who corralled the governor's advisory commission, while the same was on its brief but stealthy visit of 'investigation,' the night before last, do not represent the people of Victor in asking for the state soldiery, the necessity not existing for troops, and the people have not asked for them. Instead of being a lawless community, as a few high-toned anarchists seem to want the outside world to believe, the Cripple Creek district is one of the quietest and most peaceable, for its size, of any community in the country.

"Two comparatively trifling incidents of lawlessness have occurred in the whole camp since the miners' strike was declared, but all fair-minded people will agree these are liable to happen at any time and any place.

"We deprecate the strike that is now on, and upon this occasion do not want to go into the merits of the unfortunate controversy but we do wish to express our confidence in the ability of our county and city officials to maintain law and order and protect life and property."

At Cripple Creek, a similar mass meeting was held, presided over by Attorney Frank J. Hangs. (Mr. Hangs played a prominent and very commendable part in the strike, of which I will speak later.) Resolutions condemning calling out of militia were adopted. Major J. M. Brinson and former Attorney General Engly made addresses. Mayor Shockey was asked to address the meeting but refused.

The District Trades and Labor assembly, representing the entire aggregate of organized labor of the district, met in Victor Sept. 6, and passed even stronger resolutions than the foregoing.

CITY COUNCIL PROTESTS.

"As members of the city council of the city of Victor we take this opportunity to express our condemnation of the recent action of F. D.

French, mayor of the city of Victor. He has willfully misrepresented the conditions existing in this city and we are informed has, as willfully, misrepresented the desires of the citizens. He left the council chamber when the council was in session, to meet the advisory committee, without asking·for an expression from any member of the council, as to whether his contemplated action would meet approval. His action was taken wholly upon his own motion and without knowledge or consent of any member of the council. We condemn it now and would have condemned it then, had we known his intention.

"The conditions he represented do not exist and have at no time existed. The laws of the state and the ordinances of the city are and have been lived up to and respected by the citizens and property owners, and fully enforced by the officers of the law .

"JOHN TOBIN,

"H. HEALY,

"DAN GRIFFIS,

"JERRY MURPHY,

"J. W. WILLIAMS."

There were so many resolutions passed by fraternal orders about that time that it is impossible to reproduce them all. No one living outside will ever realize the strong feeling that existed against the troops being sent into the district.

Sept. 7, was Labor day and if anything had been needed to convince the mine owners and outside public generally, that organized labor was in the fight to win, that evidence was supplied on the foregoing date. There were nearly 5,000 members of organized labor in the parade in the city of Cripple Creek. Over an hour was required for the throng to pass any point on Bennett avenue. As the men marched, banner after banner of the different unions was cheered by the thousands that lined the sidewalks. There was over 3,000 Western Federation men in line. I will not give the number from each union of the district as I must press on, but I will make special mention of Victor Newsboys Union No. 32, which carried off the honors for appearance. Forty strong, the little fellows made a touching picture in their pure white duck suits and were heartily cheered.

Sept. 10, Chas. G. Kennison, president Miners' Union No. 40, was arrested while riding on an early morning train. There were a number of men on the train on their way to work on some of the unfair mines. Kennison got into an argument with a man by the name of T. J. Sturdevant, who was working on the El Paso and at that time was on his way to the mine. Sturdevant immediately became insulting to Kennison and finally struck him in the mouth and on the head. Kennison was reported to have drawn his revolver and attempted to strike Sturdevant over the head, when the gun caught in the bell cord in the car. Passengers on the car immediately interfered and stopped the trouble. Kennison got off the train at Elkton, where he was going, and attended to his business there and then went back to Cripple Creek and notified the sheriff's office where they could get him. He made no attempt to get away or avoid arrest. General Bell had a detachment of militia out all the forenoon and part of the afternoon looking for Kennison. After he was placed in the county jail, a detachment of troops was sent to investigate. They found him there but made no demand for him.

THEN CAME CONFLICT OF AUTHORITY.

Under Sheriff Gaughan said in relation to the matter that the military had no right to interfere with the procedure of the sheriff's office and if they took Kennison into custody they would exceed their authority so far as he was informed. But as to authority, what authority had they in the district at all? This was only "the beginning of the end."

Lieutenant Wahm, with a squad of six soldiers, rather surprised the miners at union headquarters in Cripple Creek by stationing his detail in front of the hall. Two of the men were deputed to go up stairs and make a search for the president of the union, but as he was not in evidence they soon repaired again to the street. Lieutenant Wahm was informed that a warrant had been sworn out by some person unknown, for the arrest of Kennison by the sheriff's office, and was asked if he would take Kennison in custody in any event.

"Certainly I will take him," he answered, "even though he is released on bond. If he is not released on bond and is confined in the county jail I will go back to the camp and will secure sufficient force to get him anyhow."

The Denver papers of Sept. 10, in speaking of the arrest of Mr. Kennison, said in part:

"C. G. Kennison, president of Miners' Union No. 40, was arrested about noon today and placed in the county jail on the charge of carrying concealed weapons.   In an interview with our correspondent he said:

" 'I am guilty of the offense charged.   I carried a weapon for the sole purpose of defending my life.   The guards at the El Paso mine said that they would stretch me up to an electric light pole.   Manager Sam McDonald of the Strong and Gold King properties told me on Bennett avenue that I would be in my grave before the strike was over.   I was brutally assaulted this morning and shamefully abused by a lot of scabs and I drew a revolver in defense of my life.   I do not care to say any more about the matter at the present time.   No, I am not a deputy sheriff.   I had a commission but I surrendered it some days ago.' "

C. G. Kennison was released Sept. 11, at 4 o'clock from the county jail on bond.   The charge against him was ''assault with intent to kill.''   He gave bond in the amount of $500.   Mr. Kennison was in jail just a day when released.   The men who assaulted him were never arrested, the reader will take note of that fact.   Bell stated that the militia came to preserve order and serve everybody alike, even if the mine owners did put up the money to pay the freight.   How perfectly ridiculous?   We all knew what they came for in a few days after their arrival.

After the action of the military in the Kennison affair, the following telegram was sent to President Moyer at Denver, Sept. 10 and the original cannot be improved upon by the writer:

"The victims of the corporations' tyranny greet you in the greatest gold camp in all the world.   (N. B.–Quotation from K. P.)

"The civil power has been supplanted by military despotism.   The laws of the state are overridden with impunity and the powers that be are using the glorious American flag to cover crimes against the constitution of the illustrious state of Colorado, and the 'Bill of Rights' of the United States of America.   The rights of property has supplanted the rights of the individual and a lawless mob (militia) are arresting citizens without authority at their pleasure.   Please arouse the citizens of the state and save us from this anarchistic anarchism, militaryism, un-Americanism, blatherskiteism and Bellism.

"THE VICTIMS OF MILITARY DESPOTISM."

By September 10, guards were stationed practically all over the district, at all large mines where union men were out on strike and on the public highways.   By that time the citizens began to realize the inconveniennce of having to produce a pass every time they had business to use a public road leading to or from the cities of the district.

The guards stationed over the district were growing more particular each day. At the Strong mine the wagon roads were rendered useless for the reason that the guards would not allow teams to pass that way. There were so many camps established by that time that the soldiers branching out from each of them had the district practically covered. A man living near the Strong mine was forbidden, Sept. 9, the privilege of going to his own home because it was within the guard line. **Is a "man's house his castle?"**

There was a constant rumor of martial law, bull pens and almost anything else, being established. Of course, the people at that time could hardly believe this would be done, there were also those who thought that a part of the program, and pointed to the bringing of the troops here in the first place without any cause. Yet, there were still, at that time, a few that believed they were in "free America," where we have always prided ourselves on **liberty, free speech and the rights of the individual.**

Sept. 13, the rumored "bull pen" was found to be an established fact. It was found that a military prison, to be known as the "bull pen" was in truth a stern reality. The first surprise to the people of the district was the coming of the military. That was considered an outrage on the people here, but that disgrace to the Cripple Creek district was insignificant in comparison with the "bull pen." We were beginning, by the above date, to realize that while the militia was in the camp we could expect almost anything. When we retired at night, we did not know whether a stray bullet from a reckless soldier's gun would hit us, or whether possibly, we would be called from our bed and family at midnight, and taken in charge to serve time in the "bull pen." Governor Peabody told us that the troops did not come to the district to supplant the civil authorities, but to assist them.

The public at this date wondered whether they were to consider the governor joking. The words regarding the militia's purpose here had hardly left his lips when three men were arrested, apparently without cause, and lodged in the "bull pen" and all the consolation the people got out of it was to be told that if they were good they would prove to the public that the troops were not needed and that they would finally be rewarded when they had suffered all the humiliation known to man, by the withdrawal of the troops. Such conditions were, indeed, discouraging. We seemed helpless. It was apparent that we must not express our views for fear the general in charge would call it "intimidation" and our arrest might follow.

September 13 found the military in complete control of the entire district. The troops dominated everything. A "bull pen" was established. Men were taken from home and families at dead of night, made to get out of bed and go with the militia and placed in the "bull pen" without explanation. They were not allowed defense and there were no charges preferred against them. Union meetings were, from the date given, broken into and obstructed without apparent cause.

One among the first shocks dealt the people of the district was September 12, when it was announced that the leaders of the military had ordered the arrest of Sherman Parker. It was learned that the order had been executed shortly after midnight, when Mr. Parker was at home asleep. At 12:20 Friday night, September 12, Mr. Parker was awakened by a knock at the door. He went to the door and answered the call. He was told that the gentleman calling had a note from a man by the name of Jack Minor to present to him in the way of introduction. Mr. Parker stepped nearer the door and was immediately placed under arrest and taken from his family without further explanation and lodged in the "bull pen," which was established near the Strong mine.

This was the opening chapter in a persecution against citizen rights which is without parallel in the history of the United States of America.

Sherman Parker is, and has always been, a peaceable citizen. There is probably none better in the county, but he was a member of the strike committee, and after the troops were here at the instigation and for the assistance of the mine owners, they were to arrest anyone that stood in their way of running affairs with an unlimited high hand. He was forbidden consultation, it is stated, with an attorney, and was simply told to "lie there and take what he was given."

By September 12 the action of the military attracted so much attention that even the miners almost forgot they were out on strike. The district before was quiet and very dull. From the above date until December 25 there was amusement in abundance afforded the peaceable citizens by the maneuvers of the state militia.

On September 11, Lieutenant Greenwood of Colorado Springs, was leading a squad of troops over the hills in the vicinity of the Eagle sampler when his horse ran into a prospect hole. The horse fell to the bottom and the rider was severely injured about the hip but soon recovered. Upon this General Bell announced, while rather warm under the collar next morning, that he would issue an order to all people owning mining property to close up the prospect holes and if they gave the answer that they could not get men he would arrest them and put them in the "bull pen." This was to apply to leasers, mine owners, or anyone having charge of property. Why did he not send for the searchlight corps of the army of Colorado?

At the present writing Pike's Peak still stands, not having as yet been torn down to fill prospect holes by order of Sherman Bell.

There was a story published about this time that a man by the name of Minford had been beaten up at Goldfield. The militia at once rushed to the supposed scene of action and made several arrests but had to release the men taken to the "bull pen" as the fake was exposed and the facts in the case were that the man was in a low resort quarrel and got a little the worst of the deal. There were no strikers implicated in any way whatever. We, however, held our breath and expected martial law to be declared at once.

One of the most ridiculous things that occurred during the strike was the operating of a searchlight. The light was moved from one mountain to another and turned on the various little cities of the district. Another ridiculous thing was that the citizens of the law-abiding community were given the opportunity of seeing a Gatling gun. One was taken from Camp Goldfield to Beacon hill in the afternoon of Sept. 11. It was probably the one that was borrowed from Wyoming to help out Colorado in the great war of the Cripple Creek district. At any rate the Gatling gun was here and was hauled from place to place as the great "rebellion" went on.

The direct state telegraph line between the adjutant general's office and Camp Goldfield, was overworked Tuesday, Sept. 11. From early in the morning until late at night General Bell and Governor Peabody were corresponding over it. The first telegram sent over the wire from Denver was from Governor Peabody, in reply to the telegram received from General Bell on the 10th.

"Denver, Colorado, September 10, 1903.

"Sherman M. Bell, Adjutant General, Camp Goldfield, Victor Colorado:

"Telegram this date received. I congratulate the people in Teller county upon the reported condition. Peace and prosperity will surely follow law and order. May both continue to exist throughout this commonwealth.   JAMES H. PEAEODY, Governor."

No greater parody on the sentiment of patriotic Patrick Henry, or liberty-loving Washington ever disgraced justice and debauched the name fellowmen than the above "congratulation" by the oath-bound "servant of the people."

Our ancestors were surely wrong in educational policy, for by it they have placed humanity above social gold idolatry. Shakespeare is dead, this is no rhyme—Byron, too, is dead—before his time.

Sept. 15, the militia aroused the people of the district when a company of cavalry marched to the residence of Patrick J. Lynch of Victor, and who is chairman of the board of county commissioners of Teller county, and, without doubt, as peaceable a citizen as lives in the state of Colorado, arrested and marched him before Generals Bell and Chase. Nothing since the strike started so thoroughly aroused the people of the county as this outrage Sept. 15. Mr. Lynch was presentd with no papers. He was given no reason for arrest. He was simply taken from his table while dining, and marched to Camp Goldfield.

A troop of about twenty men marched down Fourth street

across Portland, where Mr. Lynch resides. They immediately surrounded his residence, going into the back yard and into the alley, then an officer approached the house and arrested Mr. Lynch. He was rudely seized and taken out forthwith. He was not allowed to return to his residence, but soldiers were sent back for some purpose.

Mr. Lynch was ordered to mount one of the horses and was surrounded by troopers. Two were kept on foot also to guard him. As the procession marched along the street to the camp, hundreds of people lined both sides of the thoroughfare and the expressions that were uttered were possibly the strongest that had been heard. Others laughed at the folly and the absurdity of the action was ridiculed from every source.

Mr. Lynch was immediately ordered before Generals Bell and Chase when he reached the camp. He was told that it had been reported to them that he had criticised the soldiers and exercised the privilege of every American citizen in urging men not to return to work. This Mr. Lynch denied emphatically, and, turning to General Bell and pointing his finger at him, said: "There is a man who has known me for ten years, and he knows that I am as peaceable a citizen as lives in the state of Colorado." After a few other remarks Mr. Lynch was released and allowed to return to his home and partake of another meal by his own fireside, though the military bravos were still in the district.

On the morning of September 15 the following protest was issued by an organization composed of men who had at one time been real soldiers and who had seen service in the defense of their country—the Grand Army of the Republic:

"In the Denver News of this morning, appears a report of a visit of several members of the Grand Army Post of Victor, to the military camp yesterday, in which it says that the old soldiers asked that their compliments be extended to the governor for his worthy and prompt action in ordering out the National Guard among us in this time of emergency.

"Now this is a lie out of the whole cloth. If said at all it must have been by an individual, and not authorized by word or voice of us veterans, neither was it in our presence. We were not then, and we are not now in favor of the militia being here, nor do we believe that they themselves take any pride in it, but being here, we are in favor of their being treated with courtesy and respect.

"We are thankful to both officers and soldiers of Camp Goldfield for the courteous and soldierly-like manner in which they received and treated us, and we hope that they may soon be relieved from their unpleasant and distasteful duties in this district.   (Signed)

"I. N. BERRY, Post Commander,
"MICHAEL DONNOVAN,
"J. H. DAVIS,
"JAMES MAHONEY,
"J. H. DUNN,
"HENRY NEARGARTER,
"W. H. TOPPING,
"SAMUEL HEWITT."

JUDGE SEEDS ISSUES WRITS.

District Judge W. P. Seeds, September 15, granted writs of habeas corpus directing Generals Bell and Chase to bring into court the four prisoners confined in the military guard house and to show cause why Messrs. Parker, Campbell, Lafferty and McKinney were deprived of their liberty. Before reading the application of the court, General Engley said: "The matters set forth in the opening of the petitions may not seem applicable to the questions at issue, but they will be found to constitute the reasons which have led up to the circumstances of which we here complain."

At the conclusion of the reading of the application, Judge Seeds said: "It seems to me that you have set forth a large number of matters which are not pertinent to the question of the relief asked for." General Engley asked: "Then, your honor, you will not issue the writs."

Judge Seeds replied: "I will issue the writs as prayed for but I want it understood that upon the hearing at the return of the writs no matters will be allowed to be gone into except such as are connected with the question of restraint."

"The writs were made returnable Friday morning at 9:30 o'clock, September 18. Sheriff Robertson's demand for the prisoners was formally refused by Chase.

The petition for habeas corpus in the case of Sherman Parker was a lengthy document, signed by Christian Kagy as petitioner. The other petitions were practically identical with it. It set forth that Parker was a citizen of Teller county, a miner, and was unlawfully imprisoned, detained, confined and restrained of his liberty by Generals Chase and Bell.

The facts of the strike were set forth; that the Mine Owners' Association appointed an executive committee that had announced that it would destroy the Western Federation of Miners and would not confer with any labor organization. It alleged that the Citizens' Alliance was in a conspiracy with the Mine Owners' Association to compel and force the miners to return to work; that by a conspiracy these two organizations prevailed upon the governor of Colorado to send the National guard to the district to aid and abet in the intimidation of the officers and members of the Western Federation of Miners. It alleged that these two bodies reported to the governor that a state of lawlessness existed and that the commission appointed by the governor to investigate and report upon conditions in the district was influenced by the Mine Owners' Association and the Citizens' Alliance, to report that a state of disorder existed, over the protest of the sheriff of Teller county.

The petition further stated that the National guard was not sent to the district to prevent or suppress any riot, or to aid the civil authorities to suppress any tumult, but on the contrary in the sole interests of the said mine owners and at the expense of the state, for the purpose of compelling the miners to return to work; also to arrest and imprison without process of law the officers and members of labor unions, especially officers and members of the Western Federation of Miners, to arrest and imprison without process of law every one actively and peaceably engaged in supporting and advocating the rights of labor.

Further it said that the Mine Owners' Association had selected and given to the officers the names of forty miners, peaceable and law-abiding citizens and directed their arrest and imprisonment by said National guard to the end that the labor organization might be crushed and employes forced back to work; that troops under the orders of military officers were making visits and searching the habitations of law-abiding citizens at all hours of the night. That these citizens were subjected to brutal and inhuman treatment, that troops had intimidated the civil authorities and had picketed and closed public highways, and the officers of the National guard had arrested and intended to continue to arrest without process of law, citizens who had committed no offense, refusing to release them or to deliver them into the custody of civil authorities and at the behest of the Mine Owners' Association and Citizens' Alliance, Sherman Parker was at that time unlawfully imprisoned; that the petitioner believed that the National guard had no jurisdiction or legal authority to arrest or imprison the said Sherman Parker and so believed that his imprisonment was illegal.

The petitioner asked that Judge Seeds command the officers of the National guard to produce said Parker and restore him to liberty.

The Rocky Mountain News contained the following article, about September 14:

"BELL SHOULD BE REMOVED.

"Adjutant General Sherman Bell should be relieved and removed from command of the troops at Cripple Creek. His mental characteristics are such as to make him an unsafe and even dangerous person to hold that position. This has been shown by his conduct since he went to the district in his disregard of the law and the most ordinary rights of citizens.

"The troops have been used to make domiciliary visits, to enter peaceable meetings by force of arms and to make arrests without warrant or indictment and without giving information to the persons arrested or to the public of the reasons of the arrests. Some even are being held forcibly in durance without charge of any kind against them.

"Granting that the governor was sincere in the belief that the troops were necessary in the district, his first great mistake was to consent that the cost of sending them should be paid by one of the parties to the controversy. The officer in command looks upon himself and his troops as in a sense the employes of that party, and it is not to be doubted that the mine owners have driven Bell to do illegal acts which have marked his sway. He and they protest that there is no martial law; while martial law prevails in fact almost to the last extreme. When men are arrested and placed in confinement without charges against them, solely by the order of the general commanding, it is martial law.

"The troops of the state when called out on such occasion, should act solely as assistants to the civil authorities in preserving the peace. The officer in command has no right whatever to undertake to set aside civil authority and make his own whims the sole law.

"The officer in command in Cripple Creek should be calm, self-controlled and responsible, and as Bell is not qualified in any of those particulars, the governor should repair, so far as possible, the harm already done by removing him at once. A man of demonstrated unfitness should not occupy a place of such great trust at a time when so much is involved as is the case in the Cripple Creek district at the present time."

PREPARATIONS TO FIGHT A NATION.

On September 15, Bell announced that he would appear in person before Judge Seeds, Friday, September 18, with his attorneys and answer as to his reasons for arresting and holding men in the military prison. But military activity continued as if the whole state of Colorado was in a state of armed rebellion; a first consignment of 1,000 Krag-Jorgensen rifles from the United States government arrived and were given the troops. All companies of the First regiment, except E, G, and L companies not having Krag-Jorgensen rifles, were given Winchesters. Besides the new rifles, 60,000 rounds of ammunition were also received. This was the first new equipment to be sent to Colorado under the Dick bill.

The signal corps commenced to establish a great many important (to them) signal stations. Telegraph stations were established during the day-time on Bull Hill, Squaw and Nipple mountain, Gold hill and Raven mountain. The night lanterns to be in constant communication with Brigadier General Bell's quarters. With the aid of search lights it would be absolutely impossible for any person to approach or escape from camp, as they would make objects plainly visible for miles around. Telegraph stations were installed on Bull, Mineral and Beacon hills, being connected by direct lines with Denver and all parts of the United States. Official messages were to have precedence at all times. Field telephones were installed in every camp. Also on Tenderfoot hill, Battle mountain and Cow mountain. These telephones were directly connected with officers' quarters and the guard tent. At any moment that a meeting of the Western Federation of Miners was reported a general alarm could be sounded throughout the camp. The new solar lamp which operates the heliograph at night was to be stationed on the following mountains: Cow, Pisgah, Straub and St. Peter's Dome. All

heliograph stations were equipped with signal flags for wig wag-
ging purposes on cloudy days. The signal corps was equipped
with twelve powerful telescopes of the latest design, as well as
binoculars. The use of cipher messages were used in communication between commanding officers and their superiors. Now,
reader, what do you think of that outlay for a **peaceable community?**

THE PRESS COMMENTS EDITORIALLY.

The unwarranted, warrantless and arbitrary military arrests,
the vicious use of state force and power, armed against the masses,
called forth at this time the editoral condemnation of all the
influential papers of the state, whose views were expressed similar
to the following from the Denver Post and News:

"DOES GOV. PEABODY REALLY KNOW WHAT HE IS DOING?

"The present attitude of Governor Peabody is that organized labor is
treasonable. The situation at Cripple Creek is a reminder of the fact that
the President of the United States and governor of a state have unlimited
power in emergencies—but if they exercise it wrongly upon their heads
be it; that is to say, the politician or the political aspirant who uses the
supreme power of the state and it turns out to have been unnecessary, is
destroyed by his mistake. All law and government are, of course, based
on force. That is to say a government which cannot maintain itself, is
necessarily no government. And so the most ordinary every-day processes of civil law are respected, because behind them is the entire force of
the community, the state and the United States. And certainly there must
be some finale and that tremendous power is lodged in the governor and
the president.

"But there is nothing the governor of a state or the president of the
United States tries so earnestly to avoid as the exercise of the power now
being used by Governor Peabody. Seldom has it been used, and, indeed,
the most odious conditions have been tolerated rather than exercise naked,
undisguised force. So all the presidents of the United States and all the
governors of states have hesitated long and well, and, indeed, there is
no modern example of the thing Peabody is doing, save Cleveland's famous
act in Chicago. The pretext there was that the United States mails had
to be moved. The excuse for martial law at Cripple Creek is that there
is conspiracy against the law. The real reason in Chicago was that President Cleveland decided to put an end to the railway strike and likewise the
real reason at Cripple Creek is that the governor *proposes to crush the
miners' strike.*

"In Cripple Creek the thing at which Peabody has struck with all the power of the state is not physical, as in Chicago, but in the air. That is to say, men said they were afraid to go to work; but there were no criminal acts. The governor's excuse for his action is that he levels the armed force of the state against fear. To the man who cares nothing, sympathetically, one way or the other, but who has a regard for law, the view of the matter is that the governor should have refused to act until there was evident lawlessness and disorder.

"The fact of the business is that the reasons for Peabody's action would justify the seizure of all union labor leaders on the charge of treason, regardless of any strikes. In fact, it may be doubted if the governor realizes what he is doing. The real, vital interest in the thing is that Governor Peabody of Colorado, has cast a dye which, unless he backs out, to use plain words, means that organized labor is treasonable and, if his attitude is accepted, will mean the crushing of labor organization by the government as being a society or organization which challenges the supremacy of government. As soon as the country realizes what is being done in Colorado it will be recognized as a national issue.

"The outcome of Governor Peabody's action may bear results of which perhaps he never thought or dreamed. Whether he is killed politically or his party is destroyed are results insignificant beside the issue of what the law may finally do.

"Only one thing was ever settled in this country by any process, save that of law, and that one thing was slavery."—Denver Post.

"LIABLE IN DAMAGES.

"There seems to be little doubt that suits can be maintained against Governor Peabody, Generals Bell and Chase and the other officers immediately connected with the arbitrary arrests of citizens in the Cripple Creek district.

"From Bell's published statements, he was sent to the Cripple Creek district with discretion in the matter of arrests. Governor Peabody is commander-in-chief of the militia in the field, and when he trusted discretion to his adjutant to make arrests, he became personally responsible in damages for all unlawful arrests made by his subordinate.

"Not a respectable lawyer can be found who will say that there is a shadow of legality in the arrests made at Cripple Creek under General Bell's orders up to the present time. The military has surrounded homes, taken out the inmates and carried them by force to military headquarters, and either sent them to the 'bull pen' where they are yet held, or, with an admonition, set them at liberty. There has been no pretense of a charge of violation of the law having been filed civilly against these people, and those who are yet confined are held wholly at the will of Bell, with the approval of the governor.

"When the fever for this military foray to Cripple Creek has died down and men resume their sober senses, the utter blackness of these military arrests will become apparent and the juries will not be slow to mulct the offenders in heavy damages. It is gratifying to know that Commissioner Lynch and Justice of the Peace Reilly have determined to bring suits for false imprisonment against this military combination, and to lay their damages at $100,000. Every man who has been unlawfully arrested or imprisoned up in Cripple Creek, should pursue the same course.

"Peabody and Bell may have an exaggerated notion of their own magnitude while they are raiding the homes of private citizens with the military force of the state behind them, but when they face juries in the district court, presided over by an honest judge, to defend a dozen suits for damages, they will sink to the littleness of their true statues and leave the courts poorer but wiser men."—Rocky Mountain News.

"GOVERNOR DENIES RESPONSIBILITY.

"Denver, Sept. 16.—'I can hardly credit the statement that County Commissioner Lynch and Justice of the Peace Reilly intend to bring suit against me for damages because of false imprisonment. Everyone knows of the orders I have issued, and they know that I have always said that the civil authorities were supreme, if they tried to enforce law and order,' said the governor in an interview. 'Governor Bell was only sent there and I told him so, to aid the civil authorities. I hardly see that I have anything to do with this suit, even if one is really brought. I didn't arrest them and I didn't give the order to arrest them. As a matter of fact, I do not believe they would have a standing in court. I don't even know they were arrested, and it is probable that they were not. They might have been taken to headquarters to confer with the general, and they thought it was arrest.' "

Attorney General Miller, however, had another opinion:

"I can't talk about this, of course; I don't know anything about the merits of the case. But if they do bring suit it will be a good thing in one way. It will absolutely settle the question of just what right and authority the militia has when ordered out. The bringing of suits against individuals is exactly the right course to pursue. They have a chance of winning that way. While if they had sued the state the suit would have been thrown out of court at once. I do not care to talk about this part of it," said Attorney General Miller. "I am out of it and no one is better pleased with it than I. I'm heartily tired of the whole business. Why, I never heard of the military exerting such authority as they have in this case, except in the Coeur d'Alene during the big strike there. General Merriam took charge of that with United States soldiers and established practical martial law, but even that, I think, was illegal. The trouble is these military fellows go ahead and do just as they please, whether it's according to the law or not. They say it's a military necessity, and trust to luck that they get out of it all right."

STATE FEDERATION OF LABOR AROUSED.

During the week of September 14 to 19, the Colorado State Federation of Labor was in session at Canon City, and realizing the oppressing domination of Colorado militaryism and understanding that all organized labor was in imminent danger of military suppression by the determined and lawless methods used

Illustrating Military Authority Over Civil.

to crush the Western Federation of Miners, passed unanimously resolutions condemning the action of Governor Peabody in sending troops to the Cripple Creek district as well as the action of sending the militia to Colorado City in the spring to assist mill managers there. The Colorado State Federation of Labor also adopted a strong resolution commending Judge Owers for his action in the Idaho Springs affair. A copy of the resolutions were forwarded to Judge Owers under seal of the organization.

FIFTY - ONE STRIKE BREAKERS ARRIVE IN DISTRICT.

On September 18 the much heralded strike breaking miners

from the "East" arrived in Denver on their way to the district under heavy guard.

When the train carrying these men reached Cripple Creek the soldiers abandoned them, but the mine owners had places provided for their comfort. The newsboys followed them down the street and cried, "scab." This frightened the mine owners and a detachment of troops was immediately sent from Camp Goldfield to Cripple Creek, going over on the 9 o'clock electric low line from Victor. These soldiers were soon joined by two other companies of infantry and they lined Bennett avenue from First to Third streets and guarded the alleys more particularly. The soldiers' headquarters were made at the Mining Exchange building, from where they received their orders. Citizens walking along the streets were told to move on and not to loiter. Finns and Norwegians constituted most of the men brought in—in fact, there were only two Americans among them, and very few who could speak English. The ones who could speak English stated that conditions had been misrepresented to them. They had just finished their work in the harvest fields of northern Michigan and were told that a new gold field had been opened here and that the mine owners wanted men badly. They were informed that in order to get men at once they would pay $3 for eight hours work and that the first men who responded would get the jobs. They were told further that if they did not like the work they would pay their expenses back to their homes and that it would not cost them a cent to get to the district. There were eighty-seven in the crowd when they reached Denver, but twenty-six of the number pulled away in that city and about nine quit at Colorado Springs, leaving fifty or fifty-one to arrive in the gold camp.

STRIKE BREAKERS CONVERTED TO UNIONISM.

Eighteen of the men shipped into the district from Michigan were at union headquarters Friday night, September 18, and stated they would not go to work under the conditions here; that matters here had been grossly misrepresented to them. The balance of the fifty-one were taken to the Independence mine in the morning under heavy guard, but when they got to the mine they refused to go below. They were kept there all day and fed at Camp Goldfield.

On Saturday morning, September 19, while the remaining twenty-three imported laborers were being escorted along Bennett avenue, Cripple Creek, by the military, the first shot of the "Cripple Creek District War" occurred when Lieutenant Hartung of company B, took a shot at one of the imported Finns, Emil Peterson, who had been drawn off by the unions.

"County of Teller, State of Colorado, Emil Peterson, being duly sworn, upon his oath, says: 'I am twenty-four years of age. I reside in Denmark; that is my native land. I came to America February 23, 1903. I then went to Fairchilds, Wis. I am not an American citizen. At Fairchilds the Lester Lumber Company paid only $26 per month. On the 8th of September I went to Duluth to get work. At Duluth B. B. Gilbert & Co., labor agents, 5 South avenue, west, employed me to go to work in the Colorado gold mines. I was to get from $3 to $5 per day to fire boilers in the mine. I was shipped here from Duluth. Mine owners of Cripple Creek advanced me $18 for car fare. The company would pay this if we contracted to work a month. About seventy-five men were shipped from Duluth. I don't know how many quit on the way. Others joined at St. Paul, making near 150 altogether. I think that about eighty of these, of whom only five had ever worked in a mine arrived last night, Friday, September 18. B. B. Gilbert & Co. told us there was no strike in Cripple Creek. They had a newspaper in the office, saying: 'No strike in gold camp; all men go to work.' At Colorado Springs we discovered there was a strike. Men with spectacles on who said they were mine lessees met us in Colorado Springs and came on with us. I stayed last night at the Rhodes house with a party of ten. We took breakfast and then went to a building near where the shooting occurred. Here there were many others. The men were lined up and an officer said: 'Come on, boys, go to work.' I said out loud in Spanish, 'Don't go to work,' I started to run and he fired at me with a pistol. I ran zigzag to avoid the bullet. He fired once. I got away."

"Subscribed and sworn to before me this 19th day of September, 1903.

                                        "ABBY C. COLWELL,
"My commission expires June 29, 1904.   Notary Public."
    (Signed)   "EMIL PETERSON.
                                         "CARL HANSON."

Peterson's companion, Carl Hanson, made an affidavit to the effect that he had accompanied Peterson from Fairchilds to Duluth and from there to the district and that he saw the soldier shoot at

Peterson, etc. E. D. Whitney also made an affidavit that he saw the shooting and that Peterson had made a correct statement. This goes to show what the Mine Owners' Association would resort to in order to accomplish their purpose. Import men here by false representation and after they arrived and discovered true conditions and refused to work, try to force them at the point of bayonets to work when all other efforts had failed. There were many other cases like the foregoing, but I give this in detail as a fair illustration of their attempts to secure men to take the places of union miners. As time went on and attempt after attempt failed, they grew more desperate at their failure.

By Tuesday, September 22, all remaining Finns escaped from the mines where they were forced to work at the point of bayonets, had left the city at the expense of unions, be it recorded to the foreigner's credit. That set of imported men were not naturally born "scabs," union men are born—not made. To the writer's mind a natural born "scab" will leave a good union job and work for less, in order to be what he is naturally—a "scab" on the face of humanity.

Friday, September 18, was the day the prisoners were to be produced by the military. The writs issued by Judge Seeds being returnable on that date.

Tom McClelland appeared in the district court that morning to represent Generals Chase and Bell, who were not present, and asked for a continuance of the habeas corpus cases for five days. This was refused by Judge Seeds, on the grounds that the respondents had made no return upon the writ, neither producing the prisoners in court, nor showing cause why the order of the court had not been complied with. McClelland then stated to the court that if given until 2 o'clock in the afternoon, he would make a return on the writ and then argue the question of continuance. When court convened at 10 o'clock McClelland arose and, with folded arms, addressed the court, stating that he represented the respondents, Chase and Bell, and on their behalf asked for a continuance. He said:

"A great many questions are involved in this case, and owing to the duties of the military camp I have not had the time to prepare such an) answer as I would like to present to this court. Under this statute it is discretionary with the court to allow five days for an answer. I would, therefore, ask until Monday morning or longer to do so."

General Eugene Engley, counsel for the prisoners, objected. He said:

"There has not been sufficient showing to warrant the continuance sought by Brother McClelland. The statute is very clear on this point. It says that only upon the return of the writ a day shall be set for a hearing. A continuance must be made after a return of the writ, which has not been made. Whether an imprisonment has been made by the military forces or by civil officers, that person ought to know before making an arrest what is the authority for doing so, and he should be ready at any time to make a showing of his position."

McClelland said that upon the return that day the court might make an order for continuance, either for making a return or for a hearing.

John Murphy, general attorney for the Western Federation, said:

"The order of this court was to produce these prisoners. The respondents are in contempt because they have not done so, and have given no reason to the court why they have failed to produce the prisoners. Without warrants, citizens of this commonwealth have been thrown into prison. The military is only the reserve police of the state, and cannot hold a man longer than absolutely necessary to take him before a magistrate." The court said that section 2108 of the code contemplates a return of the parties to whom a writ is directed. He added: "That would be a foundation for the court to consider the questions at issue. Upon that the court would be advised that there are matters subject to trial. It would then be within the province of the court to fix a time for a hearing. Moreover, it is the judgment of the court that, on proper showing, the time of the return may be extended, but that the showing must be one upon which the court should be advised that more time may be necessary. Mr. McClelland's showing is not sufficient. It should be supported by facts and circumstances."

McClelland stated that if a continuance was given until 2 o'clock he would make a return of the writ. The court said: "Very well, I will grant a continuance to that hour. I think the parties who instituted these proceedings are entitled to a return. I will give the respondents until 2 o'clock to make it." At 2 o'clock the court convened again and the military attorney was not ready but entered a plea for further delay, and Judge Seeds again granted his request, this time giving him until Monday, September 21, at 9 o'clock. This delay aroused considerable speculation as to the cause and outcome.

The largest crowd ever assembled at a hearing in the Teller county district court room had assembled on this date to see what the outcome would be. Every seat in the court room was occupied.

Sherman M. Bell.

At 9:30 o'clock, a. m., September 21, Judge Seeds was on the bench, the sheriff at his station and court was duly in session—but Chase, Bell and the prisoners were not present. Tom McClelland, however, appeared as counsel for Chase and offered argument as to the non-appearance of Chase and his prisoners.

Counsel for the prisoners demanded that the prisoners be brought into court and Judge Seeds sustained them. Attorney Murphy presented a motion that an attachment for John Chase be issued directing the sheriff to arrest Gen. Chase and bring him into court, on the ground that he had failed to produce the prisoners in court and was therefore guilty of contempt.

Mr. Murphy read the statute relating to refusal of officers to obey a writ of habeas corpus. He said it was stated in court Saturday, Sept. 19, that the military was here to aid the court and civil authorities and desired to assist them. "If this is true," he said, "that they are here to obey the mandate of the court, there is nothing for them to do but to bring the prisoners into court, just as the sheriff would obey a writ of habeas corpus.''

McClelland replied that his position raised all these questions and he desired to present his case. Judge Seeds interrupted saying:

"The court cannot agree with Mr. McClelland. These men are entitled to be heard as to themselves. In order to avoid any misunderstanding, I called upon General Chase Saturday and told him to appear in court Monday morning, September 21, and produce the prisoners, but he has not done so. The court will not proceed in this case until the petitioners are in the court room. It is due him and it is due you, in obedience to this court, that those men be present, and the court will not conduct any proceedings in their absence. It is just as imperative that you produce the bodies of the prisoners as directed in the writ as that you make a return on the writ. The points are one and inseparable."

Judge Seeds asked McClelland if there were any preliminary matters he desired to take up before arguing the motion of petitioners to quash the return of the writ. McClelland said he desired to go on with the argument, and would like to take up the issue then.

Judge Seeds replied:

"The court absolutely refuses—unless it is compelled to by conditions beyond its control—to listen to any arguments in the absence of the prisoners."

Lieutenant McClelland requested permission to file an amendment to the return setting forth that arrest and detention of the prisoners had been the result of the judgment of the commanding officer in putting into effect the order issued by the governor placing the troops in the field. The court granted this permission and McClelland stated in reference to the order of the court regarding the prisoners that he would communicate that to the commanding general whom he represented.

A recess was taken to 2 p. m.

After Judge Seeds' decision all the military officers were closeted for two hours, discussing the situation and talking with Gen. Chase by telephone and S. D. Crump, who was associate counsel in the case. It was decided to comply with the order of the court and General Chase announced that he would go over on the train with the four prisoners, Parker, Campbell, McKinney and Rafferty, in time for the assembling of court at 2 o'clock and that he would bring them under a strong escort and send a detachment of cavalry to act as guard in the vicinity of the court house.

At about 1 o'clock p. m. the people saw that preparations were being made for the arrival of General Chase and his prisoners. A blare of trumpets, the thunderous sound of dashing troops, the rumbling roar of wheels, quick, fierce and stern commands of "Halt!" "Clear the street!" "Guard that alley!" "Guard that street!" "Ready, load!" "Sharp shooters seize the vantage of yon roof!" "Seize this," seize that," "seize any old thing!"

By the time the people realized that the fierce and mighty onslaught was not the arrival of Gabriel and the avenging hosts, they had been pushed, "yanked" and prodded from the streets; women were hysterical; children were screaming from fright; refuge had been sought by them in saloons, doors, stores and hallways—and then Cripple Creek had been captured! Sharpshooters had bravely and in the face of fearful odds gained possession of every point of advantage, the roof of the National hotel, near the Court House, swarmed with them, gallant soldiers with loaded and bayonetted muskets paraded the sidewalks, death-dealing Gatling guns (late of Wyoming), commanded the streets. The hospital corps with stretchers, lints and all were there in readiness for the ghastly duties and superhumanly wise was the man, woman, child; aye, even mouse, bird, or yellow dog who could move a lash or pick a feather unless detected by the vigilant eyes of fighters of Colorado's "bloody wars."

But why was this? Why this military coup? Can't you see? Don't you understand? The brigadier general, the mighty warrior was coming (at last) to deliver the bloody-minded, bloody-handed, crime-conceiving and committing anarchists to the "poor unprotected court" in answer to a "dinky" little old writ of habeas corpus!

At 1:30 p. m. Chase arrived with the prisoners. But what an arrival!

This is supposed to be a free Republic and never before in the annals of time have prisoners been escorted to a court of justice in such a manner as were Sherman Parker, Lafferty, Campbell and McKinney. Readers of this book should bear in mind well how these citizens, not one of whom had had a complaint lodged against him, was arraigned in court.

Search the pages of history and nothing can equal it.

Two troops of cavalry came dashing down Bennett avenue in full field equipment, jangling, glittering sabers, loaded sidearms, belted and arrayed for bloody conflict. Guards were hurriedly rushed to every entrance. Ah! ha! another brilliant coup! the court was safe! the prisoners would be safe and now would the general deliver the prisoners in answer to the writ!

The prisoners arrived on the 1:30 train and much was the surprise of the people to see instead of four bound, shackled and handcuffed assassins and robbers, anarchists or desperadoes, four ordinary miners, tired and dusty, for whose appearance all this military bravado and brilliant display had been made, marching up the street between a file of grinning young fellows with guns on their shoulders and dressed in the blue supposed to be the uniform of the American soldier.

But the court room! Freeman, its like has never been seen in this Republic.

There sat the court supported by his sheriffs—all that had been needed, but aside from this, twenty armed men, cavalry, side arms and carbines or worse, stood in solemn phalanx with their backs to the court and arms at present.

Outside all the cavalry of the militia were in waiting. Waiting for what?

To shoot down citizens if so ordered and to intimidate the court.

Hardly had the cavalcade started on Bennett avenue when the order was given to put bullets in the guns.

When court convened at 2 o'clock Lieutenant McClelland took the floor and argued that martial law existed here as soon as the governor issued his order sending out the troops and from that standpoint he practically occupied the attention of the court the entire afternoon. The court adjourned at 6 o'clock to convene at

9:30 the next morning. The prisoners were again marched to the "bull pen."

The next morning (Tuesday) it was reported the military had decided to recognize the civil authorities to the extent of turning over to them three of the four prisoners. The three to be proceeded against criminally and affidavits to be filed with the district attorney on which to prepare informationns and have capiases issued. The announcement was made in court Tuesday morning by counsel for the military. It was not stated which of the prisoners was to be given to the sheriff, and none of the officers would give any information on the subject, but it was understood that Campbell, Lafferty and McKinney were the three and that Sherman Parker would be produced in court on the habeas corpus contest and.the hearing would be proceeded with. Court did not convene until nearly 11 o'clock and the delay was occasioned by complications of the military counsel on the move it proposed to make.

When the hour for opening the court passed and Chase had not appeared with his prisoners and escort, there were rumors that the military had decided to defy the court and decline to proceed further with the habeas corpus proceedings; but after court opened the examinations were made. After much argument by attorneys for military and prisoners Judge Seeds ruled that unless three of the men were turned over to the sheriff by 2 o'clock he would proceed with the hearing in all four cases. Counsel for the military said they would have the affidavits ready for the district attorney not later than 12:30 or 1 o'clock, and that it would then be "up to him" to prepare the information and secure capiases for the accused.

The court then adjourned to convene at 2 o'clock. At 2 o'clock the streets were lined with people and the court room was crowded but no officers and prisoners arrived. Later Judge Seeds received a message from Camp Goldfield to the effect that the officers could not get their evidence together until 10 o'clock, Wednesday, the 23rd, and again the court granted them time.

The gaudy glare of war and the apparent domination of the military powers were again in evidence upon the opening of court

Wednesday morning. Bennett avenue was again crowded with cavalry troopers and infantry. A Gatling gun was stationed with its muzzle pointing toward the Midland depot. A detail of sharp shooters, who are recognized as the most expert marksmen, was placed on the roof of the National hotel, four stories above the grade of Bennett avenue. These men perched upon the cupolas stationed at intervals on the roof of the building and had their guns pointed toward the streets for immediate use. The court house was guarded by men who confronted intruders with bayonets, and the citizens who attempted to cross the lines were brought face to face with the power which the militia saw fit to exercise. As soon as the train rolled into the depot half of the troopers dashed up the street with General Chase at their head and threw their lines across the frontage of the Midland depot. The prioners were escorted to the court room with two files of infantry on either side. The troopers followed. The court room was crowded with spectators and soldiers with bayonets glistening wickedly. The fact that the court should again tolerate a display which had so thoroughly angered the citizens, stirred the wrath of General Engley. He informed the court that he would not proceed because of the intimidating forces present in and about the court room. He characterized the court as an armed camp and stated calmly that the constitution provides that the "court shall be free and untrammeled and open to everyone for the transaction of public business." He said:

"There has befallen my duty to make the closing arguments for the petitioners. When I filed the application for writs of habeas corpus and invoked the jurisdiction of this court for the issuance for the highest writ of right known to law, I supposed that these proceedings would be heard under constitutional guarantee; but it is not so. The court may say that it is, but the facts remain that the forces of intimidation are present. The constitutional guarantee that the court shall be open and untrammeled has been invaded.

"This is no longer a constitutional court. It is an armed camp. The court has been surrounded by soldiery."

After long and sharp colloquies by all attorneys, Judge Seeds adjourned court until Thursday morning and back to the "bull pen" went the prisoners.

Judge Seeds Thursday morning notified General Chase to be present in court with his prisoners before 2 o'clock in the afternoon, as promptly at that hour he would render a decision in the habeas corpus case. Chase stated that whatever the decision of the court might be, he would certainly take the prisoners back to Camp Goldfield unless otherwise ordered by the governor of Colorado. At 1:30 the military appeared with the same old pomp, minus the Gatling gun. (Formerly of Wyoming.)

After listening for several hours, Judge Seeds ordered the prisoners released and handed over to the civil authorities and

Where Sharpshooters Were Stationed on Roof.

gave reasons for his decision in a long and carefully compiled argument, from which I quote:

"If the court shall err in its conclusions, it will be no fault of the able counsel who appear for and against the prisoners. Extraordinary industry has been displayed by counsel in the production of authorities, and the questions involved have been discussed with unusual ardor, eloquence and logic. As the result of counsel's labors, and the great attention and consideration the court has given to their arguments and authorities, it feels clear in its conclusions, and can announce them without any misgiving.

"The importance of the question cannot be overestimated. They embrace not only the power and authority of the commander of the military forces of the state over the freedom of the citizens in times of local disturbances that may more or less imperil life and property, but also the very fundamental principles of American liberty. * * *

"For the reason that the governor recites in the order (see page 94.), he directs the brigadier general commanding the National guard to forthwith order out the troops, etc., specified, to properly enforce the constitution and laws of the state, and to prevent the threatened insurrection and to protect all persons and property in said county from unlawful interference, and to see that threats, intimidations, assaults and all acts of violence cease and that public peace and order be preserved. I take it that all these commands mean is that the brigadier general should, with the National guard, support and enforce the laws within the prescribed district. That the case presented by the petition required that the habeas corpus should issue as prayed admits of no question. The question is, does the executive order, admitting all that it recites as the basis for it to be true, and that General Chase arrested and detained the prisoners by virtue of that order, constitute a justification of the act." * * *

"The threatened insurrection referred to in the order was in connection with a strike in the Cripple Creek district by the metalliferous miners. It is not denied that they quit work peacefully; but it was feared by some and claimed by others that in the course of the strike persons would be injured and property destroyed, and that the insurrection was threatened by an organization known as the Western Federation of Miners, to which the striking miners belonged. Whether the fear was well or ill founded, it is not for the court to say. It will accept the statement in the executive order as the truth. It feels bound to do so from the respect which one of the co-ordinate branches of the state government should always entertain for the other two. * * *

"I take it to be fundamental that, except a state of war exists, a state in which all civil authority is overthrown, what is known as 'martial law' cannot exist or be declared under our state constitution. * * *

"Anderson's law dictionary defines martial law to be 'the law of military necessity in the actual presence of war, administered by the general of the army; it is arbitrary; it is the will of the general who commands the army; it supercedes all existing civil laws; the commander is the legislator, judge and executioner; there may or may not be a hearing upon charges, at the will of the commander; it is built upon no settled principles, but entirely arbitrary in its decisions. In reality it is no law, but something indulged rather than allowed as law.' This definition is fully sustained by a multitude of authorities, and none conflict with it. * * *

"Then if the civil power must prevail, except, possibly, in the extreme case of actual war, and for self-preservation, can the right to the writ of habeas corpus be impaired and can a citizen be deprived of his liberty for an indefinite period of time by the will of a military commander exercised under the authority of such an executive order as respondent's return sets forth? The constitution of the United States declares that 'the privilege of the writ of habeas corpus shall not be suspended unless when in case of *rebellion or invasion* the public safety may require it.' This is, in effect, the same as the habeas corpus provision of the Colorado constitution. This writ is the remedy which the law gives for the enforcement of the civil right of personal liberty, and any other person whomsoever, upon any pretense whatsoever, has a right to have this writ issued by a court commanding the person holding him in custody to bring him before the court for inquiry as to the cause and legality of his imprisonment, and if illegally restrained of his liberty, the prisoner is entitled to his discharge. * * *

"Were this court to admit that civil power is overthrown in Teller county, it would be in conflict with its unaffected consciousness to the contrary. Its courts are open; its decrees are respected; its officials are capable, earnest and law-abiding persons, and no evidence has been brought to the court's attention that the violators of the law will not be proceeded against with vigor and promptness. Though there were evidence of some indifference or neglect in the performance of duties by some of the officers of this court, that would be no proof that civil power within the county was overthrown. Were it so, civil power would be overthrown in too many states and counties of the country. The constitution of Colorado declares 'that the military shall always be in strict subordination to the civil power.' Not *sometimes*, but *always*. There could be no plainer statement that the military should never be permitted to rise superior to the civil power within the limits of Colorado. * * *

"The soldier, as well as every other citizen, is subject to the law of the land. The militia have no other or different powers than peace officers by law have under the same circumstances, except that they may act as an organized body. That an act was done by military order or order of a governor is no defense unless the order itself be one conformable to law." * * *

"I cannot and will not subscribe to such a doctrine. For me to do so would make me *particeps criminis* in the overthrow of a free government in Colorado, and to substitute for it an absolute monarchy. I do not say that when called into the field by the governor in an emergency, the military commander may not arrest those who are participating in lawlessness he is directed to suppress; but I do say that when such an arrest is made the prisoner must, with reasonable speed, be turned over to the civil authorities, with the cause of his arrest made known, that the civil authorities may proceed against them under the forms prescribed by the constitution and laws for the prosecution and punishment of his offense. * * *

"I cannot close without reference to the military display committed with the hearing of this case. It was offensive to the court, and, in its opinion, unwarranted and unnecessary; nevertheless, I tolerated it because it was by the National guard, and if I had insisted upon its withdrawal, a conflict would have probably arisen with the entire National guard of the state upon one side and a mere *posse commitatus* upon the other. The hearing of the case would have been necessarily indefinitely delayed, a great wrong to the prisoner and a denial of the justice to which he was entitled. I trust that there will never again be such unseemly intrusion of armed soldiers in the halls and about the entrances of an American court of justice. They are intrusions that can only tend to bring courts into contempt and make doubtful the possession of that liberty that is the keystone of American governments. It follows from what I have said that, in the opinion of the court, upon the facts stated in said petition and the return of the respondent, the return ought to be quashed, and that the said Parker ought to be discharged from custody, as in said petition prayed, and it is so ordered.

— AND THEN HIS PIPE WENT OUT !

"The cases of James Lafferty, C. H. McKinney and Charles Campbell, relators, vs. the same respondents, by stipulation stand decided as the case of Parker and the said James Lafferty, C. H. McKinney and Charles Campbell are ordered to be discharged from custody as in their respective petitions prayed.

"WILLIAM P. SEEDS, *Judge.*"

Judge Seeds' decision was read to a crowded court room. Immediately after the decision was finished Chase arose and notified the court that he would not abide by the order of the court and facing his soldiers, he commanded them to take the prisoners. Later in the evening, however, about 8 o'clock the military authorities released Sherman Parker, Campbell, James Lafferty and C. H. McKinney from the "bull pen." No explanation was given. The men went straight to their homes and did not even tarry at union headquarters. This news came as a startling surprise to everybody, since just a few hours before the officers had defied the order of the court and refused to release them. The supposition is that this was done in compliance with a telegram from Governor Peabody instructing Chase to comply with the order of the court.

Mrs. Sherman Parker, who sat by her husband during the reading of the decision, screamed and grasping her husband, fainted. The soldiers immediately grabbed Parker and pulled him away from his wife and created one of the most heartrending scenes ever witnessed in a Teller county court room. Mrs. Parker was in a dead faint for twenty minutes and her husband begged to be permitted to remain by his wife, whom he declared to be dying, but was refused by Chase, who also, refused her medical assistance, laughingly claiming that she was alright and would soon recover. Senator Patterson was near and admonished the soldiers to leave the man with his wife until she could recover, which a lieutenant in charge of the prisoner finally agreed to do. The court room was then cleared and Mrs. Parker finally recovered and her husband was taken back to the "bull pen."

Tears came to the eyes of many who witnessed the scene and it was with difficulty that order was restored, which was accomplished by the suggestions of Mr. Patterson.

In what country do we live? Surely not in the United States, and yet the governments of Russia or Germany or Turkey or Austria would break the swords and strip the epaulets from the shoulders of the officers who would dare to commit such an outrage upon their people.

Think for a moment. Suppose the story came from England or France or Germany that because the workmen of some province had gone out on strike, without disorder of any kind, troops were hurried to the locality and the province was harried by them. That the homes of the citizens were invaded by the sol-

diers at will; that the commandant caused dozens of workmen to
be arrested and cast into prison without charge or offense; that
the halls of the workmen were broken open and invaded; that the
citizens were forcibly carried at midnight to the commandant's
tent to be warned that they must not express displeasure and
then insultingly dismissed; that when the courts sought to inquire
why innocent men were held in prison the courts were invaded by
scores of armed men who sat throughout the sessions with bayonetted and loaded guns in hand to intimidate the judge; that
they threw lines of soldiers across the streets and sildewalks, allowing no citizen to pass except permission from an officer was first
obtained; that they planted Gatling guns in the center of the busiest thoroughfares to menace the public; that they stationed
trained sharpshooters on the tops of buildings ready to pick off
some chosen victim; that the court, after patiently hearing and
delivery of a sober and unanswerable opinion, ordered the prisoners to be given their liberty, the commandant defied his order and,
with Gatling gun and clanging sabres, marched with the prisoners
out from the court—what would we Americans have thought and
said? We would have thanked God that we lived in free America
under a written constitution that contained a bill of rights which
is supposed to make such doings impossible. We would recall that
in free America every man's house is his castle; that his liberty
is held more sacred than any number of dollars, and that, except
when found in the commission of an offense, no man dare deprive
a citizen of his liberty without charge or warrant. We would
denounce the government that permitted such outrages as a despotism that should be overthrown if relief could be had in no
other fashion.

The rot of it all is an unholy and dastardly contract between
the governor of the state and a dozen wealthy mine owners to
turn over to them the full, strong arm of the military's power to
crush out—not disturbance, for there has been none; not insurrection, for there has been none; not a conspiracy to in anywise
impede the due execution of the laws of the state, for there has
been none; but to stamp out the life of as legal an organization
as ever existed in any country and whose members are the strong,

courageous, industrious men who have brought the wealth of the mountains to the markets of the world, and who, in case of menace to the government from without, would comprise the front ranks of an army pledged to die, if necessary, to preserve it.

There is not a man or woman in Colorado who loves the state and its free institutions, but should condemn the crimes against law and peace and personal liberty, that have been perpetrated hourly and daily in Teller county, with the connivance and approval of our governor.

FORCED FROM SIDEWALK BY FEAR OF DEATH.

One of the greatest, I will not say the greatest, there were so many indignities offered the citizens of the Cripple Creek district, was on September 20, when there was, on a beautiful Sunday afternoon, hundreds, and I might say thousands of men and women and children out driving or walking in the streets of Victor. A couple of troops of cavalry under command of General John Chase, escorted to the Gem restaurant about a dozen imported non-union men to feed them as if they were cattle. The people that were out noticed the troops in front of the building and, out of curiosity, of course, walked in that direction. We had grown accustomed to these military exhibitions and had learned that a gathering of this kind usually meant the imprisonment of someone closely in touch with the forbidden faith— unionism. So the reader will at once realize it was only natural for us to want to know who the latest victim was. The writer, among the others, was out that day and with the rest of the curious crowd moved toward the fast gathering throng. Suddenly the military charged upon the mass of men, women and children and herded them like wild beasts upon the sidewalks. Then the militiamen not satisfied with this galloped down the pavements, horses prancing and rearing, and forced the people before them. The people ran for their lives; hurried up stairways, into saloons, billiard halls and every available place to avoid being trampled under foot by the horses, maddened by the yokel's spurs. The writer, with her husband and many others, ran into a billiard hall to get out of the way, and even then for a time it seemed as if the soldiers would ride into the building. I, an American born woman, was an actual eye witness to this scene, in the streets on a Sabbath afternoon, in a town in the United States of America, and all done in the name of law and order and by order of the governor of the state of Colorado—is it possible—I can never expect people who did not see the act to believe it. I, for one, would not have believed that American born citizens could control themselves and stand by and look at such a sight. There was one thing in particular that caused my southern blood to boil, there was an old man—yes an old soldier—in the street, and when the crowd was being hurried down the street at the point of bayonets, the old fellow could not move as fast as the militia thought he should, so one of them drew his sword and ordered him to move faster, and in order to hurry the feeble but REAL soldier, pricked him a few times in the back. I tell you I felt every drop of blood in my body boil. Ye Gods, how could these good, true, law-abiding men —mostly union men—control themselves? But they did, and went quietly home with their families. I marveled at what I saw that day. There were many people from other towns on the streets who witnessed the foregoing. One man, from Florence, in speaking of this episode, said that he had never seen anything so outrageous and that the miners were sure to win; as that proved beyond a doubt that the law-breaking was on the other side and that the people here had demonstrated to him that they were the most law-abiding he had ever met.

The end of this disgraceful chapter of one of the many uncalled for exhibitions of brutality of the military was that a dozen non-union men came out of the restaurant and were marched like so many criminals, with the state troops on either side with General John Chase at the head of the procession, off to some mine, not to break ore, but to try to break the strike. The officers of the militia and the mine owners knew the union men of this district too well to ever think they would harm one of those strikebreakers. There could have been but one reason for the military escort furnished the non-union men, and that must have been that the mine owners had secured the most of them by misrepresentation and guarded them lest they get a chance to escape. The owner of the restaurant was out of town at the time and upon her return secured possession of her building by legal process. The military, it is claimed, "captured" the building by force of arms to feed non-union strike-breakers.

REPELLED THE CHARGE OF A BURRO.

One of the laughable incidents of the "Rebellion" occurred September 21, when one of the sentries near Strong's camp saw an object approaching him in the dark. He called "halt," but the supposed enemy did not halt and he opened fire. Other sentries joined him and in all about twenty-five shots were fired before it dropped. Upon investigation they found it to be a burro (Rocky mountain canary) that had been wandering around, but while they were shooting they created great havoc in Strong's camp. One house had at least four bullets put through it, and another had three. Both the houses had people in them, and of course they were badly frightened.

The affair created so much amusement that it was immortalized by the muse in a poem of four verses by Mr. McCormick, I quote the last verse:

Ah! General Chase, a horrid case,
    This murder dark and bloody;
A sentry from his lurking place
    Has shot a "wanderin' Cuddy."
No doubt you'll call it "martial law,"
    'Twas foul ass—ass—ination.
Because Ned did not cry "He-haw,"
    You turned him into "ration."

MILITARY ARRESTS BECOME NUMEROUS.

From September 18 it was impossible to keep a record of the arrests and releases. A. J. Frey, a member of 32, but working at the time as a clerk in the Union store, was dragged to the bull pen, as was Emil Johnson, Chas. Beckman and Victor Poole. (No charge.) They were released September 21. On September 22 the roster of the bull pen was Sherman Parker, Pat Mullaney, H. H. McKinney, —— Campbell, C. G. Kennison, Thos. Foster and James Lafferty. Joe Lynch, marshal of Independence was arrested September 25 and released the next day. (No charge.) William Dodsworth, newly elected president of No. 32,. was the next victim. His home in Goldfield was surrounded by the militia but they were refused admission. They evidently feared to break into the house. They accordingly stayed there all night and waited for him. Dodsworth, thinking that it was possibly a case of being starved out, became impatient and walked out and allowed them to take him. He was hastened off to the bull pen, but on the 26th was released and allowed to go home. (No

COLORADO'S GREAT WAR CHIEF.

charge.) His first impression was to make them break in to get him, but it grew monotonous and he finally decided to see what they wanted and would do with him, and therefore surrendered.

A grand military coup was planned to capture some of the Altman miners, (No. 19). The plan was to wait until about 9 o'clock, when the largest attendance would be present, and rush up, surround the hall and arrest the whole union. The plans were carried out except that when 200 troopers reached Altman, they found the hall well lighted, and hastily surrounding the place, the guards were stationed at every entrance and a detail of officers and troopers were dispatched up-stairs. What did they find? That's the question to ask them. The miners had evidently out- witted them. Some one had whispered the secret and when the kidnappers reached the door and rapped, they heard not a sound or whisper. Trying the door they found it unlocked, and with fixed bayonets they charged into an empty hall room. The miners had been there and held their meeting and adjourned, and there was a sorrowful lot of soldiers there for a few minutes. It was their intention to arrest certain men and spirit them out of the district, since the courts here would not allow them to hold the men unlawfully. "The best laid plans of mice," etc.

BELL ANNOUNCES SUPERIORITY TO COURTS.

General Bell, on September 26, announced that he would obey no more orders of the civil authorities unless otherwise ordered by Governor Peabody. This announcement came as no surprise to the public, for it was well known that he could not hold down to such a strain as to obey the civil authorities. He believed that he was the whole thing, and he proposed to follow his own desires in the matter. It was generally believed, though, that when the governor sent the order to obey the law that he meant what he said, and that the district would not be dis- graced with any more such proceedings as were enacted around the courts a few days before.

DEMOCRATS CENSURE MILITARY.

The Democrats of Teller county met in convention on the 26th, and nominated candidates for county offices. I quote in part, the resolutions adopted:

"Under the Democratic banner is the natural place for the common people. An object lesson is found at our threshold. The Democratic party gave the state an Orman, and the threatened trouble at Telluride and other places in the state was averted without bloodshed and in justice to opera- tors and miners alike. The Republican party, aided by a few mercenary masqueraders in workingman's garb, gave the state a Peabody, who, in a little over eight months, has called out the National guard twice to aid his plutocratic friends.

"Those who believe that the affairs of the state should be administered

for all the people alike; that the National guard should only be called out
when necessary; that the purposes of the militia are primarily to aid and
assist the civil authorities in the maintenance of public peace and enforcement of the laws, as declared by our constitution, and not for the purpose
of superceding and over-riding them. That the sending of the state
troops under existing circumstances, is a lamentable prostitution of the
purposes for which the National guard was organized.

"The Democratic party of Teller county, being in a position to know,
hereby solemnly declares, for the benefit of those who have been misled by
false statements sent broadcast, that this is, and has been a peaceable community; that the presence of the military was not necessary, and that the
foulest sort of slander upon the good name of the district was resorted
to in an attempt to justify the call to arms; that there have been no crimes
committed here that the civil authorities have not been capable of handling,
and we denounce the many acts of the military officers, who, in their
recent martial display on the public streets and in the courts, have outraged public decency, and offended the dignity and intelligence of all fair-
minded citizens.

During these strenuous times the muse was frequently called
to express the sentiments of the general public to the actions of
the military. I reproduce the following:

OUR LITTLE TIN GOD ON WHEELS.

Colorado can boast of her climate and springs;
Of her scenery we love to tell,
But our adjutant general's our crown and **pride,—**
The world renowned Sherman Bell!
Hooray! Hooray! To our joy today!
We've a little tin god on wheels!

The United States is his stamping ground
And "Teddy" runs quick to his call,
While Governor Jim wriggles under his thumb:—
He bosses them one and all.
Watch out! Be sure and shout
For the little tin god on wheels!

It was he who flew to suffering Cuba's aid,
And pushed the 13th out of the way—
'Twas he alone charged up that bloody San Juan
And saved the whole country that day.
Oh! Despair! If he hadn't been there!
Our little tin god on wheels!

Who stood by long suffering, down-trodden MacNeil,
(Was it made worth his while, do you 'spose?)
When the plutocratic workmen made shocking demands,
And threatened to tread on his toes!
"Arbitrate? H——! I'm Sherman Bell!
The little tin god on wheels!"

A SHATTERED DREAM !

At St. Louis our glorious adjutant shone
With his colonels in glittering array.
If he went to the club with his spurs upside down
Why, he probably preferred them that way.
'Bout face! My! the gold lace!
Our soldierly god on wheels!

Oh, a self-made man is our General Bell,
A detective but a short time ago.
When he murders his English, we ne'er crack a smile—
For he surely must think it a foe.
A sleuth, raised forsooth,
To be Adjutant General Bell!

VICTOR DAILY RECORD FORCE KIDNAPPED.

Tuesday night, September 29, at 11:05, the busiest hour on a morning paper, the Victor Daily Record, which had espoused the cause of the striking miners, was raided by the militia, and the entire force at work was "captured." The linotypes were humming, "catching the elevator" on every line, the foreman was fuming and "rushing" proofs, for "first side down" and first "forms" must go to "press" at 11:30. Suddenly the door of the composing room flew open and in stalked Tom McClelland with the air of a "conquering hero," followed by a file of yaping yokels dressed in the garb of soldiers and armed to the teeth. "Halt!" yelled the fierce Tom. "Ground arms!" "Fix bayonets!" "Guard the entrances!"

"What the h——!" says the foreman, "having a fit?"

The operators merely shifted quids, "brought down" a period and "sent in" the line.

"Private————step forward!" roared "Thomas of the shining tin," "identify the force!" A long, lank specimen of the genius homo, red headed, with a scraggly, three week's growth of red fuzz that might have developed into red whiskers, had the soil from which they sprouted been fertile, shuffled from the ranks and in a hang-dog manner pointed his grimy finger at the foreman and the two linotype operators. This aforesaid specimen had been in the office the night before and had claimed to be a printer; and from his conversation he might have been at some time a janitor in a "print shop" or a roller washer in a press room—but printer—oh, no. He was informed in plain, understandable English that if he had business to make it known, if not, conversation was a waste of time. He left and the "force" all said, "we're spotted for the 'bull pen' sure."

"You're all prisoners of war!" bellowed Thomas, but the "mills" kept "turning over."

"Get up!" hissed the major of majestic mein.

"Who the ——— are you?" calmly gurgled one of the operators.

"I'm Major Thomas E. McClelland, of the Colorado National Guard."

"Oh, my, does it hurt so very much?" in pitying accents from the operator.

"Sergeant, seize that man!" gasped Thomas of the guard.

The "sergeant" pushed a wicked looking bayonet toward the operator's neck, and he had to "send in" a "short line."

Mr. Kyner, the managing editor, then stepped into the composing room, and asked what was wanted. McClelland stated that he had arrested the "force" and wanted him, too. "All right," said Mr. Kyner, "I guess you have me."

"Me, too," said Mr. Sweet, the circulator.

"That's all," said the "genius homo."

"Well, it's a clean sweep," said Mr. Kyner, "May I telephone my wife?"

"You'll have to hurry," quoth pompous Mac.

"Who'll get out the paper?" asked Richmond, the foreman.

"McClelland laughed and said, "We'll send printers down from the camp and get it out for you."

"Oh, no you won't," said Richmond, "It takes printers, and printers don't bunch in your corral."

With that the Record force was marched to the "bull pen" under an honorary guard of two companies of infantry, two troops of cavalry and perhaps the Gatling gun (late of Wyoming).

At that time I was at home in bed and Mrs. Kyner came to my home and rapped at the door. I opened the door and she asked me if I had heard the latest. I replied that I evidently had not, and she informed me of the arrest of the Record force, and asked, "What shall we do?"

"Do!" said I, "get out the paper, of course." "Just the thing," said Mrs. Kyner, and away she flew in the darkness. I realized instantly that a strong effort had been made to suppress the liberty of the press, and determined forthwith that the entire military force of Colorado should not keep the Record from making its appearance as usual.

I believe I broke all records in dressing, for in less than two minutes I was running through dark alleys on my way to the Record office, five blocks away. On the way I kept a close lookout for soldiers. I did not know how I would get into the office. My one thought was that I would get in in spite of all their efforts. Under the belief that the pressman had been arrested with the others, I planned to take "stone proofs" of the "forms" and save the issue in that way. I also thought of the Teller County Banner office, and had the emergency demanded, would have broken in there, printed a Record on the "job" press and so saved the issue.

I was much relieved when I reached the office and found that I had arrived there before the militia had completed arrangements for guarding the plant, and with the aid of Mr. Miller and Mr. Conrad, the pressman, who had been summoned, was quickly inside.

We locked, bolted and barred the doors. This was not accomplished an instant too soon, for in another minute we had the satisfaction of seeing soldier faces peering through the window panes. In vain they pounded on the doors demanding entrance "in the name of the governor of the state of Colorado." They were informed that the "governor of Colorado" was not running the Record, but in the absence of Mr. Kyner, we were, and that they would not get into the office unless they broke in, which they did not attempt to do.

This well repaid me for my flight through the streets attired in a thin dressing gown and unlaced shoes, with no wrap of any kind. It was bitter cold here, too, at that hour of the night.

I quickly "manned" one of the linotype machines and set type to the last moment. (I had set three "galleys" in the afternoon and my husband and brother-in-law had "gotten up" all the "grape vine" before the raid.) Mr. Miller made up the forms and—the pressman did the rest. At three o'clock a. m., a fairly good issue of the Record lay before us, and above all, ON TIME. Across the top in big, black letters, appeared the very forceful legend:

"SOMEWHAT DISFIGURED, BUT STILL IN THE RING."

I then went to my home and prepared a lunch for Mr. Miller and Mr. Conrad, which I took to the office. I then took a paper fresh from the press and went to Mrs. Kyner's home and everything being still and dark, I pushed a copy under the door, so that when she awoke she would know that the Record had been issued. I then returned to the office and found that the carriers, finding the doors locked, had left. I immediately hurried out and ran down the alley, finding two of them several blocks away. I told them to tie their horses some distance from the office, get the other boys and quietly slip in, as the paper was ready for delivery. I returned to the office and reported to Mr. Miller that I had secured the carriers.

Now that everything was safe, as far as the paper was concerned, I went to my sister's (Mrs. F. W. Langdon), home and awoke her and told her the news. By this time dawn began to break and I bethought me of my appearance, bareheaded, hair down, in loose dressing saque and unlaced shoes.

I hurried home, dressed myself in street attire and returned to the office

Through it all my one thought was how glad Mr. Kyner and the imprisoned force would be to see the Record at 6 o'clock, and I determined to get through the guard line and deliver it to them myself.

I took the papers and stuffed them into my waist, my sleeves, under my belt and in the lining of my jacket, and started for Camp Goldfield, where the force, including my husband, was imprisoned. I arrived at the guard line just as the Gold Coin whistle blew 6 o'clock.

I heard, while standing at the guard line, one officer say to another:

"There's one good thing, that d— Record will not come out this morning"

"Why?" the other officer asked in surprise.

"We have the whole —— —— force in the 'bull pen' and we are going to keep them there, too," was the reply.

These tinsel heroes evidently had no respect in their choice of language in the presence of a woman. I could not stand this talk any longer, and spoke up and said that I guessed that he had not seen the morning paper.

"Oh, yes," said he, "we have the Morning Times."

"I mean the Record," I said.

"I guess you are not aware that the entire Record force is in the 'bull pen' " he answered.

I said that I was very well aware of that fact, "and allow me," said I, "to present you the Morning Record for yourself and men."

The officer took the paper, and looking it over, finally broke out with another volley of oaths, beginning with "who the h—," but before he had time to finish the sentence, I answered:

"I did, and I expect I shall be your next victim."

I had just overcome the formalities of getting through the lines when I received a message from my husband that they were

RECORD FORCE IN BULL PEN.

*Left to right, F. W. Langdon, Linotype Operator; Chas. G. Langdon, Linotype Operator;
Geo. E. Kyner, Managing Editor; W. L. Sweet, Circulator; H. J. Richmond, Foreman;
Soldiers with loaded winchesters on guard.*

all ''O. K'' and that I should ''waste no time trying to see them, but to get back to that office and get the Record out in spite of everything.''

I knew that they were depending on me, so I hurried back and started composition on another issue. I worked continuously until 2 o'clock that night, when the ''regular'' force came into the office, having been released and again ready for business.

Now I will invite the reader to take a trip to the military prison and see how fared the Record prisoners.

These prisoners were marched unceremoniously to the bull pen. Armed thugs forced them into a filthty and squalid little tent, absolutely barren of furniture or bedding, where they were told to stay under penalty of having their heads blown off if they appeared an inch outside of the entrance.

The night was bitterly cold and on that frigid mountain side, under the intimidating guard of a horde of armed assassins, the working force of the Victor Record passed a night of torture equal to anything ever devised by the Spanish inquisitors. The entire force will bear testimony that the treatment accorded them was so inhuman and revolting as to surpass the belief of American citizens.

The ''bull'' tent had just been vacated by a number of drunken soldier prisoners, who had vomited all over the interior. The stench was sickening, but there they were forced to lay, without even so much as a gunny sack to protect them from the cold. Shortly after sunrise they were told to come to ''breakfast.'' Emerging from the filthy kennel they were escorted to the mess table a short distance away. A dozen guards kept them covered with guns loaded with riot ammunition while two grimy negro cooks dished out a little slop on tin plates and told them to eat. There were no knives, forks or spoons at hand. ''Use your fingers,'' said the head negro, when remonstrance was made.

Beneath the table were a number of wash boilers and buckets filled with the accumulated garbage of several days and the stench arising therefrom was nauseating enough to insult the gizzard of a buzzard. It is quite needless to state that they did not eat.

They returned to the tent hungrier and more distressed than ever. The day was raw and cold and they were chilled to the marrow. Faint and sick, Mr. Richmond approached the captain of the guard and implored him for God's sake to obtain some blankets. His appeal was cut short with an oath from that dignitary.

A little later a murderous looking Gatling gun was drawn up,

trained on the prisoner's tent, and they were subjected to the nerve rending ordeal of posing as targets. The excitement attending this outrageous intimidation completely unnerved some of them.

Attorney Tully Scott, formerly of Kansas, succeeded in getting them liberated through some legal procedure, and after unwinding a few miles of military red tape the commanding general turned them over to Sheriff Robertson of Teller county, when for the first time they learned they were defendants in a libel case.

It was a deliberate plot to suppress a paper for telling the truth about the uniformed hirelings who were guilty of the outrages above mentioned.

The excuse for the taking of the Record force was that in the issue of the day before, there was an article of about six lines which referred to two tools of the mine owners as ex-convicts. It was learned that in the case of Vannick it was true, but Scanlon, with all his faults, had not, as yet worn the stripes. However, there was a correction coming out the following morning. The whole truth of the matter was that the military was watching every movement of the Record for a chance to raid the office. The **real** reason for the military raiding the office at that hour, was to suppress the official organ of the Western Federation of Miners. The district had only the one paper that stood up for the cause, and of course, the enemy did not have a very warm feeling of friendship for the Record. The reader will at once realize that even had the editor been guilty of criminal libel the operators or the mechanical force could not legally be held responsible. But when the military endeavored to suppress the Record they reckoned without their host. Again the writer will quote: ''The best laid plans o' mice,'' etc. The writer would advise the warrior Chase, when he again undertakes to suppress the press, to not only arrest the force at work, but every living printer in the county—and it wouldn't be a bad idea to guard the cemeteries, 'for the press is a hard game to beat—even by a warrior of the ability of Chase, as he has doubtless discovered.

The act of the military in their attempt to throttle the free speech and liberty of the press was condemned by the entire press of the United States.

The editor's desk was simply ''snowed under'' with communications from far and near denouncing the disgraceful act. I, myself, received hundreds of letters from all classes of people from all parts of the United States. To me, my work at the linotype seemed the most ordinary and natural thing to do. I had but one thought and that was to please the management of the paper and go to their rescue when I imagined I was needed, at the same time assist the miners by defeating the military in their efforts to stifle the voice of the Western Federation of Min-

ers. Mr. Miller is an "all around" good printer, but not a linotype operator, and, as I was able to start the machinery to work,
I was proud of the opportunity to do so. But the simple little act
was heralded from coast to coast and made much of by the entire press—while I was still at the machine unconscious of anything except that the Record force had been somewhat reduced by
"military necessity."

I have been praised by the press of the land for a spontan-
eous action which was in accordance with my nature; I acted on
an impulse not to be defeated or see my friends defeated. From
my infancy I have been taught to love freedom and liberty. I
**believe the liberty of the press and freedom of speech the greatest
boon and only salvation of the common people against a natural,
but perhaps, unrecognized oppression of concentrated wealth.**
Let wars go on, let corporations strive for complete mastery, let
labor struggle for its betterment, but in justice to all, labor,
wealth and corporations, let the press be free to praise, educate,
criticise or condemn. Let God-given speech be not muzzled, that
but one grievance be given voice or one side of vital questions
heard. The press should give to the world both sides of all controversies. If dear old Mother Earth were but one sided instead
of a rounded, balanced whole, how soon would she leave her orbit
and become a wandering danger to God's universal plan—the
same with humanity, if one side is crushed, distorted or made so
as to be unknown or unheard, how soon would the other, unsupported or unbalanced, become chaotic in its sphere?

The act was not an act of bravery; it was exhilarating desperation that caused me to offer my services where I believed they
would be of some good. My life has been in common walks, my
education gained in the printing office. The press, the printing
office, my school room, my teacher, the principle by which I gauge
all honorable life—liberty and freedom—was being crushed. Not
by honorable contention, not by argument, not by public sentiment, but by brutal, physical force, by force of arms, by the very
power that should protect and sustain, rather than tear down and
destroy.

The action of the press of the country showed how sentiment

is growing. The public outside of the Cripple Creek district really did not know to what extremes the military was going up to that time. The newspaper reports were not what they should have been in many cases and the outside public was misled, but the action of the military in raiding the Record aroused these papers to the gravity of the situation.

This act of suppression, if tolerated, gives the governor and his generals absolute dictatorship over the press. It was a vicious stab at free speech. The question was first fought out in England under the reign of James II and William and Mary of Orange, under the championship of John Milton and Charles Blount, in opposition to the censors Robert Lestrange and Edmund Bohun. Freedom of the press has ever since been a recognized principle of right.

Governor Peabody, with his armed force, may invade the sancitiy of the home, take therefrom husbands and fathers without warrant or specific charges, and consign them to the "bull pen." He may surround the court house with cordons of soldiery, denying citizens admission to the temple of justice. He may openly defy the judgment of the civil courts. He may, without process of law, put editors and printers in the "bull pen."

He may do these things, for a time, but he can not throttle the press.

Free speech and a free press are guaranteed to the people by the national and the state constitutions.

The Record force had good, congenial company while "guests" of the military at Camp Goldfield, as Messrs. C. G. Kennison, Davis and Foster and a few other good union men were taking a vacation and had decided to be "entertained" by the mine owners and Citizens' Alliance for a short time. This, too, was caused by "military necessity."

Typographical Union 275 published a formal protest against the treatment of its members, as did many sister typographical unions

DENVER TYPOGRAPHICAL UNION CONDEMNS.

At a session of the Denver Typographical Union, No. 49, Sunday, October 4, the following resolutions were adopted:

"Whereas, The occupation of the various towns and cities in the Cripple Creek mining district by the Colorado state militia has resulted in the unlawful and illegal application of martial law, with all its attendant disregard for the rights, privileges and duties of American citizens, vouchsafed by the constitution of the United States. Arrests have followed freedom of speach; arrests have awaited the legal assemblage of citizens in union meetings; arrest has followd any communication by union men with strike breakers; the pomp of officers and the rattle of musketry have invaded the sacred precincts of the court (the only safe refuge of the innocent citizen); and, worst of all, arrest without warrant of law has followed newspaper expression, thus destroying the palladium of liberty, the freedom of the press, and

Whereas, The apprehension of the editor of the Victor Daily Record was followed by the arrest of members of Victor Typographical union at work on that paper, who are innocent of any wrong, or attempted wrong; therefore be it

Resolved, By Denver Typographical Union No. 49, the pioneer labor organization in Colorado, that we reaffirm our loyalty and fealty to the law of the land, knowing, as we do, that personal safety vouchsafed to the people through the application of legal processes is the net result of centuries of human struggle against the despotic rule of might. We deplore and denounce the subversion of laws by the military arm of the state government, and declare it to be wholly in the interest and at the behest of the few rich and strong, and we declare the use of such force to be against the best interests of the masses of the people of the state.

"Resolved, Further, That we urge upon the officers of the International Typographical Union to take active and immediate steps looking toward securing proper redress for the unlawful arrest and incarceration of the members of our sister Typographical union at Victor, and to that end the secretary of this union is hereby instructed to forward a copy of these resolutions to international headquarters at Indianapolis."

GOLD COIN AND ECONOMIC MILL MEN OUT.

On the evening of September 30, the Gold Coin mine and Economic mill shut down. Both are properties of the Woods Investment company.

As the men came out of the mines they were met by Mr. Woods, who stated that while he was desirous of keeping as many of his employes as possible, it would be necessary hereafter for men working in the Gold Coin to dissolve relationship with the Western Federation of Miners. Of the men thus approached, not one would agree to drop his membership in the Federation. A committee then went to the Economic mill and the men employed there were notified of what had occurred at the mine, and were asked to quit work. The request met with prompt compliance, not one remaining in the mill. It had been expected that whatever might have been the personal inclination of the owners of the Gold Coin, sooner or later, the Mine Owners' Association would compel them to shut down or work the property with men not affiliated with the Federation. The Woods people were loth to part with the men, but were compelled, by their affiliation with the Mine Owners' Association, to do so.

MacNeil objected to the miners interfering with the men on strike at his mill, even of they did belong to the Western Federation, and the mine owners all said "sympathetic strike." But when the Woods people expressed satisfaction with their union force the Mine Owners' Association, to which they belonged, forced them to discharge the union force, the shoe was on the other foot; but did they call it a "sympathetic" lock-out? Oh, no.

"O, consistency, thou art a jewel."

BULL PEN PRISONERS RELEASED.

Paddy Mullaney and Thomas Foster, two of the "guests" at the military bull pen at Camp Goldfield, were released from custody Sept. 30, by orders from headquarters. With the release of Mullaney and Foster followed by the giving of the Record force into the custody of Sheriff Robertson, but two civilian prisoners were left to enjoy the hospitality of the state troops. These were Chas. Kennison and W. F. Davis. Mr. Kennison, president of Miners' Union, No. 40, has many arrests and releases to his credit. On Sept. 18 he was arrested for the second time. He had gone to the Independence mine to get clothing he had left there, and after leaving the mine, was talking to some friends, when the military arrested him for carrying concealed weapons, and he was taken to the bull pen. His wife made many efforts to see him, but was repeatedly denied by the military. His last arrest caused his detention until October 2, when he and W. F. Davis were turned over to the civil authorities.

"TO HELL WITH THE CONSTITUTION."

"To hell with the constitution. We are going by the governor's orders," said Major McClelland, acting judge advocate and counsel for the military authorities, according to the statement of Attorney John M. Glover.

"I was in the office of District Attorney Trowbridge when Tom McClelland and Willis V. Elliott were preparing information against Editor Kyner for libel. Referring to the seizure of the office of the Victor Record, I said to McClelland, 'Your people apparently have not much respect for the constitution. That was a blow at the freedom of the press," to which McClelland replied: "To h— with the constitution. We are going by the governor's orders.' To which I replied: 'We will have some of you fellows pleading for your liberty before a jury where the governor's orders don't go.' McClelland replied: 'We will take care of that when we come to it.' Elliot was present and heard this conversation."

Immediately upon the appearance of the foregoing, McClelland denied that he made the remark that he was not going by the constitution, which at once brought forth the following from Mr. Glover:

"Cripple Creek, Colo., Oct. 5, 1903.
"Editor of the Daily Record, Victor, Colo.:

"Dear Sir:—The conversation reported in your issue of October 4, as having occurred between Thomas McClelland, judge advocate of the National Guard and myself, took place explicitly and exactly as stated by your correspondent. My version of the matter will be accepted by the people of this section and by any jury before which McClelland shall be tried. I repeat that this conversation took place in the immediate presence and hearing of Willis V. Elliott, also an officer of the National Guard, and I cherish the hope that Mr. Elliott has too much regard for his honor and his uniform to join in McClelland's denial.

"Very truly yours,
"JOHN M. GLOVER."

FARCIAL COURT MARTIAL MANEUVERS.

October 3 Chase was summoned to Denver to appear before the "Czar of Colorado." At once there were rumors of court martials and denials of the same. There were rumors to the effect that Chase was to be superceded, that he would return and that he would not return. Statements that there was friction between him and some of the subordinate officers, against whom, it was alleged, he made charges of irregularities. Hints of padded pay rolls were brought out, also intimations made that women were mixed up in the case, and various other matters came before the public in connection with the affair. The officers were "gagged" when asked questions, no one in camp seemed to know why Chase was called to Denver. Scandals were made public which neither the officers nor the mine owners appreciated; the officers did not relish the publicity given the scandals, while the mine owners hated to lose a subservient tool. Peabody and the mine owners, it was said, did their best to keep peace between the "tinsel ornaments" but failed. It was said by many that had it been possible to keep the "czar" of the "empire" of Colorado in the same mind forty-eight hours, the trouble might have been avoided. Close friends of the governor labored with him to help him to "release the tail of the bear," but to no avail. However, that may be, detailed charges and specifications were filed with Governor Peabody against practically all heads of departments of the Colorado National guard. The military court was to act as a kind of state grand jury and all charges that were made against the men and officers and all allegations that were made were to be considered by the court.

In connection with the investigation of the hospitals the charges of cruelty made by Monroe Kanouse and others who returned ill from the camp, were to be investigated. A searching inquiry was to be made into the death of the soldier who died on his way from Cripple Creek to a hospital in Colorado Springs, etc.

There was brought to light many cases of neglect and cruelty among the private soldiers.

Bell said, in an interview in regard to conditions that existed October 7:

"I have no apologies or excuses to make to the Lord or anybody else for the manner in which the campaign has been conducted. Everything has been done to the best of my ability in the effort to properly care for the men, through both the commissary and quartermaster's departments. I am responsible for my assistants, and not only they, but myself, as well as every officer and soldier in the field, have been practically on duty both night and day. I am running the adjutant general's and quartermaster's offices, as well as the commissary department, and no one else is running them for me. There have been accusations made on the one hand that the troops were not properly fed and clothed, and on the other hand, that they were extravagantly fed and unnecessarily provided for in clothing. Whatever the opinions of the public are, individually or collectively, in both instances, I want the people to hold their breath an hour or two and listen to this statement:

"I am responsible to the state and officially and personally am conducting these departments with the assistance of those who have been acting for me, and there is no one else either responsible, liable or otherwise conducting these departments in the past, in the present or the future. Therefore, others need not claim any credit for what has been done, and neither will they be held liable for conducting the campaign, so far as my responsibility goes."

Another statement of Bell's on the same subject would really do credit to a sane man, and was as follows:

"I offer the following moral to the Citizen's Alliance, the Mine Owners' Association, the Western Federation of Miners, and all other organizations: Moral—"Attend to your own business affairs and don't in any manner or way interfere or mix in the military operations and conduct of the troops, and, incidentally, with the management and operation of the military affairs in the Cripple Creek district."

Bell said those organizations could pin that moral in their hats.

On October 10, Governor Peabody appointed a general court martial to convene at the capitol building at 10:00 a. m., October 19, 1903, or as soon thereafter as practicable, for the trial of such persons as might properly be brought before it.

October 19 the court martial began to grind and it continued until October 31. It is useless to waste space to go into detail in regard to that ridiculous farce played by the officers of the National guard, with Peabody, Bell and Chase in the leading roles. It was a very exhilarating performance in which the governor acted as director. Bell aspired to the role of heavy villain and Chase the martyr (?). The majority of the officers in the field including the "parlor" colonels were all given minor parts.

The only points brought out in the trial, which lasted twelve days, was that there were certain jealousies existing between the officers in Camp Goldfield. That Bell disliked Chase from his hat to his shoes, although he had publicly stated what a "warm" friendship existed between him and Chase. At the court martial it developed that they had had trouble in regard to which was superior from the very first. The public became aware of this fact when Bell charged Chase with perjury. There were many disgraceful acts that had taken place at Camp Goldfield brought to light that otherwise would not have become public property, had not Bell and the other officers tried to give Chase the worst of it. He (Chase) refused to resign, and was acquitted of the charge of perjury.

Then came the other charges of disobedience and many other allegations.

It was believed that the court would find a verdict of guilty on the specifications, but not the charge of disobeying orders. In other words, he was technically guilty, but not wilfully so.

While the trial for other charges than perjury was being continued, Bell left no stone unturned to convict General Chase, and in his attempt to do so, a few little things much like the following were charged against Bell by the press of the state:

That General Bell violated his oath of office and the orders of Governor Peabody in going to the Cripple Creek district. That he issued executive orders without the sanction or knowledge of the governor. That he exceeded his authority by issuing commands to the brigade of General Chase.

That he issued orders direct to officers without sending them through brigade headquarters. That he forged the name of General Chase to passes through the lines. That he removed Colonel Louis Barnum from the court martial because he would not agree to vote for a conviction of General Chase. That he coerced and rewarded witnesses in the case of General Chase. That he approached members of the court martial to influence them to vote against Chase.

That he destroyed important records that would have vindicated Chase and substituted incorrect copies to be introduced as evidence.

After spending the entire day of November 2 in secret session, reviewing the evidence in the charge of disobedience of orders of the governor, the court martial announced that General Chase had been found guilty of disobedience by a vote of four to six. The punishment was not fixed.

The arguments still went on for several days. There were many scenes during the trial, blows being threatened, and many times the court room was cleared to avoid the crisis being reached. The lie was passed by the gold lace followers of Bell. Men were called scoundrels and curs and other names for which men used to kill. Finally, after the trial had absorbed the public attention for nearly thirty days, the verdict was announced and turned over to Governor Peabody to fix sentence. General Bell and his followers used every power possible to influence Peabody to give Chase a dishonorable discharge. Public sentiment was with Chase, for the reason that it was plain to be seen that the whole affair was a matter of jealousy and supposed to be a plot to dispose of Chase. Prejudice predominated in the court martial and public sentiment naturally grew in favor of Chase. Attorney Elliot worked very hard for Chase, and more than once held Bell up to ridicule. Once, in the heat of argument, he called Bell a cowardly cur. He was ever ready to correct and defy the opposition to Chase.

November 7 the controversy came to an end, so far as the public was concerned. The news of the acquittal of General Chase of the charges preferred against him, for which he was tried, rather amused the citizens of this district. The people were eagerly waiting to see what the governor would do with the proposition passed up to him by the military board. They heard from him and noted that he made a bold straddle of the proposition. Public opinion was too strong to "fire" Chase from the National Guard, so the governor, in order to pacify Bell, approved of the verdict but did not discharge Chase from the guard.

Governor Peabody's decision was typewritten, covering some

four pages. He agreed with the court that General Chase had disobeyed executive orders, but, "in view of the fact of his long and honorable service, in the militia of both Colorado and Michigan, the verdict of the court was set aside."

The ruling of the governor was in every way a vindication for General Chase. His handling of the court's verdict was done in complete detail, every point raised by the defense and prosecution being covered.

The verdict amounted to this: "Mr. Chase, you disobeyed an executive order. My dear sir, never let this occur again. You will remain in command, because I have confidence in you."

Apparently, it appears that the governor refused to be dictated to by Adjutant General Sherman Bell.

The governor did not make up his mind as to what the verdict would be until November 7. He spent the evening in going over the evidence and conferring with friends of both factions.

"I am going to return this verdict in accordance with the law and facts, no matter who it hits," said the governor.

Early in the morning he was at his office in the capitol building, and, calling his stenographer into his room, started the task of dictating his opinion as to the finding of the court. The governor called attention to the law and commented to some length on all points. In closing, his decision, which was signed "James H. Peabody, governor and commander in chief," set forth the different charges.

"The charge of perjury. Charge, not guilty. Specifications, not guilty."

"Charge No. 2.—Disobedience of orders. Charge, guilty. Sentence, dismissal. The sentence is set aside."

And the governor wound it up with a comment on the bravery of General John C. Chase.

So, after nearly thirty days consumed by the court martial, the result (aside from the amusement it furnished the public, which by the way will cost the taxpayers dear, as shown by one item alone, which I hereafter cite), nothing was really accomplished.

The striking miners, however, were benefited as it gave them temporary respite from military persecution as General Bell's attention was given to trying to convict General Chase in the hope that he would be dismissed from the service. There was much conjecture as to what was the real cause for the enmity of Bell against Chase. Some claimed it was jealousy, because Bell recognized Chase's superiority as a commanding officer, and therefore wanted him out of the way as Bell himself desired to be the "whole thing." My personal opinion for the cause of the court martial is that General Bell, being desirous that in his war (mimic), which he considered of even greater importance than the war for Independence, and himself the Washington, desired

THE STRIKING MINER: "TO THE DIVIL WIT' WOR-RK, WHIN I'VE SICH A FOIN SHOW TO LOOK AT!"

that nothing be overlooked that usually goes with real war, consequently deemed a court martial a necessity. Trust General Bell not to overlook anything in connection with military affairs.

The court martial was a thirty days' picnic for those participating, the amount of champagne and high-priced cigars consumed, at the expense of the state, not to mention luncheons, was something astonishing. Here is the amount of one voucher alone, being bill presented by the Brown Palace Hotel Co. for luxuries furnished members of the court martial: "Voucher No. 4,987, $1,930.60."

The press of Colorado contained daily comment and amusing

criticism upon the court martial. The foregoing cut is one of the many cartoons portraying the situation.

These conditions the miners enjoyed. They made the best of them as a means of amusement, and the question of moment each day was inquiring for the last sensation among the soldiers. The miners cared little about going to work while they could enjoy such high-class entertainment without cost.

WOMEN'S AUXILIARIES.

During the month of October the women relatives of the union men of Cripple Creek district combined and formed what was known as Women's Auxiliaries to Organized Labor. These auxiliaries were organized, one each in Cripple Creek, Victor and Anaconda. They were chartered by the Colorado State Federation of Labor.

The women were organized but a short time when they made themselves felt. They refused to patronize business men connected with the Citizens' Alliance, and it was not long before many communications were received by the auxiliaries from store keepers notifying the women that they had either no connection with the Citizens' Alliance or had severed their connection therewith. The women were very active in furnishing relief to sick and needy women and children of the strikers. In fact, so active did the women become through their organization, that several months later, General Bell was heard to say that the members of auxiliaries had caused him more trouble than all the 3,000 striking miners.

ORGANIZED LABOR COMBINES POLITICALLY.

One of the greatest victories scored by organized labor in the Cripple Creek district, was on November 3, at the general election, when P. J. Devault was elected to the office of county assessor.

Through inability to "get together" on some of the candidates, Mr. Devault, a union musician and ex-secretary of the Colorado State Federation of Labor, was placed on an Independent Citizen's ticket by the organized labor element of the district as their recognized candidate, and although both the Democratic and Republican conventions had placed in the field strong tickets and worked hard for them, Mr. Devault was elected by an astounding majority, being supported by the unions of the entire district.

Organized labor joined forces and put their shoulder to the wheel to elect a union man, regardless of party politics.

The union men were jubilant over this victory, as they claimed that it demonstrated clearly that they were not dead and that they still have fight in them.

The auxiliaries of the district worked faithfully and enthusiastically for Mr. Devault, who gave the ladies much praise.

To the writer's mind, labor's victory awaits them at the ballot box. Let us formulate a plan—a plan whereby labor will receive its fair wage, whereby capital will receive its due—and justice will be given to all. Then let organized and unorganized labor stand shoulder to shoulder and not be divided on election day by the honeyed words of the professional politician, nor the lamentations of the professional office holder.

A great many working men object to taking their politics into their unions and lodges. But what will be the end of those who toil if they do not meet at the ballot box as a unit and vote for the interests of their class? Aye, politics has placed the state of Colorado where it "politically" stands in regard to organized —yes, and unorganized—labor, and it is labor's duty, and they will make it their **business,** to be a "political" unit as well as a "laboring" unit.

CORPORATION CONTROLLED.

Both the Democratic and Republican parties, in the state campaign of 1903 advocated and pledged their candidates, their leaders and their beneficiaries of public favor, to an eight-hour law, if the people of the state amended the constitution of the state authorizing its passage.

The people did so—urged by the "politicians" of both parties, who said it was good and wise.

But the legislature, elected under that pledge, refused to pass the law.

The part played by corrupt politics was that, to carry an election, it had no conscience, but seized any and all campaign material, regardless of the consequences to the people.

And when the legislature disobeyed the will of the people and the promises of both parties, and obeyed the corporations who did not want an eight-hour law, "politics" skulked and did nothing.

The legacy of trouble drawn up by "politics," and signed, sealed and delivered by the legislature, has already cost millions and millions.

What the subsidiary and connecting losses amount to nobody knows, or ever will know.

More loss of production, more loss of wages; high prices for coal—all in the legacy left by "politics" and its agent, the legislature.

And politics skulks and the members of the legislature are able to pay for drinks with money that should scorch their fingers, and the people of Colorado hold the legacy that is not riches, but is ruin.

Should labor, organized or unorganized, throttle "politics?" Should we take politics into our halls and lodges, strip it of its heinous power, and force it to act, as it has promised, for the good of all? I say yes.

THE COAL MINERS ON STRIKE.

From November 8, through the entire month, the strike of the coal miners in the southern and northern fields of Colorado held the attention of the public. November 9 found the tie up of the coal mines almost complete. At Trinidad, when the whistle blew, there were but an inconsiderable few who responded, and the tie-up in Las Animas county was declared complete.

November 11 found ninety per cent of the miners out on strike and that per cent had been previously organized and were strictly union.

Thousands of coal miners were out before the governor realized what had taken place. Arrangements were made at once by the officers directing the strike to send many of the men away—over 1,000 departing at one time—500 of whom were sent to Thurber, Texas, and many others to the Iowa coal fields. At both places the conditions, wages and hours of work were vastly superior to those of the southern fields.

A coal strike with such capitalists as the men that control the Colorado Fuel and Iron Company and the Victor Coal Company on one side and the United Mine Workers, led by John Mitchell, on the other, is one, the effect of which can hardly be estimated.

A settlement of the difficulties in the northern fields was soon made, whereby the miners received all and more than they asked for, and work was renewed under far more favorable conditions.

"Mother Jones" played a very commendable part in the labor troubles in the coal districts and needs no introduction to the laboring classes by the writer.

Governor Peabody made a statement November 11, in an interview on the coal strike, which read in part, as follows:

"I hold that every man has a right to work, whether he is union or non-union. When a man is ready and willing to work and is interfered with, I will furnish him the protection that he, as an American citizen, is entitled to.

"Up to the present time I have received no request for troops. Regardless of the statements that have been made, I have not been approached by the Victor Fuel company, nor by the Denver Tramway company for troops to go to Leyden Junction, or elsewhere. I wish my attitude to be understood. I have no objection to unions. Every man has a right to join unions if he wants to, the same as he may join a church, a lodge or any organization, civil or religious, so long as union members do not interfere individually or collectively with the action of other men, they are all right. I have always maintained that when a man wants to work that that is his privilege, and no one shall stop him. On the other hand, a man cannot be compelled to work unless he wants to. There must be no coercion either way.

"When I receive assurance that a body of men want to work, union or non-union, I shall extend to them that protection that is in my power This is my position in this matter."

Will the reader take note that Governor Peabody says the principles that caused him to take the actions he has are that law and order shall be maintained in this state and that men shall have the right to work or not as they see fit.

Will Governor Peabody be honest and tell the public why he

has allowed the militia, with his connivance, to openly violate the laws of this state, by arresting innocent men without warrant or due process of law, and against whom no charges have been brought.

Will Governor Peabody explain why he allows printers who are at work and want to work, to be dragged with insult and degredation from their labors and thrown into a vile "bull pen" and subjected to mental and physical torture, not excelled by the finished product of the Spanish inquisition?

Will Governor Peabody explain why he permits his "law preserving" military to desecrate funeral services and with the assistance of an ex-convict drag a citizen from his brotherly duty to the dead and confine him with no due process of his much upheld law?

Will Governor Peabody explain why he permits his "law preserving" military to shoot at a man with apparent intent to kill, because he refuses to work because he has been lied to in order to secure his services?

Will Governor Peabody explain why he permits his "law preserving" military to desecrate the home of a grief stricken widow of two days and threaten to drag from her side her ten-year old son, frantic with woe by the loss of a dear and loving father, to be frightened and terrorized by a martial display, the reason for which his young and tortured mind can not fathom?

Will Governor Peabody explain why he permits his "law protecting" military to enter the home of a woman, drag her therefrom, tear her clothing from her body, and with brute force, oaths and villification force her to walk over rough granite roads between two cities because she has incurred their displeasure by resenting their intrusion of the sanctity of her home?

Will Governor Peabody tell the public why so many of the strikers were kept in the bull pen and only liberated when he dare hold them no longer without coming into conflict with the courts and perhaps the federal authorities? Will the governor tell the public why the strikers have not as much right to life and liberty as have the "scabs?"

You say, governor, that labor has the right to organize, yet you **know,** and every person in this community knows that you did all in your power to deny them that right.

Governor Peabody, you stand condemned at the bar of public opinion as a corporate vassal who is ever ready to sacrifice the liberty of the people of this state at the behests of your masters, and the public want no canting hypocracies or platitudes from you. The least said about **law** and **order** after the exhibition of it, as seen in the Cripple Creek district, the better the public will be pleased.

Back, back, Governor Peabody, back to that dear Canon City, back to the more fitting occupation of your nature. Back, I say, to the clipping of coupons, the hoarding of the yellow boys; back to where your brain may shrivel and your sense become dumb to all but its natural sphere; back to the bars of your protected bank; back to the place where your fingers may develop unrestricted into the yellow and gnarled tallons of the pictured money monger, the accursed of Christ. Desert you the misoccupied chair of justice arbitrator, the position that should be occupied by honor and contaminate not the air of heaven with the name of liberty, freedom and **justice** befouled by your construction.

PEABODY CALLS FOR HELP.

A dispatch from Washington, November 19, made known the fact that President Roosevelt had received a dispatch from Governor Peabody, asking that General Baldwin, commanding the department of Colorado, be instructed to supply such troops as may be necessary to preserve order in the Telluride district.

After a consultation between the President and secretary of war, Governor Peabody was advised that it did not appear that the resources of the state had been exhausted, and therefore, the request for troops was denied.

Upon the appearance of the foregoing, it leaked out that Governor Peabody and General Bell—beg pardon Sherman—I mean Adjutant General Brigadier General Sherman M. Bell of Colorado had offered the state militia, 2,000 strong, to fight the battles of the United States in Panama. The letter follows:

"Denver, Colo., November 9, 1903.

"Theodore Roosevelt, President:

"Commending your action in the Panama question, and having in mind the possibility of military service, I desire to tender you the services of the National Guard of Colorado, 2,000 strong, now fully armed and equipped and organized under the provision of the Dick bill, who can be ready on twenty-four hours' notice.

"JAMES H. PEABODY, Governor and Commander-in-Chief,

"SHERMAN M. BELL, Adjutant General,

"J. Q. MACDONALD, Military Secretary."

The secretary of war answered in the most polite manner possible which ended as follows:

"I beg to express the appreciation of the government of the United States for the patriotic spirit which prompted your offer. Fortunately there is at present no reason to anticipate the calling out of any part of the militia of the United States, but should the occasion arise at any time the readiness of the militia of the State of Colorado to serve their country will not pass without notice.   Very truly yours,

"ELIHU ROOT, Sec'y of War."

Governor Peabody in a mild way had made for himself the butt for gibes and jokes in the war department. From the foregoing correspondence it will be seen that he and Sherman Bell tendered the state militia, 2,000 strong, armed and ready to set sail for Panama on twenty-four hours notice; while in the next breath the governor demanded federal troops, declaring that this same state militia was wholly inadequate to cope with the "lawless" element of Colorado.

In addition to this, Secretary Root modestly reads the governor a lecture on his ignorance of law, and showed that he had not commenced to make out such a condition as the law requires to permit the President to order federal troops to interfere.

This little farce comedy on the part of Sherman Bell and the governor was apparently an effort to saddle the expense of the "war of Colorado" (guarding the property of the mine owners against imaginary depredations), upon the United States; said war having already cost the state of Colorado in the vicinity of $500,000 (if we should permit the legislature to pay the mine owners' bills), and no blood shed in combat but that of a poor little burro.

Some have been so cruel as to hint that if Bell and Peabody could volunteer the services of 2,000 armed militiamen (the entire fighting force of the state of Colorado), to go to far distant Panama, there could surely be no necessity for them in the state of Colorado.

DEATH OF WILLIAM DODSWORTH.

A very sad death must be recorded in these pages as subsequent proceedings in connection with it are almost beyond belief.

On November 20, the highly honored and ever-respected president of Victor Miners' Union No. 32, William Dodsworth, was almost instantly killed in the Delmonico shaft, one of the Stratton properties. He, in company with David Reed, were engaged in mending a steam pipe which was connected with some machinery which he had installed at the Delmonico mine. The men were standing on a plank which was balanced on two cross scantlings when Dodsworth stepped out near the end of the board, which broke, precipitating him to the bottom of the shaft. When picked up and taken to the surface, he was in an unconscious condition, from which he did not recover, until death came as he was being carried into his home at Goldfield.

Mr. Dodsworth was universally respected, and for the greater part of his life had been identified with trades unionism.

NO RESPECT FOR THE DEAD.

While the last sad rites were being paid to the dead at Miners' Union hall, Victor, Sunday afternoon, November 22, the military interrupted the ceremonies. While the services were being conducted over the remains of the beloved president of Miners' Union No. 32, where the unions and auxiliaries of the entire district had gathered to pay their last respects to the dead, a squad of cavalry, including several officers, galloped up to Miners' Union hall and laughingly dismounted. The notorious ex-convict, Frank Vannick, headed the file of officers, and with him as a leader they proceeded up the stairway to the hall of the sacred dead.

The officers, with covered heads and clanging sabres boistrously entered the hall where every head was bowed in deepest sorrow. After this display of military rule in the glorious "land of the free," Vannick advanced nearer the grief-stricken mourners and pointed out C. G. Kennison, president of No. 40. Whereupon Kennison was at once taken from the hall where he was paying his last duty to a deceased brother, and marched to the bull pen.

Men present simply turned white with rage, and God alone knows how they restrained themselves. And yet the miners are lawless, vicious criminals. Verily, were they not martyrs to abide by such an insult, not only to the living, but to their respected dead.

Mr. Kennison could not have left the building without being captured had they cause for arresting him. He had no intention of leaving the district and could have been taken at any other time.

CONSPIRACY TO IMPLICATE UNION MEN.

After a lull in military circles for several weeks, and the citizens having begun to recover from the effects of past military operations, the military again scented crime and again got busy.

November 17 there was much activity displayed in the "gold lace" circles.

A rail on the F. & C. C. railroad, just out from Anaconda, and on a high embankment, was released from the ties by someone removing the spikes. This was done sometime on the night of November 16, before the 3 o'clock suburban, carrying about forty union and non-union miners came along.

The engineer, Wm. Rush, claimed that he had a "tip" that the rail had been removed, and for that reason he stopped his train before he reached the spot and got down to make an investigation, finding the rail loose and all the spikes removed. He called a number of the passengers and the train crew to make an examination for their own satisfaction, and they verified his statement. The matter was reported to the military and General Bell detailed about thirty of his men in citizen's clothing to search the district for information regarding the matter. About noon November 17, twenty cavalry and twenty infantry, under the

command of Majors McClelland and Naylor went to the house of
Charles McKinney and placed him under arrest. He was taken
to the Independence guard house and left surrounded by soldiers.
The detachment then started for Altman and met P. H. Mullaney
on the road and placed him under arrest. Mullaney was then
taken to Camp Goldfield and placed in the bull pen, and McKinney was brought down from the Independence guard house. While
the troops were in Altman they went to the home of Thomas
Foster and Mrs. Foster refused them admission. They then broke
down the door, but Foster could not be found. A search was made
throughout the district for him, but to no avail.

Foster, when he found that the military were searching for
him, it was stated, went to the sheriff's office and turned himself
over to the sheriff and asked protection from the military and the
bull pen.

The military authorities made the claim that a like attempt
was made to wreck an electric car near the Economic mill; that
in this case the rail had also been loosened, and that it was discovered just in time to avoid a wreck.

General Bell talked freely on the subject and among other
things said:

"The prisoners will be protected, though even every man in the
Cripple Creek district made an attempt to secure custody of them, and
every man who makes an attempt to get to the prisoners will be promptly
shot. None will escape should a forcible attempt be made to secure possession of the prisoners. The men are not only under a heavy infantry
guard, but there is a double cavalry patrol, and the men are absolutely
safe from any violence. The lives of every member of the National Guard
in Camp Goldfield will be sacrificed to protect the two prisoners."

Protected from whom? Not their brother union miners, the
writer hopes; and as the military claimed that the miners were
the only lawless element in the district, who else could have
harmed the prisoners? Surely the mine owners would not have
committed such a lawless act; and the Citizens' Alliance was never
accused of being lawless by the military—then who could have
harmed the prisoners?

There was not a person in the district who was not in favor
of seeing the guilty punished, no matter who it happened to be.

No one in the district was more anxious to see the guilty punished than the members of the W. F. of M. The unions, however, grew very tired of the contemptible insinuations continually hurled at them—they were crucified at the behest and in the interest of the mine owners until it grew absolutely unbearable.

Some people suggested that it was done by someone having a grudge against the railroad and they took advantage of this opportunity to get revenge when they would be least suspected. Others claimed that it was a scheme on the part of the military or mine owners to cast suspicion on the unions, and to create the impression in the mind of the general public that it was necessary for the military to remain in the district to prevent wholesale murder and crime.

THE VINDICATOR HORROR.

A terrible disaster occurred at the Vindicator mine in Independence at about 11 o'clock a. m., November 21. Charles McCormick, superintendent, and Melvin Beck, shift boss of the mine, were killed almost outright by a terrific explosion at the 600-foot level of that property.

The news of the explosion spread over the district in a very few minutes and hundreds of people hastened to the scene. Troops were brought from Camp Goldfield and at once surrounded the mine.

Previous to descending to the place of their death, Beck was heard to say to McCormick that there was something suspicious about the appearance of things at the 600-foot level, but further than that the conversation was not heard before they went below.

As soon as possible help was sent to the 600-foot level, where a horrible sight met the eye. The bodies of McCormick and Beck were found, badly mutilated. McCormick was still alive, but unconscious. He lived twenty-five minutes. Beck was alive and conscious, and his last words were: "I want everything to go to my daughter." He lived fifteen minutes.

Immediate investigation was made as to the cause of the explosion. It was surmised that an infernal machine had been set in the following manner:

A quantity of dynamite had been placed at a certain place, and a loaded revolver rigged so that its discharge would explode the dynamite. One end of a wire was attached to the trigger of the revolver and the other end fastened to the guard rail so that in raising the rail the revolver would be discharged. The conclusion that an infernal machine as above described had been prepared was reached from the fact that broken parts of a revolver and a wire were found at the place where the explosion occurred.

The people advanced many theories and suppositions, but at this writing there has been nothing proven further than the fact that the accident happened, but prejudiced individuals, who rarely know anything of what they talk about, at once passed judgment and denounced it as a cold blooded murder. Experience has taught, however, that there are people who are not above making capital out of misfortune.

The coroner's jury, with officials of the mine, made a careful examination of the mine and premises. At the inquest, which lasted several days, many witnesses were examined. Footmarks were found near where the explosion occurred of a No. 8 shoe that appeared to be new. The verdict reached, was as follows:

"That Charles McCormick and Melvin Beck came to their death on the 21st day of November, 1903, at 11 o'clock a. m., from the effect of an explosion at the station on the sixth level of the Vindicator mine, located in the Cripple Creek mining district. From the examinations made at the mine, and the evidence introduced, the jury is unable to determine the exact cause of the explosion. In testimony whereof the said jurors hereunto set their hands the day and year aforesaid.

"JOHN KETELSON,
"JOHN HARPER,
"W. S. ELLIOTT,
"W. J. DONNELLEY,
"JACOB NEIMAN,
"J. L. WOOD."

After the explosion at the Vindicator, the military again assumed the role of the famous Nick Carter, and from Saturday, the 21st, to Tuesday, the 24th, arrested eighteen respected citizens.

No warrants or charges were brought against the men arrested, it was presumed by all interested, that they were to be charged with the dynamiting of the Vindicator. However, it was not so stated. Nearly every union miner in the district that happened to wear a No. 8 shoe, was arrested. Among the first men arrested and consigned to the bull pen were Sherman Parker, H. Chase, Link Bolson, W. B. Easterly, W. F. Davis, John Schoolcraft, Gus Johnson, J. B. Isibell, R. Bolan, William Beecher, Victor Poole, Mr. Fleming, H. P. Jones, C. G. Kennison, C. H. McKinney, Bob Adams, P. H. Mullaney and Frank Campbell.

Some of the foregoing were soon released and some were never at liberty any length of time thereafter. When the military were forced by law to release either Davis, Kennison or Poole, there was soon some unreasonable excuse found to take them again.

Don't forget, indulgent reader, that even had any of these men been guilty of any offense, the most the military could have lawfully done would have been to file charges and turn them over to the civil authorities. By what right of law were these union men confined in the military bull pen without a scintilla of evidence produced against them? It appeared from time to time as if the military officers were trying their best to create riot in the district. No doubt they lived in fear of losing their positions at any time and wanted to keep something going on. The mine owners' papers cast dirty insinuations at the "inner circle" of the Western Federation, which were very hard to bear, in regard to the Vindicator explosion. The union men could, with equal right, have accused the "inner circle" of the Mine Owners' Association with being responsible for every mishap that occurred to union men after the strike started. There were some very suspicious cases of union men's houses having been burned, particularly those at Beacon hill and near the Santa Rita mine, that would have borne investigation. True there were criminals brought into the district, and who was responsible for their being here? The mine owners. Who gleefully gave it out that they were bringing tough men into the district to create "rough houses?" The mine owners. In whose employ was K. C. Sterling and ex-Convict Vannick? Any unprejudiced person knows who committed all manner of depredations on innocent men, aye, and women too, in the community.

It must not be forgotten that we are all Americans and imbued with the American spirit. The finest steel blade may be bent until it snaps in twain.

MILITARY THREATEN TO ARREST CHILDREN.

Not content with having added a goodly percentage of the population of the hill to the roster of the bull pen prisoners, the military began a campaign against the children. Five boys, ranging in age from 9 to 14 years, were arrested and taken to the prison at Camp Goldfield, but later in the evening of November 23 were all released.

One incident in connection with the arrests of children which provoked great indignation occurred on the foregoing date. A crowd of soldiers was passing, more than a block away, the home of the late William Dodsworth, where the two Dodsworth children, aged 7 and 10 years, in company with other children were playing. None of the party on the porch, according to the best people in Goldfield, made any demonstration or offered any remark which could be heard by the soldiers or passerby; but suddenly three cavalry troopers detached themselves from the squad and rode directly to the house. The soldiers dashed up and ordered the oldest little fellow to fall in line. This the child refused to do, and he ran into the house. The doors were at once locked. The soldier led his horse up to the very door and demanded that the boy be given into custody, but was met by an emphatic refusal by Mrs. Dodsworth, who promised him a warm reception should he attempt to take the child by force. Argument and command failing, the soldiers desisted and returned to their company.

After the departure of the soldiers, Mrs. Dodsworth was completely prostrated and had to have medical aid. Following closely upon the tragic death and burial of the husband and father, the incident aroused deepest indignation in Goldfield, and upon every hand by unionist and non-unionist.

M'KINNEY TAKEN TO CANON CITY.

November 23 Charles McKinney was taken to Canon City and placed in the Fremont county jail for "protection," so said Sherman Bell; but there was probably no more danger of a lynching of McKinney in Teller county than there was one of the most innocent people in Denver, were any of them to come here. It was, however, a good play for effect, and to work additional injury on the name of the Cripple Creek district.

The action of the authorities in taking him to Canon City could meet but with ridicule from the people in the district. The very people that claimed they wanted him taken away for the sake of protection, were the ones that would not have cared much if he was lynched if they believed him guilty of the crime they claimed to hold against him. McKinney was at no time in danger here, and the report that a certain number of citizens had a rope, etc., preparatory to stringing him up, was false in every particular.

MORE WRITS OF HABEAS CORPUS.

November 30 writs of habeas corpus were again issued by Judge Seeds. The writs called for the persons of Sherman Parker, W. F. Davis, Victor Poole, W. B. Easterly, C. G. Kennison and Patrick Mullaney, and were returnable Thursday, December 3, at 1 p. m.

December 2 the military powers filed with the clerk of the district court answers to the writ. The answer recited at length the authority of the respondents for seizing the prisoners and explained in Blackstonian parlance that the honorable district court has no jurisdiction in the premises. It set forth that the governor's orders endow the military authorities with supreme power in this territory.

Another chapter in the miner's strike was reached December 3, when three military officers, one ex-convict and one detective produced P. H. Mullaney, W. B. Easterly and Victor Poole before Judge Seed's court in answer to the writs I have previously mentioned.

The capactiy of the court room was overtaxed by the throng

of interested spectators. On behalf of Colonel Verdeckberg, Captain Naylor and Major McClelland, Attorney Crump addressed the court, stating that he desired to file returns on the writs in all cases. Attorney Hangs, having filed motions to quash in the cases of Mullaney, Easterly and Poole, Mr. Crump was willing to comply with the court's orders affecting these three men, but in the cases of Davis, Parker and Kennison, Mr. Crump stated that informations had been filed charging them with attempted train wrecking, and these prisoners would be held until they were demanded by the sheriff on proper capiases. The sheriff can have these men at Camp Goldfield, or they will be delivered here, added Mr. Crump. The court then ordered that the military deliver the prisoners to the sheriff at the county jail, upon the presentation of capiases.

Judge Seeds ordered the release of Easterly, Mullaney and Poole at 1:30 o'clock. Colonel Verdeckberg announced to the military escort that the men were free. Mullaney and Poole started down stairs, but just as they reached the foot of the stairs Poole was rearrested by the militia and detectives who were in waiting, and he was promptly returned to the bull pen.

Sheriff Robertson and Deputy Hi Wilson arrived at county jail with Davis, Parker, Kennison and Adams, the prisoners having been surrendered by the military authorities. Sheriff Robertson expressed himself as fully competent to take care of the men.

The information based upon the sworn allegations of Manager Campbell of the Vindicator mine, was not filed in the district court until shortly before noon, December 3. It charged Steven Adams, W. F. Davis, Sherman Parker and Charles G. Kennison with the murder of Chas. McCormick and Melvin Beck.

D. C. Scott, special agent for the F. & C. C. railway took the cue from Manager Campbell and filed a couple of affidavits against the bull pen prisoners. Sherman Parker and W. F. Davis were implicated by Scott in the attempt at train wrecking at Anaconda. A strong effort had been made to fasten he crime upon McKinney, Foster, Parker and Davis. It was expected that Victor Poole would be implicated.

MARTIAL LAW IS DECLARED.

Martial law was declared in Teller county, December 4, 1903.

The "military operations" being so frequently interrupted by writs of habeas corpus, capiases and other civil procedures, the commander-in-chief performed a brilliant coup against the "desperadoes" of the district and decided to declare the much threatened "martial law." It was such a simple thing that the wonder is that it was not done before. Eight "whereases" relating the horrors of the district, the intimidation or unfitness of the civil authorities, the bands of armed and desperate men threatening life—no, taking life and destroying property, and, for all the "denizens" knew, the fear that the future bloodshed might drown all the little fishes in the mountain streams, or some other frightful disaster, and perhaps an etc., or so, and one little "Now, therefore, I James H. Peabody, governor of the state of Colorado, by virtue of the authority in me vested, do hereby proclaim and declare the said county of Teller, in the state of Colorado, to be in a state of insurrection and rebellion." The signature of the governor, perhaps a few blue ribbons and the seal, and then the long suffering Cripple Creek district was "up against the real thing."

The Victor Daily Record was notified by Major Naylor that it would have to refrain from publishing the Western Federation's official statement, and an editorial that had been written and was in the forms was ordered not published. The management was further notified that if any criticism appeared in the paper that was not acceptable, such as the editorial that had been written concerning the military, that the paper would be suppressed and put out of business. In order to protect the legal issue of the paper and be allowed to do business under the martial law reign in the county, the news that appeared in the columns of this paper was published under the military censorship during the time of the military rule. The Record, it seems, was the only "outlaw" paper in the district and the military must "protect" the good people from the "contaminating influence" of its editorials.

The announcement of martial law was made to the people of Victor at about 5 o'clock in the afternoon when Majors McClelland and Naylor, at the head of a detachment of cavalry, halted at the corner of Third street and Victor avenue and Major McClelland read the proclamation of the governor. The same formality was gone through with on the streets of Cripple Creek.

The reader will realize that "martial law" is a very serious thing, and, of course, calls for many proclamations, orders, instructions, etc., "by order of," "signed, sealed, witnessed," etc.,

MAJOR H. A. NAYLOR.

in order to give it the dignity due it. Of course, these were forthcoming, and in sufficient number to suit the occasion (also to fill the pages of this book). One of them was the "surrender your weapons" affair, and in consequence no little amusement was derived by the delivery of weapons that were and weapons that "had been."

Taken all in all, however, martial law did not disturb the people generally as much at they had feared it would. Of course, it was very irritating to the inborn independence of American citizens, to see, day after day, armed guards parading the streets when they knew there was no necessity for it, and they felt it rather as an insult to their patriotism than any actual discomfort.

THE CORONER'S JURY SERVES WRITS.

Application for a writ of habeas corpus for the person of Victor Poole was made in the district court December 9 by Attorney Frank J. Hangs. The defendants in the case were Colonel Verdeckberg, Majors Naylor and McClelland and Sheriff Robertson. Inasmuch as the sheriff was custodian of the prisoner, who was confined in the county jail, it devolved upon Coroner Doran to perform the delicate task of serving the writs.

Coroner Doran obtained service upon Colonel Verdeckberg and Major Naylor. The writs were returnable Friday, Dec. 11. By virtue of the recent declaration of martial law it was anticipated by many that the military authorities would cooly ignore the court's orders.

On December 10 the governor issued a proclamation, one calculated to suspend the writ of habeas corpus and remove a most sacred right of free citizens. It was sort of an eleventh hour proclamation, having been issued but a few hours prior to the filing of an answer to the writ in the case of Victor Poole. The proclamation was lengthy and cited many authorities, but the cause was in the last paragraph, which I quote:

"Now, therefore, I, James H. Peabody, governor of the State of Colorado, by virtue of the authority vested in me by the constitution of the State of Colorado and the laws thereof, do hereby declare and proclaim that, in my judgment, the public safety especially requires that the privilege of the writ of habeas corpus be suspended in this case, to-wit, in the case of Victor Poole, aforesaid, and I further direct that the said writ of habeas corpus be suspended in his case until further orders by me.

"JAMES H. PEABODY."

Attorney Crump, accompanied by the military officials, appeared in court promptly on the morning of Dec. 11, and holding in his hand the return made, explained the attitude of the respondents and said the court was bound to take cognizance of the condition of the law of his district, and that Colonel Verdeckberg and Majors Naylor and McClelland set up the claim in their return that they are in full control of the troops in the district and maintain that their only authority was the governor, and that they would elect at that time to hold the body of the prisoner.

Judge Seeds stated that the case would be continued for further hearing on the motion to quash the writ until 2 o'clock, and also gave the respondents until that time to file criminal information against the prisoner.

Judge Seeds said: "Knowing as I do that the civil courts of this county are earnest in their efforts to do their duty well and faithfully, I desire that you come into court at 2 o'clock tomorrow for a further hearing in this case."

At 2:30 Attorney Crump, for the respondents addressed the bench upon the motion to quash the return of the writ. He referred to the argument used by the opposing counsel as "ingenious" but that it failed to prove that the military power is subservient to the civil authorities.

The court finally interrupted Mr. Crump with the remark that "There is an unbroken line of opinion regarding the existence of martial law, and all showing that such a state has not existed in this country except in case of actual warfare."

With but a few moments deliberation the court rendered his decision and issued the following order:

"State of Colorado, County of Teller, ss.
    "In the District Court.
"Victor Poole, Plaintiff, vs. Colonel Edward Verdeckberg, Major H. A. Naylor, Major T. E. McClelland, as Members of the State Militia of the State of Colorado, and H. M. Robertson, as Sheriff of Teller County, as Defendants:
    "This matter having come to be heard this 12th day of December, A. D. 1903, upon the returns of Colonel Edward Verdeckberg, Major H. A. Naylor and Major T. E. McClelland, and the separate return of H. M. Robertson, as sheriff of Teller county, on the motion to quash said returns.
    "The court, after listening to arguments of S. D. Crump, in behalf of the respondents, and Frank J. Hangs, in behalf of the petitioner; and,
    "Being fully advised in the premises, doth find that the motion to quash should be sustained.
    "Wherefore, it is ordered, adjudged and decreed by the court that the motion to quash the returns herein be and is hereby sustained.
    "And it is further ordered, adjudged and decreed by the court that

the respondents, and each and every one of them, do forthwith discharge the petitioner herein from custody.

"And it is further ordered, adjudged and decreed by the court that the petitioner herein do have and recover of the respondents his costs herein expended and have execution therefor.

"Done in open court this 12th day of December, A. D. 1903.

"By the court.   WILLIAM P. SEEDS, Judge.

"State of Colorado, County of Teller, ss."

The military refused to release Poole, and on December 14 Governor Peabody stated that the state would not appeal the case. Attorney Miller said that Poole and the miners could take no appeal in the matter, as they won in the lower court, and therefore would have no standing in the higher court. Attorney Samuel D. Crump gave it out as his opinion that the state would appeal in a short time.

VICTOR POOLE CASE IN THE SUPREME COURT.

On the morning of December 16 the supreme court heard the preliminary arguments in the application for writs of supercedeas for the prisoners and issued two writs made returnable in five days, for Victor Poole and A. J. Paul, both of whom were held by the military in defiance of the civil authorities. The court decided no question in granting the application for the writ. It reserved all decisions as to its power to make jurisdiction in the cases, the right of the governor to issue a proclamation suspending the writ of habeas corpus in the case of Poole and all other questions involved.

After Attorney Hawkins had finished reading the petitions and made a short argument in the matter, Attorney General Miller was called upon by the court to express his views. He said: "There is no truth in the affidavits sworn to by these gentlemen. The worst crimes ever committed in the state have been done in Teller county and have gone unpunished. Criminals are arrested time and again and turned loose. It is nonsense for a man to stand up here before this court and make such statements. Ever since the county of Teller was a county, lawlessness has held sway there. There has been no law and order there."

Attorney Hawkins was so surprised at the attack of the attorney general that he did not seem to realize for a moment the full import of the words. He then arose and said: "This is an unnecessary insult to me and to the court of Teller county. The statement of the gentleman is on a par with the way the military has done things in the past. It is in justice to Judge Seeds that I speak. Such an attack is little more than slander on the court of Teller county. Judge Seeds has the privilege of being defended when he is set upon in such a manner. It is absolutely untrue that notorious criminals have gone unpunished. The attorney general is evidently misinformed concerning the conditions in that part of Colorado, and his statements will not be borne out by the facts in the case."

If General Miller thought his statement would go unchallenged as to the conditions in the Cripple Creek district, he was mistaken. Affidavits were made out by public officials and prominent men of Victor and Cripple Creek to the effect that the courts were open before the military came and that justice was administered properly, that the laws were enforced without favor and that the public safety was maintained in all quarters.

Saturday, January 2, was the day set for the hearing, but the case was dismissed from the supreme court for the reason that the governor fearing the decision of the court had ordered Victor Poole turned over to the civil authorities.

The military and mine owners' attorney, when they found that the supreme court would be forced to a decision, and knowing and fearing that the decision would be adverse to their stand and necessarily in favor of Poole, sought some means to get rid of his custody. They sought relief in Justice Harrington's court, and through one S. R. Lack (or Leck) filed charges of assault to kill in the dim distant years of yore, by Poole, causing warrants to be issued and turned over to the sheriff to serve. Poole claimed to have forgotten the incident upon which the civil arrest was based.

It is needless to state that the sheriff had no trouble in securing the custody of Poole. His trial for this forgotten alleged offense was set for January 9, on which date Attorney Crump order for the release of Poole from custody followed forthwith.

uance of ten days, claiming by affidavits that he was unable to secure the necessary witnesses.

Justice Harrington promptly decided that the whole affair was "horse play," and denied the motion for a continuance. The order of the release of Poole from custody followed forthwith.

JUSTICE HARRINGTON.

This abrupt termination of the sensational case was not unexpected by those familiar with its various stages. It was instituted for the sole purpose of preventing a final decision by the supreme court on the extent of the authority of the military in the Cripple Creek district. The legal representatives of the mine owners' were forced to evade the issue of habeas corpus. It was necessary to resort to subterfuge to accomplish this purpose, as it was decided to bring trumped-up charges against Poole. Attorney Crump used Leck as a complaining witness and resorted to a justice court to carry out the miserable design. The scheme worked admirably. On the flimsy pretext that serious information had been filed against Poole, the military succeeded in preventing a decision which they mortally feared.

But what of Poole? Arrest, confinement, insult. Dragged from bull pen to jail, from jail to bull pen. Subjected to every humiliation that could be devised by persecutors. Innocent, and known to be innocent. Supposed to have the rights that are guaranteed to every freeborn American citizen. He was used by what should be the **support of freedom,** for the purpose of **crushing** the very name of justice. Verily is the state government of Colorado in a fair way to make of **men** anarchists; and **law,** despotism.

UNION MINERS TO BE VAGGED.

January 7 was the day the military had set apart to put into force a "vag" law. January 6 was said to be the last day of grace allowed to the idle in which to go to work or leave the district. It was understood that a general "clean up" of dissolute citizens of the district would be inaugurated. The military authorities did not divulge their proposed modus operandi though it was given out that they would not maintain a boarding house at Camp Goldfield. Those under the military ban were to be taken in by guards of soldiers as fast as possible and escorted to the camp, where they were to be given the privilege of leaving the district at once or entering the dreaded bull pen. When a sufficient number of prisoners were thus rounded up it was proposed to take them under military escort to the limits of Teller county and force them into exile. But when the day arrived the miners remained as usual. Three or four union men were told to go, but they remained as they had always been— law-abiding citizens of the Cripple Creek district.

The Western Federation issued circulars and distributed them over the district, urging the men to refuse to be driven from their homes. It follows:

"NOTICE—To all members of the W. F. M. of the Cripple Creek district—It has been decided in many courts that members of organized labor are not vagrants. Keep your union cards and refuse to be driven from home. If compelled to leave by force of arms, union men are advised to return immediately to the Cripple Creek district. The Western Federation of Miners will provide for all striking miners' families.

"CHAS. H. MOYER, President.

"WM. D. HAYWOOD, Sec.-Treas. W. F. M."

Immediately after the above notice was distributed on the streets of Victor the military got immensely busy in a vain effort to "suppress" them. They searched Miners' Union hall, but could not find this "terrible literature," but they scared the Record into stopping the press that was turning them out and also arrested a boy who was distributing them. They also tore down all that they could find tacked up on bill boards and telegraph poles.

R. E. CROSKEY DRIVEN FROM THE DISTRICT.

In the early part of December, R. E. Croskey, first vice-president Colorado State Federation of Labor; secretary District Trades and Labor Assembly, and the author of the "official statement" issued by the Executive Committee District Union No. 1," had business in Denver and quietly left the Cripple Creek district. He has always been a recognized leader of organized labor in the district, and therefore it was announced that "military necessity" made it imperative that Mr. Croskey should be exiled to the bull pen. The military scoured the district for this recognized enemy of the mine owners, but while they were doing so, he was taking a quiet little walk over the Rockies out of the district. In an interview in Denver December 10, Mr. Croskey said in part:

"I do not fear the 'bull pen.' It has no terrors for me. I am no better than others who are now in it. It is a part of my duty to go there, and I shall. I will spend my time in reading. I want to read again Thomas Payne's 'The Rights of Man.' I will enjoy it there under the tent of Peabody's tyranny. Then I expect to again read the Declaration of Independence, Lincoln's inaugural address and his Gettysburg speech, and other *fiction* so dear to the hearts of Americans."

"Mr. Croskey emphasized the word 'fiction' and flashed his sharp eyes for the instant upon the catechist, to see if the chosen words had gone home.

"Then, too, I may read the constitution of the United States, if I am permitted to do so by the powers that rule over me. I shall not worry about my fare or how long I will be held. After all, it is but a little while here. I want Governor Peabody and General Bell to know that we are not afraid of their jails. I want them to know that we will go in and come out by the same door. They cannot crush out the spirit of freedom that dwells in the hearts of the men he is persecuting. That, you know, was tried long ago, and it failed."

Mr. Croskey returned to the district in a few days after the interview, but never occupied the bull pen. The opposition recognized in him a formidable and dangerous "enemy," but "kept their hands off."

FIRST BLOOD OF THE CRIPPLE CREEK "WAR."

The first blood of the "Cripple Creek War," (with the exception of the burro) was on December 28, when John M. Glover issued an inflammatory defi to the military authorities in regard to giving up arms. The cause of the excitement was the following letter which Mr. Glover turned over to a representative of the Denver Republican:

"Cripple Creek, Colo., December 28, 1903.

"I observe that Colonel Verdeckberg issued still other proclamations calling for more arms and detailing the strenuous things he will do if they are not surrendered. Tell the colonel that there are two guns in my office and they are not registered; they are mine; the constitution gives me the right to carry them; they are loaded to the brim. The colonel can have them when the supreme court ratifies his criminal usurpation against the liberties of the people of this county, and before that whenever he is brave enough to murder under his illegal orders.

"I look to see the supreme court ransom this people and all the active agents in this conspiracy against human rights sent to the penitentiary, where they belong.

"A disorderly and lawless governor, who prostitutes the military arm to crush one side of an industrial controversy—I don't care which side— is the chief anarchist in the state. Where agitators make single socialists he makes them in shoals. Tell the colonel to come when I am at home and to come at the head of his squad. If, whenever a governor is base enough to tell a transparent and wicked lie about a community, he can by virtue of that lie, wipe away all my constitutional rights and put me under the government of a San Hedran of wild asses' colts, like Bell, Chase and McClelland and company; I am ready to pass in my chips at any time.

"As for unionism, it is stronger today than ever. It is bulit on a basic principle of human nature. It can't be stamped out by the military heel. Persecution strengthens it as it strengthened the early church.

(Signed)   "JOHN M. GLOVER."

MR. GLOVER'S STATEMENT.

"The soldiers came to the office and demanded entrance. I refused and barricaded the door. After an hour I heard boring at the lower right hand corner of the door. I looked through the glass (upper half) and found a soldier crouched there. They were, in fact, afraid to enter, and were tying up the door to starve me out. I did not know this, and thought he was affixing something to the door to blow or force it open. After warning him twice, I began to shoot. The soldier swore afterwards that I fired three times. At any rate the return fire, twenty-five shots, riddled the office and one bullet caught me in the left arm, cutting the ulnar nerve, paralyzing the left arm for many days and the right hand temporarily, so that I could not pick up the gun (a sporting model Winchester), which had fallen to the floor. I then began to appreciate the beauties of peace and surrender. I was thrown into the county jail, which had been seized by the military. The next day I was released, and went to St. Francis' hospital, Colorado Springs, having signed the following parole:

" 'I accept my release from confinement in Teller county on the following conditions, which I pledge myself, as a gentleman, to follow strictly:

" 'First—I shall return to the Cripple Creek district and surrender myself to Colonel Verdeckberg, or any other officer in command, when requested to do so by such officer.

" 'Second—That until I have placed myself in the custody of such officer, or other proper authority, the sheriff, etc., I pledge myself to not talk or write for publication nor institute any proceedings legal or of any other kind.

" 'As soon as the wound passed the danger of blood poisoning (which would have been a sure thing in the microbe-ridden jail), I returned to Cripple Creek and notified the commandant that I would no longer be bound by the parole, and would prosecute him and his accomplices, and he sent a file of soldiers and arrested me at once, and, after holding me in jail for two days, threw me into the military prison and held me for sixteen days. The blankets were so filthy that if you slept in a clean shirt one night it looked next morning as if you had worn it six weeks. The wound, which had been open and treated daily, was deliberately neglected and closed over the dressing and the inflammation of the injured nerve intensely increased, so that I could only sleep in snatches from sheer exhaustion. After eleven days I was taken twice to Cripple Creek to have the wound dressed by my surgeon, but I would not agree to trade the right of free speech for the right of humane treatment, and that was stopped. As a consequence of the first eleven days' neglect, the arm seems to have stiffened permanently in an unnatural (bent) position. Meanwhile, two informations had been prepared, one for shooting with intent to kill Soldier Smith, and the other for the same as to Soldier Dittemore. Tried on the last charge, the judge, a Republican, and appointed by Peabody, instructed that the soldiers had the right to take the guns, and I had no right to resist. I defended myself, scared the governor unmercifully, and got a compromise verdict of simple assault, penalty $100, or six months in county jail, motion for new trial pending. Nothing the matter with this verdict except that the information states no offense, one-half of the instructions are erroneous under Colorado decisions, and there is no evidence to show that I shot at Dittemore, though much to show that I shot at Smith, who was crouching at the door. It will last about as long as the proverbial snowball in the regions below, when it reaches the supreme court. Tried on the Smith charge, I got an absolute acquittal on the ground that I was in jeopardy already in the Dittemore case. I am now about well. I intended by precept and example to cause a general forcible resistance to the disarmament order. The certainty of this killed the plan dead. Behind it there was, to my certain knowledge, a scheme to which Peabody was a party, to deport 1,500 or 2,000 striking miners who were living on the proceeds of their own toil, as vagrants. It was perforce abandoned when the disarmament failed. As the troops were only used to 'job' the strikers, there was no further use for them, and so they went out. I had an inspiration that all this would follow. If Peabody had attempted the same lawless game in any county in Missouri, his army would have been shot and himself hung to his own door-post within a week.

"The pacific fight of the unions was too strong to be beaten except by the unlimited and unscrupulous use of the military arm. In attempting to crush them, Peabody made slaves of us all."

STATE FEDERATION CALLS CONVENTION.

December 30 there was issued a call by the Colorado State Federation of Labor for a mass convention to go into session January 11 to consider the welfare of organized labor throughout the state. I give the official call complete, which explains itself:

"TO THE UNIONS THROUGHOUT THE STATE OF COLORADO: OFFICERS AND MEMBERS, GREETING:

"Denver, Colo., December 30, 1903.

"A crisis has been reached in this state which demands that the members of organized labor shall no longer remain mute and silent. The rights, the liberties and the citizenship of labor have been assailed with a wanton, cold-blooded, premeditated brutality that finds no parallel in the crimsoned pages of Russia's blood-curdling history. 'The land of the free and the home of the brave' has been converted into a Siberia, where gubernatorial czarism has climbed to the loftiest summit of despotism; where military might rides rampant over the constitution and the laws.

J. C. SULLIVAN, President Colorado State Federation of Labor.

The laborer's home, which is the castle of the poor man, is no longer sacred. The hearthstone, the family fireside, is invaded and desecrated by military outlaws, and citizenship subjected to all the indignities, humiliation and reproach, which corporate cunning and power can suggest and devise, and which armed infamy can execute; civil authority has been strangled, and a free press and free speech have been suppressed. The member of organized labor who strikes has been declared a vagrant and to be a union man, merits the dynamite of the corporation to destroy his home and the penalty of incarceration in a military 'bull-pen' without charge, warrant or due process of law. Never before in the history of this country have such scenes been witnessed as here in the heart of the Rocky mountains.

"Courts of law are no longer recognized as temples of justice, and the manifestation of that spirit of patriotism and independence that fired the brain and nerved the arm of our ancestry of '76 is met with bristling bayonets of a military mob. The Patrick Henrys, the Washingtons and the Franklins of the Eighteenth century heard the haughty mandate issued from the lips of king-hired Hessians: 'Disperse, ye rebels,' and now in the early morn of the Twentieth century, after more than a hundred years have elapsed since the Declaration of Independence was baptized in the blood of valor and heroism, we hear the exultant shout of military—fortified plutocracy—calling upon the hosts of organized labor to disband, and bow the knee in cringing sycophancy as slaves to tyrants and masters. In the lexicon of freedom there is no such word as surrender. Brawny arms and brave hearts will not retreat before the pitiless monsters of incorporated greed, backed by the state militia, recruited from the slums and riff-raff of humanity. The uniform of the soldier in the State of Colorado has become, through a Republican administration, the emblem of disgrace, and the garb in which anarchy masquerades as law. The time has come when labor must speak in no uncertain tones, for upon the dauntless courage of the working men of this nation depends the life and liberty of the citizen and the stability of the government. In the language of the Revolutionary hero, 'these are times that try men's souls,' and the day has passed away when the 'summer patriot' and the 'sunshine warrior' can hug delusions to his breast. 'Eternal vigilance is the price of liberty.' And the time is now when the clarion voice of labor must be raised and heard in every city, town and hamlet in the state, calling a halt to military imperialism. Every union throughout the State of Colorado, regardless of the affiliation with the national or international bodies, are earnestly urged to send one or more representatives to a convention that is to be held in the city of Denver, Monday, January 11, at 10 o'clock a. m., in Waiters' hall, Club building. The strike of the miners in the Cripple Creek district, Telluride and the coal fields, has resolved itself into a battle, which leaves no longer room for doubt that every craft and department of unionism are threatened with annihilation. The gauntlet has been thrown down, we must take it up, pledging 'our fortunes and our all,' as did the sires of the Revolution when driving the tyranny of king-rule from the shores of young Columbia.

"Let no union in the state fail to send one or more delegates. Bring credentials from the union, properly signed and sealed. All officers and representatives of national or international bodies are eligible to seats in the convention and are respectfully requested to be present.

"J. C. SULLIVAN, Pres. Colo. S. F. of L.
"HARRY B. WATERS, Secretary-Treasurer."

In answer to the above call by the State Federation of Labor, more than 350 delegates assembled in the city of Denver, January 11, to consider ways and means to meet the emergencies that are arising from present industrial conditions. The ringing addresses that were delivered by the prominent men and women in the convention, and the Niagara of applause that greeted the thunderbolts of indignation that were hurled at Colorado's despot, demonstrated that organized labor in the state is aroused to the necessity of action to relegate the present administration to political oblivion. When the convention was called to order by J. C. Sullivan, the president of the State Federation, the Waiters' hall in the Club building was crowded to the doors, and the earnest and eloquent words that fell from the lips of the chairman impressed the delegates with the fact that the time had come in the history of the state, when the brawn and muscle of the citizenship should "hew to the line, let the chips fall where they will."

Mr. Sullivan said in part, as follows:

"Friends and Fellow Citizens, I Greet You:

"An industrial condition that makes necessary the assembling of labor's hosts in special convention is certainly significant, and, if the facial expressions of firm determination that are stamped on the countenances of this magnificent audience correctly reflects its feelings, there is still hope that 'liberty' and 'justice,' though banished from this centennial state of ours, 'by order of a political accident,' and citizens forced to leave their homes and firesides at the bayonet point in the hands of 'our' modern 'Hessians,' for the sole and only reason that they refuse to join forces with our 'modern Tories,' and say they will not sell their manhood on mammon's greedy altar nor bow the knee in cringing sycophancy to the aristocratic anarchist, though he be clothed with brief official authority. This, my friends, is a gathering that, if each and every delegate here assembled does his full duty to his country, to his fellow man, to himself and to the posterity of mankind, this meeting will go down in the annals of history as the most important gathering that has ever been held in Colorado up to this time. But if, for any reason, you fail to do your duty, you will, by that failure, assist the modern Tories and the mine operators' hired Hessians to banish the lovers of liberty from their homes and firesides, and establish in their stead willing corporate vassals, to whom manhood is an unknown quality, to whom justice is a myth and liberty an illusion. The time is *now*, my friends, when not only labor's voice must be heard, but labor's hosts must act, if necessary, if justice is to be again enthroned in the fair State of Colorado."

The selection of a temporary chairman and secretary resulted in the unanimous choice of President Sullivan as temporary chair-

man, and H. B. Waters of Denver, as temporary secretary. Both
were later made permanent.

Secretary Waters then read the call for the convention and
the 350 delegates listened with serious faces to the arraignment of
capital and state officials. The strong and vigorous language
brought forth bursts of applause.

"The uniform of the soldier through the Republican administration in Colorado has become the garb of tyrants and of disgrace, in which anarchy stalks in the garb of law," read Mr.
Waters, and the audience thundered approval.

Then followed appointments of committees on rules of order,
credentials, resolutions and press, with other routine convention
work.

When the convention resumed its labors Monday afternoon,
the secretary read the following telegram from "Mother Jones:"

"Trinidad, Colo., January 11, 1904.
"State Federation of Labor, Convention Hall, Denver, Colo.:

"To the Delegates of the State Federation of Labor, Greeting—Let
your deliberations be tempered with a high sense of justice for all mankind—malice toward none, for you are the bulwark of the nation. The
day dawneth when you shall get your own.
"Fraternally in the cause of labor,
(Signed)   "MOTHER JONES."

The convention, by a motion that was carried unanimously,
instructed the chairman and secretary to answer the telegram
of "Mother" Jones. The following is a copy:
"To 'Mother' Jones, Trinidad:

"The greatest labor convention ever held in the state sends you greet-
ing and wishes you health and God-speed.
(Signed)   "J. C. SULLIVAN, President.
"H. B. WATERS, Secretary."

The following resolution was adopted and sent to Senator
Patterson:

RESOLUTION.

"Whereas, The convention, representing 35,000 members of organized
labor in the State of Colorado, has been called to take cognizance of industrial conditions and the course followed by Governor Peabody.

"Resolved, That the situation in this state is so grave that the facts
should be laid before the nation in an authoritative manner. To that end

H. B. WATERS, Sec.-Treas. Colorado State Federation of Labor.

we urge the immediate passage by the United States senate of Senator T. M. Patterson's resolution, directing the senate committee on judiciary, or a sub-committee thereof, to come to Colorado and make a searching inquiry into the conditions existing in this state. Organized labor courts an investigation, and we feel sure that we are voicing the sentiments of every labor organization in the state when we promise the senate committee our hearty co-operation.

(Signed)   "J. C. SULLIVAN, President."

The committee on resolutions brought in the following report which was adopted with but two dissenting votes on a roll call, which was asked for by Charles H. Moyer, president of the Western Federation of Miners:

RESOLUTION.

"Denver, Colo., January 13, 1904.

"Whereas, Organized labor in the State of Colorado is fighting a deathless battle for the right to organize and live; and

"Whereas, The chief executive and the state administration have conspired and entered into collusion with the Mine Owners' Association, the smelting trust, the Colorado Fuel and Iron Company, and the commercial allies known as the Citizens' Alliance in defeating the political mandate of the people, as expressed at the polls in November, 1902; and

"Whereas, The state militia has become corporate hirelings and resolved themselves into a military mob to annihilate organized labor, to train Gatling guns upon the temple of justice, to defy the courts, to invade the sanctity of homes, to arrest without warrant or process of law, and incarcerate in a prison, known as a military 'bull-pen,' men who have committed no crime save to clasp hands under the banner of unionism; and

"Whereas, The governor of this state has declared martial law in Teller and San Miguel counties, and, with the power of armed might, deported law-abiding citizens and branded them as vagrants and outlaws; and

"Whereas, To quote from the Declaration of Independence—'That to secure our rights, governments are instituted among men, deriving their just powers from the consent of the governed; that, whenever any form of government becomes destructive of these ends, it is the right of the people to alter or abolish it, and to institute a new government, laying its foundation on such principles and organizing its powers in such form as to them shall seem most likely to effect their safety and happiness. Prudence, indeed, will dictate that governments long established should not be changed for light and transient cause; and accordingly all experience hath shown that mankind are more disposed to suffer while evils are sufferable than to right themselves by abolishing the forms to which they are accustomed. But when a long train of usurpations, pursuing invariably the same object, evinces a design to reduce them under absolute despotism, it is their right, it is their duty, to throw off such government and to provide new guards for their future security.' And

"Whereas, Free speech has been strangled, the press muzzled and the writ of habeas corpus suspended by military imperialism, backed by bristling bayonets; and

"Whereas, The presence of an armed soldiery in Teller and San Miguel counties was for the sole use and benefit of the Mine Owners' Association in their warfare against organized labor, and not to preserve law and order, as neither was being violated; now, therefore, be it

"Resolved, That the delegates and representatives of organized labor in convention assembled, condemn and denounce the assaults of the state administration upon the rights and liberties of citizenship by trampling under the iron heel of military despotism every principle of the organic law of the state.

"Resolved, That we demand the immediate withdrawal of the troops, so that law and order may again prevail in Teller and San Miguel counties.

"Resolved, That we are unalterably opposed to placing upon the shoulders of the tax-payers the expense incurred by the state militia while quartered in the strike regions during the years 1903-1904.

"Resolved, That the membership of this convention, representing 50,000 members of organized labor in Colorado, will vote for no candidate for the Fifteenth General Assembly who will not pledge himself, in the event of his election, to use his vote and influence against any and every measure looking to the payment of a single dollar of the expenses referred to.

"Resolved, That when the reign of military anarchy is at an end in this state, we urge the membership of organized labor throughout Colorado to come to the aid of the martyrs of 'bull-pen' imprisonment, so that the wrongs and outrages from which they have suffered may be righted in the courts.

"Resolved, That we commend and admire the gallant and unflinching battle of the Western Federation of Miners and the United Mine Workers of America, who have bared their breasts to corporate power, and who are now forcing greed to hoist the white flag.

"Resolved, That we urge the membership of organized labor to establish co-operative stores wherever possible, in order that unionism may successfully measure steel with that band of brigands and pirates who have registered their names upon the roll of the Citizens' Alliance.

"Resolved, That we call upon the membership of organized labor in every city, town and hamlet, and every liberty loving citizen of the state, to march to the polls in November, 1904, and bury the present administration so deep beneath an avalanche of ballots that a million blasts from Gabriel's trumpet will not be able to awaken it from political oblivion.

"(Signed)

> "F. W. HYNES,
> "CHAS. DELOCHTE,
> "J. R. HERMAN,
> "P. J. DEVAULT,
> "W. D. HAYWOOD,
> "M. E. WHITE,
> "JAS. T. SMITH,
> "JNO. OLIVER,
> "A. S. LEWIS,
> "WM. M'ALLISTER,
> "MRS. ADA B. HANNA,
> "F. E. M'CAFFERTY,
> "JOHN M. O'NEILL."

Many resolutions were introduced and adopted by the convention. John Oliver, Denver Typographical Union No. 49, introduced a resolution in regard to this work, which was as follows:

RESOLUTION.

"Whereas, Mrs. Emma F. Langdon, representing Victor Typographical Union No. 275, in this convention, when the employes and editorial force of the Victor Daily Record were thrown in the 'bull-pen' for defending the rights of organized labor, in an effort to compel the suspension of that paper and throttle the friend of organized labor in that district, did jump into the breach, and alone and unaided did issue the paper; and

"Whereas, Mrs. Langdon is now compiling a comprehensive history of the strike in the Cripple Creek district, which will be a true and concise resume of events from its inception to the close of the aforesaid struggle, be it

"Resolved, That this convention does endorse said history and recommend the same to the public in general and to organized labor in particular, so that they may know the facts as they exist."

The above resolution was adopted unanimously.

COMMITTEE CALLS ON GOVERNOR PEABODY.

A committee of the State Federation of Labor called on the governor Thursday, January 14, and made the following requests:

That the troops be withdrawn.

That the vagrancy order be rescinded.

That the deported men be allowed to return to their homes.

The governor gave a specific reply. He promised "justice" to all the miners, etc.

The report of the committee was made by Chairman Thos. Hyder, who spoke of the governor as "wearing a smile that never comes off." Among the things the governor offered against the Telluride miners was that he had "only deported foreigners, ex-convicts, etc., most of whom bore assumed names." The writer, at the very moment the chairman of the committee was making the report, had the honor of occupying a seat next to Guy E. Miller, president of the Telluride union, who had been deported by order of the "czar." I made inquiries of Mr. Miller, "Guy" as he is commonly called, as to his convict number, and also as to

what his real name was, but for the reason that at birth he had
been christened Guy E. Miller and for the additional reason that
he had never been to the penitentiary I could obtain no satisfactory reply to my question.

JAMES H. PEABODY.

While the committee was still reporting the good promises
made to them by the "czar of Colorado," how each and every
man would have "justice," etc., there came a message to the convention from the Cripple Creek district that Sherman Parker
had again been arrested by the military and again confined in the

military prison. The message aroused the indignation of every delegate in the convention. Much discussion followed.

The convention was in open session at the time the message was received. A motion was made that another committee be appointed to wait upon his excellency and **demand** the release of the much persecuted Sherman Parker. Previous to the motion for a committee, Guy E. Miller made a motion that the convention wait upon the governor in a body and demand the release of Parker. The appeal made by this loyal union man, who had suffered arrest three or more times, incarceration in the bull pen and finally deportation, will ever remain fresh in my memory; the eloquence of his address not having been surpassed by any orator I have ever heard. However, I realized then as I do now, that the calling upon the governor in a body could not have accomplished anything. The motion so ably placed before the convention by Mr. Miller lost, and a committee was appointed to see the governor the following morning.

The committee on the following morning, January 15, met and invited A. W. Ricker and the writer to accompany them to the capitol. We were not kept waiting long before the governor rushed on the scene like the hero in a play. He still wore "the smile that never comes off," and greeted us very cordially. The chairman presented our **demand** in typewritten form, which stated our mission. He answered without hesitation that he positively refused our request. We then asked that he at least make known why no charges had been preferred against Mr. Parker. This he stated would all come in time, also that Parker would, at some future time, be given a hearing in the civil courts. He also stated that Parker was a criminal. That but for a few "agitators" the trouble would have ended long ago, etc. Whereupon a member of the committee reminded him that there were "agitators" on both sides.

Sherman Bell, minus his military uniform, was present, but was unrecognized by the committee. He was dressed in civilian clothes, and the writer, not having seen him when not on dress parade, and being so intent on studying the features of the governor, only glanced at the intruder, and if I gave him a thought at all, I thought he was the janitor.

However that may be, the members of this committee expressed their feelings very strongly, also politely, to the governor. I did not say much to him. I did not go to talk. I went to form an estimate of his character. I failed—because I found he had no personality of his own. I believe, from my study of him, that he is simply a tool in the hands of a few corporations that dictate his policy.

The reader will please forgive me for drifting so far from my subject—the convention. But to return: To the writer's mind the greatest work accomplished for the good and welfare of those oppressed, was the appointment of a committee to be known as the Ways and Means committee. By a unanimous vote this task was placed in the hands of the chairman, J. C. Sullivan. After the chair had made his appointments from all parts of the state, by motion it was voted to make Mr. Sullivan president, and H. B. Waters, secretary of the committee, which was carried unanimously.

The convention, after a session of four days, adjourned sine die Thursday evening, the 14th. The convention, in all probability, was one of the most important labor meetings that ever assembled in the city of Denver. The lines which have been drawn between the various crafts of organized labor in the past are rapidly disappearing, and the many logical and forcible speeches that were heard by the convention will have the effect of cementing the different unions in the state into a solid phalanx which will cause the advancement of the class that is now struggling to maintain the rights and liberty of citizenship from the relentless assaults of despotic greed. The Ways and Means committee has appointed subordinate committees to act in conjunction with it, and in a few months the laboring people of Colorado will be standing as a unit against corporate tyranny and oppression. Never in the history of this state have the laboring men and women been aroused as now, and the near future is bound to show results from unity of action, that will bring the human family closer to the dawn of a day when wage slavery and capitalistic oppression shall go down to their eternal death.

Among the great workers for the cause of unionism in the convention the writer enjoyed hearing John M. O'Neill, editor of the Miner's Magazine, and one of the leading spirits of the Western labor movement; a gifted author and scholar. He has spent most of his life in the mines and is one of the most expert workmen that ever handled a drill. He is a quiet and modest man in his demeanor, with a heart as gentle as a woman's but with a latent fire that, once aroused, moves multitudes to action. He wields a forceful pen, and his literary ability is needed so much at headquarters that he has little time for platform work.

The Telluride Strike

By GUY E. MILLER.

The Telluride strike was the result of a demand for an eight-hour day for the mill men working in the jurisdiction of that union.

The present strike is so closely connected with the strike of 1901 that a resume of the situation is necessary to an understanding of the conditions in that camp.

On the 1st of May, 1901, a strike was declared on the Smuggler-Union properties for the abolition of the contract system. This system was introduced by Manager Arthur Collins, a man whose hate of unionism seemed innate and who fully believed that corporations had the right to prescribe the conditions under which the workers would be permitted to live without a word of protest on their part.

Under the contract system the miner boarded at the company's boarding house, was furnished powder and tools; at the termination of his contract the expenses incident to his work, board, powder, etc., were deducted from the amount owed him by the company—a stated sum per fathom. Under this system piece work applied to mining, the price per fathom was steadily reduced and the exactions of the company increased. At its inception the miner was only required to break the ore, but before the strike he had to reduce the ore to a suitable size and throw it into the mill holes.

Some men made fair wages; others quit work in debt to the company.

During the strike the company employed thug deputies, although the union had offered to guard the property and guarantee its protection without expense to the company. Union men were beaten up whenever opportunity offered. The trouble culminated the 3rd of July, 1903, when the deputies opened fire on a band of union men, instantly killing John Barthell. The fire was returned and in the fight which followed two of the scabs were killed and a few men injured; among them Charles Becker, superintendent of the mine.

An agreement was reached between Manager Collins and the

GUY E. MILLER.

union under which the contract system was continued in a modified form. The company or the individual had the right to terminate a contract at any time, but the contractor received at least wages for the time he was employed.

In the campaign of that year Vincent St. John, president of

the union and leader of the strike, was the Democratic nominee for sheriff. He was most bitterly opposed by the mine managers who formed a close alliance with the Republicans, who nominated Cal Rutan. Rutan was elected by a small majority, and has obeyed his masters with more than assinine docility.

During the strike and throughout the campaign, the Telluride Journal, long known as an enemy of organized labor, attacked it and St. John with all the malignant hate that base natures can feel for those who would be free. Assassins and murderers were its favorite terms in characterizing the union men.

On the 1st of January a boycott was put on the Telluride Journal that for more than a month was better kept than the ten commandments. The Journal was tottering to its fall. Mr. Collins succeeded in organizing a Business Men's Association to sustain the sheet. It has since become a Citizens' Alliance—the concrete expression of the Journal's hatred for organized labor. From the day of its birth to the present these twin devils of hate and greed have sown the seeds of discord and now strong men, tender women and helpless infants are reaping the harvest in an exile's camp.

On the 20th of November one of the direct tragedies recorded in the history of metalliferous mining occurred at the Bullion tunnel of the Smuggler-Union mine. The tram house at the entrance to the tunnel caught fire. A carload of baled hay had been dumped at the mouth of the tunnel. On that cold November day the warm air of the tunnel formed a perfect chimney for the smoke and gas. Mr. Edgar Collins, superintendent of the mine, directed fitful efforts to stop the flames, then gave his attention to removing Winchesters and munitions of war from their close proximity to the flames. It is no more than charitable, perhaps only just, to state that he did not understand the significance of his action in attempting to save arms rather than men.

The fire had made great ravages before any attempt was made to warn the men in the mine of their danger. When a messenger was sent he attempted to bring the men out by the same entrance he came in, instead of another, nearly a mile distant, from the flames. All who followed his lead lost their lives, as did many others.

The fire soon attracted the notice of men on the Tom Boy, and a group of them, headed by the foreman, Wm. Hutchison, soon arrived. On viewing the smoke pouring into the tunnel, Hutchison at once gave orders to blow up the mouth of the tunnel. Had that order been given as soon as it was apparent that the fire could not be extinguished, all would have been saved.

As soon as the fire died away a rescue party began the work of removing the debris from the mouth of the tunnel. All that night in the flickering light of a gas jet we worked to bring our brothers to the light. The first rescue party were driven back by the smoke and gas and several narrowly escaped suffocation. Twenty-five men perished; sixteen union men were buried at one funeral.

I have heard the miners accused of being cold-hearted and unfeeling. I have never heard a charge more basely false. The mines were all closed on the day of the funeral and the mining population of the hills with delegations from surrounding camps followed our brothers to the grave. There were but few cries, but gloom sat on the brows and grief clutched at the hearts of those men who saw the interment of a sacrifice. Well they knew that "someone had blundered."

It was a colossal sacrifice to the weakness and inefficiency of a man who should have been wise and efficient. For such blunders—worse than crimes—no one seems to be blamed, least of all the directors who would seem to owe some duty to the men who risk their lives in the creation of dividends. It would seem that they owe the duty of appointing men to places of trust for their efficiency rather than their connections, and the further duty to provide at least all the safety appliances prescribed by law. Neglect of such duties renders them liable, morally, for the consequences resulting therefrom. Place the list of such victims by the list of offences, crimes if you wish, charged against the union, and the latter fade into insignificance.

I might mention here that it is only crimes in which they think there is a possibility of implicating the union or a member of it that are heralded abroad. There are some prominent Citizens' Alliance men that don't care to have Jim Clark's murder investigated. Sam Huston, a union man, was shot under an electric light a few months ago. But little was said or done. The disappearance of men has been charged to the union persistently months after the alleged victim was seen on the streets of Denver. How many alleged union crimes exist in the bloody imaginations of that band of men who have organized vigilant committees to dispose of objectionable men, but who have never had the nerve to call in person?

A year after the Smuggler-Union fire, the community was shocked by the report that Manager Arthur Collins had been shot. He died a short time after. The assassin had stood near a window and fired a load of buck shot into the back of the victim. It was a loathsome, horrible crime. None regretted it more than union men. He had not gotten along well with the union. I should not judge that he was well calculated to make friends with working men anywhere. The old idea of master and servant was too strongly in evidence in his treatment of them. But men do not commit murder for any such reasons. It is not the clash of principles nor the question of manner of an individual that will explain the commission of such a crime. Only a weak, unbalanced mind, smarting under the sense of personal wrong and without the courage to meet the wrongdoer face to face, could have been guilty of such a cowardly crime. Manager Collins had made enemies, but he had the respect of the miners. He always fought in the open. He stood without equivocation. He represented the interests of the company and used the methods he deemed best adapted to serve their interests. It is the camp follower and not the soldier who commits the crimes at which the common insincts of humanity revolt. Such was the murderer. Such deeds are in direct conflict with the spirit of unionism, its principles and its methods.

On the last day of February a snow slide occurred on the property of the Liberty Bell, destroying considerable property and the lives of seventeen men. This was the accident explained by Adjutant General Gardner as an evidence of the "wrath of

God" and a visitation of his justice on the Telluride union. Men acquainted with the general say that his conduct does not evince any close communion with the Almighty. Men who search for natural causes explain it by saying that the trees for a long distance on the mountain side had been cut by the company for mining timbers.

Other accidents might be mentioned, but these are sufficient to show that the lives of working men are subordinate to other considerations with the companies and all have conspired to intensify the bitterness existing between the mining companies and the miners.

The failure of the legislature to pass an eight hour law after the amendment had been passed by such an overwhelming majority, was a great disappointment to organized labor everywhere. It seemed clear to them that neither the solemn sanction of an oath nor the unmistakable mandate of the people could direct legislators under the seductive influence of corporate gold. The lawmakers were against them. If they were to better their conditions they must take by organization that which they should have enjoyed by legislation.

The annual convention of the San Juan District Union met the 1st of August and passed a resolution demanding an eight-hour day for the mill and smeltermen in their jurisdiction, to take effect not later than September 1, 1903. A committee from the millmen of the Telluride union was chosen, their demands formulated and presented to the Telluride Mining Association. The association replied that some of the men included in the demands were under a contract that had more than a year to run and that the scale submitted by the committee called for the same wage for an eight-hour day as was formerly paid for ten and twelve hours. A meeting of the union was called and the demands modified. All men under contract were to work as before. There was a general reduction of 50 cents per day in wages. Men working for $4 were to get $3.50, and the $3.50 men were to get $3. $3 to constitute a minimum wage.

The committee from the union met a committee from the association composed of Bulkely Wells of the Smuggler-Union,

Cooper Anderson of the Nellie and A. C. Koch of the Alta. Mr. Wells acted as spokesman. He stated that he would submit our demands to the association. No reply was ever received and a few days later the San Juan Mining Association was formed.

The mill men under the jurisdiction of the Telluride union were notified to quit work on the 1st of September. They obeyed. The miners were all "laid off" excepting a crew for development work on the Tom Boy and the Smuggler-Union, which continued to operate the mill with the office force and a few scabs, Manager Wells himself donning overalls. A few days later the Federal Labor union ordered out the cooks and waiters on the Smuggler-Union properties. The miners were discharged. The shut down was complete.

The strike had been on some three weeks, when a member of the Socialist Labor party, Philip Veal, was arrested; his place was immediately filled by Frank Jordan, a Socialist, who was also arrested. Arrests followed quick and fast until some six or eight had been made. The defendants were all acquitted or dismissed with the exception of J. C. Barnes, whose case was continued. The Citizens' Alliance, with the mine managers as silent sympazizers and assistants, was very active in the prosecution.

The Tom Boy mine had increased and diminished its working crew several times, and always, it seemed, for the purpose of securing men who considered their job first, the union an afterthought. The force had reached nearly a hundred men, there was an immense ore reserve, the bins being filled. If any employe expressed sentiments favorable to the union, he was promptly "sent down the hill." The mill was put in readiness and the mill men who were willing to accept the company's terms brought in. Men were to be put to the test. The company had decided on a meeting night to talk over the situation with its employes. The union held a meeting and considered it unwise to permit the company to further discriminate against union men or to break ore for scab mill men to treat. The men on the Tom Boy were ordered out on the 21st of October and every man obeyed the call; and later, when the company desired to start up with scabs under military protection, the foreman and nearly all the shift bosses resigned their positions. It was a decisive victory for the union.

Pickets were now placed at Conn's Japan store. This store is practically surrounded by Tom Boy property. Deputy sheriffs tried every means to provoke a quarrel. One night they had been particularly offensive, throwing several volleys of stones at the store and, when one of the pickets stepped outside, fired a shot and called him vile names. They were going to force a fight. The militia was expected daily. The next day four men were sent "up the hill" to change the picket's headquarters to Conn's Smuggler store, where the deputies could not well disturb them without becoming trespassers. The pack horses were loaded with bedding, etc., and the men were proceeding down the hill, when the deputies began making arrests. They pulled one man off his horse and struck him over the head with a revolver and struck another a vicious blow in the back with a Winchester, though he dropped his gun and threw himself on the ground when he was ordered to surrender. That was a lively night in Telluride. Deputies and Citizens' Alliance men were standing on the principal street corners with shot guns and Winchesters ready and expecting to do business. It is also said that each of them carried a revolver. Bulkely Wells came out of the Journal office with a sack of rifles. After all their preparation to commit murder, no excuse was offered them for its commission and they were compelled to glut their vengeance on the prisoners who were arrested that night and the next day. Those at the mine on a charge of trespass and conspiracy, those from the town on the charge of conspiracy alone. The trespass consisted in traveling over a road that had been in constant use for more than twenty years. They were finally released under $750 and $1,000 bonds.

For some time preceding these events the Liberty Bell company had been driving a tunnel, one of their machine men quit and a Tom Boy miner who had been discharged on account of his union sentiments, applied for a job. The foreman stated that he wanted a man, asked his name and stated that if he was not on the list he would give him a situation. He did not get the job, and found that no one who had been discharged by the Tom Boy company, or who had obeyed the union call to quit work, was eligible for employment. This was blacklisting with a vengeance. At the next meeting of the union, it was voted to call out all the men on the Liberty Bell mine.

The calling out of the men on the Liberty Bell and Tom Boy mines was bitterly denounced by the mine managers as a violation of the contract entered into November 28, 1901, expiring three years later. From the standpoint of union men, neither an individual nor an organization is under any obligation to commit suicide. In each case there was discrimination against union men that soon must have led to the disruption of the organization and at the Tom Boy there was a further attempt to use union men to defeat the strike by the production of ore for the scab mill men. Further, the essence of this contract has been violated from its inception by the mine managers. Under the contract the price of board had been raised from 90 cents to $1 per day, the only consideration so far as the miners were concerned was the privilege of boarding where they chose. Some men who were exercising that privilege at the Tom Boy mine were notified by the foreman and shift boss within a month after the contract went into effect that they would have to board at the company's boarding house or quit work.

President St. John protested against this violation. Manager Herron said in reply that all men found it necessary sometimes to make contracts which they knew they could not keep. Violations more or less flagrant were made by all the companies.

About the 1st of October the writer learned that the mine managers were not pledged to refuse an eight-hour day, but simply to grant no concessions that would increase the cost of milling. An interview with Manager Herron soon resulted. A few days later we took the same train to Denver and arrived at a fair understanding. The interviews were continued in Denver with the addition of Messrs. Chase and Wells from the mine managers, and Secretary Haywood and Attorney Murphy for the Federation. Good feeling seemed to prevail—the first essential to a lasting settlement. Attorney Murphy and myself for the Federation, and the mine managers with Mr. Atchison as the representative of Mr. Herron, and Mr. Melville, a personal representative of the governor. The mine managers at this time seemed willing to grant more than we demanded. In broad, general terms eight hours was to constitute a day's work about the mines and mills and $3 a minimum wage. Such a settlement would have given Telluride industrial peace for years. Manager Wells, when asked by Mr. Melville if he were willing to pay the same money to three men working eight hours each that he had paid to two men working twelve hours each, replied that it was not to be considered. "I know that I can't get my old mill men back for less than $3.50 per day." Later at a meeting of the Citizens' Alliance, Mr. Wells stated that if the whole watter was left to himself, Chase and Melville for the mine managers; Miller and Murphy for the miners, the whole thing could be settled in an hour. This on Mr. Melville's authority. It was not to be; the influence of the Citizens' Alliance prevailed. No further negotiations were made. A delegation importuned the governor for troops and they were sent.

Almost immediately after the arrival of the troops thirty-eight men were arrested on the charge of vagrancy, nearly all were found guilty and given two days to go to work or leave. Nine were rounded up and commenced a jail sentence of from twelve to twenty days. One of the boys had $140 on his person at the time of his arrest—it did not save him from doing time. Writs of habeas corpus were served in the vagrancy and conspiracy cases. Judge Wardlaw decided that if there were no legal defect in the papers, the commitment was legal and he would not inquire into the evidence. That you have committed no offense is not a defense—if anyone swears you did and makes no mistake in the complaint or service—you will serve your sentence if you are a striker.

On the 23rd of December, eighteen men, the writer among them, was thrown into jail on a charge of "intent to intimidate." I had been thrown into jail with the "conspirators" for talking to the prisoners from the window of the county judge's office. As I was brought in Sheriff Rutan said, "you must have had your feelings pretty badly hurt," alluding to the damage suits that had been filed against him. At 8 o'clock that night we were brought before Justice Holmes and asked to plead. J. C. Barnes and O. M. Carpenter asked to give bond, $250, the justice was too sleepy to fix the bond. At 4:30 eleven of the men were called out, Barnes and Carpenter among them, taken to the special and thrown into jail at Montrose. When the time for preliminary hearing arrived the prosecuting attorney ordered the cases nollied —though he had sworn out the information. While the men were going to Montrose they were called one at a time—most of them had been arrested for conspiracy—and offered their liberty and assured that all charges would be dismissed if they would not return. None availed themselves of the opportunity. Some were threatened with death if they returned.

The first Sunday night of 1904, witnessed the proclamation of martial law in Telluride; the censorship of the press, telegraph and telephone, and the deportation of thirty-one men.

The strikers were conducting a literary when a group of soldiers strode into the hall, set down their guns with a bang, the officer in command stepped under the electric light and read the proclamation in a voice trembling with emotion. Why he should have trembled I could not imagine. Was it fear? A large portion of the audience were women and children. Was it a sense of his own importance in the game being played? Or did the ghost of his dead manhood rise up and protest against the brutality of his act?

Among the deported were J. C. Williams, vice president of the Western Federation, who had been looking after the finances, and Attorney Engley, who had conducted the striker's defense. We were paraded through the streets under military guard, a squad of cavalry occasionally dashing by; drawn up in front of military headquarters and singly taken before his majesty, Major Zeph T. Hill, where we were asked the following questions: "How long have you been here? What is your occupation? Where were you born?

Thirty-one men, in addition to the seven incumbents, taxed the capacity of the jail, but in the opinion of our generous authorities nothing was too good for a striker, so we took our medicine. The following morning we were given a sandwich and cup of coffee, after which the militia guarded us to the train, preventing the Citizens' Alliance renewing their acquaintance with us; cutting short the "good byes" of husbands, fathers and sons.

We were given a military escort to Ridgeway, where we were lined up on the sidewalk and informed that we were taken out of San Miguel county because we were not wanted there. (We had guessed as much before, but this made it certain.) If we returned we would be thrown into the bull pen and kept there indefinitely. If we showed any signs of disrespect to the militia we would be immediately re-arrested.

We proceeded to Montrose and established headquarters for the deported men. Other deportations followed, one of which is best described by the Denver Post:

SIBERIAN EXILING SCENES.

"Telluride, Colo., Jan. 15.—Tears, curses, maledictions and prayers were heard at the depot this morning when the train pulled out of the station having on board six union miners, who were being deported by the military. The men were given breakfast early, the meal being served from the Sheridan hotel, after which the wife of one of them was reluctantly permitted to visit her husband in jail. At 8 o'clock a bunch of bluecoats, under the command of Captain Scholz, marched to the court house and the prisoners were taken to the county jail and formed into line, ready for the march to the station. A woman with a small child attempted to fall in line with her husband, but was brutally prevented by the soldiers, who forced her back on the sidewalk. With a face drawn with bitter agony and grief she endeavored to keep up with the soldiers as they marched down the streets, but the prisoners had reached the train long before she had gone a block.

"At the depot the men were immediately put aboard the train and two soldiers stationed at the car windows. The relatives of the men were allowed to talk to them, and for a moment the air was filled with tearful good-byes and well wishes. Fifteen minutes before the signal was given to start three women came running down the track. One of them, Mabel Marchinado, a mere girl, hardly 17 years old, weeping bitterly, rushed over the icy platform to the window in which one of the men was sitting, and exclaimed: 'Oh, papa, what are they going to do with you?'

"Her father, Tony Marchinado, endeavored to comfort her, but the girl continued sobbing pitifully. The sympathy of the entire crowd at the depot went out to this girl, and some turned away. Then the soldiers ordered her to move on. The girl suddenly ceased weeping and, turning to those standing, and in a voice loud enough for the military to hear, said: 'I think it's a living shame for men living in this country to be treated in such a manner.' She was not arrested.

"The woman with the small child in the meantime reached the depot almost exhausted. She purchased a ticket and boarded the train on which her husband was about to be sent into exile. She cried bitterly and her baby was blue with cold. 'I am too sick to work and look after our baby alone, and I am going with my husband, if it means the jail,' she moaned. If ever volumes of mute sympathy went out from a crowd, it went out to this woman, whose mental and physical sufferings seemed to grow greater as she bent down her head and fondly kissed the lips of her offspring, in a vain endeavor to hush its cries from the biting cold. It was by far the saddest incident yet recorded in the military occupation of Telluride and the subsequent deportation of striking miners."

The deported men were Tony Marchinado, Tony Sartoris, Leuis Sartoris, F. W. Wells, Matt Lingol and Battiste Monchiando.

My story is done, though the strike still continues and men remain in exile because mine managers feel that it will help them to win the strike. Any comment on the methods used would be superfluous. "The end justifies the means," nay, more, it determines the means. When the rights of the many are to be subserved in the interest of a few, a combination of force and fraud is necessary. The combination has been effected and used, whether successful or not, and if so, how long belongs to the future.

To the future I respectfully dedicate the Telluride strike.

Respectfully,

GUY E. MILLER.

THE MINE OWNERS' STATEMENT TO CONGRESS.

In the fifty-eighth Congress, second session, senate document No. eighty-six, the mine owners made, through their secretary, and introduced by Senator Scott, of Virginia, what was called a review of the labor troubles in the metalliferous mines of the Rocky Mountain region. The document commences with the following vituperous language:

"During all these years an alleged labor organization, known as the Western Federation of Miners, has been endeavoring, with considerable success, to obtain a hold on this particular industry through the unionization of these mines, and the history of this campaign, with its record of murder, arson, dynamiting and riot, to say nothing of the more petty crimes, such as assaults, intimidation, threats and personal abuse, all committed for the purpose of intimidating and coercing men engaged in earning a livelihood, is enough to shock humanity.

"No parallel can be found for it in the labor history of the world, unless it be in the Molly Maguire organization, which maintained a reign of terror in the Pennsylvania coal fields prior to 1877. During times of comparative peace the career of this organization has been marked by nocturnal assaults and secret assassinations, while now and again they have broken out into open warfare amounting to insurrection. Whenever a mine owner has assumed to stand against their aggressions or to employ as laborers men not members of this organization, his life and his property have been the forfeit. Criminal, cruel, untiring, militant, political parties have obeyed their behest, honorable judges have been retired to private life for decisions to them, obnoxious courts have yielded to their mandates, and sheriffs and other peace officers, often selected from their own number, have been their willing agents. When an executive has been found big enough and brave enough and patriotic enough to rise above political expediency and take a firm stand in favor of law and order and the preservation of those rights guaranteed by the Constitution, as did Governor Sternberg, in Idaho, in 1899, and as Governor Peabody is doing in Colorado today, protests such as that embodied in the resolution under consideration have gone up from certain quarters, either inspired by sympathy with the acts and purposes of this organization or with the hope of obtaining some political advantages through them, or, as we trust is the case with the present resolution, by ignorance of the facts which have engendered the condition.

"On account of the machinations and methods of the Western Federation of Miners, the metalliferous mining industry of the West has been in a chaotic state for a period of years. That a person was operating his property one day under satisfactory conditions was no guaranty that he would be able to do so the next. To make a contract with the Federation has always been a mere form, for this organization knows nothing of the sanctity of such an obligation. Continual aggressions have been supplemented by open outbreaks of alarming frequency."

A careful perusal of the pages of this work—which is true, and which is carefully compiled and with much labor in ascertaining facts, dates, etc.,—will demonstrate to the reader the manner in which an "executive big enough and brave enough to take a firm stand in favor of **law and order and the preservation of those rights guaranteed by the constitution**" construes law and order and the constitution. I refer you to the arrest of the Record force, the arrest of Dodsworth, the "nocturnal" visits of the "**constitution preserving**" military to Sherman Parker's home, the arrest of children, the intimidation of courts, the attempted murder of Emil Peterson, the refusal of Chase to abide by the decision of the court, the assault on Mr. Glover, and I might add, the murder of the burro.

As for the charge that "a person was operating his property one day under satisfactory conditions was no guaranty," etc., I refer you to the Portland and the statement of the "**biggest**" **and most honest one of them all—Mr. James F. Burns.**

"In 1901 the Smuggler-Union mine, at Telluride, Colo., became involved in trouble with the Western Federation. The mine was using what is known as the contract system, i. e., the miners were paid according to the amount of ground broken, instead of by the day. It was admitted that a man who was willing to do a fair day's work could earn the union scale, which means a minimum of $3.00 per day for eight hours' work, but nevertheless the Federation demanded that system discontinued. The management refused to abandon the contract system and the strike followed. Some non-union men were put at work, and on July 3 an armed body of union men attacked the mine, killed and wounded several persons, dislodged the non-union men, and took possession of the property. The non-union men were driven into the hills, and with their wounded companions were compelled to find their way on foot to places of safety."

As to the truth of the above statement, I refer you to the "Telluride Strike," by Guy E. Miller.

"So that it will be seen that in all these strikes the Western Federation has not only indulged in coercion, picketing, threats and intimidation, but has resorted to riot, arson, bloodshed and general disorder as well, and in all of these localities, in times of outward quiet, assaults, intimidation, and even murder, have been committed for the purpose of forcing men into the union. There can be no individual freedom where this organization gains a foothold.

"During the past few months the Cripple Creek district has been the center of the disorders generated by the Western Federation, both because it employs more labor than any other mining camp in the state, and because the Federation looked upon it as one of its strongholds and the best place to strike a decisive blow.'

If the above is a fair picture of the construction put upon the strike in the Cripple Creek district, by the Mine Owners' Association, I can say, and say truthfully, that their eyes, in looking at the strikers, were covered with gory goggles, while the eyes with which they viewed their own actions, carried out by the misapplied militia of Colorado, could have been located no where else than in the soles of their feet!

Ye Gods! let us recapitulate!

"Riot." **References:** I desire to call the attention of the reader to the fact that eighty-nine men were arraigned before the courts to answer to the charge of riot, many of whom are prominent mine owners of Clear Creek county, Colorado. These eighty-nine men are the "law and order" brigade who made "nocturnal" assaults upon fourteen members of the Western Federation of Miners and drove them from their homes at the point of deadly weapons!

In Telluride Bulkely Wells, the manager of the Smuggler-Union mine, after securing five rifles from the office of the Telluride Journal, headed a mob and marched down the streets in company with Meldrum and Runnels, desperadoes, who glory in their criminal records, and who feel flattered in being recognized as the partners of Tom Horn, who was executed in Wyoming for the murder of a little boy!

At Dutch Flat, California, several months ago, three members of the Western Federation of Miners were met by a mob, who, at the instigation of the mine owners, tarred and feathered their victims, solely because they delegated to themselves the right to organize a local union!

Local references: Herding citizens of all unions, like cattle upon the streets, Sunday, September 20, 1903.

Breaking up of the high school dance by drunken militia.

Rotten-egging the Novelty theatre by militia-men, December 29, 1903.

"Arson!" **Local references:** The burning of Dennison's (a union man) house on the night of September 2. Incendiary!

Burning of a union man's house in Santa Rita in September. Incendiary!

The incendiary burning of three union men's homes in Cripple Creek in December.

"**Coercion!**" The forcing of the imported Danes to work at the point of bayonets early in September!

The forcing of the Record to cease publishing the official statement, December 5, and on!

The forcing of Glover to refrain from being interviewed!

"**Intimidation!**" The military capture of Judge Seeds' court, September 21.

The suppression of the Record's editorials, December 5.

The threat to shut off the supply of ore from the Dorcas mill, in November.

The arrest of C. G. Kennison while at a funeral, November 22!

Stationing sharpshooters on the National hotel, September 23!

The threats to "blow the Record force's heads off," September 30!

The declaration of martial law, December 4!

The enforcement of the "vag" order, January 7!

The threatened arrest of R. E. Croskey, December 5.

"**Dynamiters!**" **References:** The public might inquire as to who was the most interested in the blowing up of the assay offices in the Cripple Creek district in 1902; where ore thieves, it is said, deposited their high grade.

Who was responsible for the dynamiting of houses of prominent union men who reside at Newcastle, Colorado?

The Western Federation of Miners has been charged with the explosion which occurred at the Vindicator mine, which resulted in the death of two men. The mine, at the time the explosion occurred, was surrounded by the state military and no union man was permitted to come within close proximity to the property. The secret of the explosion could probably be told by the superintendent of the property, and the men who lost their lives on the 600-foot level of the Vindicator.

The Western Federation of Miners was charged with conspiring to blow up the Sun and Moon property at Idaho Springs, and a court and jury have exonerated every member of the organization from that charge.

The Federation has been charged with the blowing up of the

Strong mine, in the Cripple Creek district, in 1894, in which mine Senator Scott is largely interested. Two of the members of the Federation were convicted by a judge and jury in Colorado Springs, the city which has won the title of "Little London" on account of the English aristocrats who have camped under the shadow of Pike's Peak. These two men served but a short time in prison when it became apparent that they were convicted through prejudice, and a Republican governor granted them a pardon. If Senator Scott and the Mine Owners' Association of Colorado believed these men were guilty why was it that Samuel Strong, the original owner, was afterwards arrested and charged with the crime, and why was it that such strenuous efforts were made by Senator Scott and the stockholders of the property to convict Mr. Strong of the crime of dynamiting?

I would like to hear the mine owners answer the foregoing.

"**Murder!**" **References:** In Scofield, Utah, some three or four years ago, nearly three hundred miners were killed by an explosion, which resulted on account of the failure of the mine owners to comply with the law governing ventilation!

In May, 1901, a disaster occurred in Fernie, British Columbia, one hundred and thirty-seven men lost their lives and a coroner's jury brought in a verdict of **culpable negligence against the company,** and this "**murderous**" organization, the Western Federation of Miners, immediately sent a representative with $3,000 for the relief of the widows and orphans. Before the bodies were removed from the mine, Manager Tonkin reduced the wages of those who survived this blood-curdling disaster.

Within the past ten months there have been two explosions in coal mines which cost 528 men their lives—338 in Wyoming and 190 near Pittsburg.

In Park City, Utah, at the Daly-West mine, thirty-five miners were killed by an explosion of giant powder, that was stored in the mine by the company contrary to law and to every safeguard which common sense should suggest!

In November, 1901, twenty-two miners lost their lives by being suffocated on account of a fire which destroyed a boarding house that was connected with the tunnel of the Smuggler-Union

mine, a property that was then under the management of Arthur
Collins. (See Telluride Strike.) The law had not been complied
with, for the doors of the tunnel were not so adjusted as to prevent the flames from entering the mine!

Fifteen men were hurled into eternity at the Independence
mine, in the Cripple Creek district, through defective machinery,
and an incompetent engineer who was imported by the Mine
Owners' Association as a strike-breaker, and in whose ignorant
keeping, for mercenary reasons, was placed the lives of all the
four or five hundred men in the mine. Scarcely had the Associated Press sent out the report of the horrible calamity, when the
Mine Owners' Association, together with Bell and Peabody, intimated that a crime had been committed and that the Western
Federation of Miners was probably responsible. I refer you to
the coroner's verdict in "The Independence Horror."

Again let us recapitulate: In Scofield, 300; Wyoming, 388;
Pittsburg, 190; Park City, 35; Telluride, 22; the Independence,
15; Fernie, B. C., 137; total, 1,087! Nor is this even a beginning!
Let us again recapitulate. **"Accidents" charged to the Mine
Owners' Association, backed by the dead and by jury's verdicts, 1,087! Charged to the Western Federation, backed by
coroner or jury 0!**

O, sweet charity, draw the veil!

If the members of the Western Federation of Miners are men
with criminal records, why has their membership been permitted
to register their names upon the rolls of the various fraternal organizations, such as the Masons, Knights of Pythias, Red Men,
Woodmen, Maccabees, Yeomen, Elks, A. O. U. W., Odd Fellows,
etc., and how was it that Sherman Bell, adjutant general of the
state, was proud to accompany the drill team of the Knights of
Pythias of the Cripple Creek district, which won the world's prize
at the encampment at San Francisco, and who were nearly all
members of the Western Federation of Miners? Why was it, if
the members of the Federation were criminals and law-breakers,
that the mine operators have frequently declared that the miners
of the great gold camp were the best in the world, and why have
they made such strenuous efforts to influence these **"criminals"**

to return to work? Search the records of every penitentiary located within the jurisdiction covered by the Western Federation of Miners, and you will find no member of the organization behind the walls of a prison, and you will find no man serving a sentence on account of his affiliation with the Federation or on account of his connection with any strike. The mine owners document charges the Federation with "**murder, arson, dynamiting and riot.**"

It would seem unnatural, nay, a brutal state of public conscience that these mining accidents—let us call them accidents—can go on regularly and not excite an indignation that would remedy this state of affairs.

Let a girl or a young woman be murdered under suspicious circumstances and the blood hounds of the law and the vigilantes of the press pursue the matter to the last extremity. Column after column is used, the whole matter illustrated for weeks, but let a score of workmen meet their death, through some unlawful act of their employers and after a little squib, oblivion is reached in the matter.

No man is allowed to practice law or administer medicine unless he is declared competent by a proper tribunal. This is done to protect the lives and property of the people from incompetent persons. Why should not the same rule apply to mining? If the law can protect people from quacks and pettifoggers, why should not the mine workers be protected from the ignorance of their fellows? It is true that a pick may strike a pocket of gas and cause a disaster, but nevertheless no man should be permitted to enter a mine until he had shown that he was not a constant menace to life and property because he knew nothing of the perils which lurk in a mine. They tell us these men are overpaid. That their demand for decent wage and safe conditions imperil the prosperity of the country!

Merciful God! The prosperity that demands a constant repetition of these horrors is not fit to survive an hour!

A BRIEF SUMMARY OF "LAW AND ORDER" NECESSITIES AS YET UNCHRONICLED IN THESE PAGES.

The Citizens' Alliance held a weekly meeting in the Alliance hall on the night of. December 8, pursuant to a signed call by the secretary, L. F. Parsons. An astonishing feature of the call was the concluding paragraph which read word for word as follows: **"We herewith inclose you a list of the firms that do not belong to the Alliance. You can govern yourselves accordingly."** Then followed a list of seventy business firms of Cripple Creek. By reference to the constitution and by-laws of that organization, the inconsistency of the Alliance becomes apparent at once. Article II reads as follows: "Section 1. The objects of the Alliance are: 1. To promote the stability of business and the steady employment of labor, whether organized or unorganized, by encouraging friendly relations between employers and employes; and to discourage lockouts, strikes and **boycotts and all kindred movements which savor of persecution.**"

In the first part of this work in recording the forming of a Citizens' Alliance in Cripple Creek, I said be it recorded to the credit of Victor's merchants that the. Alliance proposition was turned down. I am now compelled to record that at about this date (they were not proud of the institution and did not publish their organization), a few of Victor's merchants were led into the erroneous belief that it was a good thing to divide their business and lose the steady union trade they had been enjoying and hustle for the non-union trade. They succeeded in losing the union trade, all right, but as for getting the non-union trade—well, indications are that the non-union workers scattered their trade and the merchants that would not be forced into the Alliance secured the greater per cent of both union and non-union customers.

Reckless Shooting.—December 21, all citizens of Cripple Creek were frightened by volley after volley being fired at the corner of Second and Carr. It was claimed that the shots were fired by the military and it is said it was done for the purpose of creating excitement and a cause for being here.

Broke up Union Meeting.—December 19 a squad of soldiers

under McClelland and Hoag demanded entrance to a meeting of No. 32, W. F. M. They arrested James Baker. (No charge or warrant.)

Search the Trains.—December 19, Captain Hoag in charge of a detachment of troops, guarded the Short Line depot and searched the Short Line train upon its arrival from Denver, for President Moyer and Secretary Haywood of the Western Federation, with the intention of arresting them in the event they came to the district. The soldiers also searched all trains that entered Cameron.

Arrest Portland Representative.—Mr. Charles Reimer, special representative of the Portland Mining Company, was arrested January 6, by the military at the instigation of Scott and Sterling, local railroad sleuths.

Arrest Organizer White.—Mr. M. E. White, of the executive board of the American Labor Union, arrived in the district from Denver December 23. Mr. White has complete jurisdiction in Colorado and has devoted the past thirteen years to the advancement of organized labor in this state. He had hardly arrived when he was "military necessitated," lay in the "bull pen" two days, "verminized," escorted to the train, told that no organizing of unions goes in the Cripple Creek district and told to "never come back." (No charge.)

Bold Robbery by Soldiers.—A daring robbery occurred on Meyers avenue, Cripple Creek, on December 14. James H. Smith of Denver, was the victim, and his assailants were Frank Boyle and a Mexican known as Jose, both members of company H of Cripple Creek. These two "law preservers" tried to "dope" Smith in a low resort, but failed, as he was suspicious and hurried from the place. He had not proceeded far when he was overtaken by the "soldiers" who held him up and forced him to turn over his valuables, consisting of $40 in cash and a certified check on a Denver bank for $300. The blue-coated highwaymen successfully eluded capture.

Nasty Gun Play.—December 4, Patrick Mullaney was the maddest Irishman this side of Dublin. Mullaney has no love for the militia. He had long been in durance vile for no other offense than refusing to salute and kotow to passing blue-coats. He had just been released and when interviewed he stated that shortly prior to leaving camp for Cripple Creek, on the 3rd, an attempt was made by the soldiers on guard to create a fight with prisoners. The blue-coats persistently taunted and intimidated the "bull penners," threatening to shoot them without provocation. The sergeant of the guard leveled his gun at Mullaney and told him to close a window through which he was peering or he would "let daylight through him." At this juncture, Mullaney alleges, a superior officer came along and warned the guards not to get too close to the prisoners, as they were a desperate lot and might take the guns away from the captors. No charges of any nature have ever been preferred against Mullaney, yet he was twice taken prisoner and subjected to the most inhuman treatment by the "constitution preservers."

A. G. Paul "Necessitated."—December 10, A. G. Paul, secretary of No. 40, W. F. M., was transferred to temporary quarters in the county jail by "military necessity." Paul was guilty of the heinous crime of being secretary of a union. Such being the case, he had to be placed in the safety deposit vaults for "safe keeping" and the "preservation of the constitution."

Justice Courts Put Out.—December 4, "military necessity" demanded the closing of justice courts, so Justice Harrington and Justice Patrick "necessarily" closed up. On the 5th, however, Colonel Verdeckberg called up justice Harrington by 'phone and informed him that he could resume business, but admonished him to confine his judicial actions to civil and minor criminal cases. Criminal cases of any gravity must be turned over to the military. And the judge hung out his permit to do business as a justice. "This court is now open for business. C. S. Harrington, J. P."

In Justice Patrick's court the following sign greeted the eyes of all inquisitive visitors: "This court is out of business, by order of the governor."

Military Break up Dance.—New Year's night, while the young people of the P. W. C. club were enjoying a social club dance, several "law and order" preserving militiamen with six-shooters strapped on their hips and accompanied by a couple of Casino women made their appearance at the entrance and demanded admission and that the women be allowed to dance. The request being refused, they stated that they would break up the dance, and they did. The music was stopped and the dancers left the hall, where the intention was to dance until 3 o'clock. But rather than allow the music to continue and be forced to witness the soldiers and their two well-known companions on the floor, the original dancers decided that they had had enough dancing and went home. "Military necessity" being in operation, of course Peabody's "constitution preservers" received no punishment for this brave defense of the constitution.

Military Steals Water.—January 1, the military came to the conclusion that it was easier to steal water than to buy it, so they "necessitated" six or eight million gallons from reservoir No. 8, from which Colorado Springs is supplied. A squad of cavalry and infantry went to the reservoir, locked up the watchman and turned on the water. Colorado Springs was horrified and very indignant, but then a little thing like eight million gallons of water is nothing when compared to "military necessity."

D. C. Copley "Necessitated."—On December 12, D. C. Copley, member of the executive board of the W. F. M., going to his home in Independence from Denver, after an absence of weeks, and while eating a lunch which his wife had prepared for him at 1:30 a. m. the door was broken open, the military entered and without explanation or charge, dragged him away to the "bull pen." In this crowded den he was thrust to keep company with drunken militiamen. Here he spent the night, blistered on one side by the red hot stove and frozen on the other by the raw mountain wind. In the morning each inmate stripped stark naked, and, going to the stove, raked the lice off their tortured bodies. Later they were marched out in the cold and given a scanty breakfast. Mr. Copley was kept in the "bull pen" for twenty-four hours and then told to get out of town and "never come back."

Soldiers Egg an Actor.—December 29, a gang of a dozen or more militiamen gathered around the entrance of the Novelty theatre just before the 8 o'clock performance, begging the doorkeeper to let them in free of charge, and making themselves so generally obnoxious that they were forcing the patrons of the theatre to turn away from the entrance. Manager Smith courteously invited the whole crowd to come in and witness the performance free. They all went in, and with them went numerous eggs of maturity and many in the stage of second childhood. An Irish comedian by the name of Baker had been cracking jokes, one of which ridiculed Peabody or Bell, and when he appeared the "rookies" began pelting him with the eggs of ancient pedigree, spoiling the scenery and demoralizing the performance. The military authorities failed to punish any of the contemptible perpetrators of the outrage. Doubtless it was a "military necessity" for disposing of rations.

M. W. Shelly Refuses to Move.—January 4, Jovial Mike Shelly was notified that the atmosphere his body displaced was essential to the preservation of the "constitution of Colorado and to hie away to denser air." Shelly's health requires rarified ozone and he decided to consult his own inclinations and welfare and remain near the pearly gates located slightly above Victor; so when the military were resting from their labors, feeling secure in the fact that a man "answering the description of Mike Shelly in every particular" had been seen in the neighborhood of Skagway and had inquired the way to the nearest route to the F. & C. C., the cause of their serenity still enjoyed Victor weather and the society of his many Victor friends, although in a different rooming house.

Discourteous Treatment of a Lady.—Sunday, January 17, a squad of militiamen under command of Lieutenant Gunn, surrounded the home of Mrs. Mart Morrison and demanded entrance. Mrs. Morrison was alone and opened the door. They entered and searched her home. The lieutenant began questioning Mrs. Morrison in a "military necessity" tone of voice and finally he and one of the "constitution preservers" seized her and dragged her from the house, in doing so, tearing the sleeve from her waist. With oaths and villifications she was forced to walk from Independence to Victor over rough granite roads with her clothing in the torn condition. She was placed in the custody of Officer

Printy and charged with "disturbing their peace!" To the credit of Colonel Verdeckberg, he immediately released the lady but of course the "constitution must be preserved" and the perpetrators of the outrage are immune by reason of "military necessity."

THE INDEPENDENCE HORROR.

A horrible accident occurred at the Stratton's Independence mine at 2:35 a. m. January 26. Through carelessness, it is said, Engineer Gellese lost control of the engine and the cage loaded with sixteen men ran into the sheave wheel with tremendous force and hurled fifteen of the passengers into eternity. The fifteen men had no warning of the approaching danger and were hurled to their death almost instantly.

The victims were mostly men of family, and a majority of them were new men in the district. Early in the morning hundreds of people rushed to the mine to ascertain if their relatives were among the victims. There was little information obtainable for some time as the military were hastened immediately to the scene and took complete control, not even allowing press representatives near enough to gain facts. As near as the writer could learn particulars they are as follows:

Frank T. Gellese, engineer from Cour D'Alene, was on duty during the night and had experienced no difficulty with his engine, he stated, and at 2:30 he started to hoist the machine men from the sixth, seventh and eighth levels. Sixteen men were on the cage and started for the top. At the seventh level the men noticed that the cage was acting peculiar, and it appeared as if the engineer had lost control of it as it advanced in an unsteady manner. They soon reached the top and were hoisted about six feet above the collar of the shaft and suddenly lowered about thirty feet, then up they went to the sheave wheel and the disastrous accident was the result.

It is believed that the men were thrown against the top of the cage, from the force of the sudden stop, that they were knocked unconscious and knew but little, if anything, after that took place; that in the drop of the cage the speed was so rapid that through the force of the air pressure they were thrown out against the walls of the shaft, which caused them to be literally torn to pieces. When the cage struck the sheave wheel it not only threw Bullock (the only one saved) out, but also threw out a man by the name of Jackson and killed him.

No one aside from the engineer saw the accident. A miner stepped into the shaft house just after the accident and saw a number of hats laying around. He then looked up and saw Jackson in the timbers with the sheave wheel on top of him.

The military and Manager Cornish were immediately notified and hastened to the mine. Engineer Gellese was arrested and held for investigation.

The remainder of the force, numbering about 200 men in the mine, were obliged to be taken out on a small cage that would accommodate but two men at a time, and they did not all succeed in getting out until about 6 a. m.

Most of the men killed fell to the sump below and it was twenty-four hours before all the bodies could be found. There were portions of them found from the top to the 1,400 foot level. The bodies were almost all beyond recognition, heads, legs and arms being torn from the trunks. It was a grewsome sight.

Engineer's Union No. 80, as did other unions, offered their services to render all the assistance possible until the bodies could be brought to the surface. Coroner Doran made all possible haste to find the bodies. He ordered the machinery left untouched until he could have the conditions thoroughly investigated.

The Mine Owners' Association and Citizens' Alliance did not neglect trying to make capital out of this great disaster by trying to place the blame upon the strikers. It was given out that the machinery had been tampered with and other accusations all of which were disproved by the verdict of the coroner's jury.

The coroner's jury consisted of six men beyond reproach. After a thorough investigation and the examination of many witnesses the following verdict was rendered:

"We, the jury, find that the above men came to their deaths at Stratton's Independence mine, January 26, 1904, by the engineer, Francis T. Gillese, losing control of the engine there in use, and pulling the cage into the sheave, thereby parting the cable and precipitating the cage, loaded with the above named men, down the shaft to their deaths.

And we further find that if the management had not neglected the usual necessary precautions, the said casualties might have been reduced, if not avoided. The usual precautions referred to, which were not taken, are as follows:

"First—No man is required to preside at the collar of the shaft while hoisting men.

"Second—No safety device was in use on the cable to prevent the over-winding of the same.

"Third—Men were loaded and unloaded without placing the cage upon the chairs.

"Fourth—The disc brakes of the hoisting engine were detached from their usual positions and were useless.

"We, the jury, would recommend that all safety appliances and the precautions herein named and recommended be adopted and used, not only by the Stratton's Independence mine, but all the mines in the district, not now using the same, thereby reducing to a minimum the damage to life and limb that men working in mines are subjected to.

"We further recommend that a competent extra man should stand near the engineer while he is hoisting or lowering men, whose duty should be to render assistance needed.

(Signed)   "THOMAS M. HAMILL, Foreman,
"FRANK AKINS, Clerk,
"JOHN HORGAN,
"T. S. LELAND,
"R. W. REED,
"J. L. TOPPING."

There was an attempt made by a man in the employ of the Independence to influence the jury. He made the proposition to Rev. T. S. Leland, pastor of the M. E. church of Victor, a man who has the respect of everyone who meets him. It is needless to say that the attempt was exposed and also denounced. In the Cripple Creek district could not have been found six men more thoroughly conscientious and responsible than the six comprising the coroner's jury.

THE WRITER RECEIVES A PLEASANT SURPRISE.

On the evening of February 19, the writer, while busily engaged in compiling these pages, received the most pleasant and appreciated surprise of her life. About 6 o'clock in the evening,

I responded to a ring at the door, a party of about forty of my friends filed into the house, all loaded with the necessaries for a splendid spread. By the time I had recovered they owned the house and had proceeded to entertain themselves. I did the best I could, but my friends were the entertainers, not I. For three hours I was in ignorance of the occasion and was only apprised of it after a splendid banquet which they had brought with them. Then it was that Dr. Hopkins, as master of ceremonies, informed me that the meaning of the unceremonious raid was in appreciation of an act that I had performed and for which I was entitled to much credit, and that they were here to deliver to me the testimony of appreciation of the residents of the district. Such talk from my old tried and true friend was very pleasant to hear, and as he continued I thought of the pleasure of having friends such as these. Dr. Hopkins introduced Mr. Frank P. Mannix, our county clerk, who, he said, would further enlighten me. I quote Mr. Mannix, who I know as a member of my own union and a strong, firm and conscientious worker in the interest of right and justice; not because of the praise he bestowed upon me, but because of the deep, manly and American spirit of justice he so fearlessly expounds in his honorable resentment of oppression by military despotism. Mr. Mannix spoke as follows:

"Mrs. Langdon:—An incident occurred during the 'late unpleasantness' in which you played an important part, and which deserves commemoration. I use the term 'late unpleasantness' to designate a page in the history of the Cripple Creek district which has been blotted and besmeared by Governor Peabody's martial outlawry; a period in which more crimes, under the guise of law, were committed against the peace of the public and the rights of the individual, than the history of American communities records. I say 'late' because we are told by the governor that the 'war' is over; that 'law and order' has been restored. In this the governor reminds me of the woodpecker that Lincoln told about. The bird was plying his usual vocation on the main body of a big tree. He was pecking and pecking away when the wind blew down the tree. The woodpecker always believed that he pecked the tree to the ground. But let's not talk about the governor. When we can't say anything good about a person, as in this case, it is better not to say anything. For my part, I am willing to wait until next November—when Governor Peabody will be tried before the bar of public opinion—for a correct estimate of his merits and demerits as a public servant. If the verdict shall be 'well done,' then I will have to confess that a residence of twenty-three years in Colorado has not familiarized me with the true sentiment of the people of this state.

"On the night of September 29, 1903, after the military had invaded the Victor Daily Record office and taken to the 'bull-pen' almost the entire editorial and mechanical force, for the plain purpose of preventing the printing of the paper which was friendly to the striking miners and opposed to Peabody's brand of legalized outlaws, you stepped into the breach and set the type, causing the Record to come out as usual the next morning.

"Thus the diabolical attempt to smother the press was thwarted—and by a physically frail woman.

"Of course, the principal actor in the tragedy which is being played on the industrial stage is man. But woman's influence over man, for good or for evil, is great, and the outcome of the struggle between man and mammon depends largely upon the efforts of the fair creatures.

"While history records some notable exceptions, as in the case of Jezebel, whose wicked advice caused her king husband's death and her own, the influence of woman is usually on the side of God, justice and decency.

"All that is admirable in the character of Henry VI was the reflection of his good wife, Margaret; Justinian, the Roman emperor, confessed that most of his wise laws were inspired by Theodora; Andrew Jackson, warrior and president, received his chief reinforcement from his plain and unassuming wife; Washington, who burst the shackles which bound this country in foreign vassalage, himself wore a chain around his neck from which was suspended a miniature likeness of her who, whether in the snow drifts of Valley Forge or in the presidential chair, was Washington's chief inspiration.

"Mrs. Langdon, a few of your friends have gathered here this evening to assure you that your influence is being exerted in the right direction.

"The pluck and ability you displayed on the night in question, in getting out the paper after your husband and the rest of the force had been marched to the 'bull-pen,' and in the face of the despotic military edict that the paper MUST NOT BE PRINTED, have not been without influence in the local struggle, and I believe your work will have a national scope.

"You are a heroine, though doubtless it was from a sense of plain duty, rather than from any thought of achieving glory, that you acted.

"While recognizing your modesty in this matter, we desire to consider your conduct as of the heroic kind. Therefore, a few friends, representing the entire community, it might be said, have gathered here for the purpose of formally expressing their respect, gratitude and appreciation in the form of a gold medal, suitably inscribed, on the face being 'Mrs. Emma F. Langdon. For bravery in defeating military suppression

of the press, Sept. 29, 1903,' and on the reverse being, 'From friends of
the Cripple Creek District, Feb. 19, 1904;' which I have the honor of
now presenting to you. May you wear it with as much pleasure as your
friends feel in presenting it to you."

To say that I was pleased, surprised and proud does not express my feelings. I was dazed. I replied as best I could, but
speech fails to express the pleasure I felt in the knowledge that in
the medal presented lies testimony of true friendship that no
wealth can buy, no misfortune turn aside, nor tongue of envy
tarnish.

In these pages I wish to thank my friend Mrs. S. D. Hopkins,
for her unselfish labors and her pure friendship as chairman of
the committe in preparing a surprise, the result of which I prize
beyond the power of wealth.

PERSECUTIONS OF SHERMAN PARKER, W. F. DAVIS, C. G. KENNISON AND THOMAS FOSTER.

Throughout the pages of this work is chronicled the various
illegal arrests and brutal treatment of these honest, law-abiding,
patriotic, strong and firm American citizens, but a brief resume
before the trial at which they were all completely vindicated is not
out of place. In the case of Parker, which is very similar to that of
Davis, Kennison and Foster, all innocent of any crime or intention of crime—he was first arrested at 12:30 at night, September
11, by militia, without charge or warrant or any process of law;
dragged from his bed at the dead hour of night, thrown into a
filthy tent, fed on nauseating viands, insulted by negro cooks,
called murderer, dynamiter, rioter, anarchist, traitor and coward!
He was, with the others, released September 24, by writ of habeas
corpus from Judge Seeds' court under an aggregate bond of
$20,500. Fourteen days incarcerated amid the vilest surround-
ings, subjected to insult and degradation that would shame a
sultan as a novice in torture—and for what? For being an
American citizen! A believer in the principles of our forefathers, a supporter of the constitution of the state and the United
States! During his bonded freedom the victim of continued military oppression, hounded by the sleuths of the Mine Owners' As-

sociation, arrested whenever seen by the military, declared to have forfeited his bond, continually dodging the hell hounds of Bell, Peabody and the Mine Owners' Association, regardless of the guaranty of his bond. Again arrested November 22, without warrant or charge, confined in the "bull pen," subjected to the same indignities for fourteen days more! Delivered to the sheriff December 2, on capias charging him with blowing up the Vindicator, held in the county jail until January 14, the victim of vituperations unmentionable by the press, absolutely controlled by the interests of his persecutors, the Mine Owners' Association, aided and abetted by that deadliest foe to **American independence, a prejudiced governor and the Citizens' Alliance!** Released January 14, under $19,000 bonds, charged with pulling railroad spikes to wreck a train and destroy hundreds of human lives, many of his own union brothers! Was free just twenty seconds; arrested by the military on the court house steps without warrant or charge, taken back to the "bull pen," repetition of the same and even more indignities and torture! Held a military prisoner without bail until January 20! Then brought to Cripple Creek and released from Justice Harrington's court under $1,500 additional bond! Dodged the militia, who were on hand to arrest him, escaped to his home, kissed his wife and caught the train to Denver. Was arrested in Denver as he stepped from the train by a sleuth under military orders, was released by Chief Armstrong, who informed Bell that "military warrants didn't go in Denver." Arrested January 22, in Denver, charged with "harboring 'Slim' Campbell." (Campbell murdered a dance hall girl in Cripple Creek October 2.) Was brought back to Cripple Creek, dodged the military in order that he could get into the justice court to be tried, was dismissed from Justice Harrington's court because Attorneys Crump and Temple (who had made the charges), did not appear to prosecute! Was immediately rearrested by the military, taken to the "bull pen" and held until February 2, when he was again released under an accumulated bond of $28,000 and charged with almost every crime or breach of peace committed in the Cripple Creek district since the inception of the strike or, for that matter, since the district first became a gold camp.

Foster, Davis, Steve Adams and Kennison underwent similar persecutions—were tortured in the "bull pen," released on bond, re-arrested, confined in jail, released by habeas corpus, charged with train-wrecking, charged with murder, and finally held for trial for their life and liberty for crimes of which they were innocent, crimes which their persecutors **knew** they were innocent of, crimes conjured and planned by hired sleuths to railroad them to the penitentiary, crimes that only existed in the fetid minds of men of many aliases, self-confessed criminals, who would do murder to hundreds for a few paltry dollars; men who, like bustard carrion crows, live and thrive in filth and decay, and who, to fill their greedy craws in their banquet of putridity, would make of society complete debauchery; of honor a childish story; of justice a hollow mockery, and of truth a living lie!

And why this vicious persecution? To satisfy justice? No! To do honor to our laws? No! To mete out punishment for crime? No! But to crush out the true spirit of the manhood of the west; the spirit of freedom and liberty inherited from our forefathers, inherited from the exterminators of King George's Tories; the spirit of our constitution framers; that spirit of opposition to oppression which created a nation at whose voice the world trembles and whose basic principle is **justice, liberty, freedom and honor!** And by whom? By these scullion sleuths? No! By the cringing, cowardly, perjured witnesses? No! By the deluded non-union men who fail to see that their employers laugh at their claims of freedom? No! A thousand times no! By the former union men who have broken their oath, betrayed their manhood, lied to themselves, their God and their fellow man? No! Then who are the instigators of these wicked, vile and unjust persecutions? I, a frail woman from the south, a woman who has seen in the last six months atrocities perpetrated in the name of law and the constitution that make me shudder when I gaze upon our glorious flag and think of the crimes against manhood and honor committed in its name and beneath its sheltering folds! I will tell you. The Mine Owners' Association—aided and abetted by a military crazed political accident in the mis-occupied governor's chair, ably assisted by a frenzied, ambitious adjutant general and applauded, eulogized and endorsed by a slave producing and serf-creating Citizens' Alliance! Yes, this association of millionaires, and their kowtowing lackeys have created unto themselves a court of aristocracy to which a comparison with the debauched court of Louis XIV would insult the history of France! Not satisfied with untold wealth, dug from the bowels of the earth by the brave brawny arms of organized labor, they would crush, mutilate and destroy the very brawn that created their affluence.

But I, a woman, will make the prophecy that from the ashes of the fire of the tribulations of these heroes, aye martyrs: Parker, Davis, Kennison, Foster Adams, deported miners, imprisoned Record force, military oppressed patriots all, in the Cripple Creek district and Telluride, will rise a phoenix of united labor, brain and brawn, that will destroy this military oligarchy and cause the glorious emblem of red, white and blue to once more proudly wave "o'er the land of the free and the home of the brave."

DISTRICT UNION LEADERS ON TRIAL.

Friday morning, February 19, was the day set for the trial of Parker, Davis and Foster, charged with train wrecking, conspiracy, murder, in fact, the writer cannot keep track of what they were not charged with, but suffice it to say that there was no crime committed or alleged to have been committed in the district, but what every effort was made by the mine owners and their agents to saddle it on these innocent men.

The court room was crowded with interested spectators and the trial was attended by crowds until its completion. Attorneys Crump and Temple were for the prosecution and Attorneys Hawkins and Hangs for the defense. The main witnesses for the "persecution" were Chas. McKinney, D. C. Scott, Sleuth Sterling, Gleason, Mrs. McKinney and a fellow named Beckman and his wife. Witnesses for the defense were over forty in number, inclusive of the defendants. McKinney, the star witness for the "persecution," was claimed to have turned state's evidence. He is not and the records show that he has never been a member of the Western Federation of Miners, but when he was arrested the

Federation rendered him every assistance in its power, because they thought him innocent of the crime for which he was arrested, and in charity tried to shield him from persecution! The writer believes that McKinney was not in the scheme and that he did not help the sleuths pull the spikes, but was induced to make false testimony in the hope of reward and like the traditional viper, turned his poison on those who had warmed and fed him! That he became entangled with Scott and Sterling and for a paltry money consideration, entered into the plot to send innocent men to the penitentiary **after** the alleged "attempt" at train-wrecking.

McKinney's record is alleged to be a cattle thief in Kansas and Nebraska, run out of Utah for horse stealing, the blood of one man on his hands, a traveler under God knows how many aliases, a self-confessed perjurer, a self-confessed maker of false affidavits, a conscienceless liar and a self-confessed thief. As a witness he proved himself a monster, utterly without conscience, and was shown up to public view as a human weakling, a mental and moral degenerate. He is more to be pitied than censured, for it is utterly impossible for this miserable, trembling creature to tell an intelligent lie, and he is apparently irresponsible for his speech and actions. His only hope of escape from the penitentiary seems to be in the promises of Sleuths Scott and Sterling, who are alleged to have promised him a pardon through the influence of the Mine Owners' Association with Governor Peabody and $1,000 in cash for trying to swear away the liberty and manhood of the union leaders. Poor, miserable McKinney, whose oaths would make him contaminating company to the society of the penitentiary and who by suicide could only partially oblige humanity by his retirement to oblivion!

McKinney's testimony drew Sleuths Scott, Sterling and Beckman (all star witnesses in the "persecution"), into the meshes and showed them up to appear as arch conspirators in a premeditated attempt to railroad innocent men to the penitentiary! He testified that he and Beckman attempted to wreck a train, and that Beckman advised administering poison to the "scabs," thereby suggesting wholesale murder! .Attorneys Hangs, Richardson & Hawkins demanded the arrest of Beckman as a conspirator and protested to Henry Trowbridge and J. C. Cole, district attorney and his deputy: "We protest against the partiality shown in this case and demand that you do your duty at once."

On Tuesday, February 23, Chas. Beckman testified in the "persecution" as star witness No. 2 in the most contemptible plot that blackens the history of Colorado. Beckman succeeded in convincing all who heard him that he "is the most despicable and contemptible specimen of humanity—a sneaking, cowardly spy, a traitor, a betrayer of his oath, a wanton liar and a mercenary criminal with instincts that would cause a yellow cur to commit suicide from appreciation of his own debasement." He admitted his participation in the dastardly attempt to precipitate a loaded passenger train down a three hundred foot embankment! That he joined the Western Federation of Miners to become a spy in the organization! That his testimony was paid for by the Thiel sleuth agency! He admitted nearly evey detail of the dastardly plot entered into with McKinney and showed his contemptible cowardice by attempting to throw the responsibility upon his miserable partner in crime!

The only deduction that can reasonably be made from Beckman's testimony is that he is a natural born crook and scoundrel who plies his vocation under the guise of a detective, and in his profession of spy and sleuth, is not even respected by members of that fraternity, owing to his prostitution of his questionable trade to the filthy channels of divorce business—putting up dirty jobs to sever marital relations and breaking up happy homes! Verily the noose is already tightening about his miserable neck.

On February 24, Beckman implicated Sleuth Sterling as connected with the plot, stating that he had prearranged signals with Sterling whereby he could watch himself and McKinney pull the spikes in the hellish scheme to send martyrs to the penitentiary !

Mrs. McKinney, star witness No. 3, in the "persecution," assisted very materially in exposing the nauseating plot. Her face was alternately suffused with blushes and blanched to marble whiteness as her relations with the sleuths were uncovered. She proved a more artful liar than her miserable poltroon husband, yet she was forced to acknowlege the wanton falsity of her statements, and when cornered she simply admitted that she lied, and with every such confession her eyelids drooped with shame. She admitted that Sleuth Sterling had "kept" her, paid her expenses, bought her meals, slept in adjoining rooms, swore that her husband gave her no money, and when cornered as to where she got the money to pay for $4 meals for herself and Sterling, swore her husband gave it to her! But she is a woman, and in charity I say no more of her—suffice it that when the ordeal of cross-examination was finished she left the court room with shame-flushed face and downcast eyes, closely followed by Sleuth Scott.

On the 25th Sleuth Sterling was placed on the stand and proved himself skillful in refraining from incriminating himself by adroitly fixing the responsibility for dirty detective work on Sleuth Beckman. He tried hard to shield Mrs. McKinney, but did not spare her husband. His evidence was clearly presented and conflicted but little in a few details. Sleuth Scott was called to the stand and sorely disappointed the "persecution." His direct testimony showed a careful and studied comparison with Sterling's, but on the cross-examination he became sadly mixed. He admitted that he lied to Sheriff Robertson, to Judge Seeds, to President Jesse Waters and to many others. Sleuth Scott left the witness box a self-confessed liar.

Hard words, these, but true. The testimony of these self-confessed conspirators and apparently unprincipled sleuths and their accomplices was intended by the "law and order" "persecutors" to send to the penitentiary honest men, known by them to be **innocent!**

But now came a sensation and a bombshell to the "persecution"—the testimony of an honest man! W. W. Rush, who was at the throttle of the "ill-fated" train the night of the "wreck." Under cross-examination the nervy engineer fatally contradicted stories sworn to by Sleuth Scott and startled court and spectators by declaring that Scott had approached him some time **before** the "attempted wreck" and told him that it would be "pulled off." Scott further asked Mr. Rush where he considered the best location for a wreck. Rush answered that the overhead bridge would be the most dangerous place. The "attempt" was later made at the **identical place suggested by Rush!** This blow paralyzed the "persecution," and Judge Lewis immediately ordered the jury to bring in a verdict of "not guilty" in the case of Davis and "not guilty" on one count against Foster.

After months of imprisonment, innumerable indignities and persecution, but little freedom under an exorbitant bond of $15,-000, W. F. Davis, an innocent man, was liberated and free, now fully vindicated and by the very witnesses who were summoned to railroad him to the penitentiary. No witnesses were necessary to vindicate him. No witness was questioned in his behalf. No lawyer's plea made to defend him. Not one scintilla of evidence produced against him. He, as the reader will well see, was the innocent victim of one of the most damnable and foul pieces of jobbery in the annals of degenerate sleuthdom. How plainly did the **jobbers overjob themselves!**

Friday, February 26, the examination of witnesses for the defense began, and then came revelations of the utter debasement of hired fiends who would have perpetrated a crime upon Colorado's fair name that time could never eradicate. The testimony of dozens of unimpeachable witnesses proved clearly an absolute alibi for Parker and Foster. The testimony of Victor Mathers proved conclusively to any mind that the foul conspiracy and alleged crime was carried out by Sleuth Scott with Sleuth Sterling a close accomplice! Section Foreman Powers measured the tracks in the snow the morning of the bungling job and his testimony proved a most perfect link in the unbroken chain of evidence against Scott and Sterling as the actual perpetrators of the alleged "attempted wreck." Under the positively unimpeachable evidence of the numerous witnesses for the defense, the "persecution" utterly collapsed.

Saturday, February 28, witnessed the complete demolishing of every scintilla of every suspicion, let alone of evidence, against the defendants, and the diabolical jobbery of ambitious sleuths and spies and the wholesale perjuries of the star witnesses for the "persecution" had been thoroughly exposed and nothing but the formality of absolute acquittal **by the jury was necessary to** legally establish the innocence of the victims of one of the most heinous plots ever conceived in the minds of persecutors.

On Wednesday vindication came, and on the first preliminary ballot of the jury! The corrupt house of cards has fallen— shattered by honesty and truth! And now I am **proud** to give to the world the verdict of the jury of peers, as follows:

"The people of the State of Colorado vs. Sherman Parker and Thomas Foster—No. 785. Verdict—We, the jury, find the defendants, Sherman Parker and Thomas Foster, *not guilty*.

"E. A. EISWORTH, Foreman.

"The people of the State of Colorado vs. Sherman Parker—No. 784. Verdict—We, the jury, find the defendant, Sherman Parker, *not guilty*.

"E. A. ⌐ISWORTH, Foreman."

The above verdicts were reached by the unanimous agreement of the jurors, after a single ballot had been taken, within five minutes from the time the jury retired! "Out of courtesy to the court," as one of the jurors expressed it, "we remained out nearly an hour before announcing our verdict."

Before the jury came in the cases against Sherman Parker, C. G. Kennison, W. F. Davis and Steve Adams for the alleged murder of Superintendent McCormick and Shift Boss Beck, of the Vindicator mine, November 21, 1903, were nolle prossed by Assistant District Attorney Cole. At the same time he nollied the cases against W. F. Davis, who was accused of pulling spikes in the alleged attempted train wrecks of November 13 and 17. He also said that he would nolle prosse the cases gainst Thos. Foster and Sherman Parker, which he did on March 7.

Thus have the despicable machinations of the Mine Owners' Association and Governor Peabody's "constitution preservers," aided by that workingman's foe—the Citizens' Alliance—fallen to the ground! Out of the hundred or more arrests, villainies unsurpassed in the history of the United States, not one conviction secured! The Record forces' cases all nolle prossed and all other cases either nolle prossed or found not guilty by a jury of peers! An expense to Teller county of over $8,000; an expense to the state of over half a million; a loss to the mine owners of many millions; an unremovable smirch on the fair name of Colorado and an expense of thousands to the Western Federation.

And what has been accomplished? It has been proven that the Western Federation of Miners is composed of men of honor, that their leaders are patriots and martyrs, that crime is foreign to their nature and that they have suffered as did the Christians in the time of Nero!

That the Peabody administration is a remorseless enemy to labor, a supporter and abettor of injustice, no respecter of the courts or laws and a militant usurper of the constitutional rights of the masses!

Oh God, workingmen, union or non-union, will we endorse such atrocities, such unjustness in our high places of honor, such tyrannical treatment of our brother man, such despotism, such serf-creating usurpation of our constitution of liberty, to the foul ends of such a class of greed and corruption? No, a thousand times no! Will ALL labor unite and forever overthrow by peaceable ballot an oligarchy that dooms us to slavery? Yes, a thousand times, yes!

Edward Boyce, Ex-President W. F. M.

WESTERN FEDERATION OFFICERS.

Mr. Edward Boyce, who was president of the Western Federation for six years and a member of the first executive com-

Mr. Maher, Ex-Secretary W. F. M.

mittee, is a man loved and honored, not only by his brothers of the unions, but commands the respect of every man who has ever had the pleasure of his acquaintance. He was president so long and (as a member expressed it), fathered the Western Federation so long that when he was forced by ill health to resign, the members felt as though no one could ever take the place and fill satisfactorily the position held by Mr. Boyce. He has always used his wonderful personality for the benefit of the W. F. M., his fellowman and humanity in general. Mr. Boyce at this writing is in Florida for his health, but while absent in person, his goodwill and influence which will always remain is ever present.

Mr. Maher is another of whom nothing but the best can be said. What more could the writer say of either Messrs. Boyce and Maher than to repeat the language of a prominent man, when showing me pictures of them: ''These men are the makers of the Western Federation.''

Mr. Charles H. Moyer was elected president to fill the place Mr. Boyce had filled so ably for six years. I have the honor of knowing Mr. Moyer personally and can do no more than say that the Western Federation has found that they have another man that has proved himself capable of handling their affairs successfully. Mr. Moyer thinks deeply, considers well, weighs all matters fairly, and when he takes a step it is always forward and never backward—at the same time he is not a man that would tolerate a proposition to retract an action once taken. A member of the executive board in speaking of Mr. Moyer said in part: ''When Mr. Boyce had to resign on account of ill health, I wondered who, in the Federation, was big enough to take his place: I could think of no one that I believed capable. But Mr. Moyer has proven big enough and in every way a revelation to us.''

Mr. Wm. D. Haywood, as secretary-treasurer has filled a position that few men could fill so well. There are not many men that could and would feel the same personal interest in every member's own personal welfare that Mr. Haywood does. He is at all times ready to sacrifice his own pleasures, not to speak of time (he never has any) for the members and friends of organized labor—I say sacrifice his pleasure—but it appears that his pleasure is to please and serve his fellowmen. With Mr. Chas H. Moyer as president; Mr. William D. Haywood as secretary-treasurer; Mr. John M. O'Neill as editor of the Miners' Magazine, and the executive board now serving, at the helm of the Western Federation of Miners, the organization could not be less than it is—the grandest organization of the Mighty West.''

I fail here. I may possibly be able to explain to the reader conditions and occurrences in the Cripple Creek district in a way to be understood; I may be able to describe scenes to which I have been an eye-witness; I may do these things in a way; but to at-

Charles H. Moyer, President W. F. M.

tempt to explain or picture to the reader the many good qualities of the Western Federation of Miners is too much for me—I am not capable. Mr. Moyer, as president, and Mr. Haywood, secretary-treasurer, have urged at all times, to all members the necessity of "keeping cool" and not to be hasty; at all times to **observe the law and not to lose patience.** The reader will well understand by

William D. Haywood, Secretary-treasurer W. F. M.

this time that there were times when it appeared that "patience
had ceased to be a virtue." The leaders, however, being conscientious, intelligent and capable men in the proper place, set
the example, and the others, having confidence and respect for the
brothers they had elected to these positions, followed that example.
The mine owners, or one prominent member of the association,
in talking to the writer, referred to the prominent members of the

W. F. M. as "red-handed leaders," and yet, with all their efforts for the past six months, not to speak of the half million the tax-payers are supposed to pay out in the future—have failed to show anyone now a member of the Federation was even within a mile of the place where a crime was committed! I have felt many times as though it was almost cowardly for us to calmly submit to the insult we have without resistance. I say **us** because I would as soon be stabbed in the back myself, as to stand idly by and see a coward stab a brother in the back, and they **are brothers,** because I am a member of Typographical Union No. 275; they are not members of my one particular union, but the only reason we are not members of the same union is that I use a printer's "stick" and they a miner's "pick" and I have an editor for a "boss" and the brother miner a superintendent. We are both subjected to the same conditions He is on strike today, I may be tomorrow. We both stand for the same—**unionism.**

The people of this nation for a century and a quarter have celebrated the anniversary of that great epoch in American history, and dedicated with parade and speech the memorable Fourth day of July, in commemoration of the notes of liberty that rang from the old casting suspended in the tower of Faneuil hall, signalizing the birth of a republic whose people had groaned beneath the yoke of king-rule. Each succeeding year the people have gathered in city, town and hamlet and boasted of the justice and freedom contained in the Declaration of Independence.

The eloquent tongue and the poetic pen have paid tributes to our liberty and made us feel that here in this country where Columbus planted the cross, the emblem of Christianity, men were kings and women were queens, armored and shielded with a panoply of sovereignty that proclaimed defiance to every species of despotism. Hearts that beat for a broader liberty in the kingdoms and monarchies of the old world longed to leave the crumbling dynasties of regal oppression and tyranny, and cross the trackless deep and build homes upon the bosom of a nation whose constitution was built upon the shattered ruins of deposed imperialism. The scourged and downtrodden of bayonet-bristling

Europe, as they trod the decks of ocean ships mounting wave after wave bearing them nearer and nearer to the land of promise felt and believed that here in a new world where royal domination

James M. O'Neill, Editor Miners' Magazine.

was strangled to death, manhood would develop, and citizenship would be forever fortressed by the inalienable right of "life, liberty and the pursuit of happiness." The great mass, upon whose shoulders rests the stability of this nation, has been lulled to sleep and while they slept in the belief that human liberty was safe, a silken thread was woven which today has become a mighty cable which the power of a Hercules or a Sampson cannot break. On the soil of boasted freedom has risen an oligarchy of wealth that knows no law, that recognizes no liberty save the unbridled licenses of the mercenary brigand. The charter of '76 is as lifeless as the dust of the patriots that sleep in the voiceless tomb, and that document which called to arms the patriots who consecrated its every word in a baptism of blood has been torn from the hands of the subjugated slaves in the isles of the Pacific and stamped with the brand of sedition and treason. The sacred souvenirs of American liberty have been desecrated by the polluted and sacrilegious hand of lawless monopoly, and individual liberty, clad in the shoddy fabric of wage slavery, has been sentenced to death. For more than half a century the domain of human rights has been contracting under the arrogant and untrammeled sway of corporate might, and pirates of the sea of commercialism, drunk upon the wine of opulence, have a vision of the flecks of foam that can be seen upon the rising billows of hungry desperation, threatening to engulf a world in an ocean of blood. We have thrown wide the gates of this republic and beckoned to the millions of European brawn and brain, who were chanting requeims over the grave of buried liberty, to come to our shores and dwell in this paradise where humanity has been taught that "all men are equal," but now in the morning light of an infant century, liberty is a corpse, assassinated by the dagger of military anarchy.

Upon the industrial battlefield for a quarter of a century in this country has been heard the dying wails and groans of labor. The pistol of the hired corporate murderer and the rifle of the uniformed soldier have poured their missiles of death into the ranks of labor, and moneyed nobility has applauded with cheers the wanton slaughter. The soil of every state in the union has been wet with the blood of labor's martyrs, to appease the thirst of soulless greed. The commandment, "Thou shalt not kill," has found no place in the lexicon of commercial avarice. The "government of the people, by the people and for the people," has become the government of trusts and corporations, and citizenship without property has no protection under the constitution of state or nation!

The labor history of Pittsburg, Homestead, Lattimer, Chicago, Couer d'Alenes and the usurpation of civil liberty in the Cripple Creek and Telluride districts of Colorado proclaims beyond the question of a doubt that the reign of justice has passed away and that corporate wealth, backed and supported by all the awe and intimidation concentrated in the machinery of military power are to be used in crushing the rebellion of organized labor against the invasion of solidified commercialism. The Dick military bill, which was written upon the Federal statutes appropriating to the president of the United States far more power than was ever enjoyed by a Russian czar, might well cause the people to ponder and ask themselves, "whither is the republic drifting?" A civilization that demands the implements of war to protect it is doomed, and the great mass whom plutocracy has destined to bear the brunt of conflict will not be carried off its feet by a patriotism that establishes commercial supremacy at the expense of human life. That a nation is only strong whose yeomanry basks in the sunlight of a liberty that is free from the noxious effluvia of an atmosphere that breeds in the human heart the germs of murder. Wrong was never righted by the bullet or sword. The savage and barbarian who use the club and spear have as high a conception of justice as so-called civilized society, that slakes its thirst for blood through the polished steel of Gatling gun and cannon. Wrong maintained and perpetuated by all the modern machinery of war may have a temporary triumph, and right may be put in prison, but the spirit of justice that will be as eternal as humanity itself, shall repeat its demands until the thundering voice of the mighty millions shall shake the pillars of a system that has moulded and invented the machines of blood and carnage! The poverty of the world born in greed shall weld together the links of a chain that shall circle the globe, and the plebian disinherited mass shall come together in a fraternity, whose brotherhood shall sweep from the face of our planet the last vestige of that tinseled pageantry that marked the era of war, bloodshed and murder!

CONGRESS ASKED TO INVESTIGATE

Senator Patterson introduced a resolution in the United States senate demanding an investigation in the Cripple Creek district that will always be remembered, not only by the friends of labor, but by the opposition as well. At once the Citizens' Alliance sent up a wail that could be heard from coast to coast.

Why this agitation? Is it possible that the Citizens' Alliance, who claim to be the only law-abiding people in the district, were afraid to have an investigation? Is it not a fact that they knew they would be shown up in their true light? It seems that they have a very guilty conscience and a "guilty conscience makes cowards of us all."

The Western Federation wants it, understood that they stand for law and order and courted a thorough investigation. They had nothing to fear. Only the guilty need fear. They were willing to let the public be the judge.

Senator Patterson knew the conditions and was true to his fellowmen; true to his state; true to his principles of manhood, and true to the constitution when he asked for an investigation of conditions in the district. The Western Federation courted and demanded an investigation. The mine owners, Citizens' Alliance and their followers **dared not permit the investigation—they also knew the true conditions.**

CONCLUSION.

One last appeal to the voters! Working men and women wake up to the necessity of casting a ballot in your own behalf! The ballot is the only remedy for those who toil and delve. Meet me at the ballot box in November—I will be there—and cast your ballot for your own and your brother's interest, not only then, but **forever hereafter. It is the only salvation of the laboring people.**

Press reports on the strike were not what they should have been in most cases. The Associated Press reports went out from military headquarters and not from officials of the city or county. Had the press reports been fair or just, **this book would never have been written.**

Before making my closing remarks I wish to call the attention of the governor of this state to a statement in the Declaration of Independence. It says, with reference to King George: **"He has affected to render the military independent of, and superior to, the civil power."** It would be well for Governor Peabody and his subordinates to carefully read the Declaration of Independence, the constitution of the United States and the constitution of the state of Colorado.

The time has come when I must close. I do so with reluctance. Much more could be written and every page, as are these few, confined to truth.

I have a few apologies to offer—not for anything I have said, far from it. But for the appearance of this work. It is the work of **one woman—only an apprentice on the linotype.** I have compiled the work, set the type, read the proofs, made the pictures from which many of the illustrations are made, folded the pages and while getting out the work have taken care of my work as usual, doing my own sewing, baking, washing and ironing and other work that falls to the lot of woman. Outside of that I have worked at my trade sufficient to pay the greater part of the expense of halftones and press work. I attended the trials of my union brothers and fulfilled my duties as secretary to orders and membership on committees. I have in all my work on the book searched diligently for **facts.** I have been handicapped by getting the work out in a small office and entirely alone, and more especially by a lack of finance—a very necessary perquisite. I have not slept the full number of hours necessary for rest, I will admit. Therefore I say to you reader, be charitable in criticism of the mechanical part, typographical errors, mis-spelling, etc., but as to the **facts, I would not unsay one word or one phrase recorded on these pages.**

To the management of the Cripple Creek Times, Mr. Griffith, I owe a vote of thanks for several favors extended me by the gratuitous loan of material, also to his foreman, Mr. Foster, for courtesies extended.

Mr. Steele, the greatest cartoonist of the West, on the Denver Post, is entitled to my best wishes for the courtesy extended in permitting me to reproduce the cartoons drawn by him, which you find in these pages.

My story is ended—the strike still goes on. **Reader you have the facts. Weigh them well and be yourself the judge and you may answer from your heart—the right will and must predominate in our glorious state. Therefore the Western Federation of Miners, representing Education, Organization and Independence will win the victory.**

PART TWO

INTRODUCTION

TO PART TWO

WHEN the first edition of "The Cripple Creek Strike" was bound, the work was a complete record of those dark days. At that time I felt that nothing could take place that would surpass the outrages that had been perpetrated upon the citizens of Colorado.

Since that time the corporate tool of the Mine Owners' Association and the Citizen's Alliance—Governor James H. Peabody—and henchmen, who under the brazen claim that they were acting in the interests of law and order, have committed every crime in the category from petty larceny to cold blooded murder.

Governor Peabody had then gone far in his invasion of the peoples' liberties. He had then declared that a strike, for the enjoyment of constitutional rights (which he had sworn to preserve and protect), was an "insurrection against the state," thus placing the workers outside the protection of the law. He had then gone so far that men wondered what new crime he could commit or outrage commend against workingmen. The strikers had borne oppression with such fortitude, and insult with such patience, that people wondered what new act of theirs could win a wider sympathy; what new devotion could claim the gratitude and love of all who would be free.

The governor gave an order revoking martial law in Telluride, when a vigilance committee was organized, armed with state guns and led by men who held military commissions (chief among whom was the present adjutant general of Colorado, Bulkely Wells), and allowed them to work their will not only upon the miners but their sympathizers as well; when deported from their homes, a judge issued an injunction for their protection and they prepared to return, he sent additional soldiers, again declared martial law and restored to the leader of the mob the power of the sword.

He saw a mob stirred to madness at the atrocity of a crime directed and paid for by the men whose servant he was, refused to consider the information that would probably have led to the arrest and conviction of the guilty parties, saw, practically commanded the arrest of innocent men and their incarceration in a vile prison subjected to all the indignities and insults that corporate henchmen could devise; suspended the writ of habeas corpus, and, through the prostituted action of Judges Campbell and Gabbert of the Supreme Court, prevented the exercise of the writ until Moyer's case was taken to the Federal Court. In the meantime, this modern Nero boasted of his success in subverting the Constitution until he feared a collision with the Federal Court, then ordered Moyer's release, and attempted to justify his action by statements so far removed from the truth that Annanias should no longer head the list of liars. His mendacity was only equaled by his cowardice.

The foregoing facts are but a few of his spectacular exploits in support of the corporation brand of "law and order."

Men have been torn from their families and exiled from the homes they had worked years to acquire; assaults innumerable have taken place; the liberty of the press has been muzzled; constitutional right of free speech denied; one man chained to a telephone pole in a bitter snow storm until nearly frozen, because he refused to work on the street by order of the military; women and children intimidated; property confiscated; the homes of union men have been dynamited; union men murdered while defending their families; in all of which the governor of the state and the lawless element behind him acquiesced.

As a climax, through the corrupting influence of the same element responsible for these outrages, over sixty per cent of the citizens who voted in the last state election, November 8, 1904, were disfranchised by reason of the man whom they had elected governor being unseated by vote of a legislature under their control.

The author, for over three months traveled over the state of Colorado, spoke to the people of a hundred towns and cities, in the interest of a political movement to oust from the gubernatorial chair the tyrant, Peabody. This movement was launched by those who had been on the "firing line of progress," in the battle for industrial freedom and the right to organize.

I sought opinions from all classes—laborers, farmers, merchants, professional men, men in public life and men in the privacy of their homes. Everywhere I met a strong feeling of resentment to corporation methods, and was urged to complete this record of the industrial conflict in Colorado. Personally, I felt it should be done. It was due to the men and the women who had struggled so bravely, that their deeds of sacrifice, suffering and martyrdom should be chronicled to serve as an inspiration and a warning for the future.

The age is pregnant with mighty changes. The deeds of these days demand an historian. If right shall ever rule it will be largely because strong men stood for the right to organize, stood for their self-respect and independence as men, and remained firm as the granite hills for their liberties. If the present invasion of constitutional rights continues, if these aggressions but mark the coming despotism of the dollar, it will be left to the workers of some future time to renew the conflict in the spirit with which their brothers have battled and continue it until "no man shall be master and no man slave."

"Freedom's battle bequeathed from sire to son,
Though ever lost, is ever won."

PART TWO

HEN I closed the first edition of this work, which forms Part I, it looked as if the industrial conflict might continue for weeks, months or even years, without either side obtaining a victory or anything happening other than recorded in Part I. However, important events have occurred causing me to again use pen, paper and scissors for the purpose of recording events to the close of the gubernatorial contest.

I closed the first edition on May 1, 1904. I have kept in close touch with conditions and happenings since that date. Nothing worthy of recording occurred in the state up to June 6, with the exception of the famous Moyer habeas corpus case, some matters in connection with the coal strike and incidents taking place at Telluride, the latter being ably covered by Guy E. Miller, president of the miner's union of Telluride, who was one of the first deported. All of the foregoing will be treated in specific articles, in this, Part II.

The conditions in the Cripple Creek district greatly resembled that of two hostile armies before a battle.

The union miners and mine owners were engaged in strengthening their forces and maneuvering for position. A dead calm had settled over the camp, which in itself was ominous, owing to the intense strain under which both sides of the controversy were laboring. One could feel that almost anything was possible, and that it was only the "calm before a storm" and this, unfortunately, was verified.

The golden rays of the rising sun of June 6, 1904, with mocking brightness, brought to light the site of one of the most cowardly crimes ever perpetrated in this, or any other, country—the blowing up of the Independence depot platform with its human occupants, the conception and execution of which it is hard to believe that a human being could be guilty.

This occurrence in the great gold camp marked a new era in connection with the strike. Up to that time we had hoped to see the "Star Spangled Banner" again waving its protective folds over the district, guaranteeing to all the inhabitants the protection it implies. Many people, who like to look on the bright side of things, still maintained that Colorado was in America.

Before giving full details of the explosion and events resulting therefrom, I will first report some incidents in connection with the coal miner's strike, Telluride strike, and a history of the famous Moyer habeas corpus case, these events having taken place prior to the Independence Explosion.

In Part I, I have made no attempt to enter into details of the coal strike. At that time I knew very litle of the causes leading up to the controversy. The strike had not been in progress long when I wrote the brief article, although even at that date the strike in the "Northern fields" had been settled. I shall not at this time offer the following as a complete history of the coal strike, but knowing something of the heroic struggle made by the rank and file of the coal miners, I feel this work would be incomplete if a few pages were not devoted to the coal strike.

November 9, 1903, the strike of the coal miners of District No. 15, United Mine Workers of America, comprising the states of Colorado, Wyoming, Utah and New Mexico, was called and was not declared off until early in 1905.

Officers and members of the organization for months before the crisis used every means to avert the anticipated trouble. But all operators except those of the northern district of Colorado refused the union representatives a hearing.

As early as August, 1903, efforts were made by committees of the organization to have the differences adjusted and grievances complained of considered. The committees went so far as to invoke the aid of the governor and labor commissioner, both of whom responded, and, September 8, sent the operators and superintendents of mines an official communication requesting a conference. In response to the invitation, many of the operators from the northern district were in attendance and waited for representatives from the other districts of Colorado, but as they did not attend, the meeting adjourned to meet one week later—hoping that influence could be brought to bear to induce the managers of the larger southern companies to send representatives to the conference.

The second meeting had in attendance a very conservative committee from the miner's unions of the north and the representatives from the principal mines of that district, in addition to the governor and labor commissioner. After much discussion, the conference adjourned without result. The governor and commissioner promising to do all in their power to bring about a meeting of the operators of the southern fields and labor committee, but were unable to do so.

Later, however, a representative of the Colorado Fuel and Iron Company and the Victor Fuel Company, with legal representatives, with labor commissioner held a meeting in the governor's office. At this meeting it was asserted that the companies had nothing to arbitrate and would not treat with a committee from the United Mine Workers, neither would the companies recognize the organization in any manner.

Affairs, practically, were the same as stated when the cutive board of the United Mine Workers of America held a meeting in Indianapolis, Ind. The matter was brought before the board. The deputy labor commissioner appeared before the board with a written report and endeavored to show the members that a strike at that time was inauspicious and would be erroneous. The result of this was that the matter was referred to the executive officers of the organization, Messrs. Mitchell, Lewis and Wilson.

Before the above meeting there had been a convention of delegates, elected by the locals of District 15, held in Pueblo, September 23-26, at which sentiment was strongly in favor of calling a strike in the southern fields. The delegates believed that a strike would be the only way in which the miners could be reached for organization, and that four-fifths of the miners would respond to a call for a strike that had the endorsement of the National board.

The substance of the demand of the miners was as follows:

An increased scale of wages of 20 per cent, as paid by other districts.

An eight-hour day.

No discrimination against members of the United Mine Workers of America.

A bi-monthly pay day.

A fair system of weights.

April 27, Unions of Superior, Erie, Marshall, Louisville and Lafayette, of the northern fields, made a demand for the eight-hour day. The demand was not granted at that time but the operators informed the unions that other operators were to be consulted and their refusal was not to be taken as final.

Those who opposed the strike and believed that it would prove a failure appealed to President John Mitchell to come to Colorado to use his influence to prevent the strike. It was said that after the adjournment of the National Civic Federation convention, which he was attending, business of importance kept him from visiting Colorado for some time. "Mother" Jones and other representatives came to the state and made efforts to bring about a settlement if possible, but regardless of all efforts, it seemed utterly impossible to gain recognition or have a conference.

At the time the strike was called Wm. Howels was president of District 15, and was notified that the national executive board had carefully considered the advisability of calling the strike and had decided upon the only alternative—to call the strike. The official communication pledged the national organization to render all possible assistance and was signed by President Mitchell, Vice President T. L. Lewis, and Secretary-Treasurer W. B. Wilson.

The call affected about 22,000 persons in the district. I may mention here that the entire membership of District 15, voted to strike or not to strike and the result of the vote was practically unanimously in favor of calling the strike.

October 31, 1903, the miners of the northern fields requested a conference with the operators to take place at Lafayette, November 3. Both sides were well represented. At this meeting a scale of prices was presented for all classes of work performed about the mines, which was discussed. While not agreed to, it was specifically understood, that the question of an eight-hour day was to be dropped for awhile without definite agreement. The meeting adjourned to meet November 5, at the office of the Northern Coal and Coke Company, in Denver, the operators to pay expense of the delegation to that city and a large attendance was guaranteed.

In accordance with the foregoing the meeting was held and the operators were well represented. Attorney Blood, their representative, explained the position of the operators in reference to a request that had been made by the union at Lafayette. Mr. Struby read a reply of the operators, explaining same and attempted to show why it was impossible for the operators to grant the demand made by the miners. The meeting adjourned. When the committee reconvened much discussion was indulged in but nothing definite was arrived at.

November 6, the committee for the unions decided to re-submit their proposition in reference to price per ton to be paid according to thickness of vein, waiving the twenty per cent advance asked for on yardage and machine work. The union, however, still insisted on the eight-hour day and a check-off system.

The operators replied that they would not grant an eight-hour day at that time and that when the state went on an eight-hour basis, they would grant the same. They claimed that it would mean financial ruin to them and the shutting-down of their properties.

Many meetings were held and finally, the operators submitted a written proposition to the union committee which included an eight-hour day, the eight hours to commence and end at the time best suited to the operators, the following was the section in agreement referring to hours:

"That except as hereinbefore qualified the present scale at all of the mines in the entire Northern lignite field, including the Erie district shall remain and continue as it now is.

"That while the eight-hour day is in effect, as hereinbefore stated, there shall be no reduction in pay of the day men by reason of the reduction in hours, and that they shall receive the same pay for eight hours' work that they have heretofore received for ten hours' work.

"The eight-hour day above referred to, so far as the Northern Coal and Coke Company is concerned, shall, for the present, consist of the following hours: From 7:00 o'clock a. m. to 11:00 o'clock a. m., when work shall cease thirty minutes for lunch, and from 11:30 o'clock a. m. to 3:30 o'clock p. m.

"If, however, said company shall find the hour of commencement of work is too early for the successful operation of its mines, then the said eight-hour day shall, if mutually agreed upon after conference, commence at 7:30 o'clock a. m. and continue until 11:30 o'clock a. m., at which time work shall cease half an hour for lunch, and then from 12:00 m. until 4:00 o'clock p. m.

Many meetings of the miners and operators were held in November but no definite action was taken until November 21, when the miners voted 228 to 165 not to return to work. The presence of brilliant and forcible orators, who used their gift of eloquence against returning to work were given the credit for the foregoing vote. The result of the vote was surprising to the more conservative members as the action was taken after receiving a written request from John Mitchell, national president, to accept the terms offered by the operators and return to work. The conservative members claimed they had been granted all and more than they had asked. Members in favor of returning to work felt that another meeting would bring results more satisfactory and efforts were made to arrange another meeting with the end that November 28, the miners met and again cast their ballot, this time the result being 483 to 130 in favor of going to work. This vote put to work 1,270 men, who produced 7,000 tons of coal a day, which helped to avert the threatened coal famine.

This settled the strike in the Northern fields. So far as I am informed, the eight-hour day has been observed; the scale as adopted paid. Arbitration was the means by which the Northern strike was settled and had the operators in the Southern fields shown the same disposition to confer with their workmen, the strike could have been averted and the state saved millions in loss of production, not to mention the misery and suffering that resulted.

As previously stated, the Southern operators refused in any manner to recognize the miners and all efforts to adjust matters proved futile.

When the men responded to the call they practically suspended every mine in the Southern fields. The operators were dumbfounded at the success of the union in closing the mines.

After they recovered from the shock they sent out agents all over the country, enlisting new men, deputy sheriffs were employed by hundreds. Notwithstanding all this, the strike progressed without any lawlessness, which proved a surprise to many who had predicted all kinds of trouble in the "South." The companies became desperate at their failure to secure men to work their mines. Deputies and thugs were employed to beat and intimidate the striking miners. Men were offered as high as $100 of a bonus to go to work, but refused; the union miners were offered big wages to break the ranks of the union, but stood as one man for the terms asked when the strike was called.

Then it was that the imported tools of the corporations resorted to the beating system, law was not taken into consideration and force was established by the companies. Men appealed to the courts in order to retain their homes and in many cases where the courts ruled in favor of the party taking such action, regardless of the decision of the court, the coal companies would throw the men with families out of their homes. Union men were forbidden to drive over public roads.

November 19, C. Demolli and William Price, organizers, were going to Scofield, Utah; when a short distance from the town a mob, composed of members of the Citizens' Alliance boarded the train armed, and forced the train crew to take them back. December 6, 1903, Luciano De Santos and Joseph Vilano were killed by deputy sheriffs at Segundo. William Maher and Henry Mitchell were badly beaten at Engleville, Colo., January 24, 1904, by the deputies, for having gone to the town on union business.

December 17, the houses of five union miners were blown up
at New Castle, Colo. One of the homes dynamited was that of W.
G. Isaac. The night his home was blown up he was in Glenwood
Springs, about twelve miles from New Castle and did not return
to his home until summoned on account of the explosion. Had
Mr. Isaac been at home, the two children would have been killed.
The children slept in the front room, but on account of the absence
of their father, they slept with their mother and, before the family
retired, the mother moved the bed from the wall and called the
old watch dog in. Some time in the night the explosion occurred,
the dynamite set the house on fire and Mrs. Isaac saved the children and herself from being burned to death by crawling through
the broken window and taking with her the two children. Next
morning the watch dog was found, his nose between his front
paws, dead, as if he had never moved, beside the couch on which
the children slept when Mr. Isaac was at home.

And yet, reader, can you believe me, when I state that the
coal companies had the callousness to declare that Mr. Isaac and
others whose homes were dynamited were the guilty parties?

How easy for a corporation to point a finger of suspicion at a
working man and accuse him of attempting to murder his beloved
wife and little ones.

How easy for the masses to accept their decree. It appears
that the great coal barons can not understand that W. G. Isaac
could have the same feeling of affection for his frail little wife,
that proved herself an heroine, and climbed out a broken window
and walked with bleeding feet and carried the little ones in her
arms to a neighbor's, for assistance, that the owner of the coal
mine felt for the, perhaps, helpless wife of his own, that no doubt
in the face of a similar case would succumb to circumstances; that
the little ones were just as dear; that the humble home was as
much home to them as Osgood's mansion to him.

If the truth were to be told, the answer from the employer
would be like the verse in the song:

"You are not supposed to have a heart."

I believe the hirelings of the corporations dynamited the homes of the five union coal miners.

In February, Organizer Wardjon was attacked by three deputies. A striker of Sophris was beat up by Deputy McPherson. February 14, 1904, William Farley and James Mooney, national organizers, were caught by seven of the Reno gang, one mile east of Trinidad, and badly beaten. A union miner was killed by a deputy at Dawson, New Mexico.

March 14, an Italian striker was shot at Pryor, Colo. He was driven from his home and when attempting to run away was shot in the back. Shortly after, John Faletti was beat up at Glenwood Springs by a gang of Reno's men. R. L. Martell, chief secret service man for Reno, figured in the deal. Faletti was district organizer.

There were many cases like the foregoing, men taken from trains and severely beaten; shot in the back; homes dynamited; thrown in jail and all kinds of outrages that could be conceived in the fertile brain of a demon. **All unchronicled by the Associated Press.**

March 23, the militia was sent to Trinidad and martial law proclaimed and the work of confiscating firearms commenced. Midnight searches for weapons was common; men, women and children were dragged from their beds at all hours of the night and taken to the barren prairie to be threatened and in some cases tortured, to try and force them to disclose where guns were hidden.

A. Bartoli, an Italian typesetter of District 15, was arrested March 25, 1904. The following day the Italian paper was suppressed. The same day "Mother" Jones, national organizer, William Wardjon, Joe Poggiani and A. Bartoli were deported from the county and with much abuse they were told never to return.

"Mother" Jones was given five minutes to dress and get her clothing packed and taken to the depot by a rough squad, who forgot they owed their existence to a mother.

"Mother" Jones was quarantined in Utah, April 16. The following day she made her escape, going away with the strikers,

April 19, eleven strikers were arrested at Brodhead. They were deported to New Mexico. April 11, John Simpson, secretary District 15, visited Segunda, and was taken up by the militia and sent out of town on the first train. While there M. Simpson saw ten strikers doing scavenger work under guard.

April 27, fifteen strikers were arrested and deported to New Mexico. All of the deported were presidents, secretaries or commissary committees.

J. D. Ritchie was arrested the same day for returning to the county without a permit from the military. Don't overlook the fact that Mr. Ritchie's home, wife and children were in this county. John Lawson was shot by a mine owner, P. Coryell, at New Castle.

Were I to undertake to enumerate the many tragic events in the coal strike it would make a volume larger than this entire work. Miners were driven from homes they had built on company ground and non-union men and negroes were allowed to confiscate these homes under protection of the military while the builders were living in tents; some were deported and in these cases the militia herded them in droves like cattle and they were driven over the prairie, and if thirsty forced to drink from troughs provided for horses by the roadside, similar to Siberian chain gangs exiled by order of the Czar of all the Russias. I have been told of cases where the miner on foot, growing tired, lagged behind and was pricked by the military bayonet and thus forced to keep pace with the guard on horseback.

Remember, reader, Governor Peabody said that he was not opposed to unions, "all men had a right to belong to unions if they wished, the same as a church; it was no one's business"; also, that he was not fighting unions, "only the Western Federation of Miners and Socialists."

Why, do you suppose, did he allow the United Mine Workers of Colorado, who were **neither W. F. M. men nor Socialists**, to be subjected to such as I have described? I do not need to answer; you know; yes, and **he** knows—**they were union men**; they would not go to work without their demands being granted and the corporations wanted to dispose of them, and they knew the banker from Canon City—James Peabody—would do their bidding.

As time went on, many conventions were held at which the advisability of continuing the strike was discussed. In every case, when the vote was taken it was in favor of continuing the strike. When the strike became, apparently, hopelessly lost, the national organization withdrew financial support. This action was severely criticised by many. The author not being posted in all the details of the financial matters will not attempt to discuss the merits or demerits of the action of the National in withdrawing financial support.

District 15 held a convention in Pueblo, September, 1904, and the writer had the pleasure of attending the convention. Before the convention adjourned I was honored by being made an honorary member of District 15, U. M. W. of A.

No badge of honor on the shoulder of a brave knight ever conferred greater pleasure than this recognition of services rendered the cause of unionism by men who had themselves battled bravely in defense of their homes and constitutional rights.

June 6, 1904, martial law was revoked in Las Animas county. The strike was not officially declared off until early in this year, 1905.

It is to be regretted that the strike of the coal miners was not successful, in obtaining for the strikers the improved conditions they had struggled for. Surely the fight and sacrifices they made, and the suffering they underwent without a murmur was worthy of victory. The writer knows personally of families who subsisted cheerfully on macaroni and water rather than to surrender.

Too much praise cannot be given the Italian miners for their loyalty in the cause of unionism. I am convinced that the rank and file of the strikers would have held out indefinitely on a fare of bread and water, but, when even that meager fare was withheld for want of funds and by military confiscation, there was no alternative but to surrender.

During the strike the Ways and Means Committee contributed considerable financial support. In some instances supplied the families of the strikers with shoes and clothing. No discrimination was made by the committee in issuing relief as between the striking metalliferous and coal miners, the committee endeavoring to distribute the money at its command to those who were most in need of immediate assistance.

After the strike of the coal miners was declared off, there was much suffering among the miners and their families, especially among those who had been most active during the strike, for the reason that they were blacklisted by the coal operators. To some extent to relieve this situation, the national organization arranged to transport as many of the blacklisted miners for whom work could be procured, to other states.

Although temporarily defeated, the sentiment, at this writing is that the coal miners of District 15 will yet be victorious in procuring the conditions for which they went on strike, for it was clearly demonstrated that there existed great dissatisfaction among the miners with present conditions; from the fact that fully seventy-five per cent of the miners responded to the call when the strike was declared, although less than fifty per cent of them were organized. Steps have been taken to fortify the ranks of the miners for a renewal of this contest in the future.

The result of this strike should demonstrate how impotent are the efforts of organized labor in gaining better conditions when relying solely upon the strike in a contest with organized capital in control of the state government. It should teach the wage earners the necessity of not alone depending upon organization upon the industrial field but of active participation in the political field, so as to, themselves, control the state government or at least, through legislation, make it impossible for the corporations to use the power of the government to further their private interests.

> "Truth forever on the scaffold,
>   Wrong forever on the throne,
> But that scaffold sways the future
>   And behind the dim unknown
> Standeth God within the shadow,
>   Keeping watch above his own."—*Lowell.*

Men who have brains to think for themselves and eyes to see into the future feel that there is an invisible power which stands on the side of right and finally carries it forward to success. The enemies of human liberty may seem to succeed for a time, but when they meet this power they are swept aside as autumn leaves before the storm.

The ranks of organized labor contains no more ardent, faithful, self-sacrificing and unselfish worker than "Mother" Jones. No more appropriate name could have been given her than that of "Mother." She considers all working people her children and would gladly, at any sacrifice to herself, take them all under her sheltering wing.

In her denunciation of the oppressors of labor she is merciless. The enemies of organized labor fear her. The union men and women love her. Would there were many more like Mother Jones.

Julien Hawthorne paid the following tribute to Mother Jones, which appeared in the Philadelphia North American:

"I met today Mother Jones. She is a woman of the people, fearlessly fighting the battle of the class she believes to be wronged. She is the strong pedestal of industrial politics. While she lives America can count among her fair daughters one who will ever defend liberty, right and justice. She will be found on the side of the weak and crushed."

With her usual goodness of heart, Mother Jones has kindly contributed the following on the Colorado coal strike:

EXPRESSION FROM MOTHER JONES.

"The coal strike of 1904, in Southern Colorado, with all the brutal methods used by public officials, professional and business men to subjugate these poor slaves of the caves has passed into industrial history. The generations yet unborn will read with horror of the crimes committed by the mine owners of Colorado, with their hired blood hounds aching to spill the blood of their slaves. In the home of religion and civilization they held up the God-cursed dollar and saw on its face the words: 'In God we trust.' The big henchman of capitalism said so when he sent out the guns to kill these wretches. Then he yelled "law and order" to the teamsters of Chicago. Yes, his law and order—the law and order of thieves. Roosevelt went out to hunt four-legged bears, but when the two-legged bears were driving men, women and children from their homes, he had nothing to say. Defeated? No, you cannot defeat such brave men and women as entered into that frightful struggle. They have just retreated. They will unfurl their banner to the breezes of industrial liberty in the near future. The commercial pirates of the Colorado Fuel and Iron, the Victor Fuel Company, with all their degraded curs will go down before an outraged people in disgrace. They will yet call on the mountains to cover them from the indignation of the people.

"You will ask why the miners did not win. First, the generals in charge of the field of battle were not accustomed to deal with great industrial conflicts. Their mental ability was not trained in that line. Some of them could tell you about benevolent feudalism, all about Herbert Spencer, but they had no grasp of the weak points of the enemy. In fact, they remained in their rooms and were not out in the field watching the pirates.

"The men, themselves, were unorganized. It was a new move on their side. They had not learned to do their own thinking. The railroads were in close quarters for coal; in fact, they were stealing cars of coal from each other wherever they could grab one. The coal famine was taking place in the state; industries had to be closed; the people were squealing for coal, when a shrewd, cold-blooded corporation lawyer made a move to settle the strike in the Northern field. That was the first blow the strikers received. I felt then, and have not yet changed my mind, those who were instrumental in settling the strike in the Northern fields were responsible for the defeat of the miners in the Southern fields.

"Working men, regardless of who their generals are, must learn solidarity. They must learn to move as a body. Not one portion to furnish the robber with the leash to whip him and his craft. True, they could get coal from Kansas; but, bear in mind, by the time it reached Colorado it would have cost the consumer a nice price. For the information of future generations, I wish to state that as a body there could not be found more loyal men and women than the Mexicans and Italians were; they deserve the support of every man and woman in labor's ranks. The

"MOTHER." JONES.

world will never know the wrongs those brave men and women bore for a cause they loved. Every depraved cur that the sheriff could muster into service had no more regard for the life of one of these poor wretches than he had for a dog. In fact, he was a sanctified cannibal.

"Before I close I wish to refer to two of the district officers.

"During the five months that I spent in the state, I was in close touch with both those men. I observed their actions, while I realized the conflict was more than they were able to intelligently deal with, yet I know that both John Simpson, as secretary-treasurer, and William Howells, president, are conscientious, honest men. These men will live in history when the savage beast—Peabody and his dog of war Bell will be no more. The sanctified pirate knows no remorse. Brown said, 'Man's inhumanity to man makes countless thousands mours.'

"O, God, that flesh and blood should be so cheap!"

"MOTHER" JONES.

The Telluride Strike

By GUY E. MILLER.

IN concluding the narrative of the Telluride strike no attempt will be made to narrate all the incidents, nor to give them literary form—simply an unvarnished statement of the facts. There is a family likeness running through all the attempts of the corporations assisted by the governor and local officers to crush out and destroy the unions.

It is my aim to recite sufficient instances of violations of the law and the constitution that the reader may not only know who the real law-breakers are, but may also realize the despotic nature of the methods employed, the substitution of corporate rule, backed up by the militia, for the authority of the law and the regular administration of justice in the courts.

From the deportations following the declaration of martial law on the 3d of January, no event of special interest occurred until the first of March, when thirty-four men were arrested in the justice court on the charge of vagrancy, twenty-seven of them were fined $25 and costs and given until two o'clock the next day to pay their fines, leave the county or go to work. Sixteen reported for work the next day, they were taken to the jail by Willard Runnels and put to work on the sewers of the town. One of the men, Harry Maki, refused to work. Runnels led him to a telephone pole, compelled him to put his arms around the pole, then fastened handcuffs on his wrists. The wind was blowing a gale and the snow filled the air. He was left standing chained like a beast for several hours. After many protests had been made against this cruel treatment Runnels took him to the jail where he was kept thirty-six hours without anything to eat.

It might be proper to state something of the men whom the mine managers brought in to lead the fight against the miners.

Willard Runnels and Robert Meldrum were imported from Wyoming by the mine managers for the avowed purpose of discovering the murderer of Arthur Collins. But their only contact with the union was when some man was held up on his way to town and searched for stolen ore, without warrant or any process whatever. Runnels and Meldrum were pals of Tom Horn, the leader of a band of desperadoes who had been hired by the cattle ranchers to fight the sheep ranchers. Horn was hanged at Cheyenne, Wyoming, in November, 1903, for the murder of little Willie Nickell, the twelve-year-old son of a sheep rancher. The evidence indicated that he received $600 for the murder. It was characters like these who lead the "law and order" brigade for the Mine Owners and Citizens' Alliance—men skilled and reckless in the use of the gun. When a corporation pays fancy prices for skilled labor of any kind—carpenters, electricians, engineers or man-killers—it expects the employe to give value received for the wages paid, and they never pay for anything they do not expect to need.

An appeal was taken from the decision of the justice of the peace in the vagrancy cases to County Judge Wardlau; the men had on their persons and produced in court $1,148.25, besides having the union at their backs. The cases were instituted at the instance of Attorney Howe, who at the time was in the employ of the Tom Boy Mining Company, and has shown a disposition to be useful to his employers, though he prostituted his office of deputy district attorney in his eagerness to serve. Judge Wardlau discharged the prisoners.

During the trial, Attorney E. H. Richardson, who had conducted the defense of the miners, was quite severe in his cross-examination of Walter Kinley, a man who had served a jail sentence a few months before for assault with intent to do bodily harm. The examination revealed that he was in the employ of the mine managers. As the attorneys were leaving the courtroom for the hotel E. H. Richardson and A. H. Floaten were assaulted by Kinley. Richardson had a number of teeth loosened. The act met the full approval of the Citizens' Alliance and was favorably commented upon by their organ, the Journal, which also approved the act of handcuffing Maki to a telephone pole, in the following language: "A portion of the men fined for vagrancy on Monday were put to work on the streets today under a military guard. One fellow refused to toil while the others entered upon their task with zeal. Officers intimate that with a few days disciplining the obstreperous individual will be willing to do his part.

The Cosmopolitan saloon, the back part of which was occupied by the Miner's restaurant, was closed by order of Captain Wells on the 24th of February. Later the proprietor opened up and was thrown into jail for disregarding orders. Eventually all the saloonkeepers friendly to the union were compelled to quit business. Friends of the Citizens' Alliance run without let or hindrance.

The affidavit appended below tells its own story of intimidation.

AFFIDAVIT.

State of Colorado, County of San Miguel, ss.

I, the undersigned A. A. Pratt, make the following statement under oath: On or about February 26, 1904, I was in Denver looking for work. A man by the name of Johnson told me I could get work as a miner in Telluride; that the strike was off and there was no martial law; that the soldiers were all withdrawn, and that transportation was furnished free. I concluded to go, and a Mr. Snodgrass gave me a ticket to Telluride. When I arrived at Telluride, on the evening of the 27th, I was met at the depot and taken to the Victoria hotel to stay all night. The next morning a horse was brought to the hotel for me to ride to the Smuggler-Union mine, about four miles away. On the way to the mine we passed soldiers standing guard. When I got to the mine I made inquiries and found out that the strike was on, that the district was under military rule. As the conditions had been misrepresented to me, and I did not want to work under these conditions, I told the boss that I had forgotten something in town and thus obtained a pass to present to the soldiers between the mine and the town. In Telluride I was arrested on a warrant sworn to by Bulkely Wells, manager of the Smuggler-Union mine and commander of the militia, charging me with obtaining money under false pretenses. He appeared as a witness against me, although there had been no agreement made with him, nor with any one else, that I was to pay anything for fare, hotel or horse hire. These were furnished me without me asking for them, and he admitted that he had no agreement with me. There was no one but myself that knew anything about the matter, so the justice found me not guilty, but it shows to what measures they are willing to resort.

I do solemnly swear that the above statement is true to the best of
my knowledge.   A. A. PRATT.
Sworn and subscribed to before me on the 3rd day of March, 1904.
                       ALBERT HOLMES, Justice of the Peace.

The facts in the Telluride strike show that at all times,
Bulkely Wells, manager of the Smuggler-Union Mining Company,
and military commander E. E. Howe, attorney for the Tom Boy
Gold Mining Company, the sheriff and his deputies, aided by the
city administration, acted as a compulsory employment agency
for the Mine Managers' Association and the Citizens' Alliance.

Among all the brutal acts charged to the account of the Citizens' Alliance none stands out in clearer relief than the deportation of eighty-one citizens on the night of the 15th of March. It
was the result of a carefully-laid plot and beyond doubt Governor
Peabody was chief of the conspirators. Martial law was revoked
in Telluride on the 11th, but Governor Peabody had prepared an
order revoking it several days prior to that time and had intended
making the announcement at a banquet of the mine owners; other
influences prevailed, the order was recalled; in the light of subsequent events, it would seem because his friends were not ready to
derive the greatest possible advantage from it.

Almost immediately after the strike had been called, the
unions in a mass meeting decided to compel the enforcement of
the laws against gambling and so notified the council; they reluctantly stated our order as a request. All the gambling house
keepers except two bitter members of the Citizens' Alliance complied with the request. The committee proceeded to the office of
Prosecutor Howe and asked warrants for their arrest; he insisted
that the warrant be accompanied by a signed request to the sheriff
demanding the enforcement of the law, the warrants only to be
served in case the gamblers refused to comply. It was done, they
kept on playing, the warrants were served, the men were arrested
and fined $25 and costs, payment suspended. The action caused
bitter feeling, not only among the gamblers, but among the mine
managers and Citizens' Alliance. They knew that the miners
would be able to hold out much longer with their wages in their
own pockets instead of in the gamblers.' Men stood five and six

deep about the tables when the keepers were arrested and the games stopped. For the first time in Telluride's history as a mining camp gambling had ceased. It was not a moral question— simply one of self-preservation, so far as the miners were concerned, yet they accomplished that which the church and reform element had been unable or unwilling to do.

When martial law was declared gambling was closed and remained so until the order for its revocation. Gambling was opened immediately. About the last act of the military authority, before revoking the order, was to search the homes of the miners for arms. Doors were broken down and trunks broken open, but few arms were found; these were confiscated—notwithstanding that provision of the constitution which declares that "the right to keep and bear arms shall not be infringed."

With their victims naked and defenseless the brave mob was ready for its task. All elements were aroused, for as soon as gambling had re-opened the miners began the work of collecting evidence, assisted by lawyer Kinnikin.

The nature of a conflict can be pretty accurately determined by the class of people whom it calls to its aid. In all battles between the capitalists and the workers the thug, the gambler and the prostitute are ever the allies of the forces engaged in beating labor to its knees.

The Citizens' Alliance organ, the Journal, in its evening edition, stated that there would be a meeting of great importance to citizens and taxpayers. It was a stormy one, completely dominated by its most radical members, such men as A. M. Wrench, cashier of the First National Bank—short, suave, urbane, treacherous, vindictive, malignant in his hate of everything connected with unionism—the man of whom Assistant Attorney-General Melville, after hearing him harangue the Citizens' Alliance, said: "That man is a genuine anarchist. Take away his polish and education, put him at work among the miners and he would blow up the county roads." Another was Chas. F. Painter, proprietor of the Telluride Journal, a man whom brother Masons on a grand jury were compelled to bring in an indictment against for insuring property and converting the premium to his own use;

a man whose scurrilous screeds and bitter invective of unionism and union men is born of his own slimy heart and whose vicious influence is only limited by the putrescent mendacity of a degenerate intellect. These were the men whose words contributed very largely to move men to madness. They went to their homes or stores for arms and met again at the First National Bank armed largely with the weapons of the local military company. The elite of labor's enemies were there, as were those whose support comes from the half-world. John Herron, manager of the Tom Boy, Bulkely Wells, manager of the Smuggler-Union and military commander, Chas. Chase, superintendent of the Liberty Bell; Shockley of the Four Metals; W. B. Vannatta, Kracan, Rittmaster, Adams and others, leading business men, Walt. Kenley and Willard Runnels of the sheriff's office—these are illustrative of the mob of a hundred men who drove men from their wives and homes with jeer, and curse and insult. Antone Matti was compelled to get up from his bed, his wife insulted before him.

When a group was gathered together they were taken to a store that had been used as a commissary by the military and put under guard there. The mob rained curses upon the men and frequently dealt blows. But one mask was seen; many seemed proud of the part they were playing. Sackett, proprietor of the foundry, said that the cooler ones had great difficulty in preventing a wholesale killing. A. H. Floaten's account of his deportation gives a very clear idea of the mob spirit:

"On Monday night I was at home with my wife. She had retired, and I was partially disrobed. I had taken off my shoes and was just getting ready for bed when I heard the knock on the door. I knew what was coming, for I had heard a number of men in the alley at the rear of the house. The man did not knock at the door with his hand, but with the butt of a gun. They broke in the glass panel of the door, and then my wife, who was upstairs, demanded to know who was there. The people outside said they wanted the man who was in the house. When my wife demanded to know who they were and what they wanted of me, they gave her no reply, but broke the lock open and came in, searching the house. I stepped into the bedroom downstairs, and then into the clothes closet, in hopes that they would not find me. I was discovered by Walter Kenley, who shoved a revolver into my face. I said: 'For God's sake, have you come to kill me!' Kenley, who is the same man who assaulted Attorney E. F. Richardson a few weeks ago, answered: 'You get up and come with us.' I asked him if he had a warrant for me, and he answered that he had. I told him to read it, and then he said that he did not need any warrant for me; that I would have to come anyway.

"He and his companion pushed me out of the bedroom into the hall. I asked him to let me put my shoes on. Then without warning he struck me over the head with a revolver, cutting a gash about an inch deep in the left side of my head, at the same time telling me that I did not need any shoes. They then pushed me out onto the sidewalk, and my wife came out after them, begging to let me put on my shoes and hat. She had my shoes and hat in her hand, but they would not allow me to put them on. Just as my wife was trying to give me my shoes someone in the crowd, which had gathered, struck me on the head again with a gun. Kenley then took me by the arm and marched me up the alley from my house to a vacant lot near the city hall. The ground was frozen with mud and ice, and my feet were bleeding before I had taken a dozen steps. I was being pushed by one man and then another.

"Before we had gone a block we came to a large pool of water in the alley, and someone in the crowd yelled: 'Shove the —— —— —— through the water!' which Kenley did. When we got to the first street I asked them to let me walk on the sidewalk, but they continued down the alley. At this time Kenley was walking directly behind me.

"Again without warning he struck me on the head with a revolver, and at the same time someone yelled: 'Shoot him!' with an oath. When we got to the vacant lot near the city hall I found that there were a number of others there in almost my predicament. We were surrounded by armed men, some having guns, some revolvers and some both. We were forced to remain there until midnight. Then we were taken to an empty store room, where we were kept until 1:30 a. m. By this time over sixty men had been gathered there, and we were all marched to the depot, where a special train was waiting for us. As I entered the car, bleeding profusely, with my head tied up in handkerchiefs, someone shouted: 'If that fellow tied up in white ever comes back to this town he will be hung.'

"When the train started a fusilade of about 200 shots was fired by the mob as a parting salute. Fifteen members of the mob accompanied us to Ridgeway, forty-five miles out, where we were ordered to get off the train. Fifty-three of us then walked from Ridgeway to Ouray, a distance of eleven miles, where we arrived at 6 o'clock in the morning. The other men remained at Ridgeway, being unable to continue on the journey.

"There is but one reason why I did not defend my family and my home, and that is because of the union rule which was laid down at the beginning of the strike, to the effect that we must submit and not resist, so as to give them no excuse to do violence. There has not been one cent's worth of property destroyed during this strike."

Stewart Forbes, the secretary of the union is a graduate of Queens College, one of the colleges of great Cambridge university. His wife and three children are in Telluride.

Floaten, Matti and Forbes came to Denver as representatives of the union; for three days they attempted to get an interview with the governor, without success. They appealed to Attorney John H. Murphy, who used the telephone with the same result; he then wrote the governor as follows:

James H. Peabody, Governor of the State of Colorado:

Dear Sir—Yesterday I endeavored to get into communication with you over the telephone, but failed to reach you. The object of my 'phoning was to ascertain whether or not you would give audience to three of the men who were driven out of Telluride by a mob on the night of March 14, and who, with a large number of other citizens driven out at the same time, are still prevented from returning to their homes on account of the threats of the same mob, that if they do return their lives will be taken.

As I understand from the three individuals, they simply desire the audience with you for the purpose of laying before you the facts relating to the outrages perpetrated upon them. Yours most respectfully,

                                          JOHN H. MURPHY.

Three days later the governor stated that he was without "official information." The newspapers were full of the story, they also related the visit of the committee. His attitude is further illustrated by his comments on a Durango telegram sent the day following the mob:

"Does not the situation at Telluride warrant and demand that you send troops there under command of an officer not identified with the mob who last night outraged law and constitution, and that you instruct for protection of citizens against mob rule and for establishment of bull-pen accommodations for those guilty of this midnight raid and outrage? Kindly wire reply at our expense." "The dispatch does not warrant a reply," says the governor, "and none will be made."

And thus it ever was. The straining muscles of the worker pushed back the frontier, subjugated the desert, gave a continent to civilization; his bloody sweat reared and cemented free institutions, but no law is written in legislative halls to protect his bread, and in the temple of justice his cry is unheard. In the gloom of the mine, the isolation of the farm or the glare of the furnace, his work is done—his reward a crust of bread. The primeval curse rests on him and his; in the sweat of his unrequited toil the idlers of the world are fed. And if he rebel, if he strikes, if he throws down his tools and demands that before he uses them again his life shall know more of the sunshine, his wants be better supplied —then poverty pinches the face of wife and child and feeds on his own heart. If he still stand, Spartan-like, the state comes to complete hunger's conquest and sends him back to his task subdued, submissive to those who dole out his bread, hoping faintly that in another world he may rest and enjoy as a divine gift the things his toil should have secured in this.

It is this interference on the part of the state that he resents most bitterly, and yet he has learned to expect it. Experience has taught him that it comes whenever the employer becomes too impatient for dividends to await starvation's slow palsy of conscience and arm. He finds himself a part of things, an unconscious part it is true, until a policeman's billy or a soldier's bayonet awakens him; then he realizes that his interests and welfare are no more considered by the state than at the factory or mine. The directors only consider their dividends, not his needs. He feeds the machine, the machine feeds him; there is perfest reciprocity between them. The machine is oiled to keep it from wearing out too soon, he is paid wages to enable him to feed himself and reproduce his kind—neither get any more than is necessary.

The machine is a social product, made possible and perfected through the co-operation of the workers, but it is used in a non-social way, for it is used to create dividends for its owners instead of for the benefit of its users. Each new machine is a social menace instead of a universal blessing so long as it is individually owned. In every age men have exercised the power they held for their own advantage and to the world's detriment. The owners of the factories and mines have only been repeating history.

The class that owns the machine controls the state and uses it to protect profits as the machine is used to make them. While the worker struggles to increase his portion through the strike it will be in vain. His employer can wait longer for dividends than he can for dinner. The rifle's crack will down his child's cry. So long as he is willing to accept a slave's life a slave's portion shall be his. So long as he demands less than justice he is content with injustice and should bear it.

The last dregs of the cup of slavery is at the worker's lips and a night more agonizing than that of Gethsemane is falling upon him.

Newspaper correspondents had been warned away from the scene the night of the mob and all persons who were not known to be in sympathy with it were ordered from the streets. J. M. Wardlau, county judge, editor of the Examiner and correspondent for Denver papers, was notified that it would not be necessary for him to send out any news concerning the Telluride situation. There are many reasons in the history of the Citizens' Alliance why they prefer darkness rather than light. The censorship of the press was removed in theory; in fact it was extremely rigid.

Extra policemen were sworn in and from fifteen to twenty citizens patrolled the streets, keeping a sharp lookout for any of the deported men. The number was constantly added to.

Attorney Murphy notified Judge Stevens of his intention to apply for an injunction protecting the deported men in returning to their homes. The men were preparing to return. Governor Peabody, when interviewed concerning the matter, spoke as follows:

"There is one thing, however, upon which I shall insist most firmly as long as I am governor of this state. This is that armed men will not be allowed to parade in this state unless authorized to do so by proper authority. The constitution and laws do not permit the mobilization and marching of armed bodies of men without the sanction of the governor, and I certainly shall exert all the authority I possess against such procedure. The law will be maintained in Colorado."

This sounds strange in the face of his connivance at the infraction of the law and his violated oath to support the constitution.

Judge Stevens granted the injunction late on the night of the 23d; at 3:30 the following day the bugle sounded calling troop A into service. Censors were placed at the telegraph and telephone offices and at 4:40 martial law was proclaimed. The proclamation follows:

"State of Colorado, Adjutant General's Office, Denver, Colorado, March
23, 1904. General Order No. 15:

"The following proclamation is issued from these headquarters for
the information and guidance of all concerned, and it will be obeyed and
respected accordingly:

"Whereas, There exists in San Miguel County, Colorado, a certain
class of individuals who are acting in conjunction with a certain large
number of persons outside of said county who are fully armed and acting
together; and,

"Whereas, Open and public threats have been made to resist the laws
of this state and offer violence to citizens and property located in said
San Miguel County; and,

"Whereas, At divers and sundry other times various crimes have been
committed in San Miguel County by or with the aid and under the direction
of said vicious and lawless persons; and,

"Whereas, It is stated by the sheriff of said San Miguel County that
these forces, within and without said county, are about to join forces
within the said San Miguel County for the purpose of destroying property
and for the purpose of inflicting injuries upon persons in said county; and,

"Whereas, By reason of such lawlessness and disturbances and threats
and acts of violence, the civil authorities are unable to cope with the situation, now, therefore,

"I, James H. Peabody, governor and commander-in-chief of the military
forces, by virtue of the power and authority in me vested, do hereby proclaim and declare the said County of San Miguel, in the State of Colorado,
to be in a state of insurrection and rebellion.

"JAMES H. PEABODY, Governor and Commander-in-Chief.
"SHERMAN BELL, Adjutant General."

Troops were sent to Trinidad and martial law proclaimed
there also. In regard to the payment of the troops it might be
noted here that before the troops were first sent to Telluride the
Mine Managers' Association and the Citizens' Alliance put up
$155,000 in collateral securities to guarantee their payment. This
made the militia the hired men of the mine managers and they
were used accordingly. Some of them even went to work in the
mines; whether they drew pay from two sources or not, I cannot
say.

Immediately after the declaration of martial law the pass
system was put into effect and every person found on the streets
after 9 o'clock was taken to the guard-house and asked for an explanation. Many families voluntarily left Telluride in the week

preceding the declaration of martial law; the Finlanders were especially in evidence. Twenty men and women left on the morning of the 24th. And thus the hopes of men who had fled from the despotism of the Tsars were blasted under the stars and stripes.

On March 24th President Moyer sent a telegram to Governor Peabody asking him if he would insure the men protection upon their return to Telluride; he received the following in reply:

"Answering your telegram of yesterday, I have no disposition to interfere with or intercept the movements of unarmed citizens going from place to place in a lawful manner, but armed bodies of men will not be permitted to march in any portion of the state other than the state militia.

"JAMES H. PEABODY."

Interviewed in regard to their return, he said:

"As for the deported men," said the chief executive, "I understand that a dozen of them have returned to their homes. They can all return as long as they behave themselves. There will be no rabid talking, however, and there must be no criticism or threats against the military. Men who make threats or don't behave themselves will not be tolerated."

On April 8th sixty-eight men, who had been formerly deported, returned to Telluride; they were met at the depot by General Bell with about one hundred soldiers and two hundred armed citizens, who were on duty in the town, and marched to the Red Men's Opera House. There they and their baggage were searched for weapons, relieved of their cash, then they were fed. More than one thousand people were present when the train arrived. The crowd pressed forward until the soldiers warned them back. Among them were the wives and children of the deported men, watching for the return of husbands and fathers with white, strained faces and tear-dimmed eyes. No greetings were permitted. That night they were marched back to the cars from which they had alighted. General Bell took command, accompanied by Captain Wells and thirty troopers. The men were unloaded at the Dallas divide on the extreme northern line of San Miguel county, and warned not to return.

The facts in the deportation and redeportation of the men furnish sufficient comment upon Governor Peabody's pretensions as an upholder of law and order. In their light, men might well be wary of reposing any confidence in his promises.

This was the last concerted attempt of the men to return. Individuals and small squads returned later; they were always sent back. Others were added from time to time to the list of men who were personna non grata to the mine managers. To note them all would only weary the reader.

On April 30th the remaining union men in Telluride were advised by Captain Wells that it would be best for them to leave town as he could not guarantee them immunity from personal violence in the event of another raid by the citizens. The Citizens' Alliance resumed the night patrol and Major Rogers swore in the three hundred members as special policemen.

Viewed from another standpoint Judge Stevens' peremptory adjournment of the May term of court emphasizes the contempt which the Citizens' Alliance has ever shown for all authority which it could not control. When the judge arrived at the depot all the soldiers in the camp were present, jumped on the cars, jostled the people in their search for returning deportees and by their conduct generally showed their contempt for civil authority.

When the sheriff opened court the following day Judge Stevens delivered the following order:

"Gentlemen of the bar, I came here yesterday for the purpose of opening court and transacting such business as I felt the conditions would justify.

"I find a different condition here than what I had expected. The demonstration at the depot last night upon the arrival of the train could only have been planned and executed for the purpose of showing the contempt of the militia and a certain portion of this community for the civil authority of the state and the civil authority of this district. I had always been led to suppose from such research that I have been able to make that in a republic like ours the people were supreme; that the people had expressed their will in a constitution which was enacted for the government of all authority in this state. That constitution provides that the military shall always be in strict subordination to the civil authorities. It is doubtless construed differently, however, by the executive, who has declared this county to be in a state of insurrection and has declared martial law within its limit. In effect, therefore, the executive has said that there is no law in this county, except the military commander.

"I can only believe from the indications, from the demonstrations that have been made, and the conditions which seem to exist here, that the executive and the militia and a portion of the people of this county are willing that this court should be opened and such business transacted and such orders of the court executed as meet the approval of the military commander and a portion of the people of the county, may be executed; but that such portion of the orders of this court, or the decrees of this court as do not meet with the approval of this militia and the people of this county, may not be executed. Under such circumstances the court would not be in a position to enforce its lawful orders, or what it conveys to be its lawful orders.

"Such being the case, it would simply be a farce to attempt to enforce the civil law in this county. It seems to the court, further, that the members of the bar of this county, with a few exceptions, have become imbued with the military spirit to such an extent that they would not feel right assisting this court in the proper transaction of the business of the term. Under such circumstances the court will be greatly hampered should it attempt to do business. For that reason I have decided that until a different condition exists, until the supremacy of the civil authorities is acknowledged in this county, I shall not attempt to transact any business within its limits.

"It is, therefore, ordered that all matters pending and undetermined in this court be continued until the next term.

"It is further ordered that court be adjourned sine die."

The reader should remember that the machinery of deportation during these weeks when nothing is said was in constant operation, the order to depart being usually given by Captain Wells. The following instance is typical:

Tony Ralla, a property holder, who formerly owned the Senate saloon in this city, was today notified by a deputy sheriff that it would be best for him to leave the county. When he attempted to argue the matter with the officer, he was referred to Captain Wells. He had an interview with Captain Wells later, but it ended without any definite understanding whether or not Ralla would be compelled to leave the county. But for the delicate condition of his wife the man would have been deported with others a month or so ago. Ralla states that he will not go unless positively compelled to do so by the authorities.

The latter part of June Harry Floaten was compelled to leave town for the second time. In the absence of his brother he was manager of the People's Supply Company, carrying a stock of $25,000. The only accusation was one by Captain Wells, stating that he received funds of the Miners' Union on deposit. His statement covers many instances:

"Having been compelled to leave my home and business in Telluride I will give the public a statement of facts in my case. I am secretary of the People's Supply Company, doing a general merchandise business in the city of Telluride. On June 3, I was notified by Captain Bulkely Wells that I must leave on June 7. Several of my friends went to Mr. Wells and protested. I had a talk with him also and told him I was going to Denver on the 15th, but intended to return by July 1. He said that would be all right. On the 15th martial law was declared off in San Miguel County. When I had transacted my business in Denver I made up my mind to return home, as I thought civil rights would be respected once more. Before I left I called upon Acting Governor Haggott and stated my case. He assured me that I could go home and there would be no interference. I arrived in Telluride on the night of the 23rd, and, in stepping off the train, was told by the night marshal that I was under arrest. I asked what the charge was. He said: 'You will find out.' I was taken to the sheriff's office and told to remain there. After a while I requested the sheriff to show cause for my detention. He told me to wait a few minutes, and when the minutes were up told me I could go. At my home in the evening later I was waited on by a committee of five. They stated that but for their interference a mob would have had me before this time, and advised me not to stay, but if I would leave on the morning train I could stay over night. I took their advice.

"What are things coming to in this state? I have lived in Telluride over thirteen years, and there isn't a person that can point out that I ever disobeyed any law. All I have on this earth is there—my home, my wife, child and business. They say I have been doing business with the union. It is true, but is that a crime?

"The Citizens' Alliance has boycotted our store, and now they ask that we discontinue to sell to people that will patronize us. As for the miners' union, let me say that that body of men has shown the most exemplary conduct during the strike. Goaded to desperation through tyrannical oppression, they have not resisted and have never interfered with non-union men. The lessons the union has received from this strike must be demoralizing to them. It shows that when they are using force in a strike they win. When they are law-abiding and the other side is using force, they get the worst of it. But the only solution of it is peaceable means. Workers, do your duty next election.

"(Signed)   HARRY A. FLOATEN."
Ouray, Colorado."

The Smuggler-Union mine closed down the first of July. For many months it had been reported that they were running behind from $10,000 to $15,000 per month. Manager Wells in issuing his statement said that they could not secure sufficient skilled labor from the fear that a tragedy would befall the men who took the miners' places. Mr. Wells simply made the mistake of calling loyalty to unionism, fear. It is certain that the skilled men could not be secured. A few weeks later the men on the Mayflower, a mine employing about thirty men quit work because the management leased a mill and put on twelve hour shifts. Incidents like these reveal the devotion of men to their union, and the fundamental mistake of the corporations in considering the eight-hour day a demand made by agitators instead of the desire of the men.

Marshal Geyer escorted Grover Skelton, a 19-year-old lad out of town and told him to go on; instead he returned to his mother's home in Pandora. Geyer learned of his return and went to his home after him. Grover was at supper. Mrs. Skelton stood in the doorway as Geyer came up and when he went to enter she put up her hand to keep him out or ward off his blows. Geyer struck her over the head with his revolver, knocking her down. From his advent on the premises he had been using the vilest and most abusive language. A sister of Skelton's, Mrs. Bacheller, heard the disturbance and abuse of her mother. She came—a cripple —Geyer knocked her down on the porch, then kicked her off. Young Skelton was then handcuffed to Dan McMillan and taken back to the edge of town. Geyer was one of the bulwarks of the Alliance from the inception of the strike.

The Alliance hounded Cory, whom the people elected marshal and who refused to do their dirty work, until he resigned his place. Geyer took it and has worked in perfect accord with his masters

The only respect for property on the part of the mine managers, is that which they happen to own or control. On August 21st John Herron, manager of the Tom Boy, David Herron, supererintendent; W. T. Tobin, bookkeeper; Willard Runnels, deputy sheriff and an office man of the company named Stevenson, rode over the range from the Tom Boy mine to the property of the

Black Bear Mining Company. The entire party threw stones down the air shaft and rolled them against the shaft house till the men on the inside rushed out. They were lined up and four of them, staunch union men, were marched over the range to Silverton. All of them were stockholders in the company whose property they were developing.

But all things finally come to an end and thus the Telluride strike. The latter part of November the large mines posted notices stating that the eight-hour day would go into effect the first of December, together with a scale of wages practically identical with that which the union had demanded fifteen months before, and which the mine managers had practically agreed to more than a year before when the troops were secured by the Citizens Alliance.

The new scale is given here:

Underground, Eight-Hour Shifts—Miners, $3; machine men, $4; trammers and shovelers, $3; drivers, caring for horses, $3.25; drivers, not caring for horses, $3; timbermen, $3.50; timbermen, helpers and laborers, $3; nippers, $3; hoisters, engineers, $4; station tenders, $3; cage tenders, $3.50.

Outside of Mines, Eight Hours—Engineers, $3.50; engineers if hoisting men, $4; firemen, $3; blacksmiths, $3.75; blacksmith helpers, $3; tool sharpeners, $3.25; laborers, $3.

Tramway, Eight Hours—Gripmen and loaders, $3; brakemen, $3.75; linemen, $4.

Mill, Cyanide Works, Etc., Eight Hours—Crusher men, $3; battery men, $3.50; battery men helpers, $3; Huntington and Chile mill men, $3; concentrator men, $3.50; concentrator men helpers, $3; engineers, $3; firemen, $3; blacksmiths, $3.75; carpenters, $3.75; laborers and shovelers, $3; canvas plant employes, $3; solution men, $3.50.

Boarding Houses—Head cook, if over 100 men, $100 per month and board; night cook and baker, if over 100 men, $90 a month and board. If over 175 men, the head cook will be furnished with a meat cutter at $80 a month and board. Second cook, $65 a month and board; waitresses and dishwashers, $60 per month and board.

The San Juan District Union concluded its session in Ouray November 29th, when the strike was declared off. President Moyer, who was at the conference, stated the position of the union very concisely: ''We have called the strike off, because we take the position that the issues involved have been conceded by the mine owners and operators in the Telluride district in that they recently posted notices to the effect that after December 1st they would grant an eight-hour workday in the mills and a minimum wage scale of three dollars. These were the demands we made over one year ago.''

The Telluride Miners' Union No. 63 made a statement of conditions which was endorsed by the District Union. Much of it is already familiar to the reader, that part which refers to the attitude of the union is a temperate, well-considered document, worthy of a place in the minds of men ever ready to denounce the union as a lawless aggregation.

After fourteen months of industrial conflict, for which the Citizens' Alliance is solely responsible, the mine managers have discovered that the interests of the Citizens' Alliance are not the interests of the mine operators and that the Citizens' Alliance is not a promoter of peace, but of strife. The mine managers have accordingly posted notices at their various properties, conceding the eight-hour day and the minimum wage of $3 per day, which was all that was asked before the strike was declared on September 1st, 1903.

"We would infer from the action taken by the mine managers in granting the eight-hour day and a satisfactory wage scale that it is their desire that peace and normal conditions shall again prevail in San Miguel County.

"We, as members of the Western Federation of Miners of the San Juan district are in hearty accord with this sentiment. The issues involved in the controversy having been adjusted, we have no desire that any conflict shall be continued, but in the language of our preamble, 'to use all honorable means to maintain and promote friendly relations between ourselves and our employers and endeavor by arbitration and conciliation, or other peaceful means, to settle any difficulties which may arise between us. It will require a large number of practical mine and mill men to successfully operate the mining properties of Telluride and place them upon a paying basis.

"As such men return to Telluride, we will expect the mine owners to co-operate with us to prevent the Citizens' Alliance from continuing assaults upon the rights of men "to work when, where and for whom they please" and reside in any community which they may select as an abiding place.

"We demand that the Citizens' Alliance shall be prohibited from employing armed forces and murderous thugs, contrary to the laws of the state. We shall expect that the laws shall be made effective and that the restraining order of the district court shall be obeyed.

"As members of organized labor, we have endured untold sufferings through unlawful imprisonment, through invasion of our homes, through confiscation of our property and to deportation by Citizens' Alliance mobs. We can not forget the brutal and barbarous indignities that have been heaped upon us; but we will endeavor to endure these cruel memories now that our demands have been granted and we have the opportunity of resuming our vocation on an eight-hour basis.

"Indorsed by the San Juan District No. 3 this 29th day of November, 1904.   "FRANK SCHMELZER,

"President San Juan District Union No. 3.

"SECRETARY CLIFFORD,

"San Juan District Union No. 3."

The policy of intimidation did not stop with the strike. The first of December Runnels and Meldrum remarked to three men that no one who spoke against Peabody could remain in San Miguel county, escorted the men to the depot and they left; nine men were treated similarly the next day.

Doubtless the story of the Telluride strike will be read by many who are unacquainted with the metalliferous miner. I know him in his every vice and virtue, know him with the intimate knowledge that comes from membership in his class, toil at his side, struggle in a common cause, know that his vices are not different from other men's, unless it be that he takes less trouble to conceal them.

Given the conditions under which men work, and any intelligent man could give the characteristics of the class that would result. The needs and wants of a man are not supplied in bunkhouse life; men herded together, none of the refining influences of women's society; newspapers, plenty of them, but no books, save an occasional cheap novel; in his poor, mean pleasures there is nothing of science, nothing of poetry or song in his desolate life, empty of joy as the dreary arch of the winter sky above the barren sweep of storm-swept peaks.

It was a homeless man who wrote "Home, Sweet Home." I am sure if the miners' critics could know the hunger, the unsatisfied longing for life's beautiful things that these men, whose only shelter is a roll of blankets, feel, they would be kinder, more just in their criticisms. They would realize that when feeling becomes too poignant, too bitter, the natural thing is to take an anaesthetic, and that at last the power to feel, to be, is dead. The individual has committed against himself the wrong that society in every age since history began has committed against the working class. Silent through the ages, the ruins of extinct civilizations are the dumb witnesses of labor's immemorial wrongs. The greatest gift the years have brought him is increased power to suffer that may awaken him at last.

Fortunate indeed it is for the world's vampires that he has drank of the cup of forgetfulness so long, else they had ceased to prey upon his vitals. An hour of consciousness on his part would end his wrongs forever, for once aroused, he will never sleep again until his chains lie rusting in the museums of the past—till the means of life are common property and no man controls another's bread.

The Telluride strike has made its contribution to this result—the rule of man uncontrolled by men. The world might well learn a lesson from the grim patience of men who stood with folded arms and waited for the mine managers to operate the mines in compliance with the constitution.

The spirit with which they met oppression, their fidelity to the cause of unionism—seventeen members were false to their obligation—is their contribution to the world-emancipation of the workers.

The Telluride strike has passed into history; between the worker and the goal of his desire stood all the forces that feed upon and are supported by him; he passed on, unawed by the malignant hate of corporate and business interests supported by the sinister power of the state, refusing to be provoked into violence or driven into crime, submitting to the grossest indignities, the most brutal outrages in the spirit of men who, in other ages, stood while the fagots were piled at their feet, serene, above the flames, above the mob's brutal cries and appealed to the centuries for history's verdict.

Fraternally,

GUY E. MILLER.

Moyer Habeas Corpus Case

ARTIAL law declared in Colorado.

Habeas corpus suspended in Colorado.

Free press throttled in Colorado.

Soldiers defy the courts in Colorado.

Wholesale arrests without warrant in Colorado.

Union men exiled from homes and families in Colorado.

Constitutional right to keep and bear arms questioned in Colorado.

Corporations corrupt and control administration in Colorado.

Right of fair, speedy and impartial trial abolished in Colorado.

Citizens' Alliance resorts to mob law and violence in Colorado.

Militia hired to corporations to break the strike in Colorado.

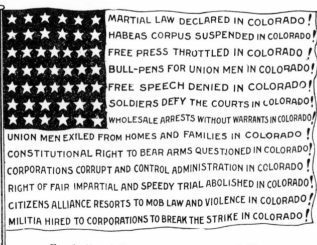

Facsimile of the so-called Desecrated Flag.

For the publication and distribution of foregoing flag by the Western Federation of Miners, President Moyer was arrested and held in the "bull pen" or jail over one hundred days. The flag was a mere pretext for holding President Moyer, the Mine Owners' Association hoping that with Moyer behind the bars the cause of the strikers would be weakened. Every possible effort was made by the W. F. M. attorneys to have Mr. Moyer either brought to trial or released on bond, but without avail. This finally led to the famous habeas corpus proceeding before the state supreme court, which resulted in the majority of that body handing down a decision giving despotic power to a governor in America, heretofore enjoyed only by rulers of absolute monarchies.

Is Colorado in America? If you consult the map you will find it there. If you read the facts in this recent industrial struggle in the light of American history and traditions, you will find nothing to recall memories of our country's youth or the hopes that led strange people across the sea to stretch wider the boundaries of a land where none were so strong as to be above the laws and none so weak as to be beneath their protection. There is nothing in recent history, save by the way of contrast, to recall the fact that ours is the Centennial state marking more than one hundred years of progress under the idea that "all men are created free and equal with certain inalienable rights, among these are life, liberty and the pursuit of happiness."

It is an unpleasant awakening from thoughts like these to a realization of such facts as were inscribed upon a symbol of the flag and burned into the hearts of thousands of Colorado's citizens.

Desecration of the flag? Was it not the deeds done under it and not the truths inscribed upon it that constituted the desecration?

THE ARREST OF PRESIDENT MOYER.

Moyer was arrested on the 26th day of March, 1904, at Ouray, and taken to Telluride, charged with desecration of the flag. He was released under $500 bond only to be immediately re-arrested by the military authorities. A warrant was also sworn out charging Secretary-Treasurer Haywood with the same offense, but before it was served a similar one had been sworn out in Denver and Haywood remained in custody of the Denver officers. Governor Peabody, when interviewed concerning the re-arrest of Moyer, disclaimed any knowledge of the facts, but stated that it was the intention to rearrest Moyer every time he secured his release on bonds.

When the state, in order to secure the conviction of a prisoner or his detention, must violate the laws and regular procedure in such cases, it must be because it lacks the evidence necessary to the conviction of a crime or the fact of crime itself is wanting and the state desires not the administration of law, but an abortion of justice.

The return for the petition of the writ of habeas corpus was made returnable on April 11th. There was no answer to the petition nor return of the writ; the court considered the petition confessed and the facts therein stated to be true, ordered the release of Chas. H. Moyer and commanded that an attachment issue against Sherman Bell and Bulkely Wells in the sum of $500 for contempt of court.

The military defied the civil authorities, and the case was taken to the Supreme Court in Denver before which Moyer was brought on April 23d.

SECRETARY HAYWOOD ATTACKED BY MILITIA.

A clash occurred between Secretary Haywood and the military upon Moyer's arrival in Denver. Haywood went to greet Moyer at the depot; he had just grasped his hand and started to walk along with him when Captain Wells stepped forward attempting to push the two apart; Haywood turned; it seems uncertain whether he struck at Wells or not; at the same instant a trooper struck Haywood with the butt of his rifle, he fell and in an instant almost the entire military detail were on top of him, and those who could not get on top were endeavoring to use their guns.

Mr. Haywood made the following statement:

"The detachment walked me up the street to the Oxford hotel. Wells told off the soldiers, and a detail was instructed to take me back into the recess. I was standing where I had been ordered, when someone commanded me to sit down. I replied that I did not want to sit down. Then he drew his revolver and attempted to strike me on the head.

"Ten or twelve soldiers crowded around me, and nearly all of them, so far as their cramped position would allow, were trying to jab or strike me with their guns. Several had their guns leveled and would probably have fired upon me, but some officer whom I did not recognize, said: 'Don't shoot him, don't shoot him.' By this time Walter Kinley, who was one of the nearest to me, got room to swing his arm, and struck me over the head with his heavy revolver, knocking me down the steps that lead to the basement. When I came up, the officer told the men to fall back. Extremely weak and exhausted from loss of blood from this murderous attack by the military, I sank into a chair, while further negotiations for my disposal were pending."

Haywood's wounds consisted of cuts and contusions necessitating the service of a physician.

For a time it seemed that there might be a conflict as to who should hold Haywood, the military or the local authorities; it was finally decided in favor of the local authorities.

HABEAS CORPUS CASE IN SUPREME COURT.

The attitude of the prosecution was very concisely stated by Attorney Waldron in his opening remarks before the supreme court:

"The writ which your honor issued required the production of Chas. H. Moyer before this court. The executive and respondents have produced the body of Mr. Moyer, not because they recognized the court's power to interfere, but on the contrary, they expressly deny at the very outset that this court or any other tribunal in this state has power to interfere while insurrection has not been suppressed. But bearing in mind the respect which the chief of one branch of government should show to another branch, they have produced the body of Mr. Moyer. He is now in charge of the officials of the National Guard of Colorado."

It may be worth while to briefly note the history of the habeas corpus act that we may understand the significance of the governor's attitude.

In English-speaking countries men have been so long accustomed to constitutional safeguards that, for the moment, they hardly realize what it means to have them swept away. Safeguards that the wisdom and struggles of the centuries had reared against the invasion of personal liberties. Men dreamed that they were potent to protect all that the past had bequeathed and preserve it as a part of the inalienable right of the humblest man. They reckoned without a knowledge of the forces contending against them. They were sufficient to curb the caprice or passion of governmental power in the hands of a despotic king or liberty-loving president, but they seem ineffective as against the greed of corporate wealth, blindly seeking to destroy whatever limits or seems to limit its profits.

The history of the writ, like many another of today, is lost in the mists that veil the cradle of civilization. It was known to the Romans when they first visited and conquered the skin-clad savages of Britain. The Saxons brought it from the shadowy glades of their native forests. When the Conqueror parceled out the lands of England among his followers and substituted the power of the Norman sword for the immemorial rights of Saxon freemen, he could silence but he could not kill a people's aspirations, aspirations that one day achieved historic recognition. From the day when the barons and common people humbled old King John on the field of Runnymede down to the present it has remained the mightiest bulwark of Anglo-Saxon liberty, the most precious jewel in the crown of a people's strength. The conflicts, oppressions, tyrannies of seven hundred years have but broadened its base and endeared its guaranties to freemen, the waves of despotism have dashed over it but the absolutism of kings has not displaced it, and parliaments have rarely limited its operation.

When our forefathers landed on these shores, they brought with them the rights of Englishmen; when denied those rights they rebelled. In framing the constitution they remembered the ancient writ in words that can not be misunderstood: ''The privilege of the writ of habeas corpus shall not be suspended, unless when in cases of rebellion or invasion the public safety may require it." The provision in our state constitution is practically identical.

Chief Justice Marsh said of the conditions under which the writ might be refused:

"If at any time the public safety should require the suspension of the powers vested by this act in the courts of the United States it is for the legislature to say so."

Chief Justice Story said:

"It would seem, as the power is given to congress to suspend the writ of habeas corpus in cases of rebellion or invasion, that the right to judge whether exigency had arisen must belong to that body."

In an opinion as attorney-general of the United States, Caleb Cushing said:

"And it may be assumed as a general doctrine of constitutional jurisprudence in all the United States that the power to suspend laws, whether those granting the writ of habeas corpus or any other, is vested exclusively in the legislature of the particular state."

The author has no ambition to write a law book; a volume could be compiled further illustrating and elucidating the principles involved. Still other constitutional guaranties were violated by the action of the governor and the decision of the court.

The reason assigned for the denial of the writ of habeas corpus was the governor's proclamation declaring San Miguel county to be in a state of insurrection and rebellion. That there was a strike, a refusal to work until the constitutional amendment granting the workers in the mines, mills, etc., an eight-hour day, is not denied. But since the emancipation proclamation of President Lincoln there is no class who are bound to work for another class on any terms the latter may prescribe with the obligation on the part of the government to compel the acquiescence of the workers. To constitute a rebellion there must certainly be armed resistance to the lawfully constituted authorities, which they are unable to put down except by force of arms, and the deeds of some individuals at least must have been so notorious as to furnish ample evidence for their punishment. At the November term of court in San Miguel county every case against the members of the union for crimes alleged to have been committed, was stricken from the docket on the motion of the prosecution. It was not because they did not deserve a conviction. No man prominent in the union had left the county except upon compulsion of men acting under the authority of the governor or with his connivance. They sent no man from the district whom they could have sent to prison.

It takes more than a proclamation to make a rebellion. Even Governor Peabody can not call a revolt into existence as the Almighty God did light.

After stigmatizing a class as criminals in his proclamation, he further states:

"That these forces within and without said county are about to join forces within said San Miguel County, for the purpose of destroying property and inflicting personal injuries upon the citizens of said county."

"A guilty conscience makes a coward heart."

The second proclamation declaring martial law was in answer to a petition by the Citizens' Alliance of Telluride. The larger part of the petitioners, practically all of them, were participants in the mob that drove eighty-one men out of the county. There is no color of law in that action, though the governor had made things extremely convenient for the mob. When sixty-eight of the men returned, they were re-deported by the military whom Peabody had sent into the district to maintain "law and order." A deed done for another without his approbation, but afterward adopted by him, becomes to all intents and purposes his deed, as if he had originally authorized it. Peabody, by sending the troops to maintain the results the mob had accomplished, indorsed their work, and, by the principles of law, (principal and agent), stands forth as the sponsor for, and the principal in, a crime whose enormity is only exceeded by the one committed against everyone in the suspension of habeas corpus on the word of a man who has sworn to execute the laws, performs his duty by the suspension of them.

During the entire period of martial law a rigid censorship of the press, telegraph and telephone was maintained. There is but one reason for a censorship, whether in Russia or Colorado, and that is that the world may not know the crimes committed against humanity in the name of law.

This itemized statement of crimes committed against free institutions by the governor and those acting in accord with him may well be closed with an extract from the executive order sending the troops to Telluride:

"Report forthwith to the sheriff of San Miguel County, Colorado, and that you use such means as you may deem right and proper, *acting in conjunction with or independent of the civil authorities* of said San Miguel County as in your judgment and discretion, conditions demand, to restore peace and good order in said community, and to enforce obedience to the constitution and laws of the state."

Ostensibly the purpose of the troops was to restore such conditions as would enable the civil authorities to bring offenders to justice, for the constitution says: "the military shall always be in strict subordination to the civil power." Yet one of their first acts was to defy the order of the court releasing Moyer and the attachment against Bell and Wells.

The constitution further states, Article 2, Section 7:

"That the people shall be secure in their persons, papers, homes and effects from unreasonable searches and seizures."

Yet it was the military who searched the persons and baggage of the returning miners, robbed them of everything of value, denied them the privilege of even greeting their wives and children, took them out of the county, violated their homes and inflicted every indignity a senile soldiery could conceive. Five of the men were detained and put to work on the streets. J. C. Burns refused to work. The guard threatened to shoot him. "Shoot away," he said. The threat was ineffectual; he was taken to the jail, put on a bread and water diet and later, again deported.

In a battle of principles, we sometimes forget the men involved; we only hear the cannon's roar or hear the bugle call; only see the pall of smoke, "funeral wreath of a world"; the plunging horses, the fierce, tense faces of the combatants, the windrows of the dying and the dead. The spirit of conflict rages in our veins; its pathos is lost to us. We do not hear a brother's last broken prayer nor the death rattle in his throat; we do not see the desolate homes and the anguished hearts that that day's work has made. In this weary world when a blow is aimed at a man it usually falls on a woman's naked heart. Moyer was a sick man, suffering from throat and lung troubles; the filthy atmosphere of the jail is not conducive to recovery; once when he requested that his cell be cleaned the hose was turned on him. He was jeered at, maltreated that in a fit of anger he might give his guards an excuse to murder him. At the close of his trial before the supreme court he was brought out past his wife, he stopped and extended his hand, but Wells, who was behind him told him to "move on."

The court denied the writ, Judges Campbell and Gabbert concurring. A paragraph from their decision is given:

"The arrest and detention of an insurrectionist, either actually engaged in acts of violence or in aiding and abetting others to commit such acts, violates none of his constitutional rights. He is not tried by any military court, or denied the right of trial by jury; neither is he punished for violation of law, nor held without due process of law. His arrest and detention in such circumstances are merely to prevent him from taking part or aiding a continuation of the conditions which the governor, in the discharge of his official duties and in the exercise of the authority conferred by law, is endeavoring to suppress."

A few remarks from Justice Steele's dissenting opinion follows:

"I know of no authority that vests in the governor the power to arrest one who he may think will commit an offense. No such power is granted by the Constitution nor bestowed by statute. The courts of the state are open and in the unobstructed performance of their functions. Most persons would regard restraint of liberty for the period of nearly ninety days as a punishment; and when the court says that the petitioner, by his detention, loses none of his constitutional rights, it ignores, it seems to me, that section of the Constitution which provides that no person shall be deprived of his liberty without due process of law. For, suppose it should transpire that the petitioner is not guilty of any offense, would not his imprisonment without charge and for the purpose of preventing him from committing an offense be an injustice? The court has presumed that this man is an insurgent; the presumption of law is that he is innocent. He asserts that he is not guilty, and no one has charged that he is guilty. The only statement made which in any way implicates him is that of the adjutant general, who says that he became convinced by inquiry that he was the leader of a band of lawless men.

"When we deny to one, however wicked, a right plainly guaranteed by the Constitution, we take that same right from everyone. When we say to Moyer: "You must stay in prison, because if we discharge you you may commit a crime," we say that to every other citizen. When we say to one governor: "You have unlimited and arbitrary power," we clothe future governors with that same power. We can not change the Constitution to meet conditions. We can not deny liberty today and grant it tomorrow; we can not grant it to those theretofore above suspicion and deny it to those suspected of crime; for the Constitution is for all men—"for the favorite at court; for the countryman at plow" —at all times, and under all circumstances.

We can not sow the dragon's teeth, and harvest peace and repose; we can not sow the wind and gather the restful calm.

Our fathers came here as exiles from a tyrant king. Their birthright of liberty was denied them by a horde of petty tyrants that infested the land—sent by the king to loot, to plunder, and to oppress. Arbitrary arrests were made; and judges, aspiring to the smile of the prince, refused by "pitiful evasions" the writ of habeas corpus. Our people were banished; they were denied trial by jury; they were deported for trial for pretended offenses; and they finally resolved to suffer wrong no more, and pledged their lives, their property and their sacred honor to secure the blessings of liberty for themselves and for us, their children. But if the law is as this court has declared, then our vaunted priceless heritage is a sham, and our fathers stood "between their loved homes and the war's desolation" in vain.

President Moyer was taken back to Telluride and lodged in jail. On June 15th, the military authorities delivered him to the sheriff. An hour later he was re-arrested on a warrant sworn out by Deputy Sheriff Runnels charging him with having committed murder in San Miguel county on or about October 15th, 1903. The party alleged to have been murdered was not mentioned. He was held two days on this charge and then surrendered to the officers of Teller county on a warrant charging him with complicity in the Vindicator mine explosion. It might be mentioned that the prosecution have dropped every case ever brought against him.

A tale hangs upon the release of Moyer by the military authorities; a revelation in acrobatic mendacity performed by the gubernatorial accident in his endeavors to keep the puppet crown placed on his head by the mining interests of the state from too rude contact with the law. After the adverse decision of the supreme court, application for the writ was made in the federal court at St. Louis, before Judge Thayer. When he commanded that Moyer's body should be brought into court, Peabody ordered his release before service could be had.

The facts are so well stated in an editorial of the Denver Times that it is worthy of being reproduced here:

"Neither the good Lord nor good people like a prevaricator, especially if his prevarications relate to public matters. It will be noticed that pains are taken not to use the good old English word that expresses more distinctly the kind of man that is in mind. The reason is that the governor of Colorado is in and respect for the office he holds proves a wholesome restraint. Now Governor Peabody has been doing his dead level best, since yesterday at 4 o'clock, to convince the credulous that the action of Judge Thayer at St. Louis, had nothing to do with his order withdrawing martial rule from San Miguel County and the turning of Moyer over to the civil authorities. But to give this attempt an appearance of even seeming plausibility has required such windings in and windings out that the prevarication hangs over every outer bend of the serpentine procedure. It would be too tedious a matter to follow out every footprint of the governor's retreat. For illustration he said never a word yesterday to the reporters about the matter, until after Judge Thayer's action became known. Reporters for the afternoon papers haunt the executive chambers for fresh news items every forenoon. Again the people of Telluride and Captain Wells, the governor's commander at that strategic center, received notice first of Judge Thayer's order and then of the governor's action. But the statement in the Republican (Denver), of times and purposes as given by the governor himself is such a mass of quibbles, notice that the good old English word is not yet used—that well, the governor should be ashamed of the showing himself. The Republican, after assuring its readers that the order to turn Moyer over to the sheriff had been 'phoned to the commanding officer at Telluride at 10 a. m., proceeds to relate how, because of the news from St. Louis, the governor contemplated withdrawing his order until he should hear directly from the court. This is the Republican's story:

"The governor considered abrogating martial law until after he had heard from the Federal Court, but this was impossible for the reason that he had ordered the prisoner turned over by telephone in the morning. He consulted with Attorney General Miller on the subject and was advised that if the order had been put into actual effect before the time specified in it, nothing could be done to stop it."

"Now what are the facts as to the time the order about Moyer was telephoned to Telluride? The Times called up Captain Wells, the military commander at Telluride, and put the question to him direct: At what time did you receive the telephone order to turn Moyer over to the civil authorities?"

To this Captain Wells gave the explicit answer:

"Between 3:40 and 4 o'clock this afternoon."

"Like a good soldier Captain Wells immediately on receipt of the order, carried it out and at 4:15 o'clock in the afternoon escorted him from the military prison to the jail of the county and delivered him to the sheriff.

"From this it is perfectly apparent that the story quoted from the Republican is hot air. Governor Peabody should cultivate not only truthfulness, but moral courage. He should be willing to admit the true cause for an official act. At least he should not give out a false one."

The measures taken by the governor show that he found the action of a court that took its law from the sources of American jurisprudence, not at all in accord with his ideas. The decision of the Colorado court is in striking contrast with our ideals. As Judge Steele said: "But if the law is as this court has declared, then our vaunted priceless heritage is a sham and our fathers stood 'between their loved homes and the war's desolation in vain.'"

In obtaining the decision from the supreme court of Colorado, it is said Peabody's head swelled several inches and in self-exaltation he added an additional red carnation in his buttonhole boquet. His attitude seemed to say: "Who so great as I?" Three great presidents of the United States tried to suspend writs of habeas corpus on occasions during their administrations, but their action was never sustained. With the grin of an ape on his insignificant countenance, Governor Peabody, of Colorado, the one-horse country banker who prostituted the office of chief executive of the state to the basest uses as paid agent of the Mine Owners' Association, boasted that what the supreme court of the United States had refused to do for the three greatest presidents the world ever knew, had been done for him and his owners by the supreme court of the hell on earth in which it and he reigned as the chief imps.

Independence Explosion

T about 3 o'clock on the morning of June 6, a mine
of dynamite was exploded by means of an infernal
machine, placed underneath the station platform
at Independence and thirteen men were instantly
blown to fragments and many others mutilated
and maimed for life.

The men were blown in all directions, and some of them were
so horribly mutilated that identification was extremely difficult.
Quivering arms and legs and other portions of the mangled miners
were picked up after the explosion several hundred feet from the
station.

The terrific crash awakened everybody in the camp, and within
in a short time the scene of the horror was alive with human beings. The awful circumstance which brought the crowd together,
and the dim, half-light of the early morning combined to make the
scene one of almost indescribable horror. By the aid of flickering candles the mangled remains were gathered together and aid
was rendered the wounded. The groans of the injured, mingled
with the cries of the men, women and children who stood about.
Some of these were relatives of the dead and injured miners, and
their grief was pitiful to behold.

Some two yards in from the track and about four yards from
what had been the end of the platform at the Florence & Cripple
Creek depot, was found a deep hole, clear cut and expressive of
volumes. It was the place where the dynamite had been placed.

All windows of the depot were broken, the large foundation
posts sprung and the entire front of the west end of the structure
blown in. The entire basement was a mass of broken timbers.
The roof was pierced in many places, huge pieces of timber were
thrown hundreds of feet in all directions, the houses in the vicinity telling a sad tale of confusion and flying missiles.

The basement of the depot was most favorable for the purpose
of such work. The running doors opened onto the platform

INDEPENDENCE DEPOT AFTER THE EXPLOSION.

below. The north side of the interior was simply a wall of earth formed by the slope of the hill at this point. From the inside, access could be had up and under the platform above. It was by means of such that the criminals accomplished their purpose.

WHAT INVESTIGATION REVEALED.

As soon as the light of day had made it possible to distinguish passing forms, a thin, strong steel wire, the kind used to fasten stove pipes, was found running from the heap of broken boards, out and down over the freight platform and along a switch track for a distance of fifty yards. On the end of the wire was a chair leg, the wire securely wrapped twice around and tied.

The apparent method of procedure was that when the men gathered on the platform and the train hove in sight, the dastardly fiend probably grasped both ends of the piece of wood, gave the wire a sudden jerk which pulled the trigger of a revolver and discharged the leaden messenger into the dynamite.

What the feeling of that coward may have been as he pulled the wire and reeled from the shock of the explosion which had sent thirteen men into eternity is not given to the power of human tongue to express.

The death-dealing fiend chose and executed his plot in a most cunning manner. The straight track afforded a most favorable place to stretch a wire which could be pulled with a decided degree of certainty. The place he selected from which to perpetrate this deed was concealed so that when the train rounded the curve the light of the headlight was cut off by the dump of the Delmonico mine.

Terrible as were the results of the explosion they would have been infinitely more so had the perpetrators of the deed waited but another moment. The train was only about two hundred feet from the depot when the mine was fired, and in another instant both it and all its occupants would have been blown into fragments.

The dead and wounded composed the night shift of the Findley mine, with two men from the Deadwood property. They were

all non-union men. They numbered about twenty-five and immediately after leaving work they, with men from the Shurtloff
and Last Dollar, made for the depot to take the train, which was in
waiting. The depot is just below the Findley mine, and probably
fifteen men were on the platform when the train, which had been
lying about two hundred feet from the depot, whistled and started
up the track toward the Independence station. Some of the
miners rushed to it and boarded it. Others, who had not reached
the platform, raced with their dinner pails in their hands, fearing
that they would miss it. The waiting men scattered over the platform and chatted as the train slowly drew near. Suddenly there
was a terrific explosion. The platform was lifted from its foundation and whirled with its human freight into a shower of debris.
The depot building heaved and swayed and then fell into a splint-
ered mass. The train stopped short, the whistle of the locomotive
shrieked and the train crew and the miners on board jumped to
the ground. For a few moments they were too dazed to act. Then
the truth dawned upon them, and they rushed to the rescue. Cries
of the wounded guided them, and while they were carrying the
mangled away from the scene men and women came from the
nearby mines and dwellings. The confusion was great, but after
some minutes there were cooler heads took charge and a systematic
search was made for the dead and wounded.

It was claimed that a man was seen running down the hill
from near the depot a few minutes after the explosion. A miner
who had just left the Vindicator saw the fellow, but decided that
he had been scared by the crash and was rushing to a place of
safety. He was not near enough to distinguish the man's features.

With the arrival of daylight, appeared an engine from Cripple
Creek, in charge of Trainmaster Middaugh, and bringing to the
scene Sheriff Robertson, Undersheriff Burton, Deputies Underwood and Wilson, A. E. Carlton and others. Immediately a rope
was stretched about the place. Undersheriff Burton and others
spent some time looking for parts of the infernal machine but
only to find the wire.

Officer George Wright, of Cripple Creek, guarded the wire

and its all-important handle that day and allowed no one to go near it, pending the arrival of blood hounds that had been ordered from Palmer Lake and Trinidad early in the morning. The writer might here state that from the dissemination of the news of the outrage at the Independence depot serious trouble was predicted. It appeared as if nothing could stay the impending clash between the union miners, who were at once charged with the responsibility of the atrocious crime, and the non-union miners, the imported thugs and deputies, who were urged on by the mine owners and Citizens' Alliance. Threats of wholesale lynching and deportations were freely made on the streets. As if by magic, headed by C. C. Hamlin, secretary of the Mine Owners' Association, S. D. Crump, attorney for the mine owners and ex-Convict Vannick, appeared on the scene and formed a vicious army of blood-thirsty humanity.

As to who was probably to blame for the explosion and who would have the most to gain thereby, I will later on recite facts as to conditions prior to the explosion and leave the reader to judge.

It is needless for me to say that Colorado, yea, the whole of the United States, stood appalled at this terrible crime. That the men lost their lives, as a result of a carefully planned, and perfectly executed plot, there is not the shadow of a doubt, and the whole state cried out for vengeance—a reparation that should be terrible, and a warning to dynamiters that would be remembered for all time to come. This feeling was shared by all classes and none were more emphatic in their denunciation than the unionists of the state. Never before in the history of Colorado has there been a crime of such fiendishness perpetrated, and never before has there been a crime committed the effects of which were so far reaching. For out of this wholesale murder of innocent men grew many crimes scarcely less enormous— property was wantonly destroyed, other murders were committed, and a wild, frenzied mob held full sway in the Cripple Creek district for several months.

Following the explosion the mines of the district were shut down and great crowds of excited people gathered, principally in Victor. During the morning it was rumored that C. C. Hamlin and others would address a mass meeting in the city of Victor in the afternoon.

DENIAL OF THE W. F. M.

"The local committee of the W. F. M. authorizes me to say that they deplore the diabolical murder committed yesterday morning. They regret that thoughtless persons should charge this crime to the W. F. M., and say that the W. F. M. did not have a thing to do with it. They are as much shocked as the rest of the community. No man, who deserves to live, could, or would approve the awful deed. The fiends who planned and carried out the devilish crime should be detected and punished to the full need of their guilt. This crime must be unearthed and the perpetrators punished. The committee and all members of the local W. F. M. are ready and willing to assist in uncovering the guilty ones. We will use every endeavor to assist the authorities in their efforts and we here tender the services of all our members. We will also join in the offering of a suitable reward for the arrest and conviction of the guilty persons.

District Union No. 1, W. F. M.
By Frank J. Hangs, W. F. M. Attorney."

The local military were called out, pending the arrival of General Bell. Thus began a reign of terror that would shame the darkest pages of mediaeval history.

TROUBLE OVER BODIES.

The remains of the dead and the mangled bodies of the wounded were placed in the cars and carried to Victor. The former were laid on the Victor depot platform until taken to the Dunn undertaking parlors in ambulance, express wagon and railroad trucks, and the others were removed to the Victor and Red Cross hospitals. It was a grewsome sight which met the eyes of the early morning risers as a white covered truck was propelled through the streets drawn by men.

The first open demonstration of strained relations as a result of the morning horror occurred at 10 o'clock, when Superintendent John Murphy of the Findley, Engineer Silvers, Undertaker Hunt and several others marched into the Dunn undertaking parlors, where Coroner Doran's office was located. It seems that it had been reported that Coroner Doran had spoken of the explosion as an accident. Doran was asked if he believed and called the early morning happening an accident. The coroner replied that he had simply casually referred to it as an accident, but did not consider it as such, no more than would any other sane man.

Murphy then stepped forward and said that the bodies would be moved. This was done, and the remains were removed to the Hunt undertaking parlors.

ROPE FOR SHERIFF.

Sheriff Henry Robertson was met on Victor avenue, Victor, shortly before noon, by a committee who requested him to accompany them to the headquarters of the Citizens' Alliance on North Third street. The sheriff promptly consented and upon arriving, he was met by a body of men who peremptorily demanded his immediate resignation. Robertson demurred most strongly and flatly refused to surrender his authority. He was then advised in strong language that unless he consented to resign without further parley he would soon be dangling at the end of a rope.

"You will have to show me the rope, boys," replied the sheriff.

From behind his back one of the spokesmen produced a grewsome looking hempen cord, with noose already tied, ready for grim business.

"We mean business, sheriff," said the man with the rope.

Robertson immediately saw the futility of further argument, and said:

"All right, boys, I'll quit right now. That noose looks pretty wicked to me."

With that he placed his signature to his resignation which had been previously prepared by the mine owners.

The board of county commissioners held a special session in Victor a few minutes after this incident and appointed Ed Bell sheriff pro tem.

About two o'clock Marshal Michael O'Connell attempted to enter Armory hall, the military headquarters, for the purpose of securing aid to disperse a mob that was gathering on the corner of Victor and Fourth. He was refused admittance and was forced to retire, not without first having earnestly pleaded from the stairs, that the proposed mass meeting be abandoned, as he feared trouble would result therefrom.

Having been refused assistance at Armory hall, Marshal O'Connell appointed about ninety men as deputies and later supplied them with white ribbon badges, inscribed with the words, "Special Police." The special police assembled at Fourth and Victor and were sworn in and armed with such weapons as could be procured, shot guns, rifles and revolvers. They remained there until later dismissed by the marshal.

After the swearing in of the deputies, Marshal O'Connell, at the request of Mayor French, and in company with Sheriff Bell, went to the city hall to hold a conference. O'Connell was asked to resign, but refused, and was then dismissed by the mayor, who suspended him temporarily, which would have held until the city council could take some action on the matter.

O'Connell went back to his men and stated what had happened, and advised the men to take off their badges, which was done in most cases, while a few of the union miners went to their own hall, carrying with them both badges and guns. Here I might state that few union men were to be seen, many of them being at home hoping to avert trouble.

MASS MEETING AND RIOT.

At between three and four o'clock a crowd assembled at the corner of Fourth and Victor avenues, in response to the call for the mass meeting that had been previously announced. Those in attendance were composed in the main of members of the Citizens' Alliance, Mine Owners' Association, strike breakers (many of whom were recruited from the slums of large cities), paroled and ex-convicts, "gun fighters" who had been arriving in the district in large numbers during the past few days, and a few daring spirits, members of the miners' union, whose curiosity was stronger than their prudence. It was evident, from the element, antagonistic to organized labor, making up the larger part of this gathering, that they could easily be turned into a blood-thirsty mob, a law unto themselves, unopposed by the military, and used to wreak vengeance upon every person known to be-long to a labor organization. For in the eyes of those opposed to organized labor, to be a union man was sufficient excuse to treat him worse than a criminal.

Taking advantage of the reckless mood of the crowd, Clarence C. Hamlin mounted a wagon, which was used as a platform. He was accompanied by S. D. Crump, attorney for mine owners, and ex-convict Frank Vannick.

C. C. HAMLIN.

Mr. Hamlin opened the meeting and his opening statement was:

"United States citizens must arm themselves and drive these Western Federation men to the hills."

In the course of Mr. Hamlin's remarks, he further said:

"For the blowing up of those brave boys fifty union men should be shot down like dogs and as many more swung to telegraph poles. Every Federation man is a criminal, and it is up to you men to drive them over the hills with your guns."

At this a union man in the crowd (many claim it was one of the Miller boys), asked Mr. Hamlin who he meant by "them."

The answer to this was cries of "lynch him," "kill him," "hang him," etc.

Mr. Hamlin called to the crowd to catch the man that had asked the question and to hold him. Hamlin's words seemed to be a signal, for no sooner were they uttered than the shooting commenced.

Hamlin's speech has never been equaled as an inspiration to riot, implying by his words that the W. F. M. was guilty of the crime at the Independence depot. He urged his too willing audience, to drive out the union men. He used every fiery denunciation he could command against the Western Federation of Miners to inflame the mob, reason and judgment became dethroned. He urged the men assembled to "drive them out, drive them over the hills." The hired rioters, armed to the teeth, and inflamed by the foul speech of Hamlin, only made, too evidently, for this purpose, began their bloodthirsty assaults upon the union men and their sympathizers. Thus it was that the Independence explosion furnished excuse for re-opening the fight against the strikers, which resulted in death, deportations, incarceration in military bull pens, the abuse and terrorizing of helpless women and children—deeds that will forever be a blot upon this civilized community.

I wish at this time to call the reader's attention to the fact that every act performed by the mob on this momentous day was evidently premeditated. Many people marveled how it could be that this vast horde was so quickly assembled and carried out the orders of the leaders so implicitly, unless it was that the deed was anticipated and the adherents of the Mine Owners' Association and the Citizens' Alliance had been previously instructed. All deeds perpetrated against organized labor, was merely the carrying out of a prearranged and well defined system. Immediately after the explosion mines were closed down and the non-union miners were assembled at Victor armed, under instruction of the mine bosses. In fact, scarcely had the dismal echo

died away, scarce had the groans of the dying ceased, when the
mine operators, the commercial brigands—the Citizens' Alliance,
and the strike breaking thugs, equipped and armed appeared as
a well organized army, ready to obey the behests of those who
were interested in forever destroying organized labor.

DETAILS OF RIOT FOLLOWING MASS MEETING.

When the question was asked of Hamlin by the union man
who he (Hamlin) meant by "them" he was struck over the head
with a revolver; a shot was fired, which seemed to be a signal for
attack upon the union men in the crowd. Guns were drawn and
a number of sharp reports were heard. "Roxie" McGee, a non-
union miner, fell to the ground with a bullet through his heart.
John Davis, a machine man, employed at the Vindicator mine, was
badly beaten over the head and shot in the back. He died an hour
later, in the hospital. Peter Chrisman was shot through the left
cheek.   Fred A. Studevoss, an engineer, was shot in the left
side, J. P. Murphy, a friend of organized labor, chief of the
Victor fire department, was shot in the back, the bullet entering
his right shoulder and coming out over his right breast, almost
in line with his heart. He was standing beside Michael O'Connell
and it was believed this bullet was intended for the brave deposed marshal. The local militia, that had been previously assembled at Armory hall, arrived on the scene and proceeded to
disperse the maddened throng.

Sheriff Bell assured the union men that were on the streets
that if they would retire and not cause any trouble he would
compel the other element to keep within the limits of the law.
Upon this assurance the union men in the crowd, wishing to avert
any further trouble, went to their headquarters, taking with them
the arms given them by the marshal when sworn in as deputies.

Instead of making good this promise, that union men would
not be molested if they would retire from the streets, soldiers
were immediately posted upon the roofs of buildings opposite
and commanding windows of Miners' Union hall. Others were
posted on the bank building next to the hall which was higher and

commanded the skylight of the miners' hall. After having posted his men at all advantageous points, Bell entered Miners' Union building and asked them to surrender their arms and go home. The union men remonstrated with Bell, telling him that their hall was. their home, that they owned the building and if they left the hall and went to their homes they would be murdered single-handed by the mob. They also told the sheriff they would harm no one if not molested and would only act in self-defense against any attack upon them by the insane mob. Upon refusal of the men, Bell stated he would take them by force. Bell retired and immediately a fusilade of shots were fired into the windows and through the skylight of the union hall.

Press reports stated that shots were fired from the hall at the sheriff and his deputies. Upon investigation I found this to be positively false. **There were no shots fired by the miners.**

Firing by the militia continued for some time, when the miners felt the best thing to do to save further trouble was to surrender. This they did. The flag of truce being a white handkerchief, and even after the flag was shown, shots were fired from the ranks of the enemy, the handkerchief used as a flag of truce was riddled.

The miners, not too seriously injured, then emerged from the building in twos and threes, each man holding his hands above his head. They were lined up on the sidewalk, relieved of their arms and marched in a body, about sixty in all, to Armory hall, where they were held as military prisoners.

An inventory of Miners' Union hall after the surrender of its inmates disclosed the havoc wrought by the military. Every pane of glass was shattered into fragments and the woodwork and walls were literally perforated with leaden pellets. That a score or more of the miners were not killed is regarded as miraculous.

The following members of the miners' union were quite seriously wounded: Arthur Parker, Thos. McManus, Edward McKelvey and Peter Calderwood.

The following as told by Arthur Parker, while lying on a cot at the hospital, shortly after the riot, will help the reader to realize the cruel treatment given the union men:

"I was among the number who left the lot and adjourned to the hall. We heard the armed scabs over in the Armory building discharging their weapons and yelling, and knowing they were bent on creating trouble we went over to our hall to keep out of it. There were some twenty-five or thirty men in the hall and while we determined to keep the mob out, it was understood by all present that if the militia demanded an entrance, no opposition would be offered.

"Directly we heard a noise at the foot of the stairs leading up to the hall, and, looking out, we saw a crowd trying to force an entrance. We warned them they were not wanted, but not once did we fire a shot. After awhile we decided to lock up the place and go to our homes. We left the windows and all of us were crowded at the head of the stairs preparing to descend when we were shot at from the outside. Then for the next few minutes a perfect hail storm of bullets were fired at us from the front, sides and through the skylight of the building. All we could do was to run alongside the walls or fall to the floor in order to protect ourselves from the terrible shower of lead.

"After awhile the firing ceased and one of our men ran out a white handkerchief as a sign of surrender. When that was done the mob and militia, who were at the foot of the stairs, ran up the steps and called upon us to throw up our hands. Such of us as were able, did so. The wounded were treated shamefully. They shoved a pistol down Ed McKelvey's throat, cursing and saying, 'Say its good, you —— —— or we will blow your brains out!' One of the non-union men abused Peter Calderwood and started to finish him with his six-shooter but was prevented by the militia, who, by this time, were swarming into the hall. I verily believe we would have been murdered had it not been for the timely intervention of the militia. There was not a single shot fired from our side and had we started five minutes earlier we would have been out of the hall on the way to our homes."

Mr. Parker's statement was verified by others who were in the hall during the attack.

After the trouble at Miners' Union hall there was no more shooting. Many arrests of innocent persons were made without resistance.

A detail of soldiers went to the Miners' Union store, where they arrested General Manager John Harper and all other union men connected with the store. They marched them up the street, where the captured miners from the hall were lined up. Shortly after the Record office was visited and the printing force was placed under arrest and marched up to where the other prisoners were held. Later, George Kyner, editor and publisher of the paper, was taken from his residence on South Fourth street by the soldiers.

S. D. CRUMP.

The regular police force was suspended by Mayor French and Major Naylor, an ardent union hater, was appointed marshal. Shortly after the attack on Miners' Union hall, former Marshal O'Connell was placed under arrest and marched up Fourth street with his hands above his head. He was placed with the other prisoners, who, in the meantime, had been moved to Armory hall. Numbers of other union men were taken in from time to time in this manner. All were quartered in Armory hall. By nine o'clock, p. m., June 6, there being about 200 men under arrest, including twenty-five arrested at Goldfield, a suburb of Victor.

It is said by men who have been engaged at mining for many

years, that all previous strike troubles in the great gold camp were as mere skirmishes in comparison with June 6 and the dark days that followed.

TROUBLE AT CRIPPLE CREEK.

Before going more deeply into occurrences in the city of Victor and other towns in the district, let us for a moment see how fared the population of Cripple Creek.

June 6, found excitement as high in Cripple Creek as I have described in Victor.

June 7, was without doubt one of the most strenuous days in the history of that city. The spectacle of large bodies of armed men, many mounted, parading the streets with members of the Western Federation of Miners and other members of organized labor as prisoners, kept the populace on the qui vive all day.

The first noteworthy occurrence of the 7th happened sometime between twelve and two o'clock, a. m. An excited, apparently insane mob of nearly two hundred men made an assault on the hall of Miners' Union No. 40, on Bennett avenue. Fortunately the building was not occupied at the time. Not finding members of the union in the building, the mob satisfied themselves with completely destroying the handsome furnishings, smashing in the windows of the reading room and secretary's office, breaking in the doors in the interior and demolishing the typewriter and everything that could be destroyed. A few special police officers reached the scene of the attack, but they were powerless to cope with the superior force. The mob finally dispersed and no arrests were made.

The hall presented a sorry aspect after the visit of the mob. The battered structure was guarded by a couple of soldiers who had positive orders to admit no visitors or curiosity seekers. Acting under orders from Sheriff Bell, Deputy Tom Underwood searched the building thoroughly and confiscated the charter of the union and all printed matter that could be found. A dray was backed up in front of the hall and loaded with paraphernalia belonging to the union and Trades Assembly. This material was stored at the headquarters of the Citizens' Alliance. A number of charters of other unions that met in the hall were taken to the First National bank, where they were carefully scrutinized by a curious crowd.

MINERS' UNION HALL, WHERE MINERS WERE WOUNDED.

The union store was destroyed in the same manner as were the Victor, Anaconda and Goldfield stores.

At the first break of dawn little groups of men began to gather on the avenue and bright and early the streets were crowded with people who assembled purely out of curiosity to witness expected stirring scenes. And they were not in the least disappointed.

The town was virtually in control of a large force of armed deputies under the direction of Tom Underwood and Henry Benton, who searched every nook and corner of both business and residence sections in quest of union men who were slated for deportation from the district. Hundreds of non-union miners were pressed into service as deputies. The homes of many union miners were visited and searched for male occupants. A dozen or more arrests resulted, the prisoners being taken to the county jail pending final disposition of their cases.

Committees were appointed to call on Chief of Police Graham and Night Captain Fred Harding and demand their immediate resignations from office. The committee found Chief Graham at the city jail and briefly stated the object of their call, at the same time presenting a written resignation for him to sign. Graham lost no time in appending his signature to the document. Harding was seen by the committee a few minutes later and was likewise relieved of his job. The committee which waited upon the officers was composed of Cliff Newcomb, cashier of the First National bank; Broker Harry Shepherd, John Russel, Dr. Funk and Editor W. H. Griffith of the Cripple Creek Times.

The demand for a change of administration extended even to the judiciary, Justice of the Peace C. M. Harrington being selected as the first victim. Harrington was waited upon by a committee composed of Sam Vidler, Frank Pinson, Dr. McCowan, J. Gaffney and an old soldier named Harcourt. It was stated that Sam Vidler held a revolver against the judge's abdomen as he presented the demand for his resignation. The judge reluctantly acceded to the demand, his protests being unavailing. Justice Thomas of Victor, was deposed from office in a similar manner.

It was stated by the Citizens' Alliance committee that Albert F. Frost, county judge, and Frank P. Mannix, county clerk and recorder, who were then in attendance at a Democratic convention which was in session at Pueblo, would be compelled to likewise give up their offices. This applied to Deputy District Attorney J. C. Cole, who was also out of the city.

On the night of June 7 the city council of Cripple Creek accepted the resignations of Chief of Police Graham and Night Captain Harding. Charles Crowder was elected to succeed Graham; a successor to Harding was found in C. E. Wiley. The mayor had previously appointed Floyd Thompson as night captain, but he was later seen by a committee from the vigilantes who objected to Thompson. Accordingly Wiley was substituted. Mayor Shockey laid particular stress upon the fact that the appointments were only temporary.

Secretary R. E. Croskey of the Trades Assembly, who was supposed to have made his escape from the district after being apprised that he was booked for deportation, was arrested by a number of deputies and taken to the county jail with the balance of the union prisoners.

A few days before the army of militia, deputies and strike-breakers, gained complete control in Cripple Creek, under instructions of the tool of the mine owners, Governor James H. Peabody, A. E. Carlton, president of the First National bank of Cripple Creek, and a shining light of the Mine Owners' Association, approached City Marshal Wm. Graham, and said:

"Billy, you and are warm friends, and I come to you as a friend to tell you to resign and the sooner the better. I know you have been fair through this strife in the district and have not at any time shown partiality to either side. I feel this is a great injustice to you, but we, the Mine Owners' Association and Citizens' Alliance, **do not want a neutral man as city marshal.** Our faction will not be responsible for you a minute. The marshal we choose must be in sympathy with us completely. We have outlined work for him that would not be agreeable to a man like you or any other except the kind we appoint."

Carlton then offered him $100 and a ticket to Kansas City, stating that many hard things would be done from that date on.

Bear in mind, reader, this conversation took place a few days before the explosion.

DESTRUCTION OF ENGINEERS HALL.   Threat written in blood of one of the victims can be seen on blackboard.

The foregoing tragic events and many others of a like nature made a dark page in the history of the city of Cripple Creek.

MORE VANDALISM.

While the mob at Cripple Creek destroyed all valuable property of the Western Federation, in Victor property was also either totally destroyed or confiscated.

June 7, Engineer's hall No. 80, W. F. M., was visited and the entire furnishings destroyed, including charters of many organizations that met in the hall. A beautiful new piano that was the pride of the Maccabees, was totally destroyed, being turned over and the sides smashed in. Many magnificent portieres were stripped from the windows, and after being torn in rags were piled in a heap on the floor.

The library in this elegant hall was estimated at $1,000. The entire contents of the bookcases were hurled from the windows to the sidewalk below.

The brussels carpet and rugs on the floor were torn and bayonetted, chairs broken, banners torn in shreds, and all charters made into fit material for the "rag man."

The engineers owned a beautiful silk banner which cost $185, and was prized very highly by the local. This artistic piece of work was made a special target by this destruction dealing mob.

In the reading room and secretary's office, desks, chairs and tables were overturned and demolished. All official records and books of Engineers No. 80, W. F. M., and other organizations that met in the building, were taken to military headquarters.

On the blackboard in the reception hall of the building, after the horde had left the hall, was found the following threat, written in the blood of one of their victims:

"For being a union man, deportation or death will be your fate.   "Citizens' Alliance."

Reader, keep this in mind—this destruction was wrought by the National Guard of the fair state of Colorado by a "law and order" for what they claimed was a "military necessity."

Women who were members of fraternal societies that held meetings in the hall, took heart-broken looks at their cherished banners, that, in many cases, represented months of tedious needle work, thus ruthlessly turned to mere useless rags, and many were seen to shed bitter tears.

Will the reader be surprised if I add, that so many things of an even more serious nature were being perpetrated in different sections of the district, that the foregoing seemed to appear common place to the majority.

The co-operative store in Victor was raided by a mob and totally destroyed, groceries torn from the shelves and thrown into the streets, coal oil poured over the flour, sugar and other groceries that could be destroyed in that manner. The groceries that were not rendered useless were "confiscated" by the Citizens' Alliance.

Many people who witnessed this disgraceful scene say that Newcomb, cashier of the First National bank, led this lawless crowd of military and civilians. The other co-operative stores were raided in a similar manner.

James H. Murphy, superintendent of the Findley mine, was the chief of the mob that tyrannized over women, children and unarmed men in the little towns of Altman and Independence. Murphy was seen to tear a woman's clothing from her body and then kick her until half dead because she was known to be a union sympathizer. A fine specimen of the Peabody gang that has stained the name of Colorado and trampled under foot the document our forefathers gave their lives to establish.

A. E. Carlton, banker, led the mob that destroyed the union hall in Cripple Creek, and vented his spleen by kicking out windows. Fine work for a would-be representative of "law and order."

But even worse was to follow, as succeeding pages will show.

By the evening of June 7, 150 men were prisoners and 100 others had been arrested and released and twenty-seven shipped out of the district.

Miners' Union hall, owned by local No. 32, was among the

property partially destroyed and furnishings confiscated. The building itself cost $30,000. The hall was rendered absolutely useless. It was one of the most handsomely furnished halls in the state and was occupied every night as a meeting place for some fraternal society. Later on the military moved from their former quarters, Armory hall, and turned Miners' Union hall into an armory. Reason given—more comfortable quarters.

Among the effects confiscated from Miners' Union hall and taken to Citizens' Alliance headquarters, were a number of photographs of miners. There were about forty of these pictures altogether and they were marked and checked up so as to show who in each picture were the non-union men. Over each non-union man was placed a number and on the back the name of the man was written with the corresponding number. This was at once claimed by the mine owners and Citizens' Alliance to be damaging evidence against the union miners, as they claimed that the persons represented by the photographs of the non-union men were marked for death by the striking miners. The truth of the matter was that the Western Federation of Miners had for many years adopted the system of photographing the miners in union camps in groups. This included the union and non-union miners, the purpose being that in the event of a union miner proving a traitor, his picture was reproduced in the Miners' Magazine as a notification to miners in other union camps.

A meeting of the Citizens' Alliance was held. Some of the union miner prisoners were examined.

Frank Cochran, secretary of No. 32, Victor, was brought in under heavy guard. He declared that he did not know who the men were or when the pictures were taken; that they were all taken before he became a member of No. 32, and that he knew nothing of any man ever being marked for slaughter.

"Make him confess," yelled a man at the meeting, and things became exciting. Two new ropes with running nooses, lay on the table before Cochran.

"Put a rope around his neck," called out another, and similar remarks were heard all over the room.

Cochran protested, saying that all he knew about the photographs was that they were taken for "scab" pictures and that in this way the non-union men could be kept track of. He could not be coerced into changing his story.

Other miners were brought in and underwent a similar sweating, with the same results.

K. C. Sterling, secret service officer for the mine operators, sweated several union men during the day and as a result claimed that he had secured valuable testimony. What this testimony was he would not divulge, nor has he up to this day made use of this supposed evidence. This proved, what at that time was surmised by the strikers, that his claim of having secured evidence was done for effect.

On this date news that a deportation was being arranged by the Citizens' Alliance meeting spread and the crowd increased to an immense size as the afternoon wore away. The state armory that had been converted into a "bull pen," at Third and Diamond avenues, was surrounded with sightseers. There was frivolity and sorrow, tears and jeers, and with every phase an extreme emotion was shown in the vast crowd. Wives and sisters and children of the imprisoned miners were lined up opposite the armory watching their friends and relatives who crowded the windows and smiled and looked seriously on the upward gazing crowds below.

The men were well fed, many of their wives bringing them good meals. Dan McPhee, one of the prisoners, was quite ill, and Mrs. McPhee brought him hot coffee and rolls and a warm blanket. Judan Pha was mourning his fate. He said he was a Spaniard and arrived in Victor Monday, to look for a long lost brother, when he was seized in Goldfield and taken to the bullpen.

Two shots were fired about four o'clock, and for a moment another riot was feared, but the shots were only to keep the crowd back. Then the train, consisting of a single coach, was drawn up, and Sheriff Bell took a paper with a list of names, and the men who were to be deported were lined up. With blue-coats on every side, they marched silently down out of the armory to the train between immense crowds. Every hill and neighboring building was black with spectators. Everything passed in silence as the men mounted the steps of the train; the militia on each side and it steamed away, destination then unknown. The next day it was learned that they landed safely in Denver.

At seven o'clock in the evening, the same day, the usurper sheriff with a number of guards, loaded fifty men on a F. & C. C. train and took them to Cripple Creek, where they were held at Citizens' Alliance headquarters until the mine owners and this "law unto itself", the Citizens' Alliance, would decide whether to release, hang, torture or deport them.

I will not give the names of each of these men and what they were forced to undergo, but among the fifty was the deposed marshal of Victor, Michael O'Connell.

MARTIAL LAW PROCLAIMED.

Sometime during the night of June 7, armed with a proclamation of martial law, issued by Lieutenant Governor Haggott, who was acting while James H. Peabody was enjoying life at the World's Fair in St. Louis, General Bell arrived in Victor. Bell was instructed to issue the proclamation if he found conditions such as to make it absolutely necessary. I have so often introduced this "tin God on wheels"—Bell—to the reader, and so often spoken of Bell's love of war (on unions), that it is unnecessary for me to state that the general found it necessary and the proclamation went into effect at 2 a. m., June 8. The proclamation follows:

"State of Colorado, Executive Chamber, Denver.—Proclamation.

"Whereas, There exists in Teller County, Colo., a large number of armed persons acting in conjunction with a large number of persons outside of that county, who are fully armed and acting together for unlawful purposes; and,

"Whereas, Open riot and insurrection now exist in said county of Teller and felonies and murders have already been committed by such persons, who are still threatening to commit murder and felonies and are offering violence to the citizens and property of said county, and are resisting the laws of the state of Colorado; and,

"Whereas, At divers and sundry other times various crimes have been committed in said county of Teller by and with the aid and under the direction of said vicious and lawless persons and the security of persons and property are now threatened in said county; and,

"Whereas, Threats, intimidation and violence are threatened and believed will be resorted to by said lawless class of individuals; and,

"Whereas, It is represented to me by the sheriff of said Teller county that the civil authorities within said county are unable to enforce the law and to secure peace and order in said county and that it is necessary to put the military in said county for the purpose of enforcing the law and restoring peace and order;

"Now, therefore, I, Warren A. Haggott, acting governor and commander-in-chief of the military forces of the state of Colorado, by virtue and authority in me vested, do hereby proclaim and declare the said county of Teller in the state of Colorado to be in a state of insurrection and rebellion.

"In testimony whereof I have hereunto set my hand and caused the great seal of the state to be affixed at Denver, the state capital, this 7th day of June, A. D., 1904.

(Signed)   "WARREN A. HAGGOTT,
                                                "Acting Governor.

"Attest: JAMES COWIE,
                "Secretary of State.
                        "TIMOTHY O'CONNOR,
                                        "Deputy.

"By command of
                                "WARREN A. HAGGOTT,
                        "Acting Governor and Commander-in-Chief.
                                "SHERMAN M. BELL,
            "Brigadier General, Adjutant General, State of Colorado."

Bell, in an interview with reporters early in the morning of June 8, said:

"We will not bring any troops here from the outside unless the situation becomes more serious than at present. These fellows (meaning union miners) did not appreciate the treatment given them when the soldiers were here before. No resistance will be tolerated now, and, if necessary, they will be shot down."

THE BATTLE OF DUNNVILLE.

All who read the daily papers during the troubles in Teller county will remember the thrilling, blood-curdling accounts of a battle at the little camp called Dunnville. This little place was about fourteen miles south of Victor, on the F. & C. C. railroad in Fremont county. The population consisted of a few prospectors who lived in tents. The camp was composed almost wholly of miners that had been on strike since the inception of the troubles in the Cripple Creek district who were doing a little mining for themselves.

A few weeks before the explosion at Independence a rich strike had been made and the little camp had been "boomed" by the press. As I have before stated, Sherman Bell has a wonderful imagination and his specialty has always been discovering plots of terrible crimes to be committed and preventing the same from being executed.

On the morning of June 8, Bell claimed that he had received a message that a force of union miners, "armed and provisioned", had entrenched themselves on the mountain side just above the little camp of Dunnville, which lay in the valley below.

The great (?) warrior declared he would raid the camp and take captive the population, which he prepared to do. Calling together a squad of deputies and militia and taking a special train about three o'clock in the afternoon, Bell left Victor to capture what he designated as "the anarchists and dynamiters."

The special train carried Bell, about two hundred non-union deputized miners and two companies of militia. Bell permitted newspaper men to go along and each wore a white ribbon badge to distinguish them from the "army." The obvious intention, undoubtedly, being that after the battle, when the dead and wounded were gathered up, the reporters could be identified. As you can see, General Bell, as becomes a great warrior, (?) never overlooked any details.

After a cautious journey, advance scouts being thrown out, they discovered three men going up the mountain. The train was ordered stopped about seventy-five yards from the tents at Dunnville. Orders were given to hurriedly load, leave the train and line up for battle. The non-union miners, who were acting as deputies being more savage than the rest, pushed ahead and fired into the tents as they hurried on in advance. Upon orders of General Bell, the militia fired upon the three men seen going up a gulch in the mountain side, and for several minutes a storm of shot fell in the direction of the "rebellious army of three."

The press, in reporting the engagement, described a fierce onslaught by the entrenched miners. Sherman Bell said that there was a regular hailstorm of shots fired at him by the miners; that the earth was actually "ploughed up" around him or words leaving that impression. The train crew stated that not more than one shot was fired by any one except the crowd that went on the special train. They stated further that the one shot had lost all force by the time it reached the valley.

A press reporter stated that he stood within fifteen feet of Bell and did not hear any bullets flying by or see the ground torn up by bullets. It has been implied that the general, in the excitement of the engagement, used his spur-be-decked feet with such effect, that, like all pugnacious roosters, dirt and gravel flew in all directions and rattled on the general's sword and the windows of the train, giving him the impression that "shot and shell" from the enemy was raining all around him.

A reporter who accompanied the "army" stated that at least 500 shots were fired by deputies and militia. Imagine the surprise of the prospectors to hear such a cannonading in their quiet little camp. They were not offered an explanation or given an opportunity to surrender if they wished. The writer interviewed many in regard to the Dunnville battle and by one it was stated that the miners, when they saw the armed force approaching, fled to the hills, and, if this was true, the reader could not censure, for they were not armed except with dinner pail and prospector's pick and shovel.

I would not blame a man for getting behind a rock if he saw he was about to be shot down in cold blood by an excited man in charge of a Krag rifle.

Bell finally gave the order to cease firing to give the miners a chance to come down from the mountain. The men at once came down with their hands up and even then they were prodded and guards made talk of shooting off fingers from hands that were elevated, and one militiaman fired three shots at a man with his hands up, trying to shoot his thumb off.

John Carley, a member of the I. O. O. F. and of the Miners' union was shot in cold blood. He was one of the three men first seen going up the mountain. His comrades saved their lives by jumping behind a rock .

The result of this grand raid on the little camp was John Carley murdered; the capture of sixteen union miners; one twenty-two calibre target rifle; one old-fashioned shotgun; one forty-five calibre revolver and about thirteen picks and a few jack knives; possibly a miner's shovel or two. Upon the miners being searched, a can of sardines was found on the person of one. This was at once conjectured to be a bomb, but upon cautious investigation by a non-partisan, proved to be sardines, long since dead, and therefore, harmless. I believe it was also said that in some of the tents was found a can of potted ham. This Bell at once declared to be a plot to commit murder (or suicide), f r the reader will remember that during the Spanish-American war a number of soldiers lost their lives by eating canned beef or corned can beef.

To show how brave some of the members of the guard are, I might mention that during this "fierce battle" I have described, a lieutenant made an excuse to return to the car for something and never found it, at least, he remained in the coach. Another member of the party was seen hiding behind a tent and when the train was ready to return to Victor, came forth trembling. Other cases of the same kind came to the writer's attention. This led me to wonder what the action of Bell's army at various times would have been were they compelled to face armed men in an actual engagement.

As is usual in war, the victorious general gave orders to destroy the stronghold of the enemy, so the little tents of the miners and their simple contents were rendered useless.

This, dear reader, is a brief but true history of the much spoken of Dunnville battle. History records many brave and valiant deeds performed by military commanders, such as Napoleon crossing the Alps, Sheridan's march to the sea, but according to Bell and his admirers, the general's Dunnville battle far excels all military achievements recorded in history. I have been told, but can not vouch for the truth of same, that upon the return of Bell's triumphant legion to headquarters, the band played, "See the Conquering Hero Comes," and "Hail to the Chief," and that, at the suggestion of Bell, a subscription was taken up in order to present him with a medal in commemoration of his bravery and military genius. That there can be no question of General Bell's high opinion of himself as a military commander and his desire that the public might have an opportunity of sharing in this opinion, he undertook to have a history of himself written, but owing to him and the man he hired to write the history disagreeing, the work has not yet appeared.

He arranged with Willard P. Hatch, a graduate of the University of Colorado, a man of much ability, to write this history, Bell to furnish some of the manuscript. Mr. Hatch and the general had a falling out on account of Bell's failing to keep his agreement as to finances. This caused considerable hard feeling between the two. Bell, as usual, made some sensational statements to the press regarding this matter. Mr. Hatch retaliated by giving a full statement of the transaction to the public. In this statement, Mr. Hatch said that the general had furnished him with manuscript for the history claiming that he (Bell) was the greatest living military commander of the age, and much other similar rot. The author was to say that Bell was the equal of Napoleon, and in fact greatly resembled that famous general.

Mr. Hatch is a man of high standing and would not make this statement unless it was true; in fact, he offered to go before a notary public and take oath as to its truth.

On the same day, the 8th, the militia and deputies were kept busy hunting down union men and their sympathizers placed under the ban by the mine owners. Squads scoured the hills in all directions hunting for those who were attempting to leave the district.

Along about this date five out of six members of the city

council of Goldfield were taken to the bull pen and later were forced to resign. Goldfield was left without a legislative body for a while.

Lieutenant Harley Keegan was appointed night marshal of Victor.

Coroner Doran of Victor, was also forced to resign on the 8th, but before he resigned he had impaneled a jury to investigate the Independence horror, which was his last official act in the capacity of coroner. George R. A. Hall was appointed as coroner.

VERDICT OF CORONER'S JURY.

"An inquisition held at Cripple Creek, in Teller county, on the 9th and 10th of June, 1904, before George R. A. Hall, coroner of said city, upon the bodies of Gus Augustine, Arthur Muhlise, Henry Hagg, Ernest McCoy and others there lying in death, by its jurors, whose names are hereto inscribed, said jurors, on their oath, do say that said persons came to their death by an explosion of dynamite or other explosive at the Florence & Cripple Creek depot, at or near the town of Independence, Teller county, Colorado, on the morning of June 6, 1904, about 2:30 a. m.

"We further find that said explosive was exploded by an infernal machine purposely and artfully set and discharged by some persons to jury unknown, for the purpose of wilfully, maliciously and feloniously killing and murdering said persons and others; that said crime is one of similar crimes designed and committed in the Cripple Creek district during ᴜₕe past few months for the purpose of killing and intimidating non-union miners and thereby preventing them from working, and that said crimes are the result of a conspiracy entered into by certain members of the Western Federation of Miners, and known, incited and furthered by certain officers of that organization."

The verdict of the coroner's jury is not surprising when it is known that the jury was composed of men strongly prejudiced against organized labor. The legitimate coroner himself being forced to resign, the following composed the jury as impaneled by George R. A. Hall, coroner, appointed to fill Doran's office: ᵀ E. Pruett, J. D. Kingston, R. L. Davidson, E. C. Newcomb, Walter F. Block and C. D. Hall.

By order of Provost Marshal McClelland, eight members of the Woman's Auxiliary were brought before him to be questioned, and after being asked many questions and warned not to be guilty of "agitation" were allowed to return to their homes.

KANGAROO COURT.

June 8, Adjutant General Bell instituted a so-called military commission, composed of seven civilians of the most bitter and prejudiced enemies organized labor ever had, corrupt politicians every one, real estate sharks, mine managers and their attorneys. This bogus commission, drum head court martial, exercised all the functions of a banditti chieftan, ordering peaceful law-abiding, hard-working citizens and tax payers to appear before them, consigned to jail or deported, as their pleasure dictated, thus making a door mat of the constitution of the state and nation, and over-riding all law.

The men appointed were as follows: F. D. French, Nelson Franklin, J. B. Cunningham and T. J. Daltzell.

The obvious intention of this commission was to supplant the regular instituted courts and to give a semblance of justice to what followed.

After having instituted this commission, in order to perfect the inquisition, General Bell appointed Major Thomas E. McClelland as provost marshal for the district, whose duty it was to arrest and bring before the commission all persons placed under the ban by it.

The board sat the same day of its appointment and recommended the deportation from the district of one hundred men. They continued in session for several weeks during which time they carried things with a high hand, regardless of all law and decency. Much indignation was aroused throughout the state and nation. Many private, personal grudges against citizens of the district other than the strikers were satisfied by means of the military commission. Persons known to be friendly to the Mine Owners' Association or the Citizens' Alliance, who desired vengeance against any person, known to be friendly toward the strikers, had only to send in the names to the commission, when the victim was dragged before that "honorable" body and sum-marily dealt with by them.

This commission and the acts performed by it will live long in the memory of its victims as one of the most heartless and cruel indignities perpetrated upon an American community.

RECORD PLANT DESTROYED.

June 8, at 10:45 p. m., the Victor Daily Record office, on South Fourth street, was wrecked by unidentified men. Eight heavily armed men did the work. It could not be seen whether they were militiamen or deputy sheriffs, as they had no outward marks of identification. They walked boldly into the composing room in the rear of the office building and with rifles and revolvers drawn ordered Walter Sweet, the foreman; F. W. Langdon, a linotype operator; John Dannenfeld, the pressman; Art Caldwell, an apprentice, and a printer named Gribben, to line up and hold up their hands.

The men obeyed at once and were then driven from the office and ordered to leave the district immediately.

While this proceeding was passing two of the armed men, who carried sledges or double-jacks, proceeded to beat the two linotype machines to pieces.

They wielded the big hammers with a vengeance and soon had the type setting machinery practically ruined. The job presses were then attacked and broken up. The forms on the composing stone were hurled to the floor and thrown about the office, the telephone was smashed, a typewriter was demolished, and as much other damage as was thought necessary to complete the destruction of the office and equipment.

No clew to the identity of the men who did the work was possible at the hands of the employes who saw it accomplished. None of the employes recognized any of the faces of the armed force, although they were not masked.

Editor and proprietor George Kyner and his reporter, Edward Mannix, were not in the office when the eight men came in.

Kyner and his employe were taking luncheon at the National

restaurant and did not know of the destruction of the office until they returned there about half an hour after it happened.

The damage to the plant prevented the same being used for further publication of the Record. The paper, however, did not suspend publication, as through the courtesy of the management of the Cripple Creek Star allowing Editor Kyner the use of their plant, he was enabled to get out a small sheet.

The Star was soon notified that if they persisted in assisting Kyner in publishing the Record, their plant would receive the same treatment as the one just destroyed. By this time, however, Kyner had repaired sufficient machinery to be able to get out a very small paper by hand composition.

A significant fact in connection with the attack and demolition of the Record office is that H. J. Richmond, the Record correspondent located in Cripple Creek, was ordered to leave the district on pain of death, by parties whom he claimed were bitterly opposed to him because he had taken pains to criticize them rather closely in a criminal charge pending in the district court at Cripple Creek.

The day after the printing office was destroyed, F. W. Langdon, linotype operator, met and recognized the leader of the mob who was serving as a deputy, and walked up to him, and said:

"You are the man that led the raid on the Record." The man turned pale but did not answer. Later steps were taken by Langdon to have him arrested, and the military promised to see to it that he was brought to justice. The following day, after the meeting I have described, it was found the man recognized was still at liberty, and the military, upon being asked what they intended to do, stated:

"We have no authority to arrest that man as he is a deputy sheriff." So far as the writer has been able to learn, no effort was made to arrest the perpetrators any more than a great deal of talk and insinuations. The following night, Langdon was given instructions to leave the district inside of forty-eight hours.

Up to the date of the destruction of the Record the paper had been recognized as the official organ of the miners' union and other unions of the county. Through the editorial columns of the paper, Editor Kyner had vigorously denounced the acts of the military, early in the strike, in raiding homes and in many ways over-riding constitutional rights of the citizens. In Part I, the reader will find that on the night of September 29, 1903, the entire force of this paper was taken to military headquarters as prisoners, details of which I chronicled under "Record Force Kidnapped."

The Independence explosion was denounced in the same manner as other lawless acts and the perpetrators spoken of as assassins.

The day chosen to destroy the Record plant was opportune for the effect that undoubtedly was intended by the mine owners and Citizens' Alliance. The last issue of the paper, before the plant was destroyed, run a long editorial headed, "Call the Strike Off," which was a plea that the W. F. M. at once issue an order calling off the strike.

It was generally believed that the instigators expected that the public would at once blame the strikers for the destruction of the plant as a matter of retaliation and the enemies to all organized labor in the district at once seized this opportunity of venting their hatred of a year's standing against the paper that had so many times past denounced the high-handed methods of the Citizens' Alliance.

In expecting that the public would believe the strikers guilty of destroying the Record office, they were disappointed. I will state that at no time did I hear any person say that they believed any of the strikers guilty.

I may here state that a matter that greatly surprised people of the district, especially the union people—Editor Kyner's editorial policy changed from the date of the destruction of the Record plant. He, who had so vigorously denounced the policy of the Citizens' Alliance and Mine Owners' Association, from that date was one of their strongest supporters and gave the support of his paper during the state campaign for the re-election of James H. Peabody.

People wondered at this change of heart, but the mystery was later solved when it was learned that he had received $4,000 from the state fund, charged up to the military indebtedness as damages for the wrecking of the Record plant. As the actual cost of repairing machinery did not exceed $1,000 it is evident that the other $3,000 was indirectly paid him to change the editorial policy of his paper.

PORTLAND MINE CLOSED.

Perhaps the event of the greatest importance in the district after the destruction of the Record plant, was the closing of the Portland mine. The reader is familiar with conditions existing at the Portland mine as I gave the Portland a great deal of space in Part I on account of the conduct of the management in 1894 and up to the strike of 1903. Briefly, since the strike of 1894 Mr. Burns worked the mine on what he considered the "open shop" plan. He did not concern himself as to whether or not the miners applying for work were union or non-union, all he required of his employes was that they be sober, capable miners and they were employed. In Mr. Burns' statement, wirtten for Part I, he says:

"In the present force of union miners I have a force of about seven hundred of the best miners in the Rocky mountains."

However that may be, Mr. Burns did not discriminate against the W. F. M., and refused to join the Mine Owners' Association and if not the entire force, at least, the majority of men employed on the Portland were union miners.

As the Portland owned a mill of its own for the treatment of its own ore, it was not necessary for the Portland to ship to any of the unfair plants placed under the ban by the Federation. At the beginning of the strike matters were easily adjusted between the W. F. M. and Mr. Burns, for the Portland company. The result was that the Portland ran the ten months of the strike previous to the Independence explosion and the stockholders of the company received their dividinds without intermission. Any friction that arose was not between the Portland management and the union, but between Mr. Burns and other mine operators. They insisted that he discharge the union miners. He replied: "**I will not discriminate. So far as the Portland is concerned, I am satisfied with the treatment accorded it by the Federation. I am trustee for the stockholders of the company, and it is my duty to operate the mine to the best advantage, and that I propose to do.**"

Thus the Portland ran along until the horrible disaster on June 6. The mine operators determined then to take advantage of the indignation the crime aroused to accomplish the purpose announced when the strike first occurred—to force every Federation miner to either surrender his card in the union or leave the camp.

Mr. Burns, aflame though he was in common with the others of the district over the atrocity of June 6, could not and did not blame any of his men for the crime. He said the union miners employed in the Portland were mostly men with families and were neither "**agitators nor criminals,**" so he refused to discharge them, being unwilling to punish innocent men for a crime committed by others.

In order to accomplish the mine operators' object, General Bell, acting in conjunction with S. D. Crump, issued a proclamation on the 9th, ordering the Portland closed, and the arrest of all men therein who were "dangerous to the community."

Bell's proclamation follows:

MILITARY HEADQUARTERS, Victor, Colo., June 9, 1904.—Proclamation: Whereas, The governor of the state did, by proclamation issued on the seventh day of June, 1904, declare the county of Teller therein to be in a state of insurrection and rebellion, and the territory comprising the said county is now under the rule of military law, and now being held and occupied by the militia of said state; and

Whereas, A reign of lawlessness, violence and crime has existed in said county for several months last past, inaugurated, encouraged and carried forward by certain evil-disposed persons, resulting in wholesale assassinations of many peaceable and law-abiding citizens; and

Whereas, Said reign of violence and crime still exists in said county so that the peace of the community is threatened, lives and property of the citizens are menaced and mob rule and violence now threaten to override the law; and

Whereas, The Portland mine, situated in said county is, and for a long time has been engaged in employing and harboring large numbers of dangerous, lawless men, who have aided, encouraged and given comfort and assistance to those who have so been guilty of said crimes and outrages, so that said mine has become and now is a menace to the welfare and safety of the good people of said county and a hindrance to the restoration of peace and good order;

Now, by the power conferred on me as commander of the military force in said county and as a military necessity, it is ordered that the said mine be at once closed and all men found therein or thereabouts who are dangerous to the community be arrested and held until further orders.

SHERMAN M. BELL,

Brigadier General, Adjutant General State of Colorado, Commanding Military District, Teller County, Colorado.

Bell carried out the order in the afternoon of the 9th, with the aid of one hundred or more of his soldiers, but strange to say, he did not arrest a single one of the men in the mine. This fact alone is sufficient to show that he did not believe that the miners at work on the Portland were dangerous or lawless, and that the statement was but a necessary pretext upon which to vent his order to close down the mine.

The only dramatic feature of the occasion was that as the military force advanced up the hill an American flag rose to the top of the staff over one of the shaft houses.

The sequel to the foregoing is this: The mine operators do not propose to allow the Portland company to work its mine as the company may prefer.

It isn't possible that the Citizens' Alliance will deny a man's right to work? Some walking delegate of the unions must have called a strike on the Portland mine.

It was at once announced unless he carried a card in the Mine Owners' Association he could not work. They caused the mine to be closed down to force out the union men employed in it, against the will and protest of the owner, and proposed to continue the management of that mine by saying whom its owner should and should not employ to work it. And yet from the very inception of the strike Peabody was ever ready to proclaim: "A

man has the right to work for whom, when and where he pleases,''
etc. ''O, consistency, thou art a jewel.''

Mr. Burns was very indignant at the arbitrary action in
closing down the Portland and about a week later brought suit
in the circuit court of the United States in the name of the Portland company against Governor Peabody and others, to be allowed
to conduct the mine in his own way for the best interests of the
company.

The suit, however, never came to trial, for the reason that
influence was brought to bear on the board of directors of the
Portland Gold Mining Company. On June 20th, a special meeting of the directors was held at which they compelled President
Burns to withdraw the suit. Mr. Burns protested vigorously,
but without avail, as the majority of the board was against him.

At this meeting of the board of directors it was decided to
start up the Portland with non-union miners, and this was done
immediately.

BLACKLIST INSTITUTED.

On the morning of June 9th, two committees appointed
by the Citizens' Alliance circulated the following agreement
among the employers of the district:

"We, the undersigned merchants of the Cripple Creek district and employers of help, hereby agree not to employ help of any kind that is in any
way connected with the trades assembly or the American Federation of
Labor or the Western Federation of Miners or kindred organizations."

All employers were urged to sign the agreement which was
typewritten. All complied, with the exception of the Atlantic
Tea Company and George A. Childers both of Cripple Creek.
Later on in the day when it was ascertained that the enforcement of this rule would prevent the publishing of the daily
papers, as the printers were affiliated with the American Federation of Labor, and non-union help could not be procured to
fill positions, the ban was removed from the American Federation of Labor unions and American Labor Union organizations
substituted.

From the time of this petition being circulated, it was necessary for those belonging to organizations boycotted by the Citizens' Alliance to either surrender their positions or take a card or permit issued by the mine operators. Many employes refused to take out a card and were discharged and deported.

Following is a fac simile of permit card issued by the Mine Owners' Association in this section of "Free America."

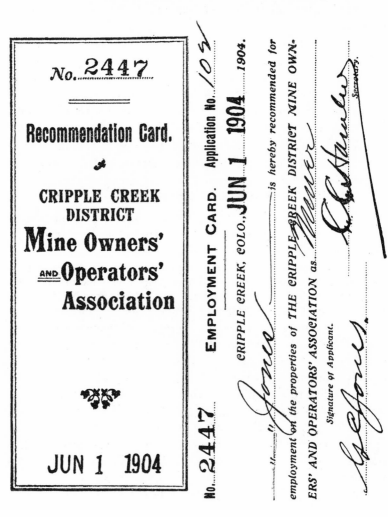

VICIOUS VERDECKBERG.

The following order which was sent to Secretary-Treasurer Haywood, is self-explanatory. It puts Colonel Verdeckberg exactly where he belongs—in the rank of the beast and the brute. Needless to say the suffering miners' families were well supplied with relief by the Western Federation of Miners.

"Headquarters Teller County Military District,
"National Guard of Colorado.
"Victor, Colorado, June 15, 1904.

"Wm. D. Haywood, Secretary and Treasurer, Western Federation of Miners, Denver, Colorado.

"Dear Sir:—The enclosed order is for your guidance and information. I have the honor to remain,

"Very respectfully yours,
(Signed) "EDW. VERDECKBERG,
"Colonel First Infantry, N. G. C."

"Headquarters Teller County Military District,
"National Guard of Colorado.
"Victor, Colorado, June 14, 1904.

"SPECIAL ORDER NO. 19.

"No organization will be allowed, while this county is under military control, to furnish aid in any form to the members of any organization or their families in this county, unless the same is done through military channels. Major Thos. E. McClelland is Provost Marshal of this military district and he stands ready to receive from any person or organization any money or other supplies which are for distribution to any person rendered needy by reason of the military occupation of this county for the suppression of insurrection, and all money and other supplies so furnished will be applied to the relief of the persons above referred to.

(Signed "EDW. VERDECKBERG,
"Colonel First Infantry, First Brigade, N. G. C.
"Commanding Teller County Military District in the absence of Brigadier General Sherman M. Bell."

The cause for the above order is due to the fact that after the union grocery stores in the district were closed by the military, the Western Federation of Miners, through its officials in Denver, made arrangements with the grocery house of John Kettelsen in Victor to furnish supplies to the destitute or needy families of miners' union members who were deported from the district.

Shortly before the order was issued the sum of $1,000 was sent to Victor to be distributed among the needy families. If the military imagined that the Federation would, after the foregoing order was issued, forward money to them in lumps of $1,000 at a time to be distributed by them to the strikers, they were disappointed as willing hands were found to distribute food and money without first having a permit from the military. Many women of the district braved the anger of the military commanders and did the work secretly that had been done openly before the order was issued.

The writer does not doubt the wisdom of the Federation in not heeding the order as the money would probably have been used by the military, as they openly boasted of eating the most delicate viands prepared and carried to the military prison by loving mothers, wives and sisters.

To feed and clothe the families of the deported miners was not on the program of the military junta. The plan was not to deport them with their supporters, for to thus publicly outrage women and children would create so hostile a sentiment that even the Mine Owners' Association and Peabody and his band of military rough riders could not withstand it. It was to starve them into departure from Cripple Creek, to go—it made no difference where, nor how they suffered, nor how or whether they survived.

Here are two items of news that were printed in the Denver papers of June 16th, that show that the foregoing statement is not in the least exaggerated, nor the cruel plans of the junta in the least magnified:

"Two women were brought before the military board last evening, Mrs. Margaret M. Hooten of Anaconda and Mrs. Estella Nichols of Cripple Creek. These women had been distributing supplies to union families and were warned that this would not be tolerated in the future. They were released after promising that they would cease helping the families of the deported miners.

"J. W. Ganley and J. W. Kettleson, grocers of Cripple Creek and Victor, were also brought before the military board and instructed not to sell any more groceries on Western Federation orders. These grocers had been honoring such orders when presented by the wives of deported miners. It was decided that henceforth all supplies must pass through the hands of Thomas McClelland, provost marshal of the camp.

"Here is a situation that should appeal not only to every individual mother of the state, but to the woman's clubs and the other woman's organizations. It is inconceivable that such brutalities should go unrebuked by Colorado's brave but tender women, however the hearts of Colorado men may be steeled to the cruel wrongs done to their helpless sisters."

APPEAL MADE TO RED CROSS SOCIETY.

The ways and means committee of organized labor of the state of Colorado sent the following communication to the Red Cross Society:

"Denver, Colo., July 18, 1904.

"Mrs. John A. Logan, President National Red Cross Society, Washington, D. C.:

"Dear Madam—As you are no doubt aware, Mr. James H. Peabody, governor of the state of Colorado, has at numerous times during the past fifteen months declared various counties in Colorado to be in a state of insurrection, and has called out the state militia and inaugurated war in said counties. At this time such a state of conditions prevails in Teller county. The fact is that, although the governor has placed Teller county under martial law, and has waged a relentless war against a class of citizens therein, no act upon the part of members of organized labor (whom we have the honor of representing), justified him in so declaring or doing.

"While the governor persists in declaring Teller county in a state of war, this war, is entirely one-sided, being carried on by the militia and others who are opposed to organized labor, the sole purpose being to terrorize union men and their families so as to compel them to sever their connections with the unions.

"However, be this as it may, truth is that our people are being subjected to all the cruelties that usually exist during actual war, the powers that be resorting to methods of abuse that would not be tolerated even against a foreign enemy in time of war. They do not hesitate to make war against defenseless women and helpless children in their mad desire to exterminate the unions. To this end, after having deported from their homes the husbands and fathers, they now refuse to allow relief in the way of food and clothing to be issued to the wives and children, unless it be through the hands of the military authorities. In proof thereof, I herewith submit copy of special military order No. 19, issued by Col. Edward Verdeckberg.

Special Order, No. 19, as printed above, followed.

"Now, since they have resorted to this method, which was entirely

uncalled for, and which we believe was done for the sole purpose of breaking the spirit of the fathers through the sufferings of their wives and children, we do not feel justified in trusting the matter of relief to the military, feeling satisfied that owing to the hatred they have shown to our
people they would not faithfully carry out this great trust.

"Now, therefore, we knowing it to be the mission of the Red Cross
Society, of which you are the official head, to take charge of and as much
as possible eliminate suffering caused by the cruelties of war, we earnestly
appeal to you to arrange to have your noble organization take charge of
the distribution of food and clothing to the families of deported citizens
of Teller county. We will furnish all necessary supplies, and only ask that
your organization take charge of the distribution of same.

"Hoping you will not turn a deaf ear to this appeal, but that you will
give it your immediate and favorable consideration, I am, very truly yours,
(Seal.) "H. B. WATERS,
"Secretary-Treasurer Ways and Means Committee.
"Room 504 Exchange Building, Denver, Colorado."

No action was taken by the Red Cross Society.

The following telegram was sent by Secretary-Treasurer
Haywood to President Roosevelt:

"Hon. Theodore Roosevelt, Washington, D. C.:

"A duty devolves upon you as President of the United States to investigate the terrible crimes that are being perpetrated in Colorado in the
name of law and order. We will render every possible assistance to the
proper authorities in such an investigation, to the end that the people of
the country may realize the outrages that are being inflicted upon innocent
persons by those in temporary official power.
"W. D. HAYWOOD,
"Secretary-Treasurer W. F. of M."

The above was not the first or last telegram sent to the
president, but all received the same treatment—no action.

From the 6th day of June to the 20th it is impossible to
chronicle all that occurred exactly as they happened for startling
events followed so fast that to record each in its proper date and
place would be impossible. Many city and county officials besides the ones named were forced to resign; all property belonging to the W. F. M. was either destroyed or confiscated.
Deportations became numerous, train loads of union men were
lined up, photographed and then loaded on the train like so
many animals and taken to remote parts of the state and in

many cases to Kansas or New Mexico. Those left in the district were confined in stuffy bull pens, sweated, tortured by hanging and it was said hands were even placed in vises to force prisoners to give the desired information.

Following close upon the separation of husbands from their families came despair and hunger, to say nothing of the tacit understanding that after the co-operative stores were closed, no Citizens' Alliance merchant would supply the necessities of life to the luckless wives and babes of the beleagured or deported miners. Merchants not identified with either the Citizens' Alliance or the Federation, on offering to supply means of subsistence, were compelled to withdraw the offer on threats of violence.

GIVE ME LIBERTY OR GIVE ME DEATH.

Even in the face of the outrageous proceedings of deporting men from families, there were phases that would have been comical had they not been so tragic. In one case a special deportation train was unloaded on the barren plains of a neighboring state and after the men were all out of the train and the militia and others in charge were ready to start back to Victor, one man shouted defiance at the soldiers by saying: "Ten to one we beat you back to Colorado."

At another time when another deportation train had been unloaded just on the border of New Mexico, a similar scene took place.

Standing on the stone that marks the line between the state of Colorado and the territory of New Mexico, Charles Anderson, raised half a loaf of bread aloft and shouted defiance back at General Bell's soldiers: "Give me liberty or give me death."

Another deported Cripple Creek miner, who stood near him, started to sing: "Sweet Land of Liberty, of Thee I Sing." Others took up the words—just those two lines—without a tune, and they watched the soldiers and deputies from Cripple Creek who walked back over the alkali plain to their train, which was waiting a mile away.

One train carrying about fifty union miners was unloaded thirty-five miles from Tres Piedras, New Mexico, and six miles from Antonito, Colorado.

One train arrived at Canon City. Many people met the deportation train with baskets of dainty food and fruit for the prisoners, but the military forbid it being distributed.

Bell said, after sending out a train of union men, "They need harvest hands in Kansas, and they can get eight weeks' work there and they can't come back here."

One of Bell's orders follows:

DEPORTATION ORDER.

"Headquarters Teller County Military District,
"National Guard of Colorado,
"Victor, Colo., June 10, 1904.

"Special Order No. 6.

"To Colonel Leo W. Kennedy: You will proceed by the Colorado Springs & Cripple Creek district railway to Colorado Springs; thence via the Atchison, Topeka & Santa Fe railway to the east line of the state of Colorado, taking with you the parties on list herewith attached, and there deposit them without the state of Colorado, returning at once to these headquarters and make due report to me. By command of

"SHERMAN M. BELL,

"Brigadier General Commanding Teller County Military District."

BELL GIVES REASONS.

Relative to the deportation of miners from the Cripple Creek district, Adjutant General Bell issued a long statement. Among other reasons for his acts at Cripple Creek, are these:

"I deported these men from the Cripple Creek district because in my judgment it was a military necessity.

"I sent them to the Kansas line because I believed it to be the most effective method of ridding Teller county and the state of Colorado of an organized gang of assassins, dynamiters, anarchists and lawbreakers.

"More than that, I sent them out of the district for their own safety. Martial law and the presence of the military is all that has prevented these men from being lynched by the indignant citizens of Teller and El Paso counties. My men have even taken ropes from their necks and saved them.

"The deportation was the quickest way of restoring peace. I don't want these men in Colorado. They are the leaders and participants in the insurrection now existing in the Cripple Creek district and it is my business to break that up. That is exactly what I propose to do.

"What steps I take as military commander concerns nobody but myself and my commander-in-chief, the governor of the state.

"For ten years they have had this county terrorized. Since the beginning of the strike last August thirty-eight non-union men have been murdered. They have dynamited the Vindicator mine and caused two deaths. They placed 300 pounds of dynamite under the Independence station and murdered fourteen men and hopelessly crippled twenty others.

"They tampered with the machinery on Stratton's Independence mine, an English corporation, and dropped fifteen men 1,140 feet to the bottom of the shaft. The remains were picked up in little pieces. All of the men killed in these instances were men who would not affiliate with their organization, and all of the mines damaged had refused to employ members of the Western Federation of Miners.

"I took charge of the district last week and I proceeded to clean it up.

"I had more than 300 men thrown into the bullpen, and I had every one of them put through the 'sweatbox.' The confessions they made were appalling.

"Today I have absolute proof that will send a dozen local federation leaders to the scaffold, and twice as many to the penitentiary.

"The men I deported were indirectly concerned in these crimes. Those I am keeping are directly concerned."

From the above, it is clearly demonstrated that Bell's ability as a **vindictive, malicious liar** is possibly only exceeded by his conceit as a would-be military hero. In fact, it is hard to determine in which capacity he excels—that of a **professional liar** or a parody on a general.

Let us to some extent analyze his statement. He says that his militia prevented strikers from being lynched and that they had even taken ropes from their necks and saved them. This is a bare-faced falsehood as it is well known that in every instance where strikers and their sympathizers were led to lonely places, horse whipped and robbed of what valuables were on their person and compelled to travel afoot out of the district, members of the militia invariably took a hand. In not one instance did the militia prevent the lynching of any striker.

Every accident that happened in the district during the strike was by Bell laid at the door of organized labor. Take the incident of Stratton's Independence mine, where the cage dropped and killed a number of miners. Of this, Bell accused the strikers, in spite of the fact that the coroner's jury placed the blame to carelessness of the engineer and the neglect of the mine management in having failed to comply with the state law in providing proper safety appliances.

As to his statement that he has absolute proof that would send strikers to the penitentiary; suffice it to say that this proof never materialized and in not one instance has a single striker or union man been convicted of any of the crimes charged against them by Bell and others.

He states the truth, where he says: "I don't want these men in Colorado." The mine owners certainly did not want these men in Colorado; Bell being the instrument of the mine owners, naturally was inspired by them.

When the Independence horror occurred June 6th, the Western Federation of Miners were holding their annual covention in Denver, which had then been in session since May 23d. The writer went to Denver on the same train with the delegates to the convention from the district, among them being C. G. Kennison, Sherman Parker, and others prominent in the local organizations of the district.

Immediately upon the convention going into session June 6th, the explosion was discussed at length, and the Federation at once offered $5,000 reward for the criminals. The convention was unanimous in expression of right and denouncing the crime in strong language and the reward offered by the Western Federation, in convention assembled, was the first; others, however, followed the example later.

Notwithstanding the fact that Kennison left the district May 22d to attend the convention which went into session Monday, May 23, and continued until Thursday after the explosion.

Monday, June 6th, he was arrested in Denver, charged with murder. In the face of the fact that the prominent members of unions in the district were being deported, many of them were arriving in Denver at different times, the delegation to the convention remained in Denver, hoping that conditions would soon change and that they could return to their homes and families. However, that may be, it was announced that the entire executive board of the W. F. M. and many others were wanted for the blowing up of the depot.

June 13th Kennison was arrested in Denver by a deputy from the district. He protested and was very roughly handled. He was held for a short time and then taken to Teller county and put through the same "sweating" process as others that had won the same amount of hatred of the enemy. Mrs. Kennison and the babies were in Denver and the arrest of Kennison almost prostrated the wife, her health at that time being poor.

All kinds of rumors were sent out by the press in regard to treatment of prisoners—in many cases the worst was true. It was widely circulated that prisoners were tortured by being hanged until nearly dead, hands placed in vises until the prisoners were almost demented with pain, and it was said that some were even subjected to the "water cure." As to the truth of the latter, I can not say, but I know of sufficient cruelties to prisoners to make me believe that if the Citizens' Alliance did not use the "water cure" on prisoners it was not because of their goodness of heart, but because it did not happen to enter their heads when they were doing the sweating they so openly boasted of. C. C. Hamlin proudly stated in public that he held the rope that was used to force Sheriff Robertson to resign.

Friends, in Teller county, we had a revival of the tortures of the Spanish Inquisition, yea, and for the same purpose—to torture innocent men into confession of crimes of which the torturers themselves were guilty.

June 6th the following statement was given out by Frank J. Hangs, attorney for the Western Federation of Miners:

"The members of the local committee of the Western Federation of Miners authorize me to say that they deplore the diabolical murder committed this morning. They regret that thoughtless persons should charge this crime to the Western Federation of Miners, and say that the Western Federation of Miners did not have a thing to do with it. They are just as much shocked as the rest of the community. No man who deserves to live could or would approve the awful deed. The fiends who planned and carried out the devilish crime should be detected and punished to the full need of the guilt. This crime must be unearthed and the perpetrators punished. The committee and all local members of the Western Federation of Miners are ready and willing to assist in uncovering the guilty ones. We will use every endeavor to assist the authorities in their efforts, and we here tender the services of all our members. We will also join in the offering of a suitable reward for the arrest and conviction of the guilty persons.

(Signed)   "DISTRICT UNION No. 1, W. F. M.
"By FRANK J. HANGS."

While the second week after the explosion was not marked by bloodshed, or any special disaster, there was plenty doing in military circles and with the mine owners and Citizens' Alliance to break the monotony. The chief events of the second week were about as follows:

Monday, June 13th—The arrest and imprisonment of Frank J. Hangs, attorney for the Western Federation of Miners, on the charge of "stirring up strife." He was held for some time and the only reason given was "military necessity." General Bell considered Mr. Hangs dangerous to the peace of the community, because of the fact that he was constantly advising the strikers.

Tuesday, June 14th.—Thirty-six men deported to New Mexico and there unloaded from their special car, and left to make the best of their environment.

Wednesday, June 15th.—The camp was visited by Henry George, Jr., of the Hearst syndicate, who expressed himself as being displeased with methods adopted by the Citizens' Alliance and its allies in disposing of so-called agitators.

Thursday, June 16th.—Moyer was released from the military prison at Telluride, turned over to the civil authorities and ordered to Cripple Creek for "safe keeping."

Friday, June 17th.—Orders issued from military headquarters for turning in all arms, ammunition and supplies in the hands of unauthorized persons. Charles G. Kennison, president of No 40, W. F. M., at Cripple Creek, confined in the county jail there. had a serious attack of illness on account of treatment received there.

Saturday, June 18th.—Board of Inquiry moves its head-quarters to county jail.

Sunday, June 19th—Was quiet, nothing more than the reg-ular sweating of prisoners occurred. Crump announced that he was continuing his work of sweating the members of the W. F M. in county jail and making good progress and hoped to be prepared to produce some startling evidence when the time for the inquiry into the Victor riot came.

Thus ended the second week. It might be well to mention here that a county warrant for $2,000 payable to S. D. Crump had been ordered drawn by the county commissioners. This was the first of a series of five similar warrants which would have to be drawn to make up the $10,000 fee which Crump was to receive as remuneration for prosecuting the perpetrators of the Independence depot outrage, those who started the shooting and the persons who destroyed the Record plant.

A. E. Carlton and H. L. Shepard, a prominent mining broker and operator, went on S. D. Crump's bond in the sum of $10,000 for the faithful performance of his duties.

DEATH OF EMIL JOHNSON.

June 23.—Breathing a curse against Governor Peabody, Ad-jutant General Bell and the state administration which, by exer-cise of its despotic militarism, had driven him from his wife and babies, Emil L. Johnson, one of the miners recently deported from Cripple Creek, ended his life in the morning by inhaling gas.

For some time he had been despondent because the military refused to allow him to return to his family, and when he went to his room at 1646 Larimer street a short time after midnight he disrobed, turned on the gas and laid down on the bed to die. He was discovered about 9:30 by his brother, John T. Johnson, and Police Surgeon Holmquist was summoned. Despite the heroic efforts of the physician, Johnson died a few minutes after the arrival of the police ambulance. He was removed to the morgue.

The case was one of the most pitiable ever brought to the

attention of the coroner. Johnson's wife and children, at Altman, had been refused provisions because of an order issued by
General Bell. When Johnson heard of this he was driven almost
to the verge of madness to think his innocent family should be
made to suffer so much on account of his insisting on his rights.
He brooded much over this, at times laboring under the hallucination that his family was starving.

The oldest child was six years of age. The youngest was
only four months old and was the pride of its father's heart.
Often while brooding over his troubles Johnson would bury his
face in his hands and weep bitterly, pausing now and then to
speak of the manner in which his four-months' old child would
pull his hair and pat his face, and, although so young, calling
"Da-da," and laughing in baby glee. Johnson applied to the
military for permission to return to the gold district, but this
was sternly refused. The suicide was the result.

When the union miners were started for the New Mexico
line, Johnson was rudely awakened from his bed at his home in
Altman at an early hour in the morning. Some soldiers entered
and, intruding into the privacy of the family bedroom, roughly
ordered Johnson to dress himself. When his wife attempted to
kiss him good-bye she was seized by the soldiers and told to
get back into her room and not to interfere.

Johnson was hurried from his home, half dressed, and with
the despairing cries of his wife and babies ringing in his ears.
They never saw him alive again, and it was stated that when his
wife had inquired of him from a soldier she was told that he
had been given lashes over the back and sent across the line into
New Mexico. The fear that his wife would end her life in despair
was one of the terrors which haunted the persecuted man.

Johnson had lived in Altman for seven years, and was regarded as one of the best miners in the district. He had worked
in several of the mines there and bore a good reputation as a
citizen; he had never before been arrested, and enjoyed the regard of all his neighbors, as well as the city officials of Altman.

He was about thirty-two years of age and came to Colorado from Minnesota about ten years ago.

WRIT OF HABEAS CORPUS APPLIED FOR.

June 28th.—In order to ascertain whether the men arrested were held as military or civil prisoners, Attorney Hangs, for the W. F. M., made application before Judge Seeds, of the district court, for a writ of habeas corpus, in behalf of L. R. Jenks, who had been secretly confined in the city jail for several days. At Victor the evening of June 28th, thirty-nine of the prisoners who had been confined in the bull pen were hurriedly placed on board a train and deported. This deportation caused much suffering to the relatives as the deportation was so hurriedly, so secretly carried out that they were not given an opportunity to say good-bye.

An attempt was made to land these men at Colorado Springs but upon the city officials objecting they were landed at Palmer Lake. Arrangements were made at that point to transport the men to Denver, where they arrived the following day. They were met at the depot by the officers of the Western Federation who had been notified of their coming, taken in charge and cared for. From that date as long as deportations continued many exiles made their way to Denver, some later on sending for their families who were all provided for by the W. F. M. The state ways and means committee provided the exiles with headquarters.

Mr. M. C. Parish, a retired farmer, related an experience he had with the militia, as follows:

"I can't say anything as to the merits of either side in Cripple Creek, for I don't know, but I do know of a few outrages the militia has perpetrated. The other day they came over to Mount Pisgah, where my wife and I had gone to visit our son. They said they were searching for guns and men. I don't know who any of the soldiers were, but the man in charge was called captain. The school teacher had closed her season's work and was en route to the railroad to take a train for home, but had stopped over night at the ranch house I speak of. The soldiers entered her room, looked under the bed, searched everywhere and commanded her to open her trunk.

"She insisted that it contained nothing but her personal effects, and asked the men to desist from going through a lady's wardrobe under the pretext of looking for guns. This was in Park county, too, mind you.

"Without further parley the order was given, a soldier took an ax and chopped off the lock of the trunk, and when it was opened it was turned bottom side up, the contents dumped on the floor and scattered.

"She begged them not to molest her letters, and they paid no attention. The captain read the letters and put some of them in his pocket.

"When they got through one of the soldiers told her she could pick up her belongings when she chose, and they left for Teller county.

"The same party held up my seventeen-year-old son, searched his room and took with them his target rifle and some cartridges he had brought out from Iowa.

"Military rule may be all right—I am not prepared to say; but this sort of thing is wrong in any land."

INFORMATION FILED.

July 2.—Informations against forty-eight leaders and prominent members of the Western Federation of Miners were filed in the district court of Teller county, consequent upon the findings of the coroner's jury in the inquiry into the death of Roscoe McGee and John H. Davis who were killed in the Victor rioting on June 6. Sheriff Bell filed two direct informations in the district court charging murder, conspiracy to murder and assault to kill.

In the first complaint the men arrested were charged with the murder of Roscoe McGee, June 6, and the defendants in this case were Charles H. Moyer, president Western Federation of Miners; William D. Haywood, secretary-treasurer Western Federation of Miners; John C. Williams, vice-president W. F. M.; J. T. Lewis, L. J. Simpkins, James P. Murphy, D. C. Copley, James Kirwan, James A. Baker, members Executive Board Western Federation of Miners; John M. O'Neill, editor Miners' Magazine; Michael O'Connell, Charles Kennison, Sherman Parker, W. F. Davis, L. R. Jenks and about forty others.

The second information was filed against the same parties and charged them with intent to kill one Fred Studavoss.

CORONER'S VERDICT.

"An inquisition holden at Cripple Creek, Teller county, state of Colorado, on the 27th to the 30th days of June, 1904, before George Hall, coroner of this county, upon the bodies of Roscoe McGee and John Davis by the jurors whose names are hereunto subscribed, said jurors, upon their oath do say:

"First—The jury finds that said Roscoe McGee came to his death in the city of Victor, in the county and state aforesaid, on the 6th day of June, 1904, by means of a gunshot wound inflicted, as the jury believes, by one Albert Bilat, fired by him, the said Albert Bilat, with felonious intent, he having been aided, abetted and encouraged in said crime by others as in this verdict hereinafter stated.

"Second—We find that the said John Davis came to his death in the city of Victor on the 6th day of June, 1904, by means of a gunshot wound inflicted by one William Boyle, and fired by him, the said William Boyle, with felonious intent, he having been aided and abetted in said crime by others as this verdict hereinafter states.

"Third—The jury further finds that upon the said day an armed body of men, about ninety, members of the Western Federation of Miners, assembled at Victor, in the said county, in the afternoon, pursuant to a prearranged plan, understanding the conspiracy, from different parts of said county, principally the city of Victor, the town of Goldfield, the town of Independence and the town of Anaconda.

"That said body of men so assembled were appointed special policemen for the city of Victor by one Michael O'Connell, the then marshal of said city, and were by him and through his influence furnished with badges of office, firearms and ammunition.

"That, while the act of deputizing said men gave them temporarily a color of office, the same was done and said body of men congregated and armed themselves for another and unlawful purpose, namely: to commit acts of violence, to override the law and to take human life; and that, in fact, the men so armed and deputized constituted an unlawful assembly or mob.

"That before the death of said Roscoe McGee and John Davis and before the commission of any overt act by said mob the said O'Connell was removed from office by the mayor of said city, and said mob were by the sheriff of said county publicly ordered to disperse and go to their homes, notwithstanding which a portion thereof, armed as before stated, and being about fifty in number, secreted themselves in and upon a building in said city, and used and occupied for the Miners' Union hall. That certain other members of said mob stationed themselves at different points on the streets and other places in said city, including the store operated in the interests of said Western Federation of Miners.

"That about 3 o'clock on said day a public meeting was in progress upon a vacant square in said city midway between Union hall and the said union store.

"That a riot was started by a member of said mob, to-wit: one Alfred Miller, when he attempted to shoot and kill C. C. Hamlin and others who were engaging in said public meeting, that thereupon many shots were fired, principally by the members of said mob, both from the front windows and roof of said union hall and from the front part of said union store and different points on the street, and that certain of such shots took effect, as hereinabove stated, causing the death of said Roscoe McGee and John Davis.

"That eight or ten other shots took effect in the bodies of as many citizens, grievously wounding them; in almost every instance said victims having been shot in the back. That the members of said mob who had gathered in and upon said union hall were under the immediate command of one Peter Calderwood, aided and assisted by P. J. Hall, G. M. Hooten, Mike Hannigan, William Johnson, W. E. Haskins, A. M. Weir, William Welsh, James Tedrow, J. R. Shoemaker, C. H. Say, Jack Cheby, Frank Chelan, D. T. Mitchell, Jerry O'Brien, Peter O'Neill, Tom Nolan, Lyman Nichols, Mark S. Nichols, P. J. Murphy, D. A. McCloud, Fred Minister, Thomas F. Lloyd, F. H. Greffer, John Brogan, Nick Voyle, William Voyle, Albert Bilat, D. A. Cameron, William Graham, J. I. Jenks, James Whalen. That during the progress of said riot the said Michael O'Connell, feloniously, wickedly and of his malice aforethought, fired upon and shot one J. J. Hosmer in the back with the intent then and there to take the life of the said Hosmer.

"That it was the evident intention of the leaders and members of said mob, as shown by the testimony and their own declaration, to shoot down and take the lives of citizens, called by them the mine owners.

"We further find from the evidence that the officials of said Western Federation of Miners are primarily responsible for the crimes committed as aforesaid.

"That by incendiary, unlawful and seditious statements officially promulgated and published they have incited, encouraged and abetted acts of violence and crime on the part of their members and officials and are chargeable with the said unlawful and criminal assembly and the crimes resulting therefrom.

"That among those who aided, abetted and incited the commission of said crimes are Charles H. Moyer, William D. Haywood, John C. Williams, J. T. Lewis, D. J. Simpkins, James P. Murphy, D. C. Copley, James Kirwan, James H. Baker and John M. O'Neill, and that each and every member of the said mob organized and armed by Michael O'Connell are jointly and severally guilty of the acts of violence committed in the said Victor, state of Colorado, on the 6th day of June, 1904.

"In testimony whereof the said jurors have hereunto set their hands the day and year aforesaid.

(Signed)

"H. P. REITON, Foreman.
"F. A. PHIPPS, Clerk.
"R. ARNOLD.
"P. L. THORSEN.
"G. C. BLAKEY.
"D. BERNARD.

"G. A. R. HALL, Coroner."

This same day, July 2, five more men were deported by order of the military commission. This made a total of one hundred and eighty-eight persons who had been deported by direct orders of the military commission.

At least five hundred others had left the district, some of whom had been warned to leave by members of the Citizens' Alliance and the hired thugs of the Mine Owners' Association; others left taking their families with them fearing they would be subjected to indignities at the hands of the would-be "law and order" elements.

On July 4th warrants were served by Sheriff Bell of Teller county, upon Charles H. Moyer, J. C. Williams, vice-president W. F. M., and James Kirwin, assistant secretary of the Federation. They were released on bond of $5,000 each. Other warrants were out against all persons charged by the coroner's jury as being implicated in the Victor riot of June 6th.

The warrants were made returnable to the district court of Teller county, September 20th, 1904.

ANOTHER SUICIDE.

W. H. Morgan, an assayer from Cripple Creek district, president and general manager of the Grouse Mountain Mining Company, committed suicide in Denver on the afternoon of July 4th. Letters left behind by him showed that he had been hounded and threatened by the military.

Morgan was one of the first men to be deported from the district. Although not a union man, he had been an employer and sympathizer with all organized labor.

Deportation so preyed upon his mind that when the statement was made by General Bell through the daily press, he determined upon suicide. This was ascertained through letters left by him. He accomplished this end by swallowing cyanide of potassium and then shooting himself through the heart.

This man's death was undoubtedly due to Colorado's militarism.

WHIPPED AND ROBBED.

July 8th, C. M. Tully, president of the retail clerks union, D. C. O'Neill, secretary of the same union, Fred Warburton and G. C. Fraser, members of No. 32, W. F. M., were cruelly betrayed by deputies into the hands of a mob, by whom they were beaten and robbed. Three weeks previous, Mr. Tully returned to the district on a pass issued by General Bell at the solicitation of Dr. Latimer of Victor. Mr. Tully had left the district for the reason that his wife was in a delicate condition and he feared for her safety if he became involved in trouble.

Mr. O'Neill was among those deported to Kansas on June 10th. A few days previous he succeeded in securing a pass from General Bell to return to Victor in order to collect his personal effects. Mr. Warburton had returned to Victor on a pass issued to him by Colonel Verdeckberg. Mr. Fraser also had a pass signed by Bell.

All these men were arrested and taken to the Mine Owners' and Citizens' Alliance headquarters where, upon producing their passes, they were released. They were later arrested by Deputy Sheriffs Kid Waters and William Dingman.

Sam Larson, William Miller and Ed Wilder assisted Waters and Dingman. The prisoners were taken to the Baltimore hotel and confined in a room. As the prisoners were being conducted through the streets to the hotel they were seen by dozens of the military officers to whom they called that they had passes from Bell, but none made any attempt to rescue them. They were held in the hotel until ten o'clock that night. At that hour Waters rushed into the room exclaiming, "For God's sake, get these men out of here."

Mr. O'Neill, when interviewed, spoke as follows:

"We knew we were up against it then. They rushed us out the rear way to the alley and marched us down the alley to the F. & C. C. tracks and continued still in the alleys between Sixth and Seventh streets to Wilson's creek. Here, a question of the road to take arose and Waters decided the men should take the main road although they wanted to go around by the railroad tracks. At this point Waters lighted a number of matches for the double purpose, we believe, of searching the road for fresh tracks and to signal the mob leaders of our whereabouts. He was apparently satisfied with the search, for he soon gave the word to go on, and with one deputy guarding our rear and Waters leading, we proceeded. We had gone one hundred yards when the mob broke upon us. They had a few words with Waters and he promptly stuck his guns in his pockets. They paid little attention to the other deputy, who promptly turned his back and went back in the direction of Victor. During our march out of town Tully asked Waters why he did not turn us over to the military, as they were close at hand and could protect us? Waters replied: 'That would make a pretty fix, wouldn't it? Having the soldiers shooting their own people.'

"After the mob had sent Waters and the other deputy away they ordered us to step forth. I was the first one, They gave me a crack over the back with a club and then one of them took out a long blacksnake and began on me. He must have given me about fifty lashes, but the blow in the small of the back is causing me the most inconvenience, although my body is covered with stripes."

When O'Neill paused for a moment Fraser took up the thread of the story. He is a powerful man, well dressed and has the stamp of intelligence. He said:

"While they were flogging O'Neill three of them set on me and I was knocked down with a Winchester. I tried to get up, and three times they floored me. They beat and kicked me when I was down, and when they finished lashing O'Neill they turned to me with the blacksnake."

Warburton and Heeney escaped with floggings and verbal abuse. Tully was not assaulted, one of the mob explaining to him: "You weak-looking little—— —— ——, we won't do anything to you this time, but if you come back, we'll hang you."

After the business of the floggings and assaults had been completed, the five men were faced up against the wall of the mountain and ordered to throw their hands in the air.

O'Neill continued as follows:

"They then made a run for us to go through our pockets. There did not seem to be any leader, but every member of the mob acted on his own responsibility.''

Following is the haul which the mob secured:

D. C. O'Neill—Fifty dollars in cash, fountain pen, pocket comb, papers and letters.

Fred Warburton—Diamond, valued at $50 or $60; watch, $65; fob chain, $35; railroad ticket to southern Kansas, $20; check on Colorado Springs bank, $30; $11 in cash, pocket knife, pocketbook, letters and papers.

J. C. Fraser—$39 in cash, letters and papers.

From the two other men they secured nothing of value except that each one was robbed of his pass signed by Bell. During the search O'Neill turned his head to get a better look at the thieves who were going through him, when one of them dealt him a savage blow on the head. Fortunately, he wore a stiff hat, which broke the force of the blow.

The men were then marched about 100 yards farther, when they were released with the warning never to return, emphasized by several volleys fired in close proximity to their persons.

O'Neill and Fraser seemed to be the objects of the mob's particular hatred. Curses and foul names accompanied the parting words which were delivered to the men. ''If ever you come back here,'' said one of the mob to Fraser, ''we'll hang and quarter you. You——, I've a notion to kill you now.''

It was about eleven o'clock that the lame and sore quintet began the weary march across the hills to Canon City. They were suffering from hunger and ready to drop from exhaustion when they reached the home town of Governor Peabody at seven o'clock in the morning. After staying in Canon City all day they boarded a Rio Grande train for Denver on transportation which had been wired them by the Western Federation of Miners.

The men were advised not to give out the names of the persons they recognized in the mob, but they could swear to the identity of at least a dozen of them. The case of Mr. Tully was particularly pathetic. His wife was still in delicate health, and the shock of the outrage on her husband, it was feared, would have a serious effect upon her.

General Bell, when questioned in regard to the men being assaulted after having received passes from him, expressed himself as follows: **"They just wanted to find out what would happen to them if they returned to Cripple Creek and I am glad they found out."**

July 8th a committee from the Citizens' Alliance of Victor went to Cripple Creek to demand that the board of county commissioners appoint a successor to Frank P. Mannix, county clerk and recorder, whom they were trying to force to resign. At seven o'clock, p. m., Mr. Mannix, while at supper with his family, was arrested and taken to the Mine Owners' Association room and later brought before the military commission. He was questioned at much length regarding his attitude during the strike troubles. After nearly an hour spent in examining the prisoner, he was requested to hand in his resignation as clerk and recorder. This he refused to do, stating that he had done nothing that would justify his resigning by force or otherwise, and that there was no legal basis or any just cause for enforcing his resignation. He was released and demanded military protection from General Bell, fearing that he would receive violence. Bell furnished Mr. Mannix with a guard.

On the following day Mr. Mannix, accompanied by General Bell, Major McClelland, General Reardon and two private soldiers went to Canon City. Mr. Mannix, in speaking of the affair said that he had not been deported but left because of imminent trouble in the district. Discussing his reasons for leaving Victor Mr. Mannix said:

"I had no idea that the situation was as bad as it is. No one can comprehend the state of affairs unless he sees things for himself. The military almost admit that the armed thugs are beyond their control, and I felt that one of these might do me harm if I remained. There is no telling what they will do to other union sympathizers in the district, as the military is powerless to restrain their reckless acts. It is quite likely that we will hear of more dastardly acts on the part of the members of the Citizens' Alliance.

"Every effort was made to make me resign from the office of county clerk, but I went back to the district determined that no kind of threat would induce me to give up the office. A proposition was made to me that if I gave a deputy power to act and went back to my ranch I would receive the salary from the office just as heretofore. I told the person who made this proposition that I would sooner resign than consent to anything like this.

"It is all plainly a game of politics. The mine owners and members of the Citizens' Alliance realize that without the office of county clerk they will be greatly hampered in stealing the election in Teller county this fall. * * * It is the desire of the mine owners to register all the strangers they have brought into the camp, and as they can not be qualified voters on account of their short residence, it is necessary to Republican success that the mine owners and members of the Citizens' Alliance have full possession of the office of the county clerk. I will go back to my ranch at Montrose tomorrow and stay there until I think I can go back to the Cripple Creek district and live in peace. I did not take my wife along with me. She is in bad health, and it was more on account of her condition that I left the district than any other reason I can assign. I feared that some violence would be attempted at my home, and General Bell will keep a guard there until my wife can join me at Montrose."

Mr. Mannix is one of the best known Democrats in Teller county and has always been very popular. He is a member of the Typographical union and has a very wide acquaintance throughout the state.

General Bell in speaking of the Mannix affair said he was sorry that Mannix was compelled to leave the district on account of the danger he was in, but he did his best to do things right for him, and added that it was all because of personal friendship.

Pity others did not enjoy the friendship of Military Dictator Bell, who, might thereby, have been saved beatings and humiliations.

From July 11th to 20th the people of the district were kept on the qui vive both day and night on account of the many arrests and frequent deportations. No person, unless an adherent of the Citizens' Alliance or Mine Owners' Association felt safe from molestation.

Squads, under orders of the military commission, inspected all persons arriving in the district. Strangers were hauled up before the commission, made to give an account of themselves, and, if the account was not satisfactory, were forced to leave or thrown in the "bull pen." An interview with Mr. Franklin, ex-mayor of Victor, a member of the military commission, by a Rocky Mountain News reporter will enlighten the reader as to how that body was conducting things at this time. Mr. Franklin said:

"While things are quiet now, deportations are going on just the same as before. We are not telling who is deported at present. The committee simply works on the list, and then the men are deported without anything being said."

July 20, the Portland mine was closed by the military for the second time. The close-down was due to the arrest by the military of nearly all of the mechanical force of 500 employed on the surface in the three shaft houses. This comprised engineers, firemen, master mechanics and men in other departments. All of the men arrested were miners' union members who refused to take out working cards in the Mine Owners' Association.

The action taken against them constituted one of the most specific phases that developed during the strike. It was expected for nearly a week, and if it had not come up that night, the next morning the men who were arrested would have quit their positions at the Portland, thus saving the military the trouble of arresting, imprisoning and finally sending them out of the district. As a matter of fact, the union men arrested continued to hold their jobs in the expectation that the Mine Owners' Association would demand that they take out association cards or suffer arrest. It was believed by the miners that military action would occur at that time but when it did not materialize at the time expected the decision was reached by the men to cease work, take their wages and leave the district forthwith.

When the Portland was closed by General Bell, which occurred about one month before, it was understood that no union men would be re-employed unless they should surrender their allegiance to the Western Federation of Miners and take out Mine Owners' Association cards. The majority directorate of the Portland Gold Mining Company, however, in order to retain the services of the splendid force of miners which it had prior to the closing down of the mine by the military, decided for the time being at least, to allow a certain number of the old force to go back

to work without first compelling them to take out the Mine
Owners' Association permit. This course was especially applicable to the engineering and other departments, and the result was
that substantially all of the men employed in those branches remained with the Portland company.

Between 11 and 12 o'clock details of military were sent out to
Goldfield and Cripple Creek and to other points for the purpose of
making arrests of Portland miners who worked on the day shift.
One military attache stated that it was not the purpose to deport
the men, and the same authority remarked later that the whole
scheme was a conspiracy to shut down the mine.

July 29, the attorneys for the Western Federation of Miners
won their first victory in their efforts to procure the release of the
men incarcerated, charged with the Independence disaster and
the street riot in Victor June 6, for whom bail had heretofore been
refused. Bonds were fixed for forty-six men, charged with these
crimes, bonds ranging from $1,500 to $10,000 each. Among the
men for whom bonds were secured was Michael O'Connell, the deposed marshal of Victor.

DEATH OF O'CONNELL.

Upon the release of Mr. O'Connell, he went to Denver. He arrived in that city August the 5th. On the following evening he
met his death by falling from a window of the fourth story of the
Markham hotel. The cause of his fall from the window was
shrouded in mystery. Some advanced the theory that his mind
had become partly unbalanced on account of the indignities he
suffered while an inmate of "bull pen." Others entertained the
opinion that his death was an accident, but a large majority of the
deported miners then in the city, openly charged that he had been
deliberately murdered by a paid assassin.

The untimely death of Mr. O'Connell was deeply regretted by
all who were acquainted with him, with the possible exception of a
few people who were interested in the Mine Owners' Association
and Citizens' Alliance. Mr. O'Connell, while acting as marshal,
won the esteem of all persons with whom he had dealings on ac-

count of impartiality and a desire to maintain the law, regardless
of who were the offenders. It was on account of this well-known
trait of his character, that he was deposed from office and persecuted, as it did not suit the purposes of the element, carrying
things with a high hand in the district, to have a marshal who was
impartial and would enforce the law and protect the interests of
all alike.

The Miners' Magazine of August 18, 1904, contained the following eulogy upon the life of Mike O'Connell:

"Michael O'Connell, the deposed marshal of the city of Victor, is now
numbered with the silent majority, who are wrapped in the somnus of
death. The good, brave and generous man who came to Colorado with the
blush of boyhood on his cheek, is now numbered with the thousands who
sleep in Evergreen cemetery, in the City of the Clouds. For sixty days he
suffered all the humiliation which a Mine Owners' Association and a Citizens' Alliance could heap upon him in a bull pen, and when his friends secured the bonds which liberated him from persecution and imprisonment,
he was forced to leave his home and family under threats from a hired,
blood thirsty mob. He was even denied the right of an American citizen,
to remain at his home. We are told that a man's home is his castle, and
that no man or party of men, has the right to invade or trespass upon the
sacred precincts of the home. But the Mine Owners' Association and a
Citizens' Alliance have no reverence for the sanctuary of a home, no sympathy for the breaking heart-strings of a woman's holy love for her husband
and no pang of pity for the flowers of childhood that bloomed in the once
happy home of Michael O'Connell.

"We have known the dead man for fifteen long years. We are proud
of the honor of having been numbered among his friends. The Great Ruler
of human destiny and Creator of human life only ushers into existence in
a generation a few men like the departed Michael O'Connell.

"He was the soul of honor, a prince among men—one of those grand
characters, whose every act in life soared in an atmosphere of moral
grandeur where dishonor could not live. In his death, another sacrifice of
human life lies indirectly at the door of the governor of this state. There
was no protection for the brave and heroic marshal of Victor. He had
sinned against the governor, because his heart beat in sympathy with the
cause of the striking miners. He was a law-breaker and an insurrectionist,
because his honor and his manhood scorned to bow in submission to the
Mafia, that has been backed and supported by the armed power of the state.
In the years that are to come, if a conscience returns to the chief executive
of Colorado, the memory of Michael O'Connell's death will rise up like a
ghost, to haunt him in his midnight dreams.

"In the Cloud City the brave man has been laid to rest. All over the jurisdiction of the Western Federation of Miners the untimely death of Michael O'Connell will be mourned, and the keenest sympathy and sorrow will be felt for his bereaved wife and fatherless children."

MASS MEETING OF CITIZENS.

July 26, a mass meeting was held in Cripple Creek at the headquarters of the Mine Owners' Association for the purpose of considering the advisability of recommending suspension of martial law to Governor Peabody. So much pressure had been brought to bear by conservative citizens of the state against martial law and acts growing therefrom, being continued, and the campaign for the state election being about to open, and the maintenance of martial law in the district, it was feared, would weaken the chance of Republican success, it was deemed policy on the part of the powers in control to have martial law suspended.

In accordance with the desire of this mass meeting, on the 28th, Governor Peabody issued a proclamation suspending martial law in Teller county.

General Bell said that he looked for trouble to start as soon as the troops were withdrawn, intimating that the strikers would cause trouble, when the facts were that all the trouble and violation of law under the reign of martial law, was committed by the henchmen of the mine owners and Citizens' Alliance, ably assisted by the militia. The General further stated that the troops had been kept in the district to protect the union miners and their friends. The reader can judge as to how successful Bell and his "army" had been in protecting these people from the facts previously recorded.

The suspension of martial law put an end to the famous military commission. The commission, in winding up its affairs, made the following report:

"The military court was appointed June 8, and assembled at once and elected H. McGarry as president and Nelson Franklin as recorder, and proceeded to examine all parties appearing. The number of those appearing was 1,569; the number of those recommended for deportation was 238; the number of those recommended for trial in the criminal court was 42; the number recommended for release was 1,289.

"Of those recommended for deportation the list was composed of agitators, ore thieves, keepers of fences for stolen ore, habitues of bawdy houses, saloon bums and vagrants. The examination was conducted along the line of desirability of those examined for residence in the district, with a view to peace and law observance, and no other purpose was had in view of the recommendation."

The reader can form an opinion of the vindictiveness and untruthfulness of the foregoing report when it is borne in mind that among those deported by that body were people in all walks of life, other than union men, among them being respected business men, attorneys, one former attorney-general and they did not even draw the line at ministers of the gospel.

While it is true that some of the people referred to above were deported after the military commission had suspended, it is nevertheless true that the gentlemen(?) that had comprised the same took a conspicious part in the deportations.

The suspension of martial law and the military commission made very little difference in the treatment of union people and those suspected of being friendly to them. The only difference being that instead of being deported with a military escort, victims were led up the mountain trail by mobs, beaten, robbed and compelled to make their way afoot over the hills.

At 9:15, p. m., of the same day martial law was suspended, John and Joseph Fisher, John Schmidt and John Miller were made victims of a mob. July 31, under promise of protection, by Sheriff Bell and Adjutant General Bell, John Harper and T. H. Parfet, former managers of the co-operative stores in the district, made arrangements to re-open the stores. How faithfully this promise of protection was kept the reader will learn from what follows:

On August 9, John Harper was seized by eight masked men at his home and driven from the district. The seizure was made about 8 o'clock p. m. Harper was taken from his home without hat, coat or vest. The sheriff's office was notified. Undersheiff Underwood with four deputies started out with the avowed intention of rescuing him but needless to say the rescue was a failure. Mr. Harper, after being beaten by the mob and released, made his way on foot to Canon City, from which place he took a train to Denver.

On August 10, five masked men went to the home of George Seitz, at 11 o'clock at night to deport him from the camp. They were met with a fusillade of shots. The fire was returned but no blood was spilled. Seitz held the fort. Seitz lived with his two children, both girls—one about twenty years old and the other about nine—was called to his door by a loud knock shortly after 11 o'clock. He asked who was there. The reply came:

"Never mind. We want you."

One of the men opened the back door and stepped into the kitchen. Seitz ordered the masked man out. He refused to go, but fired a shot. Seitz in return fired three shots. Then a fusillade of bullets was sent into the house.

Officers were quickly on the spot and carried Seitz down to the city jail for protection. He told a representative of the press that he had not taken out a mine owners' card and that he would not.

Former Mayor W. J. Donnelly, a hardware merchant of Victor, and the Rev. Mr. Leland were notified by a mob to leave the district. Mr. Donnelly's offense was that he had gone on bonds of some of the strikers and Mr. Leland was guilty of preaching a sermon in which he denounced the outrages perpetrated by the brigade of thugs that termed themselves the "law and order element." Both the gentlemen appealed to the sheriff for protection and were given a temporary guard.

DISTRICT OFFICIALS ISSUE PROCLAMATION.

So much indignation was aroused in the state over the frequent assaults and deportations in the district that the conservative element discussed the advisability of forming a vigilance committee to enforce **real law and order.** This, together with the protests appearing in the daily papers, compelled the authorities of the district to make an attempt to put an end to lawlessness. To that end Sheriff Bell issued the following proclamation:

"Whereas, Many evil-disposed persons have assaulted citizens of Teller county, taken them from their homes, forced them to leave the county, indulged in incendiary talk and in other ways continually agitated the unhappy condition of affairs existing in our county for months past; and

"Whereas, Many citizens are carrying arms; now, therefore

"All citizens of Teller county will refrain from carrying concealed weapons. They will, likewise, refrain from congregating on the streets and in public places and from in any manner using language that may tend to cause violations of the law. Each and every citizen, whatever his position may be, will be governed by this proclamation.

"The law will be enforced without regard to party in respect to these matters, and the lives and property of all citizens of this county shall and will be protected. The deputies of this office will strictly follow these instructions, and I urge all parties residing within and without the county to refrain from in any manner doing anything that will cause or incite trouble in this county.

"Issued from the office of the sheriff of Teller county, this 11th day of August, 1904."

Mayor Shockey of Cripple Creek and Mayor French of Victor issued the following statement:

"We, the undersigned, mayors of the cities of Cripple Creek and Victor, hereby pledge to the sheriff our hearty support and the support of the police departments of our respective cities in carrying out the spirit of the above proclamation, and all police officers of both cities are hereby required to carry out the sheriff's proclamation and co-operate with the sheriff's office to enforce the law.

"W. L. SHOCKEY, Mayor of Cripple Creek.
"F. D. FRENCH, Mayor of Victor."

From the foregoing it would appear that the officials had finally determined to make an effort to suppress lawlessness. Whether they were only half-hearted in this or that the tough element, whom they had been instrumental in bringing into the district had gotten beyond their control, I do not know. Certain it is, however, that the proclamation issued by the officials had little, if any, effect. Lawlessness continued as the following will show.

MORE VANDALISM.

August 20, a wholesale deportation took place. The co-operative store in Cripple Creek, that had been opened under new management, was closed and partially destroyed. The authorities seemed powerless to do anything to restore order.

Between 5 and 8 o'clock p. m., above date, a mob of fully 1,000 armed men took possession of the store and the authorities. All the afternoon men had been congregating on the streets of Cripple Creek.

A little after 4 o'clock the various shifts of non-union miners gathered in the town and took places at the corner of Second and Bennett avenues. Everyone seemed to be in the dark concerning the purpose of the crowd. All were armed and it was easy to surmise that something more than ordinary was about to take place, although few words were spoken.

At 5 o'clock a crowd swept up Bennett avenue, like a great wave, toward the union store, that was just a half block away. No attempt was made to stop the rush of men on the store, which the mob soon reached. The leader yelled that the time had come for a final clean-up of the Cripple Creek district. That was their determination and if they did not carry it out, at least they showed their good will to do so.

The mob dashed into the store from the front and rear, ordering every one in the store to hold up their hands. The command was obeyed quickly, and within a very few minutes the employes of the store, together with General Eugene Engley, were led out prisoners. At once the work of destroying the store commenced. Canned goods were hurled through the plate-glass windows, all shelf goods were either thrown in the street or on the floor; all canned goods were in this manner either destroyed or carried away by the crowd that gathered. A car load of flour and almost as much sugar was totally ruined by being either poured out or saturated with coal oil.

No masks were worn by any member of the crowd. As they approached the store a couple of those inside attempted to escape by running up the stairs of an adjoining building, but they were soon caught. Mr. Heinerdinger, the manager of the store, was in the sheriff's office, a few doors above but on the other side of the street, at the time, and told Undersheriff Parsons the store was to be raided. Undersheriff L. F. Parsons immediately left the office and went over to the store. He was quickly seized. Two guns were drawn on him and he was not permitted to go in. The undersheriff did not even have an opportunity to address the crowd, which he claimed was his intention. He was taken up the street about one hundred feet, where he was detained. His guards then took him down the street to the corner of Second. There he was left and immediately retired to his office, where he found Frank J. Hangs, attorney for the W. F. M., who asked him for protection. At this time Mr. Parsons was told that he was wanted in the rear office. No sooner had he entered the rear office than he was seized by a couple of masked men, who took him into the private office in the rear, where he was held a prisoner for over an hour. During the time the undersheriff was held prisoner the crowd began the work of searching for all the men marked for deportation. Committees were sent hither and thither to locate them. The men taken out of the union store were marched up Bennett avenue toward the county jail, where seventeen men were still confined for complicity in the riot in Victor June 6. In the middle of the block they were halted, and the crowd was ordered to fall back. Other searching parties began to return with other prisoners, and it did not take long to decide upon which road the men were to be taken out of the district.

A photographer stood opposite the county jail and attempted to take pictures but was prevented.

Michael O'Neill, the deputy county clerk and recorder, was one of the men sent for, and he, with others, was deported.

J. C. Cole, former deputy district attorney, surrendered to an officer, who guarded him to the best of his ability. Several men tried to take Cole from the officer, but he would not give him up, and finally reached the sheriff's office with Cole in custody. There he asked for protection, but the undersheriff was powerless. Attorney Cole was taken to where the other prisoners were. General Engley, while being marched between armed men, smiled a bitter smile at intervals, and occasionally strongly denounced those in command.

The first party deported was composed of the following distinguished gentlemen: General Eugene Engley; J. C. Cole, former deputy district attorney; Frank J. Hangs, attorney for the

W. F. M.; H. N. Heinerdinger, James Redd, J. W. Higgins and others. The party, which was composed of about ten, was escorted a distance of about four miles from Cripple Creek and there left. Before reaching the place where the mob halted, they discovered that Mr. Higgins had a revolver and began to assault him. Higgins drew his gun to defend himself but before he could use it he was struck over the head with a gun and otherwise badly injured.

The spokesman of the mob warned the men in the following language:

"You have been disturbers! If you come back, there will be a bullet or a rope ready for you. Keep on going. **Remember, you are not coming back!**"

Some demon, in human form, in the party suggested that the men being deported should be forced to remove their shoes but another objected.

T. H. Parfet, the former manager of the union store at Cripple Creek, Michael O'Neill and F. J. Hall composed another party of victims, they were taken another route.

Undoubtedly the cause for the foregoing despotic action, was the fact that it was reported in the district that Messrs. Hall and Heinerdinger, managers of the Interstate Mercantile Company, of Butte, Montana, were backed by the Western Federation of Miners. A few days previous, the two papers of Cripple Creek had refused advertising space to the company, one of the papers accepted advertising matter and the next day refused to run the matter. By the above the reader can plainly see that the merchants who belonged to the Citizens' Alliance, were afraid to compete with a co-operative store and employed radical methods to prevent the same being re-established. It would probably be well to mention here that when the store was wrecked the second time and during the trouble that followed, Sheriff Bell was out of the county. Not only was this the case on this date but it either was deliberately planned so or by chance, that on other occasions he returned just a few hours too late to prevent trouble.

Many of the mob that resorted to the lawlessness I have attempted to portray, wore buttons upon which were the words:

"You can't come back."

The men deported August 20, reached Denver sometime during the following day. They were all tired, but Mr. Higgins was especially so, being very weak from loss of blood caused by the wound on his head. After being refreshed and somewhat recovering himself he talked of the affair. In order that the reader may realize the brutality of the methods adopted and show clearly **who the anarchists were,** I could not do better than to run the following statement made by Mr. Higgins which appeared in the Rocky Mountain News August 22:

"I was at home, when my little girl came in and said there was trouble in town, and I went down to see what it was. When I walked up to the crowd A. E. Carlton, the banker, pointed at me and said: 'There is one you want,' and the next instant they had me fast. Carlton and Nelson Franklin were directing things.

"About a week ago Carlton came to me and asked me to withdraw from the bond of William Graham, one of the imprisoned miners, and I refused to do so. This is the offense for which I was deported. J. K. King, a well-known man there, shoved a gun in my face and told me not to make any resistance. William Carruthers, deputy county clerk, was also leading the mob. It was a little after 5 o'clock when the mob got me and about 6 o'clock when the leaders started up over the mountains. They rode along with guns, talking in insulting language, saying: 'Have you the ropes?' 'How many ropes do we need?' 'Oh, one is enough.' 'Will it be hanging or shooting or dropping them into a pit?'

"We walked along silently, and had gone most of the distance, when two of the guards saw my gun. I had not tried to use it when they jumped on me, although it was reported that I tried to do so. One of them grabbed at me and the other the gun. He did not quite get hold of it, and I reached for it, too, and had I secured it I would have begun shooting. One of them struck me with a six-shooter. I tried to aim, but they got the gun away, struck me on the head a fierce blow, hit me on the shoulders and chest and kicked me. They did not help me in any way after I was wounded, and as I walked along I bled profusely from the cut, the blood running down my clothes and into my shoes. When we had gone out three or four miles they stopped on the crest of a hill, and the leader, said: 'Gentlemen, this is the last time we will ever give you any show at all. If you ever return it will be a bullet or a rope.' They went off yelling:

" 'They can't come back!' " * * *

Former District Attorney J. C. Cole, made a similar statement as to the treatment accorded the party by the mob. **He,** also, stated that Carlton and Franklin were directors, and that a number of deputies and ex-militia were recognized among the whitecappers.

When General Bell was seen in Denver and the foregoing related to him, he took a long breath, assumed the air of a Napoleon and said he had not been ordered to mobolize troops, that he had not been **officially** notified and knew nothing of it except what he had seen in press reports.   He concluded:

"Those fellows up there can shoot and kill each other and hang a man to the nearest lamp post every five minutes if they want to, and I can do nothing to prevent it.   Until there is a request made on the governor by the civil authorities for troops I have no authority to order any military to the district, and none will be sent."

Governor Peabody had been absent from the capitol for awhile and chanced to return on the same train that the deportees were on.   The governor had a good deal to say about the condition that existed in Cripple Creek.   But he, too, said he did not know whether the matter published by the press was true or not and ended by saying: **"I have not been officially notified of the need of the military to protect the men that are being deported. There has not been an official request for troops."**

The indifference of the governor to what was taking place in the district, can be readily understood, as the mob was only continuing work formerly done, to a large extent by the governor's "army."   If it had been the strikers committing these lawless acts the governor would not have waited for what he termed **"official notice."**   But would have hurried the troops to the district on a special train.   That this is true, former acts of the governor in sending troops to Telluride, Trinidad and the district, presumably to maintain the law, proves.   A saloon row or an ordinary fight such as is of daily occurrence in any community, if participated in by strikers was sufficient excuse for his ordering out the troops, providing he could thereby accommodate the Mine Owners' Association.

August 30, A. G. Leduc, a union miner of Cripple Creek district, reached Denver, bruised, limping and very weary. His experience with the desperadoes in Cripple Creek was terrible. Mr. Leduc had been out of the district on account of poor health and was returning to his home when a neighbor called to him and requested him to stop in and eat supper which he did. While still at his friend's home some one rapped at the door and upon answering the knock Mr. Leduc was asked for. Leduc went to the door and the visitor said the whitecappers were after him (Leduc) and that the sheriff had sent for him and would give protection. Leduc said he would go but first wished to go to his cabin, and the two started in that direction. The man that called for Leduc said his name was Sharpe and that he was a deputy sheriff.

Before Mr. Leduc reached the cabin door a mob of men who had been in hiding rushed out and seized him. They searched him and took from him a pocketbook containing $45. He had no arms of any kind upon him. The crowd then told him to move on, and pushed him on ahead to a point two miles away from his home.

On the way the members of the mob would say to each other: "Who's got the rope?" "How deep is the shaft?" "Thirty feet," would be the reply, and then came the grim rejoinder, "Oh, well, that's deep enough to hang him." "Hang him! What do you want to do that for? Let him down and leave him there. He'll be dead soon enough."

When the mob finally stopped, Mr. Leduc was ordered to take off his coat. He did so, and several of the ruffians then lashed him with blacksnake whips till the blood flowed from the lacerations. Several times the whips were reversed, and he was beaten over the back with the butts till his body was a mass of blood and bruises.

When this cruel orgy was ended one of the men stepped up to him, and after helping him on with his coat, pointed out the road to Canon City, saying:

"There is your road. Take it, you ⸺ ⸺ ⸺, and if you ever come back to this place you'll hang as sure as ⸺."

Almost fainting at every step, Mr. Leduc painfully made his way to Canon City, and later was able to travel on to Denver where

he was properly taken care of. He was in a critical condition
when he reached his destination. He showed his bruises to many
people in proof of statements he made as to the cruelty to which
he was subjected, so that more than one person knows, as dreadful
as it seems, that the foregoing was an unvarnished fact.

REV. LELAND ARRESTED.

Many different versions of the trouble at the Leland home
have been told. As I have already stated in the foregoing pages
that Rev. Mr. Leland was not in the least influenced from the path
of right and justice by the Citizens' Alliance and the band of
whitecappers that had made life uncomfortable for so many, had
no terrors for him. When he was told to leave the district or he
would be roughly dealt with he simply told them they would find
him ready for them. They did not go until they were certain that
Leland was absent, choosing Sunday evening during the hours of
service at his church to make the raid on the Leland residence.

Fearing an assault from a mob and determined to resist the
same, Rev. Leland had for several days been assisted in guarding
by Arthur Parker and L. R. Jenks, who were glad to avail themselves of the protection of Mr. Leland's home, as they had also
been threatened.

On Sunday evening, August 28, Mr. Leland was at the Metho-
dist church conducting the evening service, Jenks and Parker,
who remained to guard the house observed a number of men
stealthily approaching. Believing them to be whitecappers, the inmates warned them not to come any nearer. Some one in the
crowd said: "We want to see Leland."

Upon being informed that Leland was at church they wanted
to know who was in the house. To this the men in the house replied: "It is none of your business."

Upon the crowd drawing nearer, Mr. Parker recognized
Sheriff Bell as one of the party. He notified Jenks and they then
informed Bell that they would open the door and hear what he
had to say.

Parker had a double-barrel shot-gun in his hands, cocked in

anticipation of trouble; unfortunately, in lowering the hammer while opening the door the gun was discharged accidentally.

Sheriff Bell then demanded the surrender of those in the house which they immediately did. They were placed in the county jail and charged with **"assault to murder."** Mr. Leland was notified of what had taken place and hurried to his home where he was also arrested and placed in jail.

Rev. Leland was released within a few days, but Parker and Jenks did not regain their liberty for several months, when they were released on bonds.

The time has come when it is impossible for me to devote space to the details of other cases of the same character as the ones I have described in preceding pages. Suffice it to say that outrages as previously recorded were of daily occurrence. The district was in complete control of a mob, intoxicated with brutal power. I realize that to portray each or even half of the cases of whitecapping and other lawless acts would fill many volumes. I, therefore, reluctantly conclude this part of this history by stating briefly that these conditions continued until after the state election of November 8, 1904.

A few days or perhaps a week, the district would be quiet and we would hope that peace had come at last, but to our disappointment another home would be raided. Some person obnoxious to the mine owners and their Klu Klux mob would appear in the district and another outbreak would follow. Many good citizens, business men, attorneys and former officers of the law in no manner whatever connected with the W. F. M., any more than that they were heard to express sympathy for the abused union miners and families, were compelled to leave the district on account of the persecution of those opposed to the W. F. M. W. J. Donnelly, a hardware merchant, at one time mayor of Victor, was a case worthy of mention. His life was threatened and finally a committee from the "law and order" brigade told him to leave the district. His home was guarded at times to protect him from whitecappers and finally he grew tired of having his life made unbearable and he announced his intention of selling out his business at a great sacrifice. The cause of Donnelly being persecuted was that he was a wealthy man and knowing the miners to be innocent of the crimes charged against them he had gone on the bond of some of the men. Frank Mannix, the clerk and recorder at that time was a case similar, only in his case, it was not because he went on bonds for the strikers but because he was a member in good standing of the Typographical union of Victor, and from the very inception of the strike to the date of this writing, he stood as firm as a stone wall against the despotism of Peabody and the lawless methods adopted in Teller county. Mr. Mannix is not the kind of a man that would be called an "agitator" but at the same time if you want to know on "which side of the fence" he is to be found, he will tell you—**unionism.** While the Citizens' Alliance failed in their efforts to force Mannix to resign, at the same time they were the direct cause of him later leaving the district. In the first place, his life was not safe there. Second, his life was made so intolerable that it would only have been a question of time when he would have to sacrifice his property and leave the district.

During the "strenuous" days in the district Mr. Mannix spent much of his time either on his ranch or in Denver. But, when the Citizens' Alliance undertook to force Mr. Mannix to resign they met defeat. He held his office to the end of his term and while out of the district placed someone in the office as his deputy. At this writing Frank Mannix has severed his connections with Colorado and now resides in Bullfrog, Nevada, where he has established the pioneer paper of the new gold camp, which he calls "The Miner." He is still a taxpayer of the state and will undoubtedly be taxed to help pay the million dollar war debt, caused by the military being sent to Teller county.

"YOU CAN'T COME BACK.

The entire front page of the Cripple Creek Times, July 12, recognized as the official organ of the Mine Owners' Association, contained the following "garble" set to music, with headlines in large type, printed in red ink:

"*CRIPPLE CREEK'S LIBERTY ANTHEM.*"

One, Two, Three—Now altogether,
    You can never come back—No, Never.
You can never come back, no never,
    We will follow your track forever.
Though you promise and plead
    We will give you no heed,
For to this we're all agreed forever.

CHORUS

You can never come back, boys, never,
    The game's all up with you forever,
We treated you square,
And the pay was fair,
And all would be yours yet,
    But now you'll beware
The W. F. M. is fated,
    And you'll stay there, you bet.

You had better keep away,
    Without test,
For here you cannot stay
    With any rest.
Cripple wants you no more,
Even though you are sore,
As we are tired of this gore,
    And that's no jest.

To that murderous crowd
    We do swear,
In words both strong and loud,
    You beware.
If you return
Well, a lesson you'll learn.
You may have a bad turn,
    So, take care.

Your venom is vain.
    No ember
Of it shall remain—
    Remember.
    Stay away and keep still,
For we mean it and *will*
From December until
    December.

APPEAL TO FEDERAL COURT.

On August 23, H. N. Heinerdinger, manager of the Inter-state Mercantile Company, which had some time previously, taken the control of the union stores of the district, applied to Judge Riner and Judge Hallett of the Federal court, first for an injunction restraining any one in the Cripple Creek district from interfering with the operations of the store; second, for damages against Teller county and certain individuals for the wrecking of the store, and third, individual suits for personal damage brought by Mr. Heinerdinger and F. J. Hall, citizens of Montana, who purchased and owned the store in Cripple Creek.

The Mercantile Company applied for the aid of the Federal court because it was a corporation organized under the laws of Montana, which made it a citizen of another state than Colorado. It was the diversity of citizenship between the company and the defendants which gave the Federal court jurisdiction to act. Most of the other deported men being citizens of Colorado as well as the deporters, the Federal court could not act for them.

On September 7, the court granted the injunction prayed for and on the following day Deputy United States Marshal Francks arrived in the city of Cripple Creek to serve the temporary writ of injunction issued by Judge Marshall in the United States Circuit Court in Denver in the case of the Interstate Mercantile Company against the men alleged to be the leaders of the mob that deported the union men and their sympathizers.

The text of the writ follows:

"United States of America, District of Colorado, ss.:

"IN THE UNITED STATES CIRCUIT COURT FOR THE DISTRICT OF COLORADO.

"The President of the United States of America:

"To Ernest A. Colburn, Clarence C. Hamlin, Gail S. Hoag, Thomas E. McClelland, Albert E. Carlton, E. C. Newcomb, Edward Bell, Nelson Franklin, R. P. Russell, John Sharp, John Dalzdell, Henry P. Dahl, William N. Bainbridge, Samuel D. Crump, H. L. Shepherd, Julius Kirby, Z. E. Funk, A. B. Shilling, F. M. Reardon, W. E. Dingman, S. A. Phipps, Clarence Fitch, K. C. Sterling, Daniel McCarthy, A. T. Holman, Frank M. Woods, J. B. Cunningham, Thomas Scanlon, Frank Beagle, Charles Huggins, William Carruthers, W. E. Driscoll, Frank May, Henry Waters, H. McGarry, L. E.

Smith, Harry Moore, Frank D. French, Edward Coplin, Philip De Wild, and all others associating with you, and to your attorneys, solicitors, agents, employes, and servants and to each and every one of you, Greeting:

"Whereas, It has been represented to the Honorable, The United States Circuit Court for the District of Colorado, on the part of the Interstate Mercantile Company, complainant, in its certain bill of complaint exhibited before said judges, and filed in said court against you, the said Ernest A. Colburn and others, respondents, to be relieved, touching the matters and things therein complained of.

"In which said bill it is stated, among other things, that you are combining and confederating with others to injure the complainant touching the matters set forth in said bill, and that your actions and doings in the premises are contrary to equity and good conscience.

"In consideration thereof, and of the particular matters in said bill set forth, you are hereby strictly commanded that you, the said persons before mentioned, and each and every one of you, do absolutely desist and refrain from in any wise or manner interfering with the said The Interstate Mercantile Company, complainant aforesaid, or with its employes or agents, in and about their prosecution of its business affairs in taking possession of its said premises and of its said goods, wares and merchandise or in or about the purchase of other supplies and the delivery to it thereof in or about the sale and disposition thereof, and wholly to desist and refrain from in any wise or manner banishing or deporting from the said county any of the employes of said complainant or from in any wise or manner apprehending, arresting, or imprisoning or proceeding against its or any of its said employes or agents, save by due process of law, as provided and required by the statutes and the constitution, and wholly to desist and refrain from denying it the equal protection of the laws of the land. And also to wholly desist and refrain from seizing, interfering with, injuring, destroying or taking the property, goods, wares and merchandise of said complainant, The Interstate Mercantile Company, or from preventing its carrying on and conducting its business in said county and state, until this Honorable Court, in Chancery sitting, or a judge thereof at Chambers, shall make other order to the contrary: Hereof fail not under penalty of what the law directs.

"To the Marshal of said District, to execute and return in due form of law.

"Witness, the Honorable Melville W. Fuller, chief justice of the Supreme Court of the United States of America, and the seal of the said United States Circuit Court, at the city of Denver, in said district, this seventh day of September, A. D. 1904, and of the Independence of the United States the 129th year.   A true copy.

(Seal U. S. Circuit Court.)   "*ROBERT BAILEY, Clerk..*

"Attested: *ROBERT BAILEY, Clerk.*"

The injunction granted by the court put a stop to further interference with the union store. The mob did not dare to disobey the court's order as it would have meant the sending of Federal troops to enforce the court's order. The powers in control in the district knew full well that they would find the Federal troops quite a different proposition from Peabody's "warriors."

While the state was much disturbed over the many outrages being perpetrated on citizens in Cripple Creek during the month of August, after martial law had been suspended and it appeared that the citizens of other parts of the state would likely take "strenuous" steps to put a stop to mob rule, the governor, in order to make it appear that he would make an effort to maintain law, sent the following communication to Sheriff Bell, of Teller county:

"State of Colorado, Executive Chamber,
"Denver, Colo., Aug. 27, 1904.

"Hon. Edward Bell, Sheriff of Teller County, Cripple Creek, Colorado:

"Sir—Upon Saturday, the 21st inst., there was assembled in Teller county a disorderly mob of men. This mob destroyed private property and maltreated and drove from the county a number of citizens and other persons.

"Teller county has been a source of much anxiety to my administration. Order has been restored there at great expense to the state, and the militia, after a protracted service, rendered with the single purpose of making life and property secure, had only recently been withdrawn.

"Your county had been freed, as I hoped, from criminal disturbers of the peace; the civil offices of your county are now filled, as I am informed, by incumbents who desire to extend to all citizens the full protection of the law. I recalled the troops because I believed and was informed that your community was once more safe in the hands of such officers. If I am right in so believing, there should be no occasion for lawless outbursts such as that of Saturday last.

"I am recently informed that a similar mob of men have in contemplation another and still further outrage. I am convinced that you, as sheriff, having the full sympathy and support of the civil authorities, can and should maintain peace and lawful order. I therefore desire to say that should you not be able, with the means at your disposal, to successfully cope with the situation and maintain law and order in Teller county, I am ready to again place at your disposal the militia of this state.

"Our paramount duty at this and at all times is to uphold the law and its safeguards, without distinction of interests or of individuals.

"I will thank you for an early reply, and am, respectfully yours,
"JAMES H. PEABODY, Governor."

August 30, Sheriff Bell replied to the governor's letter as follows:

"To His Excellency, the Governor of Colorado, James H. Peabody, Denver, Colorado.—Honorable Sir: Your kind communication of recent date at hand, and contents carefully noted. I have felt at all times perfectly competent to handle the situation here, and I believe that most of the disturbances occurring recently in this district have been occasioned by the united efforts of the Western Federation to create an impression of alarm regarding life and property in this locality and bring disrepute and odium on my administration of the sheriff's office. I find that many of the reports as to the possible deportation of this or that person living within this district are entirely without foundation, and are without any standing in fact. On tracing down the origin of these reports I find that they emanate directly from an organization known as the Woman's Auxiliary, which is an adjunct of the Western Federation, and as an evidence of how far these people will go, the attempted assassination of myself and deputies Sunday night is in itself of sufficient evidence to substantiate all the facts of the case.

"I therefore must decline your kind proffer of troops, believing that the best interests of this county and state will be subserved through the determination of the sheriff's office and the will of the best people of this district. You can rest assured that no stone will be left unturned, no risk will be considered too great, nor any clew too trivial for me to follow with the best energies of my office."

The foregoing correspondence was simply intended as a "grand stand play" and was so understood by the public. The reader will notice the inconsistency of Sheriff Bell in stating that he was competent to handle the situation, when every day flagrant violations of the law were taking place under his very nose, which, if he was capable of controlling, he certainly did not make good. It is evident that the beating and robbing of union men or sympathizers was not considered a violation of law by the **good (?)** sheriff of Teller county.

As to his statement in his communication to the governor, of the attempted assassination of himself and deputies, this referred to the incident at the home of Rev. Leland.

ALLEGED CONFESSION OF ROMAINE.

On September 9, much interest was awakened over the news that came from Topeka, Kansas, of an alleged confession of one B. F. Slagel, alias, Robert Romaine, then a prisoner in Shawnee county jail, of complicity in the explosion at Independence. Romaine's confession was made before the county attorney and sheriff and sworn to before a notary public. The confession was lengthy, giving full details of how the plot was carried out, the explosive procured, etc., and implicated a number of prominent union leaders in the district.

There was talk of bringing Romaine to Colorado to stand trial. General Bell said that Romaine was one of the men wanted. Romaine was never brought to Colorado. Many people wondered why the mine owners and authorities of Teller county, who seemingly were so desirous of capturing and punishing the perpetrators of this most fiendish crime, were so lax in the matter. However, it later developed that the Romaine confession was planned and paid for by agents of the Mine Owners' Association in order to have an excuse for holding in "durance vile" members of the miners' union. Evidently they feared exposure if Romaine's confession was tested in the courts.

The following letter was received by John I. Tierney, staff correspondent for the Denver Times, who had interviewed Romaine, shortly after his confession had been made public in Topeka. Romaine in that interview had promised Mr. Tierney that he would write him a letter at some future time concerning his confession. He kept his promise. Following is a portion of the letter:

"Sheafer came to me and made the proposition of making up the big fake. He said there was money and freedom in it for me if I would do as he said. He furnished me with all necessary dates and names, and told me to weave as good a story out of it as I could. He also gave me $5 and the promise of more, which, I regret very much to say, I did not get. I am sorry that I had anything at all to do with it, as I only got hurt myself by doing so and no one else. I am reaping the fruits of my follies here in the coal mines at three and three-quarter cents a day—truly a magnificent sum compared to what I could have been making in the Creek.

The Sheafer, spoken of in the letter, was Frank Sheafer, a deputy sheriff of Cripple Creek.

The reader can judge from the foregoing to what desperate straits the agents of the Mine Owners' Association were driven and to what length they were willing to go in order to fasten this terrible crime upon people whom they must have known were innocent.

LIBERTY LEAGUES.

During the months of June, July and August the State Ways and Means committee, that had been created by the mass convention of organized labor, held in Denver in January, 1904, in order to carry into effect resolutions adopted at said convention, to prevent the re-election of Governor Peabody, sent out over the state organizers for the purpose of·organizing anti-Peabody political clubs. The political organization was incorporated under the name of "The Colorado Liberty League." One hundred and thirty local leagues covering all parts of the state were organized and chartered by the State Ways and Means committee within a few weeks.

Meanwhile, the Ways and Means committee had been greatly strengthened by the appointment of sub-committeemen. Sub-committeemen were appointed in all the principal cities, towns and camps, care being taken to appoint only such persons as were known to be capable and in thorough sympathy with the movement.

The author volunteered her services to organize Liberty Leagues, and although having had no previous experience in this line, is proud of the success made, having been successful in organizing a League in every town and camp visited.

During my experience in organizing Liberty Leagues, I was impressed, on account of the number of people outside the ranks of organized labor, who enrolled themselves as members. These embraced people from all walks of life, lawyers, doctors, business men and farmers. Numerous persons at my meetings arose and stated that they had been life-long Republicans, had never voted any other than Republican ticket, but for once in their lives they would vote against their party in order to defeat Peabody.

It was clearly evident that in the state election, party lines would be eliminated, and that the issue would be Peabodyism and anti-Peabodyism.

That the formation of the "Colorado Liberty League" was not in vain is evidenced from the overwhelming defeat of Peabody, at the election of November 8, the League being no small factor in bringing about this result.

It is to the everlasting disgrace of Colorado and an object lesson of what little avail is the will of the people, when the corporations desire otherwise, that the choice of the people for governor, the Honorable Alva Adams, was unseated after having been elected by over 10,000 plurality. But more of this anon.

THE LIBERTY LEAGUE ADOPTS POLITICAL POLICY

Having created the Liberty Leagues, the question arose as to what would be the best policy to pursue in order to carry out the purpose of the League—**the defeat of Peabody.**

Some favored forming an independent party, others thought the surest means of success would be to support the Democratic candidiates. In order to best learn the desires of the Leagues on this important matter, they were requested to get an expression from the members and send in their recommendations to the state committee.

July 2-4, a meeting of the State Ways and Means committee was held to take final action on policy to pursue. After several days' deliberations the committee adopted a preamble and platform and decided to submit same to the State Central Committee of the Democratic party, and, providing they approved the platform and would make it a part of the Democratic platform the Liberty League would support the Democratic state ticket.

A committee was appointed to confer with the Democratic State Central Committee in regard to the proposition, which was as follows:

"PLATFORM.

"1. An eight-hour law must be passed in accordance with the constitutional mandate of the people expressed by fifty thousand majority in the free exericse of the right of franchise.

"2. A direct legislation measure must make it possible for the people to pass directly upon the laws and policies of government, thus forever precluding the lawless overthrow of democratic government, which for two years has made Colorado a hissing and a stench among the sisterhood of states.

"3. That our demands may not be misunderstood and our responsibilty absolute, we hereby pledge our honor and the good faith of the labor party of Colorado to the following specific purposes:

"(a) The Republican party has proved unworthy of the support of fair minded men; therefore, THE REPUBLICAN PARTY MUST BE OVERTHROWN.

"(b) A certain and specific eight-hour law and direct legislation bill are herewith submitted and no man shall receive our suffrage who does not unequivocally pledge to support these measures intact without modification or amendment.

"EIGHT-HOUR BILL.

"*A bill for an act to regulate the hours of employment in underground mines and workings, smelters, chlorination or cyanide ore reduction works and blast furnaces, and to provide penalties for the violation thereof* * * *

Then followed the eight-hour bill.

"DIRECT LEGISLATION BILL.

"*A bill for an act to submit to the qualified voters of the state of Colorado amedments to Article V of the Constitution of the state of Colorado establishing the principle of direct legislation by the people.* * * *

The direct legislation bill was lengthy so I only produce the enactment clause.

"(c) We demand that a constitutional amendment be submitted to the people of Colorado, taking from the governor the more than despotic power lodged in his hands by the decision of the Supreme Court in the Moyer case. Such an amendment should in specific terms absolutely forbid the suspension of the writ of Habeas Corpus, except by a three-fourths vote of the general assembly in regular or special session; also that the existence of a state of insurrection shall be made a question of fact, to be decided by the courts in the orderly discharge of their functions, and not left to the judgment or imagination of a chief executive too apt to be swayed by partisan prejudice, and a stranger to judicial impartiality.

"(d) We uncompromisingly oppose the effort of the corporate interests of Colorado, to saddle upon the already overburdened taxpayers, the million-dollar campaign graft of the Peabody-Mine Owners' tinsel war,

Illegally contracted in the service of criminal individuals and corporations, these same beneficiaries of a prostituted militia service, should not be allowed to foist upon the entire state the private tribute of enormous bills, incurred by and therefore justly due from private and corporate interests.

"(e) We demand the legal exemption from taxation, of personal property to the extent of two hundred dollars ($200.00).

"With a firm reliance upon the righteousness and reasonableness of each and all of the above demands, we submit our contentions to the people of Colorado. We are content to be tried before the tribunal of the whole people, confident that the state, to whose material and social greatness we have so generously poured out our labor, our love and our lives, will not be deaf to our plea for justice and liberty. Let the real men and women who have hearts and consciences take back into their own clean hands, the economic and political power yielded in one cataclysmic moment, to the industrial scavenger and political mountebank, and we will cheerfully abide their decision.

(Signed)   "J. C. SULLIVAN,
                    "Chairman State Ways and Means Committee.
(Attest)   "H. B. WATERS,
                "Secretary-Treasurer Ways and Means Committee."

The Democratic State Central Committee and other prominent leaders of that party who were consulted, practically agreed to the platform with the exception of plank "c" repudiating the Peabody war debt. They substituted the following in lieu thereof, which was agreed to by the committee representing the Liberty League:

"That no repudiation plank be put into the platform, and that our opposition take the following course:

"First—That the platform charge illegality in the method of contracting said indebtedness.

"Second—That we charge irregularity and dishonesty in the disbursement of state funds.

"Third—That the demand be made for a legislative commission to thoroughly investigate the military expenditures and to shift the grafting from the bona fide accounts.

"Fourth—That we secure through deals in senatorial and legislative districts a general assembly that will refuse to expend the money of the taxpayers in paying any illegally acquired indebtedness."

The committee further reported as follows:

"It was also agreed that the platform shall be in effect and essence an absolute repudiation of Peabody and Peabodyism.

"The candidates for governor and lieutenant-governor shall be acceptable to the labor people.

"The labor people are to go into the primaries and conventions of the democratic party and lend practical aid in carrying this agreement into effect.

"Your conference committee believes that the above agreements have been made in good faith by both parties and we recommend to the ways and means committee that immediate and energetic steps be taken to carry them into effect."

The next matter of interest was to procure the nomination of a candidate on the Democratic ticket who would be acceptable to organized labor and one who would have the confidence of the masses.

The Democratic state convention, held September 21-22, made a happy choice in nominating by acclamation the Honorable Alva Adams, a man who had twice before been honored by being elected governor, a business man of great integrity, who, as governor, had served the people with honor to them and credit to himself. The most radical Citizens' Alliance man could recall nothing to the discredit of Mr. Adams other than he was emphatically opposed to the unconstitutional and tyrannical methods of Peabody in dealing with labor unions. Mr. Adams did not desire the nomination as he had arranged to retire from active life for the remainder of his days and enjoy a well-earned and deserved rest. It was only through long and earnest persuasion of his friends and prominent citizens, who were convinced that he was the man to bring credit back to the state, that had been disgraced by the Peabody administration, that he finally agreed to sacrifice a life of ease to one of duty. Proof that Mr. Adams thought more of the welfare of the state than of the honor of holding the high office of governor, is in the fact, that although great pressure was brought to bear upon him, to resist the unjust decision of the corporation-corrupted legislature to unseat him, he decided to peacefully retire, rather than to bring on a conflict which would undoubtedly have lead to bloodshed and still further disgraced suffering Colorado.

May Colorado and the nation be blessed with many men like Governor Adams, then would justice reign and peace prevail.

POLITICAL CONFLICT.

We now come to a recital of one of the most remarkable state campaigns and elections ever held in America—that of 1904.

It was remarkable for the reason that partisanship was almost entirely eliminated. Whether militarism as represented by Peabody or constitutional methods should obtain in Colorado was made the issue. It was remarkable on account of the bitterness shown, and unprecedented, on account of the peoples' choice for governor being unseated and a man who was not a candidate being placed in the gubernatorial chair.

The element responsible for this condition of affairs was the same as had carried on the reign of lawlessness during the preceding two years, namely: the Mine Owners' Association, the Smelter trust, the Colorado Fuel & Iron Company, some of the Denver Utility corporations and the Citizens' Alliance.

A deliberate conspiracy was formed to prevent a Democrat from occupying the gubernatorial chair regardless of how many votes he received and to control the legislature. How successful this conspiracy against the will of the people proved, the following history tells:

The first step in this conspiracy was to have the supreme court issue a blanket injunction against all Democratic election officials in the city and county of Denver and to appoint supreme court watchers at the polling places. The demand for the injunction and watchers being made by Governor Peabody and Chairman Fairley, of the Republican state central committee, for the purpose, they claimed, of assuring an honest election. The **real** purpose was to have the supreme court control the election and to decide the contest they proposed to make in the event of their candidates not being elected. The excuse for the contest to be election fraud, perpetrated by the Democrats. Needless to say, the supreme court granted the injunction and court watchers applied for.

The court by granting the request virtually assumed the power of regulating and controlling the state election. This assumption of power was in direct conflict with the state laws, regarding elections.

If the intention of asking the supreme court to interfere in election had been made in good faith to prevent election frauds, which unfortunately are only too numerous under our "spoils" system of politics, there could have been no objection, but the supreme court, as later developed, was so apparently partisan, that there could be no question of justice. While the court granted an injunction for Denver county at the request of the Republican organization, it refused to grant injunctions when applied for for Teller county, which was controlled by the Mine Owners' Association; for Las Animas county, controlled by the Colorado Fuel and Iron Company; and for Pueblo county, controlled by the Smelter trust.

The Republican party, in this election, assumed to be disciples of honest elections, while it is conceded that frauds were committed in the interest of Democratic candidates in Denver and other counties, they could not at all compare with the frauds perpetrated in the counties controlled by the corporations, for which injunctions were denied.

As previously recorded in these pages under caption "Liberty Leagues," it was evident that organized labor would be no small factor in determining the result of the state election. This was recognized by the Republican campaign managers. They realized that organized labor and many citizens of the state who believed in constitutional government were thoroughly aroused on account of the high-handed and servile methods of Governor Peabody in serving the interests of one class of citizens as against another, and, as a consequence, Republican success in the state was in danger.

In order to off-set this, every effort was made to justify the actions of Governor Peabody. To this end the campaign was practically opened by a lengthy statement given to the press by Governor Peabody in which he attempted to justify his course during the labor troubles. This document of the governor's was labeled by a great many people as **"an explanation that failed to explain."**

In his statement Peabody made a great effort to make it appear that he was not opposed to unionism, in fact, that he was much in sympathy with organized labor and the "**best friend they ever had.**"

The next step in the campaign was the issuance by the Colorado Mine Operators' Association of a large thirty-two page pamphlet, bound in red, entitled, "Criminal Record of the Western Federation of Miners—Couer d'Alene to Cripple Creek—1894-1904." This pamphlet became popularly known as the "Red Book." It was widely circulated, not only in Colorado but throughout the entire United States.

The "Red Book" presumed to be a complete history of the W. F. M. from its organization on May 15, 1893, to the present date. It accused the W. F. M. of being guilty of every horrible crime in the calendar of criminology, and as a mass of vindictive, malicious falsehoods, it has never been equaled. Every mine accident in which men lost their lives, or destruction of property that took place in any mining camp in the United States where the W. F. M. was organiized, was laid at their doors. Any rash or unusual statement, made by an individual member of the W. F. M. was magnified and charged against the organization.

The document contained six principal indictments.

One of the purposes of the book was to conciliate and win the votes of what is considered the conservative element of organized labor by making it appear to them that the W. F. M. was a criminal organization that should not be sustained by the **conservative** element and that, therefore, they would vote for the re-election of Governor Peabody and thereby approve his action in making war on the striking miners. To this end the book devoted a page, printed in large type to the following:

"POSITION OF THE PEOPLE OF COLORADO

"Neither the people of Colorado nor their governor, James H. Peabody, hold organized labor responsible for the terrible crimes of the Western Federation of Miners. Neither do they contend that *all* members of this organization belongs to the vicious or lawless class.

"It would be just as unreasonable to condemn the institution known as organized labor for these crimes as it would to condemn the re-

publican form of government because of the crimes of the barbarous little
republics of Central and South America.

"It was not a question of whether corporations, mine owners, alliances
or unions should prevail; it was a question of whether or not law and
security for life and property should prevail.

"The people of Colorado believe that the long record of outrage and
crime given in this pamphlet justifies the following conclusions:"

Then followed the six principal indictments, which I produce
later.

The "Red Book" instead of being a vote-winner as was intended, proved, on account of its vindictiveness, to be a boomer-
rang which recoiled upon its authors. It brought forth much
criticism from prominent people all over the United States.

The Western Federation of Miners replied to the Mine Operators' "Red Book" by publishing a pamphlet of similar size bound
in green. This became known as the "Green Book." Many
thousand of the "Green Books" were circulated.

The "Green Book" answered every accusation contained in
the "Red Book and among other things charged the Mine Operators' Association with the responsibility for the death of eight
hundred and fifty men in less than four years.

The "Green Book" as near as possible, followed the style
adopted by the authors of the "Red Book," it, too, devoted a page
in large type under the caption:

"POSITION OF THE PEOPLE OF COLORADO.

"Speaking for 72,000 citizens of the state, we charge organized capital
with being responsible for the most horrible crimes that have ever been
perpetrated in this nation.

"We charge organized capital with bribery, and brazenly purchasing
legislative bodies.

"We charge organized capital with the responsibility for defeating
the eight-hour law, and every measure that has for its object the betterment of the conditions of the masses of the people.

"We condemn organized capital in its attempt to fasten upon the
taxpayers of the state Peabody's war debt, created in an effort to crush
organized labor."

I here reproduce the six indictments contained in the "Red
Book" and the answers thereto as published in the "Green Book:"

INDICTMENTS.

"That a large number of criminals and lawless men have been welcomed, supported and sheltered by the Western Federation of Miners.

"*That a large number of ex-convicts, gamblers, desperadoes and other criminals have been and now are, knowingly employed and paid by the Colorado Mine Operators' Association and the Citizens' Alliance in Cripple Creek, Telluride and elsewhere in the state as deputy sheriffs, guards, detectives, etc.*

"That the officers of that organization and a large number of the members, while perhaps not committing crimes themselves for which they can be prosecuted, do directly and indirectly advise or encourage the lawless among them to commit crimes.

"*That the officers of these organizations and a large number of their members have not only committed crimes themselves, for which they could and should be prosecuted and punished, but the organizations as such, have directly and openly aided and abetted the same, and their members have boasted and approved of such crimes.*

"That these officers and this element preach disrespect for the law and contempt for the lawful authorities and openly and publicly, as individuals, approve of and gloat over the slugging, dynamiting and murdering of non-union men by their criminal associates.

"*That the association and alliance, while shouting hypocritically for "law and order," have openly defied the courts, destroyed the liberty of the press, invaded the sanctity of the home, caused arrests without warrant, imprisoned men without charges of crime, driven men from the county after robbing them, and while declaring such men to be criminals of the deepest dye, have, without compunction, dumped them on neighboring communities. They have tortured men and intimidated women and children in order to obtain confessions, and openly and publicly boasted and approved such crimes, as organizations, by adopting and publishing resolutions commendatory of them.*

"That where this organization has had its members in local public offices, or where it has had the power to influence peace officers and courts in this state, it has paralyzed the hand of justice and made it next to impossible to convict members of the federation caught in the act of committing crimes.

"*That wherever the association or alliance have not had their members in public office, they have, whenever deemed necessary, compelled by violence and intimidation, the resignation of duly elected public officials and the appointment of their own creatures to the so-called vacancies.*

Wherever their members or tools are in office, or where they have had the power to influence peace officers and courts in this state, the law, as established since Magna Charta, has been subverted by decisions which have made the state subject of derision to the entire country, the hand of justice has been paralyzed, and it has been futile to attempt conviction of their members, although caught in the act of committing crime and openly confessing and boasting of it.

"This charge is supported and proven by the decisions themselves and by the following facts. The informations for riot and conspiracy which a court compelled an unwilling district attorney to file at Idaho Springs against some eighty members of those organizations, charging them as participants in a mob which had driven miners from their homes, were at the earliest possible moment dismissed by the same district attorney, and the criminals allowed to escape trial and punishment, though tne whole community could have testified to their identity. At the same time, the same district attorney, aided by the attorneys of those organizations and backed by all the money needed, made two attempts by two separate trials, to convict miners of the crimes of arson and conspiracy for which the same mob had pretended to expel them. They were each and all triumphantly acquitted without introducing evidence in their defense.

"Not one of the mob of "best citizens" who exiled miners from Telluride has been prosecuted. When Judge Stevens issued his injunction to aid the exiles in returning home, the mob appealed to the governor of the state for force to defy the courts, and he ordered out the militia, placed the leader of the mob in command, and the court stands defied and helpless to this day.

"At Cripple Creek, a mob in brass and blue, under orders from a puppet governor controlled by the association and alliance, filled the court room with armed men, and defied the court in open session. While this mob of soldiers was in the district, it aided and abetted the members of the Alliance and Association, in compelling, by force and threats, the resignations of the duly elected sheriff and coroner and other civil officers of Teller county, and the appointment of their own creatures to the so-called vacancies.

"Ever since this lawless governor recalled his mob of soldiers from Cripple Creek the reign of terror continues. Stores belonging to a foreign corporation have been looted in broad daylight by mobs led by A. E. Carlton, president First National Bank; Nelson Franklin, former mayor, and Cliff Newcomb, cashier First National Bank, and other "law-abiding citizens.' Not one of these criminals fears arrest or punishment, and daily outrages are committed with impunity, by mobs composed of members of the alliance and association, or acting under orders from them, and acting with the approval of the peace officers of the county, who they forcibly installed in office. These crimes are committed with the con-

sent and approval of the governor, who refuses to enforce the law and restore order on the pitiful pretense that he has "not been officially notified.

"That this organization, having formally and officially espoused the cause of the so-called Socialist party, is opposed to our present form of government and is aiming at its overthrow, together with the abrogation of the present constitution.

"That these organizations have formally and officially espoused the cause of the so-called Republican party, which they pretend to be still the party of Lincoln. That each of them is opposed to our present form of government, and aiming at its overthrow. To this end they have destroyed and confiscated property, destroyed the freedom of the press, defied the courts, nullified the writ of habeas corpus, exercised the right of search without warrant, denied the right of trial by jury, exercised the power of banishment, denied the right of citizens to keep and bear arms, and trampled upon every other guarantee of personal liberty made by the constitution of the state and of the United States. Besides these and other violations of the constitutional rights of citizens, they are seeking to abrogate the constitution and install a plutocracy, and to that end, have adopted as their rallying cry a phrase, classic in its terseness, and aptly description of the men and their purpose, to-wit: 'To hell with the constitution.'

"That this organization teaches its members to regard the wealth they produce from the property of others as their own, thus encouraging theft (of ore, for instance) and also inflaming the minds of its members against their employers, against the law against organized society and against the peace and safety of the public.

"That the organization mentioned teach their members that the sole aim and end of existence is to acquire wealth without producing it, and that therefore, the methods of trusts, stock watering, stealing ore from neighbors under the guise of trespass, buying the interests of widows and orphans in adjoining property without informing them of its value, and other similar methods used by predatory wealth, are respectable, when compared to the economic theory that wealth should belong to him who produces it, or to Lincoln's assertions in his message to congress in 1864, that "to secure to each laborer the whole product of his labor is a worthy object of any government," and that "labor is superior to capital and deserves much the higher consideration.

"The facts which support and prove these charges made by the Federation are within the knowledge of every citizen of Colorado."

THE CONVENTIONS.

The corporations that were being served by Peabody were in absolute control of the Republican state convention which met in Denver early in September, and nominated as their candidate for governor, James Hamilton Peabody.

The convention, in its platform indorsed Peabody's administration in the following language:

"We indorse and approve the administration of Governor James H. Peabody. We urge all good citizens, without regard to vocation and irrespective of party affiliations, to join us in supporting him for re-election, thus sternly rebuking the spirit of lawlessness which would turn popular government into irresponsible despotism, and through unprincipled agitators keep alive the fires of class hatred, lawlessness and treason. We affirm the right of every person, whether union or non-union, to labor when, where and for whom he pleases, and to enter freely into whatever contract he may choose. We recognize the right of both capital and labor to combine into associations and organize into unions for the accomplishments of lawful objects by lawful methods. We deny the right of either to exceed such bounds."

The platform contained the following pledge:

"We pledge ourselves and our candidates to restrain by all constitutional and legal methods any excesses practiced by such organizations, whether capital or labor. We stand absolutely and unequivocally for the maintenance of law and order against anarchy and lawlessness. We appeal from the utterances of the demagogue to the sober sense and right feeling of all law-abiding citizens for support in our struggle. We believe that no citizen, and least of all the citizen who lives by the labor of his hands, can prosper where disorder reigns and the protection of law is withdrawn."

Think of the inconsistency of the Republican convention, when in its platform it indorsed the policy of Peabody, which signified that they approved his actions, among other things, closing the Portland mine, as previously recorded in these pages, and in the same breath affirming the right of every person, "whether union or non-union to labor where, and for whom he pleases, and to enter freely into whatever contract he might choose."

Then again, this same body of men affirming this sacred right, knew full well at that very time working men in the Cripple Creek district were denied the right to work unless they possessed a card issued by the Mine Owners' Association. In order to show the fallacy of their affirmation of the rights of the working man "to labor when, where," etc., I will state here that scarcely had this convention adjourned when the same card system adopted in the Cripple Creek district was put in operation in Leadville. This was a political move on the part of the Peabodyites to carry the election for Peabody in Lake county. They had expected that the miners would refuse to submit to this unjust system, which would lead to a strike and would give excuse for wholesale deportation of union men and other voters known to be opposed to Peabody's re-election.

Their plans failed. The Western Federation seeing through the plot, in order to defeat it, notified their members to accept the card system.

A matter that was sure to be an important issue in the state campaign was the enactment, by the incoming legislature, of an eight-hour law, which had, at a previous state election been demanded by the voters, by the adoption of a constitutional amendment, declaring for the enactment of such a law. The failure of the preceding legislature to adopt an eight-hour law in conformity with the constitutional amendment was the direct cause of the strikes.

The Republican convention, in its platform referred to the eight-hour proposition as follows:

"We favor the enactment of a fair, just and equitable eight-hour law."

It was well understood that although the Republican convention adopted this eight-hour plank in its platform, the corporations in control of the convention were not sincere in favoring a just eight-hour law, they being the same parties, who through corrupt methods were instrumental in preventing an eight-hour bill being passed by the previous legislature. The state was so thoroughly aroused on account of the strike for eight hours, that the convention could do no less than declare for an an eight-hour law in order to be in touch with public sentiment and win votes.

The corporations had two important achievements to accomplish—first, the re-election of their instrument, James H. Peabody, governor; and the election of a legislature, subservient to their interests, so as to defeat the passage of an eight-hour bill, such as was demanded by the constitutional amendment.

DEMOCRATIC CONVENTION.

The Democratic party held their state convention September 21st. They nominated as their candidate for governor the Hon. Alva Adams. The convention in its platform condemned the Peabody administration in the following language:

"The present state administration has deliberately violated and set at naught every safeguard guaranteed to the individual by the bill of rights. Under the old plea of necessity the governor, in the name of law, has swept aside statutes and constitutions, and in the name of order has substituted disorder and passion for justice. The party has indorsed his conduct, and with characteristic effrontery demand his re-election in the name of both.

"The law of the dominant party is the unrestricted will of the executive; its order, the proclamations of the commander-in-chief and in his subordinates. This is the law of the monarch and the order of despotism. They have no place on the soil of the American Union, and Democracy repudiates them.

"Democracy is the embodiment of that genuine law and order whose ends are justice. It represents that law and order which, by conformity to established rules and usages, universally applicable and binding alike the ruler and the ruled, regulates and governs organized society. We solemnly protest against their violation, either by organizations or citizens owing obedience to them, or by officials elected and sworn to execute them.

"Every individual in the land is entitled to the just and equal protection of the laws. The right to live, to work, to acquire and enjoy property, to domicile, to follow any lawful vocation, to contract, to bear arms, to be secure from unreasonable searches and seizures, to freedom of speech, of person and of conscience, to the writ of habeas corpus and speedy trial by jury guaranteed by the national and state constitutions, must and shall be recognized and enforced in behalf of every man and woman. To deny any of them anywhere is to imperil all of them everywhere. They are protected by penalties which have been proven adequate by centuries of experience."

The convention denounced the so-called eight-hour plank in the Republican platform as a palpable and cowardly evasion, calculated to deceive and imposing no obligation upon it whatever. The Democrats adopted the following eight-hour plank:

"The Democratic party, if intrusted with power, pledges itself to enact a law, and prescribe suitable penalties for the violation thereof, for a period of employment not to exceed eight hours within any twenty-four hours (except in cases of emergency when life or property is in imminent danger), for persons engaged in underground mines or underground workings, blast furnaces, smelters, and any ore reduction works or other branches of the industry or labor that the general assembly may consider injurious or dangerous to health, life or limb."

As promised the Liberty Leagues, planks were adopted indorsing the principle of the initiative and referendum and the exemption from taxation of personal property of the value of $200.

In accepting the nomination, Hon. Alva Adams made the following speech:

"SPEECH OF HON. ALVA ADAMS.

"Fellow Citizens: I need not assure you that I appreciate to its full this distinguished compliment. It is perhaps the greatest tribute that any man has received at the hands of a Democratic convention. But I am sincere when I tell you that I wish this cup might have passed by me; that the mantle might have fallen on other shoulders.

"But the call has come and I must lay aside my personal preferences, my business interests, my home life, that I may respond to your call, which is a demand that I can not refuse. What the campaign is to bring forth no man can tell. If defeat is to come to me it is but an incident in my life and none, perhaps will mourn except myself. But if defeat comes to the principles that I am to carry in this campaign, then calamity falls upon the state of Colorado. It is your battle, as Senator Teller has told you. I will do my part the best I can, but the 30,000 Democrats who did not go to the polls two years ago must vote and determine this election. There can be no absent treatment. You can not put ballots into the box by prayer. Every citizen of this state who believes in what we believe in must work and sacrifice and go to the polls and cast his ballot. If that is done, and honestly done, then, whatever be the result, I shall abide by it, because an honest election is the voice of the people, and I shall submit, it matters not whether it is defeat or victory.

"This afternoon a Republican friend of mine told me that he wished I would take this nomination. I asked him why, and he said 'because we must have this election. Peabody must be elected, it matters not at what cost. We have all the money we want, and if necessary, can buy one-half of Colorado.'

"This is a challenge of your ability, but I have faith in the purity, the patriotism of Colorado manhood and womanhood, which I have known for thirty-four years, to believe that they will rebuke that sentiment and not indorse the sentiment that money is everything.

"There is something more than money. It is principle. There is something higher than cash. It is manhood and womanhood.

"I believe that at the next election the ballots of the people of Colorado will be a flame of fire of indignation that will consume the tabernacles of bribery.

"No, money answereth not to all. If I thought it did, I would leave the state of Colorado. I want to say to you, my friends, that if elected governor that the governor of this state will be guided by the law. When a preacher or priest tries to enforce the doctrines of the Ten Commandments, he must in his own life be an example of those doctrines.

"The law must be enforced.

"There is not one law for one and another law for another. I have never read in any statute book or constitution that preference was to be given to property or person.

"I believe that the courts of law are competent to right every legal wrong.

"The law stands for the high and the low, and every citizen of this state is entitled to its protection.

"I believe there is no conflict between the citizens of this state that can not find a way of being righted before the courts of law.

"If I have a political creed, I find that creed in the first inaugural of Thomas Jefferson, written 100 years ago. It applies to Colorado, as it applied then. It is new today, and yet old, because it is as new and old as human liberty. The sentiment that he described is Democracy itself. His definition stood for freedom of the press, freedom of speech, freedom of the individual under the privilege of the writ of habeas corpus. It stood for the subserviency of the military to the civil power, the right of trial by jury honestly selected. This is Jeffersonian Democracy, and it embodies the principles upon which I expect to stand and administer the affairs of Colorado.

"I have but one desire, and that is that when I enter official life I shall give every energy I possess, every hour that comes to me, every day of the two years which I put in at the capitol, to support by law the rights of the individual to liberty, and to make an economical administration of the finances of this state.

"These, my friends, are the sentiments to which I subscribe—to support the law, to give an honest administration and to make a fair use of the taxes of the people. And with these sentiments upon my banner, under that banner I will go. I will treat every citizen, whether he voted for me or whether he did not, as an equal before the law, as one having the same rights as every other citizen. There can be no distinction. To these things I consecrate myself, without thought of future preferment or personal ambition; with no purpose but to serve the people of Colo-

rado, .and to bring back a Democratic government and a government by
the people in the capitol on yonder hill." (Great applause.)

Although it was a presidential campaign, very little attention
was paid to National issues by the campaign orators of either
party in the state. They confined themselves almost entirely to
state issues. The principal issues between the parties was Peabodyism vs. anti-Peabodyism.

The Republican orators took their cue from the mine owners'
"Red Book," accused the Western Federation of Miners of all the
crimes under the sun; accused the Democratic party of being an
auxiliary to the W. F. M., upholding that organization in its supposed lawlessness and that if the Democratic candidates were
elected anarchy would reign in the state and that capital would be
driven out.

They attempted to make capital out of the agreement made
between the Liberty League and the Democrats regarding the
platform. They distorted the facts and gave it as positive proof
that the Democrats had, for the sake of winning votes, agreed with
the W. F. M. to support them in winning their strike regardless of
what methods they employed.

The Democratic orators reviewed the unconstitutional actions
of the Republican administration; recited high-handed methods of
Peabody in serving the interests of the Mine Owners' Association
and kindred organizations and pledged that if their candidates
were elected, constitutional government would again reign in Colorado.

The Democratic party was greatly handicapped by lack of
funds, while the Republican party had unlimited wealth at their
command. All large corporations in the state contributed to the
Republican campaign fund.

Believing in the policy adopted by the Liberty League in supporting the Democratic candidates as the safest method of defeating Peabody for re-election and obtaining relief and justice to my
fellowworkers, suffering by reason of his tyranny, I donated my
services to the Democratic party during the campaign. My first
experience on the platform was gained while organizing Liberty

Leagues. Having lived in the Cripple Creek district during the time of the excitement there and knowing the conditions thoroughly, I believed I could be of service. I am not a politician, neither have I ever been a seeker for political preferment. I have always contended and believed that woman's sphere was the home—to keep it sacred and holy. That was my faith politic. My idea of high politic power was that men who occupied the positions— men who had the confidence of the vast majority of the common people of the land—men into whose hands the law-abiding and law-respecting people of the commonwealth had placed the power of controlling the the affairs of the state were men of honor. I had always believed that the respect and confidence of the masses would and should be a boon that those high in power should and did consider as sacred as woman should her home, the child its parents, or the good citizen should his state, and that this confidence, placed by the majority was unpurchasable and unsusceptible to greed, mammon or ambition—for I believe no ambition could be more noble or more to be desired than to be the respected protector of the masses. Oh, but of politics I know very little, nor if they are habitually conducted as I have seen them conducted in Colorado for the past two years, do I care to know much of them. I have seen the expressed will of nearly 47,000 majority of the voters, the home-owners, the people of Colorado, ignored and betrayed by a legislature each and every one of whom had taken a solemn oath to God and on their honor to do as the majority dictated.

Benedict Arnold betrayed the position of a small detachment of a small army. The legislature of Colorado betrayed an entire state, a very wealthy and large state. Benedict Arnold is the despised of this nation, he was sentenced to death as a traitor. These later day traitors are, by some, honored for their treachery and even spoken of as patriots—as men. Had Washington's cabinet and the Continental Congress been composed of such patriots as the Fourteenth and Fifteenth Assembly's and James H. Peabody—instead of the stars and stripes, emblem of liberty, a banner at the sight of which tyrants have trembled and monarchs bowed their knee in awe, instead of this banner of stars and stripes being the emblem of the grandest nation on earth, we would be doing homage to the ancestors of King George and all but rebels would be declaring the divine right of his majesty to extort tea tariff and stamp revenue without the privilege of voting and our National air would be "God Save the Queen."

That is the reason I, a woman, holding the belief I have just stated—that womans' natural sphere should be the home and not public life—deemed it my duty as one having the welfare of my country and my countrymen at heart, believed it to be an imperative duty, in this the darkest hour of Colorado's history to do my mite, however little, just as did the women of '63, many of whom are recorded in history as having made noble sacrifices that our country might be free and independent. The civil war found many women working earnestly, aye, even risking their lives, that this, our beloved land, might be the home of the free for even the most humble citizen.

I was in attendance at the W. F. M. convention held in Denver, at the time the Independence explosion occurred. Upon desiring to return to my home in Victor I was notified by military officials that I had best stay away from the district. Being an exile from home, I deemed that I could devote my time of exile to no better purpose than to assist in ridding the state of an administration that was responsible for such a condition of affairs.

Too much cannot be said in praise of the noble women that remained in the Cripple Creek district, wives and relatives of the unionists, who all through the dark days of the strike, assisted the strikers in every possible way. They cared for the sick, fed and clothed as far as lay in their power the needy, secured bonds for those incarcerated in jail. They suffered hardships uncomplainingly and were a power of support and encouragement to the strikers that cannot be estimated.

THE ELECTION.

The day after election, returns showed that the state had gone overwhelmingly for Roosevelt. His plurality being over 34,000 votes. Governor Adams was elected by 11,000 majority and that a Democratic legislature had been elected.

The repudiation of Peabody could not have been stronger for the reason that the state had gone so thoroughly Republican for President, and that all the state candidates for state offices on the Republican ticket had been elected with the exception of Peabody. This, in spite of the unlimited money, expended by the corporations to insure his election.

HONORABLE ALVA ADAMS.

It is clear that had it not been Presidential election, Peabody would not have received near as many votes. The result in Fremont county, his home, was an indication of his unpopularity. It went strongly against him; although he had at numerous times been elected to various county offices.

The corporations voted their employes as they liked in Huerfano and Las Animas counties. The C. F. & I Company in Las Animas bringing in train loads of foreigners who did not have naturalization papers and voted them for Peabody. As to Teller county, the mine owners had local candidates for office in the field that they wished to elect as well as Peabody, and in spite of all plans of peace made by the unions and the Democrats in charge, Chris Miller, a well-known union miner, was shot and killed at Goldfield about 10:30 a. m. November 8, by Deputy Sheriff Warford, who also, almost at the same time, shot Ike Liebo, a Democratic election officer. Other shooting and trouble of various kinds, all caused by the mine owners and Citizens' Alliance trying to steal the election, took place. Prominent and highly respected ladies while acting in the capacity of Democratic election judges were insulted and cruelly treated by the element managing the Republican interests there.

Mr. Miller was a staunch worker in the cause of unionism and had for that reason been persecuted by the opponents. He was absolutely fearless.

The night before election Miller, Liebo, Frank Mannix and two other pominent Democrats received letters telling them to leave the district. Miller and Liebo were shot the next day and later an effort was made to deport the others.

C. C. Hamlin was a candidate for the office of district attorney and Ed Bell for sheriff. Hamlin's nomination was an insult to the people of the Cripple Creek district, but, for all that, he was elected by his own class stealing the election for him. Ballot boxes were stuffed. "Gun men" were at all the voting precincts and in some cases ballots were cast, we might say, at the point of bayonets. The union miners had been deported and many of their families had left the district.

Many of the city and county officers elected are connected with the Mine Owners' Association. The mine owners gave their men a holiday with pay on election day as an inducement to vote the Republican ticket.

PEOPLES' WILL OVERTHROWN.

As previously recorded the supreme court had taken control of the election at the request of the Republican protests and charges of fraud against the Democratic legislators, principally Denver county, whom the returns showed to have been elected, were made by the Republicans and laid before the supreme court. This body caused the arrest of many Democratic election officials and others for violation of the court's injunction and numerous other charges. The court threw out the returns from many of the precincts, which resulted in defeating all of the Democratic legislators from Denver county, and electing the Republicans.

In other parts of the state trumped up charges of fraud were made against Democratic legislators that had been elected and contests entered by their Republican opponents.

According to the election laws of Colorado these contests should be decided by the state canvassing board. The canvassing board consisted of Governor Peabody and his associates in the state administration. Knowing that the Democrats could not look for justice, the supreme court was asked to decide if the canvassing board had a right to go behind election returns. This the supreme court refused to do, thus leaving the canvassing board free to act as it pleased. It being a part of the conspiracy against the will of the people, it is, needless to say that the canvassing board decided in favor of the Republican candidates.

The control of the legislature, by the Republicans, was necessary in order to carry out the conspiracy to oust from office the duly elected Democratic candidate, Honorable Alva Adams, and seat James H. Peabody.

Governor Peabody's part of the programme was to contest the election of Alva Adams, claiming fraud. On November 12th, he took the first step by issuing the following statement to the public:

"*To the People of Colorado:*

"From the most reliable information obtainable from the several counties of the state, I am now confident that I have been fairly and honestly elected governor of Colorado. Great outrages have been attempted in some outside counties, as well as in Denver.

"Opposition to my election did not come mainly from labor unions.

"They are as much in favor of law and order as other law-abiding citizens. Neither do threats or personal violence and public disturbance, nor the stirring up of strife come chiefly from them. I am now convinced that the fight came in a large degree from a set of reckless men, both in and outside of the Republican party, who aided the Democrats, agged them on to disorderly conduct, and supplied them with large sums of money in the hope of defeating me. We shall probe the facts about the recent election in every county of the state. If it should prove that I am not re-elected, I will admit it promptly.

"I make this public statement because of an evident attempt on the part of some people, some politicians, and some newspapers, to bluff the public into believing that I am defeated, with the hope thereby of discouraging my friends and frightening me away from the contest.

"I ask the assistance and support of all. law-abiding citizens of Colorado in my attempt to honestly and fearlessly establish the facts in relation to the election of November 8, 1904.

(Signed)   "JAMES H. PEABODY."

This he followed by contesting the election of Adams before the legislature.

The Republican senate unseated two Democratic senators, through unconstitutional methods, which required a two-third vote to expel a member.

Through the action of the supreme court, the partisan decision of the canvassing board and the high-handed methods of the senate, the Fifteenth General Assembly, which, according to the election returns, would have been safely Democratic, stood in joint session, sixty-six Republicans and thirty-three Democrats.

ADAMS INAUGURATED.

On January 10, 1905, the entire preceding day having been consumed by Republican leaders, in attempting, through resolutions and protests, before the joint Assembly, to prevent the same, the Honorable Alva Adams was inaugurated.

The president of the joint session announced that Alva Adams had received a plurality of 9,764 votes. This did not include the votes he received in the city of Denver that had been thrown out by the supreme court.

In his inaugural message to the Fifteenth General Assembly which occupied less than half an hour in its delivery, the briefest address of the kind ever delivered by a governor of Colorado, Governor Adams made the following recommendations:

An honest eight-hour law, a promise made to the people by both parties, and which should be kept.

An amendment to the arbitration law requiring a compulsory submission of any grievance or difference between employer and employe to the board of arbitration.

An honest and efficient primary election law.

A law making clear, definite and limited the power of the state board of canvassers.

A reduction of the tax levy to the minimum point which will enable the state to take care of its institutions in a respectable manner.

"Enact good laws, to see that they are administered with justice and impartiality, and to collect and spend the money of the taxpayer with wisdom and integrity, are the sacred duties of the government.

"Colorado is a great state; you are its moral and material guardians. The first bill introduced, as well as the last, should recognize this responsibility. Do not wait until the last hours of the session to economize. The earliest hour is the best hour for doing right.

"Let the troubles and turmoils of the past be forgotten as we turn our faces to the future and press forward to a certain and splendid destiny.

"As citizens and official you and I must make Colorado noted as a state of wise management of state institutions, just and fair expenditure of the people's tax, equity and justice in our courts, integrity and ability in official, patriotism in citizen, purity in the election franchise, virtue, honesty and loyalty everywhere, religion respected, education universal, civic righteousness the daily thought."

An eloquent and touching tribute was paid to Senator W. S. Buckley, former Governor Eaton and Representative White, all of whom have died within the past few months and were in their lifetime connected with affairs of state.

Two days after the inauguration of Governor Adams, James H. Peabody filed his petition before the legislature, claiming that he had been defeated as a result of fraud and conspiracy upon the part of the Democratic machine and praying that body to reconsider its actions in seating Alva Adams, and, that he be declared the duly elected governor. In his petition he asked the legislature to throw out the returns from one hundred and three precincts in the city and county of Denver, claiming that the said poll had been tainted by fraud.

With his usual disregard for the rights of the people, Peabody's request meant the disfranchisement of one-half of the voters of Denver in order that he might again gain the gubernatorial chair.

On January 17th, in joint assembly, a committee consisting of twenty-seven members, eighteen Republicans and nine Democrats, was appointed to hear the contest. This was in violation of the statutes which provide for the hearing of such contests before a joint session. The Democrats protested against this action and demanded that the representation on the committee be equally divided between Democrats and Republicans. Their protests, however, were in vain.

On January 21st, Governor Adams answered Peabody's charges of fraud and made counter charges that a huge conspiracy had been hatched by the corporations and the leaders of the Republican party, to seat Peabody by unlawful means. He named the American Smelting and Refining Company; the Victor Fuel Company; Colorado Fuel and Iron Company; Colorado Mine Owners' Association; the railroads; the Sugar trusts and the Denver Public Utility corporations as being parties to this conspiracy.

The gubernatorial contest consumed two-thirds of the time of the Assembly, two months. The contest committee held daily sessions, during which time they examined several thousand witnesses. The main evidence relied upon by the attorneys for Peabody, was the evidence of a numerous staff of so-called experts on handwriting, employed to examine the ballots. These experts reported hundreds of ballots written by the same person, which were afterward proven to be genuine by the sworn testimony of persons who voted them. The report of the contest committee was voluminous, requiring fourteen large volumes, the cost of printing same being $60,000.00.

The burden of proof, according to all rules of evidence, required Peabody to show that he had been honestly elected. In this he utterly failed, though the evidence showed that election fraud was rampant, workers for both parties being guilty.

The joint Assembly convened March 3rd to hear arguments of attorneys in behalf of Adams and Peabody. The rules governing the contest allowed sixteen hours for argument, time to be equally divided between attorneys for contestor and contestee. John M. Waldron, one of the most forceful and brilliant attorneys in the state, acted for Peabody. Adams was represented by the following staff of brilliant attorneys: Ex-Governor Chas. S. Thomas, Milton Smith, Samuel Belford, John A. Rush and Judge Orr.

Mr. Waldron in his argument did not confine himself to any extent to the evidence introduced before the contest committee, but occupied his time, rather, in endeavoring to convince the joint Assembly that that body was not acting in the capacity of a jury to determine the rights or wrongs of the parties. That it was discharging a purely political duty. He declared that there was absolutely no constitutional guarantee which either ex-Governor Peabody or Governor Adams could invoke against the action of the joint Assembly in its decision of the contest, regardless of whether that decision be right or whether it be fundamentally wrong. This line of argument by Peabody's attorney was intended to quiet the scruples some of the Republicans were known to have against voting to seat Peabody when it was well known that he had not been elected

The attorneys for Governor Adams confined themselves more to the evidence and clearly showed that Peabody did not have a case. There can be no question that if the contest had been tried by a jury of twelve men, or before an impartial judge the case would have been thrown out of court. Unfortunately, partisanship and not justice, swayed the members in deciding the contest.

Attorney Waldron's argument and the action of the joint assembly was merely the climax of the conspiracy to steal the governorship that had been hatched prior to the election, the first act of which was the injunction and control of the election by the supreme court.

On the 16th day of March, having remained in continued joint session to that date, the joint Assembly, by a vote of fifty-five to forty-one declared that Mr. Peabody had been elected governor. This, however, was done with the understanding that Peabody was to resign within twenty-four hours after he was inaugurated. This understanding was brought about by twelve Republican members, who could not bring themselves to vote in favor of seating Peabody, who, the evidence so clearly showed, had not received enough votes at the state election to be elected, yet whose partisanship was so much stronger than their sense of justice, that they could not resist taking advantage of the opportunity to seat a Republican as governor. This they brought about by insisting that Peabody, after being seated, resign, which would make the Republican lieutenant governor, Jesse F. McDonald, Peabody's successor.

These twelve Republicans, holding the balance of power, were in a position to enforce their demands against the pleadings and earnest protests of Peabody and his corporation supporters. It was generally understood that the inducement that finally caused Peabody to agree to resign was the guarantee, upon the part of the corporations, to pay him the two year's salary that he would have received as governor.

To show how little confidence the people of Colorado have in the word of Peabody, the twelve Republicans that insisted upon Peabody's resignation, compelled him to write his resignation when the agreement was made, and place it in the hands of W. S. Boynton; by him, to be turned over to the secretary of state.

Upon the announcement of the vote deciding the contest, the

lieutenant governor, acting as president of the joint Assembly, announced that according to the vote he declared the Honorable James H. Peabody to have been duly elected governor of Colorado at the election held November 8th, 1904, and that the Honorable Alva Adams had been, since the 10th of January, unlawfully holding said office, and that he declared the aforesaid Honorable Alva Adams ousted from the possession of the aforesaid office.

Immediately upon this announcement of the president of the Assembly, Mr. Peabody, who had been in waiting, was escorted in and was inaugurated, Chief Justice Gabbert administering the oath of office.

Great indignation was aroused among the citizens of the state, against the action of the joint Assembly, in this, the deliberate theft of the governorship. Many life-long Republicans were loud in their denunciation.. It looked for awhile as if civil war would reign in Colorado. There is no question but what, had Mr. Adams refused to abide by the unjust decision of the joint assembly, fully sixty per cent of the citizens would have stood by him, even to the extent of resorting to arms. Much credit is due the Honorable Alva Adams, that civil war was averted. Strong pressure was brought to bear upon him by prominent citizens of the state to resist, to all of which he turned a deaf ear, preferring to retire from office rather than that blood should be shed. Mr. Adams retired from the governorship with the respect of every reasonable citizen. That he had been elected by a majority of 10,000 honest votes there can be no question. When it first became clearly evident that there was a conspiracy to steal the office from him, he might have defeated the same, by demanding that the contest, as required by the constitution, be heard in its entirety before the joint legislature and not by a committee as was done. He would not be convinced that it could be possible that a majority of the legislature could be won over by the corporations to deliberately steal the office. Feeling strong in the justness of his cause, having faith in humanity and knowing public sentiment to be with him, he had no fear of the result. Events proved that he was mistaken and that he did not fully realize the power of the great corporations to corrupt legislators. He made a clean, decent fight to have the will of the people carried out. The influence of the corporations, which decided the contest, clearly demonstrated that the corporations in their mad desire to, for selfish interests, seize the resources of the state, were not concerned with such trifles as **law, decency or justice. They violate the law as readily as any highwayman and find means of controling men in office to assist them in their robberies.**

It rests with the people to determine at the next state election if Waldron's policy of "Might makes right," will long prevail in Colorado.

Too much praise cannot be given to the thirty-one Democrats and the ten Republicans in the legislature who stood firmly from start to finish against the theft of the governorship.

From the very beginning of the contest until the last vote had been taken the entire Democratic membership of both houses was loyal and without thought of disloyalty. So undisputed was the integrity of these members that no lobbyist or corruptionist even approached them.

The ten Republicans are especially deserving of praise and of the honor which will be given to them by every honest voter in the state, no matter what his party may be. Because of their party affiliation they were made targets for assaults of every kind from the corporation lobby. Business and social pressure were brought to bear upon them. They were haunted day and night by pretended friends who talked to them along party lines and by avowed corruptionists who sought to influence them by material inducements. They were threatened with revenge.

Some of the Republican members who had promised to vote for Adams because they knew that the evidence showed his election fell before these influences, but ten Republicans who voted for Adams at the last proved themselves to be honest, brave and incorruptible.

It is a good thing for the state that it numbers such men in its citizenship. The test which they stood was a severe one. It proved the quality of their metal. They won the esteem and good wishes of all whose esteem and good wishes are worth having.

JESSE M'DONALD, GOVERNOR.

March 17th, late in the afternoon, the resignation of James H. Peabody was presented to Secretary of State Cowie, according

JESSE M'DONALD, ACTING GOVERNOR OF COLORADO.

to the plans adopted previously. W. S. Boynton had carried the document around in his pocket from the time Peabody placed his signature upon it until it was presented to the secretary of state.

Lieutenant Governor McDonald was in the capitol building and was promptly informed that if he would kindly consent to appear before a member of the supreme court and take the required oath, he might become the chief executive of the state. He acquiesed and the inauguration ceremony was of the most simple style. Mr. McDonald repeated the words of the oath in a firm voice and then turned to receive the congratulations of his friends.

"I will endeavor to give the people of Colorado a satisfactory administration," said the new governor. "Let us have peace."

Jesse McDonald, of Lake county, made the third governor Colorado had had within twenty-four hours.

As to the personality of Governor McDonald, I have nothing to say. I do not know him personally. Since his inauguration the state has been quiet on the surface and there has not been an opportunity, more than the general routine work, to require any great amount of executive skill. If I should offer any criticism of Governor McDonald it would be for accepting the gubernatorial chair under the conditions that he did. But for all that, let us hope he will give us the "satisfactory" administration he promised in his brief inaugural address.

GOVERNOR ADAMS RETURNS TO HIS HOME.

March 19th, Ex-Governor Alva Adams, accompanied by his wife, returned to his home in Pueblo. Never in the history of that city was there ever accorded to a citizen of Colorado such a demonstration as was accorded the victim of Republican infamy.

Long before the hour the governor's train was announced to arrive not only was the union depot platform crowded with an eager mass of humanity, but the streets surrounding the union depot and the immense viaduct over the tracks close by were jammed to the limit. No Roman warrior returning after victory in the field ever met with more whole-souled expressions of good will or greater loyalty than was accorded Alva Adams, citizen, and, as characterized by the speaker who presented him to the vast crowd in waiting, "the first citizen of Colorado."

GOVERNOR ADAMS' STATEMENT

Before returning to his home to take up the duties that awaited him there, ex-Governor Adams issued the following statement:

"To the People of Colorado:

"Force has triumphed. A brutal majority placed in the governor's
chair a man the people repudiated. Ninety-five per cent of Colorado
citizens know that Peabody was not elected. All of those connected
with the crime know it.

"Defeated at the polls, the conspirators started in November 9 to
seat the beaten candidate. Every conscienceless engine of corruption and
pressure has been used. Foiled in their attempt to override the constitution and hold Peabody in his seat, a fake contest was inaugurated.
This failed of its purpose, as enough Republican members would not
forfeit their manhood by voting for a man that the testimony, as well
as the election returns, said was not elected. The revolt was dangerous;
it was clear that Peabody could not be seated. A new scheme must be
devised, so that coterie of Christian utility statesmen, Hearne, Sheedy,
Chappell and Evans, met in the Majestic building Wednesday evening and
gave birth to the last plan in the ignoble conspiracy of stealing the governorship. Representatives of the anti-Peabody Republicans were invited.
A resignation of Peabody was offered and the voucher of the political
purity quartet was given that it was genuine and that he would abide by
it. A man who had held the great office of governor so debased himself
as to promise to resign at command if they would seat him but for a day.
This resignation is a confession that he was not elected and one that an
honest man honestly elected would rather die than give. Peabody is
entitled to the position for two years or he is not entitled to it for one
hour. We are given the spectacle of a man not elected being placed in
office for a day that he may resign in favor of a man who was never a
candidate.

"The McDonald promotion scheme appealed to a few who would not
vote for Peabody, but were reluctant to aid a Democrat. Most participants admit the absurdity and wrong of the situation, but for pardon
depend upon the tolerance and indifference of their constituents. One
of the main conspirators said, "The people will forget." Will they? Is
public opinion dead, or is it but a party annex? Is free government a
delusion? Is civic virtue nothing but a phrase?

"The vital principle of republics is obedience to the will of the
majority. In this faith we relied in the contest upon the honest individual judgment of every legislator, and have been met by partisanship. We expected fair play; instead the majority of the legislature has
bowed to the dictates of corporations who had selfish need of the gover-

norship. It has been declared to the world that Colorado is a province of the Fuel company, the smelter trust, the Tramway and allied corporations. These companies and their agents and tools have carried the burden of the Peabody campaign from the time they forced him upon a reluctant party at the state convention until through the last disreputable deal he has been given a twenty-four-hour tenancy of the statehouse.

"In this long campaign hundreds of thousands of dollars. have been contributed by the corporations. The cost may not be enough to stagger humanity, but it would certainly stagger the stockholders of these contributing and conspiring companies if they knew the amount and use made of the funds.

"In the eyes of the nation Colorado has been disgraced. We have won the contempt of free men everywhere. By command of the corporations a usurper has been placed in the executive chair—a new record in political infamy has been made.

"It is legitimate for a citizen or a company to support any ticket it pleases and as vigorously as each pleases up to the close of the polls. But after that to set aside the people's verdict is a crime. Certain corporate officials pretend fear of anarchy, yet pursue methods that make them masters of lawlessness. Anarchy is not practiced alone by those with the torch and knife.

"The greatest anarchists, and the most dangerous, are often the no-party, no-conscience heads of great corporations, who use the money and influence coming from the franchises and privileges that are the gifts of the people to control legislation, to dictate the personnel of courts and officials, to corrupt the ballot.

"They stand high in church and society; they drone their prayers with regularity; they are the "holy Willies"—the "holier than thou" politicians—no publican of old more pious and self-satisfied. They are full of homilies on political virtue; they preach morality and practice treason; their purse is open to the church and to the political corruptionist and lobbyist with equal liberality. For their disregard of the law there seems to be no relief, as they would have the laws so made, interpreted and executed as to exempt them from penalty.

"The investigation proved that, where under control of corporate influences, the outrages against the franchise and the election law were so gross as to make Denver repeating and fraud seem almost respectable. They preferred even the disgrace of an empty ballot box to the shameless story that the falsified books and ballots would reveal. Bosses and corporate officials dictated votes and manipulated returns.

"Under God's law, if not man's, the workman who, to save his job and earn bread for his family, obeys the command to pollute the ballot is not half so guilty and criminal as the employer who coerces him. Ten-fold more wicked is the priest who violates the commandments than is his lowly follower who forgets.

"I am calm and moderate in my statements, but do not deny a feeling of intense resentment at being robbed. From my soul I feel outraged at being the victim of a conspiracy that has brought ill fame and discredit to Colorado.

"I am but an incident in this contest. For me it is no hardship to go back to my home and my own affairs, but it is a serious matter to the state when canvassing boards are permitted by arbitrary and illegal methods to change the political character of a state senate and a partisan legislature so created uses its power to force into office a man who was defeated at the polls. Character is as great an asset for a state as for an individual, and when the will of the people is set aside and the constitution becomes the plaything of faction the character of the state is tainted. Broken laws and discordant politics do not attract the investor or the emigrant.

"The legislature's governor is welcome to all the joy that can come to the occupant of a tainted seat. Welcome to all the glory he can find as receiver of stolen property. Office is not an elixir of life. It is neither a path of pleasure nor a conservator of fortune, and unless attained with honor can add no leaf of fame, no satisfaction to an honest man. To say that merit or right guided the vote in this contest is to impeach the intelligence of the legislature. They simply followed the destructive moral and political heresy of their attorney, who advised, when he found that no case had been made, that it was not a question of moral right or wrong, but of power, of duty to the Republican party. The doctrine of might makes right has won. No fair man who heard the evidence, whether upon the committee of twenty-seven or elsewhere, but knows that the case of the contestor was a complete and humiliating failure. Most of them have admitted it, but party fealty and other influences smothered their consciences and secured the verdict making good the boast so often made prior to the election that Peabody would be seated, no matter whether he got the most votes or not. Money was offered in wager by inspired Republicans in different parts of the state upon the tricky proposition that Peabody would be governor—not that he would receive a majority of the votes. The Republican organ time and again intimated that, as the party had the state officers and the canvassing board, Peabody would remain in office without regard to the verdict of the ballots. Friends who were with the Peabody management or in their confidence told me again and again that I was up against an invincible combination—that the deal was to elect Peabody without regard to circumstances or cost. The climax of this political drama, or tragedy, throws light over many events of the long campaign. Their victory is one of the kind where to win is to lose, as no party ever long flourished on rascality.

"All honor to the patriotic Republicans who had the courage to stand for the right. Their oath to support the laws and the constitution was held sacred as against the command of the corrupt lobbyist or the party boss. Principle was preferred to party. All good citizens owe to them a debt of gratitude. Upon such independent citizenship rests the destiny of the republic. All honor to the thirty-one Democrats who stood as a single man for justice. Amid all the charges and insinuations of venality no suspicion ever touched the garment of a single Democrat. There was never a moment of anxiety as to where they stood; no guardian watched them; no briber came near.

"To the world I would say that the majority of the legislature does not represent the people of Colorado any more than falsehood represents truth; than Lucifer speaks for the angels. Fearing to offend the great companies who in this campaign furnished their party with the largest corruption fund ever used in the West, the majority of the legislature basely surrendered. It was an act of political and moral cowardice in which the people had no part.

"The 600,000 Democrats and Republicans in Colorado are honest. They stand amazed at the crime committed by their representatives and they ardently wait the hour and the day when they can rebuke the crime and those responsible for it.

"Those who have been moved to wrong and injustice by avarice or the party lash must make peace with their own conscience as best they can. Facts and truth can make no plea for them.

"Is the prize worth the cost? Is it worth a scar upon self-respect, a blemish upon manhood? Is it worth the suspicion and contempt of constituents and an entire state? Power is but a temporary lease. From the people we came and back to them and their scrutiny we must return.

"A legislature cannot repeal the decalogue. A majority cannot make stealing respectable. Where things are even we may give our party the benefit of the doubt, but loyalty to party is no apology or defense for larceny. Our party has no right to be flagrantly wrong, and when wrong it has no right to claim the allegiance of any honest man. "Many a noble neck that has bowed itself to party has found that yoke a guillotine."

"Thou shalt not steal;

"Thou shalt not bear false witness;

Are commandments that have never been amended or repealed, and apply to parties as well as to men.

"Integrity is the polar star in the moral firmament, and the state, party or individual that does not sail by it will come to wreck.

"Had this contest been tried upon merit and evidence it would have been dismissed at the end of the contestor's phantom testimony. Faith in a two-thirds partisan majority was all that kept it alive. No honest cause should require the means employed. Their overwhelming political majority was a guarantee that had their case been half way fair and decent there would have been no need to employ money, coercion, lobbyists. No occasion to threaten Republican members with social ostracism, business ruin, political oblivion, or to present tricky resignations.

"It was a dishonorable victory, dishonorably won. Let those responsible look over the cost in cash and in deed and see if they dare give the account to the public eye.

"I want to stand an honest man before the people of Colorado. Better a hundred times a private citizen than hold the highest office by such a title. The stolen presidency added no luster to Rutherford B. Hayes. A stolen governorship will bring only reproach and disaster to Colorado and Republicanism. "The theft is to the thief and comes back most to him."   "ALVA ADAMS."

"Denver, Colorado, March 17, 1905."

SUMMARY OF CONTEST

Cost of contest to taxpayers, $100,000.

Election November 8, 1904. Adams' plurality on face of returns, 10,511.

November 10, Peabody men charge fraud.

November 13, Peabody announces contest.

Actual length of contest before legislature, two months and six days.

November 30, corporations ask the supreme court to throw out all votes in precincts where frauds are alleged.

December 14, supreme court throws out precincts 8, ward 7.

December 18, four more precincts are thrown out, giving legislature to Republicans.

December 27, Adams demands that all ballot boxes be opened.

December 30, supreme court orders·a recount of all Denver ballots.

January 1, Richard Broad, Simon Guggenheim's manager, says: "Peabody will be counted in."

January 6, Peabody protests against publishing the vote of Denver and a committee of fifteen is appointed to probe Peabody's fraud charge.

January 7, Adams declared elected by the legislature on face of returns.

January 8, Adams inaugurated.

January 16, a committee rescinded by joint session.

January 17, Committee of twenty-seven appointed by joint Assembly to hear contest. Peabody demands that Denver's entire vote be thrown out.

January 18, first evidence taken.

January 20, handwriting experts begin their false claims.

January 21, Governor Adams makes specific charges of fraud in outside counties.

January 25, Peabody issued personal appeal for money to aid in contest.

January 30, handwriting experts end evidence.

February 1, 2, and 3, hundreds of citizens identify their votes, which experts called fraudulent.

Adams' plurality increased 2,730 by throwing out fraudulent ballots in outside counties.

February 19, testimony ends.

February 26, briefs filed.

March 1, four reports filed, one favoring Peabody, one Adams, third insufficient evidence to unseat Adams, and the fourth recommending seating of Lieutenant Governor McDonald.

March 1, Peabody's counsel, J. M. Waldron, tells legislature "Might makes right."

March 13, supreme court says contest is between Adams and Peabody, McDonald not to figure.

March 14, test vote showed equal strength, 48 to 48. Lieutenant Governor McDonald, contrary to rules, casts the deciding vote and enforces recess.

March 16, final vote shows Peabody 55, Adams 41. Adams unseated, Peabody declared governor.

March 17, Peabody resigns and Jesse McDonald seated as governor. Peabody goes for a trip east.

March 19, Governor Adams returns to his home, Pueblo, and is greeted by 15,000 enthusiastic citizens. Hundreds of well-known citizens draw his carriage through the streets to his residence.

March 20, the legislature takes up legislation and begins to hurry the long-delayed work.

The corporation lobbyists spent money freely and at different times as much as $7,000 was paid for the influence and vote of one man in the house, it is said. Many of them had their price and it was usually willingly paid by the corporation lobbyists. At no time was there a Democrat accused of taking bribes. The two principal grafts was the gubernatorial contest and the defeat of the eight-hour bill. In fact, money was used to such an extent to defeat desired and much needed legislation in the interest of the masses that I feel almost tempted to suggest that:

Since treachery seems to be the rule,
    Fidelity the exception;
Since money secures the passage of bills,
    Its absence their rejection;
Why not establish a "boodle" fund
From the gifts of an outraged nation,
And then go into the market and buy
    Some decent legislation.

RESUME OF THE CONSPIRACY.

The history of the time that elapsed from election day to the end of the contest may be stated very briefly about as follows:

The political complexion of the legislature and the personnel of the governor was changed by other than the will of the people as expressed at the polls election day. The supreme court was the power used to bring about the first change, when, in a contempt proceeding, it declared it possessed the power to throw out entire precincts when it was shown that fraud had been committed in the precinct. The court did not unseal the number on the ballots, nor did it summon the voters and distinguish between the good ballots and those alleged to be bad. The court held that it could not unseal the ballots because the proceeding was not a contest, it could not, under the law, unseal the ballots and reveal who cast them. It could not violate the secrecy and sacredness of the ballot. I wish to call especial attention to the fact that **the same** law which provides that the ballots cannot be unsealed except in a contest also provides that the ballot boxes shall not be opened except in a contest. But the court did open the ballot boxes and permitted the ballots to be scrutinized by so-called hand-writing experts whose testimony later given in the contest was so wild and foolish that it proved worthless. Yet their testimony, proved to be of no value, must have had some weight with the court as it ordered the exclusion of a number of precincts from the count and this exclusion had the effect of electing three Republican senators and the fifteen representatives who had been candidates for the legislature from Denver and the counties floated with it.

The next page in the history should be devoted to the jobbery executed under order of the corporations. A strange change took place in the returns from a precinct in Pueblo. The change was not questioned by the Peabody canvassing board composed of the state administration. This defeated Senator Martin and elected Senator McCarthy, a Republican. Next the Peabody canvassing board deliberately stole the seats of Senator Ward of Boulder and Beshoar of Las Animas and gave them to Milard and Barela.

The next act of this tragic performance was the illegal expulsion of Democratic Senators Born and Healy on the shameful pretext that the senate two years ago unseated—in a legal manner —two Republican senators. They failed to consider that the house two years ago had first unseated six Democratic members in the effort to create a majority to elect a Republican United States Senator.

By the foregoing methods there was established a strong partisan majority in the legislature, then it was that the Peabody- ites lodged a contest against Governor Alva Adams. The evidence which was submitted during the hearing of the contest clearly proved that Peabody had no case and he never thought he had a case but relied solely upon the partisan majority. It proved that Governor Alva Adams, under an honest count, had a larger instead of a smaller plurality than he received on the face of the returns.

This tragedy had many acts and the next was the long struggle. Corporation money in unlimited sums was put into circulation. Corporation influence was used, the influence of party bosses and of "boodle," whipped enough members into line to steal the governorship for Peabody by a vote of fifty-five (55) to forty-one, (41) ten honest Republicans vindicating their manhood by voting for Mr. Adams on the final ballot.

The last act was the working out of the disgraceful deal by which Peabody, the recipient of the stolen office passed it along to Lieutenant Governor McDonald and retired, repudiated and discredited.

POLITICAL OBLIVION FOR PEABODY.

Now that Peabody has passed into political oblivion, forever, we hope for brighter days. He was nominated by corporate power after making personal pledges to do their bidding, he was elected by the lavish use of corporation funds. Under his reign the entire United States has stood simply appalled at his violations of law. The beautiful state of Colorado has been an object of pity to the other states in the Union, pointed to with scorn as proof of the decadence of independence of our citizens.

Ex-Governor Peabody represented one class—the mine owners and corporations—to the lasting detriment of the farmer, the business man and the laborer.

He, in time of peace, hired out the militia of the state to do the bidding of the Mine Owners' Association and corporations.

He created a million dollar deficit which the farmers and business men of the state will be compelled to pay.

He sanctioned the seizure and deportation of unoffending citizens of Colorado by the state militia.

He approved the acts of the military in casting citizens of the state—untried by any court of law—on the deserts of Kansas and New Mexico without food or drink.

He authorized, without the consent of the legislature, the suspension of the writ of habeas corpus in Teller, San Miguel and Las Animas counties.

He sanctioned the payment of the troops of the state by the

mine owners to the extent of nearly a million dollars, all of which is to be made an interest bearing debt on the state of Colorado.

He depleted the contingent fund of the state by paying it out for personal expenses of Eastern jaunts.

He squandered the revenue of the state by unauthorized warrants, such as depleting the educational fund $40,000 to give himself and his World's Fair commissioners a chance to live in luxury at St. Louis.

He hired an entire floor of the Planters Hotel in St. Louis at an expense of $1,577 for six persons for one week, or at the rate of $225 a day of the hard earned money paid in taxes by the farmer and business man.

He sanctioned the surrounding of courts of law of the state while in peaceful session, with the state troops. He sanctioned their entrance into the halls of justice with triggers set and bayonets fixed.

He sanctioned the payments to officers of the national guard of vast sums run up by them in the bar rooms of Cripple Creek and Denver.

He stands arraigned for violation of the constitution of the United States by men of all parties, including such Republicans as Elihu Root, former secretary of war; Judge Dixon of Pueblo, former Senator Thurston of Nebraska, and the best Republican papers of the land.

He sanctioned the arrest and imprisonment of citizens of the state without warrant of law.

He sanctioned the destruction of the property of unoffending citizens of Colorado.

He sanctioned the refusal of a body of lawless citizens to permit the distribution of money and food to the wives and children of men who had been deported.

Political and industrial peace in Colorado will be a boon to all classes—rich, poor, organized labor and organized capital.

With Peabody in the gubernatorial chair, peace could not obtain. We want liberty more than we want peace—without liberty there can be little peace. We do not want Peabody's brand of peace and we don't want his brand of corporation "law and order."

Peabody is a stranger to both liberty and justice. We don't ask for what our forefathers sacrificed their lives to gain for us, as charity from a half dozen corporations with Peabody as their servant—we **demand liberty as our birthright and heritage; not to be given or withheld as it suits C. C. Hamlin, Craig, Carlton or some of the operators in the coal fields.** Labor has struggled for over one hundred years to establish the improved conditions that exist in many parts of the United States. The workers have accomplished much, it is true, but in the past two years they have learned a great lesson—to not alone organize industrially but politically as well. Peabody has helped to teach us this lesson.

Mr. Peabody claims he stood for "law and order" and the punishment of crime, but the punishment of crime that omits the perpetrators and reaches only the innocent, or when a body of individuals resolve themselves into a mob and act as accusers and judges and inflict penalties that are unlawful, then the procedure is neither conducive of "law and order" nor peace but savors strongly of anarchy.

Never was a truer warning uttered than by Spinosa, the Dutch philosopher, who had occasion to know the results of unwarranted and illegal persecutions. He said

"Men are so made as to resent nothing more bitterly than to be treated, without trial, as criminals and cutthroats on account of opinions which they deem true. And what can be more fatal to a state than to exile as malcontents citizens on a wholesale plan? What more baneful than that men should be taken for enemies and led off to death, and that the torture pen should become, to the signal shame of authority, the finest stage for the public spectacle of endurance and virtue?"

This was written more than 250 years ago, yet it will fit these times and scenes in Colorado as well as it did the scenes and times that gave Spinosa the inspiration to write it.

The people of Colorado have had enough of strife and we want peace, but not on Peabody's terms, we want it along lawful and constitutional lines. To expect it through the lawless violence resorted to by the henchmen of the corporations and a military battalion will be in vain; that is, unless it is the peace at Warsaw which came when the Poles had all been slain.

When the people of Colorado had an opportunity to register their disapproval of Peabodyism, at the ballot box, they repudiated him, notwithstanding the fact that he had a huge corruption fund at his back, the largest ever known to be used in a state election. After he found the people had rendered a verdict that was not to his liking he and his backers, a few corporations, sought in vain by bribery and trickery to reverse the fiat of the people. As soon as his usefulness as a tool was ended, the men he had served so well were ready to toss him in the political junk heap where he may reflect that notoriety, bought by a sacrifice of personal honor and integrity, is not worth the cost.

Peabody's example will be held up for avoidance and loathing and in the years to come decent people will draw aside their garments as he passes by.

After all, as I said in the introduction to Part I, he was simply one of the instrumentalities used. He served the corporations well, but brought misery, suffering and discredit to the state.

I do not know of one act during Peabody's administration that had a tendency to improve the conditions of the people of the state. His "business administration" has been a dismal failure; his policy ruined thousands of business men and cost the state millions of dollars, to say nothing of the undesirable notoriety to the state on account of his unprecedented actions.

Peabody's policy if followed to its logical conclusion would end in no one's life or property being safe.

"For humanity sweeps onward: where today the martyr stands,
On the morrow crouches Judas with the silver in his hands;
Far in front the cross stands ready and the crackling fagots burn,
While the hooting mob of yesterday in silent awe return
To glean up the scattered ashes into History's golden urn.
—LOWELL.

EIGHT HOUR LAW.

A number of eight-hour bills were introduced in the legislature by both Democrats and Republicans. Those introduced by the Democrats were in accordance with the constitutional amendment providing for a law making eight hours a day's work for all persons employed in underground workings, mills and smelters. The eight hour bills introduced by the Republicans were in the interest of the employers of this class of labor, aiming to limit the persons to be benefited by the eight hour law to a small per cent of those actually so employed.

The corporations being in control of the legislature, succeeded in having the eight-hour bill of their framing passed.

The bill that was passed was not at all satisfactory to union people as it was an eight-hour bill in name only and not at all such as was intended by the voters of the state when they voted for the constitutional amendment granting an eight-hour law.

For the information of the reader I reproduce the constitutional amendment for an eight-hour law as carried by the voters and the eight hour bill passed by the corporation-controlled legislature:

CONSTITUTIONAL AMENDMENT.

"AN ACT—To submit to the qualified voters of the State of Colorado an amendment to article five of the constitution of the State of Colorado by adding thereto a section, to be known as Section 25 A, directing the General Assembly to provide by law and prescribe suitable penalties for the violation thereof, for a period of employment not to exceed eight hours within any twenty-four hours (excepting in cases of emergency where life or property is in imminent danger), for persons employed in underground mines or other underground workings, blast furnaces, smelters, and any ore reduction works or other branch of industry or labor that the General Assembly may consider injurious or dangerous to health, life or limb."

EIGHT HOUR BILL

Bill as Carried by Corporations.

"Section 1. All labor of miners in underground workings, and labor directly attending blast furnaces, either in smelters or in ore reduction works, in directly attending stamp mills, chlorination and cyanide processes and directly attending smelting furnaces producing metal or matte, which labor is in contact with noxious fumes, gases or vapors, is hereby declared dangerous and injurious to health, life and limb; and the period of employment in underground mines or other underground workings, attending blast furnaces either in smelters or in ore reduction works, stamp mills, in chlorination and cyanide mills, and attending smelting furnaces producing metal or matte, shall be eight hours per day, except in cases of emergency, where life or property is in imminent danger.

"Sec. 2. Every person, body corporate, agent, manager, superintendent, employer, president or director shall, in every case of such emergency, make to the commissioner of the bureau of labor statistics, within ten days after the commencement of such emergency, a report, according to the form which may be prescribed by him, verified by the oath or affirmation of such person, employer, agent, manager, superintendent, president or director; each report shall exhibit in detail the circumstances creating such emergency.

"Sec. 3. Any violation of this act shall constitute a misdemeanor and be punished by a fine of not less than $50 nor exceeding $300."

As the reader will note the constitutional amendment provided for an eight-hour law as a sanitary measure for persons employed in mines, etc. The eight-hour bill passed by the legislature which has become a law, as it was signed by Governor McDonald, granted eight hours only to persons who were actual miners and persons directly attending blast furnaces. As a consequence, only a small per cent of persons employed in places as provided by the constitutional amendment were benefited by this so-called eight-hour law for the reason that the greater number work as helpers. The inconsistency of the bill can readily be seen, when, by reason of its being unhealthy employment it grants eight hours to men who are actually miners but denies the same benefit to others working along side of them as helpers, who are subjected to the same unhealthy conditions. The same applies to those working in mills and smelters.

This was the "just, and equitable" eight-hour plank adopted by the corporation-controlled convention.

Having the Fifteenth Assembly so completely under their control the corporations did not fail to present numerous bills, aiming to restrict labor unions. If some of these measures had become laws, organized labor would have been helpless. The gubernatorial contest having consumed two-thirds of the time of the legislature was the means of preventing the passage of these vicious measures, as the time remaining was too short to put them through.

The only bill passed that can be considered seriously against the interests of organized labor was an anti-boycott bill. This bill made it a penalty to ask people not to patronize any establishment unfair to organized labor or to call employes from any job. Attorneys claim this law is clearly unconstitutional. The labor unions will test its constitutionality upon the first arrest made.

A great disappointment to the corporations was their failure to get through a bill appropriating $800,000 to pay Peabody's military war debt. The direct cause of the failure of this bill from passing was that it was so apparent a graft, some of the Republican legislators, whose votes were necessary for its passage, believed that a large per cent should be divided among them as payment for their votes. The failure of the bill to pass was due to the fact that they could not agree upon the spoils to be thus divided. It is to be hoped that future legislatures will repudiate this so-called military indebtedness. The Mine Owners' Association being the one served by the military, should pay the bills.

I might state that as far as any legislative body passing a bill to prohibit any man or body of men from going on strike if they really wish, I do not believe it could be made effective.

We are a nation of strikers. Our independence was established by a strike. I claim the first strike that was called in the United States of America was in '76 and the leader of that strike was no one of less note than George Washington. It will be remembered that there was a Boston tea party. Property was destroyed and by the strikers, tea was thrown overboard. King George called out his red-coated military to suppress the strikers but the strikers refused to be suppressed and since that time we have had handed down from generation to generation a document that we are pleased to call the "Declaration of Independence," which was the terms on which the first strike in this country was settled.

A similar but worse condition confronts us than confronted

those patriots of '76. They struck for the abolishment of a tax and established a nation; we strike for the right to live under the banner of liberty that they fought to establish and to enjoy all the benefits it implies.

SMELTERMEN DECLARE STRIKE OFF.

The mill and smeltermen employed at the Globe and Grant smelter had been on strike for over twenty-one months prior to the passage of the eight-hour bill. The strike was called July 3, 1903, and the issue was an eight-hour workday. The men did not demand ten hours' pay for eight hours' work, but were willing to have the wage scale adjusted fairly between employer and employe.

It was not the amount of labor they did in their ten-hour shifts that caused the strike, but it was being confined so many hours in the presence of noxious smelter gases. The number of hours that were put in sent men to the grave and made many families destitute. Broken in health and spirit, the workers decided to make one last fight for their lives. While they have not won a decisive battle, they have won admiration by refusing to work without gaining at least one concession.

At a meeting of Mill and Smeltermen No. 93, W. F. M., at which a number of prominent speakers of the national organization were present, a resolution calling off the strike was adopted. The resolution stated that while the eight-hour bill did not include all the smeltermen they believed when it became a law it would give an eight-hour day to some of the employes.

SHERIFF BELL'S TROUBLES.

The sheriff of Teller county has his hands full keeping the mine owners' imported "gun-fighters" in order. Now that there are no more deportations taking place or union men to be murdered, this element had to occupy their time in some way in order to kill the monotony. Burglary and highway robbery are of frequent occurrence. Sheriff Bell is in a peculiar position regarding these men. They having rendered the Mine Owners' Association good service during the strike and election, and their services probably being needed in the near future when it is expected that the non-union miners will go on strike as it is rumored that their wages will be reduced and they will be asked to work ten hours per day. So Bell, being a mine owners' man, has to overlook a great deal from the mine owners' pets—the "gun men." As an example of how these "law and order" supporters, violate the law with impunity, I here give a little history of what took place in May.

The reader will remember a deputy by the name of Warford, who, on election day, murdered Chris Miller and wounded Ike Liebo, both union men. Warford and his partner, Kenley, were proud and boasted of having been chums of the notorious Tom Horn, professional murderer who was finally hung in Wyoming for murdering a boy.

Warford was finally arrested for the murder committed on election day and confined in jail, where he feasted royally at public expense. He was tried for murder at the February term of district court, and while the evidence of his guilt was overwhelming, he had enough of his "law and order" friends on the jury to cause a disagreement. He was returned to the jail to await another trial, but May 13, District Attorney Hamlin, who was elected on the "law and order" ticket of which Warford was a guardian angel, nollied his case and turned this red-handed murderer loose on this blessed "law and order" community.

Kenley and Chapman, another imported "gun man," were arrested on January 1 for the robbery of Daniels' assay office in Cripple Creek, and Sheriff Bell announced that he had "overwhelming testimony" of their guilt, in addition to their identification by Mr. Daniels, whom they captured when they stole the contents of his office. But both of these "law and order" shining lights had rendered the Republican party signal services in the campaign, and after lying in jail for four months, their cases were nollied by the "law and order" district attorney, without even the formality of a trial. And it is thus that "law and order" virtues are duly recognized in the Cripple Creek district.

Monday, May 15, Kenley and Chapman visited the down town office of Sheriff Bell to demand the arsenal of which each was divested when arrested. Some red hot words passed between the erstwhile "law and order" companions, when Sheriff Bell disarmed Kenley,of one gun and ordered Deputy Underwood to take the culprit to jail, a little more than a block away. The two had proceeded only a few yards, however, when Kenley drew a second gun suddenly and compelled his official escort to hold up his hands. Sheriff Bell saw the occurrence and started to the aid of his deputy, but before he had gone many yards, he, too, was invited to hold up his hands and found himself looking into the barrels of two revolvers in the hands of Warford. Then Warford and Kenley marched the sheriff and deputy to the jail, one block away, the officers trying to scrape the clouds with their uplifted hands while they marched before their captors.

After Warford and Kenley had "shooed" the amiable sheriff and deputy to jail, they bade the officials a fraternal "law and order" farewell and started towards Anaconda. Soon the sheriff and a number of his deputies, reinforced by a platoon of Chief Sharpe's cossacks, started in pursuit. The "law and order" pets of District Attorney Hamlin were overtaken about a mile south of the city, and a battle ensued compared with which the conflict of General Bell at Dunnville was a mere skirmish. The fugitives were wounded and captured, largely through the aid of Chief Sharpe's braves, and marched back to the city, where their former admiring chief loaded them with chains and tossed them into the dark and dismal dungeons of Castle Bell. There they shall remain at the expense of the taxpayers until their wounds are healed and their spirits recovered, after which, doubtless, the district attorney will recognize their great "law and order" services to himself and the other Republican candidates during the last campaign, by nollying their cases once more. The district attorney displays a keen sense of gratitude, to say the least, and he seems ready to protect the "law and order" friends to whom he owes his election, regardless of consequences.

As I am writing the closing pages of this book, it is rumored that the "gun men" of the district are determined to liberate Warford, Kenley and Chapman even if they have to take the jail by force. From the foregoing it is evident that the sheriff can expect a strenuous time so long as the men of this class remain in the district.

WHO WAS RESPONSIBLE?

Nearly all the troubles depicted in this, Part II, resulted from the Independence explosion. As previously recorded, every possible effort was made by the Mine Owners' Association to fasten this crime upon members of the Western Federation of Miners. Numerous indictments were served against members of this organization, charging them with complicity in this crime. **Each and every one of them, when brought to trial have been acquitted.** This is equally true of every case since the inception of the strike, including the Sun and Moon cases at Idaho Springs, spoken of in Part I. **Not one member of the Western Federation of Miners has been convicted of any crime of which they have been accused.** Since the mine owners and Citizens' Alliance, backed by the powers of the state, with unlimited use of detective agencies, a district attorney elected from their own organization, with all their hatred of the unions could not convict a member of organized labor for the Independence explosion, who, then, **was responsible for this atrocious crime?**

In order that the unprejudiced reader may be able to form an opinion as to which side to this industrial conflict had the most to gain from the perpetration of this terrible deed I will describe conditions as they existed just previous to the explosion.

At that time public sentiment was clearly in favor of the strikers, for the reason that the strikers had submitted patiently to all abuses heaped upon them by the mine owners, the Citizens' Alliance and the militia. In not one instance had a striker resisted arrest and in every case that came to trial where members of the unions were accused of crime, they were acquitted, in spite of the fact that the juries were composed mostly of men who were only too willing to find them guilty. The strikers were relying solely upon the justness of their cause to win and no one realized more fully than they, that the perpetration of crime upon their part, could only weaken their cause. Just previous to the explosion the supreme court had rendered its decision in the Moyer case, which decision gave the governor absolute power of life and death over persons the governor might declare in insurrection. This would serve as a check upon strikers meditating crime, as they knew they could look for no mercy. The union people of Teller county and especially of the Cripple Creek district had been taking a very active part in politics, in the hope of defeating their avowed enemy, Governor Peabody, for re-election.

At the primary elections held to elect delegates to the county conventions which would select delegates to attend the Democratic state convention, the union voters elected two-thirds of the delegates from the ranks of organized labor, thus proving conclusively that organized labor at this time was in a position to control politically.

The day the explosion occurred, a state convention of the Democratic party was being held at Pueblo, at which it was well known that strong resolutions would be adopted condemning Governor Peabody's method of dealing with the strikers. These facts go to show that the strikers had everything to gain by maintaining the law and all to lose by the perpetration of crime that would be sure to bring public sentiment against them. If the crime was committed by a union man it could only have been done by one driven insane through persecution of himself and family.

Upon the other hand, the mine owners and their sympathizers, had expended thousands of dollars, and in spite of having the aid of the militia, were at that time far from being successful in their undertaking of destroying the miners' union. They saw public sentiment against them, the majority of the people of the state and nation condemning Peabody's methods and organized labor in the county in control politically. What could change these conditions? Some crime that could be laid at the door of organized labor and give excuse for deportation. Every attempt had been made to provoke the strikers to violate the law, without success, so what more natural than to cause some crime to be committed and lay it to organized labor? Dear reader, do you believe this to have been impossible? Remember the plot that was fully exposed in court in the attempt to fasten the crime of attempting to derail a passenger train on the F. & C. C. railroad upon union men at which McKinney confessed to being hired by detectives in the employ of the Mine Owners' Association to commit this crime, in order to fasten it upon the strikers.

McKinney also testified at this same trial that he would kill two hundred and fifty human beings for $500. Remember, McKinney was at this time a free man, having been set free at the suggestion of the attorney for the mine owners. Having one such man as McKinney in their employ may they not have had others? Desperate as I know the mine owners and the Citizens' Alliance to have been at this time on account of their failure to defeat the strikers and wipe out the W. F. M. I do not believe they would have deliberately planned such a crime at so great a sacrifice of human life even to throw odium upon the strikers. It has been suggested that some one acting for the mine owners gave orders to some desperado in their employ to cause an explosion and destruction of property so as to give further excuse for persecution of the strikers and that the **hired tool overdid the job.**

It is significant that for a week prior to the explosion quite a number of toughs and professional thugs had made a re-appearance in the district who had been visitors before, about the time of the other outrages. The re-appearance of these men was quite generally remarked and wondered at by the union men. About this time railroad men had reported the arrival of large consignments of the latest improved fire arms that were taken to the Citizens' Alliance headquarters at Victor.

On the morning of the explosion it was noticed that the mine owners and their allies were in no way embarrassed but conducted their business of getting all their men together and arming them, as though the whole program had been prearranged and rehearsed. This was especially remarked and commented upon by others than union men and to say the least was very significant.

In my opinion they came near to detecting the criminal when one of the bloodhounds led the searchers to the door of the dwelling place of one of the mine owners' detectives and was at once called off of the scent. They went back and took another bloodhound and put him on the scent and he, too, went to the same house, but was called off when he reached the gate.

It is to be hoped that some day the truth of this matter will be known and if that day ever comes I am convinced the criminal will not be found to have been a union man.

A COMPARISON.

The conditions that have existed in Colorado since the strike was called in the Cripple Creek district reminds one of events that transpired centuries ago which caused the French Revolution.

Tyranny and democracy can not dwell together. The conflict between the tyrant and those over whom he tyrannized has often been long and bitterly fought in all ages. The French Revolution was an effective struggle for the abolishment of despotism. This historic event, so filled with suffering, to the modern thinker, shows the evolution of the principles that build up or wreck nations. Take the fall of the bastile for instance: At that time with four towers looking toward St. Antoine and four upon Paris, the famous French Bastile with impenetrable walls surrounded by an impassable defense stood defying with proud scorn the murmurs of the people. Though at first only a local prison, the fortress finally became the common jail for all accused, guilty or innocent. A just trial was unknown. Mere suspicion meant a life sentence. Pious priests, brilliant authors and gallant generals were incarcerated to please court minions. The great Voltaire without the semblance of a (law) trial, was committed to the dungeon, and while there he penned his famous "Henriade," which fired the hearts of thousands to resist to the death the imposition of a heartless nobility; the intrepid Labowrdrannais triumphant at Madras over his country's ancient enemy, the "Man in the Iron Mask," whose face was hidden for a quarter of a century and whose name shall remain a mystery forever—these and a host of others, innocent of wrong, imprisoned in dark loathsome cells, were lost—lost to their friends and the world, forgotten by the ruling nobility into whose hands fate had consigned the life and property of the people.

Accordingly the people came to regard the bastile as the stronghold of tryanny. What wonder then that it became the first object of attack when the populace rushed for vengeance. The king styled himself the state. The clergy and aristocracy were relieved from duty and supported by the government and were exempt from taxation, while the artisan must labor without remuneration, without protection and without hope. Peasants were robbed by the lord of the manor, by priest and king, barely existed, half starved and poorly clad.

The people began to move impatiently under this system. A revolutionary spirit was kindled. The king increased the taxation but in spite of this he could not meet the expenses; his failure to pay his soldiers and especially the rumor that he had dismissed Neckar, a minister and possible savior of France, fanned the spark.

Sunday, July 12, 1789, the cup of iniquity became full to overflowing and judgment was at hand. Busts of Neckar and D'Orleans covered with mourning were carried through the streets by a suffering throng, crying: "To arms! To arms!" The ever-increasing multitude with axes, staves and pikes, surged hither and thither, maddened by the wrongs of a century, despoiled by unjust and oppressive laws, and when darkness fell, Paris found itself in the throes of revolt and anarchy. The next morning the city awakes, not to its week-day work, but to the work of righting the wrongs of suffering humanity. The laborer turns soldier

The multitude demands its own. Hungry and bitter, with little regard for its own miserable life, it breaks through the cobwebs of artificial legislation; the hedges of authority and pretended rights fall apart like rotten timbers. Meanwhile the tide rises. The unpaid soldiery takes up the cause of the people. Not a protesting hand is raised. Justice and right was on the side of the people and woe to the nobles and the lords of the manor. A revolution can not go backward. This day ye shall do or die. "Is life so dear and peace so sweet as to be purchased at the price of chains and slavery? Forbid it Almighty God! Give me liberty or give me death."

With the first ray of light on the morning of the fourteenth, the sleepless and trembling king heard the cry now frantic and fearful. "Give us arms, a hundred and fifty thousand!" At nine o'clock the national volunteers march to get the one thing needful and the passionately desired arms are secured. Then, as by common consent, all turn toward the Bastile, the seeming incarnation of their wrongs. Like a raging lion, Paris sprang upon its hated foe.

Neither the strong defenses nor the massive walls could hold the multitude. On, on to the rescue of the innocents. The crackling of the musketry, the volley of grape shot from the castles serve only to intensify the madness. The great chain of the outer gate gives way under the fierce onslaught. Goaded by cruel wrongs and dreadful suffering, infuriated Paris halts not in her course of destruction, until the grim walls of the Bastile fall with a thunderous crash—a sound heard round the world, making tyrants quake and monarchs tremble in their capitols.

It seems but yesterday that Louis XIV reveled in careless debauchery and fancied that he was the state because he happened to stand for a short time on the throbbing necks of a patient people. But the shadow of his castle of terrors, the Bastile, suddenly crumbled and disappeared. The conceited despot had hardly closed his eyes when French aristocracy felt the ground crumbling beneath their feet. The Bastile ruins were drenched with the blood of royalty and aristocracy.

The Bastile of France is no more. But the American Bastile has come. The French Bastile stood amid a people who had come through centuries of feudal oppression. It worked noiselessly and secretly. Its victims disappeared over night and were heard from no more. Bayonets, guillotines, draconic laws, chambers of torture, and a network of police spies held down every deep breath of the people. Yet the inexorable hand of social evolution pushed new methods of production, new social classes, and new ideas into this mass of vassals, and the feudal house of cards was blown into oblivion.

The American Bastile has been erected in Colorado. Its victim is union labor. Since the French people, several years ago, overthrew the Bastile, think you that the American people of the twentieth century would be any more tolerant of its counterpart— the "bull pen?" True, we have no tyrant king in America today, but we are fast raising an element as arrogant and dangerous to the happiness and prosperity of the masses as any monarch. The gigantic and soulless trusts of today are the menace of our government, and if not restrained will bring on a repetition of the French Revolution. God forbid that day should ever come. The intelligent use of the ballot by the masses is the only remedy to restrain the trusts and corporations. It is to be hoped that the citizens of our great nation will realize this before it is too late.

IT IS TIME.

In this age, when gold is king, sitting on a brazen throne;
When it is the proper thing, rating men by what they own;
When the brute is more and more and the spirit less and less;
When the world is lorded o'er by corruption and excess—
It is time that men of worth boldly step into the van
With this message to the earth: Down with Mammon, up with Man.

We have seen the idler boast while the toiler lacked for bread;
We have seen the king and priest rob the living and the dead;
We have seen the thief arrayed in the purple robe of state,
While the honest man was made to beg succor at his gate.
It has ever been the same since our human world began;
Let us stay the sickening game—Down with Mammon, up with Man.

Earth is far too wise and old for a lordling or a slave;
For to heed a ring of gold on the forehead of a knave;
Far too old for war and hate—old enough for brotherhood;
Wise enough to found a state where men seek each other's good.
We have followed self too long—let us try a better plan,
Keep the right, subdue the wrong—Down with Mammon, up with Man!
—*J. A. Edgerton.*

THE POWER OF THE BALLOT.

It is evident that the conflict between capital and labor will, in the future, to a large extent, be fought in the legislative halls of our country. The employers of labor are and will endeavor to procure legislation restricting the rights of labor unions. They will undertake to make it a criminal offense to strike or boycott. In order to procure legislation of this nature the organized employers elect legislators whom they can control. We, working people, have been too indifferent to matters of legislation. Being vastly in the majority, we could by concerted action elect men from our own ranks as law-makers.

I, although never having taken an active part in politics, have, nevertheless been amazed at the little value placed on the right of franchise by the middle and working classes; most of us seem willing to allow the professional politician to look after our affairs politic, seeming to be glad to shirk this responsibility.

My friends, when we consider that the whole fabric of our government practically rests upon the ballot, that whether men elected to high office be fit to conduct the affairs of office in the interest of the masses of the people rests with ourselves who, by the ballot, determine who our officers shall be. I sometimes think that it would be a good thing for the working classes if they were denied for a time the right of franchise. Were it a fact that none but large property holders were allowed to vote, you can imagine what the principal agitation would be. The present day agitation for more wages and shorter hours would give way to the agitation for the right of franchise.

Probably after a great deal of effort we had again secured the right of franchise we would value this great boon at its true worth, and would never again trust our interests to the professional politicians, who invariably work in the interest of the corporations, whose only patriotism lies in the making of money at the expense of the masses.

Friends, arouse. Hold voting as a sacred duty to yourselves and your fellow workers, and be assured that if you but take proper interest in public affairs there is nothing you complain of politically or anything that you desire in the way of just legislation but what can be procured by wise and united use of the ballot, and rest assured if you do not look after your own interest the corporations will not do so for you.

I stood upon the sidewalk, and viewed the passing throng
Of union men in uniform, who proudly marched along,
    With flags and banners flying, how sweet the bands did play—
    It was a scene that once a year occurs on Labor Day,
The thousands who were looking on kept up a constant cheer
As union after union passed, how fine they did appear.
    I thought while gazing on the scene, I'm thinking yet today—
    Why don't they vote together as they march on Labor Day?
The Allied Printing Trades passed by, a splendid set of men.
Their mettle has been tested and they stood together when,
    The outlook seemed extremely dark, and yet they never flinched.
The people had a welcome for the men who build the town—
The unions in the Building Trades have often won renown.
    I thought as they went marching by, I'm thinking yet today—
    Why don't they vote together as they march on Labor Day?
The boys from mill and factory, comprising every trade
Which goes to make a city great, were in
    No one could help but be impressed at such a splendid sight.
    For all admire the men who stand for justice and for right.
Fraternalism reigned supreme, 'twould do a person good
To see the workers marching on in one grand brotherhood.
    I thought while gazing on the scene, I'm thinking yet today—
    Why don't they vote together as they march on Labor Day?
                                              —*Thomas H. West.*

THE STRIKE STILL ON.

In concluding this work I would have been pleased to record the strike at an end, and victory crowning the efforts of the Western Federation of Miners. The strike in the Cripple Creek district still continues. The miners, however, although on strike since August 10, 1903, are not discouraged. As an indication of their determination to continue the strike until victory has been achieved I reproduce the following:

"STRIKE IS STILL ON.

"Headquarters of the Western Federation of Miners.

"Denver, Colorado, April 11, 1905.

"To all Members of Organized Labor and Those who Desire to Maintain Their Honor:

"The Mine Owners' Association of the Cripple Creek District, with its lawless ally, the Citizens' Alliance, has been sending out fabricated reports to the effect that the srike has been declared off by the Western Federation of Miners. This brazen lie has been hatched and circulated by the same mob that bull-penned and deported miners, that even murdered in cold blood men who refuséd to yield their allegiance to the principles of the organization of which they were members.

"The Mine Owners' Association and the Citizens' Alliance have discovered that while thugs, gunfighters, rape fiends, outlaws and convicts from the penitentiaries may be of valuable assistance to mine operators, in upholding a reign of terror, yet these debauched and depraved degenerates are practically useless in the production of dividends.

"The members of the Mine Owners' Association and Citizens' Alliance have had an experience for which they have paid an awful price. The dividends of which they have boasted have been on paper and not in the vaults of the banks. In their desperation they are attempting to deceive through the circulation of a lie, hoping that the old miners will return to the Cripple Creek district and once more become inmates of the mines.

"The Western Federation of Miners has not declared the strike off, and never will as long as the mine operators are unfair to organized labor—as long as they continue shipping their ores to the scab mills of Colorado City, and as long as the card or blacklisting system is used to discriminate against members of the Western Federation of Miners.

"Hundreds of men have been driven from their homes in the Cripple Creek district, and are still exiles from their wives and children. Many of these men bear the scars that were inflicted by the brutal orders of a Mine Owners' Association and a Citizens' Alliance. These men and their wives and children who have borne the insults and outrages of a hired soldiery, would scorn a compromise or a surrender to that "law and order" combination that reveled in a carnival of brutality, to subjugate and enslave the best blood and brawn in the Cripple Creek district.

"Men of honor, of spirit, and of independence, will shun the mines of the Cripple Creek district as they would a pestilence.

Men who have any conception of the principles of Unionism will not be used as tools of a Mine Owners' Association to assassinate justice.

"Stay away from the Cripple Creek district, and the time will come when the miner in Colorado's greatest gold camps can enjoy some of the liberty that is guaranteed to him by the law and the constitution of the state.

"Any one who goes to the Cripple Creek district and accepts employment in the mines, will be recognized as a scab by the metal miners throughout the United States and British Columbia.

"Whenever the strike is declared off, or a settlement is effected, an official notice will be issued from the headquarters of the Western Federation of Miners.

"CHAS. H. MOYER, President W. F. M.
"W. D. HAYWOOD, Sec'y-Treas. W. F. M."

The emblem of the Western Federation of Miners is three stars which represent education, organization and independence. At the twelfth annual convention held in Denver, I was made an honorary member and presented with the emblem of the order. I value this token of appreciation more than the crown of an empress, nor would the proffer of such tempt me to part with it. I see in the emblem of the three stars all that is sublime. I have seen demonstrated under it the fortitude of the faithful followers of the single star—the Star of Bethlehem—the insignia of Christianity—the birthright of Christ—whose faithful followers, martyred followers, created and maintainel the sweet sentiment of "Peace on Earth, Good Will to Man."

When I look upon the three stars of the Western Federation of Miners, with their innumerable rays spreading Education, Organization and Independence, I feel the inspiration that from far above, He, whose mission the single star announced, looks down upon the sublime constellation of three with approval for its representation and sturdy maintenance of His divine given law, "Peace on Earth, Good Will to Man." I feel that far above another constellation of stars and stripes, representing human liberty, this land of pioneers, a constellation that has been debauched by tyranny such as the Nero attempted in extinguishing the sentiment of the single star, will again be placed in its true position—representing a brave, happy, pure and justified people by the tribulations of the sturdy followers of the three stars, as was the supremacy of the single star established and the faith of Christianity made permanent by the tribulations of the martyrs of Nero's despotism. By the emblem of the W. F. M., the three stars, I predict an ultimate victory.

The folder inserted in first part of this, Part II, shows cut of delegates attending the thirteenth annual convention of the Western Federation of Miners, held at Salt Lake City, Utah, during the months of May and June, 1905, the convention being in continuous session for about three weeks.

These are the men whom the Mine Owners' Association, the Citizens' Alliance and other enemies of progressive unionism, charge with being anarchists. Study these faces, dear reader, and see if they will not compare favorably with any body of men ever assembled, for sturdy manhood and intelligence. Certain it is that for unselfish devotion to the cause and steadfast purpose of uplifting toiling humanity they have never been surpassed.

On the faces of the delegates of the thirteenth convention, if I am any judge, I see reflected a determination to win this battle, and from the same faces I catch the inspiration of truth, honesty and justice. We need more such men—more such determination to battle for human liberty.

Someone has said:

"God give us men; a time like this demands
    Strong minds, great hearts, true faith and ready hands;
Men whom lust of lucre does not kill;
    Men whom the spoils of office can not buy;
Men who possess opinions and a will;
    Men who have honor; men who will not lie;
Men who can stand before a demagogue
    And damn his treacherous flatteries without winking;
Tall men, sun-crowned, who live above the fog

In public duty, and in private thinking;
For, while the rabble with their thumb-worn creeds,
Their large professions and their little deeds,
Mingle in selfish strife, lo! Freedom weeps.
Wrong rules the land, and waiting justice sleeps.''

CONCLUSION.

The time has come to close. Much more could be said. I have made no effort at word painting. I have confined myself to facts and made no attempt to polish them by the use of superfluous words. Perhaps at times I seemed bitter in my denunciations but if they seem so it was because I felt keenly the insults heaped upon an American populace. Fair words convey pleasure but fair words could not paint the scenes I have attempted to picture in my humble way. I have felt my blood boil many times while writing these pages and feel that I can understand why men shoulder a gun and fight when goaded beyond endurance. I believe with all my heart in the freedom of the press, religious toleration, free speech, untrammeled rights of domicile, prompt punishment of crime, innocent men should not be made to suffer for the guilty, reverence for law, that military rule in time of peace is the reign of the mob, that right of habeas corpus should be inviolate except in time of war, trial by jury is the only protection against tyranny, no war on women and children. I believe all men are equal and all should receive the same protection under the law and all punished alike for crime; one law for mine owners and miners. I do not want to see our constitutional government converted into a military oligarchy. The workers do not ask favors; we want justice.

In as much as this work has been devoted to the actual history pertaining to industrial strife, it is fitting to say a few words upon the good things as well as the bad. While the people of the state have been so unfortunate as to become involved in a bitterly fought war the past two years, I have no desire to leave the impression that Colorado is a lawless state. A half dozen corporations with as many hired tools have caused acts of lawlessness to be committed that gave the state notoriety of which we are not proud. Because we had a political accident as governor, that proved an inefficient executive, and he appointed a military crazed adjutant general, is no proof that Colorado is not one of the greatest states in the Union.

Suppose we **did** have a Peabody and a Bell. There are no more like them and we have repudiated them, and they do not make our ore less abundant nor our soil less productive. And there isn't another spot on this great round globe equal to it, either. In natural resources, in climatic advantages, in situation, in intelligent citizenship, in city building, in inventive genius, in educational facilities, in progressive politics and kaleidoscopic industrial conflicts, we lead the world.

Did you say there were some things to cause infinite regret? I do not deny that; yes, no scheme is flawless, no picture is perfect, no blade of grass but might have grown a little longer or shorter, never a mountain without a valley on either side.

Thank God, Colorado is greater than Peabody, and the corrupt corporations that were back of him. No one corrupt, tyrannical state administration should blind us to the glorious sunshine and the stately mountains, the incomparable climate and inexhaustible wealth, the almost immeasurable natural advantages and the indomitable spirit of progress, all enjoyed by the people of the Centennial state.

The curse of "bad politics and labor troubles" is not indigenous to Colorado. Each state in the Union has its share. The labor problem is a world problem. We are not in the only war zone on the map. We are not making any epochs in human history. We are not traveling any new paths. Why, the paths we are traveling in Colorado are worn smooth by the trampling feet of generations. Stop for a few minutes and reflect on how countless have been the labor wars of the past. How history is full of them. How, even now, from England and continental Europe, from Japan and Russia, from South America and Australia, from Hawaii and from far off South Africa, comes the faint echo of industrial conflict.

Some of our citizens and politicians may make mistakes, but we love dear old Colorado. We love the blue skies, the glinting sunshine, the music of her laughing streams, and the wooing tenderness of her melting distances.

> "We will press for aye those mountain peaks
> Girdled with snow by blushing morning kissed."

We believe that the great heart of the people throbs with intense desire to do the right and their very excesses grow out of their intense convictions.

That the undertow of regret exists in every life is doubtless part of a mysterious plan beyond our ken. Yet shall it never drag us from the grand harmony of the breakers and the thrilling sting of the flying spray.

"Is Colorado in America?" Yes, indeed, my dear reader. It is also on the map of the world.

List of Deported

H. A. Allen, Fred Aspgrain, George Andrews, Ernest Allen, George Anderson.

Frank Brewer, James Brown, J. J. Brothers, A. L. Bolson, Tom Brick, W. F. Benton, J. R. Bean, James Beck, John Bubolo, M. P. Basinger, John Burns, Harry Boaz, Benjamin Irwin Beatty, G. C. Briggs, W. G. Bradley.

W. J. Carter, Gus Carlson, H. Curwen, Walter Curwen, Geo. E. Cooper, John Castello, William J. Carter, Joseph T. Campbell, Joseph W. Cooper, Peter Campbell, Robert Coughlin, Patrick Callahan, M. Cloud, M. Comstock, Angus Campbell, Ed Corbett, Patrick Carey, Walter Costello, Eugene B. Cox, C. H. Conway.

T. J. Devenney, S. M. Dickey, Henry Davis, James Dennis, Richard Dunn.

Thomas W. Edwards, John Edwards, Arthur Evans, Charles E. Erwin,John Eigle, Joe Egger, alias Joe Krauz.

N. D. Frey, J. E. Fish, Frank Fayhan, Garfield Force, John Flees, Bert Fuller.

Alf Given, Joe Green, Joe Gilhooley, James Grant, Delfido Gonzales, John Gallagher, Eugene C. Gilfillan, William E. Gorman, Frank Gardner, Eugene C. Gilfillan (re-deported), Gus F. Girardot.

W. H. Hoover, George Howard, Ed Hart, Hans Hansen, Chris Hansen, L. F. Hebner, Joe Hamilton, E. A. Hess, John Hackward, John Hanifan, James-Hennessey, J. K. Henderson, Mike Harrington, Gilen C. Hard, Seligman Herz, Higby Holtzolaw, John Harper.

J. C. Jensen, Charles James, Emil Johnson, F. E. Jones, Henry Clay Johnson, Charles Johnson, Claudy E. Johnson, A. F. Jordan.

William D. Ketchum, H. P. Kean, Jerry Kelly, Joe Kreig, Thomas Kearns, Thomas Kuhlman, John S. Kelly, H. L. Kane, Thomas Kilker, Chris Keagy, Pat Kennedy, Martin Keating Buron Kohn, Henry King, Thomas Kirkpatrick, L. E. Krotz, Virgil King, Joe Krautze, alias Joe Egger.

John E. Logan, S. E. Lutz, W. T. Lynch, W. C. Ludlow, Arthur Lanterman, Joe Lemeraux, Hugh Lee, Otto Liss, W. F. Lally, J. H. Lampson, Edward J. Labitsky, Thomas Layden.

William McCall, E. L. McParland, Dennis McBride, T. L. McChesney, Sylvester McAvoy, Mike McGuire, Phi McCaughney, R. C. McCarty, Tim McCarty, P. J. McNulty, Albert McLean, Peter McDonald, R. H. McMann, Alex McIsaac, Dan McLeod, Patrick McCarvill, J. F. McGuire, B. J. McArdle, J. B. McIntyre.

Doy Miller, Sherman Miller, Walter Muir, Frank Murnane, Mike Maher, Anthony Milroy, William Murphy, Norman S. Martin, John Michael Mullen, Santiago Martinez, H. W. Moore, Thomas Marnoch, Tom A. Murphy, Jack I. Maulsby.

William Nelson.

D. C. O'Neill, James O'Neill, Tom O'Brien, Joe O'Brien, W. W. O'Bryan.

N. V. Paddock, A. J. Payner, T. I. Post, A. C. Paxson, Alfred Peterson, E. H. Parrott, Henry Paul, L. L. Palmer.

N. P. Reinhard, Frank Riley, Ed Ruet, Judge W. C. Reilly, John Roach, John Retallac, John Retallac, Jr., Max Reisener, Sam Renner, Thomas J. Rinker, Tom Rocks, Charles Riley, Joe Rigg, Harry Robinson, Thomas Rumney, Peter Roberts.

G. B. Simms, D. W. Schutt, C. A. Sullivan, John Spiker, Nick Schmidt, J. T. Saunders, Rudolph Sixteleman, James Stapleton, Harvey Starbuck, A. T. Simpson, W. H. Smith, C. S. Scott, W. A. Shafer, D. P. Sackett, Mike Shelley, John P. Shea, Mike (M. J.) Sullivan, Jim Sullivan, William Shoemaker.

W. F. Trainer, J. L. Topping, Fred Trevette, Mike Tolan, Peter Tiernan.

Howard Ullmer.

Reese Williams, J. E. Wilkins, James Wright, John H. Wilcox, A. A. West, David Ward, H. H. Wherry, Charles Weld, Walter Warner, Fred Wright, Daniel Warren, George Williams, Tom Wilson.

Joseph Zuban.

Looking Backward

With Apologies to Edward Bellamy.
(Year 1917.)

Special Correspondence to the "Weekly Public Sentiment."
Victor I, Colorado, June 10, 1917.

 E looked travel stained and worn, but withal wore a prosperous air as he stepped from the passenger coach to the platform yesterday morning. For a number of years since the declaration of the strike of 1903 he has been away from Colorado and heard little of the changes which had occurred during his absence. The detachment of military which surrounded the train had been just a little disconcerting, especially when he was ordered gruffly to salute as he stepped off. His resentment, however, was quickly overcome as he beheld on the platform a friend of former days, and in a trice the two were arm in arm exchanging greetings.

As they walked down the street, tipping their hats to occasional army officers, the traveler explained to his old time friend that since the declaration of the strike in August, 1903, he had been in the Alaskan gold fields, and later, when Goldfield was opened he went there and had acquired a fortune and was just come back to his old home, Victor. He then explained that the Western Federation of Miners had control of all the mines in Nevada and that they were conducted on the co-operative plan, and not managed as were the mines in Victor.

"Don't call it Victor," his friend interposed, "or you will do time in the military bull pen. Ever since the campaign of 1903, by order of the Dictator of the District of Cripple Creek, the city has been officially known as VICTOR I. It's a little awkward to write with the capital "I" for a tail piece, but it don't sound so bad as it looks."

"Say," said the traveler, "aint we in the United States, so what do you mean by Dictator?"

"Well, you see, it's like this," said his friend, "the Mine Owners' Association during the strike had deposed all officials elected by the people. They had ignored the regular courts and had set up a court of their own, which they called a 'commission,' Since the Association and the Citizens' Alliance were so completely in control of things, regular elections, courts, etc., would be a mere farce, so they asked and were granted a special dispensation by an extra session of the Fifteenth General Assembly, called by the Republican governor for that purpose. This dispensation granted the mine owners full possession and powers in the district. You might think that the citizens of the state protested, but, the truth was, that the Cripple Creek district, on account of the conduct of the element in control, had become a sore disgrace to the rest of the state and they were only too glad to get rid of the responsibility of carrying it as a part of Colorado.

"So then the Mine Owners' Association proceeded to select nine men to form a 'commission;' these men elected from among themselves a ruler who was named 'Dictator,' he to hold office so long as he obeyed the will of the mine owners.

"The commission makes all the laws, acts as a court of justice and equity and has the power to determine who shall be allowed to become subjects of the District of Cripple Creek."

"Has there been any trouble in maintaining this form of government?"

"Nothing very serious; there were several rebellions brought about by 'gun fighters' who had been imported into the district by the mine owners during the strike of 1903-4. They, on two different occasions, undertook to take possession of the government and name a Dictator of their own. They were, however, defeated after several battles had been fought and were placed in the military bull pen. You see the Dictator's army is composed of employes of the Mine Owners' Association, one of the conditions of employment being that they must bear arms when called upon."

"Say," said the newly arrived, "what's become of the ever-

lasting hills and the big dumps that used to be around here? The
district looks now as bare and level as the Kansas prairies.''

"Why, don't you know? You see it's this way. When General Bell and his troops first occupied the district a member of the
cavalry rode, into a prospect hole one night inflicting injury to
himself and his horse and bringing humiliation upon the flag.
The general recognized in these prospect holes a base conspiracy
of the enemy and forthwith ordered that they be filled. It took
all the scenery we had to fill them and several years' work, but
it's been done. Now when a man wants to prospect he has to start
early in the morning so that he may refill the hole by night. Of
course, with such a system of work, there are few strikes made,
but the heroes who defend the flag are safe.''

"What has become of the miners who used to be here? Besides yourself and an occasional business man, I have hardly seen
a familiar face.''

"The miners? Why, all these fellows you see in uniform are
non-union miners. After the militia had been here for two years,
with none of the strikers returning to work, a provision was
added to the articles of war making it compulsory for all able
bodied citizens of the state to do military duty for a term of five
years each, and for all soldiers during the period of their enlist-
ment to work a ten-hour shift each day in the mines. They divide
up the guard duty and other military work into shifts of four
hours daily, so they are obliged to work but fourteen hours a day.
If one of them gets drunk or violates any of the minor articles
of war he is punished by being compelled to do overtime in the
mines.

"You are no doubt surprised that the miners stand for such
treatment. Well, you see the Western Federation men would
not. They all left the county and since then the district has never
been the same. The miners that are here now are mostly men
who have been discarded by the union miners for being traitors.
The others are law-breakers from other parts of the United States
who are 'wanted' but find a safe retreat under the banner of the

Dictator, the country in general being glad to have a dumping ground for undesirable people.''

''Where is Bell now? I used to know him in the good old days when we were members together of Company Eight, which won first honors in 'Frisco. I'd like to seen him.''

''Oh, Bell's in Pueblo; been there for about five years, occupying a padded cell in the insane asylum.''

''I'm surprised; what in the world happened to him,'' asked the visitor.

''Well, you see the poor fellow was so imbued with the idea that he was the greatest general the world had ever produced, and the fact that the public would not appreciate his greatness, in spite of his never missing an opportunity of lauding himself through the press and to all who would listen to him, he finally had made, and wore, a Napoleon uniform. It got to be a common thing to see him slowly wandering down one of the principal streets of Denver, dressed in this uniform, his sword dangling at his side, his hat pulled down over his eyes, his head drooped and his chin resting in the palm of his right hand. This gave him the appearance of having grave and mighty matters on his mind, upon the solution of which rested the future welfare of our great nation. The public had for a long time recognized that Bell was a monomaniac on militarism, but so long as his mania did not take a violent form were satisfied to humor him. Of course you understand Bell's antipathy to anything that smacked of union. It was noticed that in his wanderings over the city, whenever he came to an establishment, displaying a sign such as ''Union Hotel,'' ''Union Cigars'' or the like, he would halt, draw his sword and brace himself as if expecting an attack from an opposing army. One day he posted himself before the main entrance of the Union depot as a train was unloading, swung his sword frantically and called upon his army, that his hallucination caused him to believe he still commanded, to charge the enemy. As you can imagine, this caused a panic and led to his being put in restraint. They say at the asylum that he imagines he is exiled to the Isle of Elba, and declares he will escape and will yet rescue his beloved country from the enemy—the unionists."

"I am sorry to hear all this," replied the astonished visitor, "Bell was a good fellow when he and I were in Company Eight together, his chief weakness then though, was his love of great military parades, and it must have been his craze for fame and militarism that drove him hopelessly mad."

"And McClelland, of whom I heard just after the strike began, before I shipped from Seattle? Is he here?"

"Yes, he's still here; but you'd hardly know him. He's aged terribly in these ten years with his duties as military censor of the press bearing so heavily upon him. He's finally suppressed all the papers in the District of Cripple Creek with the exception of the VictorI Bazoo, and they say that the Bazoo came near going under last week through inadvertantly using in an editorial the obsolete expression, "the rights of the people."

The former resident was amazed.

"But it's nearly noon now," said his friend. "Come with me and join the people of VictorI in their obeisance to the Dictator. At high noon each day every inhabitant of VictorI must render the military salute."

The two joined the throng in the journey to the monument, and as they came near the palace, the shriek of the Gold Coin whistle announced that it was noon all over the world, the entire populace gave the military salute.

"Well, said the traveler, "none of this for me. I'm for Denver on the first train out. But tell me before I go, what has become of Peabody?"

"Peabody, oh, he's turned hermit. You see the decent people of the state would have none of him, the mine owners having nothing further to gain from him as a tool, gave him the cold shoulder. He tried living in several other states, but was continually being pointed out as the notorious ex-governor of Colorado, so he finally retired to the back woods of Arkansas, where he is living in seclusion shunning his fellow men. They say he has been occupying his time in writing a book, entitled: "Justification of My Acts While Governor.'"

"I see Colorado has a Democratic governor now. Since when have the Democrats become the dominant party in the state?"

"Since the election of 1906. At the election of 1906 the Honorable Alva Adams was the candidate on the Democratic ticket. Jesse McDonald was a candidate for election on the Republican ticket. Adams was elected, receiving four votes to McDonald's one. At the election of 1908 the Republican candidate was again badly defeated. Since then it is a rarity to meet a voter who will acknowledge being a Republican. The Republican party sealed its doom in the Fifteenth General Assembly by stealing the governorship.

"The political party feared by the Democrats today is the Socialist party."

| | # APPENDIX | |

An account of the Moyer, Haywood and Pettibone cases—
Trial and outcome, a brief account of the rise of the
United Mine Workers with an account of the
Anthracite strike—the rise of Trade Unions,
sketching the History of the Typograph-
ical Union and other Informa-
tion of Vital interest to the
Student of Labor Conflicts.

April, 1908

*T*O the organizations that so generously
contributed funds for the defense of the
*Imprisoned Union men and to all that assisted
by moral or financial support this Appendix
is respectfully dedicated.* ∴ ∴ ∴

Famous Kidnapping Cases

THE foregoing pages have related in detail sufficient facts to convince the reader that the labor war being waged in the West is a fight not to be considered lightly by the progressive man or woman of today—and war it has been and is still—for the end is not yet. Such a struggle between two such contending forces can only be settled one way and that is the complete overthrow of the one or the other. As has already been stated elsewhere it has been a struggle between organized labor and organized capital—between the working class and monied power—right and might—for the complete control of the industrial and political mastery of the situation in the Rocky mountains. Determination to win on both sides. The miners have proven to the world they are not mental weaklings, but strong both mentally and physically—with hearts that beat for the love of justice and liberty and have faith sufficient unto the hour. These men who have explored the West and reared a golden empire know not the word compromise.

Organized capital fought a bloody fight—but employed unfair methods—illegal means under the name of law. I can admire determination and good generalship in an opponent as well as in our own ranks but not a man or party of men who stabs in the back. In spite of the fact that money in unlimited sums has been used to buy the State Supreme Court, unseat governors, hire special trains and give steady employment to Pinkerton's force of "operatives," the Western Federation of Miners still maintain headquarters. In fact, 1908 finds the organization stronger educationally and in actual membership greater than in the past, national headquarters enlarged and newly furnished with money in the treasury to continue the conflict.

No effort will be made by the writer to enter into the details of this outrage which is as dark as the other deeds of the mine owners chronicled heretofore. It is offered merely as a brief synopsis, the details properly related would fill a very large volume. Some of the most important facts for reference follow:

During the evening of December 30, 1905, ex-Governor Frank Steunenberg, of Idaho, was killed at Caldwell, Idaho, by a bomb which exploded as he opened the gate to go into his yard.

Frank Steunenberg was supported for governor by a sufficient number of the workmen's votes to elect him governor of Idaho. He was one of the old party politicians who gained the workers' votes by posing as the "friend of labor," "full dinner pail," and the promise of a "job." He at one time carried an honorary membership card in the Typographical union. He served two terms as governor of the state of Idaho. His first term being satisfactory as far as the writer has been able to learn.

During his administration, (second term,) in 1899, the W. F. M. became involved in a strike known in the history of industrial conflicts as the Coeur d'Alene strike. The "bull pen" was soon established and this was the beginning of the "bull pen" in the West and it has continued ever since up to this date. The miners were fast winning the fight and victory seemed assured when the mine owners sounded the alarm and called upon Steunenberg for assistance. He proved himself a friend and tool and was the instrument used to disrupt the union at that time. He made requisition on the National government for troops. General Merrian was given charge and with negro soldiers took charge of the district. Truthful men—men of honor, who would not lie needlessly—say hundreds were subjected to tortures and persecutions more horrible than the memories of Andersonville or Libby prison during the Civil war. Homes were destroyed and even worse occurred. Men saw their beautiful daughters forced to submit to brutal indignities from negro soldiers and were powerless to prevent. These memories will ever live a hideous nightmare haunting those who experienced the horrors. Steunenberg was class conscious and did not falter, he took his stand without hesitation.

In spite of the fact that Steunenberg was morally responsible for the outrages perpetrated in 1899, he was generally liked, especially by his neighbors, considered by his associates a "hale fellow well met," possessed, in fact, all the characteristics necessary for a successful politician.

This being the case, his death naturally created a great furor, a determination to run down and punish those responsible for this dastardly crime at any cost. Opponents of the Western Federation of Miners lost no time in pointing out the organization as being instrumental in the murder of Steunenberg. This, even before the arrest of Orchard. They undoubtedly had in mind the condition that would prevail when Orchard was engaged by them as the instrument by which they fondly hoped to once and forever crush the W. F. M. Large cash rewards were offered by the State of Idaho and individuals for the capture of the murderer.

ARREST OF ORCHARD.

Harry Orchard was arrested January 1. Immediately the press promised more sensations and from that date all kinds of hints of startling "evidence" that was soon to be made public filled the daily capitalist papers. They furnished an abundance of sensations and used a great deal of red ink in "scare heads" —the reporters poured out vitriol upon page after page of "copy"—consigning labor unions to purgatory in short order— had a few men hanged or lynched in their own putrid minds but we are still waiting for the promised "evidence" that was to convince the world that'the Federation was a criminal organization.

ORCHARD'S PART IN THE PLAY.

It was upon an alleged confession, by Harry Orchard, alias Hogan, Horsley, to Detective James McParland, in charge of the Western branch of the Pinkerton Detective Agency, that the prosecution depended for conviction of the people they so much desired to dispose of. Two days after the horrible murder of

Steunenberg, Orchard was arrested at Caldwell, Idaho. In his room was found incriminating evidence sufficient to stamp him beyond doubt as the man who constructed the fatal bomb. Pieces of dynamite littered the table, on which were standing several bottles of sulphuric acid and other chemicals that usually enter into the composition of infernal machines. In addition, there was discovered a piece of string identical in manufacture to that attached to the bomb which killed the governor. Apparently no attempt had been made by Orchard to destroy any traces of the evidence that might lead to his apprehension. Neither had he made the slightest effort to escape after the explosion of the bomb. According to the hotel employes, he "just hung around," seemingly awaiting for certain arrest, which, no doubt, was a part of the plan.

Twenty-one days after his incarceration, McParland, who had arrived from Denver, Colo., and had taken charge of the case, announced that Orchard had made a typewritten "confession" of 18,000 words, in which he declared that he was hired by Moyer, Haywood and Pettibone to kill Steunenberg with dynamite. He further "confessed" to twenty-six other murders committed by himself at various times in different parts of the country. Altogether, this "confession" was a lurid affair, and its details were grewsome enough to make the most hair-raising writer of dime novel fiction turn green with envy. With this "confession" came the arrest and kidnapping of the officers of Western Federation of Miners.

THE KIDNAPPING.

After business houses had closed in Denver, courts adjourned, lawyers were at their homes, the secret arrest of President Charles H. Moyer, Secretary-Treasurer William D. Haywood and George A. Pettibone, business man, all citizens of Denver, took place, late Saturday night, February 17, 1906.

President Moyer was the first victim, taken prisoner about 9 o'clock. Haywood an hour later and Pettibone taken from his home just before midnight.

The circumstances of the kidnapping of three of Colorado's best citizens were unprecedented and in line with other high-handed methods employed during the strikes of which these pages are a history. On February 12, 1906, O. M. Van Duyn, county attorney of Canyon county, Idaho, filed a sworn complaint in the office of the county probate judge, charging Moyer, president of the Western Federation of Miners, Haywood, secretary-treasurer, of the Federation and Pettibone with the murder of ex-Governor Steunenberg. On the same day the probate judge issued warrants for the arrest of the accused men, and several hours later Governor Gooding, of Idaho, issued a requisition upon the governor of Colorado for the three men, who were known to be living in Denver. In his affidavit and petition to Governor Gooding, Attorney Van Duyn swore "that the said appellants and plaintiffs in error were in the state of Idaho on the date of the murder of said Frank Steunenberg," and that they were fugitives from justice from the state of Idaho. In the conference that occurred in the governor's office before the requisition was granted were Gov. Gooding, Attorney Van Duyn, James H. Hawley and W. E. Borah, attorneys at law residing at Boise City, and several others. It has been stated and not denied that Detective McParland was also present.

J. C. Mills and James H. Hawley were designated to take the requisition to the governor of Colorado and receive the bodies of the men wanted. At 11 o'clock on the morning of February 15, Mills and Hawley, and, presumably, McParland, arrived in Denver, where they at once conferred with Governor McDonald and perfected the conspiracy, already begun in Idaho, whereby Moyer, Haywood and Pettibone were to be kidnapped and carried from the state.

During all of the time while these conspirators were perfecting their plan, Moyer, Haywood and Pettibone were engaged in their business, openly and above board, and could easily have been arrested at any time after the arrival of Mills and Hawley in the city. Instead, the conspirators waited all day Thursday, all day Friday, and all of Saturday and then proceeded late Saturday night to carry out the kidnapping.

The kidnapped men were taken to the county jail and every precaution was exercised to prevent either their relatives, friends or attorneys from discovering the arrest. The purpose, undoubtedly being to prevent the prisoners from having recourse to the usual legal method granted to even well-known desperate criminals, to fight the requisition.

Early Sunday morning, shortly after 5 o'clock, the prisoners were driven to a siding near the Union Depot, placed in a special train, consisting of an engine and two coaches, and whirled rapidly out of the state. No stops were made except for coal and water, and this "Kidnapper's Special" had the right-of-way over every other train on the track from Denver to Boise, Idaho. The men were heavily guarded throughout the trip by the parties commissioned by the Governor of Idaho, Adjutant General Bulkely Wells, of the Colorado National Guard and some of his troopers. Upon their arrival at Boise, were taken to the penitentiary, where they were placed in felon's cells and denied communication with the outside world. The arrest in Denver was made by Pinkerton detectives and a detachment of state troops.

Then followed more promising sensations by the press. The statement went out from the State Capitol of Idaho that the prisoners would be given a fair trial and immediately following that statement another saying that the proper authorities of Idaho and Colorado had in their possession documents which, when produced, would be sufficient to hang not only the three kidnapped, but many others who belonged to the "inner circle" of the W. F. M. L. J. Simpkins was badly wanted and others according to the reports.

ST. JOHN ARRESTED.

Vincent St. John came in for his share of their venom and immediately after the kidnapping of Moyer, Haywood and Pettibone was seized, in the darkness of night at his home in Burke, Idaho, taken to Boise and committed to the penitentiary on suspicion that he was implicated in the assassination of ex-Gov. Steunenberg. He was held in the penitentiary a period of twenty-three days, before the attorneys for the W. F. M. could secure his release upon a writ of habeas corpus.

As soon as he was liberated from the penitentiary in Idaho, he was re-arrested on a trumped-up charge of murder and taken to Colorado. Not a single particle of incriminating evidence was produced at his preliminary hearing, notwithstanding this fact he was bound over to a District Court in the sum of $10,000.

In September, 1906, his case was called and the prosecution with the hired attorneys of a Mine Owner's Association were forced to go into court and move that the case be nolle-prossed on the ground that there was **no evidence upon which to base a** conviction.

McPARLAND IN EVIDENCE.

The report was whirled over the United States, credited to Governor Gooding and other officials of Idaho, that the kidnapped men would never leave the state alive. McParland was very liberal with his interviews and filled much space with the "terrible secrets" he had "unearthed." According to his statements, which filled half the daily press, the lives of every prominent official of each state and the Supreme Court judges were in danger and he, at the last minute, had appeared on the scenes in time to avert the tragedy. According to him Denver was about to be blown off the map on account of Gabbert or Goddard residing in the city. Some way he always, for reasons best known to himself, perhaps, failed then and until now to produce this "startling evidence" which was to hang so many.

WRIT OF HABEAS CORPUS DENIED.

Februray 23, 1906, attorneys for the imprisoned men filed petitions in the Supreme Court of Idaho, asking for a writ of habeas corpus to test the validity of the imprisonment. March 12, the Supreme Court refused the writ and remanded the prisoners. March 15, the attorneys for the defense filed petitions for a writ of habeas corpus in the office of the clerk of the United States Circuit Court of Idaho. After several days' consideration, the writs were refused and the prisoners remanded. A bill of exceptions was filed, and an appeal was taken to the United States Supreme Court. The decision of the Supreme Court, handed down Monday, December 3, 1906, fully ten months after the men had been kidnapped from Colorado, sustained those of the lower Federal and Idaho state courts. This meant the legalization of kidnapping, an act heretofore considered a crime. by the highest judicial authority in the land.

If the reader will read the synopsis of Justice Harlan's opinion there can be but one impression left in the mind—that the constitutional laws are but hollow mockeries when the working men of the land test them to obtain their rights under the so-called laws of this Republic. Others will find as time puts them to the test that the constitution of our state or nation has not during the past few years and will not in the future, so long as monied interests predominates over justice, come to the rescue of any but the monied power unless, perchance, it suits the convenience of the corporate power that controls the executive, legislative and judicial departments of government of state or nation. A decision such as Justice Harlan's should be sufficient cause to shatter the reverence felt in the past for the judiciary, when it is so plainly shown they are but the willing tools of corporations to put the stamp of legal approval upon the lawlessness of the trusts and monopolies of various kinds.

Through the decision of Justice Harlan, the United States Supreme Court said to the world: "We approve of kidnapping." According to the decision, kidnapping is legal if perpetrated by the governors of two states, who have entered into a plot with a corporation, to seize in the midnight hour, the victims and spirit them away to another state, in which they have not lived, and confine them in a felon's cell. If this is not a violation of the constitution of the United States then let it be amended in such a manner as to make it a crime. If the governors can do this legally, in what manner would private citizens offend if they should follow the example of the executives of the state? Does kidnapping become legal only when indulged in by the gov-

ernors? Are men who are clothed with executive authority licensed through the positions they hold to mock laws and jeer at the lauded rights we are told are guaranteed by a constitution.
Synopsis of the Supreme Court decision follows:

SYNOPSIS OF SUPREME COURT'S DECISION.

"Looking first at what was alleged to have occurred in Colorado touching the arrest of the petitioner and his deportation from that state, we do not perceive that anything done there, however hastily or inconsiderately done, can be adjudged to be in violation of the constitutional laws of the United States."

He added that the governor of that state had not been under compulsion to demand proof beyond that contained in the extradition papers. His failure to require independent proof of that fact that petitioner was, as alleged, fugitive from justice, can not be regarded as an infringement of any right of the petitioner under the constitution or laws of the United States. He also said that even if there was fraud in the method of removal there had been no violation of rights under the constitution.

"It is true, as contended by the petitioner, that if he was not a fugitive from justice within the meaning of the constitution, no warrant for his arrest could have been legally issued by the governor of Colorado, it is equally true that after the issuing of such a warrant before his deportation from Colorado it was competent for a court, Federal or State, sitting in that state, to inquire whether he was in fact a fugitive from justice, and if found not to be, to discharge him from the custody of the Idaho agent and prevent his deportation from Colorado.

WHERE IDAHO WINS.

"No obligation was imposed by the constitution or the laws of the United States upon the agent of Idaho so to time the arrest of the petitioner and so to conduct his deportation from Colorado as to afford him a convenient opportunity before some judicial tribunal sitting in Colorado to test the question whether he was a fugitive from justice and as such liable, under the act of Congress, to be conveyed to Idaho, for trial there.

"It can not be contended the the circuit court, sitting in Idaho, could rightfully discharge the petitioner upon the allegation and proof simply that he did not commit the crime of murder charged against him. His guilt or innocence of that charge is within the exclusive jurisdiction of the Idaho state court. The question in the court below was not whether the accused was guilty or innocent, but whether the Idaho court could properly be prevented from proceeding in the trial of that issue upon proof being made in the Circuit Court of the United States sitting in that state, that the petitioner was not a fugitive from justice and not liable, in virtue of the constitution and laws of the United States, to arrest in Colorado under the warrant of its governor and carried into Idaho."

HARLAN'S SUMMING UP.

In summing up his lengthy opinion Justice Harlan says:

"Even were it conceded, for the purpose of this case, that the governor of Idaho wrongfully issued his requisition and that the governor of Colorado erred in honoring it and issuing his warrant of arrest, the vital fact remains that Pettibone is held by Idaho in actual custody for trial under indictment charging him with crime against its laws, and he seeks the aid of the circuit court to relieve from custody so that he may leave that state. In the present case it is not necessary to go behind the indictment and inquire as to how it happened that he came within the reach of the process of the Idaho court, in which the indictment is pending, and any investigation as to the motives which induced action by the governor of Colorado and Idaho would be improper as well as irrelevant as to the real question to be now determined. It must be conclusively presumed that those officers proceeded throughout this affair with no evil purpose and with no other motive than to enforce the law. **The decision of the lower court is therefore affirmed.**"

This decision caused little surprise. In this age, where corporate interests predominate over justice and right and the constitution is ignored, when it suits the interest of capital, it is not strange that the Supreme Court of the United States should have sustained the lower courts, regardless of the rights of the masses.

Justice McKenna had the courage to hand down a dissenting opinion. This opinion was, undoubtedly, such a one as would have unanimously been rendered by the United States Supreme Court if the personnel of said court were true to the constiution of these United States and were concerned in safeguarding the interests of the masses, rather than subservient to the interests of a favored class.

McKENNA'S DISSENTING OPINION.

Justice McKenna's magnificent dissenting opinion follows:

"I am constrained to dissent from the opinion and judgment of the court. The principle announced, as I understand it, is that 'a circuit court of the United States, when asked upon habeas corpus to discharge a person held in actual custody by a state for trial in one of its courts under an indictment charging a crime against its laws, cannot properly take into account the methods whereby the state obtained such custody.'

"In other words, and to illuminate the principle by the light of the facts in this case (facts, I mean, as alleged, and which we must assume to be true for the purpose of our discussion), that the officers of one state may falsely represent that a person was personally present in the state and committed a crime there, and had fled from its justice, may arrest such person and take him from another state, the officers of the latter knowing of the false accusation and conniving in and aiding its purpose, thereby depriving him of an opportunity to appeal to the courts; and that such person cannot invoke the rights guaranteed to him by the constitution and statutes of the United States in the state to which he is taken.   And this, it is said, is supported by the cases of Kerr vs. Illinois (119 U. S. 436), and Mahon vs. Justice (127 U. S. 700). These cases, extreme as they are, do not justify, in my judgment, the conclusions deduced from them.   In neither case was the state the actor in the wrongs that brought within its confines the accused person.

"In the case at bar the states, through their officers, are the offenders. They, by an illegal exertion of power, deprived the accused of a constitutional right.   The distinction is important to be observed.   It finds expression in Mahon vs. Justice.   But it does not need emphasizing. **Kidnapping is a crime, pure and simple.   It is difficult to accomplish; hazardous at every step.   All the officers of the law are supposed to be on guard against it.   All of the officers of the law may be invoked against it.   But how is it when the law becomes the kidnapper?**

"When the officers of the law, using its forms and exerting its power, become abductors? This is not a distinction without a difference—**another form of the crime of kidnapping distinguished only from that committed by an individual by circumstances.**   If a state may say to one within her borders and upon whom her process is served, I will not inquire how you came here; I must execute my laws and remit you to proceedings against those who have wronged you, may she so plead against her own offenses?   May she claim that by mere physical presence within her borders an accused person is within her·jurisdiction denuded of his constitutional rights, though he has been brought there by her violence?

"And constitutional rights the accused in this case certainly did have, and valuable ones.   The foundation of extradiction between the states is that the accused should be a fugitive from justice from the demanding state, and he may challenge the fact by habeas corpus immediately upon arrest.   If he refute the fact he cannot be removed (Hyatt vs. Corkran, 198 U. S. 691), and the right to resist removal is not a right of asylum.   To call it so, in the state where the accused is, is misleading. It is the right to be free from molestation. It is the right of personal liberty in its most complete sense; and this right was vindicated in Hyatt vs. Corkran and the fiction of a constructive presence in a state and a constructive flight from a constructive presence rejected.

"This decision illustrates at once the value of the right, and the value of the means to enforce the right. It is to be hoped that our criminal jurisprudence will not need for its efficient administration the destruction of either the right or means to enforce it. The decision, in the case at bar, as I view it, brings us perilously near both results. Is this exaggeration? What are the facts in the case at bar as alleged in the petition, and which it is conceded must be assumed to be true? The complaint, which was the foundation of the extradition proceedings, charged against the accused the crime of murder on the 30th of December, 1905, at Caldwell, in the county of Canyon, state of Idaho, by killing one Frank Steunenberg, by throwing an explosive bomb at and against his person. The accused avers in his petition that he had not been 'in the state of Idaho in any way, shape or form, for a period of more than ten years, prior to the acts of which he complained, and that the governor of Idaho knew accused had not been in the state the day the murder was committed, 'nor at any time near that day.'

"A conspiracy is alleged between the governor of the state of Idaho and his advisers, and that the governor of the state of Colorado took part in the conspiracy, the purpose of which was 'to avoid the constitution of the United States and the act of Congress made in pursuance thereof; and to prevent the accused from asserting his constitutional right under clause 2, section 2, of article IV, of the constitution of the United States and the act made pursuant thereof.' The manner in which the alleged conspiracy had been executed was set out in detail. It was in effect that the agent of the state of Idaho arrived in Denver, Thursday, February 15, 1906, but it was agreed between him and the officers of Colorado that the arrest of the accused should not be made until some time in the night of Saturday, after business hours—after the courts had closed and judges and lawyers had departed to their homes; that the arrest should be kept a secret, and the body of the accused should be clandestinely hurried out of the state of Colorado with all possible speed, without the knowledge of his friends or his counsel; that he was at the usual place of business during Thursday, Friday and Saturday; but no attempt was made to arrest him until 11:30 o'clock p. m. Saturday, when his house was surrounded and he was arrested. Moyer was arrested under the same circumstances at 8:45, and he and accused thrown into the county jail of the City and County of Denver.'

"It is further alleged that, in pursuance of the conspiracy, between the hours of 5 and 6 o'clock on Sunday morning, February 18th, the officers of the state, and 'certain armed guards, being a part of the forces of the militia of the state of Colorado,' provided a special train for the purpose of forcibly removing him from the state of Colorado; and, between said hours, he was forcibly placed on said train and removed with all possible speed to the state of Idaho; that prior to his removal and at all times after his incarceration in the jail at Denver he requested to be allowed to communicate with his friends and his counsel and his family and the privilege was absolutely denied him. The train, it is alleged, made no stop at any considerable station, but proceeded at great and unusual speed, and that he was accompanied by and surrounded with armed guards, members of the state militia of Colorado, under the orders and directions of the adjutant general of the state. I submit that the facts in this case are different in kind and transcend in consequences those in the cases of Ker vs. Illinois and Mahon vs. Justice, and differ from and transcend them as the power of a state transcends the power of an individual.

"No individual could have accomplished what the power of the two states accomplished. No individual or individuals could have commanded the means and success could have made two arrests of prominent citizens by invading their homes; could have commanded the resources of jails, armed guards and special trains; could have successfully timed all acts to prevent inquiry and judicial interference. The accused, as soon as he could have done so, submitted his rights to the consideration of the courts. He could not have done so in Colorado. He could not have done so on the way from Colorado. At the first instant that the state of Idaho relaxed its restraining power he invoked the aid of habeas corpus successively of the Supreme Court of the state and of the Circuit Court of the United States. He should not have been dismissed from court, and the action of the Circuit Court in so doing should be reversed."

ADAMS CASE.

Not many days elapsed after the imprisonment of Moyer, Haywood and Pettibone before another member of the Western Federation of Miners, Steven Adams, was arrested on his farm in Oregon, and taken to Idaho and placed in the penitentiary. McParland had another brain storm and gave the Associated Press several thousand words as to Adams' corroboration of Orchard's "confession" and how Adams would testify to the crimes that had been committed and others anticipated by the "inner circle."

Steve Adams was placed in the cell with Orchard. In

September, 1906, however, Adams, in an affidavit, which was published, swore that he was coerced by McParland into signing the confession. He declared that Gooding threatened him with death did he refuse to "confess" that he was implicated with Orchard in the Steunenberg affair, and in the other crimes revealed in Orchard's "confession."

Up to the making of the affidavit by Adams, both he and Orchard were kept in solitary confinement. No one was permitted to visit them save Gooding and McParland. The Orchard "confession" and the Adams corroboration comprised the evidence that was to take the lives of the imprisoned leaders of the Western Federation of Miners. When Adams broke down and declared he had been forced by McParland into signing a lie, he was released through habeas corpus proceedings instituted by Attorneys Darrow and Richardson, but was immediately re-arrested and charged with the murder of two men in northern Idaho, Tyler and Bóule.

Again the interests of corporations ran counter to the welfare of the people. For years great lumber companies had been plundering the common heritage. Nature's magnificient gift, the forests, protecting man's water supply and furnishing the means of shelter had been ravaged to satisfy the greed of corporations. In carrying out their nefarious work, the robbery of the people, they committed crimes ranging from perjury to murder. Their tools were men, sunk almost to the level of Pinkertons, who entered lands swearing they were for their own use and benefit, later they turned them over to the lumber companies, but bonafide settlers who had to make a living while perfecting title had entered valuable tracts—it was part of the professional perjurers work to jump these claims. The men who have developed the West place the claim jumper below the horse thief.

Tyler and Boule were found dead in the woods. They were tumbled into their graves without ceremony. Dead men can make no profits. So whether the victim meets his fate in the infamous occupations of deputy, scab, homesteader or as a man at his work, crushed on the railroad, maimed in the factory, blown up in the mine, there is the same callous indifference to his fate. Tyler was forgotten until there seemed to be an opportunity to implicate a member of the Western Federation of Miners, then the lumber companies joined with the Mine Owner's Association in using all the machinery of the state of Idaho, not to avenge him, but to plant fear in the breasts of all opposers.

After Adams repudiated his confession the remains that were supposed to be Tyler's were dug up to be used in the trial by the prosecution. About three weeks were spent in the trial. The jury was out two days when they returned into court announcing that they could never agree and were discharged. From the first to the last ballot they stood seven for acquittal and five for conviction. Adams was returned to jail to await another trial.

In November, 1907, he was again tried. The prosecution entertained the opinion that the conviction of Adams could be trusted to a jury of farmers, a change of venue was asked by the State, in order that the trial might take place in an agricultural district. In the first trial of Adams at Wallace, Idaho, in the very heart of the Coeur d'Alenes, where Standard Oil reigns supreme, the jury stood seven for acquittal, and at the second trial, held at Rathdrum, the jury stood eight for acquittal, yet Adams was still held to appease the vengeance of mining corporations at the expense of the taxpayers of Idaho.

The attorneys for the Western Federation of Miners after the disagreement of the jury the last time, secured his release on bond. Shortly after this legal procedure he was again arrested and taken to Telluride, Colo., confined in jail and it is said he is to be tried at some future date for the murder of Arthur Collins. At this writing no time has been set for the trial.

THE WORKERS BUSY.

From the kidnapping of Moyer, Haywood and Pettibone on February 17, 1906, until Haywood was acquitted in July, 1907, the working class was aroused as never before in its history. The methods used by the State of Idaho to obtain custody of the prisoners was considered indicative of the principle that would guide the court in the hearing of the case. The workers had not forgotten how the Pinkertons, through perjured evidene had hurried the Mollie Maguires to the scaffold, nor that a court had given legal sanction to the verdict of a mob in hanging the Chicago anarchists. They knew the mighty forces united for the destruction of labor's most advanced organization.

Knowing the power they had to combat, organized capital in control of all the departments of government, they prepared for the contest. Fearing nothing but falsehood, asking nothing but justice, they called the American people into court and submitted their case to a jury that only needs to know the truth to do right. As labor reared its Titanic form its shadow fell across the palace and the counting house and its voice penetrated the dim recesses where owl-like men pondered over the mouldy precedents of the past and aroused them with the call of the new day.

The way had been blazed for such a campaign. Labor was already aroused. The Colorado strike had been discussed in every hamlet. Every phase had been given on the floor of local unions, in mass meetings, before national conventions of labor bodies with the result that the workers of the country felt as if the wrongs done in Colorado had been committed against them in their own town.

Working men are accustomed to seeing laws and constitutions set aside when their interests are affected and are passed by with little thought, but deportations, bull pens and insults to women are understood by the dullest, resented by the most submissive.

In carrying on the strike the officials of the Federation had found it necessary to appeal to organized labor for funds, the necessity was even greater when the three men were put on trial for their lives, confronted by the treasury of a state as well as the wealth of the Mine Owner's Association. Obedient to the request of Gov. Gooding, the Idaho legislature appropriated

$104,000—not for the prosecution of Steunenberg's murderer, but for the prosecution of Moyer, Haywood and Pettibone. Labor rose to the needs of the hour. Protest meetings grew in number and fervor. Money for the defense and resolutions of protest poured in from all sides. The Appeal to Reason sent out more than three million copies of a single edition stating the worker's side of the controversy. No lie could live in such a light—no wrong could triumph before such a jury.

The Mine Owner's Association, standing for the capitalist class, were not prepared for such a test. They had thought to strangle these men in the dark, their best appeal is to prejudice, their reliance the Pinkerton perjured by their gold, their answer to citizens demanding constitutional rights had been the bayonet and bull pen. Their methods were disclosed, their batteries unmasked. How could they meet this new giant, an aroused working class, grown conscious of his power?

They had hoped to procure a legal assassination and justify it by labor's traducers, the capitalist press, but the light of millions of copies of the Socialist and Labor press fell upon them. They had hoped Labors groan would go out in silence, but it was transformed into speech, its cry on a world's lips.

They had thought to pillory these men but lo! Their prison became the loftiest height in the western world. Capitalism will yet climb the scaffold it erected for these men, from it one may see the light of a new day and in its shadow discern the grave of the old system.

All along the line the battle raged. Nothing that malice could invent or fraud encompass was neglected by the prosecution. The writer has only space to note a few of the sensations intended to prejudice the cause of the defendants, will only mention that every agency controlled by capitalism from Roosevelt down was used against them. Fearing that the Idaho laws gave the accused a fair chance for life, protecting them from prejudice, the legislature raised the number of peremptory challenges that could be used by the state from five to ten, bankers were remarkable for their presence and union men for their ab-

sence in the several venires called for jury duty. Roosevelt took
occasion to denounce them on several occasions and in a letter to
Congressman Sherman coupled Harriman's name with Moyer
and Haywood as "undesirable citizens." It was a blow worthy
of the man who could boast of shooting another in the back.

Friends of the accused were alarmed as to its effect on the
trial. Haywood issued a statement to the effect that the words
of the President would do more to prevent a fair trial than all
that had occurred before. The effect was overestimated. Most
men felt that passing on the guilt of the accused was not among
Presidential prerogatives. We are "undesirable citizens" became the slogan of the defense and will doubtless become the
battle cry of the workers in the campaign of 1908.

TAFT TO THE RESCUE.

During the campaign of 1906, when Governor Gooding of
Idaho, was a candidate for re-election, he made the Moyer, Haywood and Pettibone case the chief issue. Political speeches
teemed with denunciations of the defendants. Secretary of War
Taft was sent to Idaho and made Gooding's cause the administration cause. United States Senator Heyburn raised his voice and
denounced the opponents of Gooding as enemies of law and order
and friends of anarchy and crime. Gooding, by the help of
Taft and the influence brought to bear from Washington was re-
elected. He recommended that the legislature appropriate
$104,000 to prosecute Moyer, Haywood and Pettibone. The
money was appropriated unanimously.

HAYWOOD CANDIDATE FOR GOVERNOR.

The battle took on national proportions, it was made an
issue in the states of Idaho and Colorado. In Colorado the
Socialist party took up the gauntlet which capitalism had flung
down.

July 4, 1906, the Socialist party of Colorado, in convention
assembled nominated Wm. D. Haywood for governor of Colorado.

J. W. Martin made the nominating speech and the eloquence of his words will long be remembered.

The Socialist party did themselves proud when they selected the prisoner in Caldwell jail to carry the banner of Socialism—the working class party—in the state campaign. Haywood was not the first candidate of the Socialist party nominated while confined in a capitalist prison—Eugene V. Debs, the hero of Woodstock jail, was twice Socialist candidate for the Presidency of the United States.

Mr. Haywood accepted the nomination in a manner worthy of his ability, intellect, and the principles of the class which he was to represent. I quote the first paragraph of his letter of acceptance:

"Ada County Jail, Boise, Idaho, July 14, 1906.

"State Committee Socialist Party of Colorado.

"Comrades and Fellow Workers: While sitting with my lately widowed, gray-haired mother, in the shadow of this jail, surrounded by guards, I received your message notifying me that I had by acclamation been nominated by the Socialist party, candidate for governor of Colorado. After a brief reflection on the duties of a member of the party, I said to mother, 'I will accept the nomination.' The maternal love in her eyes was partly veiled with a mist gathered from the lake of tears, while, like a benediction, she spoke these words: 'It is well, my son.' Thus your notification was received and accepted."

THAT FIRE FIASCO.

Few things were more effective in arousing the indignation of organized labor than the continual postponements of the trial by the prosecution. They seemed determined the men should be punished before the trial if they could not be afterward. The Victor safe was one of these. The time set for trial was approaching, something must be done to explain the lack of evidence. The cry of fire was sent in from the National hotel,

Cripple Creek, Colo., where the Mine Owner's Association had offices. When the firemen arrived smoke was pouring from the cracks between the door and walls of the safe. The secretary of the association was standing by, the heat had not affected the lock yet he said it could not be opened.

The safe was supposed to contain acids, "Pettibone dope," photographs and evidence incriminating the accused. Certainly a strange jumble. Only men with the prescience of a Mine Owner's Association would place supposedly valuable papers in conjunction with such inflammable material. The unduly critical might suggest that such articles constituting a part of the evidence should have been in the care of the prosecuting attorney where the trial was to be held.

BLACK MAIL MOYER.

"You told a lie; an odious, damned lie;
Upon my soul, a lie; a wicked lie."

—Shakespeare: Othello.

There appeared in the Chicago Journal of May 10, 1907, an article from the pen of some tool of the combination fighting unionism, which declared Charles H. Moyer, president of the Western Federation of Miners, was an ex-convict, claiming he had served time in the Joliet, Ill., prison from 1886 to 1887. It was easy to prove that from 1886 to late in the fall of 1887, Mr. Moyer was working for J. H. Damon, in the Black Hills. Having gone to South Dakota in 1884.

This malicious report was not circulated without reasons. While a dastardly, base falsehood, it was used with the hope of blackening the name of President Moyer and to create the impression that the Federation was a criminal organization, with hope that organized labor would withdraw support. This resort to trickery was soon discovered and cooly met by a record of Moyer's residence at the date given by the false report.

KIDNAPPING CASE BEFORE CONGRESS.

Individually and as an organization the Socialists were untiring in their effort in behalf of the imprisoned men, giving their wrongs the widest possible publicity. Eugene V. Debs, that tireless worker in the interest of humanity, who has given the best days of his past life to the working class and is now the most eloquent man on an American platform, endeavored to have the facts in the case brought before Congress in an official report. He secured the consent of some of the senators to the presentation of the matter and wired the Western Federation of Miners for a statement of the case.

John H. Murphy, general attorney for the Federation, formulated the petition which completely covered the case from the affidavit made by Prosecuting Attorney Van Duyn, of Canyon County, Idaho, February 12, 1906, to the Supreme Court decision, going into the details of every illegal act. The petition asked that Congress investigate the extraordinary violation of the laws of the United States and the conspiracy fostered under the guise of law.

It was a worthy document and should have a place in these pages but space forbids.

The petition was introduced March 2, 1907, by Senator Carmack of Tennesee. Debs felt that the foundation was laid for a Congressional investigation and expressed the hope that the next session would order the same, bringing the truth before a section of the public that had not been reached.

EUGENE V. DEBS.

There could be no more fitting place to note the service of this gifted man Debs, not alone to the imprisoned men, that was but an incident in the life of this knight-errant of humanity. All who come after him will be his debtors. From the great strike of the American Railway Union, in 1894, to the present, his voice and pen have been devoted to the oppressed. Perhaps his work in behalf of the imprisoned men was his greatest service.

The love he felt for them as men gave a fiercer glow to his impassioned denunciations of oppression, his fervent appeal in behalf of men threatened with martyrdom. In special editions of the Appeal to Reason exceeding three million copies he pleaded their cause with unsurpassed eloquence, from a hundred platforms he declared: "Their only crime is loyalty to the working class," then lifted his audience to a hero's level as he thundered: "If they hang Moyer and Haywood I will make them hang me." His daring was the highest discretion. In the light of his intrepid courage men walked bravely when they might have faltered. Well he knew prison doors would fly open before an aroused working class, but if capitalism should press on, seek their blood careless of impending fate, well he knew the shadow of the scaffold he climbed would fall across its grave. In one glad, supreme moment, he would have sealed the devotion of a life.

More than any other man capitalism fears Eugene V. Debs; more fully than any other he holds the hearts of the toilers. Their dumb agony finds speech through his lips. Their bowed and broken bodies grow tall and fair in his presence. The dreams of the ages flower in the love of that lofty soul.

James Whitcomb Riley spoke in music for thousands when he said: "God was feeling mighty good when he made 'Gene Debs."

MOTHER JONES.

"Happy he
With such a mother! faith in womankind
Beats with his blood, and trust in all things high
Comes easy to him, and though he trip and fall,
He shall not blind his soul with clay."

—Tennyson.

Among the Socialists two names stand out like mountains above the plain—"Mother" Jones and Eugene V. Debs. What Holy memories cluster around the woman Re-Christened Mother in the hearts of the workers of the new world. It speaks of a service to humanity, devotion to a cause, love of individuals that can be measured only by the Infinite. Her heart is as warm as in life's springtime and her sympathies as wide as the needs of her children, notwithstanding her seventy years.

For forty years "Mother" Jones has stood in the vanguard. Her labors have covered a continent and reached every class of workers. Lavishly she has given herself, when she has given all she has yet more to give. Her speech is a summons to action. Patience with wrong is a crime. How grandly she drove that truth home throughout the imprisonment of Moyer, Haywood and Pettibone for she can "touch the hearts of men as the storm-god touches the ocean's keys."

No sorrow of humanity is alien to her. She is the incarnation of the proletarian spirit. Those who have heard her before a throng, the avenging spirit of justice, kindling dead hearts in the glow of her own, grim, relentless, implacable, as she drew the indictment of capitalism in words that roused like a bugle's call, would scarcely recognize the woman that knelt above Virginia mine workers, murdered by corporation thugs, and bathed their faces with her tears, yet it was but the expression of the Universal Mother heart. Naught but a great cause could give strength for such tasks.

"Mother" is the worker's refuge and inspiration. "Mother" is the cry when overawed by corporation hirelings they yet seek to join hands in a common struggle and "Mother" again is the cry when the troops, re-inforced by hunger, are beating them into the earth; often she has changed defeat into victory, but always her best gift is the transfused courage of her own unconquerable soul. Words are weak here. **Her work is her eulogy. Let no granite shaft rest on her, but let the flowers tell the sweetness of her life and prattling children, wrested from mine and mill and given back to childhood's joy sing her praise.**

McPARLAND TALKS.

"But still his tongue ran on, the less
Of weight it bore, with greater ease;
And with its everlasing clack,
Set all men's ears upon the rack."   —Butler.

May 7, Detective McParland, the Pinkerton on whose "evidence" the prosecution hoped to dispose of Moyer, Haywood and Pettibone had another attack and forgot "Silence is Golden." Evidently this man of Mollie Maguire fame has never made a special effort to uphold the teaching:

"The man who to the highest rung goes easiest and best
Is he who always gives his tongue vast quantities of rest."

At any rate he gave out the statement for publication that he had procured absolute evidence against Haywood that he and his associates were responsible as principals for all the crimes in the Colorado mining strikes. The "inner circle," as the officials of the Federation were called, were, according to McParland, to be exposed, and atrocious and diabolical murders fixed upon the men who managed the affairs of the miner's organization. Among the felonies McParland declared Haywood, Moyer and Pettibone to be directly connected with were the following:

April 29, 1899.—The blowing up of the Bunker Hill and Sullivan mine at Wardner, Idaho.

December 27, 1901.—Murder of Martin Gleason, manager of the Wild Horse mine at Cripple Creek, Colorado. Gleason was thrown down an abandoned mine shaft.

January 23, 1901.—Murder of J. W. Barney, non-union shift boss, Smuggler-Union mine, Telluride, Colorado. Barney was attacked in a livery stable, dragged out and never seen again.

March 2, 1901.—Murder of Wesley J. Smith, non-union shift boss, Smuggler-Union, Telluride, Colorado.

November 19, 1901.—Murder of Arthur Collins, manager of Smuggler-Union mine, Telluride, Colorado. Collins was killed by a bullet fired through a window.

July 5, 1903.—Dynamiting of Colorado Springs Electric Company's power house.

September 1, 1903.—Non-union carpenter named Stewart, beaten to death at Cripple Creek.

November 21, 1903.—Murder of Superintendent McCormick and Foreman Beck in the Vindicator mine, Cripple Creek, Colorado.

June 6, 1904.—Assassination of fourteen men at Independence railway station.

December 30.—Assassination of Former Governor Steunenberg at Caldwell, Idaho.

This is the list of crimes McParland said he had absolute "evidence" to prove the three men guilty of, beyond all question of doubt, when the time arrived for trial.

WIVES ATTEND TRIAL.

At the time the trial was opened Mrs. Chas. H. Moyer was seriously ill in a hospital, in Boise, Idaho. She had gone to Idaho soon after the kidnapping to be near her husband. The little woman made a brave fight to keep her spirits up, but knowing the confinement of her husband would have a tendency to completely undermine his health there was a continual gnawing dread at her heart that the extended confinement would prove fatal.

Mrs. William D. Haywood, accompanied by her nurse reached Boise the latter part of April, to be present at the trial. This little wife has been confined to the house or an invalid chair for eight years, but when spoken to of the cases from the first day after their kidnapping until the final outcome of the trial— her pale but bright face would light up with a glorious smile of pride and she would proudly say the prosecution could not convict any of the men and that they would be acquitted with laurels fit to adorn a martyr—her confidence in her husband's innocence never wavered. She had placed her faith in the labor movement and believed the workers of the land would help restore to her her husband. This brave little woman had taken the trip from Denver to Boise at the risk of her life. Her two daughters accompanied her—the youngest a mere baby of ten summers whose eyes had opened wide as she innocently asked the question that rang over this country from the Atlantic to the Pacific: "Will they hang my Papa?"

The meeting of this loving family that had been cruely separated for fourteen months was pathetic to say the least. The corporations can always call in the assistance of the courts to issue injunctions against strikers when they are afraid of losing a fight, but in cases like the Idaho tragedy there are no injunctions against the blow that strikes the wife's heart—no injunction to prevent her loneliness or to restrain her tears.

After Pettibone was taken from his place of business so unceremoniously, his wife went regular every morning and opened his store and remained there all day looking after his business interests. Neither Mrs. Moyer or Mrs. Pettibone had a family, so it was much less trouble for the two ladies to be near their husbands than Mrs. Haywood who was an invalid and had the responsibility of two daughters.

It requires nothing less than heroism for women to take up such a fight and keep a smiling face under the conditions these three little wives did and the men were blessed, indeed, in not having women of the clinging vine type—who were not mentally capable of understanding the cause of the inconvenience of having innocent husbands in jail indefinitely without trial.

The families of the three men were in Boise at the opening of the trial, also Haywood's gray-haired mother.

PRISONER'S TREATMENT IN JAIL.

To the query from friends as to how the men were treated in prison, the answer was always: "All right, we have no complaint, no men were ever treated better under the circumstances —the sheriff and his men have been fine to us—we have absolutely no complaint."

Moyer, Haywood and Pettibone were caged in steel at night, but their days were spent in a large room with steel-barred door and window. For two hours each day they exercised on the lawn under guard. A sheriff, and three or four deputies, tall, lithe, clear-eyed chaps, men of the West, were the alternating guards. When they were on the lawn it was difficult for strangers to distinguish prisoners from officials. Pettibone tells with glee of a farmer who mistook one of his guards for him and descanted on his ferocity and depravity. In an interview with the sheriff he said: "They are good prisoners."

After the families went to Boise they were permitted to spend a part of the day with the prisoners on the lawn under guard or in the large room. While their surroundings could have been worse it is doubtful if many would envy the prisoners their long confinement in Idaho.

The Haywood Trial

"In peace, there's nothing so becomes a man
As modest stillness and humility;
But when the blast of war blows in our ears,
Then imitate the action of the tiger:
Stiffen the sinews, summon up the blood."

—Shakespeare.

AT last the day for trial arrived. It was a measuring of the forces. The prosecution had centered its fight on Haywood. Moyer, a man of medium stature, thoughtful, reserved, taking council of all, keeping his own, devoted to his organization, inflexible in a question of right, wholly averse to the limelight. A man whose strength was only realized by his closest associates, underestimated by many of his friends and all his foes, had only been arrested to give the color of conspiracy to the case. The prosecution admitted that the case against him was the weakest of the three.

Pettibone has not been introduced to the reader in the foregoing pages of this history, while the other two, Moyer and Haywood, on account of their prominent positions in the Western Federation of Miners, have been constantly before the reader—especially President Moyer who was made a special target during the thick of the fight on account of his unfaltering loyalty. An organizer usually feels the venom of the opponents of his organization—so as such President Moyer was persecuted in every way that could be hatched in the polluted brain of hirelings of organized capital.

Pettibone was not actively connected with the Colorado labor troubles but was engaged in business in Denver. To know George Pettibone is to be his friend, jolly and philosophical. He has a droll way of expressing himself and a marked native wit. Having this happy disposition he made the best of his prolonged imprisonment and made as much fun for the others as possible. For amusement during the days when the three were together in Idaho, he took up pyrography and often sent out souvenirs to his many friends in Colorado. Just at the beginning of the Haywood trial he exhibited some of his work to press representatives and friends saying jokingly: "Mr. Darrow tells me these will be worth a great deal of money after I'm hung but I am not saving any of them." In the same interview he said:

"This day cell of ours is really the home of the Western Federation of Miners, for it was here, back in 1892, after the first trouble up in the Coeur d'Alenes, that the Federation was first proposed and discussed. You will remember that they arrested a lot of our men in 1892 and held us until the Supreme Court decided in 1893 that we were illegally in custody. While we lay here in this cell we planned the Federation. This is indeed a historic place for the old Federation. People who have not been in the Coeur d'Alenes and underground there know nothing of the frightful conditions that prevailed. We were wretchedly housed and miserably fed. A company store supplied everything at outrageous prices, a company doctor was supposed to look after us, and we were paid in scrip, if there was anything coming to us when the company got through. I've seen a company surgeon refuse to go to the home of a dying miner. Now what are men to do? Is there anything too mean to do to men who grind down their laborers under such circumstances?"

Organized labor has no stauncher friend than George A. Pettibone—that is why he occupied quarters without a permit to go and come as he desired—in a prison cell in Idaho. Corporations appreciate too well the power of such men and both fear and hate them.

President Moyer in a personal conversation with the writer, in discussing the labor movement in general, the Idaho trial in particular, characterized Pettibone as "the biggest man in the United States."

Haywood was on trial. It was for Haywood's blood that capitalism lusted. Big, magnetic, whole-souled "Bill" Haywood, terse, forceful, frank to impulsiveness, a stranger to fear, he was the idol of the crowd, the incarnation of evil to the Mine Owner's Association. Through him they hoped to discredit labor organizations, in his death to disrupt and destroy the Federation.

But little they knew of the cause of labor unions or the strength and capacity of the men whose labor opens nature's treasure vaults and pours into the channels of commerce the golden streams that turn the wheels of a world's industry. The strength of the granite hills is in their sinewy arms, the knowledge of dateless centuries in their brains, the vision of sunlit futures in their eyes—the irresistible forces of modern civilization driving them on. They know the world with the intimate knowledge that comes from doing things, their hands have taught them great lessons. They know the rough way over which Labor has borne humanity to the heights of civilization. They have the key to the world's progress and get more meaning out of their newspapers than spoiled darlings are able to get from great libraries. The world's constructive thoughts is in the ranks of labor. They know that history repeats itself in but one thing, and that is that tyrants reach the scaffold, Bastiles fall, oppressive systems die, man ever marches on to higher ground. They realize that industry has knit the bonds of a world's brotherhood that knows not the red boundary of nations, that stops not at the shore. They would gladly die that the ages' hope might live.

The day has long since gone by, if indeed it ever existed, when an individual was indispensable to a cause. A great cause develops great theories in its champions, their strength is evidence of its virility. The forces of the universe are behind the social needs of the race. The wisdom of all the past belongs to those who have grasped the processes of civilization and are able to read its history. This was the vantage ground occupied by the defense and their myriads of supporters. that made them more than a match for the combined forces of capital and government. Their thought had swept the past and forecast the future. They knew the forces that wrote history when men groped in the dark for the goal. They did not make that force, they did not enact the law of economic determinism, they did not decree the class struggle—they discovered them, knowing them, they are masters of them. They did not place employer and employee in conflict, they found them so—in the cause of evolution the master had become an employer, the slave a wage-worker, when the struggle breaks out in open revolt—the strike —Fear and Hate make earth a hell for all.

The worker's goal is always right, the means to reach it often wrong.

The trial was a judicial combat between the Mine Owner's Association standing for organized capital everywhere, directing the forces of the state and Federal government on the one side and the Western Federation of Miners on the other, supported by labor organizations, the Socialist party practically directing the campaign in their behalf.

Organization is the measure of social progress, from the clan and tribe, to the state, the nation, the world organization of capital and labor. Self-interest, which is another name for self-preservation, is the main spring of human action. Economic combination proceeds among those who have common purposes to effect, who get their living in the same way. Naturally, organization was most perfect among those who got their living from the labor of others, could give all their thought to the advancement of their economic interests. Since labor produces all wealth, pays its own wages, makes improvements and dividends, all the gains of capital are at the expense of labor. The capitalist brought a large measure of intelligence to the direction of industry while actively engaged in the management of affairs, but with the advent of the great corporation—the trust—the management was turned over to hired men—he no longer performed a social service, he drew dividends, his appetite grew by what it fed on, the exploitation of labor proceeded at a more rapid rate, men were worn out at forty-five. Experience wakens men to a consciousness of the facts of life and time teaches them to utilize their knowledge. The combination of dollars compels the organization of men. But dollars control the law. The law gives the owner of property the right to control it. Through his organization the worker seeks to exercise a joint control, regulate hours, wages, conditions—this could come only with joint ownership. He uses the strike to enforce his demand but as he is only paid a living wage when employed he soon becomes hungry, the militia is used against him, the injunction is brought into action and men are bull penned. The strike is lost. He struck at the wrong place. He asked too little. The power of the state was used against him, it must be used for him before he can succeed —that can come only through the aid of the workers, organized and unorganized. Unity of action can only be attained through understanding of the goal. The labor movement economic and political rests on the education of the worker.

Private ownership of the machine and the gifts of nature stand between the worker and an abundant life. The present rulers, owners of the earth have taken what they wanted by legal technicalities, by economic might, by the sword. The worker would not travel the old blood-stained path, he must find a new way. By what right? By the right of common heritage of the earth, creator and user of the machinery of industry. By what means? By the organization of a political party whose goal shall be the control of government and when in control, change through legal enactment the title to the productive wealth of the country.

No other movement has had a base of knowledge that grasps the universe and analyzes its processes from star dust to worlds and systems of worlds, from the amoeba to man, from the cave-dweller to Marx and Darwin, from the flint ax to the steam engine and the wireless telegraph. The future is to be shaped by the conscious action of society. Man no longer the victim of blind forces is their master. He would organize the world's knowledge to explore the unknown and widen his empire over nature, organize forces of production to supply the wants of producers, would eliminate prostitution, fear of want and dig up war by the roots.

COURT CONVENES.

Upon the convening of Court, May 9, a bill of particulars was asked for by the attorneys for the defense who explained that they had a right to know what the state had against the prisoners. Ordinarily in criminal cases there is a preliminary hearing at which the defendant is present, he sees and hears the the names of witnesses examined and on whose testimony the in-dictment was found. In this case nothing ordinary occurred. It was an extraordinary case from the kidnapping to the end. Absolute secrecy was maintained by the prosecution. They continued to declare they had unlimited evidence but refused to allow the defense to share their confidence as to the manner they expected to proceed. Senator Borah, for the prosecution said: "We are forced to move secretly as some of our most important witnesses have disappeared from Colorado."

Judge Wood withheld his decision for a few days. While awaiting the decision the attorneys continued their preliminary work. Judge Wood overruled the motion of the defense for a bill of particulars. This decision cleared away the last of the preliminary technicalities. Gladiators in the legal profession stripped for the combat and labor, with justice on its side, begun a fight against bank vaults with untold millions.

The work of selecting twelve men to act as jurors begun May 9. This proved to be a tedious task on account of the prejudice that had been created during the campaign by Gooding and associates, President Roosevelt's characterization of the men as "undesirable citizens" and false press reports.

Attorneys representing the state were James H. Hawley, of Boise, known as one of the best criminal lawyers in the West, represented the Federation in one of its greatest conflicts; U. S. Senator W. E. Borah, also of Boise; Public Prosecutor O. M. Van Duyn, of Ada County, Idaho, and George Stone, special attorney for Canyon County, in which the murder was committed. A change of venue was taken to Boise from Caldwell upon application of the defense. A fair trial at Caldwell being considered impossible.

The attorneys for the defense were: E. F. Richardson, of
Denver, Colorado; Clarence S. Darrow, of Chicago; Frederick
Miller, Spokane, Wash.; John F. Nugent, of Boise; Edgar L.
Wilson, of Boise as assistant counsel and John H. Murphy, of
Denver, general counsel for the Western Federation was on the
ground to act in an advisory capacity, his health being such as
to prevent him taking an active part.

Edgar L. Wilson is a former law partner of Judge Fremont
Wood who presided at the trial, his retention as assistant counsel
was a surprise to the prosecution.

With such talent as Clarence Darrow and E. F. Richardson
as leading counsel organized labor was ready to measure steel
with organized greed inspite of their countless millions and government machinery.

May 9, three jurors were passed by the state and defense,
panel exhausted. Special venire of one hundred ordered. Court
adjourned until Monday, 2 o'clock, afternoon, May 13. This
was the result of the first day's actual work in the trial of
William D. Haywood.

From May 9 to May 30, the work of examining jurors continued in tedious monotony. Until on the night of the 30th the
sixty-first citizen of Ada county was rounded up on the third
special venire. The examination of prospective jurors sometimes
brought out amusing as well as serious facts. At the close of the
afternoon session June 3, the jury had been completed, sworn in
and the indictment read.

Jurymen that rendered the verdict in the famous Haywood
trial:

Thomas B. Gess, farmer, 59; Finley McBean, rancher, 52;
Samuel D. Gilman, farmer, 57; Daniel Clark, farmer, 32; George
Powell, farmer, 60; V. Sebern, farmer, 52, (served on Tom Horn
jury also); H. F. Messecar, farmer, 52; Lee Scrivener, farmer, 60;
J A. Robertson, farmer, 73; Levi Smith, carpenter, 42; A. P.
Burns, retired rancher, 52; Samuel Russell, farmer, 68.

Perhaps the hardest fight between attorneys during the empaneling of the jury occurred in the case of a banker who did

not hesitate to admit he was opposed to the Federation, that he would allow that prejudice to influence him, and upon being questioned, admitted he would not want anyone to sit on a jury to try him if they had formed an opinion such as his own. This occurred on the last day. Judge Wood overruled the challenge that was raised by the attorneys for the defense. The action of the court in this instance caused fair-minded people to think the judge was showing partiality to the prosecution. The prosecution had challenged (and been sustained by the Court) for no other reason than the fact that the prospective juror admitted reading some Socialist or Labor paper. Of the large number of men that were summoned for jury duty in this trial there were few, if any, members of organized labor, yet Boise has a membership of organized workers of over one thousand. Among the men summoned for jury duty the bankers were decidedly in the majority.

The jury selected to try Haywood was not composed of men who had any particular love for organized labor. They were men whose environments, vocations in life and reading gave them wrong impressions as to the objects and aims of men banding together in labor unions. Politically, the jury stood eight Republicans, three Democrats and one Prohibitionist. Not one member of organized labor. Majority Republican—the dominant party in Idaho.

ORCHARD AS WITNESS.

"If weakness may excuse,
What murderer, what traitor, parricide,
Incestuous, sacrilegious, but may plead it?
All wickedness is weakness; that plea, therefore,
With God or man will gain thee no remission."
—Milton.

In the afternoon of June 5, the scenes were swiftly shifted and the curtain raised on another act in the tragedy. Hawley dramatically said: "Call Harry Orchard." Orchard was not far away—he had been closeted during the day three or four

hours with McParland, who, no doubt, had put him through a
rigid rehearsal. He was the star witness and through his testimony the state must either lose or win.

Orchard appeared in a few minutes and with uplifted hand
took the oath that made him a perjuror. The first question—
"where do you live" seemed to be a surprise and for a moment
unnerved him. Upon being re-assured by the state's attorneys
he told his story.

Here it would be well to mention that Detective McParland
claimed Orchard's "confession" was brought about on account
of a change of heart—he had repented of his sins and did not
hope for reward here but had "confessed" in order to be at
peace with God.

The writer regrets space will not permit the reproducing of
Orchard's testimony. The slightest intimation upon his part,
while he was telling his story, that he was actuated by compunction or reformation brought a sneer to the lips of the auditors in
the court room. He recited chapter after chapter of cold-blooded murders, without a flicker of an eye-lash a story of heartless
villainy that showed he had memorized even to the slightest detail, the story framed up for him to deliver on the witness stand.
He told without a quiver of the lips how he had gone to California to poison the Bradley family. How he purchased strychnine to place in the milk left by the milkman, that would kill a
family of four, one of which was an innocent babe. Even the
baby in its cradle did not appeal to this soulless monster, whose
own story upon the witness stand, if true, wrote his name upon
the page of history in letters of blood as the deepest dyed villain
that ever polluted the earth.

Continuing, Orchard related how he planned to kill Peabody
but failed; how he shot Lyte Gregory in Denver; how he planned
the Murder of Moffat, Goddard, Gabbert and others but failed.
He claimed the explosion that killed Wally in Denver, was caused by a bomb he had placed for Judge Gabbert. How the wrong
man had picked up the pocket-book he had attached to a wire,
which, when picked up would explode the bomb, Gabbert, accord-

ing to Orchard, passed without noticing the pocket-book. Before he left the witness stand he had charged himself with every kind of crime from bigamy to twenty-six cold-blooded murders. Some of the crimes he referred to as "jobs" he claimed to have been assisted by others—it seemed to please him especially to implicate Steven Adams. The latter, he stated, assisted him in the blowing up of the Independence depot in 1905. The dates of the murders he testified to being guilty of ranged from 1899, at Wardner, Idaho, to the murder of ex-Governor Steunenberg, December 30, 1905, in the same state. According to his testimony, at intervals between the greater crimes, he was engaged in high-grading, kidnapping children or any odd job of villainy he could find to do either for money or from force of habit. He claimed he had taken part in every crime committed in Colorado since strike troubles existed—according to his account he blew up the Vindicator mine, killing two men; the Independence depot disaster of June 6, 1904, was all his work. He told every detail with a careless air as though reciting a mere incident.

When Harry Orchard had finished his blood-curdling story of crime he made the great criminals of the world look like amateurs compared to this man who told, without a sob of ushering a score of men into eternity without provocation—just for a few paltry dollars. The writer is constrained to doubt if mere "confession" to a Pinkerton would be sufficient reparation in a case so heinous.

Orchard was thoroughly groomed and coached in all the revolting details to give an element of plausibility to his "confession." But it is safe to say that not one of the three million unionists who were watching the trial of William D. Haywood, believed any part of the story of crime as related by this degenerate. His story branded him as unreliable, a confirmed liar, a seeker after notoriety, a Nero of modern times and the Ananias of today. He was the chief instrument in the colossal conspiracy to destroy organized labor.

No one but Orchard, over-trained by a criminal detective agency, advanced any testimony that incriminated either of the three kidnapped victims. He was the tool of the Pinkerton detective agency and the same agency used him in order that thousands of dollars might flow into the coffers of a gang who make a specialty of furnishing convictions through professional perjurers.

The testimony on both sides, proved absolutely, that for years the Pinkerton agency used blood money to purchase the honor of weak men in the Federation and make them Benedict Arnolds to violate the obligation that they had taken in the sanctuary of organized labor.

Orchard, foul and infamous as he proved himself to be, said in his cross-examination that Haywood had nothing to do with the Vindicator explosion or the murder of Lyte Gregory, one of his alleged victims. He also admitted neither Moyer or Haywood advocated law-breaking during the strike in the Cripple Creek district, Colo. During his testimony he had described the blowing up of the Bradley home in California by dynamite. He had also climbed on the porch of this same Bradley home to await the milk man, his intentions being to place strychnine in the milk. It was shown the house in which Bradley lived did not have a porch. The explosion at the Bradley home was caused by gas. The statements made relative to the poisoning and later of dynamiting the Bradly home was disproved by numerous depositions taken and also witnesses introduced by the defense.

Mention should be made of the treatment accorded Orchard by the state officials after the alleged confession. He was well dressed in a summer suit, sleek, well fed, and, judging by appearances might have been a capitalist, rather than a self-confessed criminal of so many aliases that it is doubtful if his true name has been included in the list. He was treated more as a distinguished guest of the state than as the villain he painted himself when he swore on the witness stand he had murdered twenty-six people for a few dollars, he had stolen sheep, collected money on insurance on stolen cheese, deserted his wife and become a bigamist, made bombs to destroy life for a Pinkerton agency and other crimes which would brand him as the most heartless Cain that ever lived in a world's history.

Was it because the state had taken McParland's word as a fact when he sent broadcast the statement that Orchard had repented of his sins and was "as harmless as a Saint?" True it is he was well-groomed and treated as an honored guest. It has been stated and not denied to the writer's knowledge, that the widow of the dead governor had even expressed a willingness for him to go free. Presumably, this was the reward for his effort to punish some one for the crime.

OTHER WITNESSES.

The prosecution summoned about one hundred and fifty witnesses in their effort to substantiate Orchard's testimony. Pinkertons were employed to watch their witnesses. The state was forced to send an army of witnesses back home who had not been called to the witness stand. The prosecution begun to realize early in the hearing of testimony that the testimony that they had to offer would have but little weight before any fair Court. McParland was lacking in nerve when the time came for him to testify. He had experienced one siege of Darrow's rapid fire cross-examination during the Adams trial and he was afraid another grilling of the same kind would land him behind prison bars. In the slang phrase he got "cold feet." He was afraid to tell the jury what he had so often caused the capitalist press to herald to the world. He found different conditions to face to what confronted him in Pennsylvania when he caused many innocent victims murdered upon perjured testimony. He, no doubt, realized he could not murder working men in the West today as he did in the East thirty years or more ago. Notwithstanding this, however, the Idaho taxpayers will pay the debt of an enormous sum as did the small property owners pay the mine owner's war debt during the reign of Peabody in Colorado.

While James McParland, who lives by blood money as a spy, failed to testify for the mine owners—his brother who earns an honest living as a shoemaker, did not fail to take the witness stand and tell of the high-handed methods of the mine owners in Cripple Creek. He was among the deported by the mandate of a mine owners organization. He made a strong witness for the defense. Strange there could be such a contrast in the same family.

The defense introduced witnesses from all walks of life, in unlimited numbers, no ground was left uncovered. The attorneys for the defense upon cross-examination of the state's witnesses and by the introduction of scores of witnesses summoned from all sections that had been mentioned by the prosecution soon razed to the ground the conspiracy house built on sand by the mine owners and the political ring of two states, indorsed by organized capital of the United States.

NO CORROBORATION.

McParland and the attorneys for the state frequently declared that the unbelievable story of crime and bloodshed as told by Orchard would be fully corroborated but when the prosecution closed its case the perjured story of Orchard stood alone. The whole case of the state turned upon his testimony, which, under the law, had to stand or fall on the success or failure to introduce a measure of corroborative evidence. When the test came the state could not show outside of Orchard's testimony even a connecting link between any of the crimes credited to the officials at Western Federation headquarters, directly or indirectly.

PEABODY AND GODDARD WITNESSES.

Among the distinguished witnesses for the state was the name of Judge Goddard of the Supreme Court of Colorado. Conspicious in the list of witnesses for the state appeared the name of Peabody and daughter, of Colo. His former Adjutant General Bell and the present Adjutant General Wells, who had acted as escort to the victims to Idaho and many others who had acted as tools in the capacity of deputy sheriffs during the Colorado labor troubles. The writer asks the reader how you would like to see your daughter go on the stand to corroborate the testimony of such a one as Orchard?

NOT GUILTY.

Into the stillness of a summer morning—into the beautiful sunlight of a Western Sabbath day, William D. Haywood walked forth a free man, July 28, 1907.

It was after it had been out for twenty-four hours that the jury, which at first had been divided eight to four and then seemed deadlocked at ten to two, finally came to an agreement shortly after the first faint streaks of the coming day showed gray above the giant hills which wall Boise to the North and East. The weary, snow-bearded old bailiff, who had kept an all-night vigil before the door of the jury room, was startled into action by an imperative knock from within. Events moved rapidly enough after this, and when at last the principal actors in the trial had been gathered into the court room at a few minutes before 8:00 o'clock, the white envelope handed by the foreman to the judge was torn open and the verdict read:

"**State of Idaho against William D. Haywood: We, the jury, in the above entitled cause find the defendant, William D. Haywood, not guilty.—Thomas B. Gess, foreman.**"

Then came the congratulations, in the midst of which Judge Wood said:

"**The defendant will be discharged and the jury dismissed for the term.**"

"Twelve good men and true" have been the hope of justice among Anglo-Saxons for centuries—and in the twelve farmers of Idaho has been found men who place life and principle above gold. Our form of government is vindicated. It is only when dishonestly administered that the law fails.

The acquittal of William D. Haywood was accepted everywhere as the vindication of Moyer and Pettibone. In the language of John M. O'Neill: "The verdict of the jury means the most glorious battle that has ever been won by the Western Federation of Miners and puts a sparkling gem in the crown of organized labor of this country."

The verdict of the Boise jury marks a decisive stage in a serious crisis in the life of this country. For the Haywood trial was a National crisis. The struggle between the working class and capitalist class was displayed in all its tremendous significance. But a jury of twelve men, living almost on the scene of the crime, admittedly prejudiced in advance, one of them having dwelt with the murdered man for two years, after listening to the evidence, was won over to the defense. They acquitted Haywood and therefore justified our confidence in our comrades and our faith in humanity.

"Not Guilty" soon flashed over the wires, was pronounced in every nook and corner of the globe, hands were clapped and hearts rejoiced and tears of joy were shed.

The Haywood case was the greatest case ever submitted to the decision of a court; not even excepting that world-renowned one wherein Edmund Burke impeached Warren Hastings at the bar of the House of Commons. Then the prosecutor spoke for humanity, India's silent, submissive millions found voice through Burke, Sheridan and Fox. Here the contrast ends, the likeness begins, for in that historic trial all the forces that enable the strong to hold down the weak were on the side of the exploitee invested with regal power and against the robbed. Here those same forces were arrayed enmasse against the accused, the hopes of the silent ones were with him. He had helped to teach them how to strike and when. They knew he was confronting death because he had battled for them. They were looking upon what might be a sacrifice. Here was a man who had attested his faith in life, stood ready to prove it in death.

Some way his fellows had lost the submissiveness that had stamped them in the old days. Their hands were not clasped, they were clenched, they did not implore the Heavens for mercy, in tones that would not be denied they demanded justice. In every zone and tongue the protest was registered and eyes peered through the mist, saw men high in place stooping to make a mockery of the forms of law, President and perjurers alike the tool of forces that made mockery of justice, noted the gold in the scales and wondered **how much steel would be required to bal- ·ance it.**

In every land they gathered. The Alaskan gold seeker under the play of the Northern Lights wondered what new curse would be written on the rule of gold. The Englishman, walled in by conservatism, had felt the walls fall in his own country when the Taff Vale decision was handed down, saw the hands sweep backward on the Clock of Time when our Supreme Court legalized kidnapping and felt that perhaps Runnymede was in vain after all. Under the Southern Cross the Australian miner and herder looked up at the starry vault, thought how long the greed of gain had lain on the soul, over what oceans and deserts it had come to cast its shadow over all the sons of men. The German felt within him the fires of '48 as the wires brought to him the story of an autocracy more brutal than that of Germany's war lord. Only the Marsellaise could tell the revolt in the Frenchman's soul and the Italian longed for a new and nobler Garibaldi. In the silent watches the Siberian exile recalled the long, weary way, counted the miles behind and the days before him, pondered on the crimson pathway Freedom's sons have ever trod to prison and scaffold, pondered how much the Liberty of the new world resembled the despotism of the old, pondered till he fell asleep and dreamed it was Dawn.

Yea, not only from Boston to San Francisco, but throughout these wide lands the hearts of the workers were united by this menace to one of their class!

At the bar of the court the formal charge said Haywood was to answer on the charge of complicity in the murder of Frank Steunenberg, but in reality the crime was a graver one in the judgment of the conspirators. The ferocious hate borne the prisoner by the ruling class was but thinly veiled by the indictment charging him with a terrible crime. All other crimes may be forgiven but he who would teach the slave the love of freedom must bear the hate of the master through his life, fortunate if in death the odium of prison or scaffold do not fall upon his grave, blasting all who come near him in life.

Haywood had hopes wider than his own fireside, desires that could only be gratified when his fellow workers took a seat with him at the banquet of life. He had a nobler incentive than to shift the burden of his chains upon a weaker or less fortunate brother. Had he been content with a place for himself, strong hands would have lifted him up and the mercenaries of press and pulpit would have pointed out the rewards to ambition. Haywood's organization, does not exist for the benefit of the officers but for the toilers. It did not come to hide the class conflict but to end it and Haywood merely did his duty—gave the members what they wanted.

The conviction of the secretary-treasurer of the Western Federation of Miners would have been a deadly blow to the labor movement of this country and the unions appreciated the situation. They realized that organized labor would receive a staggering blow if the conspiracy was not exposed—so they rose in a body to meet the emergency and fought a legal battle and won.

It would be impossible to review the many chapters in the history of the trial. Attorneys Richardson, Darrow, Murphy, Nugent, Breen, Wilson, Miller and Whitsell covered themselves with glory and won a battle that enrolled their names on the page of history as legal giants.

DARROW DIAMONDS.

THE PLEA TO THE JURY.

"Gentlemen, I need not tell you how important this case is. How important to the man on trial and to those who still must be placed where he is today. How important to his family and his friends. How important to society. How important to a great movement which represents the hopes and the wishes and the aspirations of all men who labor to sustain their daily life. You know it! You could not have sat here day after day so long as you have without understanding it, and grasping it, and excusing us if in our haste and zeal we seemed to say things we should not have said, and forgot things we should have spoken of to you.

"And, gentlemen, we are here as aliens to you. Our client and the men who are with him down here in this jail have been brought fifteen hundred miles to be tried by a practically foreign, alien jury, a jury unfamiliar with their method of thought, a jury unfamiliar with their methods of life, a jury who has not viewed life from the standpoints of industry as these men have viewed it; I am here, two thousand miles from home, unacquainted with you, with your life, with your methods of reasoning—all of us are brought here in an alien country; before people, if not unfriendly, whom at least we do not know, and we are here met by the ablest counsel that the state of Idaho ever produced—the peer of any counsel anywhere; and, more than that, we are here in the home of the man who was killed in the most ruthless, cowardly, brutal way that any man could meet his death.

"We are here, strangers, aliens, if not regarded by you as enemies, to meet an accusation of the murder of a man whom you all know, whom many of you voted for, maybe, whom one of you at least did business with, a man in whose house one juror lived for two long years. We are trying this case to a jury that is almost the family of the man who is dead. We are trying it to a community that has no community of interest with the men whom we defend. We are defending these men for what seems to you almost an assault upon your own home, and your own fireside, and we must be contented with results. We can only appeal to you, gentlemen, to lay aside those common feelings which possess the minds of all men, to not be governed by passion or feeling or prejudice, but to look at us as if we were of you, to try to find out the standpoints from which these men acted, to give us that same fair, impartial trial that should be given to a defendant if you did not know the deceased or as if you knew the defendant and stood equally between him and the law

MEN CONTROLLED BY ENVIRONMENTS.

"More than that, gentlemen, we are all human. We have come into this court room and into this community, a community that has been deliberately poisoned for a year and a half, a community where feeling, and sentiment, and hatred have been deliberately sown against this defendant and his friends; a community where lie after lie has been sent broadcast like poison to infect the minds of men. We have come here after a year and a half of that, and must submit our case to a jury that has been fed upon this poison for all these months. We have no redress. We ask for none. You have sat here for two months, and you know the lies that have been scattered broadcast on the leaflet of every paper almost that is circulated in this community. You have heard it from the witness stand, and you know it, and they could not have failed to have influenced this jury and this court. Men cannot rise above their environments. We are all alike, and if I were to tell this jury that I believed they were great enough and wise enough and strong enough to overcome the environments in which they live, and if I were to say to this Court that he could do what no other judge in Christendom ever did, rise superior to his environments and his life, you would know I was lying to you. You would understand that, if you did not understand anything else. We are all human, we are all influenced alike, moved by the same feelings and the same emotions, a part of the life that is around us, and it is not in the nature of things that this Court or this jury would not to some degree have been influenced by all that has gone before. But, gentlemen, as men go, as we see our neighbors and our friends, I have no doubt that you twelve men before me intend to carefully guard and protect the rights, the hopes, the interests and the life of this defendant. I have no doubt that you mean to give to him the same honest trial, the same benefit of the law, that you would expect twelve men to give you, if by some trick of Chance or by some turn of the wheel of Fate your life was hanging in the balance and twelve of your fellowmen were passing upon it.

* * *

ASKS NO COMPROMISE.

"Gentlemen of the jury, one thing more: William D. Haywood is charged with murder. He is charged with having killed ex-Governor Steunenberg. He was not here. He was fifteen hundred or a thousand miles away, and he had not been here for years. There might be some member of this jury who would hesitate to take away the life of a human being upon the rotten testimony that has been given to this jury to con-vict a fellow citizen. There might be some who still hold in their minds a lurking suspicion that this defendant had to do with this horrible murder. You might say, we will compromise; we cannot take his life upon Or-chard's word, but we will send him to the penitentiary; we will find him guilty of manslaughter; we will find him guilty of murder in the second degree instead of the first.

"Gentlemen, you have the right to do it if you want to. But, I want to say to you twelve men that whatever else you are, I trust you are not cowards, and I want to say to you, too, that William Haywood is not a coward. I would not thank this jury if they found this defendant guilty of assault and battery and assessed a five-dollar fine against him. This mur-der was cold, deliberate, cowardly in the extreme, and if this man, sit-ting in his office in Denver, fifteen hundred miles away, employed this miserable assassin to come here and do this cowardly work, then, for God's sake, gentlemen, hang him by the neck until dead. Don't compro-mise in this case, whatever else you do. If he is guilty—if, under your conscience and before your God, you can say that you believe that man's story, and believe it beyond a reasonable doubt, then take him—take him and hang him. He has fought many a fight—many a fight with the perse-cutors who are hounding him in this court. He has met them in a battle in the open field, and he is not a coward. If he is to die, he will die as he has lived, with his face to the foe. This man is either innocent or guilty. If he is guilty, I have nothing to say for him.

* * *

"Mr. Hawley tells you that he is a friend of the union. There cannot be any doubt about that! He told you in his opening statement that this labor union was a criminal conspiracy from the beginning, and that Ed. Boyce, who led it in its earliest troubles, and its early triumphs, who organized this great mass of unorganized labor, that they might look up in the face of their master and demand a portion of what they earned, that he was a criminal—that he is guilty; and all you would need to do would be to go to Mr. Van Duyn and get him to sign his name, and Hawley could get him to bring Boyce in here, too, and charge him with this murder as well.

"He told us how from the beginning it was a criminal organization, and yet he organized it himself—and he admits it after we have proved it—and he organized it while the leaders of this union, or a large part of them, lived, from that day to this, down here in the jail. He organized it where for conscience sake these men were confined in the cells down below. He said to them, 'You have your poor, weak individual organizations all over; you have one in Butte, you have them in Idaho, you have them in Colorado; there is nothing on earth but to get together into one great Federation so you can fight together.' That was good advice wasn't it? And he went out here in the jail yard and he told them about it, and when he got through and they got out, released for a crime which the court said did not exist, after they had suffered eight months' imprisonment for a crime which was not a crime, there was no way to give them their liberty back, any more than there is a way to give Moyer, Haywood and Pettibone the eighteen months they have spent here in the Boise jail. These are all a part of the premium that one gets, and has always received, for his services to his fellow man. For the world is the same now that it always was, and if a man is so insane that he wants to go out in the wilderness and preach and work for the poor and the oppressed and the despised, for the men who do not own the tools, the newspapers, and the courts, and the machinery, and organization of society, these are the wages that he receives today, and which he has received from the time the first foolish man commenced to agitate for the uplifting and the up-building of the human race.

"But Mr. Hawley took their money; he organized them; he fought their battles; he was their first attorney; and he says to this jury, 'I have always been a friend of labor unions.'

"Yes, gentlemen, Mr. Hawley has always been a friend of labor unions —when they got their cash to his office first. But when they did not they had better hunt some other friends. Mr. Hawley is advising the

state in this case—he had better stick to the state and let the labor
unions be taken care of by some one of their own choice.

* * *

SOME KNOTS IN THIS STRING.

"Let us see, now, gentlemen: I will give you a specimen. When I
opened this case I said to this jury that before the first witness left the
stand I would convince Mr. Hawley that his precious client had lied upon
one important fact. Now, I want to apologize to the the jury—I did not.
That is because I did not understand Mr. Hawley. I thought he had some
sense. Let me tell you who was the first witness in this case—you may
have forgotten it, it was so long ago; it was Mrs. King. Do you remember Mrs. King? Let us hold an inquest on Hawley's sanity for a
minute, and let us see whether he is sane or insane. Now, gentlemen,
Mrs. King was a matronly woman of perhaps 55 or 60 years of age; she
was not a member of the Western Federation of Miners; she did not
work in the mines at all. She has two sons working in the mines and
they are both scabs, so she would not favor us on that account; both of
them are working there now, neither one belonging to the union or having ever belonged to the union.

"I submit there has not been a witness placed upon this stand in this
trial who had more of the appearance of truth and candor and integrity
than Mrs. King. Is there any doubt about it? Is there any man in this
jury box that would not as soon doubt his own wife, except for the fact
that she is his own wife, as Mrs. King? I do not belive it. Will you tell
me what license this lawyer has, for a few paltry defiency warrants, to
say to this jury that Mrs. King is a perjurer to get the blood of Mr. Haywood; and yet you twelve men are expected to take that sort of talk so
you can get his blood and accomodate Mr. Hawley with another scalp at
his belt in his declining years!

"Mrs. King swore that she kept a rooming house and that Mr. Sterling the detective of the Mine Owners' Association, occupied a front
room, and she saw Harry Orchard come there at least six or eight times,
and he came up the back stairs at any time, and she only saw him when
she happened to see him. She does not stand alone, for her daughter, a
bright, intelligent, comely girl, who is not a member of this organization,
swears that she saw him four or five times, and she is a perjurer, too,
and it is a wonder that Mr. Hawley doesn't swear out a warrant for them
before they leave the state; in these hot days and hot times—you could
expect Mr. Hawley to do most anything.

* * *

ORCHARD'S MOCKERY OF RELIGION.

* * * "I want to say a few words for the benefit, not of this jury, but of those sickly slobbering idiots who talk about Harry Orchard's religion. If I could think of any stronger term to apply to them I would apply that term. The English language falls down on Orchard and likewise upon all those idiots who talk about Orchard's regeneration. Now I am going to take a chance and talk about that for a few minutes.

"There is one thing that is well for them to remember right at the beginning, and that is that at least a month before Dean Hincks persuaded him to lay his sins on Jesus, Father McParland had persuaded him to lay his crimes on Moyer, Haywood and Pettibone. You might remember that in starting. It is on a par with the character of a characterless man—I am referring to Orchard now, so there will be no mistake. It is a smooth game of shifty Harry. You are asked to give him immunity and to give immunity to everyone of his kind. You are asked to say to the old and to say to the youth, you may kill, you may burn, you may lie, you may steal, you may commit any crime or any act forbidden by God or forbidden by man, and then you can turn and throw your crimes on somebody else, and throw your sins on God, and the lawyers will sing your praises. All right, gentlemen. If in your judgment public policy demands it, go ahead and do it. Don't stop for a little matter like Bill Haywood's neck.

"Shifty Harry meets McParland. He has lived a life of crime and been taken in his deeds, and what does he do? Why, he saves his soul by throwing the burden on Jesus, and he saves his life by dumping it onto Moyer, Haywood and Pettibone. How can you beat that game, gentlemen? Can you beat it? And you twelve men are asked to set your seal of approval on it and to make that contract good so it may go out to every youth in the land. You may need to do it, but it should be a mighty strong necessity that would lead you to do it, should it not?

AN ELOQUENT TRIBUTE TO RELIGION.

"Now, gentlemen, like Brother Hawley and I know like Senator Borah, I, too, have a profound regard for religion. Mine may be broader than Brother Hawley's. I don't want to say to these twelve men that I think the Christian religion is the only religion that the world has ever known. I do not believe it for a moment. I have the greatest respect for any religion or any code of ethics that would do anything to help man, whatever that religion may be. And for the poor black man who looks into the black face of his wooden idol and who prays to that wooden idol to make him a better man and a stronger man, I have the profoundest respect. I know that there is in him, when he addresses his prayers to his wooden idol, the same holy sentiment, and the same feeling that there is in the breast of a Christian when he raises his prayer to the Christian's God. It is all one. It is all a piece of ethics and a higher life, and no man could have more respect for it than I have. In the ways of the world and in the language of the world I am not a professed Christian. I do not pretend to be. I have had my doubts, my doubts about things which to other men's minds seem plain I look out on the great universe around me, at the millions and millions of stars that dot the firmament of Heaven in the night time; I look out on all the mysteries of Nature, and the mysteries of life, and I ask myself the solution of the riddle, and I bow my head in the presence of the infinite mystery and say, 'I do not know.' Neither do I. I cannot tell. But for that man who understands it all and sees in it the work of a Supreme Being, who prays to what he honestly believes to be this higher power, I have the profoundest regard; and any communion with him, any communion of that poor, weak mortal with that higher power, that power which permeates the universe and which makes for good, any communion that lifts a man higher and higher and makes him better, I have regard for that. And, if Orchard has that religion, well and good. I am willing that he should have it. I hope that he has it. I would not deny that consolation and that solace to him, not for a moment. But I ask you whether he has it, and what it means to him? I have no desire to injure Harry Orchard. I am not made that way. I might have once when the blood in me was warmer and my feelings were stronger. But I, like Hawley, have been tempered by years, and I have no desire to hurt even Harry Orchard, despicable as I think he is I have no desire to take his life. I am not responsible for his being I cannot understand the purposes of the infinite God who fashioned his head as he saw fit to fashion it. I cannot understand the purpose of that mysterious power who molded Harry Orchard's brain as he pleased. I am willing to leave it to him to judge, to Him who alone knows.

A PLEA FOR ORCHARD, THE UNFORTUNATE.

"I never asked for a human being's life and I hope that I may never ask for a human life to the end of my days. I do not ask for his. And if the time should ever come that somebody pronounces against him the decree of death and nobody else asks to save his life, my petition will be there to save it, for I do not believe in it. I do not believe in man tinkering with the work of God. I do not believe in man taking away the life of his fellow man. I do not believe that I understand, I do not believe that you understand, I do not believe that you and I can say in the light of Heaven that if we had been born as he was born, if our brain had been moulded as his was moulded, if we had been surrounded as he has been surrounded, we could say that we might not have been like him.

* * *

THE KILLING OF HEROES.

"To kill him, gentlemen! I want to speak to you plainly. Mr. Haywood is not my greatest concern. Other men have died before him. Other men have been martyrs to a holy cause since the world began Wherever men have looked upward and onward, forgotten their self-ishness, struggled for humanity, worked for the poor and the weak, they have been sacrificed. They have been sacrificed in the prison, on the scaffold, in the flame. They have met their death, and he can meet his, if you twelve men say he must. **But, gentlemen, you short-sighted men of the prosecution, you men of the Mine Owner's Association, you people who would cure hatred with hate, you who think you can crush out the feelings and the hopes and the aspirations of men. by tying a noose around his neck, you who are seeking to kill him, not because it is Haywood, but because he represents a class, don't be so blind, don't be so foolish as to believe you can strangle the Western Federation of Miners when you tie a rope around his neck. Don't be so blind in your madness as to believe that when you make three fresh new graves you will kill the labor movement of the world.** I want to say to you, gentlemen, Bill Haywood can't die unless you kill him. You must tie the rope. You twelve men of Idaho, the burden will be on you. If at the behest of this mob you should kill Bill Haywood, he is mortal, he will die, but I want to say that a million men will grab up the banner of labor at the open grave where Haywood lays it down, and in spite of prisons or scaffolds or fire, in spite of prosecution or jury, or courts, these men of willing hands will carry it on to victory in the end.

* * *

THE BULL-PEN OF THE COEUR D'ALENES.

"Now, gentlemen, I am not going to discuss to this jury whether his method was right or wrong. I believe it was wrong. I don't believe any lawyer can defend the right of any human being to indiscriminately take his fellow man without any criminal charge whatever, without any trial or any hearing, and shut him up in a pen, as was done in the Coeur d'Alenes in '99; and whatever Governor Steunenberg might have thought, and however honest and sincere his motives were at the time (and I am not here to impugn them) when he established the bull-pen in the Coeur d'Alenes he sowed the seed of more strife and contention than was ever sown by any governor from the days that this nation was founded to the present time. There was nothing to justify it. If the arm of the law was not strong enough, if the civil authorities were not strong enough, then the military authorities should have been called in to assist. But when you say that a governor or a general may reach out indiscriminately and take whom he will, without warrant, without charge, without a hearing of any kind, and lock them up as he sees fit, then you say that all government should be submerged and the only law be the law of might, and I don't think the man lives who can defend it. Doubtless Governor Steunenberg felt at the time of this crisis that there was nothing else to do—I don't propose to discuss him for a moment on that account—but I believe that large numbers of right-minded people, in labor organization and out, have always denounced that act and always will denounce that act so long as we pretend to have a government by law in these United States. It is not strange that at that time large numbers of miners and workingmen, that honest lawyers, ministers, congressmen and all classes of people protested against it as being an outrage, a crime against the liberties of man. But what had Moyer, Haywood and Pettibone to do with it? Orchard was doubtless there and he ran away.

* * *

HUNTED BY MANY, BAYED BY ONLY ONE.

After Bill Haywood becomes the secretary-treasurer of the Western Federation of Miners, and, mark you, the next thing they have against him, the very next act, does not occur until 1903, four years after the Bunker Hill and Sullivan mill has been blown up, four years after the time when he was an obscure miner over here at Silver City. In the meantime he had been one of the officers of the Western Federation of Miners for three years, and all was peaceful and serene, and they have not brought to this jury one single act up to 1903, and then they gather up another act of Harry Orchard's to charge to him. It is a strange thing, is it not, gentlemen. Here is Mr. Haywood, the secretary-treasurer of the Western Federation of Miners. Here is Mr. Moyer, the president. They have been leading a strenuous life, God knows. Their organization is a militant organization and has been from the beginning, from the time Mr. Hawley advised them how to construct it, when its officers were lying in the county jail, until now, when the hand of the powerful and the great has been raised against it. They have had to fight every inch of their way, and fight it, gentlemen, in the face of courts, in the face of jails, in the face of scaffolds, in the face of newspapers, in the face of every man who could get together a body of stolen gold to spend to fight this organization. Mr. Moyer and Haywood were connected with it for several years. Haywood has not been in Idaho since 1900 until he was brought to this state in 1906. Will you tell me where any voice has been raised against Haywood excepting Harry Orchard's? Will you tell me—where the Pinkertons, with their million eyes focused upon him, with their million ears trained to catch every sound that could come from his voice; can you tell me while the public was poisoned against him and where its captains of industry poured out there gold to compass his death —can you tell me—why it is that there hasn't been one word, one look, one letter, one circumstance that does not come from this foul creature upon whose testimony I undertake to say there is not one of you farmers but would blush with shame if you should kill a sheep-stealing dog! A man who would not give a dog a show for his life against Orchard would not be a man. Who else has said anything against him—the world of wealth, the world of power, the world of influence; the world of official-dom—and they have produced Harry Orchard and they have nòt produced another line or another letter or another word or another look or another thing. Gentlemen, another thing: In all of theiȓ unions everywhere were the Pinkerton detectives, ready to report every act, every word, every letter. They were present with them in all their trials and in all that took place. The Pinkertons were with Moyer in the bull-pen and stuck to him as close as a pull-pen tick. Why didn't they get a word out of him in the days of his unlawful imprisonment and his tribulation? Why haven't they found something somewhere that would give twelve men a reason, if they wanted it, for taking away the life of their fellow man? Why haven't they found it? And these men havę been conspir-ing, they have been talking, they have been writing, they have been work-ıng—this Pinkerton and all his cohorts—with the money of all the mines and all the mills behind them, and have produced nothing except the paltry story which you have heard upon this witness stand.

* * *

"The state of Colorado passed an eight-hour law in 1899—under the evidence in this case, 1899 is right, isn't it? And the Guggenheims fought it, and they took it before the Supreme Court—and the courts are always the last to move, and the higher they are the slower—and they took it before the Supreme Court and of course the Supreme Court declared it unconstitutional. It is unconstitutional to pass a law which won't permit Guggenheim to take ten hours out of the hide of his men instead of eight.

" 'Mr. Richardson—It was twelve hours in the smelter.'

"Mr. Darrow—Well, a man that will wòrk in a smelter ought to be worked twelve hours a day.

"The courts declared it unconstitutional. Of course they would. What is the constitution for except to use for the rich to destroy the laws that are made for the poor? That is the main purpose in these latter days. Then what did the workers do? They said, if the ·constitution is wrong, let us change it. And they·appealed once more to the state—to the people. The people are blind and stupid, but still more generally right upon an issue like this—and they put it to a vote of the people, and the people voted six to one to change the constitution which was in their way, and the new constitution provided that the next legislature should enact an eight-hour law. This was the strike which Hawley says was unconstitutional—was unwarranted. They appealed to the people, and by six to one they changed the constitution of the state and then the legislature came in in 1902, and was asked to pass that law which the constitution commanded them to pass, and what did they do? Why, the constitution is only meant to be obeyed by the poor. What is the law for if a rich man has to obey it? Why should they make it if it can reach them? Why should they have the constitution if it could be used against them? The constitution said that they must change the law— must pass an eight-hour law, and Mr. Guggenheim and Mr. Moffat and the Union Pacific railroad and the Mine Owner's Association and all the good people who lived by the sweat and blood of their fellow men—all of these invaded the chamber of the house and the senate and said: 'No, you must not pass an eight-hour law; true, the constitution requires it; but here is our gold which is stronger than the constitution.' The legislature met and discussed the matter, and these miners were there. The evidence in this case has shown you who they were. Haywood was there; the labor organizations were there and they were there pleading then, as they have always pleaded, for the poor, for the weak, for the oppressed. I don't mean to tell this jury that labor organizations do no wrong. I know them too well for that. They do wrong often, and sometimes brutally; they are sometimes cruel; they are often unjust; they are frequently corrupt; they will be as long as human nature is human nature, and there is no remedy for it. But I am here to say that in a great cause these labor organizations—despised and weak and outlawed as they generally are—have stood for the poor, they have stood for the weak, they have stood for every human law that was ever placed upon the statute books. They have stood for human life. They have stood for the father who was bound down with his task; they have stood for the wife threatened with being taken from the home to work by his side, and they have stood by the little child, who has also been taken to work in their places, that the rich could grow richer still, and they have fought for the right of the little one to have a little of life, a little of comfort while he is young. I don't care how many wrongs they have committed—I don't care how many crimes—these weak, rough, rugged, unlettered men, who often know no other power but the brute force of their strong right arm, who find themselves bound and confined and impaired which ever way they turn, and who look up and worship the God of might as the only God that they know; I don't care how often they fail —how many brutalities they are guilty of. I know their cause is just. I know that trouble and strife and contention have been invoked, yet through brutality and bloodshed and crime has come the progress of the human race. I know they may be wrong in this battle or that, but in the great long struggle they are right, and they are eternally right, and they are working for the poor and the weak, they are working to give more liberty to the man, and I want to say to you, gentlemen of the jury, you Idaho farmers, removed from the trades unions, removed from the men who work in industrial affairs, I want to say, had it not been for the trades unions of the world—for the trades unions of England, for the trades unions of Europe, the trade unions of America—you today would be serfs instead of free men sitting upon a jury to try one of your peers. The cause of the men is right.

* * *

ORCHARD'S INTRODUCTION TO HAYWOOD.

"Who was he, and what was he doing at that time? Let us see about this fellow. Harry Orchard swears that he tried first to explode a carload of gunpowder and failed, and he did not get any money for it, and then Bill Davis told him he was going to have plenty of money when they wrecked this train and it made Harry Orchard jealous because something was going on and he was not in it; to feel that anybody should explode a mine or tear up a railroad track, or kill any human being and Harry Orchard not considered. He said: Here is the union putting out their good money for a comparatively easy job; why don't they hire me? And he went to Scott. Now, do you suppose that was the reason? I don't know how anybody can tell. If you can tell, you are wiser than I, but there is one thing he did and that is sure—he did go to Scott. He went to Scott, the chief detective of the Florence and Cripple Creek railroad, and he had a conference with him, and, strange to say, the first time he ever saw Moyer or Haywood in the world he went up to Denver with a pass furnished by this detective and twelve or fifteen dollars in his pocket which this detective had given to him. Now think of it. And you are asked to believe that we are responsible for him. Before Haywood ever saw him or had heard of him, he had Scoot's money in his pocket. He was sent to Haywood with a pass and cash to get next to the offiers of the Western Federation of Miners. Whose hired man was he? Now, let me be plain about this matter.

* * *

"Orchard went up to Denver with Scott's money and Scott's pass, and there he says he saw Moyer and Haywood. Now, Scott and he do not agree. I asked Scott how much money he ever gave him, and he said forty-five dollars at the most. I asked Orchard how much money he ever got of Scott, and he says he got either twelve or fifteen dollars once, and

five dollars afterward, and that is all. They don't agree. Perhaps
neither of them tells the truth. I don't care which, or whether either of
them does.

* * *

THE ABSENCE OF JACK SIMPKINS.

"Gentlemen of the jury: Before I overlook it I want to refer to a
few suggestions made by Mr. Hawley as to Jack Simpkins and why he
is not here. I suppose the reason he is not here is because he is afraid
to be here. That is the best reason I can give. I do not propose to go
around the question or get up any fantastic reason. That is the reason.
But Mr. Hawley says to you that the fact that he ran away proves that he
is guilty beyond a reasonable doubt. With that statement I take serious
issue. If the fact that Jack Simpkins ran away proves that he is guilty,
then the fact that Haywood and Moyer did not run away, but waited in
their offices and stayed to face whatever might come, proves that they
are innocent. Neither statement is true. One is as true as the other,
but neither statement is true. I used to think that I could tell something
about whether a man was innocent or guilty by the way he acted. But I
have gotten over it. Sometimes the guiltiest wretch on earth is the coolest man. Accuse a guilty man of crime, one who has known it and has
lived in it and is accustomed to it, and he is often the coolest man you
can imagine. Accuse an innocent man of crime, a man who has lived an
upright life, and he may drop dead with fear, or he may tremble with confusion, or he may run away. No man can tell what an individual is going to do under circumstances like that. When you undertake to judge a
man's guilt or innocence by his conduct when he is accused, you are on
very dangerous ground. Mr. Hawley says that because Jack Simpkins
ran and hid himself therefore he is guilty beyond a reasonable doubt.
Now, Mr. Hawley is an expert on the subject of conversion and what it
does for a sinful man. I don't know whether he is a student of the Bible
or not. But I can call his attention to one historical illustration of what
an innocent man will do; and if he is as well posted on the acts that
prove guilt as he is upon conversion, he is making a pretty dangerous
statement when he says that if a man hides or runs away that is conclusive evidence of his guilt. There was once a great reformer and
agitator who lived on the earth and walked with men and who was a disturber in his day and generation, one of the kind of men that Mr. Hawley describes who always makes trouble wherever he is, because if a
man stands for truth and justice and righteousness he is bound to make
trouble no matter when he lives or where. There was a man nineteen
hundred years ago who stood for truth and justice and righteousness as
they understand it. And this man offended the Jerusalem Daily Adver-

tiser and the other fake newspapers which published the ads. of the
Pharisees of that time, and he offended the great and the strong and the
mighty raised a mob in Jerusalem, just as they raised a mob at Cripple
Creek and Victor, and they went out after this disturber and this out-
cast. What did he do? Why, he ran away and hid. Was he guilty?
He ran away and hid to save his life from the mob, from the righteous
mob that believed in order and law, especially order so long as they made
it. And he hid himself securely, until one of his friends and disciples,
Judas, betrayed him for thirty dollars, I believe it was. I wonder if he
was guilty! I wonder if he was a criminal because he hid himself because he did not wish to throw himself into the hands of the mob of
that time!

* * *

PERORATION.

"Gentlemen, Mr. Hawley has told you that he believes in this case,
that he would not ask you to convict unless he believed Haywood was
guilty. I tell you I believe in my case. I believe in it as I believe in
my very life, and my belief does not amount, nor his belief does not
amount to anything, or count. I am not an unprejudiced witness in this
case. Nobody knows it better than I. My mind is not unbiased in this
great struggle. I am a partisan, and a strong partisan at that. For
nearly thirty years I have been working to the best of my ability in the
cause in which these men have given their toil and risked their lives.
For nearly thirty years I have given this cause the best ability that God
has given me. I have given my time, my reputation, my chances—all
this in the cause of the poor. I may have been unwise—I may have
been extravagant in my statements, but this cause has inspired the
strongest devotion of my life, and I want to say to you that never in
my life did I feel about a case as I feel about this. Never in my life did
I wish anything as I wish the verdict of this jury, and, if I live to be a
hundred years old, never again in my life will I feel that I am pleading
in a case in which involves such momentous questions as this. You are
jurors in a historical case. You are here, with your verdict to make history, here to make history that shall affect the nation for weal or woe,
here to make history that will affect every man that toils, that will influence the liberties of mankind and bring weal or woe to the poor and
the weak, who have been striving through the centuries for some measure of that freedom which the world has ever denied to them.

"Gentlemen of the jury, this responsibility is on you, and if I have
done my part I am glad to shift it upon your shoulders and be relieved
of the grievous load.

IF CONVICTED SUN WON'T SHINE.

"I have known Haywood—I have known him well and I believe in him. God knows it would be a sore day to me if he should go upon the scaffold. The sun would not shine or the birds would not sing on that day—for me. It would be a sad day, indeed, if any such calamity could come to him. I would think of him, I would think of his wife, of his mother, I would think of his children, I would think of the great cause that he represents. It would be a sore day for me, but, gentlemen, he and his mother, and his wife and his children, are not my chief concern in this great case. If you should decree that he must die, ten thousand men will work in the mines and send a portion of the proceeds of their labor to take care of that widow and these orphan children, and a million people throughout the length and breadth of the civilized world will send messages of kindness and good cheer to comfort them in their bereavement and to heal their wounds. It is not for them I plead. Other men died before. Other men have died in the same cause in which Will Haywood has risked his life. Men strong with devotion, men who loved liberty, men who loved their fellow men, patriots who have raised their voices in defense of the poor, in defense of right, have made their good fight and have met death on the scaffold, on the rack, in the flame, and they will meet it again and again until the world grows old and gray. William Haywood is no better than the rest. He can die if die he must. He can die if this jury decrees it; but, oh, gentlemen, do not think for a moment that if you hang him you will crucify the labor movement of the world; do not think that you will kill the hopes and the aspirations and the desires of the weak and poor. You men of wealth and power, you people anxious for his blood, are you so blind as to believe that liberty will die when he is dead. Think you there are no other brave hearts, no other strong arms, no other devoted souls who will risk all in that great cause which has demanded martyrs in every land and age?

"There are others and these others will come to take his place; they will come to carry the banner when he can hold it up no more.

SPEAKS FOR THE WEAK AND WEARY.

"Gentlemen, it is not for him alone that I speak. I speak for the poor, for the weak, for the weary, for that long line of men, who in darkness and despair, have borne the labors of the human race. The eyes of the world are upon you—upon you twelve men of Idaho tonight. Wherever the English language is spoken or wherever any tongue makes known the thoughts of men in any portion of the civilized world, men are talking, and wondering and dreaming about the verdict of these twelve men that I see before me now. If you kill him your act will be applauded by many.

If you should decree Bill Haywood's death, in the railroad offices of our great cities men will applaud your names. If you decree his death amongst the spiders of Wall street will go up paeans of praise for these twelve good men and true. In every bank in the world, where men hate Haywood because he fights for the poor and against that accursed system upon which the favored live and grow rich and fat—from all those you will receive blessings and unstinted praise.

"But if your verdict should be 'Not Guilty' in this case, there are still those who will reverently bow their heads and thank these twelve men for the life and reputation you have saved. Out on our broad prairies where men toil with their hands, out on the wide ocean where men are tossed and buffeted on the waves, through our mills and factories, and down deep under the earth, thousands of men, and of women and children—men who labor, men who- suffer, women and children will kneel tonight and ask their God to guide your hearts— these men and these women and these little children, the poor, the weak, and the suffering of the world, are stretching out their helpless hands to this jury in mute appeal for Will Haywood's life."

ATTORNEY JOHN H. MURPHY.

John H. Murphy's part in the struggle is best told by a glowing tribute from the pen of the gifted Journalist and Orator John M. O'Neill, editor Miner's Magazine, which appeared in the Magazine August 8, 1907.

"THE NOBLEST ROMAN OF THEM ALL."

"While the Western Federation of Miners is being showered with congratulations, and while Richardson and Darrow, the shining lights of the legal profession, are receiving the highest encomiums of praise for their ability and eloquence as lawyers, yet, when we return to our normal condition of mind after such a grand and glorious victory achieved, we can behold the wan and wasted figure of a man looming up before us, whose very name and work are linked inseparably with the history of the Western Federation of Miners.

"The history of the labor movement of this country cannot be written in full without placing the name of John H. Murphy upon its pages. Murphy, the general attorney for the Federation, has made history in every state and territory covered by the jurisdiction of the organization. From the statute books of Colorado, Utah, Nevada, Missouri and other states, eight-hour laws arise as monuments to perpetuate the heroic energy of the man whose advice and counsel have been priceless to the organization that has faced courts, bull pens and deportation. Murphy, the attorney, is a man who has carved an enviable name and record out of the hard rock of adversity. His youth was not spent in the lap of luxury. As a boy he revelled in no dazzling magnificence, but was among the great army that was struggling for the necessaries of life. In his young manhood, with the bloom and blush of health upon his cheek, we find him upon an engine, serving in the capacity of fireman. But while he was exhausting his physical energies in the battle to secure the necessaries of life, this student upon the engine was communing with Blackstone and other great legal minds that had filled the libraries with the products of their brain.

"Murphy, the fireman, became the lawyer, and his heart and soul at once became aroused in a yearning desire to render service to the great mass that were struggling against the wrongs of oppression. In the state of Utah he made his first great fight for the constitutionality of the eight-hour law. With the ablest lawyers which corporations could secure to assassinate the validity of the Utah eight-hour law, Attorney Murphy ultimately won a decision from the Supreme Court of the United States which stamped him as a gladiator in the judicial arena worthy of the best steel.

"For four years Attorney Murphy has been in a battle against death. His close attention to his work and the long hours that he has spent in equipping himself to meet the ablest at the bar, has undermined his vitality, and he is now a physical wreck, bravely struggling against the inevitable.

"No member of the Western Federation of Miners can forget the services that Attorney Murphy has rendered to the organization.

"When the great trial at Boise, Idaho, opened, he arose from his bed of pain, and though the dew of death was gathering upon his brow, he wended his way towards the 'Gem of the Rockies' to give his counsel and advice in one of the greatest trials that has ever taken place in this country. Day after day he sat in the court room in the sweltering heat, and though he endured agony of a thousand deaths, yet his loyalty to the organization nerved him for the ordeal. The pale and emaciated face, upon which disease had written the lines of pain and suffering, lighted up with hope and joy whenever the defense scored a point in the great legal battle that had human life at stake, and the future of the militant labor organization of the West.

"When Haywood was at last liberated and vindicated by a jury of twelve men, and rushed from the court room to embrace the silvery-haired matron at whose knee he once lisped the name of mother; when he had clasped his invalid wife to his breast and folded in his strong arms his two loving daughters, in his great joy he did not forget the brave, fearless little man upon his couch of pain in the hospital who had braved death to be identified in the struggle. In that moment, when Haywood lifted in his arms the devoted attorney of the Western Federation ot Miners, and when there broke from the lips of the frail and wasted lawyer, 'Bill! In this hour of your great triumph be humble and thankful,' the great, big, whole-souled Haywood must have felt that here is a loyalty that rivals the fraternity of a Damon and a Pythias. In the years that are to come, when memory shall revert to the great trial that has taken place at Boise, Idaho, when men and women shall be paying tributes to the great lawyers who have participated in the battle, the name of John H. Murphy shall shine as 'the Noblest Roman of Them All'."

Attorney John H. Murphy passed away, at his home in Denver, March 3. His life had been one of continuous service to organized labor. In the death of this gifted attorney, the workers lost one of their staunchest and most able defenders.

HAYWOOD HOME AGAIN.

Sunday, August 4, William D. Haywood and party reached Denver just before midnight. Notwithstanding the lateness of the hour it was estimated 10,000 people had assembled and anxiously awaited his arrival to tender a welcome of cheers to the man who had spent nearly eighteen months in an Idaho jail.

It was a day long to be remembered in Denver! As the train steamed into the Union depot the thousands in waiting gave vent to their pent up enthusiasm. Carriages were in waiting and the party were escorted to the Albany hotel where a suite of rooms had been engaged for the family. When the party reached the hotel—cheer after cheer rent the air and cries for a speech followed in rapid succession. The vast assembly simply went wild over the man McParland had said "would never leave Idaho alive." Haywood, after a brief address that was drowned in the shouts of enthusiasm, mingled with the crowd and upon several occasions was lifted off his feet by the frantic crowd that yearned to grasp him by the hand and congratulate him.

No man in history was ever given a more hearty welcome than William D. Haywood upon his return home to the "Queen City of the Plains."

PRESIDENT MOYER RELEASED ON BOND.

After a delay of thirty-six hours after the verdict of the jury in the Haywood case, Charles H. Moyer was released from Ada County jail on a bond of $25,000.

President Moyer did not return with the Haywood party. An editorial in the Miner's Magazine, August 8, explained thoroughly President Moyer's attitude better than the writer would be able to do. The Editorial follows:

"Charles H. Moyer and wife did not reach Denver with the Haywood party. The president of the Western Federation of Miners did not feel that the time had come for him to receive the congratulations of his friends. He is yet facing that charge that was made by a combination that feels no scruple in putting a noose around the neck of the man who does battle for the interests of the laboring people. President Moyer has been permitted to enjoy temporary freedom under a bond of $25,000. When he has conquered his enemies and when the doors of an Idaho jail have opened to give liberty to his loyal and staunch friend, George Pettibone, Moyer will then feel that the victory is complete and will enjoy the downfall of the conspiring fiends who attempted to perpetrate the crime of judicial murder.

"The health of President Moyer and wife is not of the best, and it is probable that he will rest for several days before he takes up the active work of the presidency."

Long live the President of the Western Federation of Miners, Charles H. Moyer!

PETTIBONE REFUSED BAIL.

Formal application was made July 30, before Judge Wood to have Pettibone admitted to bail. The motion was submitted without argument and promptly denied. So George A. Pettibone still remained a prisoner in the state of Idaho. No generosity could be felt by the prosecution for the philosophical man who had borne with patience and a cheerful spirit eighteen months imprisonment. But while he was left alone in his prison cell the hearts of all organized labor was with him and pledged their "fortune and their all" in his behalf.

Steve Adams was still held to appease the wrath of corporate despotism but the Federation pledged itself to exhaust every dollar in the treasury, if necessary, in protecting his honor with the others.

The Pettibone Trial

"O, such a day,
So fought, so followed, and so fairly won,
Came not, till now, to dignify the times,
Since Caesar's fortunes."

—Shakespeare.

AFTER the satisfactory termination of the Haywood trial, the workers throughout the country seemed to fall into a lethargy of indifference, which had the effect of giving hope to the conspirators. Any one who understood the case in all its details realized it was as important to completely vindicate Moyer, Pettibone and Adams as Haywood—this was not a battle for individuals, one any more than another, but justice for all.

It was the concensus of opinion all over the land that the acquittal of Haywood was the vindication of the others and that the cases would be dismissed against Moyer and Pettibone.

George A. Pettibone suffered the pangs of imprisonment for a period of nearly two years. Notwithstanding his health was shattered, the conspirators, in cold-blooded brutality demanded that he be refused bail. So when the day dawned that had been set for the trial, he had been confined so long behind the walls of a jail that he was but a physical wreck of the philosophical Pettibone when he enjoyed good health.

Immediately after the disagreement of the jury in the Adams case in November, the Pettibone case was called and the long, tedious task of selecting a jury begun on November 27 Judge Wood announced that he would not allow the latitude of challenges that he had permitted in the Haywood trial. He also stated long sessions would be held each day in order to conclude the trial as quickly as possible.

The Pettibone trial was practically a repetition of the Haywood trial. Judge Fremont Wood presided ; James R. Hawley representing the prosecution and Clarence Darrow chief counsel for the defense.

Here I wish to mention that the prosecution during the examination of talesmen had the unexcelled audacity to ask each juror that took his seat in the box if he would convict Pettibone on the same evidence that was produced at the Haywood trial. If the juror gave a negative reply, the prosecution challenged the eligibility of the man to sit as juror.

JURY COMPLETED.

December 6, 1907, the jury to try Pettibone was completed and sworn in and were as follows:

J. H. Frazier, 25 years old, student; E. L. Evans, age 38, farmer; A. A. Tillotson, age 29, merchant; W. A..Palmer, age 40, liveryman; Wm. Stahl, age 48, placer miner; A. C. Boot, age 52, printer; Charles Wilmot, age 45, farmer; Arthur Estes, age 38, farmer; C. R. Smead, age 29, liveryman; J. H. Garrecht, age 40, butcher.

Both Clarence Darrow for the defense and James R. Hawley for the prosecution expressed satisfaction with the jury selected. The defense used but seven peremptory challenges and the state nine, each side being allowed by law ten challenges. Practically one week of actual work was consumed in empaneling the jury, and eighty talesmen were examined. In the Haywood trial it required more than three weeks to obtain a jury, three hundred and twenty men having been called. Court adjourned until Monday, December 9.

December 9, after a long conference between attorneys for the state and defense, a stipulation was signed, providing that all testimony introduced in the Haywood trial on the Bradley explosion at San Francisco, be read to the jury from the court records and that no witnesses on that feature of the case testify in the trial.

No agreement could be reached regarding the testimony on the crimes which Orchard claimed he committed in Colorado.

Judge Wood announced no testimony would be admitted concerning the deportation of miners, but practically all of those who testified in the Haywood trial both for and against the state were summoned as witnesses.

Judge Goddard of the Supreme Court of Colorado, again went to Boise, Idaho, to bolster up the confession that was framed up for Orchard by the Pinkerton agency.

When a judge on the supreme bench of a state is called on to make creditable the monstrous story of a confessed degenerate, it is needless to say that the judiciary is in need of disinfectants.

Here may be mentioned that the prosecution had a great deal to say about L. J. Simpkins, member of the Western Federation Executive board, not going forward and surrendering to the state. McParland had included Simpkins in the list of the "inner circle" that he had absolute "evidence" against. The opponents of the Federation claimed Simpkins keeping secret his whereabouts was evidence of his guilt.

Simpkins not testifying or surrendering to McParland was not evidence against him when even his former experience in the strike of '99 is known. People are not always guilty because they do not fall into the arms of their persecutors and become martyrs.

Simpkins had suffered nine months in the military stockade of the Coeur d'Alenes in '99 and to this day carries a scar on his breast from the thrust of a bayonet in the hands of one of Uncle Sam's "peace preservers." Notwithstanding his imprisonment of nine months he never had a trial. Is it any wonder Simpkins didn't seek any more of Idaho's interpretation of Justice? Does the English language contain another word that has had to bear the burden of so many crimes committed in her name as the word "Justice?"

> "Justice, while she winks at crimes,
> Stumbles on innocence sometimes."—Butler.

About December 10, Senator Borah returned from Washington and took his place with counsel for the state. Hawley stated the case against Pettibone in substance about as follows:

"Pettibone has been the paymaster into whose hands was passed the money given to the actual murderers by officers of the Western Federation. He was an actual participator in some of the crimes, and was the constant counsel, with others, engaged in the conspiracy. He operated a store in Denver, near Federation headquarters, and that store was the arsenal and the scene of the hatching of many a murderous plot. Pettibone was the most important factor in the conspiracy. He was mediator between the Federation leaders and the desperate men who made murder a trade and assassination a means of livelihood. It was Pettibone who manufactured a peculiar kind of explosive known as 'Pettibone dope' which, when thrown upon anything, causes fire which cannot be put out; it was he who sawed off the shotguns which became common weapons for the use of the assassin; he helped to make the bombs which caused a score of deaths."

For two hours Hawley spoke of what he termed the most gigantic conspiracy in the annals of crime, always keeping in the foreground the part which he alleged Pettibone took in it.

At the conclusion of the statement by Hawley for the state, Darrow calmly announced that the defense would reserve its statement until the conclusion of the state's case.

The taking of testimony was begun at the afternoon session, December 10. Two or more witnesses were heard and then Harry Orchard was put on the stand and under the guidance of Hawley retold the story of his crimes. It was the same story with but few omissions and one special addition. He went more into detail as to the manufacture of what he termed "Pettibone dope." Otherwise, the time of the court was consumed by hours in listening to the recital of Orchard's story of crime in detail. From the days of high-grading to the murder of Steunenberg. In the cross-examination by Darrow, it was brought out very clearly that Orchard had been a deep-dyed criminal, possessed of many aliases before he met either Moyer, Haywood or Pettibone, according to his testimony.

From the latter part of November to December 24, the case continued, long sessions being held. It would be impossible to go into the all the details of the testimony, the charge, the proof offered and the ultimate outcome is all the writer has made an effort to record.

The defense had filed a motion for an instructed verdict of acquittal. December 24, at the morning session, Judge Wood announced his conclusion on the question of corroborative evidence, and stated that there had not been sufficient corroboration of Orchard's testimony on the killing of Governor Steunenberg alone to warrant a conviction. He said that corroboration was necessary to establish a conviction. He also said that corroboration was necessary to establish a conspiracy and invited argument as to whether or not such corroboration had been given by the state and whether or not the defendant had been connected with that conspiracy.

This announcement created a great deal of excitement and some curiosity as to what his ruling on the motion would be.

In the Haywood trial Judge Wood held that it was necessary for the state to produce evidence tending to connect the defendant with the specific crime charged, independent of the testimony of Orchard. He stated he would rule on the motion Thursday, December 26, and directed the defense to be ready to proceed with its case at that time in the event the motion was not sustained. Attorneys for the defense offered arguments in support of the motion to instruct jury to acquit, going at length into all the technicalities of the law in the case. Senator Borah spoke for the prosecution.

December 26, Attorney Darrow, chief counsel for the defense, was too ill to rise from his chair and spoke with difficulty. By permission of the court he remained seated as he outlined his case to the jury.

On the 26th Judge Wood said he did not have his ruling ready and would be prepared by the following day, 27th. He, later, denied the motions filed by the defense that a verdict of acquittal be advised by the court. In considering the motion he

reviewed the independent testimony on each side of the crimes
confessed by Orchard and stated that in his opinion there was
sufficient corroboration of each of them to require the submission
thereof to the jury. Concluding, Judge Wood said:

"I think the facts already in evidence tend to show a conspiracy as contended by the prosecution and I think that the independent testimony sufficiently tends to connect the defendant
Pettibone therewith to require the submission thereof to the
jury."

On the convening of court in the afternoon of December 26,
Darrow again asked permission to remain seated as he addressed
the jury. This was granted. He reviewed briefly the early life
of Pettibone in Pennsylvania and of his coming West and engaging in mining in the Coeur d'Alenes, where he became president of the Gem union. In 1892, Darrow said, the defendant left
the Coeur d'Alenes and never engaged in mining again. "It was
a number of years after he went to Denver that Pettibone
heard of the Western Federation of Miners. But one day he
learned of a convention that was to be held and he attended it,
becoming acquainted with the officers and leading members. He
was later made an honorary member of the organization. He
never attended a meeting of a local union in his life, never paid
any dues and never had anything to do with forming policies of
the organization."

Darrow called attention to the alleged indignities to Simpkins in the Coeur d'Alenes bull pen, and of the bitterness that he
had always retained. He said that Haywood lived in Idaho at
the time and had considerable feeling over it, but Pettibone and
Moyer had nothing to do with the troubles of 1899 and had no
feeling in the matter. He told of the passing of the eight-hour
law in Colorado, of the Supreme Court declaring it unconstitutional, of the adoption of a constitutional amendment, of the failure of the Legislature to act, and of the smeltermen's strike at
Colorado City, Colo., and the resulting strike at Cripple Creek,
which he characterized as the greatest labor war in the history of
the country and the most disasterous to organized labor.

Harry Orchard was referred to by Darrow as a man always looking for easy money, who never stuck to anything except gambling. He told of Orchard's transferring his interest in the Hercules to Gardner, from whom he always had hopes of getting his claim back, and said the defense would show that he tried to sell this interest a year after he had disposed of it to Gardner. Darrow said the defense would prove by fifteen or twenty witnesses that Orchard swore vengeance on Steunenberg for the loss of his rich Hercules interests. Darrow declared that while Orchard was drawing benefits from the Miner's Union he was being paid as a detective for the other side and that he had claimed credit for a good many crimes with which he had nothing to do.

Darrow said that the defense would show that the Vindicator explosion was a pure accident and that Orchard went out and hunted up all the crimes he could and claimed them as his own, boasting frequently of crimes as his own which were not his.

Taking up the Independence depot explosion, Darrow said he did not wish to charge the mine owners with intentionally killing anyone —but that this explosion occurred while Orchard was working for Scott and Sterling. "Something had to be done to bring the troops back!" he said, "but they made a mistake of a few seconds and got a lot of men they never intended to."

December 27, Clarence Darrow was forced on account of ill health to retire from the Pettibone case for the time being and left for Los Angeles, California, where he had an operation performed to remove an abscess in the ear. The physicians told him after he made the opening address to the jury, that if he did not submit to the operation at once his life would be endangered.

This left Attorneys Wilson and Nugent in charge of the defense. The remainder of December 27 and 28 was consumed in reading depositions of San Francisco witnesses on the explosion in the Bradley home.

December 30, George A. Pettibone was seriously ill and court was adjourned on his account. He had been a very sick man all through the trial and had frequently been taken to the hospital at night because of his suffering but urged constantly that the trial be continued. At times his illness seemed very critical and doubts were expressed as to his being able to last through the long dreary trial.

On one occasion, while he was confined in a hospital, before his trial commenced, he left the hospital and wandered back to the jail and asked to be locked up. At this time the prosecution claimed Pettibone was not able to stand trial. So Pettibone made his escape from the hospital and returned to jail hoping to prove his health would permit the hearing of his case, thus thwarting the flimsy excuse of the prosecution.

Judge O. N. Hilton, of Denver, was entered December 30, as an attorney for the Western Federation of Miners.

December 31, when court convened Pettibone was in his place looking paler than usual from his severe attack.

After the formalities of opening court had been concluded, Judge Hilton, for the defense, announced that the defense would rest its case and offer to submit the case to the jury without argument. This announcement came as a complete surprise to the state. Judge Hilton said that he had gone over all the testimony and as the state had failed to connect the defendant with the crime charged in the indictment, it had been decided to offer no further testimony.

Senator Borah asked for a recess in order that the proposition of the defense might be considered, and Judge Wood granted the request. After a brief conference of the state's attorneys, Senator Borah stated that the question of dispensing with the arguments could not be settled until the instructions of the court had been examined. Judge Wood announced that he would have his instructions ready by January 3, 1908, and after he had instructed the attorneys to submit their suggestions an adjournment was taken.

There was nothing of special interest between December 31 and January 3. Only brief sessions being held. Judge Wood announced night sessions would be held in order to complete the case during the week.

January 3, the jury in the case of George A. Pettibone began its deliberations at 8:50 p. m. The last day of the trial was begun by James Hawley for the prosecution, and the instructions of the court. The defense carried out its announced intention not to argue the case, thus preventing Senator Borah from addressing the jury. Hawley fairly dared the attorneys for Pettibone to speak in his behalf, but they sat dumb when he concluded, and when asked by Judge Wood if any argument would be presented by the defense, Judge Hilton answered:

"Certainly not."

The courtroom was cleared before the jury retired, but the attorneys, defendant and a few of his friends waited for a time in the hope of hearing the verdict at once. No session of court was held in the afternoon on account of the illness of Juror Stahl, but he recovered sufficiently for the trial to proceed in the evening. Pettibone was very sick during the day, but insisted on the trial being concluded. It was necessary to carry him to the courtroom after supper on account of him being too ill to walk.

In closing Hawley argued that every circumstance in the evidence pointed to the guilt of Pettibone. Recalling the list of the score of men killed by Orchard, the prosecutor said that every one was an enemy of the Western Federation of Miners, and said that during that time no friend of the Federation met his death through violence; he said that while Orchard was, he conceded, one of the worst criminals of the century, he regarded those who hired him and directed him as vastly worse than he. Hawley concluded at 8:10 o'clock and Judge Wood asked Juror Stahl, who had been ill, if he felt able to proceed that night.

"Yes," answered Stahl, "I would like to hear from the other side."

This significant remark was passed and Judge Wood proceeded with the reading of his instructions.

The instructions differed to some extent from those given in the Haywood trial. Judge Wood held that on proof of the existence of a conspiracy to kill enemies of the Federation; that the defendant was a member of such conspiracy; that Steunenberg was regarded as an enemy of the Federation and that his murder was a result of the conspiracy, the defendant should be found guilty.

The jury was instructed that if these facts were proven it was not necessary to show that the defendant was cognizant of the crime charged in the indictment at the time it was committed. The jury was instructed that the accomplice must be corroborated by independent testimony tending to connect the defendant with the crime charged.

Saturday, 11:00 a. m. January 4, 1908, the jury in the case of George A. Pettibone rendered a verdict of **"Not Guilty."**

MOYER CASE DISMISSED.

The case of Charles H. Moyer was called by Judge Wood in the afternoon. James H. Hawley, representing Prosecuting Attorney Van Duyn, signified the desire of the state to have an order of dismissal entered. So the formal dismissal of Charles H. Moyer, President of the Western Federation of Miners occurred at 4:00 o'clock p. m. January 4, 1908.

"I am satisfied," said Judge Wood, "that the course taken by the district attorney and decided upon by attorneys for the state is the proper one to be taken. I have watched the evidence carefully, so far as the connecting and corroborating evidence under the statute was concerned in its application to this defendant, and certainly nothing has been developed in the two cases that would justify the court in submitting the case against him to a jury, unless there was considerable additional connecting testimony, and for that reason the case will be dismissed and an order entered exonerating the bail of the defendant."

At the request of the state the case against Dr. Magee and C. W. Aller, charged with perjury by reason of testimony given by them in the Haywood case, were also dismissed.

At the conclusion of the Pettibone case the Western Federation of Miners had expended a total sum of over $300,000, in the defense of those persecuted in connection with the conspiracy.

This ended the farce of the conspirators to murder judicially, the three men kidnapped from Colorado, February 17, 1906. The Federation after all the slander came forth from the battle grander and stronger to continue the great struggle for Industrial Liberty.

Adams is the only victim left to be vindicated. He stood trial twice in Idaho and in each case the jury failed to agree but in both instances the majority stood for acquittal. The enemies of the Federation finally came to the conclusion they could not convict Adams on the charge of being implicated in any of the Idaho cases, transferred him to Telluride, Colorado, on the charge of murdering Arthur Collins years ago. Court will convene in that district in May, 1908. A change of venue in the case of Adams will be asked. In case this is granted, his case will go over to the fall term of court. In the meantime, Steve Adams occupies a prison cell.

As this work goes to press, April, 1908, Charles H. Moyer, President of the Western Federation of Miners, is again at the helm—having assumed his duties as president immediately upon the acquittal of his friend George A. Pettibone. After the acquittal of Haywood and the release of President Moyer upon bond, the latter devoted his energies almost entirely to the Pettibone case—was untiring in his determination not to desist until the prison doors were thrown open and Pettibone walked forth a free man.

HAYWOOD ON LECTURE TOUR.

In January Mr. William D. Haywood started on an extended lecture tour through the Eastern states. Mr. Kirwan resigned as acting secretary-treasurer and Mr. Earnest Mills, executive board member of Greenwood, B. C., was appointed by the executive board to fill the position of secretary-treasurer. Mr. Mills has been closely connected with the movement for years and is recognized as a man of executive genius and ability.

Mr. Haywood was greeted in all the large cities by audiences that packed every meeting place. His Boston meeting probably ranks among the most notable of his extended tour on account of the history that has been made in the hall where the workers gathered to listen to him.

Faneuil hall, the cradle of liberty, was the scene of a historic gathering Monday night, February 17. It was the most impressive, enthusiastic and inspiring meeting ever held there. Patrick Henry, with words of fire, demanded constitutional rights. Wendell Phillips asked for the freedom of the negro. Haywood, in a speech logical, eloquent and so heartfelt that many wept, demanded the freedom of the wage slave.

Patrick Mahoney, of Cigarmakers No. 97, acted as chairman. As first speaker he introduced Joseph Spero, who did so much for the great Boston demonstration held on the Common May 5, 1907, where one hundred thousand people gathered to protest against the hanging of Moyer, Haywood and Pettibone.

Mr. Mahoney introduced Miss Luella Twining as the little woman who had come from the West and done more for the liberation of Moyer, Haywood and Pettibone than any other person. She made an appeal for Steve Adams and the miners in Goldfield. The collection was $150.

In introducing Haywood Chairman Mahoney said: "On this platform have stood many renowned men and women. Here our forefathers came to protest against the oppression of King George. They made the rafters of this hall ring for over a century. Never has so important a meeting been held here, never has so great a man stood on this platform as William D. Haywood." When Mr. Haywood, stepped forward he was given an ovation. The people of Boston had been waiting to see and hear him in Faneuil hall and they expressed their pent-up feeling in the reception they gave him.

His address was brilliant; many said the best they had ever heard in that hall. The Social Revolution is already producing its orators. He was interrupted by great applause. He made his points well and brought them out with telling effect.

A meeting had been arranged and widely advertised, permit granted and an audience of 3,000 congregated to hear Haywood speak February 5.   Delegations from all over New England
gathered and when the doors of Faneuil hall were thrown open
at 7 o'clock they poured in.   Ten minutes before the hour set for
opening, a messenger arrived with a notice to the committee on
arrangements canceling the permit for the meeting.   The crowd,
when this was explained, refused to go, and the janitor sent in a
call for the police.   For a time it looked like serious trouble, but
the police reserves were called and the crowd was literally forced
out of the hall and the doors locked.

Just then Haywood arrived and started to address the people
from the street corner.   The police threatened to arrest him, so
he advised the people to go home.   The city authorities explained
their conduct by stating they had had considerable trouble with
the unemployed and were afraid Haywood's speech would incite
them to riot.

Mr. Haywood also addressed the convention of the United
Mine Workers of America who were assembled in annual convention at Indianapolis.   This visit of Mr. Haywood's brought the
organization of the U. M. W. of A. and the Federation in closer
sympathy than ever before.   A step was taken, by the appointment of a committee from the coal miners to visit the coming
Western Federation of Miners convention to see if a joint understanding could be reached that would result in the amalgamation
of the two miners' organization.

All organized labor would be pleased to see the two great
miner's organizations united into one body—many times in the
past they have differed to a great extent as to tactics—notwithstanding this, when either were in trouble, differences of opinion
were forgotten and they were united when either was being
oppressed by their common foe.

The United Mine Workers contributed liberally to the defense fund—more than one donation of $5,000 being sent im-
mediately following the kidnapping besides the amount donated
by local unions of the organization.   It was very fitting that Hay-

wood should address the great convention at Indianapolis for the coal miners protested vigorously against the treatment accorded Moyer, Haywood and Pettibone and substantially backed their moral support with the necessary prerequisite—cash.

While Moyer, Haywood and Pettibone have been vindicated—tyrany still lives and Labor has yet to fight the battle for the Industrial emancipation of the toilers in the ranks and the complete overthrow of corporate tyranny—"Why don't they vote as they march on Labor Day?"

General Summary

THE Industrial conflict in the West while to the public at large has seemed more strenuous, perhaps, than in other sections of the country, but while that seems to be the case on the surface, the conditions that have prevailed in the West, exist to a large degree, over the entire country. The powers in control brook no opposition to their absolute tyranny. When the corporations are opposed they become insane—resort to any method in order to subdue.

The arrest and imprisonment of the president and secretary-treasurer of the Western Federation of Miners was due to an erroneous idea of the mine owners that if they could dispose of the officers of the Federation that it would disrupt the organization —they had resorted to every other means and failed. The unfaltering loyalty and eternal vigilance of these men had baffled every effort of organized capital to crush organized labor. For once the power of wealth had met opposition immovable—they had met face to face men at the head of a powerful organization, whose honor was proof against their bribes. They were accustomed to bribing judges, using governors as their willing tools, Supreme Courts to render favorable decisions for them.

The Federation has in its ranks many men who are capable and would jump to the helm and steer the Western Federation ship clear of the corporate rocks had the plotters succeeded in their plan of judicial murder. They met their Waterloo.

Upon the kidnapping of President Moyer and Secretary Haywood, Vice President C. E. Mahoney became acting president and James Kirwan succeeded to the duties of secretary-treasurer. They picked up the banner that had fallen at the prison doors and bore it on until the imprisoned men regained their freedom.

The Federation lost nothing in the efficiency of its officers. The labor movement has passed beyond that stage in which the fate of an organization depends upon one or a few men.

Whether in the work of organizing his men or conferring with the employers, President Mahoney displayed excellent judgment. At headquarters everything went smoothly under the direction of Secretary Kirwan. His genial personality, united with rare ability and unfaltering devotion to the cause of labor, won prestige for the organization and hosts of friends for himself.

The imprisonment of Moyer, Haywood and Pettibone and other members of the miner's organization marks once more the seduction of government from its primary functions as an instrument for the promotion of the common welfare of the people. It is a surrender by those in authority to the machinations of capitalist conspirators.

Organized labor nor the Socialist party do not object to punishment of crime—exactly the contrary—crime is especially repulsive if committed in the name of law. To organized labor, kidnapping is simply kidnapping whether taken part in by individuals or by governors officially. In fact, when the offender is clothed with official authority he becomes not only infamous but monstrous and inexcusable.

The beginning of the fight seemed a mere skirmish but soon developed into an irrepressible conflict between capital and labor. When the crimes recorded in the pages of the first edition failed to exterminate the miner's organization another was planned; the scene of it was laid and the conditions of its commission so arranged that when its actual execution had taken place, the world, following the accusing finger of the Mine Owner's Association, would at once fasten its gaze upon the officers of the Western Federation of Miners.

Backed by millions of dollars and the assistance of hundreds of agents, the mine owners stealthily enlisted the support of many other corporations in the concoction and execution of its final conspiracy.

This organization, through its power, political and financial, managed to reach the President of the United States. There is no question in the writer's mind as to the truth of the fact that the plutocracy and the government of two states at least, and the

National government, (at the behest of the two,) were leagued together to effect the judicial murder of the three men. Plutocracy selected the ground and laid out the campaign but the brave Spartans of labor from the Atlantic to the Pacific, from the lakes of the North to the Gulf at the South, raised its voice which said in its might to organized greed: "Beware, thou shalt not murder these innocent men! In the language of the noble Debs: "If Moyer and Haywood die 20,000,000 working men will know the reason why."

Twenty years ago brave, courageous men were hanged in Chicago, not because they committed crime, but because they stood with their faces to the foe, true and dauntless, with their hearts beating for the economic freedom of their fellowmen.

Since that judicial murder in Chicago labor has learned some lessons from the book of experience, that have enabled the wage slave class to observe more clearly the infamy of the monstrous system that sacrifices human life to perpetuate the merciless reign of profit.

The general sum total of the kidnapping cases reviewed are about as follows:

The state officials of Idaho, without the slightest hesitation, issued certificates of indebtedness to the amount of more than $50,000. When the legislature met the governor in his message devoted the greatest space to urging that body to not only redeem the certificates but advised that they make an additional appropriation, in order that the prosecution would be enabled to hang their victims to gratify a mine owner's organization and all at the expense of the taxpayers.

The governor in his zeal assured the legislature that with available funds the conviction of Moyer, Haywood and Pettibone was certain. Not only was the state looted of its funds but even the legislature was infested by a lobby that railroaded bills into law that gave the prosecution special advantages. The legislature appropriated $104,000 and that amount was practically exhausted at the end of the Haywood trial.

It mattered not that the state of Idaho paid out $40,000 to the blood-hounds of detective agencies to furnish a corroboration of the Orchard frame-up; it mattered not that $147,000 were expended in corpulent fees to attorneys and for booze and debauchery to make life one continuous round of pleasure for professional perjurers; yet the state of Idaho was again fleeced and plundered in the trial of George Pettibone. The prosecution must have known the case would end disasterously for their side of the controversy.

Trials of Colorado's citizens, most hated by the corporations; the secret kidnapping; special train to Idaho; denial of writ of habeas corpus; Supreme Court's decision; Orchard's tale of murder; a complete expose of Pinkertonism; Roosevelt's "undesirable citizen" utterance and the unexpected awakening of the workers—all these things in this particular case are now history in America's most thrilling battle of Capital versus Labor.

The writer does not suppose our children in the public schools will be told any thing of the details—our public schools will go on teaching reverence of "Old Glory," "that all men are equal," that this is the "land of the noble free"—that any poor farmer's son may become President of the United States, etc., etc. But by and by what an awakening!

Governor McDonald of Colorado in 1906, who allowed the kidnapping, and Governor Gooding of Idaho, who provided money for McParland and Orchard, the banks that floated the loans, Senator Borah and all others who gave freely their time and energy have been dealt a crushing blow, for these champions of "law and order" burned all bridges behind them in an attempt to convict.

The acquittal of Pettibone, January 4, and the dismissal of the charges in the Moyer case is a complete vindication of these men, which should compel that champion of the "square deal"—Roosevelt—to hang his head in shame for prostituting his mighty office in an attempt to sway public opinion and cover the retreat of mine owners and land thieves in the Northwest.

The cases aroused international interest and the workers in this country stormed the very White House doors with strange threats because of Roosevelt's statement.

Monster meetings and parades of workers were held every-where. In Boston alone 40,000 men and women marched twenty abreast, while 100,000 assembled on the city's historic Commons to hear the Chief Executive grilled and flayed in a dozen tongues. The mighty wave of angry protest served its purpose and a change of front was made by those who saw the growing senti-ment of class hate.

If the writer should offer a comment as to who of the three kidnapped men suffered the most in the Idaho outrage it would be from a general point of view, Pettibone. Moyer was president of an organization founded upon the principles of liberty—prin-ciples that will live through all eternity, even though the organ-ization be disrupted—Haywood in charge of the funds, what more natural than that they should be selected as targets by the enemies of organized labor.

And yet who can judge another's suffering or measure an-others happiness! To the writer, who knows each of the three men personally, there is something indescribably pathetic in the Pettibone case. Passing lightly over the manner of his kidnapp-ing from his home, wife, business, city and state, the slander of the capitalist press, the President's words of "undesirable cit-izen," we reach the acquittal of Haywood and the release of Moyer on bond. After eighteen months of confinement miti-gated, at least, by the presence of his fellow prisoners, he is left alone. He is made to endure another six months imprisonment. All the time aware the case against him cannot be stronger than that which failed to convict his comrade. Notwithstanding his health is failing every day, he is gayety personified. His spirit is at all times heroic and irrepressibly humorous. He wins the heart of every man with whom he comes in contact. During his imprisonment he refused to face the future with anything but the whimsical smile with which the heroes of Les Miserables met death behind the barricade.

Now, when, after two years of unjust imprisonment, he is acquitted by "twelve men true," his release comes to him as an expression of the world's belief in his innocence, he is broken in health by his long confinement. Here lays the tragedy! While unionism never had a more loyal friend, yet he was not even a member of the Western Federation of Miners at the time of his arrest. Years ago, Pettibone served months of imprisonment for the same principle he has served two years in jail in Idaho, later, the organization in recognition of his loyalty and indomitable spirit made him an honorary member. For the benefit of those who hate the word Socialism, the writer adds that Pettibone has never held a membership card in a Socialist local.

This man endured with a smile and a jest all an individual could be made to bear on account of his loyalty to the cause of humanity. Now that his liberty has been restored by a jury of peers, the very shadow of death seems to hover near. What can the world offer a man in return for loss of health? There is a pathos in these facts which no incapacity of the chronicler can obscure. There is a tragedy here nothing can hide!

Now that the legal proceedings are over, so far as this chapter in the class conflict is concerned, who is to compensate the victims who have been made the butt of the tyranny of the ruling class? Is Pettibone to suffer the injustice, false imprisonment, and ruined health of the past years without compensation? Is it possible that in the land of so many bitter and historical struggles for liberty and right—in the land which owes its existence as a nation to the fact of its struggles for liberty? and the proud—perhaps arrogant—position it holds amongst the so-called free and independent nations of the world, because of its demand for liberty—is it, can it be possible, that in this land whose very foundations, walls and roots are constructed out of the sacrifices made by our ancestors for that little of freedom which is left—that such things can be done?

As the last pages of this work is being completed, the very shadow of death hovers over the martyr in the case—George Pettibone. For awhile it was hoped he would recover. But Sundåy, March 15, a telegram was received at Federation head-quarters from San Diego, California, where he is confined in a hospital, announced that he was very low and not expected to recover. The telegram requested the presence of President Moyer at the bedside of his devoted friend and Moyer left at once for San Diego.

Some day, the unthinking man animal will shake himself from his long sleep and realize that his freedom is a farce, that his power is equally so and that he is but a strong man bound and when this time dawns he will shake off his fetters.

This brief history of the Idaho cases is not written for the purpose of eulogizing individuals. The acquittal of Haywood and Pettibone and the dismissal of the Moyer case has a greater significance than any consideration of individuals can impart to the drama. The verdicts of the Idaho jury mark a phase of the conflict between the employing and the working class. It is the dawn of consciousness. Henceforth he will make history as well as dividends, each page luminous with a. people's hope. The Idaho cases, like the strike at Cripple Creek, Telluride and Gold-field, Nevada, are a series of connected incidents in the class struggle.

The Mine Owner's Association, in this case, represented the employing class and was a clear forecast of the conduct of that class in many incidents that will write the history of the future. The acts of the employing class in any of the conflicts recorded are conspicious for nothing but their brutality and cunning. Capital in its fight against organized labor has depended upon money, fraud, the abuse of great power, the perjuries of convicted and unconvicted criminals, the destruction of legal safeguards to the individual, and recourse to the prejudices of men whose material interests had been menaced by the organization they attempted to disrupt.

In the Idaho cases, labor won its first great victory in a court room, won it through the aroused intelligence of the working class. The mine owner's gold weighed naught in the scales against simple truth. The plain straight-forward evidence of working men and women secured an acquittal from the jury and what is of vastly more importance, vindication at the bar of history. Ten years ago it is highly probable, the men would have been hung. We shall furnish no more martyrs. When capitalism makes the mistake of selecting a man for that role, we shall send him to the State house instead of to the scaffold. For humanity sweeps onward.

Capitalism's faith in gold is shaken, broken—labors' faith in man supreme. We need naught but light, they fear but that. By that we conquer. All the forces of the universe are behind the workers.

Had those men been hung through perjured testimony, no man prominent in labor circles could have felt secure. The course followed in this case would have been followed in scores of others. The Pinkertons could have vied with the Supreme Court for the favor of capitalists, but now they are thoroughly discredited.

There are so many salient phases of the case—so many that should not be passed lightly—one other should be mentioned in particular, briefly—the establishing of precedents.

The class in power have set precedents and examples that may some day be followed by the brain and brawn of this nation. Suppose, by way of illustration, the workers were as vindictive as the capitalist class have proven themselves to be. What would happen when the working class gain control of the machinery? They will have these precedents before them for their guidance. If they should follow the examples set by the class now in control what would prevent the proletarian government from kidnapping Justice Harlan, Rockefeller, Morgan, Harriman, or some of the lesser lights, the Rev. Buchtel, Gooding or U. S. Senator Borah, taking them on a "Kidnapper's Special," to some place where the workers control the powers of government, placing the accused on trial before a proletarian jury from which every capitalist had been carefully excluded?

Do you realize if the workers should do this at some future time, they would not establish a precedent but merely follow one recently established by the Supreme Court of the United States? The reader thinks that would be wrong—we agree with you that the workers are lovers of liberty and would be more just than the corporations have been. But the Supreme Court says this method of procedure is legal. If legal for mine owners, it must be alike lawful for the miners. So it will be seen at once a dangerous precedent has been established.

Cannot the ruling class learn something from history? Are they too dense to learn even from the book of experience? Do they imagine they will always be in control because they hold the reins today? The slave-holders had control as did their proto-types of the French Revolution. But a day of awful reckoning came when wrongs were wiped out in an ocean of blood!

The conflict between capital and labor does not cease with the vindication of the men kidnapped from Colorado any more than their liberty rights the wrongs endured by them. Every device that can be concocted by the retainers of capital will be used without scruple or mercy against those who dare to do aught to incite slaves of capital to tug at their chains. Before wage-slaves are free the list of Labor's martyrs will be a lengthy one. We must keep this tragic fact ever before us, remembering the words of a great statesman: "Eternal vigilance is the price of Liberty."

Even now, as the writer pens the closing words of this record, the country is in the throes of a financial crisis. Thousands of people who are willing to work have been thrown out of employment, leaving them penniless with families dependent upon them for food and clothing. It is practically impossible to convince a man the country is overflowing with prosperity when his loved ones are facing starvation, while he begs for the most menial labor at any wage in order to provide for his destitute family. Yet we read in the capitalist daily papers of multi-millionaires whose ambition (as expressed through the press) it is to dispose of their wealth "in order to die poor." It seems this would be easy to arrange if they were consistent. Alas, the best they offer is a Public Library, where human beings, who have

created their wealth, are perishing for bread. Books are a boon
—education a necessity. but when the pangs of hunger are unsatisfied they are scarcely appreciated. If Carnegie is consistent
in his expressed desire to die poor it could be accomplished by
ordering the great accumulation of wealth divided among the
poor slaves who produced it at Homestead.

In support of the statement that the conflict goes on and that
in every case the workers' rights to life and liberty are denied
by the ruling class we mention two mining sections of the country
several thousand miles between, that have attracted unusual attention recently. One in the coal fields of Virginia, almost unorganized. The other in the metal mining section of Nevada, thoroughly organized. The greed for profits has cost 23,000 lives in
seventeen years in coal mines alone. In Virginia in one mine
five hundred men were killed because the company found it
cheaper to murder than to properly timber and ventilate their
coal mine. A lesson of criminal profit may be found in this.
From this same mine was taken the corpse of a boy of eleven
years, a mere child. The press reports chronicled in a pathetic
way that other little trapper boys were hidden in the catacombs,
that they had never known the joys of tops or marbles—had
never been children. That the little fellow first taken out, with
his little face charred and begrimmed, was a weakling and in
life could hardly have lifted a bushel of coal. What pathos in
those words—what tragedy!

Pages could be written, yea, volumes, recording just such
incidents—this is only one individual sacrificed—thousands of
children have been murdered by greed for gold—profits. Not
necessarily in coal mines—in thousands of ways, in the factories,
department stores, the cotton mills of the South, cellars, garrets,
the cities of the United States are filled with sweatshops where
little lives are crushed out by over work, lack of food, proper
clothing, air and sunshine and all to gratify that monster
capitalism.

In the other section, Goldfield, Nevada, the miners refused
to dig the gold and be paid in worthless paper which the mine

owners would not guarantee. In defense of their position the operators said they could not get the money. At the same time they advertise a production of from $300,000 to $400,000 of gold per week. It is significant that just before the announcment of the payment of wages in scrip, the Consolidated Mining company announced it had enough money on hand to pay dividends for a year but nothing for the men who brought out the gold that created the dividends. The miners offered to wait until the operators were in a position to pay in cash or to let the ore stand as a guarantee for their wages but the proposition was refused. Troops were asked for by the governor of the state and Roosevelt rushed nine companies there. Immediately wages were reduced a dollar a day and the mines resumed with all non-union labor it was possible to secure. So the scheme of the mine owners was plain to the most dense.

The press reports have not mentioned troops being sent to Virginia to punish the operators for the disaster in the Monongah mine and it was only one of many disasters that have occurred on account of criminal neglect. Almost every day the daily papers report some horrible mine disaster and in almost every instance the cause is neglect in timbering and ventilation. Laws exist on the statute books regulating timbering and ventilation, they cost money, men are cheap. The ruling class never enforces the law against itself. Strange as it may appear to the casual observer of this state of affairs, we never read of the operators being punished. By the foregoing illustrations alone it will be seen that while the curtain has fallen on the Idaho cases, the same lessons go on, being repeated in different forms but Abraham Lincoln said:

"There are two principles that have stood face to face from the beginning of time, and they will ever continue to struggle. The one is the common right of humanity and the other the divine right of kings. It is the same principle in whatever shape it develops itself. It is the same spirit which says: 'You work and toil and earn bread and I'll eat it.' No matter in what shape it comes, whether from the mouth of a king who seeks to bestride the people of his own nation and live by the fruit of their labor, or from a class of men as an apology for enslaving another class, it is the same tyrannical principle.''

Under the operation of the capitalist system, recent calculations show that fifty-one multi-millionaires in the United States have amassed total fortunes of $3,295,000,000. Of this fifty-one, John D. Rockefeller, the oil king, leads with $600,000,000. Andrew Carnegie, the steel magnate of library fame, follows with half this amount. The secretary of commerce recently made a report showing the population to be 89,000,000. If we analyze the wealth of this total citizenship as given in his report we will find these fifty-one multi-millionaires control one-thirty-fifth of the wealth of the entire nation!

What an alarming concentration of wealth! What an alarming concentration of power! The class in control have gone insane in their frenzied efforts for the dollar. Men seem willing to sell their souls for one bright smile from the god of mammon. Money is king; money is their God; without wealth the doors of opportunity are closed; the doors of society are shut; the doors of the church do not welcome the unfortunate in rags and tatters. How will it all end? How shall this deplorable condition be changed?

The workers were united in demanding justice for their comrades, in the kidnapping case and thus saved them from martyrdom. United at the ballot box they could forever wipe out wageslavery which makes possible conditions such as portrayed in the foregoing pages, and usher in a form of government which will in the truest sense of the word be a government by the people and for the people where no man **could be master and no man slave.**

The brief history related in these pages is truly Labor's Greatest Conflict under the yoke of capitalism.

> "There is a moving of men like the sea in its might,
> The grand and resistless uprising of labor;
> The banner it carries is justice and right,
> It aims not the musket, it draws not the sabre.

But the sound of its tread, o'er the graves of the dead
Shall startle the world and fill despots with dread;
For 'tis sworn that the land of the Fathers shall be
The home of the brave, and the land of the free."

ORCHARD SENTENCED—LENIENCY RECOMMENDED.

Harry Orchard was arraigned in District Court at Caldwell, Idaho, Tuesday, March 10. He pleaded guilty of the murder of ex-Governor Steunenberg. March 18, Judge Fremont Wood sentenced Orchard in accordance with the law of Idaho in such cases, which is the death penalty. The judge in sentencing Orchard to hang May 15, 1908, recommended that the board of pardons commute his sentence to imprisonment in the penitentiary —adding that in spite of the jury's verdict in the Haywood and Pettibone cases he believed that Orchard had told the absolute truth. He stated that the state could gain nothing by hanging Orchard and on the other hand he could probably be of service in the future. The judge reviewed the cases and the substance of his decision summed up was to the effect that Orchard should be imprisoned in the penitentiary and not hanged. Will he be hung? The writer doubts it—time alone can answer.

That Orchard was promised a reward and immunity is generally accepted by thoughtful men who have made a study of the great conspiracy trial that was staged in the Courts of Idaho.

But Gooding has declared that the murder of Steunenberg must be avenged, and more than $200,000 has been expended by the state and Gooding scarcely dares to show leniency or mercy to the man who in open Court admits that he is the Cain whose hand cut short the life of an ex-governor.

Organized labor will keep its vision riveted upon the state of Idaho until the last word is written in the closing chapter of Idaho's tragedy.

REFERENCES:

The following works have been consulted in the preparation of the following articles:

History of the Ancient Working People—Ward.
Organized Labor—John Mitchell.
History of the English Language and Literature—Welsh.
Industrial History of the United States—Coman.
Class Struggles in America—Simons.
Bulletin Bureau of Labor of the United States.
Thirty Years of Labor—Powderly.
Labor Conflicts—Howells.
The Story of a Labor Agitator—Buchanan.
Mosaics of Grecian History—Willson.
Industrial Wars of Colorado—Langdon.

The Typographical Union

"Blest be the gracious Power, who taught mankind
To stamp a lasting image of the mind!
Beasts may convey, and tuneful birds may sing,
Their mutual feelings, in the Spring;
But man alone has skill and power to send
The heart's warm dictates to the distant friend;
'Tis his alone to please, instruct, advise
Ages remote, and nations yet to rise"

—Crabbe.

IT may be instructive to trace the history of a labor organization from its inception to the present time. The records of the printers are probably more complete and begin at an earlier date than that of any other organization. For this reason we will trace the Typographical union for a few years as an example of the progress of the trade union movement in general.

Historians differ to some extent, but John Gutenberg is usually credited with the invention of movable types, about 1437, but a strong contestant is Laurens Janszoon Coster, of Holland, who claimed to have invented wooden type in 1428 and at a later date metal ones.

All association among printers, prior to 1795, was temporary, having a single purpose, the compact was dissolved when its object was accomplished. When a question of importance arose a call was signed by members of recognized influence for a meeting, which was usually held at the home of a member. After a discussion, resolutions were adopted, committees appointed and frequently those present signed an agreement to stand by each other during the difficulty. Meetings were held frequently during the trouble, especially if a strike. Labor was not yet conscious; it was the age of the individual as opposed to the corporation.

The Typographical Society of 1795, lived two and a half years and raised wages to $1 per day for the New York City printers. The Franklin Typographical Society of Journeymen Printers of New York, was organized in 1799. It formulated the first complete wage scale ever adopted by the printers of New York and went on strike for its enforcement. It demanded twenty-five cents per 1,000 ems, not less than $7 per week in book and job offices and $8 per week on newspapers.

The New York Evening Post in its issue of September 19, 1803, contains the following acknowledgment: "The president of the Franklin Typographical Society, of New York, acknowledges the receipt of $83.50 from the Philadelphia Typographical Society, for the relief of such of our members as may be distressed in consequence of the prevailing epidemic." The Society ceased to exist in 1804, but the scale of prices formulated by it remained the standard until September 20, 1809, when the New York Typographical Society organized early in that year, formulated a new schedule of prices.

The Philadelphia Typographical Society was organized in 1802, and enjoys the distinction of being the oldest existing organization of the craft. It existed as a benevolent and trade society, as was the rule among the early societies, until 1831, when it became a purely benevolent association and as such exists today.

The Philadelphia constitution as adopted November 6, 1802, is the oldest constitution of a labor organization extant in the United States. It gives prominence to the fraternal features of the organization but does not conceal its industrial purposes. In addition to a sick benefit of .$10, "in every case when a member may be thrown out of employment by reason of his refusing to take less than the established prices," the board of directors "shall advance, if required, on his own security, in their discretion, such sum per week as will be sufficient to defray his ordinary expenses." If the person was unable to pay the loan, an assessment was to be levied on the membership, to this strike benefit fund was added an obligation to secure employment for members in preference to non-members; membership being conditional upon an apprenticeship satisfactory to the board of directors.

This union began expelling members for working below the scale of prices in 1806. The following year witnessed a demand for the exclusive employment of union men, the adoption of the monthly working card and a union employment bureau. The initiation fee was raised to $4 and the funeral benefit increased to $25. By resolution of the organization, monthly cards were printed by the Society, renewed monthly by the secretary for the benefit of those out of employment, stating that they were not in arrears with their dues. A fine of $1 was imposed upon any member for informing one who could not produce a card of a situation.

Provision for a "rat list" was made in 1808, by enacting that no member should teach an apprentice who was not bound before his eighteenth year, the penalty being not only expulsion from the Society, but notice of such expulsion was sent to other Societies of printers.

If the unions of today should resort to such measures, the United States Supreme Courts would soon come forward with an injunction.

A new wage scale was adopted in 1815. In the correspondence concerning its adoption, the New York employers were first to insist upon a uniform wage scale throughout the country. In the strike to enforce the wage scale of 1815, the Society again disciplined many of its members. The obligation required members to demand the scale as journeymen and pay it, should they become master printers. Such an one was brought before the Society on six counts, three of which are as follows: "First, for an attempt in combination with a few employing printers to lessen the established wages of journeymen. Second, for introducing into the printing business men wholly unacquainted with it to the exclusion of regular-bred workmen. Third, for refusing to give employment to members of this Society and employing one not a member in preference—a direct violation of the pledges he has repeatedly given us."

The experience led to amended by-laws in which they recognize "that the actions of men are influenced almost wholly by their interests, * * * as the interests of the journeymen are separate, and in some respects opposite to that of the employers, we deem it improper that they should have any voice or influence in our deliberations, therefore,

"Resolved, That when any member of this Society shall become an employing printer he shall be considered without the limits of the Society and not to vote on any question or pay any dues in the same."

In 1817, the Society resolved to keep a register of its members and their places of employment; one member was appointed to act in each printing office, "to give information as to the state of the trade and the chances of employment for more of our members." The Society made application to the legislature at Albany, for an act of incorporation, the House passed the bill, but the Senate added an amendment prohibiting it from interfering in trade matters. Two years later the act was passed with the following amendment to its constitution: "In no case shall the Society interfere in respect to the price of labor."

The New York union was the stormy petrel of unionism, but for its emasculation by the act of incorporation, it is probable that the Societies organized from 1815 to 1820, would, under its leadership, have been as distinctly trade unions as those organized from 1830 to 1850. From its organization in 1809, until it ceased to be a labor force in 1818, it enrolled 237 members. Samuel Wordsworth, author of The Old Oaken Bucket was among the founders of this union.

The first discussion on women as compositors was in the Philadelphia union in 1832. The Washington union called a special meeting January 17, 1835, because of a statement that girls were being employed in newspaper offices in Philadelphia, to break a strike. Resolutions were embodied in a circular letter sent to the Philadelphia, Boston, New York and Baltimore unions, asking if any girls were employed, if so how many, and what action these unions "proposed to take to prevent the further progress of the evil." The national convention of 1854, devoted much time to discussion along these lines; it was referred to a committee that recommended the matter be left to the local unions. The discussion continued until a union of women printers was organized in 1870 and sought admission to the international union. The convention of 1872, settled the matter by admitting women to full membership and demanding for them the same wage paid men.

Boston, Albany and Washington were organized in 1815, and the Baltimore Society is first mentioned in that year. The Washington Society was modeled after Philadelphia, at first largely a benevolent society, it still proceeded to regulate prices. It is the only one of the old. Societies that has survived until today and developed into a modern trade union, instead of a mutual benefit association

The Washington union had been waning for some time but in 1821, they made history by adding six new members and in 1822, five names were enrolled. Some improvements were noted and in 1824, the union joined in a civic parade on the Fourth of July, as a society, wearing as badges silver "printer rules." The minutes of a later meeting show the total membership took part. The printers had a press on a wagon in the parade and printed and distributed from it copies of the Declaration of Independence. This was the most notable feature of the celebration, July 4, 1824.

Free membership was a fatal mistake in the organization of the early unions. The member who paid his dues for a period, usually ten years, was freed from further payment. When this period arrived the union or Society, found itself with a free list which acted as a discouragement to new members. The early orders generally ceased to exist about the time the first list of free members appears. The Washington Society escaped disaster from this source through the shifting character of the employment. A study of the minutes of the union shows the character of trade unionism and its correspondence reveals its nature elsewhere.

The first convention of the National Typographical Society convened in Washington, D. C., November 7, 1836, and lasted five days. Delegates were present from Baltimore, New York, Washington, Harrisburg, Philadelphia, and New Orleans by proxy. Philadelphia was excluded because Washington Society proved their delegate had worked for the Duff Green establishment during the strike. Evidently the Philadelphia union did not know this when he was elected, for they at once expelled him upon his return. Duff Green was notoriously unfair. Another convention was called the following year.

The Society seems to have collapsed in 1840. September 28, 1850, the New York Union issued a call for a national convention, Boston and Philadelphia joining in the call. The National convention of Journeymen Printers of the United States, met December 2, 1850, in New York City with delegates from New York, Albany, Baltimore, Trenton, N. J., Philadelphia and Louisville. Boston, St. Louis, San Francisco, Washington and Cincinnati were heard from by letters. Discussion of the apprentice system occupied much of the time of the convention; from this time on the printers stood definitely committed against a system that had amounted to child labor.

Preparations for a general organization of the printers of the country were made at this convention. Organization was recommended on the basis of a national executive committee, composed of three members from each state, whose duty it was to carry out the resolutions of the convention, to gather information on matters of interest to the trade and to make a quarterly report of the same to the convention and make arrangements for its assembling. The convention also urged that the printers in every town containing six or more should form a union and that after February 1, 1851, no journeyman printer coming from a town known to contain an organization would be allowed to work within the jurisdiction of another union without a card.

The basis of organization for local unions consisted of seven principles. First: Regulation and adjustment of prices. Second: Traveling certificates to members in good standing, entitling them to assistance and traveling expenses from a union where they could not obtain work, provided they had not brought discredit upon themselves by intemperance or otherwise. Third: A registry of "rats" and unworthy members of the trade, with a description of them to be sent to every union in the country. Fourth: Receiving no stranger as a member without certificate of membership in the place from which he comes. Fifth: Levying a monthly contribution upon each member, sufficient to amount to $10 for each member as a reserve fund. Sixth: Giving any sister union the right to call for assistance to the extent of $1 per member, to be repaid in monthly installments of at least five per cent of the loan, beginning in one month after the difficulty had passed. Seventh: Granting certificates enabling a member to join another union without paying initiation fee.

Local unions were advised to abolish the benefit system and a plan proposed by which the combined unions of the country were to bid on the government printing.

The third day, May 6, 1852, of the Third National Convention of Journeymen Printers, which met May 3, at Cincinnati, Ohio, witnessed the formation of the International organization. There were delegates from fourteen unions, some did not seem inclined to participate. The permanent organization was formed by New York, Boston, Philadelphia, Baltimore, Cincinnati, Albany and Pittsburg.

The name of the organization was changed to The International Typographical Union June 11, 1869, at the Seventeenth annual session, held in Albany, New York.

The writer would be less than human, being a member of Denver Typographical Union No. 49, if the organization was not mentioned among the historic local unions of the International. The local of Denver, in a historic way, can claim a place with the most interesting of the Typographical organizations. In the first place, it was the very first local union organized in Colorado, if not in the entire Golden West.

Thursday evening, April 12, 1860, a few printers gathered at the home of Charles S. Semper, Terry street, Auraria, now Eleventh street, West Denver. Mr. Semper was then a member of the New Orleans union. General discussion prevailed and finally drifted to the subject of the New Orleans union. The host passed around constitutions and by-laws of the aforesaid local and the result was that it was decided to organize a Denver union. An application for a charter was sent in to the International and the original charter granted, shows the following names as charter members: John L. Merrick, president; George L. Sanborn, secretary; Charles S. Semper, treasurer. The other names on the charter are: T. C. Brown, Joe Clark and Thomas S. Tucker. The charter is dated June 9, 1860.

At the regular meeting June 6, 1897, President George Esterling in the chair, a motion was made by Chas. S. Semper, that the original charter of the union be presented to the State Historical and Natural History Society of Colorado, for safe keeping. The motion carried and Mr. Semper was appointed to take charge of the charter and deliver the same. The writer visited the state capitol building and copied the names given as charter members from the original document. It hangs in the Historical department as the first charter of a labor organization of Colorado—the custodian explained at great length all the history in connection with its origin—of which the writer was quite familiar. The charter in question had been damaged by both fire and water—a copy of it had been made which hangs in the hall where the union meets.

Hon. Chas. S. Semper, a charter member of No. 49, still lives and attends the local meetings of the union. The writer visited him and his estimable wife at their home, Semper Farm, nine miles from Denver, in search of data relating to the history of the printer's union. The pleasure of the visit was one not to be forgotten. Such a collection of statistics as this worthy man possesses—and how his face would light up with interest when asked various questions pertaining to the early history of the organization! He untiringly, told of the formation of the union at his home, explaining that the inspection of his new house was the occasion of the gathering of the men of the "rule and stick." His home was the fifth house built in Denver and the first frame house. The other buildings being ordinary log cabins of the very crudest form. He exhibited a complete file of "The Rocky Mountain News" from vol. 1, No. 1, to many years later. The first copy of the paper being dated April 20, 1859. Some of the copies he exhibited were printed on but one side of the paper and were about twelve inches long and six or less wide. This, he explained, was caused by a shortage of the necessary paper to print a full size paper. Some were printed on yellow sheets. The weekly—that was all that was published—sold for twenty-five cents per copy and the publication was awaited with deep interest by the entire population.

Mr. Semper said Eastern papers were scarce and were never sold for less than fifty cents per copy—were bought again after being read were re-sold at a gradual reduction in price as they became damaged until they were so worn they could not be read at all.

The first daily paper published in Denver was the Rocky Mountain Herald, of which Mr. Semper has a copy, very probably a file. In speaking of the printers' union he said all the members held office, and this statement brought a jolly laugh from Mr. Semper. It is little wonder, when you consider the contrast in No. 49 in the 60's with barely a sufficient number of members to hold office, the only paper with three cases of type, and now. Today the membership of the union is 475 and hundreds of linotype machines in the newspaper offices. Denver a beautiful city of 175,000 inhabitants, the equal of any city in the country, a list of morning and evening papers unsurpassed.

This veteran of the printers organization recited how the printers kept a flint-rifle standing near the case as they worked, for protection from the lawless faction which was composed principally of gamblers. The only paper had opposed the policy of the lawless element and as a result, they combined to "put the paper out of business." He said sometimes a band of the lawless crowd would ride pell-mell by the office and fire into the windows as they galloped by. So the printers kept a gun near for protection. It is certainly interesting to note the difference in convenience in newspaperdom now and the lack of proper equipment at that time. Time after time he pointed out columns of the paper where "small caps" run out and the compositor finished his copy with any "face" type left unused.

In one of the first issues of the paper it was announced that all future copies would contain a list of "immigrant arrivals." Among others published in a long list appeared the following: "Charles S. Semper, April 23, 1859, forty days from St. Joseph via Platte route."

The owner of the Rocky Mountain News owned the building in which the paper was printed, then as now—in '59 a two-story log-cabin with three cases of type and an old style Washington hand press—now a thoroughly modern building, a score of linotypes and the latest improvements in every department applying to the printing art.

Mr. Semper's home is a regular store-house of treasured documents connected with the labor movement in general— the printers' union in particular. Union cards of 1880; files of all his own job-work; files of papers back as far as 1857-8; badges, etc., etc. Among these treasures was a copy of a history of Trinidad, South America, his birth place. He showed the volume as a sample of his first effort at binding—the book was printed in 1850, many pages of history had been written in his own hand-writing and "tipped in" to make the volume more complete. The only data I wished to secure and failed, was where and when this brother first joined the Typographical union. He said he could not remember—that it was either Chicago or St. Paul and he was not certain which, but believed it was St. Paul—with this statement he enumerated the towns where he worked in those days. He was an all-around-practical-printer in 1853, when he came to the United States from

Trinidad, South America. He had been a member of the New Orleans local union some time when he came to Denver in '59. An autographed copy of Buchanan's "Labor Agitator" was on a stand in the parlor and he read the glowing tribute written to him and his wife by the author in the front of the book—explaining the warm friendship that had ever existed between him and the author, since the pioneer days in which they had been, as now, the closest friends.

The writer being a Southerner and naturally somewhat of a "rebel," mentions the fact that Mr. Semper served as a Confederate soldier in the Civil war. He established Semper Farm in '79 and has scarcely missed a meeting of the Denver Typographical union. He says that until very recent years he walked both to and home from the meetings—a distance of at least twenty miles by the road he followed. He is now past seventy years of age and at the time of the writers' visit was slowly recovering from a serious illness.

How my heart filled with reverence for this couple—sweethearts still—who are among the few surviving pioneers of the labor movement and the man a charter member of the first labor organization of the Centenial state!

The woman in this case shall not be forgotten. Mrs. Semper prepared a real "home-grown" supper—it is not polite to mention what you are served to eat—but the rule must be broken to mention the muffins Mrs. Semper makes and we will not tell the reader about all the other dainties she can prepare equally as well.

Mrs. Semper, as she walked to the depot with me, asked my opinion on the strike question. I mentioned that strikes recently, with but few exceptions, had been lost as a result of the Supreme Courts and the government itself, joining with capital against the workers. This had taught us we must fight our battles in the legislative halls and abandon the strike. She exclaimed: "That is the exact situation, now you are talking common sense!" Mrs. Semper has written many articles for publication and is a brilliant woman. The state of Colorado can justly be proud of such pioneers that have helped to rear a Golden Empire and the printers are proud to claim Charles S. Semper as a charter member.

After the formation of the International Typographical Union in 1852, the growth of the organization has been almost phenominal. As the history has been related up to and including the formation of an International labor organization it may be of interest to note the progress since '52, just a few years being sufficient to show what rapid strides were taken.

At the International convention held at Atlanta, Ga., 1890, 139 delegates were present. The membership including pressmen, photo-engravers, electrotypers, stereotypers and binders· was 24,194.

The Boston convention, 1891, 166 delegates were present and the membership had grown in numbers to 25,165. Philadelphia convention, 1892, showed a still greater increase—170 delegates present and the total membership 28,187. A similar growth continued each year, two years later, 1894, the convention was held at Louisville, Ky., and the total membership had reached 31,379, which included pressmen and all mentioned heretofore connected with the printing trade. In 1896, the convention was held at Colorado Springs. The records show the membership again reduced to 28,838, by the surrender of jurisdiction over the pressmen and binders.

In 1900 a total membership of 32,105 had been enrolled. During the year 3,000 more names were added. And so the history runs on until the Golden Jubilee convention was held in Cincinnati, Ohio. 205 delegates answered the roll-call besides ex-delegates and other visitors. 1,200 visitors registered at headquarters of which 152 were women. The membership at this time stood 38,364, without the electrotypers or stereotypers—jurisdiction over these two having been relinquished.

August 13, 1902, Cincinnati, Ohio, marked the formation of the Woman's Auxiliary to the International Typographical Union. Two years later they had forty auxiliaries with a total membership of 1,031. They have advanced rapidly ever since, growing in popularity and membership all the time.

In 1904, the International had surrendered jurisdiction over the photo-engravers and still had enrolled a membership of 46,-165. In 1905, the convention was held at Torronto, Canada, the registration showed 1,580 names and many visitors were in attendance that did not register. The membership of the International Typographical Union without the pressmen, binders, photo-engravers, electrotypers or stereotypers was 46,734, against 24,-194, in 1890, including all of the above. 46,000 seems to be its zenith, in 1908, after the close of the great strike for a general eight-hour day, the membership is between forty-five and forty-seven thousand.

It is useless to trace the progress from year to year but no doubt it would be interesting to note advances gained in obtaining better wages and shorter hours. The organization has progressed as rapidly along these lines as in membership. I shall note only the recent strike and the outcome.

In newspaperdom improvements in method was slow. But when it did arrive progress was extremely rapid. Mr. Lynch, president of the International, said in an article, published in 1906: "The newspaper industry felt the effect of the typesetting machine, and coincident with the introduction of that labor-saving device came the desire on the part of the newspaper printer that animated his forefathers of the past ages. He wanted to reduce the hours of his employment at his trade." The newspaper printer soon succeeded in this and 1906 found the eight-hour work-day established almost everywhere—in fact the rule had applied generally for several years.

The book and job field was a more difficult field for the linotype to fill. As time passed even this obstacle was overcome. Not only was the typesetting machine introduced, but other labor saving devices that could be used in the commercial branch of the printing trade. The book and job printer soon followed the example of his newspaper brother and demanded a shorter work day. As a result of this agitation the nine-hour day was established. It did not satisfy the general membership of this progressive organization that a part of its membership should have an eight-hour day and the job printers in some cities work nine hours, so a general demand was made for eigth hours where it had not already been granted.

The battle cry had been taken up in 1905: "We propose to sell to the employer eight hours out of every twenty-four, and we will do as we please with the remaining sixteen!" With this slogan, January 1, 1906, in every office where eight hours was not recognized as the maximum for a days' work the printers "put on their coats."

Many assessments of various per cents on the earnings of the membership was levied as the necessity for money in large denominations grew, but to give the reader a fair idea of the general feeling of the membership, it may be mentioned that a ten per cent assessment on the total membership was submitted to referendum for their approval or disapproval and a majority of nearly thirty thousand voted in favor of the assessment plan. Gradually, as the strike progressed and victories were won, the per cent collected from the membership was reduced until March 1, 1908, marked the complete suspension of the strike assessment —which means no more funds are needed—a complete victory fairly won and a general eight-hour day for all of the craft.

The newspaper publishers were less able to resist demands that are based on justice than the employing printers of the job offices; they may have the same inclination to resist but their business is more liable to suffer seriously by industrial strife— so it was not their devotion to the unions but their own material interest that the newspaper employers considered. The employing printer of the book and job office considers himself more as a manufacturer and is governed in the majority of cases by the methods followed generally, by the Manufactures' Association. If you follow the history of the labor movement from its inception to the present you will find in every instance, where the workers banded together for mutual benefit, their employers organized to defeat their plans. The Typographical union was met likewise by the organization of the employers known as the United Typothetae of America. This organization stubbornly resisted the demand for an eight-hour day. The employers were so foolish as to believe it would be easy to win a victory over the Typographical union and that all that was necessary was to resist. So those most opposed to the union movement, welcomed the announced intention of the union printers to demand a general eight-hour day. In a few localities, the employing printers hurried matters along by taking an arbitrary position in advance, they were so sanguine of success.

The trade union movement has seldom witnessed such stubborn resistance on the part of the employers as characterized the efforts of the Typothetae to defeat the printers. The employers were supported morally and financially by other associations of a like nature.

As is usually the case in such struggles between the employing and the working class, the former used the courts to their advantage against the workers. It has been generally admitted the strike of the printers was the most peaceable of any of the conflicts between capital and labor of recent years. The law was strictly observed by the strikers. Despite this, the printers were haled before courts in numberless instances, charged with all the crimes that usually make up the application for injunction writs filed by corporation attorneys. As is also quite common, the judges accepted the affidavits submitted by the employers' attorneys and issued temporary injunctions against the printers, prohibiting picketing and boycotting. These injunctions were later made permanent, despite any evidence that the union advanced. The Federal and state judges trampled under foot all law or sense of right and justice in their eagerness to serve the Typothetae and defeat the union. While the union observed strictly, the recognized laws it did not hold sacred the decisions prohibiting picketing but continued their "peaceful pickets" around all unfair establishments in all kinds of weather.

The printers considered the injunctions "class legislation and therefore, "unconstitutional."

Did they go to jail for ignoring the injunctions? Certainly they did—but others were willing to fall in line and continue the picketing while their brothers served the jail sentance for violating the injunctions. The various injunctions helped to prolong the strike but did not succeed in defeating the cause for which it was called. They simply served to arouse the workers to the dangers that confront them in the injunction court procedure when the courts are controlled by the trusts of this country.

A year of warfare practically won the victory for the Typographical union, although the struggle continued in some places —the majority of the shops had fallen in line and signed the contract granting eight hours before the close of 1906. The fact that the International at the close of February, 1908, discontinued the assessment upon the membership as no longer necessary in a few words means the victory has been won and that the employing printers realize that the job printers as well as those employed on newspapers will "sell to the employer eight hours out of every twenty-four and do as they please with the remaining sixteen."

The cost of the strike to the International is estimated by conservatives at three and a half million dollars and by others at five millions which does not include loss in wages.

Mr. Lynch in an article entitled: "A Struggle for Eight Hours," dated June 14, 1906, published in the Colorado Springs' Souvenir, closed with the following:

"Many people take into consideration only the cost of a strike—this or that strike cost a million dollars—or two million was expended. What a terrible waste of money. In our conflict, a conservative estimate of the loss of money paid out by the union, in money lost in wages, and in money lost by the employers, is at least five million dollars. But the cost of a strike is a bagatelle as compared to the benefits that will accrue in future years. For more than fifty years, the newspaper men struggled for equitable conditions; strike after strike occurred, but in the end industrial peace was achieved. This history will repeat itself in the book and job branch, resulting in a period of peace and prosperity that we hope will last for years.''

This article was written after six months of strike—that the printers won has become a fact since then—the financial cost was many millions if loss in wages is considered—but the victory priceless.

The printers are justly proud of their progress as an organization. In addition to the good accomplished in gaining shorter hours, better wages, etc., etc., we have the distinction of maintaining a Home for aged or distressed members, the bounty of which is unpurchasable. This Home is the only institution of the kind in the United States and as far as the writer can ascertain, the only one of a like nature in the world.

The Union Printers' Home is located at the very foot of Pikes' Peak, Colorado Springs, Colorado. The Home was built and is maintained by the membership of the International Typographical Union. In the early days it was known as the Childs-Drexel Home for Union Printers—this name came as a result of a gift by the late George W. Childs and Anthony J. Drexel, each of whom contributed $5,000 to the International Typographical union in token of their life-long friendship for union printers. This was the first money set apart to be used in some like manner that would benefit the entire organization. At first it was hard to determine in just what manner the money could be best used with the final result as stated. The printers, feeling extremely grateful and wishing to honor the two gentlemen for their gift, called the Home in its infancy the Childs-Drexel Home. Aside from the $10,000 contributed to the institution by Childs and Drexel and a small bequest by Julia A. Ladd, the money spent upon it has come voluntary from the pockets of union printers. The contribution to the support of the Home to each member of the union is but ten cents per month per member but when combined means something like six hundred thousand dollars. In a half minute each day a union printer earns what he contributes daily to sustain this beautiful Home.

The Union Printers' Home was dedicated May 12, 1893; the original cost of the main building, $70,114.44; later an annex was built which cost $20,820.54; superintendent's cottage, $3,400;

laundry and its equipments, $12,241.55; barns, green houses, corrals and other outbuildings, $10,000; fire escapes, $2,000. The tents for tubercular patients cost $2,000. The beautiful granite archway at the entrance to the grounds, cost $1,500. Many other figures of cost of various additions and improvments could be added but the foregoing will give the reader an idea of the cost of building and maintaining the Union Printers' Home, the greatest monument to unionism in the world. To appreciate the great advantages, the perfection of the plan and the enormity of the undertaking it would take a visit to the Home to fully realize. Visitors are always welcome and entertained hospitably. The Home has eighty acres of land; five hundred shade trees, seven acres of green lawns, five thousand square feet of cement sidewalks; its own conservatories; a dairy unsurpassed; poultry yards of the highest class and everything necessary to the health and happiness of those who are sick or disabled in any manner. Every year marks some decided improvement, an enlargment or addition in size or comfort of the Home. The library was made a specialty recently with the result that the Home has a splendid collection of the best books published.

In short, the Union Printers' Home is the pride of every member of the craft and justly so. The rules are broad—more so than any city or county institution—it does not require a year of "red tape" for a union printer to take advantage of the benefits of this institution of which every member is a part owner.

The management of the Home is in the hands of a superintendent and board of trustees, elected by the membership. At this writing the management is as follows: Chas. S. Deacon, superintendent; James M. Lynch, J. W. Bramwood, Thos. McCaffery, L. C. Shepard, W. J. White, Thos. F. Crowley and T. D. Fennessy, trustees. Mr. Deacon has been in charge as superintendent for many years, this fact alone, proving his able management and popularity. Mrs. Deacon is a "mother" to every inmate of the Home they will tell you.

> Where giant mountains lift their crests,
> And valleys golden secrets hold,

UNION PRINTERS' HOME, COLORADO SPRINGS, COLO.

Erected and Maintained by the Membership of the International Typographical Union.

And perfect air makes men live long,
  There stands a home for printers old.

For knights of keyboard, stick and rule,
  Whose union faith has stood the test,
If "slow" beneath the weight of years
  Or by the needs of illness pressed.

It sent our banners to the van.
  It said our brotherhood was true.
The crowning glory of the craft,
  It honors Childs and Drexel, too,
Whose names shall live in union hearts
While printers ply the art of arts.
                              —Sam Christy, Indianapolis.

1908 marks the establishment of a pension fund by the International Typographical Union. Another move in the right direction. This will mean that the superannuated members will eventually receive a pension. The apprentice question is being given a great deal of attention. Schools or unions of apprentices being taken up. These meetings are to be attended by one or more members of the Typographical union that will guide the juniors in the "straight and narrow path," educating them not only in perfecting themselves as skilled mechanics in the trade but also instilling into their minds the rudiments of unionism.

Supreme Court vs. Labor

"Tyranny
Is far the worst of treasons. Dost thou deem
None rebels except subjects? The prince who
Neglects or violates his trust is more
A brigand than the robber-chief."

—Byron.

THIS work would not be complete without some mention of the numerous decisions of the Federal and state Courts in favor of the employers and striking a direct blow to the wage workers of the land. The New York Worker recently published a compilation of decisions in favor of the trusts. The following compiled from the Worker and from various other sources, is a summary of a few of the most important anti-labor decisions rendered by state and Federal Courts, covering a period of more than six months:

In August, 1907, Judge Dean of Arizona, issued an injunction forbidding Miners' Union No. 106, each of its officers or anybody else connected or in sympathy with it to make any efforts to get workmen to join their strike and especially commanding them "to desist absolutely from writing or sending through the mails any written or printed card, circular, letter, or other communication conveying to any patron or prospective patron of the plaintiff any information of the miners' strike."

In September, 1907, a Vermont Court issued an injunction forbidding the Quarrymen's Union to try to persuade any employee of the Associated Quarry Owners to join the strike.

October 19, 1907, the United States Circuit Court of Minnesota upheld a lower Court in issuing an injunction against the Brotherhood of Carpenters, forbidding the carpenters to carry out their resolution not to use materials manufactured in nonunion factories.

October 21, 1907, Judge Thompson of the United States Circuit Court of Ohio, issued an injunction forbidding the officers of the International Pressmen's Union to pay benefits out of the union's funds or to do anything to support the union's demand for an eight hour day and forbidding the union to take a referendum vote on the question of striking.

October 23, 1907, Judge Dayton of the United States District Court of West Virginia, issued an injunction forbidding the national or district officers of the United Mine Workers to make any attempt to organize the employees of the Hitchman, Glendale and Richland Coal Companies in that state.

November 18, 1907, Judge Hazel of Buffalo, issued an injunction forbidding the Switchmen's Union to take any action toward declaring a strike for reduction of hours or increase of wages on the Lackawanna railroad.

December 13, 1907, a Circuit Court in Ohio, wiped off the statute books, the state law prohibiting the employment of young boys at night work in the mills and factories.

December 17, 1907, the Equity Court of the District of Columbia, issued an injunction forbidding the American Federation of Labor to publish in its official organ the name of the Buck Stove & Range Co., as one of the firms that workingmen ought not to patronize on account of its bitter antagonism to the labor movement.

January 6, 1908, the United States Supreme Court declared unconstitutional the Federal law making railway companies engaged in interstate commerce liable for damages in the case of employees killed or injured at their work as a result of defective equipment or negligence of fellow servants.

January 24, 1908, Judge Phillips of the Common Pleas Court of Cuyahoga County, Ohio, ordered the dissolution of the Amalgamated Window Glass Workers of America, on the ground that the union is "a labor trust, an unlawful combination in restraint of trade."

January 27, 1908, the United States Supreme Court declared unconstitutional the Federal law forbidding railway companies engaged in interstate commerce to discharge employees for belonging to a labor organization.

February 3, 1908, the United States Supreme Court rendered a decision against the United Hatters of North America in favor of D. Loewe & Co., hat manufacturers of Danbury, Conn., and indirectly against the American Federation of Labor. The Loewe concern run one of the twelve non-union hat factories in the United States, seventy being unionized. The United Hatters, in the hope of inducing Loewe & Co. to comply with union conditions of work, hours and wages, has carried on an active campaign to induce workingmen and sympathizers with the labor movement to buy only union-made hats and to particularly refrain from buying hats made in the Loewe concern. Loewe was printed in the "We Don't Patronize" list run in the American Federationist.

Loewe sued the union, its president and two hundred of its individual members under the Sherman Act. The United States Circuit Court dismissed the case as not properly falling under the provisions of that law. Loewe therefore appealed. The Circuit Court of Appeals reaffirmed the decision, but the Supreme Court reversed it, upholding the claims of the capitalist plaintiff.

Loewe alleged that his business had suffered to the amount of $80,000—that is, he thought he would have made $80,000 more profit if the working people had not been informed of the fact that his factory was a non-union place. He therefore proposes to collect from the union and its members $280,000—three times the amount of his loss, plus $40,000 for the expenses of the suit.

The Sherman Act is commonly spoken of as an anti-trust law. Its ostensible purpose, when enacted by the Republican party, was to prevent combinations of great manufacturers or traders with railroads, etc., from combining to crush smaller competitors and drive them out of business. In practice, under Republican and Democratic judges, it has been used almost exclusively against labor organizations.

At a glance the reader can see that in the decision of February 3, the Court takes the position that unions shall not boycott, that the publication of a list of names as "unfair" to organized labor is a criminal offence and punishable by law. The boycott has been used for many years as one of labor's strongest weapons. The recent decisions only tend to more fully demonstrate to the workers the necessity of filling these positions, occupied now by representatives of the trusts, by members of their own class.

Backward Glances

"They never fail who die
In a great cause; the block may soak their gore,
Their heads may sodden in the sun; their limbs
Be strung to city gates and castle walls;
But still their spirits walks abroad. Though years
Elapse, and others share as dark a doom,
They but augment the dark and sweeping thoughts
Which overpower all others and conduct
The world at last to freedom."

—Byron.

THE strike is probably the most ancient of labor's weapons, the first protest against injustice. They have continued from Pharaoh's brick yard to the present. The early history of Greece, Sicily and Rome records disastrous strikes. The strikers were made up of freemen and slaves—the latter owed their miserable condition to birth, conquest, debt or crime, the former weighed down by poverty differed from the slave only in the fact that he had no master.

One of those early strikes left an indelible mark on the pages of history. It occurred during the conflict between Athens and Sparta in the silver mines of Laurium, B. C. 413. It was a revolt of 20,000 workers condemned to the most inhuman toil. Men and women were stripped of their clothing, their bodies painted, their legs loaded with chains, driven on by the clubs of overseers.

In this condition they were set at work drilling rock, breaking it in pieces and carrying it to the mouth of the shaft. Outside were the smitheries, machine shops, etc. The money and supplies of war for Athens were made here. Their work continued three hundred and sixty-five days in the year, they received eighteen cents per day. Employers considered the wage a tempting one.

The splendors of Athenian civilization rested upon their

labors. The Athenians considered themselves kind masters because the citizens of other states treated their slaves still more harshly, the status of labor was yet more degraded.

If such was the condition of the worker among the most enlightened people of antiquity, consider how dire the state from whence labor has emerged.

The strike destroyed the supremacy of Athens and placed Sparta at the head of the Grecian states, it was a victory of aristocracy over democracy. The forces of reaction triumphed over the forces of progress.

When the strikers went over to the Spartans the latter were enthused, the former disheartened. They struck a blow that staggered civilization, but they improved, for the moment, their own condition. What else should they have considered? They were only burden-bearers of the civilization that rested upon them with such crushing weight. The doctrine of each for himself was carried out in that strike. Philosophy, literature and art suffered in consequence. What then? No civilization can endure that rests upon the misery of the worker. Labor will wage no more battles in which victory will but lengthen the night of her bondage, increase the weight of her chains.

Rome was the scene of many fierce labor wars—or strikes. There was an attempt on the part of slaves to burn the city in the year 417 B. C. Another desperate revolt occurred 194, B. C. It was caused by the appropriation of the public lands by the rich men of that time—much like the rich land thieves of today. A third of a hard-working population were being choked from the means of subsistence. The revolt was crushed by a Roman army and 2,500 public executions were its bloody fruit.

The subterranean quarries of Rome furnished stone for the public buildings were differentiated into sewers, workshops and prisons, a person, once thrown in, never again saw the light of day.

Everywhere the success of the Roman arms was followed by the enslavement of great masses of people. At long periods the workers struck back endeavoring to ameliorate their awful conditions. The names of some of the leaders have survived to the present time, but have only recently been made accessible to the general reader.

The poor and lowly have not written the records nor kept the archives of history. We should have had a very different account had it been written by the lowly. Names long revered are toppling from their lofty pedestals as mankind recognizes that they were the servitors of oppression, and others lost in the gossip of a kings debauches or covered with the opprobrius epithet of demagogue and agitators are being restored their rightful place in the affections of the race.

We can but call the roll of a few who deserve remembrance. The brothers Caius and Tiberius Gracchus who fought against a landlordism worse than that which has devastated Ireland, killed by the Roman nobility. The bondman Drimakos, Viriathus bringing the Roman armies to a halt in Spain; Eunus, a slave rising through revolt, to the rule of Sicily; Clodius an eloquent lawyer restoring to the workingmen the right of organization, and in so doing encompassing the downfall of Cicero; Spartacus, the gladiator, rising at the time the Roman nobles were attempting to destroy the right of organization among the workers defeating numerous armies and only beaten at last through divisions in his own ranks; these are a few of the names that deserve a place in Labor's Pantheon.

In this connection we might note the slow advance of labor. Conceded the right of organization among primitive people but beaten down as soon as wealth is accumulated and concentrated. Battling under the Caesars for rights fully enjoyed centuries before, suffering restrictions today unknown to our fathers. Yet enjoying rights and possessing powers to which the people of every other age were strangers. The advent of the people is a very modern event. The first public meeting held to enlighten Englishmen in regard to their political rights was in 1769. In 1795 a law was passed giving a justice of the peace power to disperse a public meeting, if it consisted of more than twelve people a refusal to dispurse one hour after being ordered to do so was punishable with death. In 1798 five journeymen printers who had been invited by their employers to meet them and discuss grievances, were upon their arrival arrested, tried and sentenced to penal servitude. For many hundred years Parliament had legislated to keep down the wages of the workers.

One of the first acts of the authorities in our own country was to determine wages—and not in the interests of the laborer. In 1633, the General Court of Massachusetts, decreed that skilled laborers, specifying the crafts of that day, were not to receive more than fifty cents per day. The wage of the better class of unskilled workers was set at thirty-six cents per day. In 1672 wages for common labor did not exceed fifty cents per day and remained almost stationary until after the Revolutionary war.

A strike occurred among the sailors of New York in 1802. The first trade union in the United States was that of the New York Society of Journeymen Shipwrights. A union of house carpenters was incorporated in 1806 and a printers union called the New York Typographical Society existed almost from the beginning of the century. The shipwrights and caulkers of Boston were incorporated under a charter granted by the legislature of Massachusetts. They were considered as a benefit society without any right to take aggressive action.

Then as now the press was unfriendly to labor. The first paper published in its behalf was the Workingmens' Advocate in 1825.

The first trade union council was convened in New York in 1833. With the improvement in facilities for communication, local unions were converted into national and international organizations.

The International Typographical Union formed in 1852, was the first national trade union in the United States. They were followed by the hatters in 1854, the iron and steel workers in 1858 and the Iron Moulders of North America in 1859.

The Civil war ushered in great combinations of capital and was followed by a more general organization of labor.

The Brotherhood of Locomotive Engineers was organized in 1863, the Cigarmakers International Union and the International Union of Bricklayers and Masons in 1864. Between thirty and forty national organizations were in existence at the close of 1866.

A working man's party was organized. A bill promising an eight-hour day was passed by Congress in 1869. The first efficient limitation of the working day for women and children was passed by Massachusetts in 1874. The limit was sixty hours per week and provided that the children should show a school certificate.

The Knights of Labor organized in 1869, maintained a precarious existence for the first ten years, had reached but 100,000 in 1885, in the following year however, it added 700,000 members. This marked its zenith. Corruption, internal dissension and the rise of a new organization, the American Federation of Labor, which was organized in 1881, hastened its downfall. One of the most important acts growing out of its agitation was the passage of the Alien Contract Labor Law. Secretary of Commerce and Labor Straus' decision, sustained by Attorney General Bonaparte, that the law did not apply to immigrants brought over by state agency has practically nullified the effect of the law. The mill owners of the South, the coal barons of West Virginia, the employing lithographers have availed themselves of this decision.

One of the first effects of a panic is to reduce wages. This was first clearly shown in the panic of 1873. Month by month wages went down. When the Centenial of the Declaration of Independence was celebrated the workers were suffering more from the tyranny of capitalism than the colonists had from King George.

The spirit of revolt spread among the workers. It reached a climax when President Scott of the Pennsylvania railroad announced a ten per cent reduction in wages that had already reached the starvation point. A train crew abandoned their train saying it was better to starve in idleness than to starve while working. The strike spread until a large part of the country was involved. The troops were called out, for the first time in America the soldier was used to suppress the worker.

A truly remarkable strike was that on the Union Pacific of May, 1884. The company posted a notice over the entire system announcing a general reduction in the wages of all employers except engineers and firemen of from ten to twenty-five per cent. Not a shop on the system was organized, yet within thirty-six hours every shop from Omaha to Ogden was on strike. The notice of reduction was posted on Thursday, the company rescinded the order Saturday and announced that on Monday work would be resumed at the old scale.

A second strike on the Union Pacific in the same year terminated successfully for the men, as did that of the American Railway Union on the Great Northern in 1894.

The list of unsuccessful strikes on the railways is a long one, no attempt will be made to give it in detail. The engineer's strike on the "Q," the one on the Gould system led by the heroic Irons, will recur to most readers as striking instances of failure.

The greatest and most disastrous strike in the railway world was that of the American Railway Union led by Eugene V. Debs in 1894. The American Railway Union was an industrial organization and when the men went out against the advice of its president in sympathy with the Pullman car employees, traffic was tied up from Chicago westward. The entire country realized the tremendous power of labor. President Cleveland and the Courts came to the relief of the corporations. Over the protest of Governor Altgeld the Federal troops were sent to Chicago. Debs spent six months in jail for disobeying an injunction. The strike was lost, thousands of men were blacklisted. They learned how not to do things—and the cause went marching on.

A large number of men scattered over a wide area are not nearly so effective in aiding their fellows in securing better contions as when restricted to narrower area. Again those whose work is rough and heavy seem most willing to strike hard blows and themselves undergo severe hardships in defense of others. The teamsters of Chicago and other cities afford an illustration of this fact.

In sympathy, interests, mode of organization and assistance to others in time of need, the coal and metalliferous miners are closely related, a short space will be devoted to their organization.

The first union of coal miners was formed in the anthracite region in 1849 but speedily collapsed. In 1869 John Siney organized the Miners and Laborers Benevolent Association. It grew rapidly until 1875 when a general strike was ordered which closed every mine in the district but the strike collapsed and the union was destroyed.

The American Miners' Association was the first attempt at organization among the bituminous miners, in 1861. It went down in the strikes of '67 or '68. It was followed by the Miners' National Association which gained a membership of 20,000 in 1874, but soon disappeared. It was followed by the Knights of Labor which spread throughout the mining regions but at last shared the fate of its predecessors. It had passed its zenith in 1885, in that year the Miners' National Progressive Union was formed. It reached a larger measure of success in the bituminous fields than any of the former unions. Joint conferences were held with the operators in West Virginia, Western Pennsylvania, Ohio, Indiana and Illinois. There was constant friction between the union and the Knights of Labor and the membership of each declined. It became apparent that the mine workers must be united in a single organization if any permanent gain was to be secured.

Assembly No. 135, of the Knights of Labor, which claimed jurisdiction over the coal miners and the Progressive Union, were consolidated in 1890, forming the United Mine Workers of America.

ANTHRACITE COAL STRIKE OF 1902.

One of the most notable strikes in the mining industry in the United States was begun in the Antharcite coal district in 1902, when, at a signal, almost one hundred and fifty thousand men and boys laid down their tools. Despite the pangs of hunger, temptations that were offered to desert the cause, only a small minority returned to work in the five months of suffering that followed.

The railroad and mining companies and their financial backers represented a capital of hundreds of millions if not of billions of dollars and their strength was used to its fullest capacity to defeat the mine workers.

The financial losses resulting from the strike showed the costliness of labor conflicts. The Anthracite Coal Strike Commission estimated that the loss to railroads and coal companies in reduced freight and coal receipts was not less than $74,000,-000, and the loss in wages to the miners of not less than $25,000,-000, the total loss being placed by the commission at $99,000,000. The strike of 1902, is memorable for the terrible hardships which it entailed.

The strike came as a culmination of development lasting through three-fourths of a century. During the last two generations a slow, stubborn contest had been waged by labor in the Anthracite coal fields against the ever-increasing power and oppression of monopoly.

Anthracite coal was first shipped to the seaboard during the War of 1812, but up to 1850, the shipments were comparatively slight. Mining hard coal was considered of little importance and the number of miners only about eight thousand. In 1850, there was no monopoly of the mines, no connection between transportation and mining companies.

It was not until after the Civil war that mining became profitable to any great extent.

After the war, although the operators made large profits, a strong attempt was made to reduce wages and break up the miners' union. From 1867 to 1875, an aggressive war was waged between the operator and the union, known as the Workingmens' Benevolent Association with the result the miners' organization ceased to exist by the end of 1875.

It was during the quarter of a Century between 1875 to 1900, that the abuses leading to the strikes of 1900 and 1902 were inaugurated. During this period of practically unorganized labor, the conditions grew more terrible all the time. The object of the operators seemed to be to prevent the formation of unions and to keep the men in absolute subjection. This they practically succeeded in doing. They were organized from time to time but as often disrupted. One section was used against the other, so that divided, all of the sections fell.

It is not strange that in this semi-unorganized state the miners were wronged, cheated and mistreated in many ways. Chief among these was the increase in what constituted a ton of coal. The size of a ton increased in weight from 2,000 to 2,800 until finally, they exacted from the miner 3,190 pounds of coal and called it a ton and he was paid the same for a ton that weighed 3,190 as he formerly received for 2,000 pounds. Where the coal was paid for by the car, the same system was adopted, and the car grew, as though it were a live oak. So a man was paid no more if three or four inches were added to its size or if he was obliged to fill ten inches of "topping" above the rail. The company adopted a system of docking, which was arbitrary, unjust and tyrannous. The Strike Commission stated that the amount docked by even fair companies diminished fifty per cent when the miners were allowed to employ check docking bosses.

As late as 1899 the idea of organizing the miners of the Anthracite region of Pennsylvania was regarded as all but impossible by all but a few of the most enthusiastic members of the mine workers. Some of the greatest difficulties being the difference in race, religion, and ideals of the twenty Nationalities in the region, the variations in the standard of living, all conspired to make them distrustful of the movement, especially so on account of the mutual distrust of the races and the failures of the different unions organized before.

The market was overcrowded with coal and the region with men. The operators were united in a bitter hostility toward any form of organization among the miners. Pioneer miners were threatened with being blacklisted. Men that had grown old in the Anthracite region, shook their heads doubtfully and predicted it would be impossible for any organization to gain a foothold in the Anthracite region. Within a year all this changed and the leaders of the organization claim the Anthracite settlement as one of their greatest victories.

The local organizations of the miners were organized under so many different names, grew then died from 1861 to the final formation of the United Mine Workers of America, it would take a great deal of space to enumerate them. Many times the organization under one of the old names in the bituminous fields, grew to a membership of 20,000 but as often the membership fell back to 8,000 or in some cases, practically a few hundred.

After the Miners' National Progressive Union and District Assembly No. 135, Knights of Labor, amalgamated, forming the United Mine Workers of America, the union gradually extended its influence and organized the Anthracite and bituminous men to a great extent. In 1894, a general strike was inaugurated in the bituminous fields and the membership was reduced to 9,000, this left nothing but history of the organization in the anthracite region.

Several small strikes took place. Early in 1900, under the leadership of President John Mitchell, an increased force of organizers were stationed in the Anthracite coal fields.

In July, 1900, mutterings were heard on every hand and it seemed the time had come for the inevitable struggle. Every means was resorted to by the unions to meet the operators but to no avail and the strike of 1900 was ordered to take effect September 17. Although the membership was only 8,000 the organization so clearly represented the attitude of the majority of of the mine workers, that from 80,000 to 100,000 men and boys quit work the first day and their number increased until it reached 144,000 employees. Fully ninety per cent of the total men employed. October 20, work was resumed, a raise of wages of ten per cent having been granted. No one considered the struggle in 1900 as conclusive.

Immediately after the men returned to work in 1900, stockades were built about many of the mines, depots were established for the storage of coal. In 1901, the union again maintained peace by a continuation of the agreement of 1900 which had been flung at them rather than granted.

In 1902, every effort consistent with the preservation of dignity was made by the representatives of the union to secure a joint conference with the operators in the hope that a strike might be averted. February 14, 1902, the officials of the United Mine Workers, addressed a letter to the various railroad presidents asking for a joint conference to be held at Scranton, Pa.,

March 12. The request was refused by the operators unanimously. The Mine Workers, in convention assembled at Shamokin,
Pa., formulated a series of demands to be presented to the operators. March 22, a telegram was sent to the railroad presidents
asking them to meet representatives of the mine workers. The
first conference was held March 26. The operators remained
obstinate. The second conference was held but the operators still
refused the demand. The union offered to compromise their
original demands by accepting a ten per cent increase in wages
instead of twenty as at first demanded, a nine-hour day instead
of eight. The peaceful attitude was mistaken for cowardice and
the railway presidents grew more obdurate.

May 8, there still lingered a hope that the trouble could be
averted and as a last resort the officials of the United Mine
Workers sent a telegram to the operators offering to submit their
demands to an arbitration committee of five persons selected by
the Industrial Branch of the Civic Federation, or, if that was not
satisfactory, to a committee composed of Bishop Ireland, Bishop
Potter and one other person whom these two might select. This
proposition was also refused. President Baer of the Reading
Coal and Iron Company declared "Anthracite mining is a business and not a religious, sentimental or academic proposition,"
etc. May 9, the District Executive Committee assembled at
Scranton and after all other efforts had failed, ordered a temporary suspension of mining to take place May 12, and issued a call
for a convention to meet at Hazelton, May 14, to determine if the
suspension should be made permanent. The convention by a vote
of four hundred and sixty-one and one fourth to three hundred
and forty-nine and three-fourths decided in favor of the strike
and the strike which has been conceded to be the greatest in
American history was declared May 15, 1902. At this time the
miners of West Virginia were also on strike, so with the calling
out of the Anthracite miners half the membership of the United
Mine Workers were on strike. The Anthracite miners hoped for
the calling out of the bituminous miners which would have meant
a general suspension of mining throughout the country. It seems
the existence of a contract between the operators and the miners

which was binding until April, 1903, was the sole reason the bituminous mines continued work. This contract was sacredly observed. A special convention was held in Indianapolis, Ind., beginning July 17, to consider the advisability of a general strike and many other important matters. The delegates voted against a sympathetic strike. The members of the organization in the bituminous fields pledged themselves to subscribe weekly one dollar or ten per cent of their earnings to a fund to be used for the relief of the Anthracite strikers; and the officers of the organization agreed to pay thirty-five per cent of their salaries for the same purpose. In this manner, during a period of sixteen weeks the enormous sum of $2,645,324.42 was collected. The bituminous miners alone paid into the relief fund an average of $7 to $16 per man. Toward the close of the strike many local unions increased their donations, in some instances members offered to pay twenty-five per cent of their earnings. As time passed the suffering of the miners and their families became acute and the publics' need of coal more pressing—the price of coal soared as high as $30 per ton, especially was this so if purchased in small quantities.

At this time the President of the United States intervened. The operators had stubbornly refused to yield to advice of friend or threat of foe; they appeared absolutely indifferent to the suffering public. The President sent an invitation to the various railroad presidents, to Mr. Mitchell, president of the United Mine Workers of America, and the presidents of the local unions of the Anthracite district to meet him in the temporary White House October 3. This meeting became historic. The President appealed to their patriotism. Mr. Mitchell proposed that all matters of dispute be submitted to the arbitration of a tribunal selected by the President. At this juncture a recess was taken until 3 o'clock and Roosevelt suggested discussion be suspeneded until that time. The afternoon session was one not to be forgotten. The operators disregarded the President's admonition and launched forth upon a series of tirades against unions and their officers. Instead of accepting the proposed plan of peace and arbitration, the operators urged the President of the Nation to send troops into the coal fields.   The attitude of the operators caused a wave of indignation to sweep over the country.   The President continued his efforts and October 6, requested President Mitchell, through the Hon. Carroll D. Wright, commissioner of Labor, to secure the return of the men to work.   On account of the complications this would have brought President Mitchell refused.   A few days after the conference with Roosevelt, the governor of Pennsylvania, ordered out the National Guard, which proceeded to the coal fields.   The operators had repeatedly stated that with the troops in the field they would resume and supply the public need.   On the day 10,000 militiamen reached the strike center the union men assembled in mass meeting and 150,000 men without one dissenting vote, voted to continue the strike until victory was won.

When October came coal had reached famine prices, the press and people in general were clamoring for a settlement of the strike.   The operators finally realized the necessity of surrendering.   October 13, J. Pierpont Morgan called upon President Roosevelt, and, in the name of the operators, offered to submit matters in dispute to a commission of five men to be appointed by the President and selected in the manner prescribed in the letter of submission.   At the time the offer was made the miners had practically won the strike.   They had more money on hand than ever before in the history of the organization and the men had demonstrated that the troops had no effect upon them and they were in a position to continue the conflict indefinitely. After it was learned the President was to have full power a convention was called to meet in Wilkesbarre, October 20.   This convention after one days' discussion, voted unanimously that work should be resumed October 23, and all questions in dispute were submitted to the arbitration commission appointed by the President of the United States.   So the strike that had endured for five months as a result of the operators refusal to arbitrate was brought to a close.

The sessions of the commission were destined to become historic.   Preliminary meetings were held October 24 and 27, 1902, and with few intermissions sat in Scranton and Philadelphia from November 14, 1902, until February 5, 1903. This period was devoted to the taking of testimony and was succeeded by five days of argument February 9, to 13th, inclusive. Attorneys represented both sides. The sessions were marked by dramatic incidents, chief among which was the testimony of little children who worked in the silk mills and coal breakers. 558 witnesses were examined, of whom 240 were called by the union, 153 by the attorneys for the non-union men who were specially represented, 154 by the operators and 11 by the commission. The testimony covered over 10,000 pages of legal cap paper besides exhibits, etc., etc. The award given March 18, 1903, was lengthy and with the exhibits appended to it made a document of 120,000 words.

The award did not give the men nearly all they were entitled to, yet it secured substantial advantages to the mine workers. It recognized the United Mine Workers as one of the contracting parties, granted an increase of ten per cent in wages, reduced the hours of engineers and firemen from twelve to eight hours without reduction in pay, reduced the hours of mine laborers from ten to nine and provided that their wages should be paid by the company instead of the miner. It further provided that cars should be equitably distributed, granted to the men the right to have check weighmen and check docking bosses and recommended a permanent board of conciliation.

The strike of 1902, probably increased the total wages of the mine workers between seven and eight million dollars annually.

EMPLOYEES VS. EMPLOYERS.

In the twenty years from 1881 to 1900, there were 22,793 strikes, involving 6,105,694 workers. The loss in time was equivalent to 194,000,000 days, or practically one month for each worker who had been involved in a strike. The loss in wages was $258,000,000; the total estimated loss to the community was $469,000,000. Contributions from labor organizations to maintain strikes amounted to $16,000,000.

Fifty-one per cent of the strikes in this period were successful, thirteen per cent partially successful, and thirty-six per cent failed. Strikes are characteristic of periods of prosperity, lockouts of periods of depression. In the boom period from 1881 to 1883, fifty-seven per cent of the strikes were successful, while sixty per cent were won in the prosperous years from 1896 to 1900.

Data is somewhat meager regarding strikes prior to 1860, 500 are recorded, the results known for 1,053. Of these thirty per cent were successful, fifteen per cent compromised, fifty-five per cent lost.

It should be remarked that the loss from strikes is more apparent than real. Periods of prosperity result in overproduction, followed by a period of depression. The markets are practically always supplied with all that can be consumed. The strike tends to put off the day when the employer must enforce a lockout.

Every attempt of the employee to better his condition has met the prompt opposition of the employer. In this matter the state has always given its assistance to the class that paid wages and in the early history of industry fixed the wage in their interest. The first strike, that of the New York seamen, though unorganized, met the immediate opposition of the merchants and ship owners. The first labor union formed in Boston brought about a union of Boston merchants who pledged themselves to "drive the shipwrights, caulkers and gravers to submission or starvation," and pledged $20,000 as a fighting fund. Seven years later one hundred and six merchants and ship owners agreed to "discountenance and check the unlawful combination formed to control the freedom of individuals as to the hours of labor."

Four hundred employers organized in New York in 1872, to combat the ten-hour movement, agreeing to contribute $1,000 each to the defense fund.

The close of the Nineteenth Century found national associations of the employers in nearly all the trades. The Citizens' Industrial Association of America, comprising sixty national and three hundred and thirty-five local associations, was organized in 1903. At the national meeting of the Manufacturers Association, held in 1907, the delegates pledged themselves to raise a fund of $1,500,000 to combat organized labor. No one can remain neutral in this conflict. A man's place is determined by his interest. When each recognizes this fact the end of a struggle that begun Centuries before a page of history was written is at hand.

"So all in vain will timorous ones essay
To set the metes and bounds of Liberty,
For Freedom is its own eternal law;
It makes its own conditions, and in storm
Or calm alike fulfills the unerring Will.
Let us not then despise it when it lies
Still as a sleeping lion, while a swarm
Of gnat-like evils hover round its head;
Nor doubt it when in mad, disjointed times
It shakes the torch of terror and its cry
Shrills o'er the quaking earth, and in the flame
Of riot and war we see its awful form
Rise by the scaffold, where the crimson axe
Rings down its grooves the knell of shuddering kings.
Forever in thine eyes, O Liberty,
Shines that high light whereby the world is saved,
And though thou slay· us, we will trust in thee!"
                                        —John Hay.

THE END.

Index to Appendix